PSYCHOPATHOLOGY

CONTRIBUTIONS FROM
THE SOCIAL, BEHAVIORAL
AND BIOLOGICAL SCIENCES

WILEY SERIES ON PERSONALITY PROCESSES

IRVING B. WEINER, *Editor*
Case Western Reserve University

PSYCHOPATHOLOGY

Contributions from the Social, Behavioral, and Biological Sciences

EDITED BY

MURIEL HAMMER

KURT SALZINGER

SAMUEL SUTTON

In honor of Joseph Zubin

A WILEY-INTERSCIENCE PUBLICATION

JOHN WILEY & SONS
New York • London • Sydney • Toronto

Library of Congress Cataloging in Publication Data:

Main entry under title:
Psychopathology: contributions from the social, behavioral, and biological sciences.
(Wiley series on personality processes)

"In honor of Joseph Zubin."
Includes bibliographies.
1. Psychology, Pathological.   I. Hammer, Muriel, 1927–   ed.   II. Salzinger, Kurt, ed.   III. Sutton, Samuel, 1921–   ed.   IV. Zubin, Joseph, 1900–
[DNLM: 1. Psychopathology—Collected works.

WM 100 H224p 1972 (P)]
RC454.P785   616.8′9′07   72-5449
ISBN 0-471-34723-X

Printed in the United States of America

10 9 8 7 6 5 4 3 2 1

Contributors

RUTH BENNETT, Ph.D., Principal Research Scientist, Gerontology Section, Biometrics Research Unit, New York State Department of Mental Hygiene; Adjunct Associate Professor, Gerontology Program, Teachers College, Columbia University; and Research Associate, Department of Psychiatry, College of Physicians and Surgeons, Columbia University, New York, New York

ARTHUR L. BENTON, Ph.D., Professor of Psychology and Neurology, The University of Iowa, Iowa City, Iowa

EUGENE I. BURDOCK, Ph.D., Professor of Psychiatry, Director, Biometric Laboratory, The New York University School of Medicine, New York, New York

SHEILA BRASS CHADWICK, M.A., Department of Medical Genetics, New York State Psychiatric Institute, New York, New York

RICHARD ALLEN CHASE, M.D., Associate Professor, Department of Psychiatry and Behavioral Sciences, The Johns Hopkins University School of Medicine, Baltimore, Maryland

JOHS. CLAUSEN, Ph.D., Chief Research Scientist, Institute for Research in Mental Retardation, Staten Island, New York

BARBARA SNELL DOHRENWEND, Ph.D., Associate Professor of Psychology, The City College of the City University of New York, New York, New York

BRUCE P. DOHRENWEND, Ph.D., Professor of Social Science, Department of Psychiatry, College of Physicians and Surgeons, Columbia University, New York, New York

JEAN ENDICOTT, Ph.D., Associate Research Scientist, Evaluation Section, Biometrics Research Unit, New York State Department of Mental Hygiene; and Research Associate, Department of Psychiatry, College of Physicians and Surgeons, Columbia University, New York, New York

JOSEPH L. FLEISS, Ph.D., Associate Research Scientist, Biostatistics Section, Biometrics Research Unit, New York State Department of Mental Hygiene; and Adjunct Associate Professor of Biostatistics, School of Public Health, Columbia University, New York, New York

BARRY GURLAND, M.B., M.R.C.P., D.P.M., Psychiatrist II, Diagnosis and Psychopathology Section, Biometrics Research Unit, New York State Department of Mental Hygiene; and Assistant Professor, Department of Psychiatry, College of Physicians and Surgeons, Columbia University, New York, New York

LOUIS GUTTMAN, Ph.D., Professor of Social and Psychological Measurement, The Hebrew University of Jerusalem; and Scientific Director, The Israel Institute of Applied Social Research, Jerusalem, Israel

MURIEL HAMMER, Ph.D., Principal Research Scientist, Anthropology Section, Biometrics Research Unit, New York State Department of Mental Hygiene; and Assistant Professor, Department of Psychiatry, College of Physicians and Surgeons, Columbia University, New York, New York

ANNE S. HARDESTY, Ph.D., Associate Professor of Psychiatry, The New York University School of Medicine, New York, New York

HOWARD HUNT, Ph.D., Chief of Psychiatric Research (Psychology), Department of Research Psychology, New York State Psychiatric Institute; Professor of Psychology, Columbia University; and Professor of Medical Psychology, Department of Psychiatry, College of Physicians and Surgeons, Columbia University, New York, New York

LISSY F. JARVIK, M.D., Ph.D., Psychiatrist II (Research), Department of Medical Genetics, New York State Psychiatric Institute; and Associate Professor of Clinical Psychiatry, Department of Psychiatry, College of Physicians and Surgeons, Columbia University, New York, New York

MURRAY E. JARVIK, M.D., Ph.D., Professor of Psychiatry and Pharmacology, Department of Pharmacology, Albert Einstein College of Medicine, Bronx, New York

E. ROY JOHN, Ph.D., Professor of Psychiatry and Physiology, Department of Psychiatry, Director, Brain Research Laboratories, New York Medical College, New York, New York

H. E. KING, Ph.D., Professor of Psychology, University of Pittsburgh School of Medicine; and Chief, Psychology Service, Western Psychiatric Institute and Clinic, Pittsburgh, Pennsylvania

SOL KUGELMASS, Ph.D., Professor of Psychology, Dean, Faculty of Social Sciences, The Hebrew University of Jerusalem, Jerusalem, Israel

PAUL F. LAZARSFELD, Ph.D., Professor of Sociology, Columbia University, New York, New York

HEINZ E. LEHMANN, M.D., Chairman, Department of Psychiatry, McGill University, Montreal, Canada; and Director of Medical Education and Research, Douglas Hospital, Verdun, Canada

SARNOFF A. MEDNICK, Ph.D., Professor of Psychology, New School for Social Research, New York, New York; and Director, Psykologisk Institut, Kommunehospitalet, Copenhagen, Denmark

NEAL E. MILLER, Ph.D., Professor of Psychology, The Rockefeller University, New York, New York

H. B. M. MURPHY, M.D., Ph.D., Professor of Psychiatry, McGill University, Montreal, Canada

ANATOL RAPOPORT, Ph.D., Professor of Psychology, University of Toronto, Toronto, Canada

MAURICE M. RAPPORT, Ph.D., Chief, Division of Neuroscience, New York State Psychiatric Institute; and Professor of Biochemistry, College of Physicians and Surgeons, Columbia University, New York, New York

GREGORY RAZRAN, Ph.D., Professor Emeritus of Psychology, Queens College of the City University of New York, New York, New York

KURT SALZINGER, Ph.D., Principal Research Scientist, Behavior Analysis and Modification Section, Biometrics Research Unit, New York State Department of Mental Hygiene; Professor of Psychology, Department of Social Sciences, Polytechnic Institute of Brooklyn; and Research Associate, Department of Psychiatry, College of Physicians and Surgeons, Columbia University, New York, New York

SUZANNE SALZINGER, Ph.D., Associate Research Scientist, Behavior Analysis and Modification Section, Biometrics Research Unit, New York State Department of Mental Hygiene; and Research Associate, Department of Psychiatry, College of Physicians and Surgeons, Columbia University, New York, New York

ELIZABETH SANCHEZ, M.A., Research Scientist, Gerontology Section, Biometrics Research Unit, New York State Department of Mental Hygiene, New York, New York

FINI SCHULSINGER, M.D., Chief Physician and Professor of Psychiatry, University of Copenhagen; and Co-director, Psykologisk Institut, Kommunchospitalet, Copenhagen, Denmark

HERBERT SOLOMON, Ph.D., Professor of Statistics, Stanford University, Stanford, California

ROBERT SPITZER, M.D., Psychiatrist III, Evaluation Section, Biometrics Research Unit, New York State Department of Mental Hygiene; and Assistant Professor of Clinical Psychiatry, College of Physicians and Surgeons, Columbia University, New York, New York

SAMUEL SUTTON, Ph.D., Deputy Chief, Biometrics Research Unit, New York State Department of Mental Hygiene; and Professor, Department of Psychiatry, College of Physicians and Surgeons, Columbia University, New York, New York

JUDITH TANUR, Ph.D., Lecturer, Department of Sociology, State University of New York at Stony Brook, New York

PETER H. VENABLES, Ph.D., Professor of Psychology, Birkbeck College, University of London, London, England

Series Preface

This series of books is addressed to behavioral scientists interested in the nature of human personality. Its scope should prove pertinent to personality theorists and researchers as well as to clinicians concerned with applying an understanding of personality processes to the amelioration of emotional difficulties in living. To this end, the series provides a scholarly integration of theoretical formulations, empirical data, and practical recommendations.

Six major aspects of studying and learning about human personality can be designated: personality theory, personality structure and dynamics, personality development, personality assessment, personality change, and personality adjustment. In exploring these aspects of personality, the books in the series discuss a number of distinct but related subject areas: the nature and implications of various theories of personality; personality characteristics that account for consistencies and variations in human behavior; the emergence of personality processes in children and adolescents; the use of interviewing and testing procedures to evaluate individual differences in personality; efforts to modify personality styles through psychotherapy, counseling, behavior therapy, and other methods of influence; and patterns of abnormal personality functioning that impair individual competence.

IRVING B. WEINER

Case Western Reserve University
Cleveland, Ohio

Preface

This volume covers a wide spectrum of topics concerning social, behavioral, and biological approaches to psychopathology, and, in a final section, mathematical description and the use of models in psychopathology. The emphasis throughout the volume is theoretical, methodological, and quantitative. The point of view is that of the research worker striving for conceptual clarity in some segment of the field in order to cope with its unresolved issues. In some chapters the source of the research question is clinical; in others the implications are clinical; in a third group both source and implications are clinical. The book was conceived as a reference work as well as a stimulus to maintain a multifaceted approach to the field for the research worker, the clinician, the teacher, and the student of psychopathology.

Perhaps to a greater extent than most books composed of chapters written by different authors, this book has been a group venture. The reason lies partly in the range of fields covered, which required technical and editorial help from colleagues more conversant in these fields than the editors. However, the main reason for the participation of so many people is that this volume was compiled to honor Joseph Zubin, a fact that facilitated the task of attracting illustrious authors to the project. These authors have generously agreed to contribute the income realized from the sale of this book to a fund for furthering Joseph Zubin's new research ideas. Therefore we thank the many people who participated in this volume, not so much for helping us, as for joining in our common goal of honoring Joseph Zubin.

We wish to thank the current and former staffs of Joseph Zubin's department, the Biometrics Research Unit of the New York State Department of Mental Hygiene, as well as many other associates and colleagues. Members of this group met together to plan the volume and to designate the editors as a committee to produce it. It is not possible to mention all of them by name because there were so many who gave time, advice, and money for the preparation of the manuscript, as well as editorial assistance. On the other hand, some should be mentioned because they did so much—Richard

S. Feldman, Joseph Fleiss, Judith Tanur, and David Jenness, who so graciously and unstintingly gave their time in the editing of the book, and Florence Schumer and Frank Hardesty, who encouraged us in the early stages.

As everyone knows who has ever tried to write or edit a book, a large burden is always borne by the secretaries who keep things organized and who do the typing of the various (often illegible) drafts of chapters. We are especially grateful to Shula Bitner and Lynn Garibaldi, who worked very hard on the enormous task of handling the correspondence and early drafts of papers during the first major phase of preparing this volume; and, as always, we were able to count on the devoted efforts of Madeline Misar, Marie Junger, and Vilma Rivieccio, of the Biometrics Research Unit, from the earliest stages through delivery of the completed manuscript. We are greatly indebted to Marion Hartung, who took on the arduous task of checking out the references and footnotes of all the chapters, and who made sure that the tables were properly placed and that the figure legends were in correct form—all thankless tasks but all necessary for producing the finished book.

Finally, a word about the multiple editorship of this volume is in order. We can truly say that this was a collaborative effort—one in which it is now quite impossible to single out the various contributions made by each of us. For this reason we chose to list ourselves alphabetically. Moreover, our collaboration was such that we have all learned from one another—interestingly enough, exactly the kind of collaboration which Joseph Zubin might have supervised and for which he certainly made us ready. So here we are again saying thank you to Joseph Zubin, to whom this book is dedicated.

MURIEL HAMMER
KURT SALZINGER
SAMUEL SUTTON

New York, New York
April 1972

JOSEPH ZUBIN—*An Intellectual Biography*

When a famous pianist was asked, after performing a piece of music, to explain its meaning, he is said to have sat down and played it again. The meaning of a man's intellectual history is no easier to explain. Perhaps here too we should seek the meaning by sitting down and "playing it again." With that in mind, we thought we could honor Joseph Zubin most appropriately by a book of this kind.

Joseph Zubin has taken on many roles in his career (he still adds a few each year)—teacher but also student, writer but also reader in wide-ranging areas of the literature, researcher but also constructive critic of research, stimulator of new ideas but also their consumer and adapter. The common concern that characterizes all of these roles stands out clearly: it is an emphasis on the importance of evaluation. This emphasis was apparent in his earliest publications on the validity of tests of intelligence and personality, and has continued to manifest itself in his appraisal of handwriting analysis and the projective techniques, particularly the Rorschach test, in his weighing of the worth of various kinds of therapy, in his evaluation of screening procedures for the emotionally maladjusted, in his appraisal of the success of psychoanalytic training, and in his critical examination of the phenomena of subliminal and dermo-optical perception. In fact, it was his creative concern with evaluation that brought him, in 1968, the New York State Department of Mental Hygiene Distinguished Service Citation for Research.

But Joseph Zubin's critical analyses have always been followed by constructive or reconstructive work. The negative findings that he unearthed with respect to the Rorschach challenged him to construct scales for appropriate measurement and to examine more closely the nature of the interview. Results indicating the ineffectiveness of various somatotherapies spurred him to sift the literature more carefully for characteristics of patients, to determine whether assigning therapies more appropriate for each disorder would produce a greater rate of recovery. Here we find him using the rating scale to bring stability to Rorschach scoring and order to the observation of patients' behavior on hospital wards. Here too we find him creating quantitative indices of prognosis. We see him working on the psychophysiology of the pupil of the eye and the evoked potential of the brain, applying his knowledge of verbal learning to analyze the effect of electroshock treatment on memory, joining behavior theory with developmental psychology to examine the genesis of speech in children. Although he feels most at home in experimental psychology, he does not hesitate to study the friendship patterns of the prepsychotic individual when he decides that these are important. Pursuing the fields of inquiry he believes to be germane to psychopathology, he is forever finding a new set of results that must be integrated into his armamentarium of tools and conceptualizations.

A field as much his own as psychology is statistics. He has contributed to it by designing new techniques, as in his pattern analysis and clustering techniques. He has also brought into psychology some of the statistical techniques that he thought psychologists should start using—for example, the analysis of covariance—even when their application has forced the abandonment of cherished hypotheses.

Since Joseph Zubin undertakes the kind of thorough evaluation which requires that the phenomena appraised be better organized, he is inevitably led to investigate the best models of conceptualizing and is thus brought to consider general questions of scientific theory. He has contributed to this area by taking diverse and seemingly unconnected accumulations of data and organizing them in ways that shed light on disorders as complex as schizophrenia. His paper on the power of scientific models brought into high relief their uses in the study of personality. The study of psychopathology, which has yielded everything from isolated facts to untestable theories, has also profited from his conceptualizations. Being partial to no single model, he has written many papers to show how various testable models can give meaning to data. He moves easily from the developmental to the learning model, from the internal environment to the sociocultural model, from the genetic to the ecological model.

Joseph Zubin's urge to make order out of the chaos of psychopathology has made him an ideal organizer of the yearly meetings of the American Psychopathological Association. All of these meetings, no matter how different from one year to the next, have borne his unmistakable stamp—the logical exposition of the problem, the new developments, and the significant controversies presented by the important figures in the field. The published proceedings of many of these meetings have become classics in their time. In recognition of his skills, the American Psychopathological Association made him its president and gave him one of its highest honors by having him deliver the first Paul H. Hoch Award lecture in 1968.

Because of his interest in organizing a field of knowledge, he is in great demand as a journal editor. Thus he has served as associate editor on eight different journals dealing with both theory and practice in psychiatry and in experimental and abnormal psychology.

His skill in evaluation has also been utilized by various agencies of government concerned with the funding of research grants. Here is additional evidence of his range of interests, for he has sat on the Psychopharmacology Study Section of the National Institute of Mental Health and on the Section on Developmental Behavioral Sciences of the National Institutes of Health. He has also been called to serve on the Board of Professional Affairs of the American Psychological Association.

His zeal in teaching and his interest in students have always endeared him to them. At Columbia University, graduate students quickly learned that Professor Zubin was always willing to talk to them and to entertain fresh ideas. The number and variety of topics of the dissertations he sponsored constitute a tribute to his range of interests. Though now professor emeritus, he has made sure that he will continue to teach and to guide students by becoming a special lecturer in psychology and psychiatry at Columbia University and adjunct professor at Queens College of the City University of New York. He continues to lecture and is invited to speak all over the world. For a period of some 15 years, the Clinical Division of the American Psychological Association invited him to conduct his famous postdoctoral institute and, in 1968, gave him a special Certificate of Merit.

We have not yet mentioned his administrative duties and abilities or his significant role in getting the New York State Department of Mental Hygiene to provide for evaluation of new programs. The establishment of his Biometrics Research Unit is concrete evidence of his vision and of his unwillingness to be bound by the artificial borders erected by jealous departmental definition. In a single group he has gathered together investigators in such fields as anthropology, sociology, neurophysiology, psychiatry, statistics, linguistics—and, within psychology, psychophysics, conditioning, and psychomotor behavior; with his gentle administrative guidance, he has elicited the best from each of them. Although knowing when to change course in research and when to direct interest to new areas, he has never demanded a change in course from anyone working for him. Unafraid of large projects or of new areas of investigation, he accepted the challenge of doing a comparative cross-national study of diagnosis involving the coordination of research teams in the United States and the United Kingdom.

To all this we must add a word about Joseph Zubin the man. Perhaps most surprising on first encountering him is his direct expression of an overriding curiosity. When he fails to understand something, he asks about it, and no matter how naive the question may at first appear, it eventually turns out to be significant. Never hesitating to rediscover the obvious, he nevertheless shapes that rediscovery into something new. Surely no friend of the shortened work week, he spends much of his currently reduced work time of 70 hours a week in self-education; he seeks knowledge from all around him, making inquiries with humor and humility. And as he accepts help, so he gives it: professor of psychology and psychiatry, chief of the Biometrics Research Unit, consultant to the Veterans Administration and the National Institutes of Health, editor of journals, organizer of meetings, writer of papers and books, researcher and integrator of research, he never closes his door to a student or staff member in need of advice or assistance, either professional or personal.

Happily this record of achievements is incomplete, for Joseph Zubin's work continues as does the recognition that he receives. To mention but the latest honors, he was a member of the American Psychological Association Task Force to prepare for the 1971 White House Conference on Aging; in 1971 he was elected president of the American College of Neuropsychopharmacology; in 1972 he was awarded the honorary degree of Doktor Honoris Causa of the Medical Faculty at Lund University in Sweden.

If there were a word that combined the areas of measurement, evaluation, anthropology, sociology, geriatrics, experimental psychology, learning and development, and others, it might describe the scope of Joseph Zubin.

MURIEL HAMMER
KURT SALZINGER
SAMUEL SUTTON

Contents

Introduction

Interest in psychopathology reflects a convergence of concerns from an extraordinarily wide range of sources: legal, medical, humane, administrative, philosophical, esthetic, psychological, social, neurological, biochemical. It would be difficult to think of a field or a viewpoint that has not touched on psychopathology. Such interest has often been intense, sometimes passionate; it is ancient and persistent.

The disciplines and viewpoints represented in this volume, although quite diverse, are all drawn from one set, with the common traditions, assumptions and goals of contemporary science taken for granted. They therefore implicitly share the assumption that all phenomena have regularities that are available to human understanding—and potentially to human alteration—on the basis of rational objective procedures of investigation and analysis. Subjective anguish or ecstasy, poetic vision, or religious inspiration are neither accepted nor rejected; their truly subjective aspects are simply not in the relevant domain, while their objective aspects are physico-bio-social events amenable to systematic analysis. The chapters here share also the assumption that such objective systematic analysis is valuable in at least two senses: first, simply that it is good to know, to understand; and, second, that such knowledge constitutes the most potent kind of tool for the alteration of undesirable conditions.

What constitutes a desirable or undesirable condition is not itself traditionally studied within the domain of science. It is perhaps primarily in this connection that psychopathology is an example par excellence of a field of study which seems likely to force the extension of a number of relevant disciplines beyond the dimensions that have defined them. Psychopathology is not unique in having a number of fields impinge upon it—so, after all, do broken legs, pollution, warfare, and orchid growing—but it may be unique in some of the ways it impinges on other fields and thus in the ways it must integrate these other fields. For example, the need for scientists to deal with human values has recently become powerfully apparent, in terms of the moral necessity of taking account of the consequences of scientific findings. The need to deal with values in the study of psychopathology, however, not only is a matter of consequences but also is deeply ingrained

1

in the phenomenon itself; it is a research necessity as well as a moral necessity. The meaning of deviance or social disruption in relation to pathology is not a semantic game to be played by others—it is a problem the researcher encounters in the very matter he is studying.

Even the question of whether the kinds of values incorporated in the concept "pathology" constitute the appropriate framework for scientific research must in some sense be coped with. The very conception that abnormal behavior is to be viewed as illness, like cancer or tuberculosis or syphilis, is itself a product of the *Zeitgeist* of the last century—and one that is already under attack. The patient is generally brought for treatment by his family or friends, and it is clear that the social mores defining normality are involved in the decision that abnormality is present. Although the psychiatrist may also see in the patient other and less obvious symptoms, our confidence in their diagnostic meaning is shaken by the knowledge that many symptoms have waxed and waned in form and frequency even over recent history, and that they vary in different parts of the world.

The psychotic patient presents simultaneously social, psychological, and physiological disturbances. While the predilections of our society tend to make us more vividly sensitive to the psychological disturbances, we need to be wary about whether this heightening is a reflection of the patient or a reflection of our habitual modes of awareness. A society with different biases might de-emphasize this level of symptomatology and be more oriented toward the social disturbances exhibited by the patient. For example, in the Soviet Union, as a by-product of a political philosophy, the social and physiological manifestations tend to take precedence over the psychological.

Similarly, by classifying abnormal behavior as illness and turning the patient over to a physician, we create the set that the physiological aspects are the fundamental source of the aberration—just as with other illnesses that are the concern of the physician. Although this may in fact be so, our attitude is based not on clear research findings but rather on implicit assumptions deriving from our mores and institutions.

Thus, for a number of reasons, the impact of values and attitudes on science arises as a specially significant question in the study of psychopathology. This is referred to, either in passing or as a central issue, in a number of the chapters in this volume.

In addition to the impact of values on science, there is a second pervasive paradox of scientific methodology that is heightened in the study of psychopathology. The fundamental proviso of classical scientific law, "all other things being equal," requires that everything not irrelevant to the question under consideration be under the scientist's control. To some extent this classical model remains applicable in physics and chemistry; it is not and never has been truly appropriate in the biological and social sciences, however, except as a methodological commitment. It is perhaps even less appropriate to problem-oriented approaches (except where they are fully defined *a priori*) than to particular disciplines. The reason for these differences has to do with the implications of treating natural (and therefore open) systems as though they were closed systems. To the extent that the aspects or variables in a situation can be handled as finite and known, it is possible to deal with any subset of them with "all other things" held in check. The study of a problem such as psychopathology, however, is interwoven in complex ways with a wide range of phenomena and involves an unlimited number of potentially relevant variables. It is not quite satisfactory, therefore, to treat parts of the problem as closed systems by treating the rest of it as finite—either concretely or in the sense that the nonspecified variables are handled as a group; and known—either concretely or in the sense that the effects of these variables are assumed to cancel each other. It is not a matter of choice whether or not to use a closed-system approach: such a treatment is indispensable to analysis, yet it is a fiction that must distort and that requires constant restructuring.

Analysis rests implicitly on closed-system assumptions; sets of events are not closed systems. Actual events are not themselves finite, in the sense of being sharply bounded, nor do they have a finite number of causes, components, attributes, or effects. The analysis of an event requires first the choosing of boundaries of several kinds on the basis of which to eliminate most of the event from consideration. What is left can then be "processed." If the internal correctness of the procedures is assumed, the validity of the results of analysis, with respect to the sets of events they refer to, must depend on the influence of what has been excluded from consideration.

Thus, in the context of a theory of a particular psychiatric disorder, only certain aspects—perhaps even ones that appear to be least dramatic—may be emphasized in order to construct a chain of evidence. This procedure rests on the assumption that only thus can a coherent explanatory structure be built which may subsequently permit the fitting in of the wider set of phenomena observed in the disorder.

The fundamental contradiction between closed-system analysis and open-system phenomena is inescapable, but there are various approaches to dealing with it, some of which may be better than others for a given set of purposes. One is a kind of ad hoc approach, which does not use well-defined criteria of selection from events, or the same criteria consistently throughout the analysis, and which can therefore bring in factors from domains outside the initial one as they seem relevant. Thus, for example, the problem of diagnosis in psychopathology, which is a recurrent thread through most of the chapters of this volume, has classically been handled in ad hoc terms. Strikingly different classes of observation and of behavior are used in the specification of the various psychiatric disorders. Prognosis may be considered as a key criterion in relation to one grouping, yet may not be deemed relevant for another. The various diagnostic groupings are rarely mutually exclusive, and regions of overlap between groups are freely acknowledged. The simple fact that a particular subdivision serves some useful clinical or research purpose appears to be a sufficient rationale for its existence.

Although the ad hoc approach rests ultimately on unspecified closed systems, the partial utilization of these systems may give the resulting analyses the appearance of being based on open systems. The disadvantages of such analyses are that they are, as totalities, unverifiable, even when each component is verifiable; that they are unique analyses, which do not lend themselves to further comparison or generalization; and that they lack power, since productive manipulation requires continuity of the rules within a system of analyses.

The ad hoc approach may be seen as a more flexible but also more ill-defined form of the explicit multiple-system approach, in which two or more closed-system analyses are brought into conjunction by explicit criteria, based either on overlapping definitions or on a sequence of expansions of the domain of each system. There are no logical limits to such overlaps or expansions, but the knowledge available at any given time may or may not make it possible to meet the relevant criteria for a particular multiple-system analysis. Although these approaches are verifiable, generalizable, and powerful, they have these characteristics for precisely the same reasons that they lack some of the flexibility of the ad hoc approach and are far less amenable to "intuitive" verification.

Another alternative is the loophole approach, which builds into a closed-system analysis one or more loci for potential penetration by or integration with other systems. Some uses of "indeterminacy" and the concept of randomness exemplify this type.

Most works of comment and criticism and, in fact, most conscious human knowledge and wisdom are based on the ad hoc approach, bringing to bear on any issue of interest whatever may seem likely to add to an understanding of it. Science is the primary user of the loophole approach; classically, science deals with a deliberately restricted set of variables, implicitly excluding almost everything else from consideration, and explicitly setting aside other sets of variables deemed relevant to the question but outside the immediate system of analysis. The boundaries of such systems are never held firm (except within a particular analysis) but usually vary only within a domain of related sets of variables. From time to time, the boundaries of parts of two or more domains come to overlap, and a "hyphenated" domain arises (such as psycho-linguistics, bio-chemistry, neuro-psycho-pharmacology) which may, for a while, utilize multiple-systems analyses until a fuller integration takes place within a new combined domain.

Such combined domains not only are potentially enlightening with respect to the questions pursued within them, but also feed back new clarifications and questions into the more traditional disciplines from which they derive. Similarly, the study of psychopathology has often contributed more to the science whose methods were applied to it than to psychopathology itself. (Kety, for example, has commented that biochemistry profited more from the study of schizophrenia than schizophrenia profited from the various biochemical theories of the disorder.)

It is of course possible that the slow development of principles and knowledge in a series of independent disciplines will eventually yield the solution of the sources of abnormal behavior. Human beings are sociocultural animals. It follows, therefore, that in studying abnormality we apply what knowledge we have of the sociocultural factors in normal human beings to "abnormal" ones as well. Human beings have sensory systems that control the intake of stimuli. This must be so in individuals with abnormal behavior as well. The human motor system has been studied in great detail and has shown lawfulness. We must investigate its role in psychopathology as well. Human behavior is integrated through an internal communication system consisting of the nervous pathways along which travel electrical impulses helped or hindered by complex biochemical reactions. If these apply to behavior in general, then they must apply to abnormal behavior as well. Any living organism interacts with its environment and is changed by that interaction; those with psychopathology are also modified by such interaction.

However, a substantive problem such as psychopathology often generates pressures that are orthogonal to the approaches of the more traditional research disciplines. Exploration of a new clinical finding may require a unique combination of several traditional disciplines; social and humanitarian pressures act as forces to seek rapid solutions. Such developments are often possible, as, for example, in the case of the discovery of insulin for ameliorating the dangers of diabetes. Yet to this day the subtleties of the complex metabolic interactions involved in diabetic illness continue to pose a challenge to research. The relatively recent widespread use of tranquilizers to ameliorate, or perhaps suppress, the more difficult symptoms of psychiatric disorder presents a somewhat less successful example than the discovery of insulin of a partial solution that precedes a fundamental understanding.

It is not only in the realm of cause that a stimulus to the involvement of many disciplines arises. The optimal treatment of an undesirable condition is not necessarily in the same domain as the cause. It is perhaps trivial, but nevertheless instructive, that a drug operating presumably in the physiological domain can relieve symptoms such as anxiety in the psychological domain. In a similar vein, behavior theorists have tended to declare their independence from the traditional problems of diagnosis and etiology by arguing that their reinforcement procedures can alter undesirable behavior, whatever its ultimate source. Within such a framework, the concept of "ultimate source" loses much of its importance, perhaps retaining its relevance primarily for approaches to the prevention of abnormal behavior. (The concept has, in any case, only pragmatic validity, where single major factors can be identified, since there are no real events or conditions with single "causes.")

In view of our continued profound ignorance of causes, and even of the basic dimensions of the problem, it becomes necessary to encourage many different approaches, for the solution may come from what appears to be an unlikely direction. Thus, although arguments may be marshalled against the view that psychopathology is exclusively defined by its use as a method of social control and repression, it is impossible at this time to dismiss such a view out of hand. As another example, the fact that Alcoholics Anonymous is at least as effective as our more traditionally derived therapies operates as an encouragement to remain open and even humble in our assumptions. In the absence of any fundamental answers, we are necessarily unsure about how to formulate the questions.

The study of psychopathology makes forceful demands for the incorporation of many sets of variables. Although our demands for comprehension—and action—will always ultimately require ad hoc integrations, it seems reasonable to expect that explicit combinations of different scientific domains can take us much further than we have come so far.

Fully developed theory approximates a closed system with explicit and well-defined loopholes. Theories of psychopathology are in a much more formative stage and generally involve quite frankly ad hoc approaches, with differing degrees of rigor in the setting of boundaries of relevance, mechanisms of connection among aspects of the phenomena, and so on. For some aspects of psychopathology, recent accomplishments in related disciplines have stimulated work across the boundaries of previously separate fields, aimed at formulating multiple-systems analyses.

The appropriate function of a volume such as this one should not be limited to informing readers of the current thinking and findings in a range of fields relevant to psychopathology. It should also involve a renewed raising of the issue of developing valid methods of conjoining these different disciplines.

In this context, something should be said about the contents of this volume. The orientation of the chapters is, by and large, theoretical and methodological. They range from the explication of potentially applicable models and the convergence of disciplines on psychopathology to proposed solutions of highly specific substantive problems in psychopathology. The first four parts of the volume proceed from higher to lower levels of organization, from the superorganic to the molecular: Part One on the external milieu, dealing with the impact and the role of social variables in psychopathology; Parts Two and Three on different levels of psychological organization; and Part Four on biochemical and physiological issues involved in the internal milieu. Part Five deals with problems of psychiatric classification which arise in relation both to research and to practice in psychopathology. The subject matter of the final section, Part Six, is mathematical description. Mathematics does not itself deal with phenomena, but rather is concerned with (approximately) closed systems some of which are applicable to analyzing the open systems that phenomena involve. The mathematical portion of this book undertakes the application of some of these closed-system formulations to open-system phenomena. The emphasis is on tools of research and on conceptual approaches of high generality.

PART ONE

The External Milieu

One of the more frustrating and intriguing problems in psychopathology is how to interpret the role of sociocultural variation among human populations, whether one is considering diagnosis, etiology, epidemiology, or therapy, and whether one is collecting or utilizing incidence figures, subjective accounts, behavioral observations, or laboratory tests. On the basis of the current status of both concepts and evidence, any or none—of a number of positions with widely different implications is defensible. These positions range from the view that mental illness is essentially independent of cultural differences, which affect the illness not at all and its manifesta tions in only trivial ways, to the polar view that "mental illness" is only incidentally "mental" and not at all "illness," but is rather a complex social response to certain culturally produced normative variants. Although neither extreme position can claim many proponents, the implicit assumptions underlying work in every area of psychopathology reflect both extremes as well as a very large variety of intermediate positions.

Probably the most commonly voiced position at present is that in most forms of psychopathology there are biological factors, which, in combination with cultural ones, produce the conditions leading to a psychiatric disorder in a given individual. The biological variables may be viewed as antecedent (e.g., genetic) or consequent (e.g., psychosomatic); the cultural variables may also be viewed as antecedent (as in culture-stress theories or the double-bind hypothesis) or consequent (as in some theories of social drift); or a more complex position involving interaction between factors of both kinds may be held. Chapter 3 by Jarvik and Chadwick and Chapter 2 by Murphy represent quite divergent approaches to studying the role of culture in psychopathology, although they have in common the use of relatively long time spans and a focus on specific syndromes. Jarvik and Chadwick elaborate a theory of interaction between a genetic factor and a culturally determined selective advantage for a paranoid syndrome; Murphy traces the detailed history of changes in two "exotic" syndromes, in relation

9

to major sociocultural changes in the societies where they occur. Both analyses are of interest not only in terms of the specifics they deal with, but also as possible methodological paradigms for other forms of psychiatric disorder. Jarvik and Chadwick take a genetic view of etiology, though culturally modified; Murphy takes a sociocultural view.

Whatever the views may be on etiology, there tends to be wide agreement that cultural norms affect psychopathological behavior and society's responses to it, and therefore the who, when, and what with which we are presented for understanding and treatment. It is interesting that one fundamental question of definition is being raised strongly in the current period. There has certainly been concern for many years over mutually exclusive definitions of the domains of sickness/health, as opposed to some pair such as approval/disapproval, expected/unexpected, normative/deviant, or conformist/nonconformist. This concern has, however, been directed largely to methodological issues, primarily involved with the "proper" identification of cases. These methodological issues have not been resolved, but more recently the issue has been explicitly broadened to question the relevance of the medical model to phenomena that are part of the domain of social behavior. That the medical model is totally irrelevant is not a commonly held position, but the view is no longer uncommon that the medical definition may be misleading to theory, research, and treatment. This is not the place to attempt an analysis of the social forces that have contributed to this change. One might speculate, however, that extensive or rapid changes in the world's societies in the past few decades, leading to publicly expressed insecurity over the special rightness of *any* society's set of social norms, bring with them uncertainty over the special wrongness of behavior not in accord with those norms, whether that behavior has previously been judged immoral, criminal, peculiar, or psychopathological. For example, the widespread use of illegal drugs among quite ordinary people has intensified the uncertainty about what is or should be meant by "pathology."

Part One contains no direct defense or dismissal of the medical model in psychopathology, but clarification of the underlying basic issues is, in different ways, the major concern of the chapters by Dohrenwend and Dohrenwend, Bennett and Sanchez, and Hammer. All three chapters share the assumption that our knowledge of what it is we are trying to study is chaotic and suffers even more from conceptual confusion than from inadequate data. In Chapter 4 Bennett and Sanchez deal with the confounding of the concepts of illness and deviance, which have been used as though they were interchangeable. They suggest methods for their differentiation and present some relevant evidence. In Chapter 5 Hammer proposes the use of less global and more precisely defined variables within the sociocultural domain in order to develop tools for dealing with the imprecision of our concepts in psychopathology. She illustrates the approach with variables defined by the structure of small social networks. The Dohrenwends set forth in Chapter 1 a multiphased methodology for empirically based clarification of our concepts, by working back and forth between information regarding the community's norms and values and the characteristics of those the community in fact "selects" as especially suited or especially unsuited for life by those standards.

Those familiar with the history of work in this area will be aware of an important shift in emphasis reflected in these five chapters. Strong forms of causal theorizing have given way to more modest—and methodologically more careful—analyses, directed to clarification of some of the complexities of psychopathology rather than to demonstration of the "key" to it. Current work tends to deal with particular syndromes rather than psychopathology as a whole, or with specified social or cultural conditions rather than more global labels (like "primitive" and "advanced" societies), or with empirical rather than a priori approaches to defining those syndromes or conditions. Strong causal theories are not rejected as a goal, but there is an implicit recognition that the foundations for valid formulation of such theory are not yet present, and a hope that deliberately more limited approaches can build the necessary foundations.

Although none of these chapters makes any generalizations about the ways in which the study of social variables in psychopathology is revealing about society as well as pathology, each of the chapters has clear implications in this direction: Jarvik and Chadwick on the social characteristics that might make a given genetic type adaptive; Murphy on the social conditions associated with historical changes in particular syndromes; the Dohrenwends on the relationship between norms of optimal performance and of pathology; Bennett and Sanchez on the social dimensions of conformity and deviance; Hammer on the structural characteristics of small social networks and some of the ways in which these may break down. Claims made in an earlier period about the value of studying society through individual pathology seem to have been too large in scope to have been amenable to serious testing. Perhaps we are now in a period in which more limited propositions of this kind can be examined profitably for both fields of study.

CHAPTER 1

An Approach to the Problem of Valid Comparison of Psychiatric Disorders in Contrasting Class and Ethnic Groups from the General Population

BARBARA SNELL DOHRENWEND and BRUCE P. DOHRENWEND

Although studies of the epidemiology of psychiatric disorder have been conducted in many different parts of the world, they have seldom been designed to collect comparable data or to use standardized techniques for combining the data into assessments of disorder. The result has been that differences in the findings reported by such studies are difficult to interpret.

A recent exception to this rule is the study by Joseph Zubin and his colleagues of first admissions to mental hospitals in the United States and the United Kingdom. In this pioneering project, the investigators developed clinical interviewing instruments aimed at providing standard data in the two national settings. Moreover, they used common criteria for making reliable diagnostic judgments from these data. With these standardized diagnoses as a basis for making cross-national comparisons Zubin and his colleagues are investigating the possibility that the populations of the United States and the United Kingdom differ in the relative proportions of persons with schizophrenia as opposed to manic-depressive psychosis, a difference that would have important implications for the etiology of these disorders.

As Zubin (1969, pp. 14–15) pointed out, however, he and his colleagues have not yet tackled two problems that are raised by comparisons of groups with different backgrounds, traditions, and values. The first of these problems is how to assess disorder independently of treatment status in the populations with which they have been concerned. Since it seems beyond doubt that there are selective factors with regard to treatment other than the presence and severity of disorder (e.g., Dohrenwend & Dohrenwend, 1969, pp. 5–7; Zubin, 1969, p. 14), indicators of untreated as well as

13

treated disorder will be needed either to study factors that affect the selective use of treatment facilities or to eliminate these factors in order to determine whether there are true differences in rates of disorder in different groups. Moreover, in developing these indicators the second unsolved problem raised by Zubin must also be tackled—the problem of the validity of the indicators of untreated disorder.

The research in which we are engaged is also focused on making psychiatric comparisons across groups, but instead of cross-national comparisons we are concerned with comparing persons occupying different social class and ethnic statuses (Dohrenwend & Dohrenwend, 1969). Although this focus is somewhat different from that of Zubin and his coworkers, we share their interest in investigating etiology; moreover, our objectives and theirs converge upon a common obstacle to such investigation—the problem of how to develop measures of psychiatric disorders that are independent of treatment status and that can be used to make valid comparisons between groups that differ in background, traditions, and values.

LEGACY OF PROBLEMS AND POSSIBILITIES FROM EXISTING "TRUE" PREVALENCE STUDIES

In the last 50 years, at least 35 different investigators or teams of investigators have attempted to count not only treated but also untreated cases of psychiatric disorder in 44 community studies. Table 1 gives some indication

Table 1. Medians and Ranges of Percentages of Psychiatric Disorder According to Geopolitical Area and Rural versus Urban Study Site[a]

Site		Area			
		North America	Northern Europe	Asia	Africa
Rural	Median	18.0	10.4	1.1	—
	Range	1.7–64.0	1.1–28.6	0.8–54.0	40.0
	Number of studies	(7)	(14)	(9)	(1)
Urban	Median	7.2	15.6	2.4	—
	Range	1.8–32.0	1.0–33.0	1.1–3.0	11.8–45.0
	Number of studies	(6)	(5)	(3)	(2)

[a] These medians and ranges are based on data presented in Dohrenwend and Dohrenwend, *Social Status and Psychological Disorder*, New York: Wiley, 1969. The number of rates on which these figures are based is 47, which is 3 more than the actual number of studies because separate rates for rural and urban sites were extracted from the African study by Leighton and his colleagues and from the study of three sites on Taiwan by Lin.

of the magnitude of the problem of cross-cultural comparison. As this table shows, the rates of disorder ranged from less than 1% to 64%. Moreover, the large variability within geopolitical areas and within rural and urban study sites suggests that the measures used by different investigators were not reliable. This suggestion is reinforced by the results in Table 2, showing that studies published in 1950 or later tend to report higher rates of

Table 2. Medians and Ranges of Percentages of Psychiatric Disorder for Studies Published before 1950 and for Studies Published in 1950 or Thereafter[a]

	Date of Publication	
	Before 1950	1950 or Later
Median	2.1	15.6
Range	0.8–9.0	0.8–64.0
Number of studies	(16)	(28)

[a] These medians and ranges are based on data presented in Dohrenwend and Dohrenwend, *Social Status and Psychological Disorder*, New York: Wiley, 1969.

psychiatric disorder than earlier studies. This increase probably in part reflects the expansion of nomenclatures after the experience with psychiatric screening during World War II.

The unreliability of measurement is not surprising when one considers that, for most psychiatric disorders, etiology is unknown. There has been, therefore, room for a considerable degree of anarchy where definition and measurement are concerned. Thus, even though Zubin and his colleagues have confined their study to hospital first admissions for schizophrenia and manic-depressive psychosis, they have found a considerable portion of the apparent variation in rates between the United States and the United Kingdom to be a function of differences in the diagnostic concepts and, probably, in the related data collection procedures traditionally used in the two countries (Cooper, Kendell, Gurland, Sartorius, & Farkas, 1969).

Furthermore, studies that are not limited to treated cases, especially hospitalized cases, are vulnerable to sources of unreliability of measurement that are controlled in hospital studies. The fact that a person is in a mental hospital, for example, indicates that he is not functioning in customary social roles: his disability is self-defined by his patient status. Moreover, the clinician diagnosing a patient has a "presenting problem" with which to start, so that the question he must answer is not *whether* something is wrong, but rather *what* is wrong. The diagnostic result of this analysis, furthermore, can be changed on the basis of repeated observations and interviews over a course of treatment.

By contrast, the investigator of disorder in general populations must work without the aids to diagnosis inherent in the clinical setting. He cannot assume that psychiatric symptoms of disturbance of cognition, affect, and volition (we will call them "mental status symptoms") are positively related to disability in role functioning in the same way that they have been found to be in hospital patients (Ginzberg, Anderson, Ginsburg, & Herma, 1959, pp. 167-193). It becomes necessary, therefore, to develop measures of ability and disability in role functioning in community settings to provide information about impairment comparable to that which is self evident for hospital patients. So far, this has not been done in epidemiological studies of general populations (e.g., Leighton, Harding, Macklin, Macmillan, & Leighton, 1963, p. 53; Srole, Langner, Michael, Opler, & Rennie, 1962, p. 57).

Another major problem with the results from the "true" prevalence studies, as compared with studies of psychiatric patients, is that the large majority of the field studies were done at only one point in time. Since most of these studies provide little information about the duration of symptomatology and its persistence or fluctuation with changes in situational context, we have no way of knowing the extent to which the psychiatric judgments were based on symptomatology that represented situationally specific and potentially transient responses to stressful events, as opposed to symptomatology that shows the intractable, persistent, or recurrent quality characteristically reported for psychiatric patients (Dohrenwend & Dohrenwend, 1969, pp. 106–109).

On the positive side, we have some consistent findings from the field studies that are all the more impressive in that they appear despite the unreliable measurements employed (Dohrenwend & Dohrenwend, 1969, Ch. 2). Thus, in 20 out of 25 of the studies that reported data on social class, the highest rate of psychiatric disorder occurred in the lowest class; moreover, this finding appears to hold for two broad subtypes, schizophrenia and personality disorder. By contrast, neurosis is not consistently related to class, and no study reports manic-depressive psychosis as being most frequent in the lowest class. Furthermore, neurosis is consistently reported as more prevalent among women than among men, whereas just the opposite is true for personality disorder. It would seem, then, that certain broad nosological types of symptoms are being meaningfully grouped together in these studies since they show consistent relationships with important social variables.

Ideally, one or more of the 44 community studies described above would provide us with valid measures of psychiatric disorder. Unfortunately, however, scant evidence for the validity of the measure used is provided by any of these studies. Analysis of the difficulties they faced indicates that major reliance must be placed on construct validation if the problem is to be solved (Dohrenwend & Dohrenwend, 1969, pp. 100–106). Therefore, we will describe an approach to developing valid psychiatric comparisons across groups which focuses on construct validity.

AN APPROACH TO THE PROBLEM OF VALID GROUP COMPARISON*

We will use as starting points for our analysis hypothetical samples of individuals from psychiatric patient and community populations selected in such a way that each patient and each community population sample is homogeneous as to class and ethnic composition. Furthermore, the patient and community population samples will be matched with respect to class and ethnic groups.

After the appropriate groups have been selected, our next hypothetical step is to administer the following items or measures to each:

1. Items judged by clinicians to describe the main types of mental status symptoms that are characteristic of disorders having no known organic bases.
2. Items designed to measure effectiveness and impairment in the performance of major life roles.
3. Indices of the incidence over a period of time of stressful events, such as a death in the family, birth of first child, serious injury to the breadwinner, or promotion, intervening between one or more premeasures and a postmeasure of the types described in 1 and 2 above.

Let us see, then, how these data would be used in our approach to the

---

* If different languages are spoken by the groups to be compared, the instruments to be used in data collection must be translated. Illustrations of the problems likely to be encountered and possible means of solving them are provided in discussions by Anderson (1967), by Jacobson (1954), and by Murphy (1969), among others. Even if the same language is spoken, problems may arise from different styles of communication, particularly in the case of cross-class comparisons. For example, there is some evidence that lower class respondents provide less valid answers than middle class respondents to open interview questions (Strauss & Schatzman, 1960) and to leading questions on controversial topics (Dohrenwend, 1970). The procedures for validation of measures that we will describe assume that the instruments used in data collection have been constructed so as to be linguistically equivalent and equally effective as modes of communication for all status groups in the study. These procedures also assume the existence of reliable diagnoses made on the basis of careful and detailed observation of the relevant groups of psychiatric patients over time. The work of Zubin and his colleagues provides some assurance that such diagnoses are possible.

problem of constructing indices with which to make valid comparisons of psychiatric disorder across status groups.

The Problem of Identity Versus Equivalence in the Content of Scales across Groups

In studies of non-Western, particularly preliterate societies, cultural anthropologists have found behavioral expressions of psychological disturbance not found in Western societies (e.g., Kennedy, 1961, pp. 411–413). Striking examples are the phenomena among Malays of *running amok* and *latah,* discussed by Murphy in Chapter 2 of this book. Such observations have alerted investigators of psychiatric disorder to look for the possibility of culturally determined differences in symptomatic behavior even where a lesser degree of cultural contrast exists. Thus, for example, in comparing hospitalized male schizophrenic patients from Italian-American and Irish-American backgrounds, Opler (1967, p. 295) found, among other differences, that none of the 27 Irish patients was an overt homosexual but 74% of the 27 Italian patients exhibited this trait; also, whereas 85% of the Irish had fixed delusions, only 37% of the Italians showed this symptom. Even more extensive contrast was found in a study of medical inpatients from three social classes who had been classified, by a combination of actuarial and clinical criteria, as depressed. Of 36 symptoms selected for study because of their association with this condition in the literature, the authors reported that "none . . . discriminated the depressed in all three classes, and only nine did so in two of the three classes [Schwab, Bialow, Brown, Holzer, & Stevenson, 1967, p. 541]." Thus, these studies clearly suggest that, in constructing nosological scales to be used in making comparisons across status groups, the researcher must be prepared to decide what to do about traits that are unique to one group or traits that are rare in one group and relatively common in another.

The same kind of problem may arise in scales designed to compare role performance across status groups. Thus, for example, in the work role self-employment is a status found largely in the middle rather than in the lower class. The problem is also illustrated in the area of marital role performance by Rainwater's finding that, whereas 88% of a sample of American upper middle class couples reported predominantly joint activities, 72% of American lower-lower class couples reported that they carried out most of their activities apart from the spouse (1965, p. 32). Differences between cultures as well as between social classes might also be expected in these and other types of role performance.

Given this problem, when the aim is to construct scales that will be valid across different status groups the investigator must take care that the pool of mental status or role performance items identified by judges as candidates for scales include those that may be appropriate to only one group as well as those that seem to be appropriate to both. Thus, for example, an investigator interested in building an index of depression to compare lower class and middle class subjects would include in the pool items on "hopelessness," "self-accusation," and "palpitations," all of which Schwab and his colleagues (1967) found to be unique to lower class depressives.

After items had been selected in this way, the scale structure of the pool of items for a given index would be tested within each status group. For symptom items this analysis would be performed on the responses of a diagnostically heterogeneous sample of psychiatric patients, and for role performance items on a sample from the general population. For any pair of status groups, A and B, this test could yield four types of items for a given scale:

1. Items that scale in both groups.
2. Items that scale only in group A.
3. Items that scale only in group B.
4. Items that scale in neither group A nor group B.

The last of these types, items that scale in neither group, would be discarded without debate. The investigator then faces the problem of what to do with items that scale in only one of the two status groups. Specifically, the question is whether scales that are not made up of identical items can be comparable and, if so, what the basis is for establishing their comparability. Both parts of this question have generated controversy.

Positions on the first part of the question range from the assumption that operational identity is necessary to ensure equivalence of measures in different settings (e.g., Duijker & Rokkan, 1954, p. 20) to the argument that use of an identical test across status groups or cultures almost always imposes "built-in criteria from the donor culture that prescribe the content of the test with reference to its own value system and at the same time grade individuals according to such criteria [Irvine, 1969, p. 30]." Since the aim is to subject the measures to construct validation, however, the question of whether conceptual identity across status groups is maximized by operational identity, by cultural relativity, or by some combination of the two becomes an empirical one. That is, identical and nonidentical sets of items for each construct will be tested to determine which yields comparable results across status groups in relationships posited to hold for that construct.

To do this, however, the investigator must decide what kinds of nonidentical items are worth testing. One position is that comparability across status groups will be achieved if items unique to one group are substituted for items whose relations to others change in the new group context (e.g.,

Gordon, 1968). Thus, for example, if a scale was constructed in one group and the position of an item in a Guttman scale, or its correlation with other items in an additive scale, changed markedly in another group, the objective would be to find for use in the second group a substitute that occupied the same Guttman scale position or yielded approximately the same correlation in the second group as the altered item did in the first group. Thus scales designed for comparisons across groups would differ in content to some extent from group to group but would be similar in structure for all groups.

Another suggestion is that the investigator should include scale items that describe the full range of the construct as it exists in one group even if that range does not exist in another group. At its simplest, this idea implies something analogous to using a longer stick in order to be able to measure height in a relatively tall population as well as in a relatively short population (e.g., Berrien, 1968). In more general terms, which do not involve the assumption of a unidimensional measure, the suggestion is that a measure to be used across groups should include attributes that fall within the domain of the construct in the second group even if they are not in this domain in the first group (e.g., Inkeles & Smith, 1970; Przeworski & Teune, 1966–67). Thus, for example, an index of depression designed to compare lower and middle class subjects might include "hopelessness" as a lower class item even though it was unrelated to other items indicative of depression in the middle class group (Schwab et al., 1967). Similarly, a scale of work role performance to be used in comparing middle and lower class groups might include "regularly self-employed" even if this status was irrelevant to the work performance of the lower class. According to some critics, however, the constructual meaning of these items in the status groups in which they were not relevant would be in doubt (e.g., Gordon, 1968).

The question, then, is whether the investigator should retain nonidentical items for later construct validation only when they are substitutes for items that do not scale in one group, or should include as well items that extend the domain of the scale in one group. Since the aim is to resolve the issue of comparability in the course of construct validation, there seems to be no reason to eliminate items on the basis of *a priori* cautions about the nature of comparability across groups. The investigator could, then, finish this stage of scale construction in two status groups with three types of scales for each construct:

1. A scale composed of items that are identical in both groups.
2. A scale composed of identical items plus substitutes in one group for items whose scale characteristics are not stable across groups.
3. A scale composed of identical items, substitute items as needed, and

items that extend the scale to include attributes relevant to the construct in only one or the other group.

Some Validation Procedures

Table 3 outlines the steps we would follow in our approach to construct validation of measures of psychiatric disorders for comparisons across two status groups. In the first step we would test the ability of each of the previously constructed scales to discriminate among psychiatric patients of different diagnostic types within each of the status groups. The aim at this point would be to eliminate scales that were, by this criterion, appropriate to only one group.

We expect that this operation would tend to favor nonidentical scales since such scales include items especially adapted to each group; conversely, this procedure would tend to eliminate scales limited to items that scaled in the same way in both groups. For this reason we suggest that the criterion for unsatisfactory discrimination be lenient rather than strict in order to retain at this point as many identical as well as equivalent scales as possible for further testing.

The Choice of Identical Versus Equivalent Cutting Points for Identification of a Particular Type of Disorder Among Patients from the Two Status Groups

Assuming that we now have a set of nosological scales that discriminate appropriately among psychiatric patients in both status groups, we are ready for the next question: will these scales provide valid comparisons across patients from the two status groups? This question is most obviously raised when a scale gives quantitatively different results for patients from the two status groups.

For example, we might find that lower class Puerto Rican patients score higher on a scale of depression than lower class black patients. The problem is whether a difference of this sort indicates a corresponding difference in the amount of psychopathology in the members of the two groups of patients (cf. Dohrenwend & Dohrenwend, 1969, pp. 84–86). It seems reasonable to assume that, if both black patients and Puerto Rican patients have been selected in equal proportions from the same diagnostic types and the same outpatient and inpatient facilities, there should be little difference in the general levels of disability in the two patient groups. The difference in the scale scores of the black and Puerto Rican patients would be hypothesized to be due, therefore, to difference in factors other than severity of psychopathology in the two groups. The question of what other factors might account for the difference leads us to undertake as the next

Table 3. Steps in an Approach to Construct Validation of Measures of Psychiatric Disorders in Two Status Groups

Line	Test	Possible Observations for a Given Scale	Decisions
1	Ability of nosological scales to discriminate within each status group among types of diagnosed psychiatric patients	Satisfactory discrimination in both status groups	Retain scale (continue to line 2)
		Unsatisfactory discrimination in either status group	Discard scale
2	Re evaluative norms concerning attitudes and behaviors described in items in nosological scales: differences in these norms in community samples from two status groups correspond to difference, if any, in scale scores between patients of appropriate diagnostic type from the two status groups	Hypothesis confirmed with no intergroup difference in norms or scale scores	Nosological scale scores of the same magnitude are equivalent in patients from the two status groups (continue to line 3)
		Hypothesis confirmed with intergroup difference in norms corresponding to intergroup difference in scale scores	Adjust scoring of the nosological scale in one patient group to compensate for the intergroup difference in evaluation of the scale items (continue to line 3)
		Hypothesis not confirmed	Re-examine or discard scale

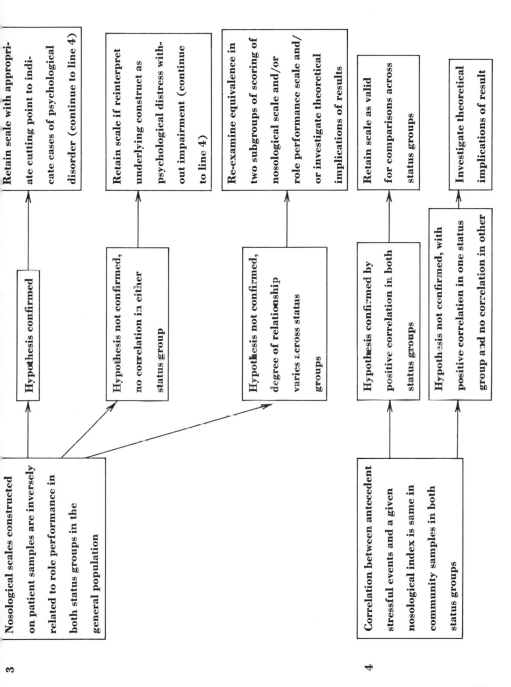

3

4

step an analysis of the relation between scale scores and norms regarding the items in the scales.

To continue our example, suppose that we ask lower class Puerto Rican and black samples from the general population for social desirability ratings of the attitudes described in the "depression" items and find that they are more strongly condemned by the blacks than by the Puerto Ricans. The implication is that the higher scores among the Puerto Rican patients may indicate a higher rate of adoption or admission of attitudes that are viewed tolerantly by the Puerto Ricans in the larger community. As noted on line 2 in Table 3, however, we would not confine this analysis to nosological scales on which the level of scores differed in the two status groups but would include as well scales that yielded similar distribution of scores in the two status groups to see how evaluations of the scale items related to scale scores in the two groups in these cases as well.

The outcome of this analysis would lead us to adjust the scale scores in one group, where necessary, to compensate for an intergroup difference in evaluations of the items in a scale. Where these evaluations were different, we would use the correlation between the difference in evaluative ratings of items and the difference in frequency of positive responses to these items by patients from the two status groups as a basis for determining weights with which to equate scale scores in the two groups. Thus, at one extreme, if the intergroup difference in community sample evaluation and the intergroup difference in patient response rates were perfectly correlated, we would standardize the scale scores so that the distribution in the two status groups would be the same, on the hypothesis that there is no true difference in the rate of psychopathology of the type indicated by this scale in patients from the two status groups. By contrast, if the correlation is zero, we would assume that to the extent that there is a difference in scale scores of patients in the two groups this difference indicates a true difference in rate of the type of psychopathology indicated by the scale. In such a case, we would want to re-examine our assumption that levels of disability were similar for this disorder in the two patient groups by comparing them in terms of more detailed data on role functioning than is self evident in their patient status.

In summary, then, this step in the construction of measures for valid comparisons across groups reduces differences in nosological scale scores of patients from the two status groups to the extent that such scores are a function of differences in relevant evaluative norms. Note, however, that this type of adjustment is not made unless the patient groups were selected so as to equate their levels of disability.

Testing the Constructual Meaning of the Nosological Indices in the Two Status Groups from the General Population

So far, any interpretation of scores on the nosological scales as indicative of psychiatric disorder in community populations would be based on indirect evidence. It would be based, first, in terms of discriminant validity, on analogy with psychiatric patients. Second, it would rest on the hypothesis that, where differences between groups in nosological scale scores are correlated with evaluative group norms, the differences in scores do not indicate differences in rates of disorder or, conversely, that items that yield similar levels of negative evaluation across groups indicate true similarities or differences in disorder. Our next step tests one implication of this hypothesis in status groups from the general population.

As we indicated earlier, there is *prime facie* evidence in the case of psychiatric patients that their social functioning is to some degree impaired. Therefore, insofar as the nosological scales are to indicate in the general population psychiatric conditions similar to those found in patients, high scores on these scales should be associated with impaired role performances. The next step in our approach to construct validation of measures of psychological disorder for use in community populations is, therefore, to test the relationship between our nosological indices and role performance scale scores in a sample from the community population within each status group.

Before performing this test, however, we will have to assure ourselves of the validity of the *role performance* scales across status groups. The steps we suggest for this purpose are outlined in Table 4. We would first test the ability of the scales to discriminate within each status group among types of respondents selected for variation in social effectiveness. For this purpose we would use three types of respondents: psychiatric patients, since the patient status is evidence of some degree of impairment in social functioning; community leaders, since eminence in the community implies that the person is performing unusually well in terms of at least some of the criteria for success in his social milieu; and a community sample, which would be expected to fall between the highly effective leaders and the impaired psychiatric patients in level of performance in various life roles. We would retain only role performance scales that discriminated among the three types of respondents in the expected way in each status group.

This evidence for the validity of a given scale within each group would not necessarily imply, however, that quantitative comparisons across groups would be valid. The possibility that a comparison is not valid is most clearly suggested when a scale that discriminates adequately within each group yields quantitatively different results in the two status groups. Such a differ-

Table 4. Steps in an Approach to Construct Validation of Measures of Role Performance in Two Heterogeneous Groups

Line	Test	Possible Observations for a Given Scale	Decisions
1	Ability of role performance scales to discriminate within each status group among types selected for different levels of social effectiveness: psychiatric patients, community sample, community leaders	Satisfactory discrimination in both status groups	Retain scale (continue to line 2)
		Unsatisfactory discrimination in either status group	Discard scale
2	Norms in status groups concerning expected role performance are correlated with status group differences or similarities in levels of role performance scores in community samples	Hypothesis confirmed when same types of respondents (e.g., leaders) have equal scale scores in two status groups	Use same cutting point in both status groups to distinguish effective from impaired role performance
		Hypothesis confirmed when same types of respondents (e.g., leaders) have unequal scale scores in two status groups	Use different cutting points in two status groups to distinguish effective from impaired role performance as indicated by data
		Hypothesis not confirmed	Discard scale

ence is illustrated by a cross-class comparison of work performance on a nine-point scale showing that, whereas 92% of middle class respondents scored 1 or 2, indicating full-time work for a specified period, only 77% of lower class respondents scored that high (Myers & Bean, 1968, p. 225). The problem is to determine whether or not this kind of discrepancy indicates a difference in social effectiveness in the individual members of the two groups.

We would resolve this question by testing the hypothesis that group norms concerning expected role performance, or, possibly, in the case of the work role group differences in occupational opportunities, are correlated with the relative level of role performance scores in the two status groups. Thus, if the distribution of scores on a given role scale is the same, the norms concerning expected performance in that role should be the same in the two groups. By contrast, where the distribution of scores differs across groups there should be a corresponding difference in performance expectations. Where differences or similarities in expectations or opportunities across groups do not correspond to differences or similarities in scale score distributions, the scale would be discarded. Among the scales retained, those on which the distribution of scores and, correspondingly, expectations or opportunities differed across groups would require adjustment of the cutting points used to distinguish effective from impaired role performance to compensate for the differences in expectations or opportunities. Thus, for example, on the basis of Rainwater's (1965) finding concerning class differences in the proportion of activities shared by married couples, and given a corresponding class difference in the frequency of positive responses to this item, one might decide that absence of such activities should be scored to indicate marital role impairment in the middle class but not in the lower class.

Assuming that the operations described in Table 4 yield a set of role performance indices that provides valid comparisons across status groups, we would be ready to test the hypothesis, presented in line 3 of Table 3, that a given nosological scale score is correlated with effectiveness of role performance in community samples to the same degree in both status groups. The finding of inverse correlations of the same order in both groups would support the interpretation that a given nosological index was in this respect constructually equivalent when applied to psychiatric patients and to a general community population.

By contrast, the finding of no correlation between the presence of symptoms and impaired role performance would clearly indicate a difference in the implications of the symptoms in the community population as against patients. A scale yielding this negative result nevertheless might be retained if the investigator wanted to broaden his study of the community population to include the construct of nonimpairing psychological distress.

Another set of possibilities arises if the outcomes are inconsistent across status groups. This would be the case either when an inverse correlation is present in one group but not in the other or when there is a marked difference in the magnitude of the inverse correlation in the two groups. In such instances of inconsistent results, the scoring of the nosological scales might be re-examined, or the equivalence of the performance scales across status groups might be reconsidered.

Although it seems likely that correlations between performance scale scores and nosological scale scores would vary across groups for one reason or another in some cases, let us assume that some nosological scales yield the same correlations with role performance scores in both status groups. Where significant inverse correlations had been demonstrated, we would set cutting points on the nosological scales to discriminate respondents showing impaired role performance from respondents showing effective role performance, labeling each of the former as a case of psychiatric disorder of the type indicated by the nosological scale. Where the nosological scale was not correlated with role performance scores, no discontinuity is implied, so we would use the continuum of scale scores as indicators of the level of nonimpairing psychological distress.

With these indices of psychiatric disorder or distress we would then proceed, as indicated on line 4 of Table 3, to test the hypothesis that the relation between antecedent stressful events and a given nosological index is the same in both status groups. That is, we would separate types of disorder or distress whose onset is related to the respondent's immediate situation in both status groups from types that appear to be independent of the respondent's immediate situation in both groups.

This step follows from our particular theoretical interest in the relation of symptomatology to stressful situations (Dohrenwend & Dohrenwend, 1969, Ch. 8). Investigators with different theoretical foci might choose at this point to study other relationships—for example, the factor structure of symptom patterns (Benfari & Leighton, 1970), or the relation of nosological indices to family history (e.g., Robins & Guze, 1970) or to premorbid social competence (Phillips & Draguns, 1969), or their relation to variables such as respondent sex which have shown consistent relationships to certain types of symptomatology (Dohrenwend & Dohrenwend, 1969, pp. 26–27). Moreover, any number of relationships can be tested: in fact, the more the better. Thus the last step in our approach differs from earlier ones in that we believe the specific steps we described earlier to be essential for the development of measures that will yield valid comparisons across status groups no matter what the theoretical orientation of the investigation. By contrast, we assume that the substance of the last step would be guided by the theoretical premises of the study for which the measures were being developed. The only principle necessarily common to all studies in this last step would be that, whatever relationships between nosological indices and other factors are posited, they must be found to hold in both status groups or, possibly, in neither, but not to vary across groups if the validity of the measure across groups is to be argued.

SOME SERENDIPITOUS POSSIBILITIES OF PROBABLE LIMITATIONS IN THE PROPOSED APPROACH

Optimistically, we think it likely that, perhaps after some backing and filling, the approach we have suggested would yield some indices of nosological types that would be consistent across status groups with respect both to the presence or absence of impaired role performance and to dependence on, or independence of, antecedent stressful events. These measures would permit not only direct comparison of rates in the status groups involved but also comparison, for example, of the development over time in two status groups of disorders with different relationships to antecedent stressful events (Dohrenwend & Dohrenwend, 1969, Ch. 8). They could also be used to make comparisons across status groups of subgroups that are homogeneous with respect, for example, to age or sex.

Along with some success in measurement construction, however, it is likely that there would be a number of negative findings concerning the similarities of the two status groups at each stage of development of the measures. We might find, for example, that a particular set of symptoms was associated with impairment in role performance in one group but not in the other, or that symptoms related to antecedent events in one group appeared to develop independently of such events in the other group. For example, Noyes and Kolb (1963, p. 456) speak of "three day psychoses" shown by soldiers in combat, and note that these symptoms are unlikely to have the same relation to disability as the same symptoms reported by chronic schizophrenics. Similarly, it is possible that some symptomatology reported by persons in certain community groups, for instance, the lower class, is also situationally specific and mimics nosological types without having the same persistent quality or implications for disability. Such findings, although raising obstacles to valid comparisons across groups, would also, we believe, provide challenges to our conceptualizations that would, in the long run, enhance our understanding of the etiology of psychiatric disorder.

ACKNOWLEDGMENTS

This work was supported in part by Research Grant MH10328 and by Research Scientist Award K5 MH14663 from the National Institute of Mental Health, U. S. Public Health Service.

REFERENCES

Anderson, R. B. S. On the comparability of meaningful stimuli in cross-cultural research. *Sociometry,* 1967, **30,** 124–136.

Benfari, R. C., & Leighton, A. H. Comparison of factor structures in urban New York and rural Nova Scotia population samples: A study in psychiatric epidemiology. In I. I. Kessler & M. L. Levin (Eds.), *The community as an epidemiologic laboratory: A casebook of community studies.* Baltimore: The Johns Hopkins Press, 1970. Pp. 235–250.

Berrien, F. K. Cross-cultural equivalence of personality measures. *Journal of Social Psychology,* 1968, **75,** 3–9.

Cooper, J. E., Kendell, R. E., Gurland, B. J., Sartorius, N., & Farkas, T. Cross-national study of diagnosis of the mental disorders: Some results from the first comparative investigation. Supplement to *The American Journal of Psychiatry,* 1969, **125** (10), 21–29.

Dohrenwend, B. P., & Dohrenwend, B. S. *Social status and psychological disorder: A causal inquiry.* New York: Wiley, 1969.

Dohrenwend, B. S. An experimental study of directive interviewing. *Public Opinion Quarterly,* 1970, **34,** 117–125.

Duijker, H. C. J., & Rokkan, S. A comparative study of teachers' attitudes to international problems and policies. *Journal of Social Issues,* 1954, **10** (4), 8–24.

Ginzberg, E., Anderson, J. K., Ginsburg, S. W., & Herma, J. L. *The lost divisions.* New York: Columbia University Press, 1959.

Gordon, L. V. Comments on "Cross-cultural equivalence of personality measures." *Journal of Social Psychology,* 1968, **75,** 11–19.

Inkeles, A., & Smith, D. H. The fate of personal adjustment in the process of modernization. *International Journal of Comparative Sociology,* 1970, **11,** 81–114.

Irvine, S. H. Factor analysis of African abilities and attainments: Constructs across cultures. *Psychological Bulletin,* 1969, **71,** 20–32.

Jacobson, E. Methods used for producing comparable data in the OCSR seven-nation attitude study. *Journal of Social Issues,* 1954, **10** (4), 40–51.

Kennedy, D. Key issues in the cross-cultural study of mental disorders. In B. Kaplan (Ed.), *Studying personality cross-culturally.* Evanston, Ill.: Row-Peterson, 1961. Pp. 405–425.

Leighton, D. C., Harding, J. S., Macklin, D. B., Macmillan, A. M., & Leighton, A. H. *The character of danger.* New York: Basic Books, 1963.

Murphy, H. B. M. Handling the cultural dimension in psychiatric research. *Social Psychiatry,* 1969, **4,** 11–15.

Myers, J. K., & Bean, L. L. *A decade later: A follow-up of social class and mental illness.* New York: Wiley, 1968.

Noyes, A. P., & Kolb, L. C. *Modern clinical psychiatry.* (6th ed.) Philadelphia: W. B. Saunders, 1963.

Opler, M. K. *Culture and social psychiatry.* New York: Atherton Press, 1967.

Phillips, L., & Draguns, J. Some issues in intercultural research on psychopathology. In W. Caudill & T-Y Lin (Eds.), *Mental health research in Asia and the Pacific.* Honolulu: East-West Center Press, 1969. Pp. 21–32.

Przeworski, A., & Teune, H. Equivalence in cross-national research. *Public Opinion Quarterly,* 1966–67, **30,** 551–568.

Rainwater, L. *Family design: Marital sexuality, family size, and contraception.* Chicago: Aldine, 1965.

Robins, E., & Guze, S. B. Establishment of diagnostic validity in psychiatric illness: Its application to schizophrenia. *American Journal of Psychiatry,* 1970, **126,** 983–987.

Schwab, J. J., Bialow, M., Brown, J. M., Holzer, C. E., & Stevenson, B. E. Sociocultural aspects of depression in medical inpatients. II. Symptomatology and class. *Archives of General Psychiatry,* 1967, **17,** 539–545.

Srole, L., Langner, T. S., Michael, S. T., Opler, M. K., & Rennie, T. A. C. *Mental health in the metropolis: The Midtown Manhattan study.* Vol. I. New York: McGraw-Hill, 1962.

Strauss, A., & Schatzman, L. Cross class interviewing. An analysis of interaction and communicative styles. In R. N. Adams & J. J. Preiss (Eds.), *Human organization research: Field relations and techniques.* Homewood, Ill.: Dorsey Press, 1960. Pp. 205–213.

Zubin, J. Cross-national study of diagnosis of the mental disorders: Methodology and planning. Supplement to *The American Journal of Psychiatry,* 1969, **125** (10), 12–20.

CHAPTER 2

History and the Evolution of Syndromes: The Striking Case of Latah and Amok

H. B. M. MURPHY

Psychiatry has made ample use of epidemiological approaches in its attempts to elucidate the etiology of mental illnesses, as numerous mental health surveys attest. Yet if one views epidemiology as being concerned with the distribution of disease through space and time, as is customary, then it must be admitted that the time dimension remains largely neglected. Change has been well documented for general paresis (Jacobowsky, 1965), but very little use has been made of this finding. Change also appears to have occurred in what we call mania, but despite the considerable theoretical importance of this it seems never to have been properly documented and analyzed. In part we can attribute such neglect to the very large volume of reading that a historic review of some syndromes would demand. There are a number of conditions, however, on which the historic evidence is reasonably limited and clear, so that a search for possible changes in incidence or in symptomatology is within modest reach.

The syndromes of *latah* and *amok,* to which my attention was drawn many years ago, fall into the latter category and have additional attractions for the researcher. Their key features are such as can be reported on as easily by the layman as by the professional; the literature on them is limited but represents many writers, so that the problem of observer bias is small; they are found almost exclusively in a single people or culture, a fact that makes them of special theoretical interest; and it needs only a brief search to reveal that quite definite changes in frequency have occurred.

In this chapter I propose to review these changes and then to discuss how such evidence may throw light on etiology.

AMOK

From the mid-seventeenth century the phrase running amuck has been current in English, and from the mid-nineteenth century or earlier the term amok is to be found in medical textbooks. Since few professional men ever encounter a case, however, the popular usage has contaminated the medical one and the word is employed by many doctors to describe any episode of homicidal mania or panic. Such episodes occur in all parts of the world, and their manifestations, sequels, and etiology are so varied that there is little point in considering them as comprising a single syndrome. In the Malay peninsula and archipelago, however, "amok" has had a much more restricted meaning, and for the nineteenth-century form the term syndrome is quite appropriate. At that time cases usually showed a prodromal period of brooding or depression, no immediate connection existed between the outbreak and any provoking situation, there were usually no paranoid delusions, the subject often had his eyes closed during the fighting, and amnesia always followed the event. It is this syndrome with which I am concerned here.

The term amok (or *amouco* in Portuguese) enters written literature in the mid-sixteenth century when European travelers began providing detailed first-hand descriptions of South Asia. Initially it referred only to groups of exceptionally courageous men who had taken a vow to sacrifice themselves in battle against an enemy, as in the following passage:

"All that night they shaved their heads (this being a superstitious practice of those who despise life, people whom they call in India Amaucos) and betook themselves to their mosque, and there devoted their persons to death . . . and as an earnest of this vow, and an example of this resolution, the Captain ordered a great fire to be made, and cast into it his wife, and a little son he had, and all his household and his goods, in fear lest anything of his should fall into our possession. Others did the like, and then they fell on the Portuguese [De Barros, 1552, quoted by Yule & Burnell, 1886, p. 13]."*

Later, the term came to be applied to an individual form of death-seeking activity, a form that earlier Europeans had found remarkable and that was specific to the Malaysian region,† not being reported from India. In this connection Nicolo Conti wrote, in about 1430:

---

* Yule and Burnell's book of Anglo-Indian words, quaintly entitled *Hobson-Jobson,* has been a most valuable source of information concerning the early usage of "amok," even though not entirely accurate.

† Throughout this paper the term Malaysian will be used geographically to apply to the whole region of the Malay peninsula, the Malay archipelago, and Borneo, while culturally it will apply to all peoples speaking a tongue related to Malay and

"Debtors are made over to their creditors as slaves; and some of these, preferring death to slavery, will with drawn swords rush on, stabbing all whom they fall in with of lesser strength than themselves, until they meet death at the hand of someone more than a match for them. This man the creditors then sue in court for the dead man's debt [Yule & Burnell, 1886, p. 13]."

Almost a century later, Duarte Barbosa wrote similarly, again not using the term amok:

"If anyone of these Jaos [i.e., Javanese] falls sick of any illness he makes a vow to his God that if he restores him his health he will seek out another more honourable death in his service; and after that he is whole he takes a dagger in his hand with certain wavy edges which they have among them of very good quality, and going forth into the places and streets he slays whomsoever he meets, men, women or children letting none go; these men they call *Guanicos* [Barbosa, 1921, p. 177]."

It is clearly this individual pattern of behavior, which by the sixteenth century had lost the name of *guanico* and acquired that of amok, that we are mainly concerned with here, but it must be understood that at this time there was justifiably recognized a connection between the two usages. The individual amoker, like the member of a consecrated band of fighters, initiated his action consciously and deliberately; he avoided attacking his own relatives and friends (unless in a preliminary attempt to save them further suffering); there is no record of him closing his eyes; it is easy to establish the connection between some precipitating event and the episode; he does not seem to have shown signs of mental illness either previously or, if he survived, subsequently; and society often gave approval to the act, with a survivor sometimes having "the fame of being an invincible hero because he so manfully repulsed all those who tried to seize him [Schulzens, 1676, p. 20]." Moreover, the term amok was not applied only to large groups or to individuals; it was applied also to two or three persons acting in consort—for instance, in revenge against a cruel master as in the legend of Hang Tuah (Sheppard, N.D.).

We have no idea of the frequency of the individual form of the condition in these early days. In the seventeenth century Schulzens (1659) reported seeing three amok-runners broken on the wheel during his few months' stay in Batavia; this seems more than earlier writers had observed at first

Javanese. This conflicts with present-day usage, which on the one hand restricts "Malaysian" to the former British territories and on the other extends it to all peoples within these territories, regardless of language and culture; but the convention is convenient for our purposes.

hand, but that is doubtful evidence. What is clearer is that by the seventeenth century the Dutch were coming round to the view that amok might be a form of insanity, perhaps caused by opium. At this time they were paying for the spices which they brought west with opium that they carried east from India (Goldsmith, 1939). Schulzens (1659) was the first to make reference to this, and the idea that some types of amok were caused by the misuse of opium persisted in Dutch writings until the late nineteenth century. The theory was never confirmed, however, and the possibility of a transient connection between opium and amok at that time is doubtful. Later, there was definitely no connection.

The eighteenth century yields almost nothing of interest on the subject, as far as I have been able to trace. In 1764 amok for the first time received separate legal recognition by the Governor General in Batavia (Van der Chijs, 1890), but insanity as a possible cause was not mentioned in the announcement, which appears to be directed mainly at combating the traditional tendency to treat the surviving amok-runner as a hero. When the British returned to the region during the Napoleonic wars, however, they were able to view the condition with fresh eyes, and their descriptions tell us that it had been changing.

For Crawfurd, the first of the nineteenth-century reporters, the characteristic feature of the condition was "the apparently unpremeditated, and always sudden and unexpected [p. 68]" manner in which it broke out (Crawfurd, 1820). He told of a petty chief who had changed sides during a small local war and had made himself very useful to his new associates. As the war was ending and he could anticipate the rewards for his efforts, he suddenly arose from his sleep one night and ran amok within the house, killing or wounding many people, the majority of whom were of his own tribe and had changed sides with him. Crawfurd, on the scene the next morning, could get no indication that the man had been angry, depressed, or sick, or that anyone could have anticipated the attack. In this case, as in the others reported by Crawfurd, a loss of honor had previously occurred and was probably a factor, though there was a quiescent interval between the time at which the loss or insult should have been recognized and the onset of the amok. Opium and physical sickness are not mentioned in these cases, and neither is fighting with the eyes closed, but the amoker's family and intimates are now as exposed to the attack as his enemies.

Some 30 years after Crawfurd's initial description, Oxley, Singapore's first medical officer, the first doctor to make a formal study of amok, and an oft-cited authority on the subject, reported on the condition. His amokers were not defeated warriors or persecuted slaves, as had still largely been true earlier in the century, but ordinary workmen and traders living in the peaceful settlements that the British had by then established. For Oxley the typical history was as follows:

"A man sitting quietly among his friends and relatives will without provocation suddenly start up, weapon in hand, and slay all within his reach. . . . The next day, when interrogated, the answer has inevitably been "the devil entered into me, my eyes were darkened, I did not know what I was about." I have received the same reply on at least twenty occasions. . . . On examination of these monomaniacs I have generally found them to be labouring under some gastric disease or troublesome ulcer, and these fearful ebullitions [i.e., the amok] break out upon some exacerbation of the disorder [Oxley, 1849, p. 532]."

Here we see that two further changes have taken place. The main underlying frustration has become somatic instead of social, disease instead of insult; and the identification with the act is now denied, the primitive impulse being attributed to the devil. Symbolizing this denial, these men now sometimes fought with the eyes closed (*mata gelap*). It is possible that these changes did not apply to the amokers who achieved death during their attack, for Oxley, like the other medical reporters after him, based his impressions on those who survived. This could have induced a distortion in the reported picture similar to that which occurred when people began interpreting consummated suicide on the basis of the characteristics of patients who had made suicidal gestures. What is clear, however, is that in Oxley's time a form of amok appeared which was different both from the earlier type and from that which later was found to be associated with psychosis. Oxley's patients conversed and behaved quite normally the day after the attack (apart from some reactive depression), and although one can infer some earlier mental disturbance in one or two cases the picture is not that of a chronic psychosis. There seems to be little doubt, therefore, that the character of amok had changed, at least among those who had elected to live peacefully by trade and labor in the protected ports rather than by war and piracy in the jungle and the narrow seas.

Since Oxley had had less than 10 years to make these observations, since the Singapore adult male Malay community at this time must have numbered fewer than 5000, and since most amok-runners traditionally did not survive to be interrogated, we have for the first time the means of making a very rough estimate of the incidence of the condition. It could not have been less than 1 per 1000 adult males per annum, and might easily have been twice or thrice that rate. Some 20 years later the famous naturalist Alfred Wallace stated that in the port of Makassar, in Celebes, "there are said to be one or two a month on average, and five, ten or twenty persons

are sometimes killed or wounded at one of them [Wallace, 1898 p. 273]."
If we give Makassar a population of 20,000, which is not unlikely for that
time, the resultant rate is similar, and there is no doubt that this frequency
was causing much alarm. Thus in the non-Europeanized areas a bankrupt
gambler and a resentful slave are known to have been killed for merely
suggesting that they might choose to run amok (Wallace, 1898), while in the
Straits Settlements the chief justice of that time announced in passing
sentence on a case that he found amok "frightfully common [Norris, 1849,
p. 461]." From Java, Swaving (1856) wrote a thesis on the legal aspects
of the condition and also remarked on its frequency. In the mid-nineteenth
century, therefore, we have evidence for a rise in the incidence of the
condition. It is my impression, however, that, at least in the peaceful Straits
Settlements, it was a transient rise that had built up during the 1830s and
1840s and was to fade away shortly thereafter, since before the end of the
century it was recorded that there had been "not more than three real cases
in the last fifteen years for the whole Straits Settlements, despite the marked
increase in the population there [Swettenham, 1900 p. 253]."

In the second half of the nineteenth century, writing on amok increased,
though with much at second hand. If we take only the first-hand reports,
however, a fairly clear picture appears. In areas remote from European
influence the condition is associated with slavery, warfare, or politics and
can still be referred to as "the national and therefore honourable mode of
committing suicide [Wallace, 1898, p. 273]." In rural Java and Sumatra,
where slavery and warfare had nominally been suppressed, there is a fairly
direct connection between amok and some obvious frustration, but now the
frustration tends to arise within the family, there is a latent interval between
the provocation and the outbreak, and some cases fight with their eyes closed
(Metzger, 1887). In neither area are insanity, sickness, or drugs alleged to
be involved. In coastal areas of European settlement, however, somatic
factors (Crawfurd, 1856), opium (Heymann, 1855; Breitenstein, 1899),
and residual insanity (Swaving, 1856; Vogler, 1853) are mentioned as
causes, while social factors tend to be ignored unless the author also had
experience in the interior. Moreover, it is suggested for the first time that
the condition may develop during the course of chronic dementia or a
febrile delirium (Vogler, 1853).

Particularly interesting, though regrettably brief (the paper seems to be
the summary of a doctoral thesis, but I have been unable to locate a copy of
the latter), are Swaving's observations at this time (1856). Some of his
cases are already showing mental disturbance (perhaps schizophrenia
simplex) before the episode; others, though previously considered normal,
report having had vivid dreams involving stab wounds or blood streaming
down their bodies—dreams which led them to wake in great anxiety and

to attack imaginary enemies. Of those who showed no mental derangement before the episodes, some now show it afterwards. As a lawyer Swaving is much concerned by the difficulty of distinguishing the genuine *mata gelaps* from instances in which it is feigned for the purpose of achieving revenge or gain, and he notes that some case studies yield the history of a man apparently taking strong drink or opium as a deliberate means of loosening ego controls. Also, he notes that most cases occur among men from the mountains who have come to the city, have little education, and apparently are of low intelligence. Thus amok is now acquiring a psychiatric character which had previously been absent. The picture is still mixed, however, and Clifford (1897) is skeptical regarding the degree to which conscious intention is absent.

By the end of the century psychiatrists had arrived in the region and gave support to the idea that amok was a mental rather than a social disorder. Van Brero (1896) is very cautious in regard to the matter and recognizes that the cases he sees in his asylum may be unrepresentative, but does tell us that family members are now the commonest victims and that dissociation from the act is customary. Ellis (1893) is bolder, though with only three cases to work from, and adds a new element to the picture by referring to a condition that is commonly called *sakit hati* (literally, "liver sickness," the liver being considered the seat of the emotions but which he calls heart sickness) and which Gimlette (1901) states is best understood as spite, envy, or being affronted. It is a form of depression, with brooding over wrongs, which was common among Singapore Malays at this time and for which running amok was viewed by some, according to Clifford (1897), as a remedy. Two of Ellis' three cases seemed to have suffered from this condition before running amok, and Clifford describes sitting up all night with a depressed Selangor noble to dissuade him from running amok after his father died. Neither opium nor somatic illness is now seen as a factor, though both are mentioned. (At this time Malaysians rarely took opium, whereas the Chinese, who used it extensively, did not run amok.) Ellis does propose epilepsy as a factor, however, and this theory, though unsupported by his own material and most other studies, was taken up by Kraepelin, introducing a new confusion.

Ellis' three cases were all that he saw in his first five years in the region; and although I have read all the annual reports that he wrote during his remaining quarter-century there, I cannot remember him returning to the subject. We may infer, therefore, that before the turn of the century amok was becoming very rare in Singapore, with the same holding true of Batavia (Rasch, 1894) and Penang (Fitzgerald, 1923). Rasch and Fitzgerald, as well as Van Loon (1922), Gans (1922), and Galloway (1923), all tell us that cases were occurring in the interiors of Java and Malaya, and Fitzgerald writes casually about "the last six persons" admitted to Johore jail for running amok; but they can gain us very little first-hand information.

There is no doubt, therefore, that the condition had become quite rare in the regions where European doctors were practicing, and such descriptions as we possess suggest that by 1920 its clinical character may have changed once more. Three of the four reports from this decade mention, quite independently of each other, a connection with malaria or other sources of acute febrile confusion. Thus Fitzgerald states that the six amok-runners admitted to the Johore jail were all tested and found to have quartan malaria in their blood, and the single case personally treated by Galloway was also suffering at the time of his amok from a malarial relapse, although it was not in the febrile phase. (Incidentally, that patient killed no one.) Van Loon groups amok with what he regards as other types of acute confusional state induced by diseases such as malaria and syphilis, and in a later paper (Van Loon, 1927) addressed to an American audience goes so far as to call it "infectious-murder [p. 437]."

In concordance with this etiological view, the three (Fitzgerald, Galloway, and Van Loon) also see the condition as treatable, with the patient recovering his normal personality when the febrile delirium is over. In their discussions of the condition, epilepsy and opium are dismissed as irrelevant, Oxley's nonfebrile somatic precipitants go unmentioned, social precipitants are discussed by Van Loon only to be rejected, and even *sakit hati* hardly receives recognition. The writers of this generation (with the exception of Gans, who saw only cases that reached his mental hospital after months or years of imprisonment) are relatively unanimous respecting the role of infection in the disorder.

By the 1930s, however, this theory was also on the wane. Amir (1939 and earlier) provides us with full clinical descriptions of five cases with which he was concerned, and in only one of these could recent infection be considered a partial factor. In most of his cases a more chronic process—organic brain syndrome or schizophrenia—was clearly of major importance, and the only patient who had no such chronic disorder developed a prison psychosis three weeks after being apprehended. To judge by these cases, therefore, amok has now become an episode in a chronic process, not appearing in persons who afterwards make a sane impression. Amir, however, was a hospital psychiatrist with a long but perhaps restricted experience, and Wulfften Palthe, the professor of psychiatry in Java, disagreed with his view, arguing that "any native [i.e., Malaysian] may react with amok if only the emotional stimulus is strong enough [Palthe, 1933, p. 137]." Unfortunately Palthe gives us only a single detailed case, omits telling us where and when he encountered others, and complicates matters by stating that the condition can occur in Chinese and Arabs. From conversation with him, however, I gather that he was wont to wander into little-changed parts of the interior of Java and Sumatra, where amok had remained comparatively more frequent. The more doubtfully genuine account of a case by Fauconnier (1930) fits Palthe's view.

Since the work of Palthe and Amir, there have been only two first-hand studies of amok in the region, although Yap (1951), Van Bergen (1953), and Pfeiffer (1971) have written on the subject from a general knowledge of the region and Burton-Bradley (1968) cites seven cases from the neighboring but non-Malaysian territory of New Guinea. The first of the two direct reports is by Zaguirre (1957), who deals with cases occurring in the Philippine army. Twelve of these soldiers actually went on a "murderous spree," while another thirteen were halted on the verge of doing so; but some or perhaps most of Zaguirre's cases did not closely fit the amok picture, being indistinguishable from instances of homicidal mania occurring in other cultures. Zaguirre is of the opinion that amok does not constitute a distinct syndrome today and that many cases showing the behavior that he calls amok have other forms of pathology. He does not give sufficient details for one to be able to judge how many of his cases did show the classical syndrome, but in one instance, in which the soldier involved had recently lost his favorite child, the picture is suggestive. An interesting aspect of his report is the use of narcoanalysis.

Karl Schmidt, the other field researcher on the subject, has collected the records of 24 cases occurring over a 10-year period in Sarawak, but at the time this is being written has not completed his paper on them, so that the information is still incomplete. From a preliminary report most kindly shown to me, it is uncertain how many of Schmidt's cases conform to the classical picture. It is clear, however, that most of them exhibited other signs of psychopathology before or after the episode and also that a family history of mental disturbance was frequently to be found. A number of his cases were soldiers suffering from homesickness and one was a woman, although running amok is usually considered a male phenomenon and no one, to my knowledge, has been able to report details of any female case.

To summarize, then, amok has shown a marked decline in incidence from the mid-nineteenth century onward, this decine being most striking in the centers of European influence where previously (i.e., during the eighteenth and early nineteenth centuries) the incidence had probably increased. Over this period amok has shown a marked shift from being a consciously motivated form of behavior to being a dissociation reaction, and probably a further shift from a dissociation reaction in an otherwise sane individual to an episode in the course of a longer mental disorder. Whether its reported associations with opium in the eighteenth century, nonfebrile somatic diseases in the mid-nineteenth century, and febrile disease in the early twentieth century represent additional shifts is more doubtful; but some changes in both character and incidence have undoubtedly taken place. I will briefly consider the possible causes of these changes after reviewing the other syndrome, latah.

LATAH*

This syndrome is less well known than amok, and it may be helpful, therefore, to commence this section with a definition and brief descriptions. First, the definition:

"Latah is an affliction or a disease, one hardly knows what name to give it, which causes certain men and women to lose their self-control for shorter or longer periods whenever they are startled or receive any sudden shock. While in this condition they appear to be unable to realise their own identity or to employ any but imitative faculties, though they very frequently, nay almost invariably, make use of villainously bad language without anyone prompting them to do so. A complete stranger . . . can induce the condition accidentally and without exercising any effort of will . . . [so that] though latah resembles hypnotic suggestion in many respects it differs from it in the important respect that it in no way depends on an original voluntary surrender of willpower [Clifford, 1898, p. 189]."

Two main subcategories of latah are recognized, though more have been proposed. One is a startle pattern that often involves coprolalia and may be induced not merely by a sudden shock but also by a key word or by the presence of a superior. The other is an imitative pattern wherein the subject seems forced to copy the actions of another person or animal, even when these are meaningless, indecorous, or dangerous.

An illustration of the first form has been provided by Ellis (1897), whose best mental hospital nurse was afflicted in the following fashion: "Whenever I have occasion to admonish her she stands trembling for a few seconds, micturates and passes flatus, and then as if startled by the sound she loudly utters a filthy word and promptly apologises for her conduct [p. 36]."

* For reasons of space I am confining myself in this paper to latah among Malaysians and am ignoring the latah-like conditions—*myriachit, yaung da hte,* and so on —which have been recorded sporadically in many other peoples. The latter are germane to any general discussion of the syndrome (see Aberle, 1952; Pfeiffer, 1971; Yap, 1952) but have been too irregularly noted for their frequency and distribution to be analyzed.

The second form can be exemplified by a case of Clifford's, that of a cook who was watching the cookhouse fire and was startled by a pot toppling over. A boy sitting with him made a grab to save the pot; but whereas the boy's hand stopped before reaching it, the cook's hand, in imitation, went into the fire, grasping the scalding metal. "With the wanton cruelty and mischief of his age, the boy once more made a feint at the smoking ricepot and again Sat's fingers glued themselves to the scalding metal. . . . Sat's fingers were in a terribly lacerated condition when at last someone chanced to enter the cook-room and prevented the continuation of Sat's torture [Clifford, 1898, p. 191]."

Latah is thus a quite dramatic condition, likely to excite comment from both medical and lay observers regardless of culture, a fact that makes the absence of descriptions before the mid-nineteenth century both surprising and significant. The word latah had been used before that time to mean jumpy or ticklish. Only one doubtful reference to a pathological state has ever been cited from an earlier date (Wilkinson, 1957), however, and I have been unable to trace the original. Normally, as in the legend of Nakhoda Ragam (Hervey, 1885), the word latah meant no more than to be easily startled.

The first description of a possible (but not probable) case does not use the word latah (Logan, 1849), and neither the author nor his Malay guide appears to have been seen anything similar before (the predominant features were tics and obsequiousness), whereas if the two had known of the latah syndrome they would probably have referred to it. In the Strait Settlements at that time, therefore, the condition must have been unfamiliar or unknown. When the word latah first comes to be applied to the syndrome in a written text, however, it is apparent that in Batavia the condition had been known for some time, since Van Leent (1867) not only refers to it as a distinct entity but also remarks that the judiciary recognized acts committed during a latah episode to be involuntary. When it became commonly known is a different matter, for Van Leent's brief note* remains unique until the 1880s, when two nonmedical descriptions appear, the one (O'Brien, 1883a, 1883b) stating that the condition is common and the other (Metzger, 1882) implying that it is not. Moreover, despite the fact that O'Brien's excellent descriptions attracted much attention from Gilles de la Tourette (1884) and others in Europe, 15 years passed before the next first-hand report.

By the end of the nineteenth century, however, latah seems suddenly to have become very common. Thus, Van Brero (1895) tells us that in western

---

* Van Leent probably provided greater details in the book that he published in Dutch the year after the cited paper, but I have been unable to track down a copy of it.

Java "the condition is so common that one can find many women with it any day in the streets [p. 940]"; Swettenham (1896) states that in some parts of Perak one or two cases are seen in every village; Bordier (1894) (though with what authority is unclear) refers to it as sometimes taking on the character of an epidemic; and Clifford describes how, within his own large retinue of servants, its dramatic occurrence in one individual led to its appearing in others. Whereas O'Brien and Metzger had seemed in 1882 to be describing every case they had known, Clifford by 1898 claims to have seen so many that he could go on giving examples indefinitely. We thus must recognize either that there was a true, marked rise in incidence at this time, or that the condition became suddenly recognized in subjects among whom it had previously been ignored. Of these alternatives the former is much the more likely, not only because the condition is a difficult one to ignore but also because a description is available of its actual spread among a group of servants, a spread that might suggest some infection had the author not shrewdly added:

"I must not be understood as suggesting that they became infected with latah, for on enquiry I found that they had one and all been subject to occasional seizures [of latah] before they joined my people. But the presence of Sat [the cook referred to previously] seemed to cause them to lose the control which they had hitherto contrived to exercise over themselves [Clifford, 1898, p. 192]."

Not all peoples within the region, however, were as yet affected; and, among those who were, our informants at this time recognized differences in susceptibility. Most vulnerable, apparently, were the Amboinese (Swettenham, 1896), people who occupied a small island that the Dutch had used, since the seventeenth century, as the center for the spice trade and who had extensively converted to Christianity. Next came the Javanese and Malays around areas of European influence. Only an occasional case was reported among the Buginese, Sundanese, and Madurese, who had been more distant from that influence, and no cases at all were reported from the Achinese, who had been well studied by Hurgronje (1906) and Jacobs (1894); or from the Bataks, among whom Christian missionaries had recently started working, or from the peoples of Borneo. The Achinese were at this time resisting Dutch penetration strongly, and the Bataks and Borneans had hardly experienced any contact at all. Apparently, therefore, the condition first became frequent in areas of European influence, though this association was later to change.

In Java latah commenced and remained almost wholly a female disorder, but in Malaya at this time almost as many male as female cases were reported. Ellis (1897) remarks that the advent of the Christian mission schools had not reduced its incidence; Fletcher (1908) suggests that it is quite as common in the educated and higher class as in the lower; and Ellis' colleague Fitzgerald claims 20 years later (1923, but based on earlier experience) that "the latah sufferer is usually intellectually superior and more alert than his fellows [p. 154]." Most medical informants note that latah is absent in mental hospital patients, though present in the attendants, and that it is unassociated with epilepsy, mental deficiency, or hysteria. All informants remark that latah subjects are normal outside of their attacks.

After 1900, first-hand papers on latah decline sharply in number and quality for a time, but from the writings of Abraham (1911, 1912), Fletcher (1908), Gans (1922), Galloway (1922), and Fitzgerald (1923), as well as from the absence of mention of the condition in some locations where one would have expected it, some tentative deductions can be drawn. One is that the average age of latah subjects in Java is increasing. A second is that the proportion of male cases in Malaya, though still higher than in Java, is declining. A third is that the condition is moving away from the centers of European influence and into the countryside. According to Fletcher's account (1908), it is now quite frequent in such locations as Pahang and Upper Perak, with cases encountered every day in the streets and courtrooms there, whereas anecdotal sketches and medical reports from Singapore, Batavia, Penang, and Malacca almost cease to mention it. These impressions, at least in regard to the age distribution and the incidence in urban locations, are confirmed in the next major paper on the subject, that by Van Loon (1924).

Van Loon circularized 600 physicians in the Dutch East Indies, inquiring for information on latah cases they had seen, and received answers from 106. This is a low figure, considering that doctors in such countries tend to feel isolated from the mainstream of medicine and hence welcome inquiries from a university, and of these 106 only 13 claimed to have seen more than two cases. This suggests a considerable diminution since the time of Van Brero and Bordier, at least in the areas in which Western-trained doctors were practicing. Of the 169 cases reported by these doctors,* all were Malaysian or part Malaysian, most had had contact with Europeans, and all but 4 were female, thus confirming earlier observations. However, the great majority were servants (something that cannot be said of the earlier cases), most were over the age of 40, and 11 showed some signs of dementia or other chronic mental disturbance—and this is new. Attacks were most common in the presence of the master of the house, obscene wishes were sometimes expressed toward him during

---

* Since there are discrepancies between Van Loon's 1924 and 1927 papers, I have used mainly the earlier and fuller version, written in Dutch.

these attacks, and in 10 cases the condition is said to have started after a frightening and frankly sexual dream. Nevertheless, the great majority of these women were reported to be intelligent, efficient servants except when in the throes of an attack.

After Van Loon a quarter century elapsed with virtually no original or useful contributions to the subject, and it therefore comes as little surprise that Yap, when he returned to the subject in his extensive thesis (1952), could report only 7 fresh cases. Latah, judging from his experience, was now disappearing, and such cases as remained were atypical insofar as his subjects did not appear to be intelligent or alert and the attacks tended to be incomplete. Yet this is misleading, perhaps because of the fact that Yap had to seek his cases in and near large towns, since the deeper countryside was still in political turmoil. Even as his paper was being published, the anthropologist Hildred Geertz was finding, without much intent or effort, some 13 cases in a small, central Javanese town (1968), and a few years later agricultural resettlement officers told me that they still regularly saw cases in some parts of Malaya. Since then Pfeiffer (1971) has written that the condition remains endemic in some parts of East Java and has reported on 22 cases in the area round Lawang; Chiu, Tong, and Schmidt have uncovered no fewer than 65 cases during the psychiatric survey in Borneo (1970); and Barnett has told me that in some parts of Malaya most villages have at least one publicly recognized case.* What has clearly happened, therefore, is not that the condition has disappeared (though it has undoubtedly diminished) but that it has shifted its location, abandoning the centers of social change where it was initially to be found, and moving into regions that previously seemed free of it, notably Borneo.

Grouping the data of Yap, Geertz, Pfeiffer, and Schmidt, one can compose a picture of the distribution of latah among the present generation which is considerably different not only from the one suggested by Yap alone but also from that reported at the beginning of the century. The picture is as follows. The condition is still quite frequent among rural Malays and Ibans who have moved into the area surrounding Kuching, the capital of Sarawak. The prevalence here seems to approach 1%, informants regard it as comparatively normal, and subjects seem relatively resigned to it. In central Javanese towns the prevalence is less and subjects seem to resist the condition more, but it still seems to affect mainly women who have moved from the countryside to the town and remains more frequent in towns than in remote villages. The areas around Malacca and Kuala Lumpur, where Yap found most of his cases, rank

---

* These last two sets of observations are unpublished at the time of writing, and I am most grateful to the observers for making the data available.

next in relative prevalence, and there, where European influence has been strong for some time, the subjects seem to fight the condition hardest, modifying it somewhat in the process. Finally, among some 4000 rural Iban in Sarawak no case at all was found, although the Iban near the town were susceptible and regarded latah as an aspect of their own culture. Virtually none of this generation's subjects had worked with Europeans and few had been servants; their attacks seem milder than those reported at the beginning of the century, but this may be because their neighbors tease them less. Meanwhile the basic constellation of symptoms remains the same.

Summarizing once more, one can say that latah appeared relatively suddenly during the second half of the nineteenth century, spread quite rapidly among the populations most exposed to European influence, and then moved in wave fashion away from these centers, so that today it is virtually absent in the locations where it was first observed but is present in more distant locations where it was previously absent. Throughout this period its symptoms have remained relatively stable; however, the earlier form in males has almost disappeared, the intensity of attacks has declined, and in areas from which it is disappearing the residual subjects seem less intelligent than the earlier ones.

DISCUSSION

The purpose of this paper has been not to review the total literature and all the theories on latah and amok but rather to explore whether the tracing of a mental disorder's distribution and characteristics through time can contribute a new tool to the science of psychopathology. Like most psychiatric syndromes, latah and amok have attracted many theories based mainly on the clinical characteristics of cases, but have elicited as yet no convincing explanation. Although the present review of only a part of the picture cannot provide such explanation, it has, I think, added a new element wherewith old theories can be tested and new ones fertilized.*

In most informed discussions of latah and amok the assumption is that those pathological syndromes are part of traditional Malaysian life now disappearing as a result of modernization. This is stated explicitly by Galloway (1922) and is implicit in the views of Van Loon (1927)

* In a paper "Notes for a Theory on Latah" read at the Conference on Culture and Mental Health in Asia and the Pacific, and due to be published in *Mental Health Research in Asia and the Pacific,* Vol. 4, the total picture of latah is discussed in relation to the foregoing observations, and a tentative theory offered for it.

and Palthe (1933). The present review has shown, however, that the assumption is wrong. Latah seems to have been absent in Malaysian societies untouched by European influence, just as it is today absent among the rural Iban, though present in their suburban compatriots. Amok, similarly, can hardly be called a psychiatric syndrome before the nineteenth century, since it is only then that cases are encountered where the conscious intent to attack is absent and where social provocations seem insufficient to explain the behavior. The syndromes are thus best conceived not as offshoots from Malaysian cultural tradition but as transitional products of an interaction between that tradition and certain modernizing influences. Why should this have been?

Amok provides the clearer clues to an answer. In its original, conscious form it was a recognized instrument of social control, restricting the abuse of power by chiefs and the wealthy (Gullick, 1958; Haar, 1948), sanctified by proverbs (Wilkinson, 1925b), and endorsed by hero worship of the man who went amok and escaped the consequences. In tale after tale one reads of the courtier, the emissary, the debtor, the vassal, the slave threatening to run amok if traditional customs of fair dealing were abandoned by some superior; and the threat was no empty one. When less drastic forms of social control were demonstrated in the European settlements and when it proved more profitable to collaborate with the European trader than to pursue traditional methods of warfare and piracy, however, recourse to amok became not only unnecessary but also repulsive, and most individuals consciously rejected it as something which they themselves might undertake. It is at this point and in this setting that the pathological syndrome first appears, with the provocation (physical sickness, domestic troubles) quite insufficient by traditional standards and with the act dissociated from consciousness, but with the same underlying meaning of escaping from distress into death while at the same time taking revenge on the society that has permitted this distress. And as other means of escaping these distresses are learned and the social tradition of amok becomes fainter in men's minds, this pathological distortion of that tradition dies away also.

For latah there is no prior model of conscious behavior that is really similar, but a widespread tradition existed of children submitting themselves to a dissociated hypersuggestibility state for the amusement of others, a state during which they would imitate whatever was suggested to them and carry out actions that would be seemingly impossible in their conscious state.* Hence hypersuggestibility was in a sense already being

* These childhood games were described by Wilkinson (1925a), Hurgronje (1906), and others around the turn of the century and have been shown by Koentjaraningrat

used for a vaguely social purpose; and my proposal is that, when it became desirable to learn rapidly some new but little understood custom, a mild degree of hypersuggestibility was again, though less consciously, called into service. It is a notable fact that, although European colonists found the Malaysians unreliable and apparently unintelligent when it came to general labor or working on their own, they admired and became greatly attached to those with whom they had close personal contact, finding the usually more enterprising Chinese and Indians quite inferior in such relationships; and I suggest that this may have been related to the Malaysian's readiness to subordinate his personal inclinations and prior training to an accepted superior. It is always easier, when called upon to learn rapidly some quite unfamiliar task, to do so by rote† or simple imitation rather than by understanding, and an ease of accepting and retaining suggestions facilitates this approach. Our data suggest that latah became most frequent when the need to rapidly learn new customs pressed heaviest on Malaysians, and I propose that it be seen as a by-product of the increased suggestibility with which many Malaysians responded to that need, one form of the disorder being merely an exaggeration of this suggestibility and another, involving coprolalia or swearing, representing in part the resentment usually aroused by such complete submission to the will of another.

That is not the whole story, either for amok or for latah. It ignores, for instance, the fact that when ego controls are partly renounced, as in hypersuggestibility, repressed desires are more likely to gain expression. Broadly, however, the combined data suggest that, when Malaysian society was confronted by certain types of social problem, it responded by exploiting personal characteristics that were only partly egosyntonic. The explosive release of repressed resentment was exploited as a check on those who too freely used their power to arouse resentment; the suppression of personal inclinations and prior training at the suggestion of a superior was exploited as a means of rapid learning in unfamiliar conditions. But because each method involved to some extent the bypassing of ego controls, each also resulted in a certain amount of uncontrolled behavior in forms that served no social function, that is, each produced some individual psychopathology. This psychopathology reached its height

(1957) and McHugh (1955) to persist in the present generation. It seems likely that they are a vestige of adult religious ceremonies which still persist in Bali but which Mohammedanism has stamped out elsewhere in the archipelago.

† Most, though not all, of the situations in which latah-like syndromes have been found present a similar picture of a people being called upon to learn new customs rapidly. In many there has also been, as in the Koranic schools, a tradition of rote learning for children.

when the demand for adaptive change was greatest; but as long as society perceived some value in the underlying characteristic it was not viewed as really egodystonic and the bearers of the pathology did not consider themselves markedly deviant, so that its presence did relatively little personal damage. Once society had mastered the problem or found more efficient methods of tackling it, however, the characteristics began to be seen as being undesirable and requiring suppression. Hence it was only when the ego was weakened by other means or when strong, repressed feelings sought to exploit the characteristic for their own ends that amok and latah still continued to be found. Moreover, in this later stage they were increasingly likely to be associated with other pathology.

But now, although the tracing of latah and amok across time and place has provided new clues to their natures, can it be said that the same would probably apply for other syndromes? Latah and amok, it might be argued, are both atypical and little known; have we any reason to think that similar results could be obtained with more typical disorders that have been more thoroughly explored? The question resolves itself into two parts, the one concerned with the approach that has been used and the other with the relationship between psychiatric symptomatology and social change to which the results have pointed.

In regard to the usefulness of the general approach the answer is, I believe, relatively simple. Once we cease to regard psychiatric syndromes as stable patterns to be found in all societies and epochs, it becomes quite easy to spot apparent shifts in incidence or in symptomatology, and the likelihood is that a study of these shifts would in some instances enlarge our understanding of the conditions involved. One such probable shift is that from the medieval acedia to the Protestant melancholia in Western Europe during the fourteenth to the seventeenth centuries. Another lies in the striking diminution of classical mania over the past hundred years or so. Yet another, only partly overlapping, involves the increased chronicity of hospitalized patients during the middle of the nineteenth century. Away from Europe and North America instances are more numerous, though lesser known. One group concerns the apparent increase of depression in many parts of Africa and Asia; another, the increase of schizophrenia in certain specific peoples, as I have discussed elsewhere (Murphy, 1968). And of course within the neuroses the changes in the diagnosis of *la grande hystérie*, neurasthenia, the cardiac neuroses, and others should be known to every scholar of modern psychiatry. Although some of these changes will undoubtedly prove to have been no more than shifts in diagnostic fashion, all deserve more attention than they have received, and I believe that some will prove to represent genuine changes in symptomatology or frequency which our current theories are poorly designed to explain.

Such changes, even when proved, need not have in any way the same sort of connection to social change that has been hypothesized here to have existed in the cases of latah and amok. On the contrary, all our knowledge argues against the relationship between psychopathology and social change being so simple that a single hypothesis could cover it. Yet this is not to say that relationships analogous to those described here will not be found. Jaspers long ago, I believe, pointed out that the pathological significance of delusional beliefs depends greatly on how they are treated by surrounding society, and more recently I have argued that in many developing countries delusional systems may provide a means whereby the public can be induced to explore new concepts or unfamiliar ways of tackling new problems (Murphy, 1967). Often, as with the Cargo Cult beliefs, those who produce socially useful delusions develop no further individual pathology but are accepted as leaders or heroes, just as the amokers were accepted as heroes if they survived, and the latah victims as clowns. When such beliefs serve less purpose, however, those who freshly produce them usually suffer from further pathology. Turning to a more familiar subject referred to above, namely, the alleged rarity of classical depression in some African and Asian groups earlier in this century and its increasing frequency in recent decades, one might also see this as the by-product of a type of social change which conditions were pressing on these people, the change from the collective superego of the tribe or family to the individual superego of modern man. And if this were the case, might one not interpret the apparent increase in depression in England during the seventeenth century as reflecting a similar shift?

These last suggestions may be treated as flights of fancy produced in response to the editors' request that I give some indication of how the conceptual approach employed in this paper might be more broadly applied "toward a science of psychopathology." It is impossible to say without a proper examination of the evidence whether a particular theory will apply in a given situation or not, and I have not subjected the evidence to such examination. I do propose, however, that our understanding of psychopathology would be increased if we reviewed the history of different syndromes with open eyes, and that it might also enlarge our understanding if we thought of mental disorder as sometimes being the by-product of social problem solving.

ACKNOWLEDGMENTS

I wish to acknowledge the assistance of the Social Science Research Institute (NIMH Grant MH-09243) and the East-West Center at the University of Hawaii in the preparation of this paper.

REFERENCES

Aberle, D. F. Arctic hysteria. *Transactions of the New York Academy of Sciences* (Series 2), 1952, **14** (7), 291–297.

Abraham, J. J. *The surgeon's log; being impressions of the Far East.* New York: E. P. Dutton, 1911.

Abraham, J. J. Latah and amok. *British Medical Journal,* 1912, **I**, 438–439.

Amir, M. Over eenige gevallen van amok uit Nord-Sumatra. *Geneeskundig Tijdschrift voor Nederlandsch-Indië,* 1939, **79**, 2786–2797.

Barbosa, D. *The book of Duarte Barbosa.* London: Hakluyt Society, 1921.

Bordier, A. *La géographie médicale.* Paris, 1894.

Breitenstein, H. *Einundzwanzig Jahre in Indien. Aus dem Tagebuche eines Militärarztes.* Leipzig: T. Grieben, 1899–1902.

Burton-Bradley, B. G. The amok syndrome in Papua and New Guinea. *The Medical Journal of Australia,* 1968, **I**, 252–256.

Chiu, T. L., Tong, J. E., & Schmidt, K. E. A clinical and survey study of latah in Sarawak, Malaysia. Unpublished manuscript.

Clifford, H. *In court & kampong; being tales and sketches of native life in the Malay peninsula.* London: G. Richards, 1897.

Clifford, H. *Studies in brown humanity: Being scrawls and smudges in sepia, white and yellow.* London: G. Richards, 1898.

Crawfurd, J. *History of the Indian archipelago.* Vol. 1. Edinburgh: A. Constable, 1820.

Crawfurd, J. *A descriptive dictionary of the Indian islands & adjacent countries.* London: Bradbury & Evans, 1856.

Ellis, W. G. The amok of the Malays. *Journal of Mental Science,* 1893, **39**, 325–342.

Ellis, W. G. Latah, a mental malady of the Malays. *Journal of Mental Science,* 1897, **43**, 33–40. (Also summary and discussion in same journal, 1896, **42**, 209.)

Fauconnier, H. *Malaisie.* Paris: Stock, 1930.

Fitzgerald, R. D. A thesis on two tropical neuroses peculiar to the Malays. *Transactions of the 5th Congress of the Far-Eastern Association of Tropical Medicine,* 1923, 148–161.

Fletcher, W. Latah and crime. *Lancet,* 1908, **2**, 254–255.

Galloway, D. J. A contribution to the psychology of latah. *Journal of the Straits Branch of the Royal Asiatic Society,* 1922, **85**, 140–146.

Galloway, D. J. On amok. *Transactions of the 5th Congress of the Far-Eastern Association of Tropical Medicine,* 1923, 162–171.

Gans, A. Ein Beitrag zur Rassenpsychiatrie. *Münchener Medizinische Wochenschrift*, 1922, **69**, 1503–1504.

Geertz, H. Latah in Java; a theoretical paradox. *Indonesia*, 1968, **5**, 93–104.

Gilles de la Tourette, H. Jumping, latah, myriachit. *Archives de Neurologie*, 1884, **8**, 68–74.

Gimlette, J. D. Notes on a case of amok. *Journal of Tropical Medicine*, 1901, **4**, 195–199.

Goldsmith, M. L. *The trail of opium, the eleventh plague*. London: Ryerson Press, 1939.

Gullick, J. M. *Indigenous political systems of western Malaya*. London: Humanities Press, 1958. (London University, London School of Economics and Political Science. Department of Anthropology Monographs on Social Anthropology, No. 17.)

Haar, B. ten. *Adat law in Indonesia*. New York: Institute of Pacific Relations, 1948.

Hervey, D. F. A. Malacca legends of Nakhoda Ragam. *Journal of the Straits Branch of the Royal Asiatic Society*, 1885, **15**, 26 (Notes & Queries suppl. No. 2).

Heymann, S. L. *Versuch einer pathologisch-therapeutischen Darstellung der Krankheiten in den Tropen-Ländern*. Würzburg, 1855.

Hill, B., & Schmidt, K. E. Amok; a description of twenty-four cases, unpublished manuscript.

Hurgronje, C. S. *The Achehnese*. English translation by A. W. S. O'Sullivan London: Luzac & Co., 1906.

Jacobowsky, B. General paresis and civilization. *Acta Psychiatrica Scandinavica*, 1965, **41**, 267–273.

Jacobs, J. *Het Familie en Kampongleven op Groot-Atcheh*. Leiden, 1894.

Koentjaraningrat, R. M. *A preliminary description of the Javanese kinship system*. Yale University, S. E. A. Studies Series, 1957.

Logan, J. R. Five days in Naning. *Journal of the Indian Archipelago and Eastern Asia*, 1849, **3**, 24–41.

McHugh, J. N. *Hantu Hantu*. Singapore: Donald Moore, 1955.

Metzger, G. Sakit latah. *Globus*, 1882, **41**, 381–383.

Metzger, G. Einiges über amok und mataglap. *Globus*, 1887, **52**, 107–110.

Murphy, H. B. M. Cultural aspects of delusion. *Studium Generale*, 1967, **20** (11), 684–692.

Murphy, H. B. M. Cultural factors in the genesis of schizophrenia. In D. Rosenthal & S. S. Kety (Eds.), *The transmission of schizophrenia*. Oxford, Pergamon Press, 1968. Pp. 137–153.

Norris, W. Sentence of death upon a Malay convicted of running amuck. *Journal of the Indian Archipelago and Eastern Asia*, 1849, **3**, 460–463.

O'Brien, H. O. Latah. *Journal of the Straits Branch of the Royal Asiatic Society*, 1883, **11**, 143–153. (a)

O'Brien, H. O. Latah. *Journal of the Straits Branch of the Royal Asiatic Society*, 1883, **12**, 283–285. (b)

Oxley, J. Malay amoks. *Journal of the Indian Archipelago and Eastern Asia,* 1849, **3**, 532–533.

Palthe, P. M. W. Psychiatry and neurology in the tropics. *Malayan Medical Journal,* 1933, **8**, 133–139.

Pfeiffer, W. *Transkulturelle Psychiatrie—Ergebnisse und Probleme.* Stuttgart: Georg Thieme Verlag, 1971.

Rasch, C. Über "amok." *Neurologisches Zentralblatt,* 1894, **13**, 550–554.

Schulzens, W. *Walter Schulzens Ost-Indische Reise-Beschreibung.* Amsterdam, 1676. (Quoted in Yule & Burnell, below.)

Sheppard, M. C. *The adventures of Hang Tuah.* Singapore: Donald Moore, N.D.

Swaving, G. Geregtelijk-geneeskundige stellingen over den moordlust of mata glap bij den Inlander. *Regt in Nederlandsch-Indië,* 1856, **7**, 125–130.

Swettenham, F. A. *Malay sketches.* London: John Lane, 1896.

Swettenham, F. A. *The real Malay; pen pictures.* London: John Lane, 1900.

Van Bergen, G. Betrachtungen über amok. *Zeitschrift für Psychotherapie und Medizinische Psychologie,* 1953, **3**, 226–231.

Van Brero, P. C. Z. Über das sogenannte latah. *Allgemeine Zeitschrift für Psychiatrie und ihre Grenzgebiete,* 1895, **51**, 939–948.

Van Brero, P. C. Z. Einiges über die Geisteskrankheiten der Bevölkerung des Malayischen Archipels. *Allgemeine Zeitschrift für Psychiatrie und ihre Grenzgebiete,* 1896, **53**, 25–33.

Van der Chijs, J. A. *Nederlandsch-Indisch plakaatboek.* Vol. 13. Batavia, 1890.

Van Leent, F. J. Contributions à la géographie médicale. *Archives de Médecine Navale,* 1867, **8**, 172–173 (these pages refer only to the note on latah, not to the whole article, which is scattered over several numbers).

Van Leent, F. J. *Geneeskundig-topographische opmerkingen betroffende Batavia, hare neede en het eiland Onnust.* The Hague, 1868.

Van Loon, F. G. H. Acute Verwardheidstoestanden in Nederlandsch-Indië. *Mededeelingen van het Burgerlijken Geneeskundigen Dienst in Nederlandsch-Indië,* 1922, No. 4, 658–690.

Van Loon, F. G. H. Lattah, eene psychoneurose der Maleische Rassen. *Geneeskundig Tijdschrift voor Nederlandsch-Indië,* 1924, **64**, 59–82.

Van Loon, F. G. H. Amok and Latah. *Journal of Abnormal and Social Psychology,* 1927, **21**, 434–444.

Vogler, W. Wenken omtrent mata-glap. *Tijdschrift der Vereeniging tot Bevordering der Geneeskundige Wetenschappen in Nederlandsch-Indië,* 1853, **2**, 95–113.

Wallace, A. R. *The Malay archipelago, the land of the orang-utan and the bird of paradise; a narrative of travel, with studies of man and nature.* London: Macmillan, 1898.

Wilkinson, R. J. *Papers on Malay subjects. Life and customs—Part III: Malay amusements.* Kuala Lumpur: F. M. S. Government Press, 1925. (a)

Wilkinson, R. J. *Papers on Malay subjects. Malay literature—Part III: Malay proverbs on Malay character.* Kuala Lumpur: F. M. S. Government Press, 1925. (b)

Wilkinson, R. J. *A Malay-English dictionary.* London: Macmillan, 1957.

Yap, P. M. Mental diseases peculiar to certain cultures. *Journal of Mental Science,* 1951, **97,** 313–321.

Yap, P. M. The latah reaction. *Journal of Mental Science,* 1952, **98,** 515–564.

Yule, H., & Burnell, A. C. *Hobson-Jobson; being a glossary of Anglo-Indian colloquial words and phrases, and of kindred terms: Etymological, historical, geographical, and discursive.* London: J. Murray, 1886.

Zaguirre, J. C. "Amuck." *Journal of the Philippine Federation of Private Medical Practitioners,* 1957, **4,** 1138–1149.

Some first-hand reports have been omitted from this bibliography since they were in essential agreement with other reports cited from the same period.

CHAPTER 3

Schizophrenia and Survival

LISSY F. JARVIK and SHEILA BRASS CHADWICK

"A tremendous amount has been written about schizophrenia . . . . Yet, despite this full measure of dedicated work, the important questions of diagnosis, prognosis, etiology, and therapy are still unanswered and constitute psychiatry's greatest challenge [Redlich & Freedman, 1966, p. 459]." To the foregoing list of unanswered questions, we have to add another, "Why does schizophrenia persist in human populations?" This question has been asked with increasing frequency by geneticists and behavioral scientists alike, for now that the importance of genetic factors in the etiology of schizophrenia is generally being recognized, a new enigma has been posed: According to the Darwinian theory of natural selection, so detrimental a condition as schizophrenia should be declining; instead, it continues to affect a nearly constant proportion of the populations examined.

Today there is still considerable controversy about the role of biological factors in the etiology of mental illness, particularly schizophrenia. This is not surprising since the peculiarities of schizophrenic behavior have so far defied explanation in terms of known organic mechanisms. As a result, psychiatrists and psychologists have emphasized psychological processes in an attempt to account for the development of the disease (cf. Cameron, 1959; Retterstøl, 1966). By contrast, geneticists have concentrated their inquiries on the biological aspects of mental illness and have applied the Darwinian postulate that disease acts as a population filter, eliminating the progeny of those biologically "unfit" to withstand the ravages of their environment and thereby leaving the species better adapted to survive—if the environment is not significantly altered.

Ernst Caspari's concept of cultural-genic feedback is a further development of Darwinian theory and may bridge the gap between the psychological and genetic approaches. Caspari (1963) proposes that inherited traits interact with the environment in such a way that there is *reciprocal* continued reinforcement for *selected characteristics* biologically needed and

57

socially valued by a given culture. From this hypothesis, which integrates the evolutionary evidence with environmental influences, it would be expected that a biologically useful and culturally rewarded selective advantage is responsible for the continued high rates of schizophrenia.

Although it is not the intent of this chapter to provide an exhaustive survey of the literature on the genetics of schizophrenia (this material is available elsewhere: see Heston, 1970; Shields, 1968; Slater, 1968; Zerbin-Rüdin, 1967), we would like to briefly consider previous hypotheses concerning biological and social advantages postulated for the carriers of the gene or genes predisposing to the development of schizophrenia.

PREVIOUS HYPOTHESES

Huxley, Mayr, Osmond, and Hoffer (1964) proposed the existence of a genetic morphism to account for the persistence of the schizophrenic genotype, the frequency of the "morphic gene" being "the result of a balance between its selectively favourable and unfavourable properties [p. 220]." They reasoned that a physiological advantage (e.g., resistance to infection) might compensate for the selective disadvantages of lower viability and fertility. However attractive this hypothesis may be, a number of investigators have pointed out the lack of corroborative evidence (Alland, 1967; Erlenmeyer-Kimling & Paradowski, 1966; Kuttner & Lorincz, 1966). To date, the existence of compensatory physiological advantages sufficient to account for the persistence of the schizophrenic gene (or genes) has not been demonstrated, although the recent work of Erlenmeyer-Kimling (1968a) on the reduced mortality of offspring of schizophrenic parents suggests the possibility that such evidence may be forthcoming.

The second hypothesis of Huxley and his collaborators (1964) states that some carriers of the gene for schizophrenia (including cryptoschizophrenic carriers, nonmanifest carriers, and some overt female schizophrenics) "may possibly have a higher than average fertility [p. 221]." In recent times, we have seen that overtly schizophrenic women, given an improved opportunity to procreate through shortened periods of hospitalization and more tolerant social climate, show increasing fertility when compared with women in the general population. This trend has been impressively documented by Erlenmeyer-Kimling, Nicol, Rainer, and Deming (1969) with data from a longitudinal study, initiated by the late Franz J. Kallmann (Erlenmeyer-Kimling, Rainer, & Kallmann, 1966), of schizophrenic patients admitted to New York State hospitals in the 1930s and 1950s.

Erlenmeyer-Kimling and Paradowski (1966) elaborated on the genetic morphism of schizophrenia and examined the idea that, historically, schizophrenics were esteemed for their mystical experiences and enjoyed privileged social status as shamans, prophets, or saints. They justly commented: "Saints and prophets not being renowned for high fecundity, the benefits ordinarily garnered by them or their isomorphs would scarcely have bestowed a reproductive advantage of the needed magnitude [p. 652]."

Hammer and Zubin (1968) suggested that creative deviation and pathological deviation rest on the same genetic base, and that the channeling of idiosyncratic behavior into culturally approved, stereotyped (but creative) roles enables individuals with deviant behavior patterns to contribute acceptably to their society. These authors propose, in effect, that the psychopathology of schizophrenia may be culturally advantageous under suitable environmental circumstances.

This hypothesis of Hammer and Zubin, like that of social advantage or physiological advantage, rests on the assumption that a biological etiology underlies the manifestation of schizophrenia or schizoid personality. By contrast, there are other psychological explanations of schizophrenia as the end result of an abnormal familial constellation in which faulty communication and inadequate role adjustment produce confused offspring with distorted perception of reality, incapable of successful interpersonal relationships, and unable to cope with various stresses. In these theories, biological factors are assigned relatively little importance and emphasis is placed on the home environment. A "mentally healthy" home should, therefore, limit or eliminate schizophrenia.

We do not wish to imply that psychoanalytic and other psychogenic theories regarding the development of schizoid and paranoid reactions are invalid. Indeed, they may explain how genetic endowment is actualized; however, we do take exception to the superficially optimistic view that environmental constellations *alone* are sufficient to account either for schizophrenia or for schizoid-paranoid personality features.

Even though there is no adequate estimate of the number of schizoid-paranoid individuals in the general population, the frequency of schizoids is far greater among the relatives of schizophrenics than in the families of other psychiatric patients; moreover, "normal" relatives of schizophrenics have a very small proportion of schizoids among their progeny. Having culled from the literature that approximately one-third of the first-degree relatives of schizophrenics are schizoid, Heston (1970) has made a good case for a continuum of schizoidia-schizophrenia. In a similar vein Rosenthal, Wender, Kety, Schulsinger, Welner, and Østergaard (1968) speak of the "schizophrenic spectrum" to describe the disorders found in abundance among biological, but not among adoptive, relatives of schizophrenics. Therefore, we must agree with Wender's cautious observation that "one cannot but conclude that the role of deviant psychological experiences in the etiology of schizophrenia has been overestimated [1969, p. 455]." Bleuler (1968), too, stresses the interplay of predisposing constitutional factors and environmental influences.

The foregoing does not contradict the descriptive evidence of the schizophrenogenic home environment and aberrant familial interaction so ably elucidated by the psychological school. It does suggest, however, that viewing schizophrenia in the broad terms of past human experience may add to our understanding, even though the broad view may not be applicable to each individual instance.

THESIS

Taking this broad view, we submit that, in addition to the psychological factors embraced by the hypotheses previously mentioned, there is a *fundamental psychological advantage* in the paranoid outlook on life which characterizes many nonpsychotic carriers* of the gene (or genes) for schizophrenia, although culturally induced phenocopies may also exhibit schizoid and paranoid behavior.

We would like to suggest that *the explanation of the ubiquitousness of schizophrenia in human populations lies not in the disease itself, but rather in the personality characteristics described as schizoid and paranoid, which are so often found in the nonpsychotic relatives of schizophrenics.*

Although others have suggested the possible psychological advantage bestowed by a high degree of creativity upon many nonpsychotic carriers of the gene(s) for schizophrenia (Heston, 1966; Karlsson, 1968), the possible survival advantage conferred by the paranoid life style itself has, with rare exceptions (Mayer-Gross, Slater, & Roth, 1969), gone unheeded. Yet it is likely that evolutionary advantages accrue to the suspicious, seclusive individuals rather than to their trusting fellow-men. In a world replete

---

* The term carrier here is used in its broadest sense, since our thesis does not depend on any given genetic model but is compatible with all of those proposed to date, whether they involve a single major gene, recessive or dominant, with incomplete penetrance, with or without modifier genes (cf. Böök, 1953a, 1953b; Elston & Campbell, 1970; Garrone, 1962; Heston, 1970; Kallmann, 1938, 1946, 1953; Slater, 1958); are polygenic (cf. Edwards, 1960; Gottesman & Shields, 1967; Kety, Rosenthal, Wender, & Schulsinger, 1968; Kringlen, 1968); are digenic (cf. Burch, 1964; Karlsson, 1964; Rüdin, 1916); or are based on genetic heterogeneity (cf. Erlenmeyer-Kimling & Paradowski, 1966; Hamburg, 1967).

with war and episodes of persecution, the wary have survived. We propose that usually these survivors have been the nonpsychotic carriers of the gene (or genes) for schizophrenia, who inherited a *psychological advantage* in their predisposition toward a *personality organization that has equipped them more effectively than others for basic survival in a threatening and competitive world.*

Attributes of the Schizoid-Paranoid Personality

The conspicuous features of paranoid and schizoid personality configurations are hypersensitivity, suspicion, mistrust, and relative seclusion. According to the *Diagnostic and Statistical Manual of Mental Disorders* of the American Psychiatric Association (1968), the paranoid personality is a behavioral pattern characterized by "hypersensitivity, rigidity, unwarranted suspicion, jealousy, envy, excessive self-importance, and a tendency to blame others and ascribe evil motives to them." The schizoid personality is described as manifesting "shyness, over-sensitivity, seclusiveness, avoidance of close competitive relationships, and often eccentricity [p. 42]." Brody and Sata (1967) state in their comprehensive discussion of schizoid-paranoid personality traits that many people designated as paranoid "share many of the traits found in the schizoid personalities." The schizoid "stands alone like an outsider looking in." Paranoids are, in addition, "distinguished by their defensive position against the world [pp. 941–943]." Are these necessarily maladaptive attributes?

Negative descriptions such as "argumentative, . . . egotistic, . . . demanding [Kolb, 1968, p. 402]" have positive correlates usually overlooked, such as "self-protective," "goal-oriented," "decisive." The "uncompromising" paranoid may also be the cautious scientist, the honest politician, the orthodox clergyman; the "hypersensitive" schizoid may be the exquisitely sensitive artist or musician or the insightful psychologist (Swanson, Bohnert, & Smith, 1970, p. 408). In other words, "it is not the personality outlook that is maladaptive but the use of these attributes in the total functioning of the individual so constituted." Schizoid-paranoid behavior patterns can be exceedingly useful under certain cultural conditions.

The Odyssean Personality

In order to escape the negative connotations associated with the terms schizoid and paranoid, we have selected the heroic figure of Odysseus (Ulysses) as the prototype of this personality.* Odysseus' character com-

---

* The authors gratefully acknowledge that Professor Steven Lattimore, Department of Classics, University of California at Los Angeles, directed their attention to the representative figure of Odysseus and to Stanford's description of him.

bined the primary advantages and disadvantages conferred by the schizoid-paranoid outlook. He was not a typical hero; Homer "skillfully succeeded in distinguishing Odysseus by slight deviations from the norm in almost every heroic feature [Stanford, 1968, p. 66]." For example, despite his ability to hold audiences "spellbound like a bard," his "habitual pose before beginning an important speech" was to "stand with his eyes fixed on the ground, his body and gestures stiff 'like an ignorant fellow's' [p. 71]." In line with Odysseus' reputation for deceitfulness and treachery, Stanford describes him as far less "intransigent" than the typical hero, ". . . prepared to . . . imitate the mole or the fox rather than the rhinoceros [p. 73]." In particular, "Odysseus's gift for anticipating dangers and his readiness to avoid them when it best served his purpose, did separate him from the normal hero of his time [p. 73]."

Stanford (1968) also stresses Odysseus' aloofness:

"There was no one, apparently, among his associates at Troy to whom he could open his heart and speak without suspicion or caution . . . . A marked degree of separateness, and often even of loneliness, is the common fate of those gifted like Odysseus with an abnormal degree of intelligence and subtlety. Friendship is naturally difficult with a person of this calibre. The razor-edge of his mind and speech, however well controlled, will be widely feared . . . . His general efficiency and success in whatever he undertakes will give an impression of inhumanity and self-sufficiency [p. 43]."

Odysseus clearly emerges as a schizoid-paranoid.

Although not always attractive, the characteristics mentioned above accounted for the survival of Odysseus in the face of overwhelming obstacles. Hence we have chosen the term *Odyssean personality* to delineate the potentially successful schizoid-paranoid individual.

The Odyssean personality may be identified by his use of the *paranoid mode of thinking*. He feels a need to be in control at all times and is suspicious of anything outside himself that might limit his control. He withdraws when he cannot assimilate a new experience or event and projects his fears to the external environment. With the "enemy" in view, he devises coping techniques.

The accuracy of paranoid perceptions and conceptualizations varies with the individual, the extent of his pathology, if any, and the external conditions. There is no doubt, however, that the Odyssean perceives events differently from the nonparanoid individual and also that he feels an innate compulsion to organize new percepts into his conceptual system, in order to deal with them. He prefers to err rather than to suspend judgment and cope with uncertainty (Abroms, 1966; Swanson et al., 1970). In primitive times, readiness to "see the worst," to take precautions against natural enemies, environmental threats, and human competitors *before* they attacked, must have afforded a potent survival advantage to individuals constituted to act unhesitatingly in such a manner. Furthermore, the Odyssean's typically maximal use of his intelligence, his careful store of information that might be of protective value to him, his oversensitivity to the motives of others, and his perspicacious judgment, so good "when it relates to situations of danger, competition or survival [Swanson et al., 1970, p. 57]," undoubtedly saved many such individuals actually confronted with real threats to life. The majority of other personalities, to whom the devious schemes of the Odyssean are ego-alien, who trust their fellow men, their social system, or their national organization, have a considerably lower probability of survival because they rarely recognize danger in time to act.

In summary, we consider the salient feature of the Odyssean to be a predisposition to suspiciousness, seclusiveness, and hypersensitivity with preferential utilization of the mechanisms of projection and self-reference.

The competitive, aggressive behavior of our times is not of recent origin. Beginning with the earliest civilization yet discovered (the Natufian, 8000–6000 B.C.), entire populations have succumbed to the "horrifying tendency of man, wearily repeated throughout the centuries, to take his neighbor's goods or country, or to 'scorch' the land for his own protection and his enemies' hurt [Glueck, 1959, p. 3]."

So long as schizoid-paranoid patterns are reinforced in a hostile environment, culturally sanctioned, and rewarded by survival, they will be perpetuated socially and genetically, as will the gene(s) for schizophrenia that directs this behavior.

The parent who teaches his child to remain distant from others, to be suspicious and secretive, will promote the development of Odyssean personality characteristics in suitably predisposed children. It is probable, however, that children not so predisposed are actually unable to internalize Odyssean behavior patterns even under appropriate parental tutelage.

The essential question is whether the schizoid-paranoid genotype is actually more capable than other personalities of responding successfully to life-threatening emergencies. No data to answer this question are available. Although concentration camp victims have been investigated (e.g., Bettelheim, 1943; Kral, 1951), as have some of the individuals who escaped internment and ultimately left Germany (Allport, Bruner, & Jandorf, 1953), the Jews who fled early because they recognized the danger posed to them by Hitler and the Nazi accession to power have not been studied. We surmise that this last group of survivors included a high proportion of Odysseans.

In contrast to the necessity for speculation regarding the frequency of Odysseans among those successful in escaping persecution, numerous reports associating vocational or social eminence, as well as success in business and certain professions, with schizoid-paranoid personality features are available (Eiduson, 1962; Henry, 1949; Menninger, 1937; Merton, 1969; Roe, 1951, 1953, 1956; Super, 1949). The Odyssean's drive to success, which we believe to be largely innate, is positively reinforced in achievement-oriented Western cultures. Culture, as a number of social scientists have stressed, is clearly relevant to survival needs (cf. Kluckhohn, 1967; Sapir, 1949) and is self reinforcing in that parents' predispositions and training direct their choices of which behavior to reward in their offspring (Gorer, 1953, p. 254).

Odyssean Creativity

Although we are inclined to dismiss the saying that genius is next to insanity, evidence is beginning to accumulate that there may indeed be a relationship between the achievement of success in a number of endeavors and the possession of genes that in other individuals seem to be responsible for schizophrenic breakdown (Hammer & Zubin, 1968).

In the Goertzels' (1962) study of "eminent" individuals, most of the parents were said to have driven their children to attainment, as well as often being, themselves, decidedly "queer," eccentric, or maladjusted. The maternal relationship particularly was often far from normal, and the dominating "totalitarian family" constellation was frequently encountered. Psychosis rarely followed in the offspring unless it had previously occurred in the family line. None of the eminent showed "ideal" social adjustment or mental health. The majority appear to have been endowed with Odyssean traits as well as the unusual talents on which their parents capitalized; they were taught to perceive the world inquisitively, critically, defensively, and/or aggressively, and to strive for successful achievement of rigorously pursued goals. Their childhood histories and later comparison with their siblings suggest important innate differences in personality; the teaching to which they were subjected reinforced their predisposition to perceive and react in the Odyssean manner (cf. Krech, Crutchfield, & Livson, 1969, Unit 44).

Karlsson's (1968) genealogical study in Iceland, concentrating on a schizophrenic kindred, revealed a high frequency of persons with "superior intellect or leadership ability [p. 85]," leading him to conclude that highly gifted individuals were also heterozygotes at the schizophrenic locus. An excess of unusually capable individuals among the biological relatives of schizophrenics was also reported by Heston (1966), who found significant musical ability and the expression of unusually strong religious feelings prominent among the offspring of schizophrenic mothers, children who had been adopted by unrelated foster parents in early infancy. The children without psychopathology were, by and large, not only successful adults but also, in comparison to a control group, were more spontaneous when interviewed, had more colorful life histories, held more creative jobs, and followed more imaginative hobbies. From their interest in music and art, their "lonely" hobbies, and their independent rather than hierarchical vocations, it is likely that many of these successful offspring of schizophrenic mothers were Odyssean personality types.

We are witnessing, then, a confluence of evidence supporting the beneficial effects of the gene (or genes) for schizophrenia when present in submaximal dose, or under suitable modifying influences, in the form of the Odyssean personality.

It is difficult, however, to resolve the paradox of schizoid withdrawal and paranoid aggression occurring simultaneously in the same individual. Clinicians have attempted to categorize each as unique, and they may indeed be discrete entities, yet clinical experience requires that we accept that they are related, not only in the patient diagnosed as "paranoid schizophrenic" but also in the relatives of schizophrenics, who are as likely to manifest schizoid or paranoid personality as schizophrenia. As early as 1938, Kallmann suggested the biological unity of schizophrenia and schizoidia. The inference that there is a common genetic basis for both schizophrenia and schizoid-paranoid personality is strengthened by the observation that monozygotic cotwins of schizophrenic index cases—who, after all, share identical genotypes—tend either to be schizophrenic themselves or to have predominating schizoid-paranoid personality features (46.4% and 41.1%, respectively: Heston, 1970, p. 252).

Since not all schizophrenics are paranoid, it may be argued that the paranoid syndrome cannot be the key to understanding the persistence of schizophrenia. This argument is not valid, inasmuch as all of the subtypes appear to be genetically related and none breeds true (Essen-Möller, 1946; Kallmann, 1938; Miller, 1941; Ødegaard, 1963; Slater, 1968). Although monozygotic cotwins, when concordant for schizophrenia, tend to manifest the same subtype (cf. Gottesman, 1968) and the same form (nuclear versus atypical: Mitsuda, 1967), Kringlen (1967b) noted: "The data lend no support to the idea that some subtypes of schizophrenia are more genetically determined than others . . . [p. 22]." Swanson et al. (1970), after reviewing the differences between paranoid and other subtypes of schizophrenia (e.g., somatotype, premorbid adjustment, age of onset, intelligence), likewise conclude that the "relationship of the paranoid process to schizoidness recurrently appears; whatever schizophrenia is, it appears to be a principal building block of the paranoid nature [p. 307]."

To describe the range of behavior along the schizophrenic spectrum, Essen-Möller (1946) and Kallmann (1938) used the term schizoidia, and today Heston (1970), who regards schizoidia as the basic inherited trait, concludes: "At the very least a prima facie case has been made for considering the whole group of schizoid and schizophrenic disorders as alternative expressions of a single genotype . . . [p. 252]." It is likely, however, that different modes of inheritance are present in different kinships (Erlenmeyer-Kimling, 1968b). As Heston (1970) has pointed out, "The mechanisms involved in a disease like schizoidia-schizophrenia will surely be found to be extremely complex . . . . But research must proceed from hypotheses based on present understanding [p. 253]." As in other conditions, observations of "similar phenotypes under varied outside influences (controlled twin studies) are certain to provide valuable clues to the recognition of disease-producing or disease-inhibiting agents which could not easily be obtained in any other manner [Jarvik, 1962, p. 21]."

A human pattern that resists all attempts at eradication clearly is an essential part of the species' endowment, whether benign or morbid. It is widely accepted, nonetheless, that fixed behavioral patterns such as we subsume under the Odyssean personality cannot evolve in different populations, because "flexibility of behavioral adjustment to different situations is likely to have had a selective advantage over any tendency toward stereotyped reactions [David & Snyder, 1951, p. 71]." Contrary to such a conclusion, we may postulate that flexibility would not, in fact, be preferred to stereotypy. Just as there are physiological patterns that are genetically programmed and that tend to be fixed rather than flexible, so many behavioral patterns should be genetically programmed and more or less inflexible, as their function is essential or peripheral to the life cycle of the organism; that is, genetic factors should have evolutionary relevance to survival and positive adaptation. Extending this argument, we propose that the paranoid outlook which characterizes the Odyssean personality is genetically programmed.

It has long been observed that paranoids differ from other personality types. According to Schwartz (1963), vulnerability to paranoid illness represents a specific risk, "determined by the relative primacy of defensive modes of operation. People have a greater or lesser capacity for paranoid adaptation, and this is relative to the characteristic patterns of their total adaptational systems of defense [p. 357]." We think that the predisposition to perceive certain incoming stimuli with caution is primarily inherited and is secondarily either reinforced by the parental-community environment in which the child is nurtured or inhibited through training and experience. However, the individual remains a carrier for the paranoid trait even when paranoid behavior is not overtly expressed; appropriate situational stresses may trigger a manifestation of the behavior in the person or his offspring.

The positive interaction between genetic predisposition, environmental reinforcement, and learning is illustrated by the dictum: "Every paranoid has a teacher."* But in addition he had the capacity, predisposition, and tendency toward paranoid thinking *before* being indoctrinated. Without such predisposition, the teaching would but rarely be successful.

The interaction of specific genotypic and environmental constellations may lead to the development of individuals representing the entire spectrum from the outright schizophrenic patient to the Odyssean personality.

CONCLUSIONS

We have proposed that the schizoid-paranoid personality, which we have termed Odyssean, has an early warning system—a built-in chemophysical device to safeguard him from danger by occasioning constant biological vigilance in the form of observable wariness and survival consciousness; these characteristic attributes are of sufficient preservative value to preclude genetic elimination in the normal course of evolution. The core of this personality is egocentric self-reference combined with suspicion and projection: the belief that others are experiencing the same feelings as oneself, and that everyone is equally competitive. The key to understanding the durability of this personality organization in its physical and behavioral manifestations has been succinctly stated by Mayer-Gross et al.: "the assumption that outside events are directed towards oneself in a meaningful way has probably been an aid to human survival, inspiring a sensitivity to the environment which otherwise might not have been given [1969, pp. 145–146]."

It may be the case that certain physiological patterns of an organism are incompatible with its individual existence but are necessary for species survival. The positive aspects of the schizophrenic gene (or genes) may relate to human survival under certain conditions despite individual morbidity when the full-blown disease occurs. The negative consequences ensuing to carriers of the gene(s) have been extensively and thoroughly discussed in the literature, whereas the positive aspects have generally been neglected, if recognized at all. In order to adjust the balance, we have

* The senior author first heard this provocative statement from Professor Roger MacKinnon of the Department of Psychiatry, Columbia University, and wishes to acknowledge the debt.

emphasized the benefits accruing to those who view the world in a paranoid manner, the nonpsychotic bearers (Odysseans) of the gene(s) for schizophrenia.

Dobzhansky (1955) reminds us of the simple solution to the Darwinian enigma "that natural selection should fail to eliminate from the population the unfit genotypes [p. 147]." Although heterozygotes are often "the fittest genotypes," because of heterosis (hybrid vigor), by Mendel's first law they would produce 50% of homozygotic progeny.

"What natural selection does is to establish proportions of the genotypes at which the average fitness of an individual in the population is the highest attainable one, but the high fitness of the population as a whole is purchased at the price of producing some genetically unfit individuals (the homozygotes). We are compelled to conclude that, with sexual reproduction, it is the Mendelian population, as well as the individual, which is the unit of natural selection and evolution [Dobzhansky, 1955, p. 147]."

Eckhard Hess may have provided us with the theoretical framework in which to reconcile the opposing views of the biogenic and psychogenic schools of thought. The contribution of ethological psychology, he says, is

"the rediscovery that man is a biological organism, that man must have a background and bring to present day species members an ancient repertoire of behaviors that have some bearing on the problem of human behavior today . . . a legacy of potential behavior patterns that at one time assured the survival of the organism . . . sexual behavior, aggressive behavior, and innate social responses [1967, p. 188]."

If, as we believe, the Odyssean personality also belongs to this legacy of potential behavior patterns, then there are two major questions we would like to ask.

1.   How prevalent is the Odyssean genotype in current societies?
2.   What is the impact of this genotype on the rest of the population?

We do not know the answers to these questions, but whatever they are, it appears that the schizoid-paranoid personality is an integral part of the inheritance of our species. We must come to terms with it.

The usefulness of the Odyssean personality depends on its role in the culture. No one would contest the desirability of eliminating schizophrenia. However, of the nonpsychotic carriers, a significant proportion may make social contributions of a high creative order, which others, not so biologically constituted, may be unable to offer to society. The instantaneous suspicion of the Odyssean and his immediate readiness to cope with emergency may often be inappropriate to the stimulus, but then again they may save his life. If he is in a position of leadership, his early awareness may also protect his group, just as his aggressiveness and projection may endanger it.

The influence of Odysseans by far exceeds their numbers, and we suspect that there are many more schizoid-paranoid genotypes throughout our communities than is currently believed. Certainly, their outsize imprint on history is undisputed, be they witless assassins of great men or religious leaders of humble multitudes.

In current times, the value *to the individual* of a paranoid constitution may be increasing; as social crowding breeds discontent and wars are waged in the name of *Lebensraum,* the ability to isolate oneself, the sensitivity to scent danger, the intelligence to plan escape are ever more valuable. But this same paranoid disposition to see evil in benign circumstances, to actualize the self *against* others, to be the first to attack, and frequently to misjudge others and act on such erroneous perceptions is exceedingly *dangerous to societies.*

"The survival of any species," Szent-Gyorgyi (1970) remarks, "depends on its ability to adapt to its surroundings [p. 13] . . . . We live in a new cosmic world which man was not made for [p. 17]." The changes from an agricultural world with its limited weapons to a technological world with its atomic bombs has been too swift for mankind to adapt. "We are forced to face this situation with our caveman's brain, a brain that has not changed much since it was formed [p. 17]." The defensive paranoid expression of the schizophrenic gene(s) may once have been useful, even necessary, to the species, but have we so institutionalized the paranoid outlook that we are "crazy apes," as Szent-Gyorgyi thinks? Certainly, in the senseless wars, increasing violence, proliferation of the tools of mass destruction, and ascription of the epithet "enemy" to all who look or behave differently than we do, we are perpetuating our paranoid inheritance.

The dog-eat-dog cultural pattern and the schizoid-paranoid personality pattern may be equally maladaptive; however, so long as the former exists, the latter may well be necessary, quite literally, for biological survival. With Munn (1938) we stress that "selection of the best adapted does not mean selection of the *inherently best* individuals [p. 90]"; where aggression is the fundamental psychic factor and the basis of the social organization, however, the vigilance of the Odyssean may be a prerequisite for survival —of some individuals at least.

ACKNOWLEDGMENTS

The manuscript was completed while the senior author was on leave holding appointments in the Department of Psychiatry at the University of California at Los Angeles and in the Veterans Administration Center for Psychosocial Medicine at Brentwood. The junior author also was on the staff of the latter institution.

The authors gratefully acknowledge the assistance of Ruth Bernstein, Karen Franck, and Sheldon Levy in the preparation of the manuscript.

REFERENCES

Abroms, G. M., Taintor, Z. C., & Lhamon, W. T. Percept assimilation and paranoid severity. *Archives of General Psychiatry,* 1966, **14,** 491–496.

Alland, A., Jr. A further note on evolution and schizophrenia. *Eugenics Quarterly,* 1967, **14,** 158–159.

Allport, G. W., Bruner, J. S., & Jandorf, E. M. Personality under social catastrophe: Ninety life-histories of the Nazi revolution. In C. Kluckhohn & H. A. Murray (Eds.), *Personality in nature, society, and culture.* (2nd rev. ed.) New York: Knopf, 1953. Pp. 436–455.

American Psychiatric Association, Committee on Nomenclature and Statistics. *Diagnostic and statistical manual of mental disorders.* (2nd ed.) Washington, D. C.: APA, Mental Hospital Service, 1968.

Bettelheim, B. Individual and mass behavior in extreme situations. *Journal of Abnormal and Social Psychology,* 1943, **38,** 417–452.

Bleuler, M. A 23-year longitudinal study of 208 schizophrenics and impressions in regard to the nature of schizophrenia. In D. Rosenthal & S. S. Kety (Eds.), *The transmission of schizophrenia.* London: Pergamon Press, 1968. Pp. 3–12.

Böök, J. A genetic and neuropsychiatric investigation of a North Swedish population. *Acta Genetica et Statistica Medica,* 1953, **4,** 1–100. (a)

Böök, J. Schizophrenia as a gene mutation. *Acta Genetica et Statistica Medica,* 1953, **4,** 133–139. (b)

Brody, E., & Sata, L. Trait and pattern disturbance. In A. M. Freedman & H. I. Kaplan (Eds.), *Comprehensive textbook of psychiatry.* Baltimore: Williams & Wilkins, 1967. Pp. 941–943.

Burch, P. R. J. Schizophrenia: Some new aetiological considerations. *British Journal of Psychiatry,* 1964, **110,** 818–824.

Cameron, N. Paranoid conditions and paranoia. In S. Arieti (Ed.), *American handbook of psychiatry.* Vol. 1. New York: Basic Books, 1959. Pp. 508–539.

Caspari, E. Selective forces in the evolution of man. *American Naturalist,* 1963, **97,** 5–14.

David, P., & Snyder, L. Genetic variability and human behavior. In J. Rohrer & M. Sherif (Eds.), *Social psychology at the crossroads.* New York: Harper, 1951. Pp. 53–82.

Dobzhansky, T. *Evolution, genetics, and man.* New York: Wiley, 1955.

Edwards, J. H. The simulation of Mendelism. *Acta Genetica et Statistica Medica,* 1960, **10,** 63.

Eiduson, B. T. *Scientists: Their psychological world.* New York: Basic Books, 1962.

Elston, R., & Campbell, M. Schizophrenia: Evidence for the major gene hypothesis. *Behavior Genetics,* 1970, **1,** 3–10.

Erlenmeyer-Kimling, L. Mortality rates in the offspring of schizophrenic parents and a physiological advantage hypothesis. *Nature,* 1968, **220,** 798–800. (a)

Erlenmeyer-Kimling, L. Studies on the offspring of two schizophrenic parents. In D. Rosenthal & S. S. Kety (Eds.), *The transmission of schizophrenia.* London: Pergamon Press, 1968. Pp. 65–83. (b)

Erlenmeyer-Kimling, L., Nicol, S., Rainer, J. D., & Deming, W. E. Changes in fertility rates of schizophrenic patients in New York State. *American Journal of Psychiatry,* 1969, **125,** 916–927.

Erlenmeyer-Kimling, L., & Paradowski, W. Selection and schizophrenia. *American Naturalist,* 1966, **100,** 651–665.

Erlenmeyer-Kimling, L., Rainer, J. D., & Kallmann, F. J. Current reproductive trends in schizophrenia. In P. Hoch & J. Zubin (Eds.), *Psychopathology of schizophrenia.* New York: Grune & Stratton, 1966. Pp. 252–276.

Essen-Möller, E. Psychiatrische Untersuchungen an einer Serie von Zwillingen. *Acta Psychiatrica et Neurologica,* 1941 (Suppl. No. 23).

Essen-Möller, E. The concept of schizoidia. *Monatschrift für Psychiatrie und Neurologie,* 1946, **112,** 258–271.

Garrone, G. Étude statistique et génétique de la schizophrenie à Génève de 1901 à 1950. *Journal de Génétique Humaine,* 1962, **11,** 89–219.

Glueck, N. *Rivers in the desert.* New York: Jewish Publication Society of America, 1959.

Glueck, N. *Deities and dolphins: The story of the Nabataeans.* New York: Farrar, Straus & Giroux, 1965.

Goertzel, V., & Goertzel, M. *Cradles of eminence.* Boston: Little, Brown, 1962.

Gorer, G. The concept of national character. In C. Kluckhohn & H. A. Murray (Eds.), *Personality in nature, society, and culture.* (2nd rev. ed.) New York: Knopf, 1953. Pp. 246–259.

Gottesman, I. I. Severity/concordance and diagnostic refinement in the Maudsley-Bethlem schizophrenic twin study. In D. Rosenthal & S. S. Kety (Eds.), *The transmission of schizophrenia.* London: Pergamon Press, 1968. Pp. 37–48.

Gottesman, I. I., & Shields, J. A polygenic theory of schizophrenia. *Proceedings of the National Academy of Sciences,* 1967, **58,** 199–205.

Hamburg, D. A. Genetics of adreno-cortical hormone metabolism in relation to psychological stress. In J. Hirsch (Ed.), *Behavior-genetic analysis.* New York: McGraw-Hill, 1967. Pp. 154–175.

Hammer, M., & Zubin, J. Evolution, culture and psychopathology. *Journal of General Psychology,* 1968, **78,** 151–164.

Henry, W. E. The business executive: The psychodynamics of a social role. *American Journal of Sociology,* 1949, **54,** 286–291.

Hess, E. H. Ethology. In A. Freedman & H. Kaplan (Eds.), *Comprehensive textbook of psychiatry.* Baltimore: Williams & Wilkins, 1967. Pp. 180–189.

Heston, L. Psychiatric disorders in foster home reared children of schizophrenic mothers. *British Journal of Psychiatry,* 1966, **112,** 819–825.

Heston, L. The genetics of schizophrenic and schizoid disease. *Science,* 1970, **167,** 249–256.

Huxley, J., Mayr, E., Osmond, H., & Hoffer, A. Schizophrenia as a genetic morphism. *Nature,* 1964, **204,** 220–221.

Jarvik, L. F. Genetic variations in disease resistance and survival potential. In F. J. Kallmann (Ed.), *Expanding goals of genetics in psychiatry.* New York: Grune & Stratton, 1962. Pp. 10–24.

Kallmann, F. J. *The genetics of schizophrenia.* New York: J. J. Augustin, 1938.

Kallmann, F. J. The genetic theory of schizophrenia. *American Journal of Psychiatry,* 1946, **103,** 309–322.

Kallmann, F. J. *Heredity in health and mental disorder.* New York: Norton, 1953.

Karlsson, J. L. A heredity mechanism for schizophrenia based on two separate genes, one dominant, the other recessive. *Hereditas,* 1964, **51,** 74–88.

Karlsson, J. L. Genealogical studies of schizophrenia. In D. Rosenthal & S. S. Kety (Eds.), *The transmission of schizophrenia.* London: Pergamon Press, 1968. Pp. 85–94.

Kety, S., Rosenthal, D., Wender, P. H., & Schulsinger, F. The types and prevalence of mental illness in the biological and adoptive families of adopted schizophrenics. In D. Rosenthal & S. S. Kety (Eds.), *The transmission of schizophrenia.* London: Pergamon Press, 1968. Pp. 345–362.

Kluckhohn, C. *Mirror for man.* New York: McGraw-Hill, 1967.

Kolb, L. C. *Noyes modern clinical psychiatry.* (7th ed.) Philadelphia: W. B. Saunders, 1968.

Kral, V. A. Psychiatric observations under severe chronic stress. *American Journal of Psychiatry,* 1951, **3,** 108.

Krech, D., Crutchfield, R. S., & Livson, F. *Elements of psychology.* New York: Knopf, 1969.

Kringlen, E. *Heredity and environment in the functional psychoses. An epidemiological-clinical twin study.* London: Heinemann, 1967. (a)

Kringlen, E. Heredity and social factors in schizophrenic twins. An epidemiological clinical study. In J. Romano (Ed.), *The origins of schizophrenia.* New York: Excerpta Medica Foundation, 1967. Pp. 2–14. (b)

Kringlen, E. An epidemiological-clinical twin study on schizophrenia. In D. Rosenthal & S. S. Kety (Eds.), *The transmission of schizophrenia.* London: Pergamon Press, 1968. Pp. 49–63.

Kuttner, R., & Lorincz, A. Schizophrenia and evolution. *Eugenics Quarterly,* 1966, **13,** 355–356.

Kuttner, R. E., Lorincz, A. B., & Swan, D. A. The schizophrenia gene and social evolution. *Psychological Reports,* 1967, **20,** 407–412.

Mayer-Gross, W., Slater, E., & Roth, M. *Clinical psychiatry.* London: Baillière, Tindall & Cassell, 1969.

Menninger, K. A. *The human mind.* (2nd ed.) New York: Knopf, 1937.

Merton, R. K. Behavior patterns of scientists. *American Scientist,* 1969, **57,** 1–23.

Miller, C. W. The paranoid syndrome. *Archives of Neurology and Psychiatry,* 1941, **45**, 953–963.

Mitsuda, H. Clinico-genetic study of schizophrenia. In H. Mitsuda (Ed.), *Clinical genetics in psychiatry. Problems in nosological classification.* Tokyo: Igaku Shoin, 1967. Pp. 49–90.

Munn, N. L. *Psychological development: An introduction to genetic psychology.* Boston: Houghton Mifflin, 1938.

Ødegaard, Ø. The psychiatric disease entities in the light of a genetic investigation. *Acta Psychiatrica Scandinavica,* 1963, **39**, 94–104 (Suppl. No. 169).

Redlich, F., & Freedman, D. *The theory and practice of psychiatry.* New York: Basic Books, 1966.

Retterstøl, N. *Paranoid and paranoic psychoses.* Springfield, Ill.: Charles C Thomas, 1966.

Roe, A. A psychological study of physical scientists. *Genetic Psychology Monographs,* 1951, **43**, 121–239.

Roe, A. *The making of a scientist.* New York: Dodd, Mead, 1953.

Roe, A. *The psychology of occupations.* New York: Wiley, 1956.

Rosenthal, D., Wender, P. H., Kety, S. S., Schulsinger, F., Welner, J., & Østergaard, L. Schizophrenics' offspring reared in adoptive homes. In D. Rosenthal & S. S. Kety (Eds.), *The transmission of schizophrenia.* London: Pergamon Press, 1968. Pp. 377–391.

Rüdin, E. *Zur Vererbung und Neuentstehung der Dementia praecox.* Berlin: Springer, 1916.

Sapir, E. *Selected writings in language, culture and personality.* Berkeley: University of California Press, 1949.

Schwartz, D. A re-view of the "paranoid" concept. *Archives of General Psychiatry,* 1963, **8**, 349–361.

Shields, J. Summary of the genetic evidence. In D. Rosenthal & S. S. Kety (Eds.), *The transmission of schizophrenia.* London: Pergamon Press, 1968. Pp. 95–126.

Slater, E. The monogenic theory of schizophrenia. *Acta Genetica et Statistica Medica,* 1958, **8**, 50–56.

Slater, E. A review of earlier evidence on genetic factors in schizophrenia. In D. Rosenthal & S. S. Kety (Eds.), *The transmission of schizophrenia.* London: Pergamon Press, 1968. Pp. 15–26.

Stanford, W. B. *The Ulysses theme: A study in the adaptability of a traditional hero.* (2nd ed.) Ann Arbor: The University of Michigan Press, 1968.

Super, D. E. *Appraising vocational fitness: By means of psychological tests.* New York: Harper, 1949.

Swanson, D. W., Bohnert, P. J., & Smith, J. A. *The paranoid.* Boston: Little, Brown, 1970.

Szent-Gyorgyi, A. *The crazy ape.* New York: Philosophical Library, 1970.

Wender, P. The role of genetics in the etiology of the schizophrenias. *American Journal of Orthopsychiatry,* 1969, **39**, 447–458.

Zerbin-Rüdin, E. Endogene Psychosen. In P. E. Becker (Ed.), *Humangenetik.* Vol. 5, Part 2. Stuttgart: Thieme, 1967. Pp. 446–577.

CHAPTER 4

Psychopathology or Deviance: Treatment or Intervention?

RUTH BENNETT and ELIZABETH SANCHEZ

Currently, the following concepts are used virtually interchangeably in the mental health profession: psychopathology, mental illness, maladjustment, behavior disorder, emotional disorder, and deviance. Several other related terms turn up in common parlance, for example, crazy, insane, nonconforming, and unsocialized. Often these labels are applied to individuals or groups of individuals with whom we do not share a set of values. Recently student demonstrators have been referred to as "crazies." It has also been easy to dismiss women's liberationists, Black Panthers, Young Lords, and hippies as deranged, while the "silent majority" or middle Americans are regarded, by implication, as mentally sound. It is apparent that terms which refer to mental illness are sufficiently fuzzy to allow professionals and nonprofessionals alike to take liberties in their usage. This practice is, at best, unscientific. At worst, it seems dangerous, particularly in times like ours in which technological change is accelerated, bringing with it changes in values, norms, and practices. Needless to say, the various labels referring to mental illness, when applied to groups or persons with whom we disagree, allow us to ignore, ridicule, or even incarcerate them.

Not only are deviance and psychopathology often equated, but also deviant sectors of society and nonlegitimated group and crowd deviant actions are often thought to result from individual psychopathology. Unfamiliar or new systems are seen not merely as repositories for individual pathology but as resultants of individual pathology as well. For example, in a recent study by Hendin (1971) of campus militants, it was found that their relationships with their families were disturbed. Although campus militants may well have poor relationships with their parents, no control groups of campus nonmilitants were studied to determine what their relationships at home were like. Given a generation gap, *all* college students may have difficulty communicating with their parents. Disturbances in individuals may possibly explain why they gravitate to militant groups, but the phenomenon of campus rebellion is a sociocultural pattern, the causes of which may be far more complex than individual psychopathology.

Not 10 years ago, a very different view of the relation between deviance and psychopathology was being taken, largely among social scientists, but also in other sectors of society. In a number of studies conducted roughly a decade ago, conformity was found to be related to factors indicative of mental illness. DiVesta and Cox (1960) found a relationship between conformity and anxiety. Breger (1963) reported a relationship between conformity and inability to express hostility overtly. Hoffman (1953) observed a relationship between conformity and lack of ego strength. On the other hand, in our own research on residents of a home for the aged (Nahemow & Bennett, 1967) a positive relationship was obtained between conformity and mental health.

Undoubtedly, the truth lies somewhere between the two extreme positions: some mentally ill people deviate from social norms, and others conform to them; also, the ill may deviate from some social norms but conform to others. Observed rates and correlations of deviance and conformity probably depend on the norms to which individuals are expected to conform and the degree of commitment that individuals have to these norms. The definitions and measures of conformity and deviance used in research may also determine the rates obtained. As far as can be determined, there seems to be no more conceptual clarity today in the study of conformity and deviance and their relationship to mental illness than existed 10 years ago.

This chapter is addressed to classifying acts of conformity and deviance according to who enacts them and the extent of group legitimation, examining current theories concerning the relationship between conformity and deviance and psychopathology, discussing the points of view of socially oriented theorists regarding the treatment of psychopathology, and making suggestions for rendering this field more amenable to research in the future.

There is, as yet, no consensus on the definitions of the concepts of norm, conformity, deviance, and mental illness, and no reliable, valid, or good methods for directly observing and measuring these concepts.

The concept of social norm is a key one in these fields. Each field has its own definition of norm, as well as its own definitions of the derivative concepts of conformity, deviance, and abnormality. Sociologists define norms as expectations for behavior to which positive or negative sanctions are assigned. Conformity is behavior enacted in accordance with norms; deviance is behavior that violates norms. It is this set of definitions that has been used in our research, as well as in the work of some other authors described in the rest of the chapter.

However, it should be noted that there are also anthropological, social psychological, and psychiatric definitions of norms, conformity, and deviance. Anthropologists, much like sociologists, see norms as culturally specific patterns of behavior. For social psychologists, most of whom work with ad hoc groups, norms represent behaviors of a majority of a group; deviance or nonconformity is taking a stand against a majority view, often when the majority is wrong and there is much group pressure to conform; conformity usually means supporting an erroneous judgment of a group majority. The psychiatric view of norms seems to alternate between accepting as a norm a statistical standard of behavior of average individuals or, conversely, defining as a norm that which is right for any individual at any given time. Little or no effort has been made to try to develop definitions of these concepts that are acceptable to members of all of the professions mentioned above.

CLASSIFYING DEVIANCE AND CONFORMITY

Both deviance and conformity may be cross classified in a number of ways. Two crucial dimensions for classifying acts of conformity and deviance are whether they are enacted by an individual, a group, or a crowd and whether they are nonlegitimated acts and nonlegitimated rituals or legitimated acts and legitimated rituals.

Using the words legitimated and nonlegitimated raises the sticky question of legitimated by whom. Usually, we think in terms of society as a whole and assume more rationality, homogeneity, and cohesion in society than is warranted. For example, we assume social agreement on the definition of a crime because such agreement is reflected in codified laws. However, it is probably true that consensus on the definition of a crime varies from state to state, subculture to subculture, and subgroup to subgroup. Whereas acts of vigilante groups toward Blacks may have been applauded in the South, they were often punished in the North. However, it should be noted that even this situation is changing, and vigilante acts toward Blacks may be coming to be regarded as criminal behavior throughout the United States.

Two other questions are raised by this conceptualization of deviance and conformity: (1) conformity to what and deviance from what and (2) who does the legitimating and nonlegitimating of behavior? As noted above, these questions may be answered tentatively by the statement that codes of behavior and legitimators of behavior vary from region to region, subculture to subculture, and subgroup to subgroup. This makes especially problematic decisions determining what is deviant, who is deviant and what should be done with a deviant. Therefore any classification of conformity or deviance must be regarded as highly tentative, culture bound, and time bound.

However, if there is concern with intervening in deviance-producing and deviance-maintaining systems, as is suggested by Scheff (1964) and those involved in community psychiatry programs such as Gruenberg (1969) and Sainsbury (1969), an effort should be made to locate such systems. It is our view that psychopathology may be generated in many nondeviant sectors of society. By cross-classifying acts of deviance and conformity according to who performs them and whether or not they are legitimated, this point may be illustrated.

Examples of nonlegitimated* acts of deviance performed by groups are gang wars, revolutionary activities, and police brutality; nonlegitimated acts of deviance performed by crowds are rioting, ritual persecutions, pogroms, and witch hunts; nonlegitimated acts of deviance performed by individuals are crimes and other forms of rule breaking. Legitimated acts of deviance performed by groups are vandalism by some groups of children and adolescents, most acts of warfare, convention behavior, and hazing. Legitimated acts of deviance performed by crowds are participation in vigilante raids and behavior during carnivals. Some examples of legitimated acts of deviance performed by individuals are mystical experiences and religious visions and acts of mischief by children and adolescents.

Examples of nonlegitimated acts of conformity engaged in by groups are superpatriotic activities; crowds may engage in nonlegitimated conformity demonstrations such as those recently conducted by "hard-hats." Individuals who exhibit blind obedience to authority exemplify a high degree of nonlegitimated conformity. Legitimated conformity on the part of groups is behavior exhibited at meetings of organizations, behavior during rites of passage, some patriotic behavior, and behavior exhibited on feast days and holiday celebrations. Examples of legitimated conforming behavior on the part of crowds are subway behavior, behavior at athletic meets, and other behaviors of large groups of spectators. Legitimated conformity on the part of individuals consists of most daily, role enactment behavior.

The problem of fitting mental illness into the tentative classification system outlined above is difficult. It is clear that most forms of deviance or rule breaking occur in groups and/or are legitimated either at specified

---

* The terms legitimated and nonlegitimated are only approximately accurate; for example, group activities such as revolution obviously have some intragroup legitimation.

periods during the life cycle or under specific conditions. This is probably true for most societies. The only category of deviance that seems to have concerned those interested in its relation to psychopathology is that of nonlegitimated rule breaking by individuals.

However, it is possible for mental illness to be expressed in the acts listed in all cells of this classification system. For example, the superpatriot or "hard-hat" may be as paranoid in his extreme conformity as the criminal is in his individual rule-breaking activity. In other words, nondeviant sectors of society may also produce and sustain psychopathology. To resolve this problem, mental health studies of superpatriots are needed along with studies of prison or hospital inmates.

ETIOLOGY OF PSYCHOPATHOLOGY AND ORIENTATION OF TREATMENT

In regard to nonlegitimated acts of deviance performed by individuals, there is virtually no agreement about causes. In general, the various authors whose work is discussed below seem to view deviance and psychopathology as indistinguishable. They differ, though, in their views of etiology. At one extreme are social scientists who virtually ignore the medical framework in relation to psychopathology and regard as deviance all behavior disorders that have an etiological basis in society. At another extreme are those postulating a medical model in which deviance and psychopathology are equated but are thought of in organic terms. Treatment, if and when suggested, may or may not correspond to the definition of or presumed etiological basis for psychopathology. With the exception of Erikson (1962) none of the environmentalists considered here proposes to treat the deviant's environment. Yates (1970) is intermediate in his views between an environmentalist and an individualist. There is some agreement that one or another aspect of environment generates deviance and/or psychopathology; however, most therapies proposed are directed at the "victim" of environment and not at the causal agents.

According to some, psychopathology resides in the eyes of the beholder and not in those whose behavior may violate social norms. If social norms change, the deviant may in time be thought of as normal. According to sociologist Erikson (1962), deviance is conventionally defined as a symptom of internal breakdown in society and as an accidental result of disorder and anomie. However, in his view this framework is too narrow because deviant activities "develop forms of organization, persist over time, and sometimes remain intact after the strains which originally produced them have disappeared [p. 307]." Erikson believes that the study of deviant behavior is as much a study of social organization as it is of disorganization and anomie. No form of behavior is inherently deviant but rather is deemed deviant by a social audience. Therefore he thinks the audience is the critical variable in the study of deviance. Society is the screening device that isolates the deviant details in otherwise conforming behavior. He considers a number of factors important to society which are "not directly related to the deviant act itself: it is concerned with the actor's social class, his past record as an offender, the amount of remorse he manages to convey and many similar concerns which take hold in the shifting moods of the community . . . [p. 308]."

Erikson notes that Durkheim theorized that deviant acts are not necessarily harmful to a society and that deviance helps keep social order intact. He suggests, therefore, that deviant behavior, by its extreme nature and subsequent interaction with social control agencies, marks the behavioral boundaries of a social system, thereby defining how much variability and diversity a system can cope with before losing its distinct structure. Erikson's research interests are to determine how persons are selected to play deviant roles and to study comparatively the soceties that allow individuals to engage in deviant behavior at specific ages or during special seasons. He notes that such societies allow deviants, upon termination of "the period of services on society's boundaries," to relinquish the deviant role wthout stigma.

A significant impetus to study the society that designates people as deviant or mentally ill came from the work of Scheff (1964). He studied some of the variations in the procedures for hospitalizing and committing persons alleged to be mentally ill in metropolitan and nonmetropolitan jurisdictions in a midwestern state. He interviewed judges, psychiatrists, and officials of 20 counties and observed proceedings in four jurisdictions. He found that in jurisdictions characterized by a small volume of cases there were only moderate public pressures against erroneously releasing patients from hospitals. Personal acquaintance with the patient or his family, little psychiatric sophistication, and, where the patient has them, resources for defending himself against allegations about him bring about "substantial rationality" in commitment procedures. On the other hand, jurisdictions with large numbers of cases, strong public pressures against erroneous releases, and lack of personal acquaintance with the persons alleged to be mentally ill, as well as limited resources whereby persons can defend themselves against such allegations, have many hospitalizations. In fact, hospitalization and treatment were found to be virtually automatic once the complaint had been brought to court. These findings suggest that in urban areas where there are large numbers of cases the relationship between urbanism and the high incidence of mental illness may simply be due to the absence of broad, rational screening processes. Scheff also suggested that the decision about diagnosis, hospitalization, and treatment is made basically by relatives or others who bring the individual to court. He concludes that to understand the incidence of mental illness one must study the operation of social control in the community.

In a later work, Scheff (1966) formulated a theory of mental illness which contains two basic components: "social role and social reaction. Its key assumptions are that most chronic mental illness is at least in part a social role and that the societal reaction is usually the most important determinant of entry into that role [p. 28]." Rule-breaking acts, responses of others, and rulebreakers' responses to others' responses constitute a social system with definite boundaries and self-maintaining properties. To treat illness means, therefore, to disrupt a chain of relationships in a bounded, self-maintaining system. Scheff points out that, in spite of large numbers of studies done on functional mental disorders, there is no substantial verified body of knowledge about them. Most methods of diagnosis are clinical and have not been verified by scientific measures. He criticizes psychiatric, genetic, biochemical, and psychological investigations on the grounds that they focus attention on individual differences rather than on the social system in which the individual is found.

Blum (N. D.) lends support to Scheff's assertion that screening processes are largely unscientific, as well as particularistic. He discusses the verdict of not guilty because of insanity (NGI), usually based on the amount of biographical data available and known to jurors. He cites a case involving a man who had regular incestuous relations with his daughter and whose wife knew of these acts. Four alternate "rules" were used to reach the NGI verdict: (1) the unfreedom rule, (2) the cultural alien rule, (3) the search procedure rule, and (4) the disposition rule. The unfreedom rule says, "Given a member's description of an act as a rule violation, any description of the actor which posits him as being chained by impulse or bound by stimuli in such a way as to be unfree to alter his action at the time of the event warrants a judgment of him as excusable [p. 28]." The cultural rule says, "Given a member's description of the act as a rule violation, any description of the actor which posits him as not knowing the meaning of his actions and hence as not being a normal, competent member of the collectivity, warrants a judgment of him as excusable [p. 29]." The search procedure rule says that jurors should search a defendant's biography on the supposition that if he is sick some biographical component, such as work history, will show this. The disposition rule allows jurors to equate mental illness with disposition, that is, to decide on a verdict on the basis of whether a hospital or a prison is more suitable for the type of person in question. When all was said and done, no positive criteria indicating mental illness were used to reach an NGI decision. The decision to hospitalize rather than imprison a deviant was not based on clear-cut signs and symptoms of mental illness.

By and large, none of the sociological theorists cited above give concrete suggestions for reducing the societal bases for deviance. At best it may be inferred that they would suggest intervention at some point in a deviance-producing or deviance-maintaining system. Erikson's allusion to societies which set aside periods for ritual deviance suggests that perhaps some sort of prolonged Mardi Gras season would eliminate some forms of what passes for mental illness in our society.

Yates (1970), whose point of view is based on learning theory and is, we consider, intermediate between the environmentalist and the individualist point of view, has experimentally altered institutional environments to approximate community environments. Through reinforcement and other learning principles, the institutionalized individuals' "wrong" behavior, which was learned somewhere along the line at critical development periods and which may be a symptom of a pathology syndrome, can be corrected. Once the symptom is "extinguished," secondary symptoms may well disappear. Behavior, not personality, is treated. The milieu of the individual deviant is revised in order to change his behavior but not to make this behavior seem less deviant.

The theorists to be discussed below view the etiology of psychopathology, or at least some forms of it, in societal terms. Those who propose treatment, however, offer suggestions for the treatment of individuals, not systems.

Szasz, a psychiatrist, wrote (1960) that the conventional notion of mental illness is derived from the idea that a discoverable defect exists in physicochemical processes and hence that mental disorders are not due to differences in individual needs, opinons, aspirations, and experiences. His criticisms of the conventional point of view imply that the converse is true, namely, that a defect or disease of a physicochemical process manifests itself in an individual other than by delusions and "belief in things." According to Szasz, mental symptoms are bound to the social context because they refer to an individual's communications about himself, others, and the world, when the observer believes them to be otherwise. This involves making judgments by comparing the "sick" indivdual's beliefs with those of the observer and society. While symptoms arise in the context of the stresses and strains inherent in social intercourse, conventional notions of mental illness use them to identify or describe a feature of an individual's personality. Mental illness as a defect in the personality is often considered a cause of human conflict; the cause of conflict is not viewed as the social situation that produces stresses and strains, but rather as the personality that does not adapt to these stresses. Mental illness implies deviation from psychosocial and ethical norms, and yet the remedy is sought in terms of medical measures, an idea that Szasz finds logically absurd. He notes that the psychiatrist's socioethical orientations influence his diagnosis and therapy. Therefore, he thinks that "what people now call mental illness are for the most part communications expressing unacceptable ideas, often framed in an unusual idiom [p. 116]." Belief in mental illness, according to Szasz, is the proper heir to belief in witchcraft and demonology. This belief acts as a "social tranquilizer thus encouraging the hope that mastery of certain specific problems may be achieved by means of a substitute . . . operation [p. 118]."

In a later and longer exposition of his theory, Szasz (1961) wrote, "When the social background of behavioral phenomena is treated as a variable, the phenomena of mental illness can be seen to appear, become intensified, diminish or disappear [p. 10]." Using hysteria as a paradigm, Szasz conceptualized mental illness in terms of (1) sign usage (hysteria-protolanguage); (2) rule following (helplessness, illness, and coercion); and (3) game playing (characterized by end goals of domination, interpersonal controls, and strategies of deceit). Hysteria, the "language of illness," is used because there is inadequate facility with another language or because it is especially useful. As rule following, illness is seen as a pattern of human action determined by roles and rules. There are two sources of rules in behavior labeled as mental illness. One is "paired activity," involving the helplessness of one role partner and the helpfulness of another. The other is the Judaeo-Christian cultural tradition, which places emphasis on helping the weak, ill, and poor, behavior that is rewarding to the helpers as well as to those helped. When viewed as game playing, illness is conceptualized in terms of goals (ends) and strategies (means). Contrasting body illness with mental illness, Szasz noted that the object of the body-illness game is bodily survival, whereas mental illness involves a heterogeneous mixture of metagames concerning how men should live. He noted:

"Socially deviant or obnoxious behavior may, in principle, be classified in many different ways. Placing some individuals or groups in the class of sick people may be justified by considerations of social expediency but cannot be supported by scientific observations or logical arguments [p. 43]."

By defining the behavioral disorder of hysteria as an illness, or any kind of suffering as illness, Szasz noted that we have lumped together A's (ill people), non-A's (which look like A's), and counterfeit A's. Hysteria (a counterfeit A) is illness-imitation behavior and to classify it as illness is to lump together an imitation and an actual item. Szasz concluded that psychiatry should be concerned with signs *qua* signs and not with signs as symptoms of something more real than themselves. He believed that psychopathology should be conceived of in terms of object relationships, sign using, rule following, social roles, and game playing and that psychotherapy should be conceived of as "a theory of human relationships involving special social arrangements and fostering certain values and types of learning [p. 297]."

The theorists whose points of view will now be briefly discussed wrote along more or less similar lines. Clausen (1968) advocated a positive approach to defining mental health, one dealing with performance, capacities, and utilization, as well as situational and contextual influence. He rejected the medical model of disease for dealing wth mental health and disorder and believed that the nomenclature and practices of psychiatry were inadequate for defining and measuring mental health. Clausen located the etiology of psychopathology in the individual, though viewed in terms of his context. He noted that the problem seems to be lodged not in the organism so much as in the person and that it is the functions of the socialized person (thought processes, beliefs, motivations, feelings, interpersonal skills) that are disordered, not those of the organism.

Presumably, if one accepts Szasz's as well as Clausen's conceptualizations, treatment for mental illness would consist of resocialization, re-education, behavior therapy, and/or persuasion techniques directed at the "sick" individual, more specifically at his personality, rather than at others in his social milieu.

For Gruenberg (1969) the secondary symptoms of mental disease may be as debilitating as the disease itself. Gruenberg referred to these secondary symptoms as social breakdown syndrome (SBS), for which there is no cure. He suggested that SBS may be prevented by reorienting both the individual and his immediate environment. Thus, although the major illness is treated medically, the secondary symptoms should be handled through social intervention techniques.

Pasamanick (1968) viewed mental illness as disease but cautioned us not to confuse it with deviance. Diseases can be treated by a variety of therapies; not so deviance, which requires social change.

RESEARCH UTILIZING INDEPENDENT DEFINITIONS OF MENTAL ILLNESS AND DEVIANCE

In order to bring about some conceptual clarity, as well as to foster research, the following suggestion is tentatively offered: define mental illness and deviance independently and hold to these definitions. If we agree to label a behavior as pathological, treatment should be aimed at the individual, his personality, his behavior, or his nervous system. However, if a behavior is viewed as deviant—and if that is deemed undesirable—then the social system may have to become the target of effort to eliminate the causes of deviance. In order to approach this goal, illness and deviance should be observed independently. The following examples from our research on the institutionalized aged (Bennett & Nahemow, 1965b; Walton, Bennett, & Nahemow, 1964) will illustrate how this can be done.

After extensive participant observation and interviews with residents of a home for the aged (selected for study because it was a clearly bounded community for the normal aged), norms were located on which there were varying degrees of consensus and which were adhered to with varying degrees of conformity. Norms were defined as expectations for behavior, on which there were varying degrees of consensus, but which were arbitrarily defined as norms because more than 50% of respondents agreed on them. Four norms were studied; three concerned interaction among residents and one concerned interaction between staff and residents, namely, tipping the help.

These norms formed the basis for constructing indices of socialization (knowledge of norms and customary practices) and conformity (behavior enacted in accordance with norms). Patterns of conformity were studied in 100 residents of a home for aged over a two-year period. One hundred consecutive new residents were interviewed on admission and after one month, two months, and two years in the home. Findings showed that conforming behavior was exhibited early. For example, at one month, 72% of the residents reported no overt conflict with their roommates, 88% reported no conflict with tablemates, 58% said they would not ask staff members for a change of room, and 74% said they tipped the help.

With time, conformity to each norm showed a distinct pattern of change. Conformity decreased on the two norms pertaining to interpersonal relations with other residents. At the end of two years, fewer residents reported that they liked or tolerated all roommates or all tablemates. Apparently, even if they intended to conform to the norm of avoiding conflict at all costs, the exigencies of group living eventually brought residents into conflict. What is interesting is that, despite increased conflict, a greater proportion of residents adhered to the norm that prevented them from asking staff members for a change of room. Adherence to this norm increased progressively, with 58% obeying it at one month, 62% at two months, and 71% at two years. Apparently, residents felt the need to avoid making any conflict public and therefore kept themselves from complaining to staff members.

Responses to the tipping norm, a subgroup norm found among residents, were also intriguing, since the conforming response was in conflict with administrative policy and with the norms of the higher-level staff.

At one month, about three-fourths of the residents gave tips; by two years, nearly everyone did. Although administrative and professional staff members tried to enforce a "no tipping" policy, they appeared to be unsuccessful in discouraging both residents and staff members from giving and accepting tips. One of the first things learned by the new resident was that he was expected to pay for many of the services he received, and numerous myths were circulated among residents about the lack of care given to individuals who had not tipped. The fact that the tipping norm was clearly operative despite the existence of an administrative policy prohibiting it indicated that residents did not blindly conform to staff rules, but were prepared to do so only when they approved of these rules or when the rules met their needs.

Mental illness was studied independently by a psychiatrist who, insofar as possible, tried to eliminate questions about current social behavior from the standard clinical examination he constructed. His work was conducted two years after residents were admitted. Residents were diagnosed according to whether they had senile dementia or functional mental disorders or were normal; the majority were diagnosed as normal. Estimates of conformity taken independently were based on self-reports of behavior enacted in accordance with norms; integration was measured on the basis of self-reports and on reports by others of involvement in activities and friendships; and evaluations were based on reports of feelings about the home. Early conformity, integration and evaluation measures did not correlate significantly with mental disorder. After two years, all mentally disordered subjects were characterized by low participation in home activities, such as clubs, games, concerts, and friendship groups. Those wth senile dementia were most like the normal aged. They evaluated the home positively and were positively identified with it. Those with functional disorder, on the other hand, evaluated the home negatively. They were the residents who had no positive affective bonds with their present environment. Failure to participate was also associated with functional psychiatric disorder. Residents with functional psychiatric disorder were uniformly maladjusted according to measures of social adjustment. There is some question, of course, about whether or not the psychiatric examination really omitted social data. On the assumption that it did, it is possible to assert that a relationship exists between functional pathology and social deviance, when both sets of measures are obtained in the same period.

The concepts of socialization and conformity refer to social processes found in any social system. However, the specific items in scales constructed to measure these processes will vary, depending on the cultural patterns of the system. Thus in one setting it may be a sign of conformity to give tips to hired help; in another, it may be deviant to do so. Although all social systems require the processes of socialization, integration, evaluation, and conformity, the emphasis placed on these processes will vary considerably. In some types of settings, therefore, integration may be thought of as central; in others, conformity to rules may be stressed.

To describe the adjustment of any one individual at each adjustment phase in a given social setting, the pattern of the group should be understood. If the normative pattern is to grow more discriminating with time in one's evaluation of a setting, then an individual who complains at a later date is not deviant even if he was a well-known "eager beaver" on entry. Group standards also should be considered in evaluating the mental state of an individual. If it is normative to be a nonparticipant in activities, then nonparticipation is not indicative of mental illness. The patterns, phases, and criteria of adjustment look entirely different in different types of residential settings. It is a credit to the adaptive capacity of most inmates of institutions that they can figure out the normative expectations of the group very quickly and, for the most part, behave in terms of them.

In a review of literature on residential settings for the aged, Bennett and Nahemow (1965a) found systematic differences in criteria of adjustment. In homes for the aged, adjustment criteria were fairly explicit and participation in formal and informal activities emerged as a major adjustment criterion. In retirement housing, participation in informal social relationships seemed an important adjustment criterion. In mental hospitals, nursing homes, and Veterans' Administration centers, on the contrary, there were virtually no social adjustment criteria. For the most part, people were expected to receive medical and nursing care passively. Our own data collected in the course of participant observation indicated similar trends. Needless to say, if the criteria of adjustment vary from setting to setting, so do the modes of adjustment found among residents. Probably it is more difficult to adjust to a setting with no explicit criteria than to one in which criteria are clearly set. Hence the apparently contradictory nature of many research findings on adjustment rates in institutions may possibly be explained in terms of institutional requirements that are rarely investigated directly, rather than in terms of individual pathology. Lack of clarity of expectations or, even, absence of any expectations for adjustment may account for the deviance or apathy found in many, if not most, mental institutions or homes for the aged.

The aspect of an institution (or of any social group) which apparently determines whether there will be complex normative expectations is the degree to which the group recognizes that it is functioning as a permanent-membership body. For example, when an institution, like a home for the aged, is explicitly structured as a terminal one, adjustment is considered critical. In fact, staff members probably evaluate themselves in terms of how well they help people to adjust. This was recognized by Geld (1964) and labeled the "principle of permanency." The way in which this principle works is illustrated in a comparison we made of an admission ward and continued-treatment wards of a large mental hospital. Our findings showed that adjustment criteria were fewer in an admission building, from which patients were sent to other parts of the hospital, than in a continued-treatment building housing patients who were chronically ill, but not violent. In the latter, some patient and staff norms were found and were explicit. Also, patients were aware of them and communicated them to the interviewers. This finding was not anticipated initially; it was thought that people who had been in a "back ward" of a hospital for many years would be much more uncommunicative than new arrivals. What was interesting was that a social system did not develop in the admission building despite the fact that many geriatric patients had lived there for as long as five years. One of the reasons that staff members kept geriatric patients in the admission building for several years was that they considered it more therapeutic. However, the knowledge that this was a temporary residence for incoming patients was powerful enough to prevent any sort of social system from developing. On the temporary ward more random acting-out, "crazy" behavior was observed than occurred on the permanent ward. Clearly, this temporary environment needed altering or treatment.

SUMMARY AND CONCLUSION

In this chapter, it was noted that accepted cross-disciplinary definitions of the concepts of deviance and mental illness are lacking and that currently the terms are used interchangeably. We attempted to classify deviance and conformity according to whether they are enacted by groups, crowds, or individuals and whether they are legitimated or nonlegitimated. It seemed possible for mental illness to manifest itself in each cell of such a classification system. However, it was noted that traditionally the only area that has been of concern to those interested in psychopathology is nonlegitimated, individual rule breaking.

Literature on psychopathology representing a predominantly environmental approach to the relations between deviance and psychopathology was reviewed in relation to proposed treatment. By and large, proposed treatment was aimed at changing the deviant and/or sick individual, rather than his environment. Even community psychiatry or mental health programs with stated aims of intervening in deviance-producing systems in the community direct their treatments at sick individuals.

One possible solution was suggested for dealing with the dilemma of deciding what is deviance and what is illness. This was to define and measure the two concepts independently and to study their interrelationships in a variety of contexts and over time. We illustrated how this was done in some of our research conducted in a home for the aged in which psychiatric examinations and measures of social adjustment were taken independently. The findings showed that only functionally disordered residents, as opposed to those with mild organic disorders, were involved in deviant behavior. Other research was described in which it was found that residential settings for the aged vary in the emphasis placed on conformity. In some settings, social interaction of any sort is valued more than conformity. Engaging in conflicts with other inmates may not be seen as deviance in such interaction-valuing residential settings.

An interesting question is whether deviants (with or without a label of mental illness) in one system, who are placed in another system in which their behavior is valued, become deviant there as well. There seems to be some controversy about this issue but no research. For example, recently we heard a psychiatrist say that a schizophrenic adolescent who had visual hallucinations remained clearly schizophrenic even in a drug-taking hippie commune. More research is needed on this problem and similar ones.

It may be concluded that, until there is some consensus and more research on the interrelationship between deviance and illness, the sophisticated practitioner as well as the enlightened layman probably will continue to label as sick any behavior which challenges their values.

REFERENCES

Bennett, R., & Nahemow, L. Institutional totality and criteria of social adjustment in residential settings for the aged. *Journal of Social Issues,* 1965, **21,** 44–78. (a)

Bennett, R., & Nahemow, L. The relations between social isolation, socialization and adjustment in residents of a home for aged. In M. P. Lawton (Ed.), *Mental impairment in the aged.* Philadelphia: Maurice Jacob Press, 1965. Pp. 90–108. (b)

Blum, A. F. Common sense conceptions of insanity. Unpublished manuscript.

Breger, L. Conformity as a function of the ability to express hostility. *Journal of Personality,* 1963, **31,** 247–257.

Clausen, J. A. Values, norms and the health called mental: Purposes and feasibility of assessment. In S. B. Sells (Ed.), *The definition and measurement of mental health.* Washington, D. C.: U. S. Department of Health, Education and Welfare, 1968. Pp. 116–134.

DiVesta, F. J., & Cox, L. Some dispositional correlates of conformity behavior. *Journal of Social Psychology,* 1960, **52,** 259–268.

Erikson, K. T. Notes on the sociology of deviance. *Social Problems,* 1962, **9** (4), 307–314.

Geld, S. Toward a definition of the modern home. In M. Leeds & H. Shore (Eds.), *Geriatric institutional management.* New York: G. P. Putnam's Sons, 1964. Pp. 389–397.

Gruenberg, E. M. From practice to theory: Community mental health services and the nature of psychoses. *The Lancet,* 1969, **1,** 721–724.

Gruenberg, E. M., Snow, H. B., & Bennett, C. L. Preventing the social breakdown syndrome. *Social Psychiatry,* 1969, **47,** 179–195.

Hendin, H. Survey of campus militants. *The New York Times Magazine,* Jan. 17, 1971, p. 16.

Hoffman, M. L. Some psychodynamic factors in compulsive conformity. *Journal of Abnormal and Social Psychology,* 1953, **48,** 383–393.

Nahemow, L., & Bennett, R. Conformity, persuasibility and counternormative persuasion. *Sociometry,* 1967, **30** (1), 14–25.

Pasamanick, B. What is mental illness and how can we measure it? In S. B. Sells (Ed.), *The definition and measurement of mental health.* Washington, D. C.: U. S. Department of Health, Education and Welfare, 1968. Pp. 29–46.

Sainsbury, P. Principles and methods in evaluating community psychiatric services. Paper presented at the 8th International Congress on Gerontology, Washington, D. C., 1969.

Scheff, T. J. Social conditions for rationality: How urban and rural courts deal with the mentally ill. *The American Behavioral Scientist,* 1964, **7,** 21–24.

Scheff, T. J. *Being mentally ill: A sociological theory.* Chicago: Aldine, 1966.

Szasz, T. S. The myth of mental illness. *The American Psychologist,* 1960, **15** (2), 113–118.

Szasz, T. S. *The myth of mental illness: Foundations of a theory of personal conduct.* New York: Hoeber, 1961.

Walton, H., Bennett, R., & Nahemow, L. Psychiatric illness and adjustment in a home for the aged. *Annals of the New York Academy of Sciences,* 1964, **105,** 897–918.

Yates, A. J. *Behavior therapy.* New York: Wiley, 1970.

CHAPTER 5

Psychopathology and the Structure of Social Networks

MURIEL HAMMER

This chapter will deal with the social component of psychopathology in terms of an approach that is in one sense overdue, in another sense premature.

"Social" is commonly used to refer to a very wide range of phenomena, including personality patterns and especially cultural norms. A "purely" social component is, however, analytically isolable from these phenomena. By purely social I mean the structure of the distribution of links among individuals and sets of individuals.

The extensive literature on social (in the broader sense) aspects of psychopathology is concerned primarily with personality (as, e.g., in many of the family background studies) and with culture (as in studies of normative disparities, etc.). The relevance to psychopathology of the "purely" social has not been analyzed. It may turn out, of course, not to be relevant, but there are sufficient implications in studies tangential to the social (as defined here) to suggest relevance. The advantages of isolating the "pure" social factor are essentially that it can provide clarity of definition for at least one part of a field whose concepts are quite confused; that it extends comparability across a very broad range of phenomena, including quite disparate cultures and nonhuman species; and that it permits the utilization of mathematical techniques of greater power than those that have so far seemed appropriate in this area.

The sense in which this approach is premature is that there is so brief a history of work on the social as such, and so little clear information, methodology, or theory in that area, that it may be foolhardy to attempt to apply it to a field of practical concern. As with other seemingly new conceptions, however, there is a long history of work with related concepts, which may be able to serve as an adequate guide.

The general question in this domain that is most closely related to other areas of research on psychopathology would be what, if any, associations (etiological, therapeutic, etc.) exist between characteristics of social networks (such as size, boundedness, interconnectedness) and characteristics of psychopathology (such as frequency, symptomatology, diagnosis, prognosis). A further question that also should be raised is whether there are pathological (rather than pathogenic) properties of networks. These are quite different questions; the justification for raising them together is that, without explicit separation, they are likely to be confounded. (Such confounding seems to exist in a parallel way in much of the literature on cultural norms in relation to psychopathology.)

In an area as ill defined as psychopathology, it seems to me not feasible to formulate clear, researchable etiological hypotheses. Among other problems, that of antecedents versus consequences of illness is not truly resolvable even in prospective studies if one does not know when the pathology really "began" or just what the pathology consists of. It may be more productive to formulate our questions in terms directed to discovering what sets of conditions—biochemical, psychological, social—are necessary to the development of publicly recognized pathology. For example, social isolation or some nutritional deficiency or heavy drug use may be the result of incipient illness, and may at the same time be necessary to the creation of that illness. Such a factor would not be etiological in the usual sense of the term but would nevertheless be part of the pathogenic process.

What I wish to suggest here is that an individual's social networks are of necessity involved in the pathogenic process for any pathology with nontrivial social aspects, a category which clearly includes much of psychopathology.

GENERAL NATURE OF SOCIAL NETWORKS

To study the social, one starts with linking behavior—interactions, sets, and sequences of interactions. Solitary behavior becomes relevant secondarily, in so far as it affects interaction sequences. Something like a map of connection densities and channels may itself constitute a description of society, involving internal interrelationships of variables defined in terms relevant to that level of description. ("Connection densities" refers to the differential distribution of relationships—if the social connections are plotted for some set of people, there will be relatively many connections at some parts of the network, relatively few at others; and "channels" refers to the paths or routes that a message or other item would have to travel to get from any one individual, X, to any other, Y—for a given

X→Y there may be no path, one path, or any number of alternative paths.) For example, size, degree of interconnectedness, and relative stability of subsets are all variables that are possible within the framework of such a description and that may be related to each other. Different kinds of channel restriction may be analyzed in terms of a concept like power, formulated at the level of that description. For example, the alteration of channel size in certain parts of a network, such as the elimination of all paths between any members except those going through a given member, Z (thus giving Z the power to control all contacts in that part of the network), may effect alteration of the sequences in other parts of the network in discernible nonrandom ways.

The kind of map I am talking about does not exist, and in the literal sense—a total map of all interactive connections—of course will never exist. An ideal network map is not even theoretically possible, since there is no logically exhaustive set of criteria for linkages. An approximation to such an ideal map would involve overlapping sets of linkages, defined by a number of different modes or types of connection, including information on frequency and intensity of activation, for all points with any linkage with each other—which presumably means for all existing human individuals. On the basis of such an overall map it would be possible to formulate and answer any purely social question about any set or sets of individuals, groups, or linkages.

POTENTIAL VALUE FOR THE STUDY OF PSYCHOPATHOLOGY OF SOME ASPECTS OF SOCIAL NETWORKS

Before considering feasible (rather than ideal) approximations to a "total map" of social connections, it seems appropriate to consider more specifically what potential value there might be for psychopathology in developing such a map. Actual data on the role of social networks in psychopathology are almost nonexistent. Using this approach on a very limited scale, with schizophrenic patients, we found that structural characteristics of the network and the patient's position in it were highly associated with the speed with which he received attention, the degree to which others would substitute for him in his tasks, and the amount of change his hospitalization made in his subsequent social connections (Hammer, 1963–64). Information on the processes most closely involved in the pathology itself is almost purely inferential: for example, schizophrenic patients reportedly have fewer and more mediated social connections, placing them in a communication system with less effective feedback than is typical for their society (Hammer, 1961); a substantial proportion of them have had loose, disrupted networks (Srole, Langner, Michael, Opler, & Rennie, 1962); incidence and type of psychopathology seem to be different for viable tight-knit communities from what they are in looser or more disorganized settings (Eaton & Weil, 1955). It is perhaps relevant that network structure seems also to affect ease of communication for normal populations (Bernstein, 1962).

The potential value of investigating this inferential material directly may be seen by considering some of the currently recognized issues in psychopathology.

If we take schizophrenia as a major example, we find that some of the more consistent findings reported in the literature* have been (1) genetic bias (Kallmann, 1938); (2) social class bias (Hollingshead & Redlich, 1958); (3) rural-urban bias (Frumkin, 1954); (4) association with geographic mobility (Murphy, 1965); (5) association with a relatively solitary mode of life (Kohn & Clausen, 1955); (6) association with marital status, especially for men (Srole et al., 1962); (7) differential incidence in different ethnic groups (Ødegaard, 1945); (8) differential prognosis for slow or sudden onset of symptoms (Schofield, Hathaway, Hastings, & Bell, 1954). Some of these findings may of course turn out to be erroneous because of serious methodological difficulties in all of this research. They have been found repeatedly, however, in a variety of contexts, with somewhat different research procedures; and for most of the studies involved, it is more likely to be the interpretations of the findings, rather than the gross data, that have tended to be misleading. Some of the more adequate studies have attempted to control for some variables while examining the apparent effect of others: for example, ethnicity and class or ethnicity and mobility or social class and social isolation. It is obviously impracticable, in any study, to control for all variables that one may have reason to consider relevant. Furthermore, in terms of understanding the results, we would be only slightly advanced if we could say with assurance that, for example, the "true" incidence of schizophrenia is inversely related to class status. Class status (or ethnicity, mobility, etc.) is itself too complex to suggest clear testable mechanisms. The major approach to clarification of some of these findings has tended to be the development of more sophisticated methods of sampling, eliciting information, and statistical processing, as well as occasionally the testing, more or less independently, of a subsidiary hypothesis, such as that of social downward "drift" for schizophrenics.

A far more powerful approach may be suggested. A large number, if

---

* There is a large number of relevant references. Those cited here are generally drawn from the earlier and better-known studies.

not all, of these findings may have one or more common components. If they do, research may be conducted that is at the same time more precise, more economical, and potentially more closely related to a possible mechanism. (This is not suggested here as a novel conception, but only as one which seems to warrant considerably more explicit attention than it generally receives.) Perhaps the best-known hypothesized common component is the psychocultural concept, stress. Stress and protection from stress may well be commonly involved in all or almost all of the findings mentioned (and others as well); the difficulty with research relevant to it is that we have no independent measures of stress. The resulting circularities of reasoning, although by no means necessarily invalid, seem particularly undesirable in an area in which there is so little firm information or conceptualization.

Aspects of social network analysis are ideal in terms of the problems so far raised: the structure of social networks is of necessity a component of any of the social and cultural variables mentioned (and may turn out to be relevant to some seemingly genetic ones as well); and although the research is costly and difficult in practice, the necessary definitions may be made with precision and quite independently of any other variables under investigation. That social network structure is relevant to psychopathology is at least suggested by the facts that the known incidence of mental illness tends to be disproportionately high in populations with unstable and disrupted social patterns—for example, cosmopolitan centers with high mobility (Faris & Dunham, 1939); migrant populations (Malzberg & Lee, 1956); ethnically marginal areas (Murphy, 1965); and groups with a high degree of in-city movement (Tietze, Lemkau, & Cooper, 1942)—and that schizophrenic patients commonly have histories of partial social isolation (Kohn & Clausen, 1955).

The simplest relationship between the sets of findings referred to earlier and social network structure would be that the same "pathogenic" network structure exists wherever a given disorder is found, and not otherwise. However, for a number of social structural and psychosocial reasons, a more complex relationship should be expected. The possible ways in which network structure might function in relation to psychopathology are essentially as a transmission structure (of behavior, goods, norms, values, language) and as a kind of security structure (positive or negative) which may "fill in" for an individual during a nonfunctional period or, alternatively, either "eject" him during such a period or direct him into more specialized institutional channels.

The characteristics of networks that must be considered are the internal structure (e.g., degree of interconnectedness, either in general or around a given individual, and, related to this, redundancy of transmission routes);

the "fit" among the several networks in which any individual is normally involved; and the "fit" between close personal networks and the larger social sets in which they operate. Furthermore, all these characteristics should be studied in terms of the whole life cycle and under conditions of routine functioning, temporary emergency, and permanent alteration. Partly for this reason, the question of the bounding of a network becomes crucial. An arbitrarily small set, such as the nuclear family, will yield insufficient information under routine conditions for adequate analysis of probable responses to emergency or altered conditions. For example, if the nuclear family group connects strongly as a unit with a larger neighborhood or extended kin group, social pressures on the unit when one member has or creates difficulty will be quite different from the corresponding social pressures if each member connects primarily with separate sets of persons outside the nuclear family. In the former case, both the pressure and the resources for maintenance of the "difficult" member are likely to be present; in the latter, the social resources are likely to be absent, and the social pressure is likely to make it easier to eject than to maintain the member.

Perhaps more significant in the present context than response to individual difficulty is the transmission pattern that may contribute to its development, and here again the bounding of the relevant networks must not be too narrow. A major fault in Bateson's double-bind hypothesis for schizophrenia, for example, or in much of the family interaction research is that the presumed pathogenic patterns are probably universal in occurrence and can be effectively pathogenic (if they are) only in a social context that enhances, rather than counteracts, them. The double bind—to pursue that example a little further—is a pair communication structure and is difficult to extend conceptually beyond isolated pairs.* Isolated pairs, however, are rare social units; pairs embedded in larger social networks participate in a communication system whose feedback to each member is likely to counteract the "bind" by a variety of techniques, all of them involving a critical "public" in the pair exchange. Thus, for the double bind to operate, a "pathological" communication network must already be present.

Social networks are the main medium for enculturation—initial training, as well as ongoing transmission and feedback—and at the same time the main outside reality with which an individual must cope. The entire tacit—

---

* Even when the double-bind analysis is extended to three-person interactions (Weakland, 1960), analysis still involves pair communication structures, with the patient as one member of the pair and the two contradictory message senders as the other member. Although the transmitter is now not one person but two, there is still only a transmitter of contradictory messages and a receiver who must act on them, with no systematic consideration of the effect that "third parties" must have.

as well as explicit—grammar of behavior is initially acquired almost exclusively through a limited set of early close networks. Even more important, the modes of acquiring new behavioral forms as conditions demand them are also acquired in such early networks. These cannot be learned as specific behaviors, but rather are learned as methods of taking in and processing cues for the revision of behavior. One would suppose that in fairly stable societies such modes would be reasonably well adapted to most of the conditions that people will actually encounter. In societies undergoing rapid change, however, this may not be the case, particularly for segments of the society whose way of life is being displaced. If the ordinary forms of social connectedness are disrupted, some interval must occur before new "ordinary" forms are established, and individuals "hit" by this process at different phases of their lives are of course differentially affected. Those without an adequate context for initial acquisition are presumably the most severely affected; those whose initial acquisition was appropriate to the old forms may not have acquired modes appropriate to entering the new forms; and so on.

It is obvious, I think, that smooth performance—and its subjective aspects—may be interfered with by lack of training or by distortion of the relevant cues, as well as by, let us say, neurological difficulties. The confusions attendant upon a realistically dis-ordered social world are surely worked through to acceptable forms of functioning by many individuals, but others who could function with well-learned patterns cannot create appropriate new ones. Individuals whose acquisition of modes of dealing with altered situations is inadequate will show behavioral and associated emotional breakdown when they confront such situations. In general, modes of dealing with altered situations are adequately acquired only by individuals who are for a long period (particularly in early life) members of several overlapping networks, and at the same time central members of small interconnected networks that are themselves connected fairly consistently with other larger networks. It is characteristically in these settings that these modes are transmitted and modified. Individuals may lack such network involvement because the appropriate networks are not available to them, or because (for many possible reasons not initially social in source) they tend to withdraw from most of their available connections and such withdrawal is not counteracted.

I will not take the space here to elaborate this speculative argument into a tighter logic with specific hypotheses (this argument is elaborated in Hammer, 1972). It will perhaps be more useful to turn now to a few issues in psychopathology in regard to which there is little clarity and to examine the possible advantages that a network approach may offer.

EXAMPLES OF SOCIAL NETWORK ANALYSIS OF ISSUES IN PSYCHOPATHOLOGY

The three issues which will briefly be considered here are (1) the possible utility of network studies of identical twins; (2) the significance of apparent social class differentials in the incidence of schizophrenia; and (3) the quasi-definitional question of whether "psychopathology" is appropriately assigned to the medical realm.

General Methodological Considerations

Certain methodological characteristics of social network analysis are generally relevant. By using as criteria of social linkage factors that are necessarily universal, such as relative frequency, it is possible to construct networks which are quite comparable despite major cultural differences. Even retrospective data are potentially usable for many purposes, since the form of the network makes elaborate cross checking of information quite feasible (an A-B relationship has as potential informants A, B, and any number of others connected with A and/or B), and since the network can be so constructed as not to be heavily affected by bias in the reporting of ties directly with any one individual (i.e., by using a selection procedure that extends the network through several steps from the initial individual, rather than intensively around that individual). Furthermore, the variable that one wishes to study can be defined with precision and universality— for example, what is a given individual's position in a network with respect to a dimension like central-peripheral, or with respect to access to the main routes of connection for the entire network; or what is his position with respect to the junctures of defined overlapping networks. In general, then, the methodological characteristics of interest involve potential reliability, precision, and comparability.

In addition to these characteristics, which are built into the procedure, there may be another which would be extremely valuable. As in other empirical realms, one expects some regularities of process and structure in this social realm. Establishment of such regularities would provide a base for evaluation of some of the material relevant to psychopathology. Such structural norms are not currently available and will therefore not be emphasized here. In passing, however, it may be mentioned that very preliminary work suggests a regular relationship between the duration of the basic connections in a network and the number and distribution of the entire set of connections. Even in the absence of clear normative information, however, it may be possible not only to detect certain "warpages" in a network but also to analyze the processes that produce them.

Network Analysis in the Study of Twins

The first issue to be considered derives from some of the more recent work in twin studies. In the past decade or so, sets of twins discordant for and concordant for schizophrenia have been intensively studied, not to establish evidence for a genetic disposition, but rather to see what additional variables are responsible for concordance/discordance. An older question in this field—never quite resolved, but more or less dismissed —is whether same-sex fraternal and identical twins are socially comparable pairs. That is, are identical twins so much more similarly treated than same-sex fraternal twins that genetic identity is only one of a number of powerful variables making for a probable common outcome?

With few exceptions, both fraternal and identical twins are reared in identical social contexts, though not necessarily occupying identical positions within these contexts. Analysis of the range of variation of social connection patterns, for pairs of normal identical and fraternal twins at different ages, should provide critical information on genetic-sociocultural interactions, as well as background for specific social hypotheses on concordance and discordance for schizophrenia among twins.

The most interesting subjects for social study are of course discordant identical twins. Although there are potentially important organic differences between identical twins (e.g., substantial differences in birth weight) that could make the expectation erroneous, one expects that the role of social variables in psychopathology should be easier to disentangle from other variables in cases of genetic identity and disparate outcome for psychopathology. Furthermore, gross sociocultural factors (class, ethnic background, geographical stability, etc.) and sociopsychological ones (e.g., general family attitudes) are also identical for twins, so that one is both permitted and forced to look at microsocial patterns like the twins' immediate networks. Unlike the grosser social variables, the immediate social networks are not likely to be identical even for identical twins. Although it is possible logically to construct networks containing identical positions—that is, within the network, for every connection involving X there is an equivalent connection involving Y—such structures are highly improbable for actual small social networks, even for the very special social conditions involving identical twins. This is true in part because, although social connections have some stability, they are not static, and even a "chance" difference at some point in time introduces non-identity, increased by any tendency for such differentials to be cumulative over time.

Any sociocultural differences between the twins must be mediated through these networks. If the network positions of discordant twins show systematic differences, the nature of these differences should provide important clues regarding the relevant processes involved in the differences between the twins with respect to psychopathology. From what we loosely know now of the social patterns of schizophrenic patients, we might hypothesize a combination of two kinds of disparity: first, within their common close network, the schizophrenic twin is a step further from the main interconnections of the set, being connected to the set more heavily through some other member (e.g., mother or twin) than is his twin; and, second, the schizophrenic twin has fewer interconnected sets of relationships outside their common set. Both disparities would tend to produce a more distorted feedback system for the schizophrenic twin. The problem of whether these disparities (or others) are involved in producing or merely in reflecting schizophrenia may or may not be resolvable. However, the likelihood of the network structure contributing to rather than reflecting pathology is enhanced if the networks that are not common to the two twins show systematic differences in structure for linkages not including either twin.

Another approach* to a resolution of the antecedent/consequence problem may be derived from the nature and range of network differences for normal identical twins, and the network characteristics for identical twins concordant for schizophrenia. Patterns that are not rare for normal pairs of twins are probably not reflections of pathology when they occur in a pathological twin. They are not ruled out, however, as etiologically relevant where there is genetic predisposition. It would then be those social characteristics of the schizophrenic member of discordant twins which are different from those of his normal twin, but within the range of normal pairs of twins, that would be implicated as relevant to the development of schizophrenia, and should then be explored prospectively for individuals (not twins) with a high risk for schizophrenia, as well as investigated experimentally for their effects on transmission and feedback.

Network Analysis in the Study of Social Class

The second issue to be considered here is the significance of apparent social class differentials in the incidence of schizophrenia. The well-known hypothesis of "downward drift" was long ago suggested—and more recently partially verified—to account for the difference. However, the overloading is not evenly distributed as one moves "down" the class structure but is found essentially in the lowest class group. The "class" in question, however, is less a socioeconomic unit with its own criteria than a "remainder," whose membership includes those who do not meet the criteria of other

* I have not referred to longitudinal prospective studies here, mainly because of the staggering problems involved in finding an effective sample.

classes. I am concerned here, not with the cause/effect question, but with another aspect of interpretation. If we are interested in applying data of this kind to point directions for studying mechanisms and processes (and surely such data are not particularly useful in and of themselves), we need to organize them by using models that are no more sloppy than the data themselves. A model of a class-status hierarchy with the people who "can't make it" dropping step by step to the bottom—with the extraordinary implicit assumption that it is easier to be poor than to stay rich*—does not seem to correspond to any reasonable analysis either of a functioning class structure or of individual performance. The individuals in that "class status" (probably an inappropriate designation) are not merely not performing in other class statuses: they *are* performing where they are. With more careful information about the distinctive social characteristics of this status, we should know more about what the individuals and groups so classified are doing (and therefore can do), not merely what they "fail" to do that would classify them elsewhere. (Perhaps it needs to be made explicit that migration rates, school dropout rates, divorce rates, and the like do not constitute adequate information about social behavior. "Migration," for example, may be alone or with others, to people one knows or to strangers, once or recurrent, etc.) If it is the case that potential patients "fall" into this status, what makes that feasible; or, alternatively, what makes them become *actual* patients *after* they enter this social class?

Detailed information of this sort should be useful in any form, and descriptive data would surely be of interest. However, the approach emphasized here, involving networks that extend through several steps, would allow more precise comparison with other class statuses—and would incidentally include information on the degree and form of cross-class connections. It may be possible, in addition, to examine the viability of the networks themselves and the question of whether hospitalization occurs primarily when the individual's behavior threatens to upset that viability. Thus one might guess that vulnerable (perhaps pathological?) networks may be likely to produce individuals considered to be pathological more often than relatively stable, secure networks, simply because the vulnerable network is less capable of maintaining itself under stress, and one means of defense against such stress is the redefinition or ejection of a potentially stressful member.

What has happened, I believe, is that indices of class have been confused with definitional criteria for class. Occupation, income level, education, and the like may be quite adequate indices for many purposes; but

* There is surely wider access to becoming a factory worker than an heir; but once having become an heir, there is no obvious difficulty in staying in that position.

they do not define the class structure, and they do not directly define any individual's position in it. (This is particularly the case for cross-sectional information with no time depth.) A bankrupt businessman and an unemployed factory worker may both be without monetary assets, but the former has a whole series of social connections that commonly get him processed in a middle class style to a slightly altered version of his position (a new business based on large loans, a partnership or managerial position in someone else's business) whereas the unemployed factory worker has a different series of social connections that commonly get him processed (through friends, in-laws, former employer, etc.) into another factory job. If both remain unemployed and are supported by kin, their positions in society come no closer together than is the case while they are employed.

To state the same thing in more structural terms, if there is a class-organized society, the complex sets of direct and especially indirect connections among the members of the society must differ systematically for different classes, since it is precisely this which constitutes class organization. To oversimplify (since an adequate development of this issue would be very lengthy and inappropriate here), if each of the major social classes is characterized by variants of a basic form of connectedness (within and between classes), except that what is often referred to as the lowest class group has several fundamentally different forms rather than variants of one form, then that "group" must properly be considered to be several groups.*

I am suggesting, then, that network analyses would reveal, first, that what we have been calling the lowest "class" must be taken to be two (or possibly several) units, not one, on the basis of the kinds and degrees of inter- and intraclass connectedness of the rest of the system; second, that the processes involved in recruitment into these several "bottom" classes are quite different from each other; third, that a change in class position is fundamentally a change in social connections, and our usual indices reveal nothing about that process; and, fourth, the aspects of this that are relevant to psychopathology may be clarified by studying these processes of change of social connections. Of particular interest in terms of the relative incidence of psychopathology would be careful information on whether class mobility, up or down, occurs on an individual basis, with attendant changes in close connections, as compared with mobility for a *group*, which thus can maintain most of its internal connections.

---

* This may well be the case for the "upper class" as well. However, if the size of the misclassified subgroup is small enough, large-scale results will not be substantially distorted.

Network Analyses on Subsuming Psychopathology in the Medical Domain

To consider now the final issue, of whether it is appropriate to define "psychopathology" in medical terms—without attempting to recapitulate the many arguments that have been raised on both sides—it is desirable to restate the question in terms that might lead to a solution.

What I assume is generally considered to be in the medical domain are phenomena that operate within an organism in ways whose primary effects concern the viability of that organism. Thus cancer is clearly medical (though it has social effects), whereas warfare is nonmedical (though aspects of it involve the medical), as are a number of other conditions that surely threaten the viability of the organism, but presumably not as the primary effect or primarily by intraorganismic processes—for example, joining an outlawed political party, robbing a bank, or being an unsuccessful artist. The question, then, is what is the primary locus of the processes relevant to psychopathology, or the locus of the primary effects?

In terms of present knowledge, it is not possible to answer this question. What we know of psychopathology relies heavily on social responses to behavior that is—circularly and literally—socially provocative. The question of whether any or all of psychopathology is "medical" may be partially answered in biochemical terms—for example, general paresis is clearly medical in some of its aspects—but which syndromes and which aspects of these syndromes are meaningfully medical cannot be fully resolved biochemically. Even now, it is not clear how much or what parts of the symptomatology even of general paresis are essentially social, despite a clear organic etiology. Obviously without discarding complementary approaches (physiological, chemical, etc.), direct investigation of the social aspects of these phenomena should help to determine a more appropriate bounding of medical relevance than is currently in use.

If this problem is translated into the concepts under consideration here, one approach would involve delineating the social characteristics associated with clear illness, and using the result as a guide to evaluate more questionable cases. Thus it would be necessary to ascertain whether there is (or are) regular alteration(s) of social linkage patterns around illness in its undisputed forms (not including psychopathology), and whether the alterations of social linkage patterns associated with psychopathology are of the same order. (All of this obviously must not include alterations that are themselves part of the medical response to illness or alleged illness.) If the social characteristics associated with clear cases of illness are essentially of the same order as those associated with psychopathology, the medical hypothesis will have been strengthened, although not demonstrated.

However, to the extent that they are qualitatively different, precise delineation of these differences may be used to provide a basis for formulating the problems of social versus medical definitions in terms that are resolvable and that can facilitate further research. Thus, if we suppose, for example, that there is likely to be severance of some connections around the key individual for both illness and psychopathology, but that the rate and the extent of severance are markedly different, or that in some cases of psychopathology but not of clear illness there is rapid inception as well as severance of connections, we are moved to consider that on social grounds we are not dealing with the same phenomenon. The issue is of course more complex than this: there are surely several social patterns around clear illness as well as psychopathology. However, systematic analysis of major types should indicate the areas where illness and psychopathology do or do not coincide by social criteria.

In no event would the results of such investigations prove the appropriateness or inappropriateness of medical definitions of psychopathology—one does not in that sense "prove" a definition—but it seems to me that considerable clarification might be achieved. Among other things, such results might indicate major distinctions between illness and phenomena not best dealt with as illness.

FURTHER IMPLICATIONS

This chapter has suggested systematic application of a narrowly defined type of social analysis to aspects of psychopathology. The issues briefly discussed here are not expected to constitute the most fruitful or the most basic examples of the potential utility of such an approach. On the contrary, they are seen only as possible starting points. If analysis in terms of rigorously defined social linkage patterns is to be a truly fertile approach, it will be so on the basis of generating new formulations as it is further developed, rather than on the preliminary basis used here, of approximate "translations" of issues that have arisen in the use of other approaches. However, even these preliminary formulations may be expected to yield some useful clarifications.

REFERENCES

Bernstein, B. Linguistic codes, hesitation phenomena and intelligence. *Language and Speech,* 1962, **5,** 31–45.

Eaton, J., & Weil, R. J. *Culture and mental disorders.* Glencoe, Ill.: Free Press, 1955.

Faris, R. E. L., & Dunham, H. W. *Mental disorders in urban areas.* Chicago: Chicago University Press, 1939.

Frumkin, R. M. Social factors in schizophrenia. *Sociology and Social Research,* 1954, **38**, 383–386.

Hammer, M. *An analysis of social networks as factors influencing the hospitalization of mental patients.* (Doctoral dissertation, Columbia University) Ann Arbor, Mich.: University Microfilms, 1961. No. 61-3883.

Hammer, M. Influence of small social networks as factors in mental hospital admission. *Human Organization,* 1963–64, **22**, 243–251.

Hammer, M. Schizophrenia: Some questions of definition in cultural perspective. In A. R. Kaplan (Ed.), *Genetic factors in "schizophrenia."* Springfield, Ill.: Charles C Thomas, 1972. Pp. 423–450.

Hollingshead, A. B., & Redlich, F. C. *Social class and mental illness.* New York: Wiley, 1958.

Kallmann, F. J. *The genetics of schizophrenia.* New York: J. J. Augustin, 1938.

Kohn, M. L., & Clausen, J. A. Social isolation and schizophrenia. *American Sociological Review,* 1955, **20**, 265–273.

Malzberg, B., & Lee, E. S. *Migration and mental disease.* New York: Social Science Research Council, 1956.

Murphy, H. B. M. Migration and the major mental disorders. In M. B. Kantor (Ed.), *Mobility and mental health.* Springfield, Ill.: Charles C Thomas, 1965. Pp. 5–29.

Ødegaard, Ø. Distribution of mental diseases in Norway, a contribution to the ecology of mental disorder. *Acta Psychiatrica et Neurologica Scandinavica,* 1945, **20**, 247–284.

Schofield, W., Hathaway, S. R., Hastings, D. W., & Bell, D. M. Prognostic factors in schizophrenia. *Journal of Consulting Psychology,* 1954, **18**, 155–166.

Srole, L., Langner, T. S., Michael, S. T., Opler, M. K., & Rennie, T. A. C. *Mental health in the metropolis: The midtown Manhattan study.* Vol. I. New York: McGraw-Hill, 1962.

Tietze, C., Lemkau, P., & Cooper, M. Personality disorder and spatial mobility. *American Journal of Sociology,* 1942, **48**, 29–39.

Weakland, J. H. The "double-bind" hypothesis of schizophrenia and three-party interaction. In D. D. Jackson (Ed.), *The etiology of schizophrenia.* New York: Basic Books, 1960. Pp. 373–388.

PART TWO

Acquisition, Maintenance, and Alteration of Behavior

Behavior is multiply determined—by the nervous system, the sensory modality, the motor system, the environment; by their interaction; and superposed on all of these by the changes induced in behavior through learning.

Chapters 7 and 8 by Miller and by Razran discuss some recent discoveries and modifications of the principles of acquisition and maintenance of behavior. Miller demonstrates the fact that visceral behavior, like skeletal behavior, is amenable to the laws of operant conditioning. Although it has been known for some time that visceral responses can be modified by means of Pavlovian conditioning (and Razran reminds us of some of the more recent experiments in this area), the fact that such responses are also conditionable by operant techniques adds significantly to our understanding of the entire area of psychosomatic medicine, for now we can delineate two mechanisms by which these peculiar maladjustments may be acquired.

Razran's extension of behavior theory has taken a different direction. He has been interested in the theoretical issue of mechanisms of integration in conditioning. Razran proposes two levels of integration: the autonomic nervous system in conjunction with the slow-responding visceral muscles, and the superstructure of cognition, which makes for more efficient learning than is found in noncognitive behavior.

These are the kinds of innovations in the area of learning that will eventually constitute new applications to psychopathology.

In Chapter 9 Chase investigates the interactions between organism and environment. Although he discusses some interactions of a purely biological type, the significance of the behavior theory variables cannot be missed. Of particular interest is the emphasis on the developing organism, which is especially sensitive to environmental insult. Chase views the environment as a modifiable variable that either expands or contracts the range of behavior of the organism on which it impinges.

Chapter 6 by Salzinger and Salzinger is a direct application of behavior theory to abnormal behavior. These authors remind us that the behavior of individuals labeled as abnormal, like that of normal individuals, is shaped by their environment. The object of this chapter is to make clear the futility of trying to study any abnormal behavior (as any normal behavior) without taking into account the impact of behavior theory variables. These variables are in effect whether or not the investigator studies them. Moreover, the authors argue that the facts of behavior theory cannot simply be equated for, nor can they be covaried out or kept constant.

That the role of learning must be considered in the study of organisms is a thread that runs through all the chapters of Part Two. When one takes a measure of someone's heart beat, one must do so with the full knowledge that not only the subject's degree of physical exertion but also his psychological state of emotion and his reinforcement history from the point of view of Pavlovian and/or operant conditioning need be taken into account. It is no longer possible to assume that a particular measure can be wholly ascribed to the functioning of the body any more than one can assume such a measure to be attributed wholly to an environmental variable. The statement that both the physiology and the environment are necessary to account for behavior has indeed become a cliché. What makes such a statement more significant today is that we now have precise ways of measuring the interactions that take place between these two significant factors.

It is interesting to note that Joseph Zubin has always made use of the fact that behavior has many determinants. Indeed, he has written numerous papers trying to account for the dynamic interactions that exist between these sets of variables (see, e.g., Zubin, J. The biometric approach to psychopathology—revisited. In J. Zubin & C. Shagass (Eds.), *Neurobiological Aspects of Psychopathology*. New York: Grune & Stratton, 1969. Pp. 281–309).

Since Part Two deals with behavior theory, it is appropriate that we comment more systematically on the place of behavior theory in psychopathology. Let us look at the areas of etiology, diagnosis, prognosis, and treatment. All of them are in a continuing ferment of controversy. In part, these debates are jurisdictional disputes and in that sense are of no interest to science. In part, however, the disputes are based on different models of behavior.

Acceptance of the behavior theory model as relevant to the description of abnormality does not automatically lead to positing learning as *the* (or even *an*) etiological factor in abnormality. No chapter in Part Two formally proposes a learning theory model of etiology. Nevertheless both Razran and Miller describe techniques of learning by which abnormal behaviors could well be acquired. Acceptance of the relevance of the model means that, whatever the cause for the emission of the peculiar behavior, we assume that this emission must interact with the environment and therefore become susceptible to modification by learning. In Chapter 18 of Part Four Mednick and Schulsinger explore the etiological significance of the inter-action between neurophysiological factors and learning.

Behavior theory allows us to make exact predictions to the extent that the specific reinforcement contingencies are known. Using a series of studies on the effect of reinforcement delivered by the interviewer to a patient, the Salzingers describe the importance of knowing the unintended effects of the interviewer in modifying the very behavior he is trying to assess. Behavior theory also makes clear that diagnosis that fails to take into account the environmental reaction to the "abnormal" behavior is perforce in-complete. Behavior theory allows us to specify critical aspects of the environment in precise and (what is more important) in functional ways (behavioral diagnosis), so that we can predict the behavior of patients (prognosis) or potential patients in specific environments. Of particular interest in this respect is Chapter 9 by Chase, in which the environment is viewed not simply as something that is there and must be taken into account but also as a treatment or supporting factor to be manipulated as a kind of behavioral prosthetic device.

Treatment is an area to which behavior theory has recently made signifi-cant contributions through the establishment of behavior therapy. All the chapters in Part Two are relevant to this area of psychopathology. Miller has provided us with a technique for the amelioration of psychosomatic disorder, which might otherwise have to be treated with the much more dangerous techniques of surgery and of drug administration. Razran's chapter calls our attention to the fact that cognition and conditionability of the internal organs ought to be used by behavior therapists to effect a more rapid elimination of abnormal behavior. Chase stresses the prosthetic effect of the environment and reminds us thereby that we must start to consider changing the community so that remitted patients are able to fare better in the setting to which they must return. Finally, the Salzingers point out that treatment is always occurring, whether it is called that or whether the environment is being changed for reasons other than the welfare of the patient. The fact which cannot be disregarded is that the environment does impinge on behavior and in so doing modifies it. We must be constantly aware of these modifications, therefore, so that they are made in the best interests of the patient.

CHAPTER 6

Behavior Theory for the Study of Psychopathology

KURT SALZINGER and SUZANNE SALZINGER

THE REINFORCEMENT CONTINGENCY: A CRITICAL BEHAVIOR THEORY CONCEPT FOR UNDERSTANDING ABNORMAL BEHAVIOR

Like normal behavior, abnormal behavior is maintained by its reinforcement contingencies (see Salzinger, 1972, for behavior theory models for different types of psychopathology). The concept of the reinforcement contingency is basic to behavior theory (Skinner, 1953). It delineates the three-part relationship existing between the emission of behavior and its controlling stimuli as follows: *Operant behavior* (behavior that operates on the environment) is emitted under particular stimulus conditions called *discriminative stimuli* and is followed by *reinforcements*, which are consequences affecting the probability of emission of additional responses belonging to the same class of behavior. The concept of drive will assume less importance in the context of this chapter for two reasons. First, it is more important in the acquisition than in the maintenance of behavior. Furthermore, it has more of an effect when the reinforcements are primary than when they are conditioned (although there is some evidence for the existence of conditioned drives for conditioned reinforcements, Eisenberger, 1970). Since the maintenance of most human behavior is largely a function of conditioned reinforcements, the importance of drive is lessened.

THE DISCRIMINATIVE STIMULUS AS A CONTROLLING VARIABLE FOR ABNORMAL BEHAVIOR OUTSIDE THE LABORATORY

Man is reinforced for different behaviors in different situations. This is critical for the definition of what constitutes abnormal behavior and for judging the degree of that abnormality. Patients, like normal individuals, do not behave in the same way with all people in all situations. The most disturbed patients do not always manifest abnormal behavior.

Identifying Discriminative Stimuli

More often than not, the therapist evaluating a patient has insufficient information about the situation in which the behavior is emitted. The therapist dealing with an outpatient must infer the discriminative stimulus for a particular instance of behavior from the patient's verbal and nonverbal behavior during the interview situation. The characterization of the discriminative stimulus in this case depends not only on the patient's memory of his past behavior in a specific situation, but also on the therapist's behavior during the interview.

One form of psychotherapy that attempts to deal explicitly with the discriminative stimulus is desensitization (Wolpe, 1958). In using this technique the patient learns to imagine the situation in which his abnormal behavior (anxiety) typically occurs. The technique assumes that stimulus generalization takes place from the imagined to the real situation. Although Wolpe argues that desensitization acts on classically conditioned responses mediated through the autonomic nervous system, others (e.g., Salzinger, 1969) have suggested that this type of therapy also conditions operant responses (primarily approach responses to feared objects and situations) mediated by the skeletal nervous system.

The inadequacies of record keeping in most state hospitals, where we care for the vast bulk of the patient population, make it impossible to describe accurately the various situations, or discriminative stimuli, that exist at the time the patient emits specific types of behavior. At best, these stimuli are recalled haphazardly by diverse staff members during the course of a case conference or are gleaned from incomplete and biased case records. On the basis of this type of information, clinicians must make decisions regarding the patient's diagnosis, his course of treatment, and his length of stay at the hospital.

Some Studies of the Effect of Discriminative Stimuli

Despite the usual difficulties in identifying the discriminative stimulus, Zarlock (1966) showed that it can have a profound effect on the behavior of even the most disturbed psychotics. He studied the effect of the discriminative stimulus on the behavior of acutely disturbed schizophrenics. They had been hospitalized at least once before, were restricted to the ward, and required tranquilizing drugs. None had pronounced difficulty with either speech or locomotion. A large room in the ward served as an experimental chamber. It was modified four times during the course of each day, for a period of 10 days. For one one-hour period the room provided "recreational" discriminative stimuli; for another, "occupational" discriminative stimuli; for a third, "social" discriminative stimuli; and for a fourth, "medical" discriminative stimuli. The room door was locked under the medical condition only. Patients received neither verbal instructions nor verbal reinforcements in the various conditions. They were assigned randomly for one hour each day for 10 days to each of the four conditions.

Zarlock observed both verbal and nonverbal behavior. Pathological verbal content included hallucinations, delusions, somatic complaints, incoherent speech, and bizarre expressions. The total number of pathology statements varied from 3 during the recreational situation, to 12 in both the occupational and social situations, to 324 in the medical situation. The four situations also produced differences in the patients' activities. They devoted 95% of their time to games in the recreational situation; 90% to work in the occupational situation; 90% to making small talk in the social situation; and, finally, 90% to a discussion of personal problems in the medical situation. The amount of time the patients spent communicating among themselves varied from 10% in the medical situation to 70% in the occupational situation and 90% in the recreational and social situations. Bizarre behaviors such as praying aloud and gesturing occurred 33 times in the medical situation, as opposed to 2 times in the recreational and occupational situations and 4 times in the social situation.

The medical situation corresponds most closely to the condition in the state hospital. We do not imply here that the hospital initiates the peculiar and bizarre behavior. It is clear, however, that the discriminative stimuli which it provides promote "sick" behavior; other situations could promote behaviors incompatible with "sick" behavior, even for such seriously disturbed patients as schizophrenics. The extent to which research findings reflect the environment of the patient must be determined and taken into account before making general inferences about the behavior of the schizophrenic.

Higgs (1970) compared a group of schizophrenics remaining in an old ward with another group shifted to a newly constructed one. He used a psychiatric rating scale and a measure of behavior based on time sampling. Three weeks after the move, 68% of the shifted group improved according to the psychiatric rating scale and 80% improved according to the behavioral observations. The group that remained in the same quarters maintained their scores on both measures. Application of the time sampling procedure eight weeks after the move showed that the change lasted, since 78% of the moved patients still manifested improvement.

The environment that acts upon patients is of course not restricted to architecture. Studies of the effect of group constitution on the behavior of normal individuals and patients (Sommer, 1967) are beginning to yield significant findings. Griffit and Veitch (1971) found that high values of temperature and population density increased the expression of negative feelings and aggressive mood on paper and pencil questionnaires.

In addition to these rather gross environmental variables, more subtle discriminative stimuli influence the behavior of schizophrenics. Braginsky, Grosse, and Ring (1966) and Braginsky, Braginsky, and Ring (1969) showed that verbal discriminative stimuli modify the amount of "mentally ill" behavior that patients emit as a function of their perception of the relationship between such behavior and discharge from the hospital. Two male patient groups (88% psychotic and 12% neurotic) were given the same 30 items from the Minnesota Multiphasic Personality Inventory. One patient group ("old-timers") had been in the hospital for more than three years, whereas the other patient group ("short-timers") had been there for less than three months. The patients received the same test in two different forms. The investigators administered the first form, the "Mental Illness Test," telling the patients that its purpose was to discover how mentally ill they were, with the larger number of "true" responses indicating greater illness and therefore a longer period of hospitalization. They administered the second form, the "Self-Insight Test," telling the patients that it revealed the extent of the patient's knowledge of himself, with the larger number of "true" responses indicating less mental illness and shorter hospitalization.

The results were quite clear. The old-timers made significantly more "true" responses for the Mental Illness Test than for the Self-Insight Test, whereas the short-timers made more "true" responses for the Self-Insight Test than for the Mental Illness Test. In addition, while the old-timers made more "true" responses than the short-timers for the Mental Illness Test, they made fewer than the short-timers for the Self-Insight Test. Furthermore, a control group of old-timers given the tests without information about the relationship of the responses to their state of health and discharge from the hospital performed the same way for the two differently labeled tests, the number of 'true" responses on each of the tests being approximately half way between the number of such responses made by the patients given the special instructions.

Unquestionably, patients are differentially responsive to instructions, again showing that such discriminative stimuli affect even seriously disturbed patients hospitalized for long periods of time. It should also be noted that the two groups of patients were influenced differentially by the same instructions, indicating that ostensibly identical reinforcement contingencies are in fact different for various groups of patients. Patients who had not been in the hospital for a long time responded to the idea of release from the institution as a positive reinforcement, whereas old-timers viewed it as a negative reinforcement. Since the different groups of patients found different types of events positively reinforcing, they acted in accordance with the discriminative stimuli for those reinforcements.

In the same context, Grayson and Olinger (1957) asked psychiatric inpatients to answer the MMPI "the way a typical, well adjusted person on the outside would do." Seventy-three per cent showed a change in the direction of more normal responses, although in fact only 11% reached a so-called normal level (cf. Chapter 24 of this volume).

THE DISCRIMINATIVE STIMULUS AS A CONTROLLING VARIABLE FOR ABNORMAL BEHAVIOR STUDIED UNDER EXPERIMENTAL CONDITIONS

Fuhrer and Baer (1970) found less differential conditioning of the galvanic skin response (GSR) in schizophrenics than in normal individuals when the conditions of the experiment were kept the same for the two groups. However, when provided with additional discriminative stimuli, in the form of instructions and some training about the differences in CS+ (the conditioned stimulus paired with the unconditioned stimulus) and CS− (the conditioned stimulus not paired with the unconditioned stimulus), the schizophrenics no longer manifested less differential conditioning than the normals.

Neale, McIntyre, Fox, and Cromwell (1969) demonstrated the effect of competing discriminative stimuli on schizophrenics' performance. When schizophrenics had to report the presence of a letter in a one-letter display, they were as effective as normals; when they had to do so for an eight-letter display, their performance was worse than that of normals. Although the authors ascribed this effect to differences in span of apprehension and one can speak of differences in information-processing time, what underlies these explanations is the increased number of different discriminative stimuli competing for control of the patients' responses. In other words, the schizophrenics were more subject to increased stimulus control by irrelevant or distracting discriminative stimuli.

The use of a disease model for abnormal behavior has led to a de-emphasis of the role of discriminative stimuli in the environment. However, the experimental literature shows that physiological measurements arc significantly affected by the environment (e.g., Shapiro & Schwartz, 1970).

Gaviria (1967) presented prerecorded sentences to normal subjects: "May I have your attention, please?" as spoken by the listener himself, his spouse, an unfamiliar male voice, and an unfamiliar female voice. The rate of habituation of skin resistance and blood pressure was slowest for the subject's own voice and the spouse's voice and faster for the unfamiliar voices. One can expect, therefore, that the instructions read to a subject in an experiment will influence his subsequent physiological behavior.

McBride, King, and James (1965) used the distance of the experimenter from a normal subject and the type of visual regard as discriminavite stimuli (CSs?). As the experimenter-subject distance decreased, the galvanic skin response increased. The increase was greatest when the experimenter approached the subject frontally.

Finally, Hicks (1970) instructed normal subjects to identify the words exposed to them in a typical perceptual defense paradigm. Some of the four-letter words shown were taboo, and some were neutral. The data consisted of detection rate, vasoconstriction, heart rate, and palmar conductance responses. The three experimental conditions may be viewed as different discriminative stimuli.

1. Automated—a sign on the door asked the subject to turn on a tape recorder, which supplied the instructions as read by an experimentally naive male. The tables were covered with surgical sheets, and the recording apparatus was connected to the subject by a male experimenter dressed in a surgical gown, with mask, cap, and sunglasses.

2. A reserved female experimenter—subjects described her as "reserved, business-like, unimpressive, and formal"; there were no surgical sheets on the table.

3. A "sociable" female experimenter—subjects described her as "amusing, friendly, surprising, indifferent, and crass."

Both the automated and the reserved experimenter's groups produced a significantly larger number of correct guesses for the socially acceptable than for the taboo words. The sociable experimenter's group, however, failed to show similar differences; the data, on the contrary, tended to reveal a higher rate of correct identification of the taboo than of the socially acceptable words. As to the physiological measures, heart rate and sweating increased for the taboo words in the automated and in the reserved experimenter's group but decreased in the sociable experimenter's group. Furthermore, vasoconstriction occurred for the taboo words in the automated group only. Thus we find that the experimenter, even though naive to the hypothesis being tested, is a critical variable not only with respect to overall level of performance but, even more important, with respect to the differences obtained among responses relative to different classes of stimuli.

REINFORCEMENT OF ABNORMAL BEHAVIOR OUTSIDE THE LABORATORY

Behavior has consequences, and these consequences influence the probability with which similar behavior will be emitted in the future. It is not sufficient to state that the reinforcement parameter is being kept constant since it may well interact with the function that one is trying to study. Experimenters sometimes state that they are leaving out the reinforcement variable by providing no consequences for patients' responses. However, a condition of no reinforcement is an extinction period, which has its own special characteristics. Extinction is usually characterized first by an increase in response rate and later by a decrease. Furthermore, extinction often generates emotional behavior. Therefore the idea that one is controlling for reinforcement is not correct; by omitting reinforcement from an experiment one is testing the behavior in question under one special set of circumstances.

The comparison of contrasting groups such as schizophrenics and normal individuals introduces still another complication. Even the delivery of reinforcement in equal measures does not guarantee equal effects, for the two groups may also differ in the way in which they respond to the same type of reinforcement.

Attention Value of Reinforcement

Groups may differ from one another in terms of the attention value of the reinforcement. Many theories of schizophrenia involve in an important way the concept of an attention deficit (e.g., Salzinger, 1971; Venables, 1964; and also Chapter 14 of this volume; Yates, 1966). The existence of such a deficit would be expected to manifest itself, among other ways, in the schizophrenic's response to reinforcing stimuli. Apparent differences in conditionability, for example, may reflect either a real difference, a difference in the attention value of the reinforcement, or even a difference in its detectability.

One solution for this problem might be to reinforce both populations to the same level of performance before bringing to bear the particular variable of interest in the experiment. This might well be more appropriate than the customary way of equating two groups, that is, in terms of sameness of procedure, independently of initial performance level.

Reinforcement History

Another important reason for a differential response to stimuli is the reinforcement history that the person brings to the situation. Ullmann and Krasner (1969) view schizophrenia as essentially the product of extinction of attention responses to social stimuli, such stimuli being of course among the most potent reinforcements for normal persons.

We must consider the relationship between the behavior reinforced in the environment in which the patient lives and that emitted during testing or the interview. Differences in test behavior are bound to reflect what is reinforced on the ward; take, for example, patients who live on a chronic back ward, where minding one's own business is the behavior most highly prized, as opposed to patients living on acute wards, where participation is more often sought.

Reinforcement during the Course of Experiments

Reinforcements administered by the experimenter are usually better specified than past reinforcement history variables, or at the very least more precisely determined before, and independent of, the behavior that the patient brings to the experiment. Nevertheless, some very important periods of time, such as those involved in bringing the patient to the laboratory, the rest periods in the middle of the experiment, the conversation which takes place in the course of inviting the patient into the experimental room and making sure that he has heard and understood the instructions, provide a great deal of opportunity for the reinforcement of various response classes in different patients and by different experimenters or interviewers.

Reinforcement in the Patient's Living Environment

Goffman (1961) characterizes the hospital, including the state hospital, as a "total institution" with the power to mete out privileges and punishments or, in the language of behavior theory, positive and negative reinforcements. He points out that some of the events that become positive reinforcements for patients do so only because they are objects and behaviors of which the patients have been arbitrarily deprived and to which they formerly had free access. In these circumstances the conditions of delivery of what is ordinarily a positive reinforcement can become aversive because they constitute a reminder of the deprivation of these reinforcements.

Interesting and successful attempts to change the arbitrary character of the delivery of positive and negative reinforcements in the total institution have been achieved by establishing "token economies" in the hospital. There are small models of relatively closed social and economic systems in which all the patients function according to the rules of the system. Token economies where reinforcements are meted out according to specific schedules and behavior contingencies are quite effective in the control and modification of the behavior of very disturbed patients (Atthowe & Krasner, 1968; Ayllon & Azrin, 1968; Davison, 1969).

The operation of the total institution differs critically from that of the token economy. In the token economy "healthy" behaviors are defined and brought under the control of reinforcement contingencies. Too often in the total institution the behavior reinforced by the staff is subservience, often involving behavior whose very emission is aversive to the patient. For example, the patient may have to ask for a cigarette despite the fact that the cigarettes were left specifically for him by his relatives or, more often than not, were even bought with his own money.

Also important is the attempt in the token economy to standardize the behavior requirements for the acquisition of reinforcement rather than to rely on the idiosyncratic and arbitrary requirements set forth by different members of the staff in the total institution setting.

Finally, both the behavior expected of the patient and the reinforcements he receives as a consequence of his behavior are essential to the patients' very existence in the token economy. Items such as bed and board are an integral part of the economy and must be earned by healthy active behavior. On the other hand, in the total institution the emission of important behaviors is usually unrelated to the custodial care of the patients.

Reinforcement of Specific Behaviors

Reinforcement procedures have proved to be effective in modifying abnormal behavior in less comprehensive situations as well. Ayllon and Michael (1959) used avoidance conditioning to increase self-feeding in a patient who suffered from a severe eating problem and a correlated delusion of being poisoned.

Ayllon, Haughton, and Hughes (1965) used reinforcement to produce the abnormal behavior of broom holding. The behavior was first conditioned and then extinguished. The psychiatrists, whose observations of the topography of the behavior alone omitted the discriminative stimuli and reinforcements operating during acquisition of the behavior, were entirely incorrect in their description of the etiology and subsequent development of the behavior. Clearly no observation of a patient's behavior that neglects to observe the stimuli preceding and following the behavior can be considered complete.

Salzinger and his colleagues (Salzinger & Pisoni, 1958, 1960, 1961; Salzinger & Portnoy, 1964; Salzinger, Portnoy, & Feldman, 1964) manipulated in an interview situation the behavior termed "shallowness of affect," which is prominent as a symptom in the diagnostic literature on schizophrenia (Zubin, Sutton, Salzinger, Salzinger, Burdock, & Peretz, 1961).

Although these studies were, strictly speaking, experiments, they are included here rather than in the following section, because the subjects considered them to be interviews and because they have important implications for the nonexperimental interview. The response of self-referred affect was reliably defined operationally as any statement beginning with the pronoun "I" or "we" and ending in a predicate referring to a state of emotion. In most of the studies, the interview was divided into three 10-minute periods: an operant level in which the interviewer asked questions of a general kind only and delivered no reinforcements; a conditioning period in which verbal positive reinforcement was delivered after the emission of every self-referred affect statement; and an extinction period in which the procedure was the same as in the operant level. The number of self-referred affect statements increased from operant level to conditioning and decreased to extinction. Thus it was clear that the degree of shallowness of affect in a patient depended on the interviewer's response to such statements. An interview cannot be considered a nonparticipant method of obtaining information; it is a situation in which the observer, by means of his own behavior, determines, at least in part, what it is he will observe.

Two other findings are important in evaluating the validity of shallowness of affect as a characteristic of schizophrenia. The first relates to normal/schizophrenic differences. No differences in affect were found between normal and schizophrenic subjects during operant level or conditioning. However, when matched for operant level and number of positive reinforcements, the patients extinguished faster than the normals. It would seem that the particular response class used in the conditioning paradigm was not as important as its interaction with the rate of extinction (Salzinger & Pisoni, 1961).

The second finding relates to the oft-cited relationship between affect and prognosis. Salzinger and Portnoy (1964) found that patients who increased their rate of self-referred affect during conditioning had a higher probability of being outside the hospital after a period of six months than those who did not. Again we find that a reinforcement contingency is critical in the conclusions drawn about a characteristic in the behavior of a patient.

REINFORCEMENT OF ABNORMAL BEHAVIOR EVOKED UNDER EXPERIMENTAL CONDITIONS

Interaction Effects Involving Reinforcement

When considering the effect of reinforcement on specific experimental behaviors, we must take into account the situation from which the patient comes.

Eisenberger (1970), reviewing studies on social deprivation and satiation, showed that the delivery of social reinforcement during experiments produced a more powerful conditioning effect on normal subjects coming from a social deprivation condition than on those receiving a great deal of social reinforcement just before the experiment. The effect of the preceding condition (deprivation versus satiation) on conditionability is not always simple and straightforward. Although its effect was clearly demonstrated on choice behavior, it was equivocal when no choice was called for.

Another interaction is found between the effect of reinforcement and the type of environmental stress acting upon subjects. In a review of studies of environmental stressors with normal subjects, Wilkinson (1969) showed that, although motivation (reinforcement) usually mitigates the effect of stress on performance, as in the case of sleep deprivation, it does not do so when the stress is noise or the intake of moderate amounts of alcohol. In fact, in the latter conditions, increased motivation appears to reduce performance level.

Another source of interaction relates to the criterion that the subject sets for himself before making a perceptual response. Clark and his colleagues (Clark, 1966; Clark, Brown, & Rutschmann, 1967) examined the measurement of critical flicker fusion thresholds in schizophrenics from this point of view. The problem of response bias versus sensory sensitivity in psychophysical measurement raises questions about the validity of many generalizations found in the literature which describe schizophrenic performance as being inferior to that of normal individuals (cf. Chapter 10 of this volume). Such experiments must be redone under conditions in which the reinforcement parameter is systematically manipulated.

In one such experiment on reaction time in schizophrenics and normals (Klein, Cicchetti, & Spohn, 1967), negative reinforcement in the form of the experimenter's verbal comments was contingent upon the subject's performance. Under this condition the widely held generalization that schizophrenics react more slowly than normals did not hold up.

Differences between normal and abnormal behavior have been produced as well as eliminated by the inclusion of reinforcement contingencies. Hare and Thorvaldson (1970) showed that psychopaths do not differ from nonpsychopaths in their tolerance level for electrical stimulation under conditions of no reinforcement; however, the inclusion of a reinforcement contingency significantly increased the tolerance level for the psychopaths above that of the nonpsychopaths.

The Effect of Reinforcement on "Basic" Abnormal Behavior

Meichenbaum (1969) showed that the presence of difficulty of communication, typically attributed to schizophrenics (cf. Salzinger references previously cited on shallowness of affect), depends on the reinforcement contingency operating on that behavior. He obtained a measure of "healthy talk" from the verbal behavior evoked in conversations and a measure of "abstractness" of interpretation from the verbal behavior obtained from proverb interpretation. He reinforced the healthy talk of schizophrenics in one group and the abstract interpretation in another in eight training sessions of 30 minutes each. He then tested for generalization between healthy talk and abstract interpretation and from these to the similarities test of the WAIS (intelligence test), to the Kent-Rosanoff word association test, and to talk between a trained and an untrained patient. The results were unequivocal. Both response classes increased in frequency. Generalization was also found between them. Finally, the proverb interpretation of schizophrenics was, after training, as abstract as that of the normal control group. Once more we find that even the most basic characteristics of psychopathology are modifiable by an appropriate environmental intervention.

SUMMARY

This chapter has argued in favor of a more comprehensive behavior theory approach to the analysis of abnormal behavior and therefore indirectly against the traditional medical model approach. It defined the critical behavior theory concept as the reinforcement contingency, consisting of the behavior itself, the stimuli that precede it (discriminative stimuli), and the stimuli that follow it (reinforcing stimuli).

This chapter discussed the control exerted over abnormal behavior by the discriminative stimulus outside and inside the laboratory. The problem of identifying the controlling discriminative stimuli for behavior was raised. A number of discriminative stimuli were cited as affecting the emission of behavior: the physical environment, the group constitution, the patient's perception of his own behavior and the behavior of others, the instructions, and the experimental conditions. It was concluded that behavior must be tested under more than one discriminative stimulus condition.

The chapter went on to discuss the control exerted over abnormal behavior by the reinforcing stimuli both outside and inside the laboratory. It pointed out that reinforcement is always a variable—that it cannot be excluded and must therefore be identified and manipulated. Its relationship to behavior is not always simple because of differences in its interaction with other stimuli and with characteristics of the subjects, such as attention value and past reinforcement history. The reinforcing characteristics of the "total institution" and the "token economy" were described and compared to explain the differences in the functioning of patients in each setting. A number of characteristics assumed to be basic to schizophrenia were shown to be modifiable by conditioning variables. And, finally, the problem of response bias versus sensory sensitivity in psychophysics was related to abnormal behavior.

We conclude that the medical model has failed because of its exclusion of the stimuli critical in the determination of behavior—and that behavior theory, in recasting psychopathology in terms of behavior, makes possible its study and its modification.

REFERENCES

Atthowe, J. M., Jr., & Krasner, L. Preliminary report on the application of contingent reinforcement procedures (token economy) on a "chronic" psychiatric ward. *Journal of Abnormal Psychology*, 1968, **73**, 37–43.

Ayllon, T., & Azrin, N. *The token economy*. New York: Appleton-Century-Crofts, 1968.

Ayllon, T., Haughton, E., & Hughes, H. B. Interpretation of symptoms: Fact or fiction? *Behaviour Research and Therapy*, 1965, **3**, 1–7.

Ayllon, T., & Michael, J. The psychiatric nurse as a behavioral engineer. *Journal of the Experimental Analysis of Behavior*, 1959, **2**, 323–334.

Braginsky, B. M., Braginsky, D. D., & Ring, K. *Methods of madness*. New York: Holt, Rinehart & Winston, 1969.

Braginsky, B. M., Grosse, M., & Ring, K. Controlling outcomes through impression-management. *Journal of Consulting Psychology*, 1966, **30**, 295–300.

Clark, W. C. The psyche in psychophysics: A sensory-decision theory analysis of the effect of instructions on flicker sensitivity and response bias. *Psychological Bulletin*, 1966, **65**, 358–366.

Clark, W. C., Brown, J. C., & Rutschmann, J. Flicker sensitivity and response bias in psychiatric patients and normal subjects. *Journal of Abnormal Psychology*, 1967, **72**, 35–42.

Davison, G. C. Appraisal of behavior modification techniques with adults in institutional settings. In C. M. Franks (Ed.), *Behavior therapy*. New York: McGraw-Hill, 1969. Pp. 220–278.

Eisenberger, R. Is there a deprivation-satiation function for social approval? *Psychological Bulletin*, 1970, **74**, 255–275.

Fuhrer, M. J., & Baer, P. E. Preparatory instructions in the differential conditioning of the galvanic skin response of schizophrenics and normals. *Journal of Abnormal Psychology*, 1970, **76**, 482–484.

Gaviria, B. Autonomic reaction magnitude and habituation to different voices. *Psychosomatic Medicine*, 1967, **29**, 598–605.

Goffman, E. *Asylums*. New York: Aldine, 1961.

Grayson, H. M., & Olinger, L. B. Simulation of "normalcy" by psychiatric patients on the MMPI. *Journal of Consulting Psychology*, 1957, **21**, 73–77.

Griffit, W., & Veitch, R. Hot and crowded: Influences of population density and temperature on interpersonal affective behavior. *Journal of Personality and Social Psychology*, 1971, **17**, 92–98.

Hare, R. D., & Thorvaldson, S. A. Psychopathy and response to electrical stimulation. *Journal of Abnormal Psychology*, 1970, **76**, 370–374.

Hicks, R. G. Experimenter effects on the physiological experiment. *Psychophysiology*, 1970, **7**, 10–17.

Higgs, W. J. Effects of gross environmental change upon behavior of schizophrenics: A cautionary note. *Journal of Abnormal Psychology*, 1970, **76**, 421–422.

Klein, E. B., Cicchetti, D., & Spohn, H. A test of the censure-deficit model and its relation to premorbidity in the performance of schizophrenics. *Journal of Abnormal Psychology*, 1967, **72**, 174–181.

McBride, G., King, M. G., & James, J. W. Social proximity effects on galvanic skin responses in adult humans. *Journal of Psychology*, 1965, **61**, 153–157.

Meichenbaum, D. H. The effects of instructions and reinforcement on thinking and language behavior of schizophrenics. *Behaviour Research and Therapy*, 1969, **7**, 101–114.

Neale, J. M., McIntyre, C. W., Fox, R., & Cromwell, R. L. Span of apprehension in acute schizophrenics. *Journal of Abnormal Psychology*, 1969, **74**, 593–596.

Salzinger, K. The place of operant conditioning of verbal behavior in psychotherapy. In C. M. Franks (Ed.), *Behavior therapy: Appraisal and status*. New York: McGraw-Hill, 1969. Pp. 375–395.

Salzinger, K. Behavior theory models of abnormal behavior. In M. L. Kietzman, S. Sutton, & J. Zubin (Eds.), *Experimental approaches to psychopathology*. New York: Academic Press, 1972, in press.

Salzinger, K. An hypothesis about schizophrenic behavior. *American Journal of Psychotherapy*, 1971, **25**, 601–614.

Salzinger, K., & Pisoni, S. Reinforcement of affect responses of schizophrenics during the clinical interview. *Journal of Abnormal and Social Psychology*, 1958, **57**, 84–90.

Salzinger, K., & Pisoni, S. Reinforcement of verbal affect responses of normal subjects during the interview. *Journal of Abnormal and Social Psychology*, 1960, **60**, 127–130.

Salzinger, K., & Pisoni, S. Some parameters of the conditioning of verbal affect responses in schizophrenic subjects. *Journal of Abnormal and Social Psychology*, 1961, **63**, 511–516.

Salzinger, K., & Portnoy, S. Verbal conditioning in interviews: Application to chronic schizophrenics and relationship to prognosis for acute schizophrenics. *Journal of Psychiatric Research*, 1964, **2**, 1–9.

Salzinger, K., Portnoy, S., & Feldman, R. S. Experimental manipulation of continuous speech in schizophrenic patients. *Journal of Abnormal and Social Psychology*, 1964, **68**, 508–516.

Shapiro, D., & Schwartz, G. E. Psychophysiological contributions to social psychology. *Annual Review of Psychology*, 1970, **21**, 87–112.

Skinner, B. F. *Science and human behavior.* New York: Macmillan, 1953.

Sommer, R. Small group ecology. *Psychological Bulletin,* 1967, **67,** 145–152.

Ullmann, L. P., & Krasner, L. *A psychological approach to abnormal behavior.* Englewood Cliffs, N. J.: Prentice-Hall, 1969.

Venables, P. H. Input dysfunction in schizophrenia. In B. A. Maher (Ed.), *Progress in experimental personality research.* Vol. 1. New York: Academic Press, 1964. Pp. 1–47.

Wilkinson, R. Some factors influencing the effect of environmental stressors upon performance. *Psychological Bulletin,* 1969, **72,** 260–272.

Wolpe, J. *Psychotherapy by reciprocal inhibition.* Stanford: Stanford University Press, 1958.

Yates, A. J. Psychological deficit. *Annual Review of Psychology,* 1966, **17,** 111–144.

Zarlock, S. P. Social expectations, language, and schizophrenia. *Journal of Humanistic Psychology,* 1966, **6,** 68–74.

Zubin, J., Sutton, S., Salzinger, K., Salzinger, S., Burdock, E. I., & Peretz, D. A biometric approach to prognosis in schizophrenia. In P. Hoch & J. Zubin (Eds.), *Comparative epidemiology of the mental disorders.* New York: Grune & Stratton, 1961. Pp. 143–203.

CHAPTER 7

Autonomic Learning: Clinical and Physiological Implications

NEAL E. MILLER

As I previously pointed out (Miller, 1969a), there is an ancient, strong, invidious distinction in our culture between the rational, voluntary behavior of the skeletal muscles under the control of the cerebrospinal nervous system and the supposedly involuntary, irrational reactions of the glands and viscera under the control of the autonomic nervous system. Thus many psychiatrists (e.g., Alexander, 1950) believe that psychosomatic symptoms of the glands and viscera are especially primitive—that they can be only direct, unlearned reflex responses to an emotional state and cannot involve symbolic representation as do other symptoms, such as hysterical conversion ones.

Similarly, the strong traditional belief of most learning theorists (cf. Kimble, 1961; Konorski, 1967; Mowrer, 1947; Skinner, 1938) has been that the autonomic nervous system is capable only of an inferior type of learning, classical conditioning, in which reinforcement must take the form of an unconditioned stimulus eliciting exactly the same type of response that is to be learned, a requirement that severely limits the opportunities for reinforcement. Conversely, a supposedly superior type of learning, variously called instrumental learning, trial-and-error learning, type II conditioning, or operant conditioning, is supposed to be possible only for the cerebrospinal nervous system. In this superior type of learning, believed to be responsible for voluntary behavior, reinforcement takes the form of a reward (including escape from punishment) which has the property of strengthening any preceding response, so that the opportunities for reinforcement are much greater. The belief that it is impossible for the stupid autonomic nervous system to exhibit instrumental learning was so strong that for more than a decade it was extremely hard for me to get any students, or even paid assistants, to work seriously on the problem. I almost always ended up by letting them work on something they didn't consider so preposterous (Miller, 1969a).

The prejudice against the autonomic nervous system has been much weaker in the Soviet Union. Following the tradition stemming from Sechenov and Pavlov, scientists there have emphasized the importance of the cerebral cortex for the regulation of all functions, including those mediated by the autonomic nervous system. The impressive work of Bykov (1957) and his many colleagues, demonstrating that many glandular and visceral functions can be classically conditioned, was one of the sources of my motivation to try the instrumental learning of such responses. But their emphasis on the technique of classical conditioning apparently prevented the investigators in the Soviet Union from trying to use the technique of instrumental training for such responses. And, as far as I know, their more recent experimental work has followed somewhat in the great Stanislavsky tradition of the theater, which emphasizes the use of various mediating responses to elicit emotions that, in turn, have an unlearned reflex effect on the viscera (Lisina, 1965; Simonov, 1962).

It is also possible to modify a visceral response, such as heart rate, indirectly, by performing a skeletal response such as running up a flight of stairs. In order to have a greater possibility for eliminating such mediating responses, I decided to work on animals.

VARIETY OF VISCERAL RESPONSES LEARNED

An early experiment, performed in collaboration with Alfredo Carmona (Miller & Carmona, 1967), illustrates a number of basic points. One group of thirsty dogs was rewarded by water every time they showed a burst of salivation; another group was given the same reward for the opposite response of going for a period of time without salivation. First the dogs were immediately rewarded for small increases or decreases, respectively, in the rate of salivation. As they learned to succeed more frequently, the criterion for reward was made progressively more difficult. In this way, they were "shaped" to make larger changes. Figure 1 shows that they did indeed learn.

Control experiments showed that the water did not have any obvious unconditioned effect of salivation. The use of the same reinforcement to produce changes in opposite directions was an additional and more powerful control against any simple explanation in terms of classical conditioning.

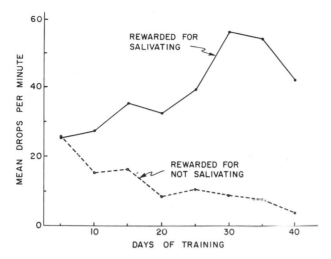

Figure 1.   Thirsty dogs rewarded by water for bursts of secretion learned to increase salivation; those rewarded for intervals without secretion learned to decrease salivation. (From Miller & Carmona, 1967)

Observe and remember that the learning was slow. The dogs were given 40 daily training sessions, each 15 minutes long.

The dogs did not obviously cheat by making panting or chewing movements. But those rewarded for increases tended to be more alert and active and showed EEGs (electroencephalograms) characterized by the typical arousal pattern of low-voltage, high-frequency brain waves, whereas those rewarded for decreases tended to be drowsy and appropriately showed EEGs characterized by more high-voltage, low-frequency brain waves. Were the differences in salivation directly learned, or were they mediated indirectly by differences in physical activity or EEG arousal? We did not answer these questions with respect to salivation, but I believe that we have answered them with respect to other autonomically mediated responses subsequently studied.

In subsequent experiments we eliminated the indirect effects of the overt performance of skeletal responses, including breathing, by paralyzing such responses by curare and maintaining the animals on artificial respiration. By recording the electromyogram we have shown that the muscles were indeed completely paralyzed. By measuring the pCO_2, pO_2, and pH of the blood we have shown that the respiration was in the normal range—something that is extremely important for consistent learning.

In our experiments on curarized rats, rewards for increases have produced large and statistically reliable increases and rewards for decreases have produced large and statistically reliable decreases in each of the following responses mediated by the autonomic nervous system: intestinal contractions; heart rate; blood pressure; vasoconstriction in the tail, in the ears, and in the stomach; and rate of formation of urine (Miller, 1969b). Work in progress by Bruce Pappas is showing similar results for uterine contractions, and by Craig Fields for the form of the electrocardiogram.

In the foregoing experiments, the fact that the same reinforcement can be used to produce changes in either direction rules out any simple interpretation in terms of classical conditioning.

The problem of mediation is trickier. As we pointed out in one of the first papers (Miller & DiCara, 1967), although paralysis by curare rules out mediation via the overt performance of skeletal responses, it does not rule out mediation by neural impulses originating from the areas of the motor cortex responsible for skeletal activity. Some of these impulses either might directly affect a visceral response, such as heart rate, or might be classically conditioned to it. But if the rats were learning to send out neural impulses for enough skeletal activity to produce large changes in the heart rate, we would expect to see the skeletal activity during a subsequent test without curare. When we gave the rats such a test, we found that a considerable amount of the heart-rate training transferred from the curarized to the normal state.* By the end of retraining without curare, the minute and highly unreliable differences in skeletal activity and breathing could scarcely account for the large and highly reliable differences in heart rate (DiCara & Miller, 1969b).

SPECIFICITY OF VISCERAL LEARNING

The strongest evidence against explaining away the autonomic learning in our experiments as a mere by-product of mediation comes, however, from experiments demonstrating the specificity of such learning. In one such experiment, Banuazizi and I (Miller & Banuazizi, 1968) recorded both heart rate and intestinal contractions but rewarded one group of curarized rats only for changes in heart rate and the other only for changes in intestinal contraction. Half of each of these groups was rewarded for increases, and the other half for decreases.

Figure 2 shows that the rats rewarded for intestinal contractions learned to contract and those rewarded for relaxation learned to relax, while neither

---

* This result is in striking contrast to the lack of transfer to the normal state of the effect of sodium amytal (Barry, Etheredge, & Miller, 1965) and *d*-amphetamine (Krieckhaus, Miller, & Zimmerman, 1965) in a different training situation.

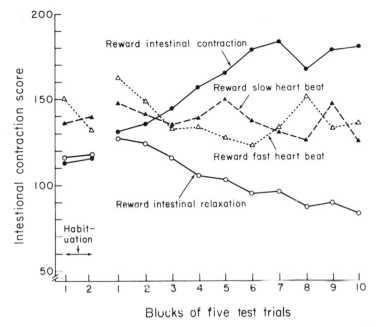

Figure 2. When increases or decreases, respectively, in intestinal contraction are rewarded, they are learned; but when increases or decreases in heart rate are rewarded, intestinal contractions do not change. (From Miller & Banuazizi, 1968)

group changed its heart rate. As Figure 3 indicates, the rats rewarded for fast heart rate speeded up and those rewarded for a slow rate slowed down, while neither group changed their intestinal contractions. Each of the 12 rats in the experiment showed statistically reliable changes of the rewarded response in the rewarded direction; for each of 11, the changes were reliable beyond the 0.001 level, whereas the twelfth little Judas showed changes reliable only beyond the 0.05 level. Furthermore, a statistically reliable correlation showed that the better the rewarded response was learned, the less change occurred in the other, nonrewarded response.

The results of the preceding experiment showed that visceral learning can be specific to an organ system, and clearly ruled out the possibility of mediation by any single general factor, such as level of activation or central commands for either activity or relaxation. Another experiment on specificity demonstrated that instrumental learning can produce changes in urine formation without affecting blood pressure or heart rate (Miller & DiCara, 1968). Incidentally, this experiment showed that the change in urine formation was achieved by specific vasomotor changes that affected the rate of blood flow to the kidneys but not to the tail. An additional

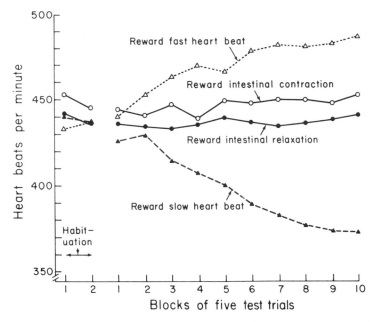

Figure 3. When increases or decreases, respectively, in heart rate are rewarded, they are learned; but when increases or decreases in intestinal contraction are rewarded, heart rate does not change. (From Miller & Banuazizi, 1968)

experiment revealed that the amount of blood in the stomach wall could be altered by instrumental training (Carmona, Miller, & Demierre, article in preparation). It is obvious that changes in blood flow to the internal organs can play a significant role in a number of important symptoms.

In regard to the matter of specificity, one experiment has demonstrated that learned changes in blood pressure can be produced unaccompanied by changes in heart rate or peripheral vasomotor responses (DiCara & Miller, 1968c), while another has shown that peripheral vasomotor responses can be learned without changes in heart rate (DiCara & Miller, 1968b). The work of Craig Fields (1970) shows that either learned increases or decreases in the p-r interval of the electrocardiogram can be produced independently of changes in the r-r interval. Finally, as Figure 4 shows, when only a difference in the vasomotor responses of the two ears is rewarded, such a differential vasomotor response can be learned (DiCara & Miller, 1968d).

I believe that it is difficult to explain the specificity of the learning demonstrated in the experiments just cited in terms of impulses to different skeletal muscles each of which elicits a specific, different visceral response. It even becomes difficult to postulate different thoughts, each arousing a

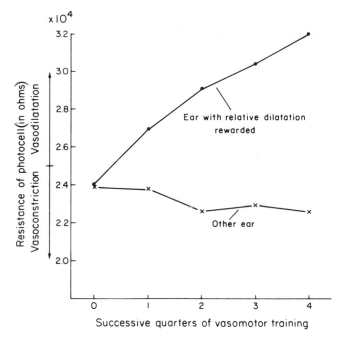

Figure 4. Specificity of visceral learning: when a difference in the vasomotor tone of the two ears is specifically rewarded, it is learned. (Data from DiCara & Miller, 1968d)

different emotion, each of which in turn innately elicits a specific visceral response—for example, blushing in one ear but not the other. If one assumes a more direct specific connection between different thoughts and different visceral responses, such as the image of warmth producing the response of vasodilatation, the notion becomes indistinguishable from the ideomotor hypothesis for the voluntary movement of skeletal muscles advanced by William James (new edition, 1950).

Although the specificity of visceral learning may surprise those who are imbued with the traditional belief in the inferiority of the autonomic nervous system, it really is not surprising in view of the evidence that various visceral responses have specific representation, roughly analogous to that of skeletal responses, at the highest level of the brain, the cerebral cortex (Chernigovski, 1960; Fulton, 1956). There may be quantitative differences between the amount of detailed representation of certain visceral organs and that of certain skeletal appendages, just as there are between the representations of the fingers and the thighs, but the difference does not seem to me to be a fundamental, qualitative one.

SIMILAR LAWS OF LEARNING

Does visceral learning have the same basic properties as skeletal learning? We have already seen that learned visceral responses can be quite specific, especially if the conditions are deliberately set up to reward only a specific response, and that there is some tendency for visceral responses to become more specific with additional training. These are characteristics of the learning of skeletal responses.

Because there are not many ways of rewarding an animal completely paralyzed by curare, many of our experiments have used the rewarding effect of direct electrical stimulation of the brain, but other experiments have shown that escape from or avoidance of mild electric shocks can serve to reward the learning of a variety of visceral responses. And it should be remembered that our first experiment, on noncurarized thirsty dogs, used water as a reward. Thus the instrumental learning of visceral responses, like that of skeletal ones, seems to be capable of reinforcement by a variety of rewards.

Another important characteristic of mammalian skeletal learning is that it is a relatively permanent effect. DiCara and I (1968e) have demonstrated the retention of both learned increases and learned decreases in heart rate over a period of three months without practice.

Although learned skeletal responses are well remembered, they can be progressively weakened or, in other words, experimentally extinguished by a series of training trials without reward. We have observed this phenomenon in visceral learning. Reward for a positive cue and nonreward for a negative one establishes a discrimination with visceral responses, just as it does with skeletal ones (Banuazizi, 1968; DiCara & Miller, 1968a; Miller & DiCara, 1967).

Furthermore, it is known that once an animal has learned to use a given cue as the positive stimulus for the performance of a given skeletal response and another cue as the negative stimulus, it is easier for the animal to learn to use these same cues in the same roles for a second discrimination involving the same reward but a different skeletal response (Trapold & Odom, 1965; Walker, 1942). As an apparently analogous phenomenon, we have found that the rats showing the best discrimination between a positive and a negative stimulus for the skeletal response of bar pressing again exhibited the best discrimination when the same cues were used as positive and negative ones for the visceral response of increased or decreased heart rate. The correlations were $+.71$ and $+.81$, respectively, and each was reliable (Miller & DiCara, 1967).

In short, all of the phenomena that we have tested thus far have been found to be similar for the instrumental learning of skeletal and of visceral responses.

SOME IMPLICATIONS

The demonstration that, contrary to the strong traditional belief, the instrumental learning of visceral responses is indeed possible has a number of clear implications. It removes one of the strongest arguments for the notion that classical conditioning and instrumental learning are two fundamentally different types of learning rather than being merely two different types of training situations. Although it does not prove that the two are fundamentally the same, it does remove the argument that there is a basic neurological difference. Perhaps other alleged differences will turn out to be the products of interaction with variables that happen to distinguish the two types of training situations as currently used, but are not necessarily unique to either of them.

The experiments of my group invalidate the notion that the autonomic nervous system is inferior to the cerebrospinal one in a fundamental qualitative way. I believe that our results force us to the radical reorientation of thinking of glandular and visceral behavior, which ordinarily is concealed inside the body, in exactly the same way as we think of the externally more easily observable skeletal behavior. In both cases, there are certain unlearned tendencies or biases, which may be more overriding with respect to some response patterns than to others, and in both cases there may be considerable opportunities for modification by learning. In the past, we probably have overemphasized the role of learning in adaptive skeletal responses and underemphasized it in glandular and visceral ones. I believe that in the long run there will be many unexpected valuable dividends from breaking the age-old shackles of the invidious dichotomy between skeletal and visceral responses and acquiring the new habit of thinking of them both as examples of behavior that follows similar laws, provided the conditions are similar.

The adaptive value of the instrumental learning of skeletal responses, rewarded by food for a hungry animal or water for a thirsty one, is clearly apparent. Does the instrumental learning of visceral responses have any adaptive function outside of the esoteric one of providing publications for a certain group of experimental psychologists? I believe that such learning probably plays a much greater role in maintaining homeostasis than we have ever realized. Such an adaptive function still remains to be proved, but DiCara, Wolf, and I (Miller, DiCara, & Wolf, 1968) have taken the first step of showing that a return to homeostasis produced by a glandular response, such as the excretion of excess salt or excess water by the kidney, can function as a reward to produce the learning of the choice of the correct turn in a T maze.

The techniques for training specific skeletal responses have been extremely useful in investigating the sensory and motor mechanisms in the brain. I believe that the controlled manipulation, by instrumental training, of specific visceral responses will be equally valuable in analyzing the neural, humoral, and biochemical mechanisms involved in visceral behavior. Instrumental training should be useful also in the quantitative measurement of the effects of drugs on glandular and visceral behavior.

In regard to a different aspect, work in my laboratory strongly suggests that, although visceral learning can be made quite specific, it also can have some interesting general emotional effects. It will be recalled that the dogs Carmona and I rewarded for increased salivation also were more active and alert and exhibited the EEG pattern indicating arousal, whereas those we rewarded for decreased salivation were behaviorally more drowsy and had the EEG pattern characteristic of early stages of sleep. Here was an interesting generalized effect of a specific type of visceral training.

DiCara observed that, when rats which had been trained to escape and avoid mild electric shocks came out of the curare, those that had been rewarded for increasing their heart rate were much more likely to squirm and squeal than those that had been rewarded for decreasing it. Therefore he and Jay Weiss (DiCara & Weiss, 1969) decided to test these rats in a skeletal learning situation, namely, shuttle avoidance. In this situation, the degree of learned performance is an inverted U-shaped function of the strength of the electric shock, so that further increases above the approximately optimal level that they were using will produce decreases in learned performance. And indeed, in this situation, they found, as they expected, that the rats which had been rewarded for increased heart rate showed poorer learning than those rewarded for decreased heart rate. This result clearly demonstrates a transfer from visceral to skeletal learning. It seems plausible that the transfer was indeed due to an effect on emotionality, but additional evidence is needed for absolute proof.

A subsequent experiment in my laboratory, by DiCara and Stone (1970), yielded additional evidence of a somewhat similar nature. In both the heart and the brain, rats trained to increase their heart rate have a higher level of endogenous norepinephrine, whereas those trained to decrease it have a lower level of this substance.

We are now starting to investigate whether there are any critical periods in the development of the infant rat, during which visceral learning will have an especially great effect on adult emotionality or on subsequent susceptibility to specific psychosomatic symptoms.

ETIOLOGY AND THERAPY OF VISCERAL SYMPTOMS

The fact that glandular and visceral responses are subject to instrumental learning, with its far greater possibilities of reinforcement by a variety of rewards (or secondary gains, as psychiatrists call them), opens up new theoretical possibilities for both the etiology and the treatment of psychosomatic symptoms. I believe that these exciting possibilities should be investigated by vigorous programs of both experimental and clinical research.

One of the first questions to be asked is: Can the instrumental learning of visceral responses be carried far enough to produce medically significant effects? Although we are just starting to design experiments aimed directly at this problem, we already have some highly suggestive incidental evidence. Whereas none of the 40 rats rewarded for speeding up their heart rate has died in the course of training under curare, 7 of the 40 rewarded for slowing it down have died. This difference, statistically reliable at beyond the 0.02 level, means either one of two things: that training to speed up the heart helps the rat to resist the stress of curare, or that the reward for slowing down the heart can be strong enough to overcome the innate regulatory mechanisms and induce sudden death. In either event, the visceral learning has a medically significant effect, namely, changing the betting odds on whether the animal will live or die.

Another question is relevant to the applicability of our results to the etiology and therapy of certain visceral symptoms: Are noncurarized men as good at visceral learning as are curarized rats? For a number of years, a small, courageous, determined, and ingenious band of workers has been investigating the possibility of the instrumental learning of visceral responses at the human level. It is not surprising that these studies have posed greater difficulties than the ones on animals, partly because of the much greater capacity of people to use various mediational responses, such as subtle changes in breathing or the tensing of abdominal muscles, and partly because of the much greater difficulty in minimizing such responses by paralysis with curare (Katkin & Murray, 1968). The results are becoming more impressive, especially as tests for the specificity of visceral learning are being added in the new studies.

Nevertheless, there remains a striking contrast between the rapid learning of changes that are large and statistically highly reliable by virtually each curarized rat and the generally much less consistent learning of smaller changes by noncurarized human subjects. The results on the instrumental learning of changes in blood pressure summarized on the opposite sides of Figure 5 clearly illustrate this difference. In A, on the left-hand side, a study on curarized rats by DiCara and me (1968c), rewards for increases in blood pressure produced large increases, while rewards for decreases

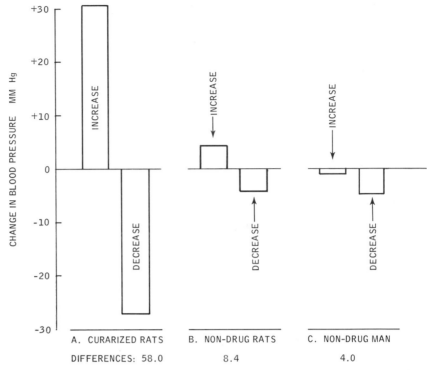

Figure 5. Whether or not training is given under curare seems to make a bigger difference than whether it is given to rats or to men. A: Data from DiCara and Miller, 1968c; B: unpublished data by Pappas, DiCara, and Miller; C: Data from Shapiro, Tursky, Gershon, and Stern, 1969. (Figure from Miller, DiCara, Solomon, Weiss, & Dworkin, 1970)

produced large decreases; the difference adds up to a total of 58 mm Hg. In C, on the right-hand side, a study on noncurarized people by Shapiro, Tursky, Gershon, and Stern (1969), rewards for increases produced a slight decrease, while rewards for decreases produced a somewhat greater decrease, yielding a difference of approximately 4 mm Hg.

I do not believe that this striking difference in results was due to any difference in investigators. A clue as to one possible cause is given by the preliminary results on noncurarized rats recently secured by Pappas and DiCara in my laboratory and represented by B in the center of Figure 5. A large part of the difference appears to be between the curarized and the noncurarized preparations, rather than between the rats and the people. Figure 5 may somewhat exaggerate the differences; in another experiment we are getting somewhat larger effects on the blood pressures of noncurarized rats, and I understand that Crider and his colleagues are now securing somewhat larger effects in their experiments also (Birk, Crider, Shapiro, & Tursky, 1966). But the essential contrast remains. The difference in Figure 5 is in line with the results of other experiments on heart rate, in which we obtained considerably poorer results when the rats were not curarized during the initial training (DiCara & Miller, 1969a). What does this difference mean? How can it be overcome short of the drastic procedure of paralyzing human patients by curare?

SUGGESTIVE THERAPEUTIC RESULTS AND A NECESSARY CONTROL

Most of the experiments on visceral learning have involved only short periods of training. Perhaps the poorer results on the human subjects that are not aided by curarization are due to a lack of sufficient practice. The results in Figure 1, it will be recalled, showed that the noncurarized dogs did not exhibit marked effects of training on salivation at first; 20 to 30 days elapsed before large effects were secured. We should not be too surprised if visceral learning, like skills in golf, tennis, or gymnastics, requires many hours of arduous practice.

When the goal is to produce a therapeutic result for a highly motivated patient, it is worth while to devote considerable time to training. Engel and Melmon (personal communication), who are pioneers in the field of applying instrumental training to the treatment of cardiac arrhythmias, have given patients from 10 to 25 sessions. The procedure is much like that used with the animals. Automatic programming equipment detects small changes in the correct direction and immediately flashes a light or sounds a tone to inform the subject that he is achieving a desirable result. This knowledge should function as a powerful reward for the patient who really wants to get well. At first small changes are rewarded; then larger ones are required. Engel and Melmon report that three of their four patients became able to sustain a significant and medically beneficial change in cardiac activity.

Similarly, Solomon, Weiss, and I trained a patient with long-standing tachycardia. During the first two weeks of one or two daily sessions of approximately one hour each, this patient showed scarcely any sign of progress. During the third week, however, he displayed much better learning and since then apparently has been able to practice by himself and to sustain his gain for a couple of months after discharge.

To date, the strategy of clinical investigations of therapeutic visceral learning has been the sensible one of first trying to achieve an effect in order to avoid wasting a great deal of time on elaborate controls for something that may not occur. As we obtain more evidence that long-lasting results can be achieved, however, it will be necessary to determine that these effects are produced by the training rather than by other features of the situation, such as the attention and hope given to the patient. A rigorous test will be to give certain control patients a sufficiently long initial period of training during which the reinforcements are programmed to occur randomly, irrespective of the changes that the subject is exhibiting.

POSSIBILITIES FOR FACILITATING HUMAN VISCERAL LEARNING

The fact that our rats learned so much faster and better under curare encourages us to hope that there may be other ways of facilitating visceral learning. One approach might be to try the effect of smaller doses of curare,* or to search for other, safer drugs that would have a similar facilitating effect. Are there any other ways?

The experiment in which DiCara and I (1969b) found that rats initially trained on curare transferred their training fairly well to the noncurarized state and gained back their generalization decrement during a second day of training gives us some hints. Curarization clearly is not absolutely essential for the good performance of visceral learning, but it does seem to be important in getting the learning off to a good start.

One plausible idea is that the curare prevents the animal from being rewarded for changing his heart rate in a variety of indirect ways, such as altering his breathing or level of muscular tension, and thus prevents his learning to do this. Although such mediating skeletal responses may constitute a quick way to obtain a few rewards, learning them may turn out to be a blind alley that interferes with the direct control that the rat really needs to learn, much like learning to cheat by copying another student's paper may produce an immediate good grade but interfere with learning the subject.

It is also possible that the noncurarized animal is confused when a small change in the correct direction, produced by direct control by the cortex of the autonomic nervous system, is overridden by a larger change mediated by skeletal activity and hence is not recorded and rewarded. Finally, it is

---

* Birk et al. (1966) provided six sessions of instrumental training to give galvanic skin responses. The seventh session was given after an immobilizing but subparalytic dose of d-tubocurarine. This dose, administered at this point in training, did not produce any appreciable change in performance.

possible that the curare helps to maintain a constant stimulus situation and/ or to shift the animal's attention from distracting skeletal activities to the relevant visceral ones.

It will be interesting to see whether effects similar to the obviously beneficial ones of curare can be produced by special training procedures which minimize the possibility that interfering responses will occur and will be rewarded and learned on the basis of their short-range effects. To achieve this goal we are trying to devise a computer-controlled routine, which we hope to be able to try out soon.

SIMILARITIES BETWEEN YOGI PRACTICES AND CURARIZATION

Those who have achieved the higher stages of Yogi training claim to have remarkable control over visceral functions. Although the temporary complete stopping of the heart sound often is produced by the trick of increasing interthoracic pressure until the venous return of blood to the heart is sufficiently reduced to muffle these sounds, while the heart continues beating (Anand & Chhina, 1961), other effects, such as slowing metabolism appreciably below the normal basal level, have been confirmed by careful physiological measurements (Anand, Chhina, & Singh, 1961b). In the preliminary states of training, the Yogis practice regular breathing, relaxation, and unvarying concentration of their attention on a single point to the exclusion of all external distractions. Our curarized animals have absolutely regular breathing maintained by the respirator, complete relaxation of the skeletal muscles produced by paralysis, and constant and unvarying stimulus conditions produced by paralysis of the eye muscles and lack of variable proprioception from skeletal movements. Although these striking similarities could be irrelevant, it should be worthwhile to try to produce similar effects by other means, such as a suitable program of instrumental training, in the hope that they will facilitate human visceral learning.

Another characteristic of the Yogi trance-like state is an unusually prominent, high-voltage, alpha rhythm (Anand, Chhina, & Singh, 1961a). It will be remembered that training in salivation modified the brain waves of Carmona's dogs. In other experiments, Carmona (1967; also see Miller, 1966) showed that direct reward for changes in the voltage of the EEG could change it in both freely moving cats and in curarized rats. Kamiya (1968) has done much imaginative work in successfully training subjects to increase their alpha activity by rewarding such increases. Korein, Randt, Carmona, and I have shown that at least some epileptic patients can learn to suppress certain paroxysmal spikes that appear in their EEGs, but we have not demonstrated whether or not this procedure can be carried far enough to have definite therapeutic results.

Human subjects can learn to control their EEGs. The Yogis apparently find a prominent alpha rhythm a part of the state that facilitates visceral control. There appears to be an incompatibility between a prominent alpha rhythm and attention to external distractions or the performance of responses, such as sudden changes in breathing, that are likely to have spurious effects on visceral responses. Therefore it will be interesting to train subjects to show prominent alpha activity and then to make continuation of such alpha a condition for achieving reward by the desired visceral response.

Yet another means of facilitating visceral learning may be to train subjects correctly to recognize visceral changes. This could be done by recording the change, having it sound a tone after a slight delay, and requiring the subject to learn to predict when the tone is going to sound.

CONCLUSION

In conclusion, I believe that the unequivocal demonstration that instrumental learning is not limited to the cerebrospinal system frees us from the shackles of viewing the autonomic nervous system and visceral functions with contempt. It forces us to think of the behavior of the internal visceral organs in the same way that we think of the externally observable behavior of the skeletal musculature. This fundamental reorientation and the possibility of using the powerful new training techniques to produce yet other unconventional types of learning open up many new vistas of basic research and therapeutic education.

ACKNOWLEDGMENTS

The research reported from my laboratory was supported by Grant MH-13189 from the National Institute of Mental Health. This chapter is based on an Invited Lecture delivered in London on July 28, 1969, at the XIX International Congress of Psychology.

REFERENCES

Alexander, F. *Psychosomatic medicine: Its principles and applications.* New York: Norton, 1950.

Anand, B. K., & Chhina, G. S. Investigation on Yogis claiming to stop their heart beats. *Indian Journal of Medical Research,* 1961, **49,** 90–94.

Anand, B. K., Chhina, G. S., & Singh, B. Some aspects of electroencephalographic studies in Yogi. *Electroencephalography and Clinical Neurophysiology,* 1961, **13,** 452–456. (a)

Anand, B. K., Chhina, G. S., & Singh, B. Studies on Shri Ramanand Yogi during his stay in an air-tight box. *Indian Journal of Medical Research,* 1961, **49,** 82–89. (b)

Banuazizi, A. *Modification of an autonomic response by instrumental learning.* (Doctoral dissertation, Yale University) Ann Arbor, Mich.: University Microfilms, 1968. No. 69-8311.

Barry, H., III, Etheredge, E. E., & Miller, N. E. Counterconditioning and extinction of fear fail to transfer from amobarbital to nondrug state. *Psychopharmacologia,* 1965, **8,** 150–156.

Birk, L., Crider, A., Shapiro, D., & Tursky, B. Operant electrodermal conditioning under partial curarization. *Journal of Comparative and Physiological Psychology,* 1966, **62,** 165–166.

Bykov, K. M. *The cerebral cortex and the internal organs.* Translated and edited by W. H. Gantt. New York: Chemical Publishing, 1957.

Carmona, A. *Trial and error learning of the cortical EEG activity.* (Doctoral dissertation, Yale University) Ann Arbor, Mich.: University Microfilms, 1967. No. 67-10, 702.

Chernigovski, V. N. *Interoceptors.* Moscow: Medgiz, 1960. (English translation edited by D. Lindsley. Washington, D. C.: American Psychological Association, 1967).

DiCara, L. V., & Miller, N. E. Changes in heart rate instrumentally learned by curarized rats as avoidance responses. *Journal of Comparative and Physiological Psychology,* 1968, **65,** 8–12. (a)

DiCara, L. V., & Miller, N. E. Instrumental learning of peripheral vasomotor responses by the curarized rat. *Communications in Behavioral Biology,* Part A, 1968, **1,** 209–212. (b)

DiCara, L. V., & Miller, N. E. Instrumental learning of systolic blood pressure responses by curarized rats: Dissociation of cardiac and vascular changes. *Psychosomatic Medicine,* 1968, **30,** 489–494. (c)

DiCara, L. V., & Miller, N. E. Instrumental learning of vasomotor responses by rats: Learning to respond differentially in the two ears. *Science,* 1968, **159,** 1485–1486. (d)

DiCara, L. V., & Miller, N. E. Long term retention of instrumentally learned heart-rate changes in the curarized rat. *Communications in Behavioral Biology,* Part A, 1968, **2,** 19–23. (e)

DiCara, L. V., & Miller, N. E. Heart-rate learning in the noncurarized state, transfer to the curarized state, and subsequent retraining in the noncurarized state. *Physiology and Behavior,* 1969, **4,** 621–624. (a)

DiCara, L. V., & Miller, N. E. Transfer of instrumentally learned heart-rate changes from curarized to noncurarized state: Implications for a mediational hypothesis. *Journal of Comparative and Physiological Psychology,* 1969, **68**, 159–162. (b)

DiCara, L. V., & Stone, E. A. Effect of instrumental heart-rate training on rat cardiac and brain catecholamines. *Psychosomatic Medicine,* 1970, **32**, 359–368.

DiCara, L. V., & Weiss, J. M. Heart-rate learning under curare and subsequent noncurarized avoidance learning. *Journal of Comparative and Physiological Psychology,* 1969, **69**, 368–374.

Fields, C. Instrumental conditioning of the rat cardiac control systems. *Proceedings of the National Academy of Sciences, USA,* 1970, **65**, 293–299.

Fulton, J. F. (Ed.) *A textbook of physiology.* (17th ed.) Philadelphia: W. B. Saunders, 1956.

James, W. *Principles of psychology.* Vol. 2. New York: Dover, 1950.

Kamiya, J. Conscious control of brain waves. *Psychology Today,* 1968, **1** (11), 56–60.

Katkin, E. S., & Murray, E. N. Instrumental conditioning of autonomically mediated behavior: Theoretical and methodological issues. *Psychological Bulletin,* 1968, **70**, 52–68.

Kimble, G. A. *Hilgard and Marquis' conditioning and learning.* New York: Appleton-Century-Crofts, 1961.

Konorski, J. *Integrative activity of the brain.* Chicago: University of Chicago Press, 1967.

Krieckhaus, E. E., Miller, N. E., & Zimmerman, P. Reduction of freezing behavior and improvement of shock avoidance by *d*-amphetamine. *Journal of Comparative and Physiological Psychology,* 1965, **60**, 36–40.

Lisina, M. I. The role of orientation in the transformation of involuntary reactions into voluntary ones. In L. G. Voronin, A. N. Leontiev, A. R. Luria, E. N. Sokolov, & O. S. Vinogradova (Eds.), *Orienting reflex and exploratory behavior.* Washington, D. C.: American Institute of Biological Sciences, 1965. Pp. 450–456.

Miller, N. E. Extending the domain of learning. *Science,* 1966, **152**, 676.

Miller, N. E. Experiments relevant to learning theory and psychopathology. In *18th International Congress of Psychology.* Moscow: International Union of Scientific Psychologists, 1969. Pp. 146–168. [Also in W. S. Sahakian (Ed.), *Psychopathology today: Experimentation, theory and research.* Itasca, Ill.: F. E. Peacock, 1970. Pp. 148–166.] (a)

Miller, N. E. Learning of visceral and glandular responses. *Science,* 1969, **163**, 434–445. (b)

Miller, N. E., & Banuazizi, A. Instrumental learning by curarized rats of a specific visceral response, intestinal or cardiac. *Journal of Comparative and Physiological Psychology,* 1968, **65**, 1–7.

Miller, N. E., & Carmona, A. Modification of a visceral response, salivation in thirsty dogs, by instrumental training with water reward. *Journal of Comparative and Physiological Psychology,* 1967, **63**, 1–6.

Miller, N. E., & DiCara, L. V. Instrumental learning of heart-rate changes in curarized rats: Shaping, and specificity to discriminative stimulus. *Journal of Comparative and Physiological Psychology,* 1967, **63,** 12–19.

Miller, N. E., & DiCara, L. V. Instrumental learning of urine formation by rats; changes in renal blood flow. *American Journal of Physiology,* 1968, **215,** 677–683.

Miller, N. E., DiCara, L. V., Solomon, H., Weiss, J. M., & Dworkin, B. Learned modifications of autonomic function: A review and some new data. Supplement I to *Circulation Research,* 1970, **26–27,** I-3–I-11.

Miller, N. E., DiCara, L. V., & Wolf, G. Homeostasis and reward: T-maze learning induced by manipulating antidiuretic hormone. *American Journal of Physiology,* 1968, **215,** 684–686.

Miller, N. E. & Dollard, J. *Social learning and imitation.* New Haven: Yale University Press, 1941.

Mowrer, O. H. On the dual nature of learning—a reinterpretation of "conditioning" and "problem solving." *Harvard Educational Review,* 1947, **17,** 102–148.

Shapiro, D., Tursky, B., Gershon, W., & Stern, M. Effects of feedback and reinforcement on the control of human systolic blood pressure. *Science,* 1969, **163,** 588–590.

Simonov, P. V. *Stanislavsky's method and physiology of emotions.* Moscow: Academic Books, 1962.

Skinner, B. F. *The behavior of organisms.* New York: Appleton-Century, 1938.

Trapold, M. A., & Odom, P. B. Transfer of a discrimination and a discrimination reversal between two manipulandum defined responses. *Psychological Reports,* 1965, **16,** 1213–1221.

Walker, K. C. The effect of a discriminative stimulus transferred to a previously unassociated response. *Journal of Experimental Psychology,* 1942, **31,** 312–321.

CHAPTER 8

Autonomic Substructure and Cognitive Superstructure in Behavior Theory and Therapy: An East-West Synthesis

GREGORY RAZRAN

Four short statements come to mind: one from Watson, one from Skinner, and two from Pavlov.

In 1928 Watson wrote: "We may earn our bread with the striped muscles but we win our happiness or lose it by the kind of behavior our unstriped muscles or guts lead us into [p. 349]." Skinner, in 1953, stated: "Reflexes, conditioned or otherwise, are mainly concerned with the internal physiology of the organism. We are most often interested, however, in behavior which has some effect upon the surrounding world [p. 59]." In 25 years, a very prestigious portion of American systematic psychology seems to have "lost its guts."

A Pavlov statement of 1911 read: "The subjective method is a method of no real causation. Psychologists' reasoning is indeterminate, recognizing phenomena but not knowing where they come from . . . psychologists' interpretations are in essence no more than fictions [p. 187; Gantt's 1928 translation, p. 164]." But in 1924 he professed: "Our subjective world is the first reality with which we are confronted and psychology has certainly a natural right to existence [1924, p. 43; Gantt's translation, p. 329]." After 13 years, Pavlov opened the door to cognition and soon began to attribute to it a role in conditioning: "School children, not being dogs,

147

should be questioned about the conditioning experiments which they undergo" (1930); "Human subjects may well inhibit conditioning when they
think about it" (1932); and "Our psychiatrists should become familiar with
empirical [read: subjective] psychology and not just rest on knowledge of
conditioned reflexes" (1934) [Pavlov, 1949, Vol. 1, pp. 98, 244; Vol. 2,
p. 415].

Three emendations to the opening chronology are in order.

1.   Watson's internal dynamics has of late (from 1966 on) been re-
deemed by Miller's discovery that gut reactions are subject to Skinner's (and
Thorndike's) reinforcement conditioning.

2.   The reinforceability of gut *reactions* is a natural complement of the
classical conditionability of gut *stimulations*, or interoceptions, first brought
to light by Bykov in 1928.

3.   Spence eventually paralleled Pavlov and in 1963 openly acknowledged "cognitive factors" in eyelid conditioning: cognition let out of
America's "First Circle."

Bringing together evidence and views is not, however, the sole aim of
this chapter. "Superstructure" and "substructure" are novel to behavior
theory and particularly relevant to behavior therapy. Regrettably, I can
only foreshadow here needed revisions of behavior therapy.

COGNITIVE EVIDENCE

"Cognition" will be used here synonymously with direct or inferred
awareness, consciousness, or phenomenal experience, but it will always be
specifically related to known or assumed higher-level neural action and
thus thought of as *neurocognition*. Its systematic evidence, from both East
and West, falls, on both methodologic and ontologic grounds, into four
ascending categories: *sensory, affective, perceptual*, and *symbolic*.

Sensory Cognition

The top panel of Figure 1 is a sample photoplethysmographic sensory
record relating vasomotor changes to the appearance of cognition in one
of three subjects. When a mustard plaster of mild concentration was applied
to the back of the subject's right hand and a control patch to her left, the
results were as follows: (I) no reaction and no special cognition for a few
minutes, (II) vasodilation of the stimulated hand, with no cognition for
another several minutes, (III) then a mild burning sensation and vasoconstriction of both hands. And when (second panel) a *cognitive* (one
sensed with awareness by the subject) flash of a blue light was paired with

the mustard in the second, *noncognitive* vasodilation stage, the subject began to blush to the light with both hands, but without mustard sensations.

The bottom panel of Figure 1 is a graphic comparison of the lapse and recovery of auditory cognition and pupillary dilation to auditory stimuli in a brain-contused subject. (The lines above the rectangles refer to cognition; those below, to dilation.) Five stages were observed: (I) total deafness and a dilation limen of 120 db; (II) continued deafness and dilation at 80 db; (III) audition at 100 db and dilation at approximately 60 db; (IV) audition at 60 db and dilation at 40 db; and finally (V) *liminal equivalence when recovery was well advanced*. The last stage is what Gershuni in the Soviet Union and Hakerem in this country normally report. And, since the Gershuni data with galvanic skin reflexes and alpha blocking normally also disclose such equivalence, there emerges the view that autonomic and neural orienting reactions normally index liminal exteroceptive cognition and, conversely, that the liminal cognition indexes the reactions. The converse is particularly challenging in the evidence at the bottom of the panel, which shows that the pupillary dilations were larger in magnitude when the contused subject was not conscious of the stimuli producing them.

To be sure, when the stimuli are interoceptive—as with subjects swallowing stomach tubes or in patients with fistulas—orienting reactions are very much ahead of cognition. But there, too, the appearance of cognition is accompanied by changes in orienting reactions. Hence comes my introductory thesis: Direct experience must neither be sacrificed on the altar of behavior, as is done by a Watson and Skinner and also Hebb and Tolman, nor be detached from it and apotheosized in the manner of autochthonous Gestaltists, unconcerned cognitionists, and what-not humanists.

Affective Cognition

Sensory cognition *per se* is, however, not a direct participant in learned behavior in the way that affective cognition *per se* is. Limbic stimulations producing cognitive affects are powerful reinforcers and punishers. Yet it is quite clear that neither the limbic system nor the affects nor, for that matter, any cognition is a *sine qua non* of learning. Figure 2 demonstrates how headless insects suspended over an electrified solution learn not to extend their legs beyond a set point. In the top left panel, *E*, an experimental headless grasshopper, shocked whenever its leg is extended, learns to keep the leg up, while *C*, a control, connected in series and shocked randomly, learns nothing. In the top right panel, the control, connected independently to the solution, becomes experimental and just as smart. The bottom left panel shows the curve of punishment learning for six headless cockroaches, with progressively fewer and fewer shocks delivered in the course of 15 minutes; the bottom right panel shows the subsequent 28

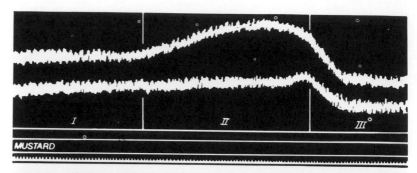

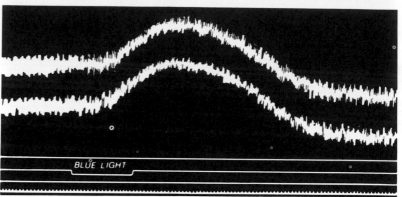

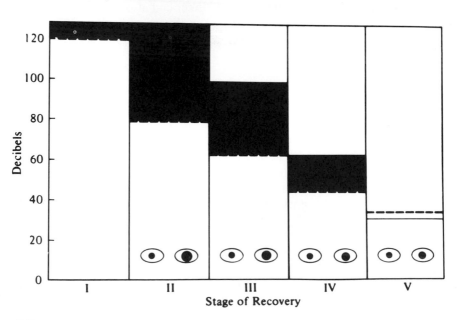

150

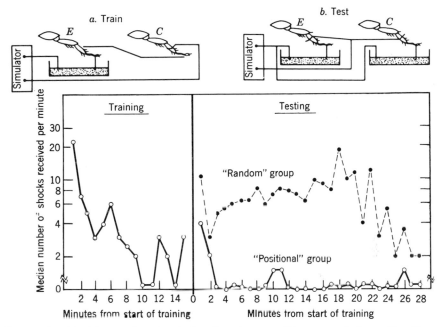

Figure 2. Punishment learning in headless insects. (Upper panels from Horridge, 1962, and lower panels from Eisenstein & Cohen, 1965)

minutes of performance of the previously trained ("positional") group and the previous control ("random") group, which is now a trained group. Note the wide difference between the two groups and the lasting effects of prior training. And while these two experiments are rather dramatic, there are scores of others to show that basic conditioning of any kind—punishment, classical, reinforcement—needs no cognition but surely is in varying degrees influenced by it when it is there—something which members of the classical-conditioning community seem readier to officially confess and profess than their operant brothers.

Perceptual Cognition

I shall not deal here with the effects of perceptual cognition on conditioning; these, I believe, I demonstrated in the early 1930s, experimenting with conditioned human salivation and surveying the literature then avail-

Figure 1. *Top and second panels*: vasomotion and cognition in response to a mustard plaster of mild concentration. *Bottom panel*: comparison of lapse and recovery of pupillary dilation to and cognition of an auditory stimulus in a brain-contused subject. (Top and second panels from Bykov & Pshonik, 1949, and bottom panel from Gershuni, 1946)

able (Razran, 1934, 1935), which at that time I thought applied only to man. What I am offering now is an essentially new systematics in the wake of subsequent developments—beginning with *new evidence of sensory preconditioning, which, I posit, is the first firm pillar of the cognitive superstructure*. Three kinds of such evidence are at hand.

1.   Thompson and Kramer (1965) used six groups of five cats each: three unoperated, two in which "all association areas were removed," and one in which "the somatic sensory cortex was ablated." The unconditioned stimulus was a shock in a Brogden-Culler apparatus, the shock-paired stimulus was a tone, and the tone-paired stimulus was a light. The results are very clear: no sensory preconditioning—no light acquiring the power to produce a shock reaction—when the association cortex was removed; full-fledged sensory preconditioning when the "sensory cortex" was ablated. In 1967, a Soviet physiologist (Sergeyev, 1967) found similar results with 10 ablated dogs. There must be something special in learning that is thus mediated, when simple conditioning is obtainable in decorticates, and there are no reinforcing and punishing loci in the cortex.

2.   The Russians have investigated sensory preconditioning in 36 chordate species, from amphioxus to man, but have reported evidence of it only in birds and mammals. Americans have obtained positive results with rats, cats, dogs, monkeys, and of course man; but Reid in England was not successful with pigeons. Yet, as is well known, classical and operant conditioning are in full bloom in fish. Again, there must be something special in what a cat can do and a fish cannot: the former commands a substantial cortex, the latter hardly a forebrain. What is the cortex for? And what may logically be the adaptive product of its several hundred million years of evolution?

3.   Recent evidence from East and West concurs in the parametric distinctness of sensory preconditioning, such as optimal manifestation with only several preconditioning pairings (Hoffeld, Kendall, Thompson, & Brogden, 1960) and little deterrence by backward sequences (Silver & Meyer, 1954). Soviet phyletic data are definitive that the general efficacy of sensory preconditioning is a positive function of evolutionary ascent —maximum retention being, for example, over a year in baboons, several months in dogs, 29 days in bats, and 15 days in rabbits (Sergeyev, 1967). Thus there is further reason to accord the phenomenon a superconditioning perceptual status.

However, lest it be concluded that I have metamorphosed into an S-S cognitionist, let me offer a counterbalancing thought. The restricted and evolutionarily recent neural basis of putatively perceptual preconditioning precludes, to my mind, its being too significant a rival of the massive neural substratum of simple conditioning in, let us say, subprimates and early human ontogeny. One must distinguish between the existence of a mechanism and its relative pragmatic role, so that rats and cats and dogs and octopuses may still be largely nonperceptual learners. Moreover, even in man, because of inattention and slow recruitment, perceptual learning is often confronted by prior nonperceptual conditioning (the preconscious?). That is to say, I am a votary of neither S-S nor S-R theory, hoping that S-S and S-R theorists will peacefully divide their psychologic territory and "in the end of days lie down together . . . not hurt nor destroy."

Figure 3 supports the second pillar of the cognitive superstructure —learned stimulus configuring: specifically, the ability of organisms to be conditioned to a compound stimulus but not to any of its components and, if the compound is a sequence, not to any changed sequence. Massive Soviet evidence has for some time revealed that this configuring is (*a*) similarly attainable to any significant degree in only birds and mammals; (*b*) similarly mediated by higher cortical regions (areas 3, 4, and 5 in cats; areas 2, 5, 7, and 21 in dogs; area 8 in macaques); (*c*) much more readily formed with ecologically related components; (*d*) prominent in primates and dominant in two to three-year-old children; and (*e*) fully evident without differential extinction of components I published a review of the topic, together with seven supporting experiments of my own, more than a generation ago. Apparently, however, the *Zeitgeister* of conditioning and configuring were then not in a "dialoguing" mood, so that only recently did a 1965 repeat review of mine manage to pierce another American "First Circle."

The upper panels of Figure 3 illustrate configuring in conditioned reinforcement of an S_1-S_2 sequence of lights preceding key pecking for food in two groups of 10 pigeons each. In Group A, the compound became significantly more resistant to extinction than either component after 2050 peckings on the fourth test, but not after 50, 650, and 1250 trials, thus *showing the effects to be due to learning*. In Group B, the compound became more resistant than either component and a reversed S_2-S_1 sequence (also a sequence with a changed S_2) on the first test, thus *abnegating the likelihood of component extinction*. Thomas et al. (1968) conclude that their results "demonstrate unequivocally the phenomenon of stimulus configuring within the conditioned reinforcement design [p. 188]."

The lower panels of Figure 3 highlight configuring with classical CERs (conditioned emotional responses of Estes-Skinner-Kamin fame) and a simultaneous light-tone compound in 30 rats bar-pressing for water. The rats were divided into three groups—A, with 4 compound-shock pairings; B, with 12 pairings; and C, with 40 pairings—after which the suppression of the bar pressing by the compound and by each component was tested twice. Note that in the 40-trial group the suppression ratio of the compound exceeded greatly that of the light on the first test and that of either component

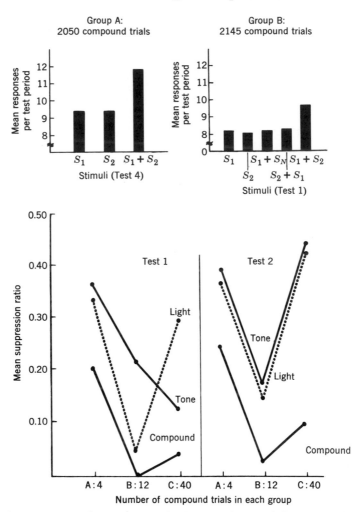

Figure 3. *Upper panels*: configuring in the conditioned reinforcement of an S_1-S_2 light sequence preceding key pecking for food in 20 pigeons. *Lower panels*: CER configuring of a simultaneous light and tone compound in three groups of 10 rats, each bar-pressing for water. (Upper panels from Thomas, Berman, Serednesky, & Lyons, 1968, and lower panels from Booth & Hammond, 1969)

on the second, while in a 60-trial group (personal communication) the compound superiority was fully evident also on the first test ($p < .01$ in all cases). This is a between-subjects design, and the problem of component extinction does not arise. The experimenters' conclusion is that "the results strongly confirm the major assumption of Razran that overtraining alone is sufficient for the formation of a configure [Booth & Hammond, 1969, p.4]."

On the other hand, Baker (1969), who obtained positive results in avoidance conditioning of rabbits with within-subjects but not with between-subjects designs, concludes that within-subjects findings are just a matter of generalization decrements or component extinction. It is clear, however, that his conclusion runs smack against not only the mass of Soviet phyletic, ontogenetic, and ablation evidence but also the plain fact that Soviet experiments disclose a total failure and not just a decrement of component CR action. Furthermore, there remains the question of why there were no such decrements in the first three tests of Thomas et al's Group A. And it is simple logic that a generalization decrement cannot occur without a differential datum between the trained and the generalization stimulus. What then, is this datum if not stimulus configuring, when pigeons in the Thomas B group respond on the first test much more effectively to a trained S_1-S_2 than to either component *and* an S_2-S_1 sequence, thus *nullifying possible differences in both quality and primacy of stimulation?*

And, of course, Baker's negative between-subjects results run counter to those of Booth and Hammond and of a related experiment by Guth (1967). To this should be added that the catch-all conjecture of the operation of a generalization decrement has for decades stymied our acceptance of Pavlov's "Law of Strength"—that the intensity of the conditioned stimulus is a significant parameter of the efficacy of conditioning —which by now is in good American standing.

There is merit in comparing the putative perceptual essences of configuring and sensory preconditioning. First, there is the consideration that configuring is a *productive* and not merely a *modificatory* kind of cognitive learning—a configuration, like a percept, being "a unitary response to a multiplicity of stimuli," whereas sensory preconditioning is a perceptual parallel of conditioned connections. Or, to borrow a term from philosophy, configuring predicates both a new *explanans* and a new *explanandum*, whereas sensory preconditioning predicates only a new *explanans* for old *explananda*. Second, there is the pragmatic fact that sensory preconditioning is so much behind configuring in expanding learning capacity. Organisms that do not configure respond to N stimuli in only N different ways; but those that do configure may respond in N-factorial ways.

My third distinctive perceptual pillar derives its strength from traditional Western "insight" learning, for which I will, however, cite a relatively recent Soviet example (Krushinsky, 1960 and elsewhere) which reports a sub-primate division in the putative manifestation of "insight" (I prefer "eduction"): crows, magpies, dogs, and cats versus rats, rabbits, pigeons, chickens, and ducks. Figure 4 illustrates the apparatus and sample results for birds. The birds feed themselves from the top of a noiselessly moving box which disappears into a two-segment, three-meter-long tunnel and then reappears. The segments are either joined (second and third panels) or have

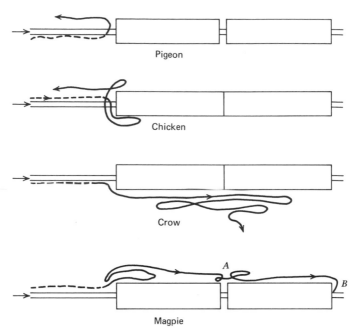

Pigeon

Chicken

Crow

Magpie

Figure 4. Sample records of the behavior of pigeons and chickens versus that of crows and magpies in a Krushinsky apparatus of disappearing and reappearing feeding boxes. (From Krushinsky, 1960)

a mid-tunnel opening of several centimeters (top and bottom panels). The irregular heavy lines show the birds' movements when the feeding box disappears. Pigeons just do not move forward; they stand for awhile and turn sideways or backwards. Chickens move along for only a very short distance. But crows and magpies (and dogs and cats) zigzag along almost the entire length of the three-meter tunnel and—most importantly—*with a mid-tunnel opening zigzag around the opening and rush to the exit to wait for the food.*

I venture to posit that the special, presumably neurocognitive, performance of these higher subprimates does not differ *qualitatively* from the more exclusive familiar feats of lower and higher primates—namely, that they all constitute a *discovery* of *new* and *unobvious* relations, whereas sensory preconditioning is an *uncovery* of existing obvious relations, and configuring is an *integration* of them. Our *higher* animal ancestry had thus, to my mind, evolved three, putatively ascending, mechanisms of cognitive learning, not one protean "insight" or a two-in-one "sign-Gestalt," and more than "lessons" and "problems" or "signs" and "solutions." The dis-

Symbolic Cognition

tinction between the existence of a mechanism and its evolutionary pragmatic role must be borne in mind, however, as well as the vast realm of noncognitive (and precognitive) learning even in man.

It seems instructive to antecede my thesis of cognitive human symboling by some hitherto unavailable and unheeded evidence of our vast quantitative and qualitative learning superiority right after birth. Figure 5 shows a sample record of conditioned prefeeding head reactions and sucking in human neonates on a four-hour feeding schedule, on the third day and, very prominently, on the fifth day of life. This appears in primates only after several weeks and even months (Voronin, 1948). Figure 6 demonstrates very clear-cut simple, discriminative, and reversal reinforcement condi-

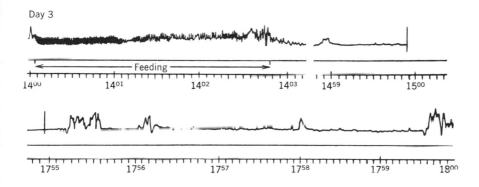

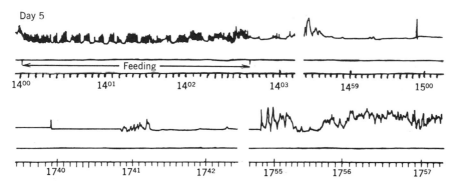

Figure 5. Sample record of prefeeding sucking and head reactions in human neonates on a fixed feeding schedule. Top lines in each panel denote the conditioned reactions, which, it will be noted, increased very markedly from the third to the fifth day. (From Bystroletova, 1954)

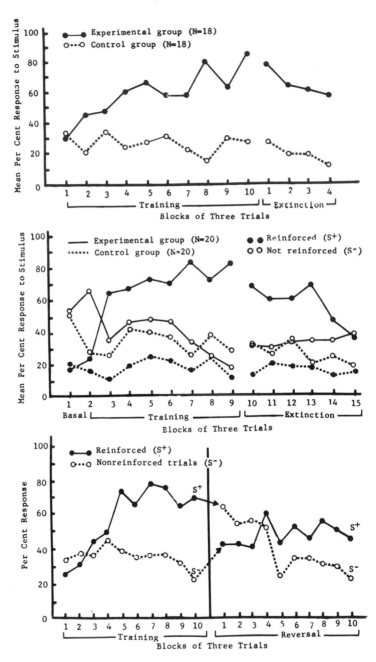

Figure 6. Simple discriminated and reversal reinforcement conditioning and extinction with auditory stimuli combined with ipsilateral touchings of one or both cheeks and varying sounds as the S^Ds. (From Siqueland & Lipsitt, 1966)

158

tioning and extinction—head turning reinforced by sucrose—in 46 neonates less that four days old. (Not very long ago Wickens maintained that neonates could not be conditioned at all.) The photographs at the top of Figure 7 (Lyakh, 1968) are a sample record of Russian three-month-old infants learning to imitate the experimenters silent articulation of "oo" and "a" and then voicing the vowels spontaneously. The bottom of the figure is a sample record of differential eye blinking in infants of the same age to the silent articulation. (Experimenters' voiced articulations interfere with training at this age: the focus is vision and motion.) And I should add the following: (*a*) Kasatkin's laboratory disclosing conditioned orientation in infants two- to three-months old, possible only in relatively mature subhumans, and (*b*) Michael Wertheimer's habituating his three minute-old daughter in seven minutes and 52 trials not to move her eyes in response to a click, which, I submit, is not only cute but uniquely human (for the granddaughter of the founder of unlearned Gestalten, at that).

Lack of space permits only three summary statements on the symboling thesis derived largely from up-to-date knowledge of the nature of conditioned semantic transfer—word-object, object-word, word-word, word-sentence, sentence-word, sentence-sentence—and comparative symboling of chimpanzees and severely retarded human beings (see Razran, 1971). First, there is the assertion that the essence and organization of man's symboling involves, in addition to simple noncognitive conditioning and

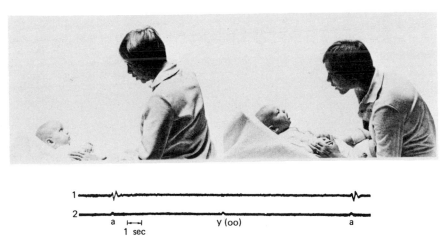

Figure 7. *Upper panel*: sample photographs of nine three-month-old infants trained to imitate the experimenter's silent articulation of "oo" and "a" (Russian, "y"), after which they voiced the vowels *spontaneously*. *Lower panel*: sample record of conditioned differential eye blinking to experimenter's silent articulation of the vowels. (From Lyakh, 1968a, 1968b)

simple cognitive configuring, a specific cognitive referential relation (meaning, *par excellence*), in which *sui generis* semantic units or "sememes" come to be subserved by manifolds of microbehavioral symbols; and, interacting among themselves, they give rise, on the one hand, to higher configured cognitions of total sentences and, on the other, to a cognitive "levelling and sharpening" of the grammatical constituents of the sentences. Second, there is at the same time a rejection of views that language organization is rooted in a *sui generis* human genetics, not only because language has been on this planet too short a time, and a modicum of it has been taught to two chimpanzees, but also because the essence of its organization is a cognitive and not a behavioral specific, and psychology has long since abandoned innate ideas. Third, the thesis offers pilot semantic-conditioning evidence that, unlike primary perception, linguistic meaning is imageless à la the Würzburg school, Binet, Woodworth, and others.*

Language and meaning are admittedly the lifeblood of thinking. I shall claim, however, that they are also the essence of "willing" and that a sharp distinction must be drawn between *conditioned* and *voluntary* control. And here I am on more specific ground. Consider the following two spectacular experiments. Kel'man (1935) classically conditioned dogs to contract their spleens at the sound of a metronome of 60 beats per minute and not to contract to a metronome beat of 170. DiCara and Miller (1968) operantly conditioned rats to "blush" with one ear at a tone of 1000 cycles and not to "blush" in "time out." Now compare these experiments with those shown in Figure 8, where Moscow University students were taught to dilate and constrict their blood vessels "at will" by correcting the students' verbal reports of the nature of their vasomotion (upper panels), and, in an old American experiment, University of Michigan students were taught to wiggle their ears by adding "voluntary effort" to the involuntary wiggles produced by attached electrodes (bottom panels: 1—involuntary wiggles, 2—voluntary augmentation, 3—voluntary resistance, 4—acquired voluntary control—this became very good at the end). In the first two experi-

---

* In other words, the thesis does not deny the naturally acquired communicative and semantic specificity of human language—only its alleged absolute Cartesian nativism (absolute unevolutionary man/brute dichotomy).

Figure 8. *First and second panels*: sample records of Moscow University students trained to dilate and constrict their blood vessels at "will" through experimenter's correcting the student's verbal reports of the nature of their vasomotion in response to vasodilative and vasoconstrictive stimuli. (From Lisina, 1960) *Next four panels*: University of Michigan students learning to wiggle their ears by adding "voluntary effort" to wiggles produced by "attached electrodes"; *bottom panel*—automatic transfer of learning to the other ear. (From Bair, 1901)

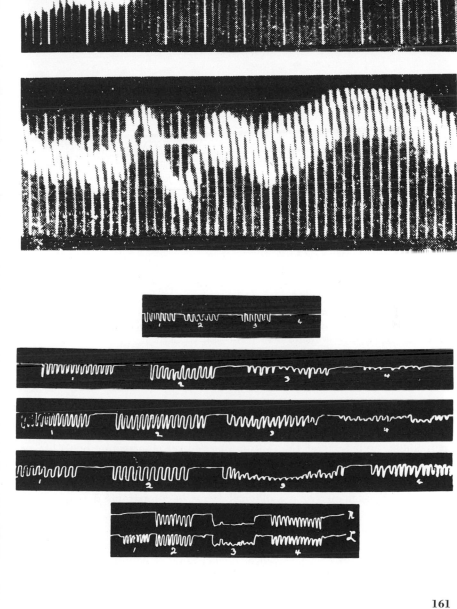

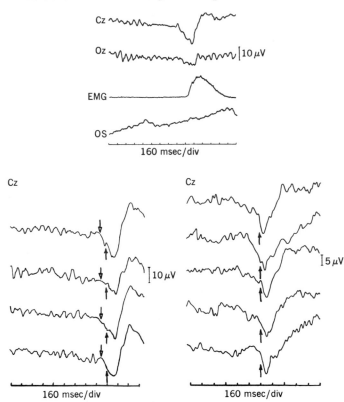

Figure 9. Summated EEGs prior to EMGs in the voluntary contraction of the extremities in seven subjects. *Upper panel*: response is dorsiflexion of the left foot; *lower panels*: response is contractions of the fist. Cz and Oz—location of electrodes; O.S.—potential below the left eye. Black arrows—onset of EMG. (From Gilden, Vaughan, & Costa, 1966)

ments, the control is linked to particular stimuli and is obviously subject to extinction and related disruptions. In the last two, it is unlinked and permanent, no less "free" than lifting one's finger, contracting one's fist, or bending one's foot, which, characteristically, modern evidence (Figure 9) shows to be accompanied by special "EEGs one second prior to EMGs"* (there are no such electrophysiological extras in comparable data of condi-

---

* Lindsley and Sassaman's report that a subject "able to control the erection of his body hairs" manifested, before any peripheral changes, "marked changes in the brain potentials . . . only over the premotor area [and] so far as he was aware the process was essentially similar to that of his initiating contraction of one of his skeletal muscles [1938, pp. 347–348]."

tioning). Pavlov switched his original stance, that type II (reinforcement) conditioning is the wellspring of voluntary movements, to the opinion that "involuntary reactions become voluntary only with the aid of the second-signal system [Pavlov, 1949, Vol. 1, p. 337; original date, May 24, 1933]. "He was right, and at 84 was evidently less atherosclerotic than American theorists of my and the present generation. And may I add that my view that symboling is a *sine qua non* to true "willing" was one of my earliest avowals (*"All voluntary behavior is symbolic . . . but not all symbolic is voluntary or will-controlling* [Razran, 1935, p. 121]" italics in original) and was not an outcome of reading Pavlov, whose change of mind was first published in 1949.

AUTONOMIC EVIDENCE

Concern with the cognitive superstructure does not lessen my commitment to the autonomic substructure cathected to a commodious triangle of interlinked evidence: (1) autonomic reactions are readily brought under the control of cognitive exteroceptive CSs and S^Ds (discriminative stimuli); (2) the CSs may be subliminal (there are no data as yet on such S^Ds); (3) autonomic as well as skeletal and verbal reactions are, to a large extent, under the control of *sui generis* unconditioned and conditioned autonomic stimulation, or interoception.

1. Evidence of the first type was already highlighted by human subjects' hand blushings at the flash of a blue light, dogs contracing their spleens to particular metronome rates, and rats' one-eared blushings at a 1000-cycle tone, the first two produced by classical, the third by reinforcement, techniques. The latter type is a Miller novelty, but the former is of course an experimental staple of long duration. Literally hundreds of experiments of classical conditioning of all kinds of cardiovascular, gastrointestinal, biliary, urinary, ureteral, uterine, and what-not autonomic reactions have been at hand for years. I certainly do not minimize the technologic serviceability of the reinforcement design, yet the classical one has the scientific advantage of trying to get at the source of the discarded "originating forces" (Skinner, 1938) of the reinforced reactions. And I might mention that Miller's conclusion (1969b; see also Chapter 7 of this volume) that his recent experiments "have deep implications . . . for the cause and the cure of abnormal psychosomatic symptoms [p. 434]" is quite comparable to Ayrapet'yants' and Bykov's 1945 statement that "interoceptive conditioned connections explain important aspects of the subconscious, giving it a vigorous scientific foundation [p. 592]" (published, incidentally, in English, in *Philosophy and Phenomenological Research*). And note also that "corticovisceral

pathology" has for decades been an active area of research and of some practice throughout the Soviet Union (there are half a dozen texts in the field).

2. There is special applied, let alone theoretic, merit in subliminal autonomic conditioning, namely, that the subject or patient has no access to the controlling stimulus. Figure 10 is a sample record of GSR and alpha-blocking conditioning to CSs 6 db below awareness in 2 of 21 subjects in Gershuni's laboratory. (To be sure, GSRs are not vital gut reactions but are of course autonomic and, incidentally, the first to be shown subject to reinforcement conditioning in the United States; see Kimmel and Hill, 1960.) And, presumably, all interoceptive conditioning equally puts the stimulus beyond the subject's or patient's control.

3. I reviewed the evidence of the behavioral role of interoceptive stimulation and conditioning in two prior publications (Razran, 1961, 1965) and will follow it up here with only four sample experiments of recent vintage, two classical and two reinforcement.

Figure 11 illustrates the apparatus for and the results of simple and differential salivary conditioning to the distention of the renal pelvis in two of five dogs. In the upper panel, note the renal and salivary fistulas, the distending solution, the manometer, and the EEG recorder. And note in the lower panel that only one of the two animals manifested a clear-cut differental CR when the ureter 5 cm below the pelvis was identically stimulated and that the magnitudes of its simple CRs were considerably higher than those of the other animal, a result that the experimenter interprets in term of Pavlovian typology: one dog "strong" in both excitation and inhibition, the other "weak" in both.

Figure 12 demonstrates interoceptive reinforcement discrimination in five macaques trained to bar-press in a Foringer chair for sugar pills on an FR25 (fixed ratio of 25:1) schedule. The S^D was a rhythmic distention of a small Thiry loop in the jejunum; the S^Δ, absence of the stimulation. The gradual development of the discrimination is very clearly evident in relating the performance of each monkey in the figure to the amount of training that it received: Charlie, 3 hours; Adolph, 4; Georgia, 6; Zsazsa, 16; Eva, 18. Interoceptive *reinforcement* conditioning was reported also by Àdàm and his associates in training five dogs to tilt the cover of a feeder with their heads in response to rhythmic distentions of their carotid sinuses.

Figure 13 discloses interoceptive-exteroceptive conditioning of alpha blocking in Ádám's two experiments. Completely habituated alpha blocking in response to carotid and renal distentions was re-established after the distentions were paired "several times" with effective auditory stimuli (cf. Miller, 1969a&b, on corresponding reinforcement conditioning).

And recent evidence supports in the main my earlier thesis that, besides

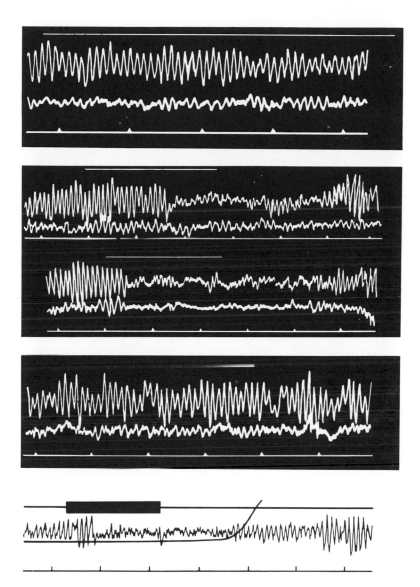

Figure 10. Sample records of conditioned GSR and alpha blocking with the CS a 6 db below awareness in 2 of 21 subjects. *Top four panels*: alpha blocking first and fourth segments—controls; second and third segments—after 30 and 20 pairings of the tone with a supraliminal light. (From Kozhevnikov & Maruseva, 1949) *Bottom panel*: alpha blocking and GSR after 20 pairings of the tone with an electric shock. (From Gershuni, 1946)

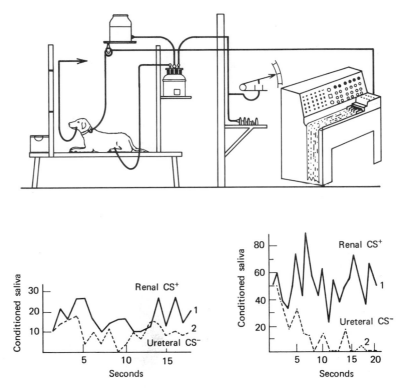

Figure 11.   Apparatus and sample results of interoceptive simple and differential salivary conditioning with distention of the renal pelvis as the CS and distention of the ureter 5 cm below as the differential stimulus in two of five dogs. (From Ádám. 1967)

being largely noncognitive, interoceptive stimulations dominate their comparable exteroceptive counterparts when the two are in conflict, do not significantly summate with the counterparts, clearly produce more widespread distal effects, and, although more slowly conditioned, are also more slowly extinguished. And it is of course generally true that interoception is (to use James's designation of another area) "sensibly continuous," whereas exteroception is (to bring in a Titchener term) "transient"; the former is an ever-present and vital background of the latter's variable functionings. (Chernigovsky's assertion, 1953, that "with very few exceptions, no autonomic organ or tissue is without its own receptors [p. 357]" is well borne

Figure 12.   Discrimination conditioning in five macaques lever-pressing in a Foringer chair for sugar pills with intestinal distention as the S^D and "time out" as the S^Δ. (From Slucki, Ádám, & Porter, 1965)

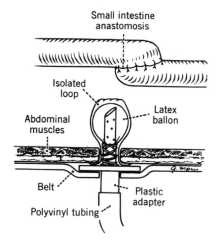

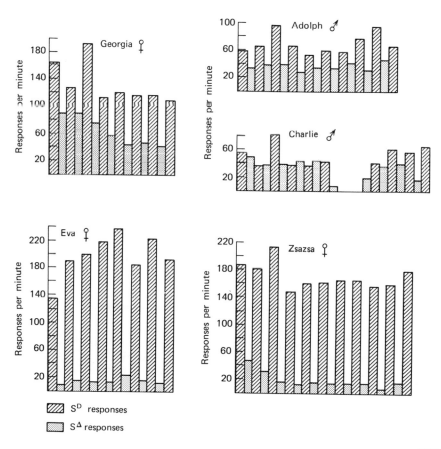

S^D responses
S^Δ responses

167

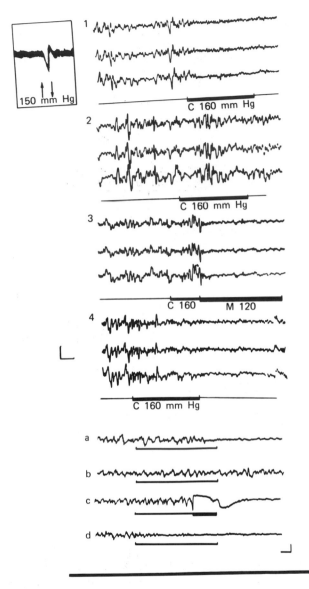

Figure 13. Sample records of conditioned interoceptive alpha blocking with an effective auditory stimulus as the US in 10 dogs. *Upper four segments*: distentions of the carotid sinus as the CS; *lower* 4 (*a, b, c, d*): distention of the renal pelvis. Thin horizontal lines—the CS; thicker lines—the auditory US. (From Ádám, 1967)

out by the later research of Ádám in 1967 and of Chernigovsky in 1960 and 1965.)

SUMMARY AND CONCLUSIONS

In fine, a collation of germane East and West evidence impels the view that the conditioned mechanisms of motor and verbal modifications are to a large extent dominated, on the one hand, by more efficacious cognitive learning and, on the other, by more ubiquitous visceral conditioning. In somewhat different terms, the learned cybernetics of man's behavior is, on the one hand, largely neurovisceral and, on the other, largely neurocognitive, each of which is in its own way more central and more integrative than our essentially peripheral neuromotor and neuroverbal outlets. More specifically, although the motor and the verbal are obviously our means of affecting the environment and each other, and although cognitive learning is perhaps less universal than noncognitive, and interoceptive less prompt than exteroceptive, it is true nonetheless that simplistic therapies in presumed eviscerated, denervated, and "decognized" human beings are too truncated to be successful in more than limited areas, and too static to be productive for long. The black box, unlike Pandora's box, should be pried open. In a recently published book of Pavlov's correspondence, a 1935 letter from Bertrand Russell extolled Pavlov's scientific approach to psychopathology vis-à-vis "the more or less mythological theories of the psychoanalysts [p. 344]." The three articles that Russell read, however, contained the novelty of "experimental neurosis," and one of them also contained the professed uniqueness of the second-signal system by itself and in interaction with the first. But, to pass from Bertrand Russell to the Good Book, I am reminded that reinforcement, after all, has operated on men and even God since time immemorial: "And God saw the light and it was good; and He divided the light from the darkness."

Regrettably, space permits only bare mention of several key therapeutic implications of my theses. (1) Behavior therapy must not wholly abandon the symptom-disease divide, even if the two lie within the same universe of deficit and deviant learning and unlearning, and "disease" is a semantic misnomer ("latent" and "manifest" or, obversely, "covert" and "overt" are closer). (2) The therapy must recognize fully that the crux of human semantic and volitional learning goes beyond the derivatives of not only the learning of pigeons and rats but also that of macaques and chimps —that cognition in general is not just another linear variable or parameter of an interstice of all-knowing and all-solving R_Gs and S_Gs. (3) Therapists, at least some of them, must begin to master the technology of autonomic

—exteroceptive and even interoceptive—conditioning and thereby come forth with a group of wanted specialists.

I must refrain from becoming involved in reforming basic principles of behavior modification proper: (a) peace between the *in utero* struggling Jacob-and-Esau twin of classical and operant conditioning and (b) separate status for punishment and *so-called* avoidance learning—in my terms, inhibitory-aversive and classical-aversive conditioning. Indeed, even evidence on the experimental divergencies in the efficacies of varying conditioning techniques, which certainly is of direct concern to therapists, must of necessity be deferred to a subsequent publication. I hope, however, that this chapter, compressed though it is, will help to narrow the all-too-common chasm between theory and practice in our field—and, of course, that the experimental basis of the theory is adequate and will be replicated.

ACKNOWLEDGMENTS

The research described herein was done under Grant MH-02196 (1957–68) from the National Institute of Mental Health, National Institutes of Health, Public Health Service, Department of Health, Education and Welfare.

REFERENCES

Ádám, G. *Interoception and behavior.* Budapest: Akadémiai Kiadó, 1967.

Ayrapet'yants, E. Sh., & Bykov, K. M. Physiological experiments and the psychology of the subconscious. *Philosophy and Phenomenological Research,* 1945, **5,** 577–593.

Bair, J. Development of voluntary control. *Psychological Review,* 1901, **8,** 474–510.

Baker, T. W. Component strength in a compound CS as a function of number of acquisition trials. *Journals of Experimental Psychology,* 1969, **79,** 347–352.

Booth, J. H., & Hammond, L. J. Differential fear to a compound stimulus and its elements. Paper presented at the meeting of the Eastern Psychological Association, Philadelphia, 1969.

Brogden, W. J. Sensory preconditioning. *Journal of Experimental Psychology,* 1939, **25,** 323–332.

Bykov, K. M., Alekseyev-Berkman, I., Ivanova, E. S., & Ivanov, E. P. The formation of conditioned reflexes to automatic and interoceptive stimuli. *Trudy III-go S'yezda Fiziologov,* 1928, pp. 263–264.

Bykov, K. M., & Pshonik, A. T. The nature of the conditioned reflex. *Fiziologichesky Zhurnal SSSR imeni I. M. Sechenova,* 1949, **35,** 509–524.

Bystroletova, G. N. Formation of conditioned reflexes to time intervals in neonates during periodic feeding. *Zhurnal Vysshey Nervnoy Deyatel'nosti imeni I. P. Pavlova,* 1954, **4,** 601–609.

Chernigovsky, V. N. Current problems in the physiology of interoception. In *The teachings of I. P. Pavlov and theoretical and practical medicine.* Vol. 2. Moscow: Ministerstvo Zdravokhraneniya, 1953. Pp. 357–382.

Chernigovsky, V. N. *Interoceptors.* Moscow: Medgiz, 1960. (English translation: American Psychological Association, 1967.)

Chernigovsky, V. N. (Ed.) *Problems of the physiology of interoception.* Vol. 2. Moscow-Leningrad: Nauka, 1965.

DiCara, L. V., & Miller, N. E. Instrumental learning of vasomotor responses by rats: Learning to respond differentially in the two rats. *Science,* 1968, **159,** 1485–1486.

Eisenstein, E. M., & Cohen, M. J. Learning in isolated prothoracic ganglia. *Animal Behaviour,* 1965, **13,** 104–108.

Gershuni, G. V. Interrelation of awareness and conditioned reflexes. *Fiziologichesky Zhurnal SSSR imeni I. M. Sechenova,* 1946, **32,** 43–47.

Gilden, L., Vaughan, H. G., & Costa, L. D. Summated human EEG potential with voluntary movements. *Electroencephalography and Clinical Neurophysiology,* 1966, **20,** 433–438.

Guth, S. L. Pattern effects with compound stimuli. *Journal of Comparative and Physiological Psychology,* 1967, **63,** 480–485.

Hoffeld, D. R., Kendall, S. B., Thompson, R. F., & Brogden, W. J. Effects of amount of preconditioning training upon the magnitude of sensory preconditioning. *Journal of Experimental Psychology,* 1960, **59,** 198–204.

Horridge, G. A. Learning of leg positions by headless insects. *Nature,* 1962, **193,** 697–698.

Kasatkin, N. I., Mirozyants, N. S. & Khokhitva, A. P. Conditioned orienting reflexes in infants during the first year of life. *Zhurnal Vysshey Nervnoy Deyatel' nosti imeni I. P. Pavlova,* 1953, **3,** 192–202.

Kel'man, Kh. B. The effects of the cerebral cortex on splenic movement. Neurohumoral connections. In K. M. Bykov (Ed.), *VIEM collected papers,* 1935, **3,** 7–15.

Kimmel, H. D., & Hill, F. A. Operant conditioning of the GSR. *Psychological Reports,* 1960, **7,** 555–562.

Kozhevnikov, V. A., & Maruseva, A. M. Electroencephalographic studies of the formation of temporary connections to unaware stimuli in man. *Izvestiya Akademii Nauk SSSR, Seriya Biologicheskaya,* 1949, No. 5, 560–569.

Krushinsky, L. V. *Formation of animal behavior: Normal and abnormal.* Moscow: Moscow University, 1960. (English translation: *Animal behavior: Its normal and abnormal development.* New York: Consultants' Bureau, 1962.)

Lindsley, D. B., & Sassaman, W. H. Autonomic activity and brain potentials associated with "voluntary" control of the pilomotors (*Mm.* arrectores pilorum). *Journal of Neurophysiology,* 1938, **1,** 342–349.

Lisina, M. I. Quoted in A. V. Zaporozhets, *Development of voluntary move-*

ments. Moscow: Akademyia Pedagogicheskikh Nauk RSFSR, 1960. Pp. 70–89.

Lyakh, G. S. Articulatory and auditory mimicry in the first months of life. *Zhurnal Vysshey Nervnoy Deyaterl'nosti imeni I. P. Pavlova,* 1968, **18,** 821–835. (a)

Lyakh, G. S. Characteristics of conditioned connections in mimoarticulatory and auditory components of speech stimuli in the first year of life. *Zhurnal Vysshey Nervnoy Deyatel'nosti imeni I. P. Pavlova,* 1968, **9,** 578–584. (b)

Miller, N. E. Experiments relevant to learning theory and motivation. In *XVIII International Congress of Psychology.* Moscow: International Union of Scientific Psychologists, 1969. Pp. 146–168. (a)

Miller, N. E. Learning of visceral and glandular responses. *Science,* 1969, **163,** 434–445. (b)

Narbutovich, I. O., & Podkopayev, N. A. The conditioned reflex as an association. *Trudy Fiziologicheskikh Laboratorii I. P. Pavlova,* 1936, **6** (2), 5–25.

Panferov, Yu. K. Chained conditioned reflexes in children. In *Theses, 2nd All-Union Congress of Physiology.* Leningrad, 1926. Pp. 153–156.

Pavlov, I. P. Basic laws of the work of the cerebral cortex. *Trudy Obshchestva Russkikh Vrachey v Sankt-Peterburge,* 1911, **78,** 175–187.

Pavlov, I. P. The latest successes of the objective study of higher nervous activity. *Izvestiya Petrogradskogo Nauchnogo Instituta imeni P. F. Lesgafta,* 1924, **8,** 43–52.

Pavlov, I. P. *Lectures on conditioned reflexes: Twenty-five years of objective study of higher nervous activity (behavior) of animals.* Translated, with additions, by W. H. Gantt, from Pavlov, 1923. New York: International Publishers, 1928.

Pavlov, I. P. *Wednesdays: Protocols and stenograms of physiological colloquia.* Moscow-Leningrad: Akademiya Nauk SSSR, 1949. 3 vols.

Pavlov, I. P. *Correspondence.* Moscow: Akademiya Nauk SSSR, 1970.

Razran, G. Conditioned withdrawal responses in adult human subjects. *Psychological Bulletin,* 1934, **31,** 111–143.

Razran, G. Conditioned responses: An experimental study and a theoretical analysis. *Archives of Psychology,* 1935, **28** (Whole No. 191).

Razran, G. Studies in configural conditioning. I. Historical and preliminary experimentation. *Journal of General Psychology,* 1939, **21,** 307–330.

Razran, G. The observable unconscious and the inferrible conscious in current Soviet psychophysiology: Interoceptive conditioning, semantic conditioning, and the orienting reflex. *Psychological Review,* 1961, **68,** 81–147.

Razran, G. The psychopathology of interoceptive stimulation. In J. Zubin & P. Hoch (Eds.), *The psychopathology of perception.* New York: Grune and Stratton, 1965. Pp. 62–82. (a)

Razran, G. Empirical codification and specific theoretical implications of compound-stimulus conditioning: Perception. In W. Prokasy (Ed.), *Classical conditioning.* New York: Appleton-Century-Crofts, 1965. Pp. 215–233. (b)

Razran, G. *Mind in evolution: An East-West synthesis of learned behavior and cognition.* Boston: Houghton Mifflin, 1971.

Reid, R. L. A test of sensory pre-conditioning in pigeons. *Quarterly Journal of Experimental Psychology,* 1952, **4,** 49–56.

Sergeyev, B. F. *Evolution of associative temporary connections.* Moscow: Akademiya Nauk SSSR, 1967.

Silver, C. S., & Meyer, D. R. Temporary factors in sensory preconditioning. *Journal of Comparative and Physiological Psychology,* 1954, **47,** 57–59.

Siqueland, E. R., & Lipsitt, L. P. Conditioned head-turning in human newborns. *Journal of Experimental Child Psychology,* 1966, **3,** 356–376.

Skinner, B. F. *The behavior of organisms.* New York: Appleton-Century, 1938.

Skinner, B. F. *Science and human behavior.* New York: Macmillan, 1953.

Slucki, H., Ádám, G., & Porter, R. W. Operant of an interoceptive stimulus in Rhesus monkeys. *Journal of the Experimental Analysis of Behavior,* 1965, **8,** 405–414.

Spence, K. W. Cognitive factors in the extinction of the conditioned eyelid response in humans. *Science,* 1963, **140,** 1224–1225.

Thomas, D. R., Berman, D. L., Serednesky, G. E., & Lyons, J. Information value and stimulus configuring as factors in conditioned reinforcement. *Journal of Experimental Psychology,* 1968, **76,** 181–189.

Thompson, R. F., & Kramer, R. F. Role of association cortex in sensory preconditioning. *Journal of Comparative and Physiological Psychology,* 1965, **60,** 186–191.

Voronin, L. G. Development of unconditioned and conditioned reactions in newborn macaques. *Fiziologichesky Zhurnal SSSR imeni I. M. Sechenova,* 1948, **34,** 333–338.

Watson, J. B. The heart or the intellect? *Harper's Monthly Magazine,* 1928, **156,** 345–353.

Wertheimer, M. Psychomotor coordination of auditory and visual space at birth. *Science,* 1961, **134,** 1962.

Note: All cited books published in the Soviet Union are in Russian.

CHAPTER 9

Behavioral Biology and Environmental Design

RICHARD ALLEN CHASE

The growth and differentiation of behavior results from a continuing exchange of structure between organism and environment. The genetic history of an animal powerfully influences the kinds of information in the environment that can influence the developing nervous system and the time periods during which specific kinds of experience can have disproportionately large effects on behavior. Brain structure affects the patterns of experience of which an organism is capable at each stage of development, and the structure of experience provided at each stage of development influences brain growth and development. Nervous systems process and generate information, and the structure of information inflow to the developing nervous system influences the future needs of the nervous system for information and the strategies that will be employed for the utilization of this information.

The human nervous system can be influenced more broadly and over longer periods of time than is the case for many other animals with simpler brains and shorter periods of socialization. Much of the early behavior of the human being consists of exploratory and play behaviors. These behaviors generate enormous amounts of information during early stages of brain development. Experiments that make use of deprivation of specific kinds of early experiences allow understanding of the crucial importance of specific patterns of experience during critical periods in the development of animals.

The marked extent to which human behavioral development can be modified by the structure of early experience represents at one and the same time an opportunity to explore the far reaches of human potential and an opportunity to produce individuals crippled in their social and intellectual behaviors because of early environmental deprivation. Biological and psychological data indicate that our ability to manipulate the early environment of the child places in our hands the most powerful single influence we can exercise on the development of broadly competent behaviors in man. This insight makes clear the importance of utilizing knowledge about early environmental influences on behavior in a way that enriches the environment of the child rather than simply adding this knowledge to our inventory of basic scientific data. In addition, this insight makes us mindful of the importance of enlarging our study of the specific patterns of interaction between children and their environments in order to expand our understanding of the early experiential determinants of developmental behavioral deficits and the early experiential determinants of optimal diversity and competence of the behavioral repertoire. The study of man in relationship to his total environment defines a new science: environmental biology; and our appreciation of the importance of applying the understanding generated within this new science defines a broad new area of work: deliberate design and evaluation of environments intended to optimize human development.

The Structure of Experience and the Development and Maintenance of Normal Brain Function

Growth and differentiation of brain cells is affected by the structure of experience and by the time in the course of development during which particular experiences occur. In addition, the continued maintenance of brain structure is contingent on the continued availability of specific patterns of experience, much as the maintenance of the total physical structure of any biological system is dependent on the continued availability of essential chemical structure. The variety and competence of the behavioral repertoire is dependent on patterns of growth and the differentiation of brain structure. The interaction between the structure of experience and the structure of the nervous system is, therefore, of direct pertinence to our understanding of the growth and differentiation of behavior. Insight into these interactions allows biology to make uniquely important contributions to the planning of the human environment (Bennett, Diamond, Rosenzweig, & Krech, 1964; Rosenzweig, Krech, Bennett, & Diamond, 1968).

Studies with a variety of mammals have shown that extreme light deprivation results in structural changes in retinal ganglion cells, cells of the lateral geniculate body, and cells in the visual cortex (Brattgård, 1952; Riesen, 1961, 1966; Wiesel & Hubel, 1963). Age is an important factor in determining the amount of anatomical change produced by sensory deprivation. Current evidence favors the generalization that the younger animal is more likely to show more marked changes in the structure of sensory systems that are deprived of stimulation. After occluding one eye of a cat with a translucent contact cover, from birth to three months of age, Wiesel and Hubel (1963) found marked changes in the cells of the lateral geniculate body that were deprived of stimulation. No similar changes were observed in an adult cat subjected to the same kind and amount of visual deprivation. In the case of the chimpanzee, extensive degeneration, atrophy, and eventual death of retinal ganglion cells and fibers of the optic nerve ensue if the animal is reared in the dark (Riesen, 1961).

Perceptual deficits also follow certain types of early sensory deprivation. In the case of cats and higher primates, visual placing reactions and avoidance of depth at an edge do not occur in animals that have been deprived of patterned vision. In addition, the following of objects, avoidance of obstacles, eye blink to approaching objects, detection of movement, and visual pattern discrimination also fail to develop in the visually deprived animal (Fantz, 1965; Riesen, 1966).

An animal acquires a perceptual map of three-dimensional space by the exploratory movements of its own body through space. The acquisition of competence in the exploration of the physical environment requires the ability to correlate parallel inputs from visual and somatic sensory systems as the organism moves through space (Walk & Gibson, 1961).

Another consequence of early sensory deprivation is serious interference with opportunities to learn the behavioral consequences and importance of stimuli. If patterned visual stimulation is withheld, it is impossible to learn the behavioral importance of specific objects and one's relationships to objects. This, in turn, prevents the development of selective attention to certain features of the environment. When the animal is restored to a normal visual environment, patterns of gross behavior reveal overcautious locomotion and failure to discriminate many behaviorally relevant visual cues.

In the case of the dog, severe restriction of early experience by rearing in cages that drastically reduce sensory input results in noticeable difficulty in learning visual discriminations (Melzack, 1965; Melzack & Burns, 1965). A wide range of objects is explored indiscriminately, without sustained attention being given to any one object. In addition, a very high level of behavioral arousal is noted. It is probable that a wide range of early experience is necessary to establish correlations of primary sensory system activity patterns and to learn the behavioral implications of specific sensory experiences. Once a nervous system has been organized to operate upon certain kinds of information, needs for continued provision of information of a similar kind are established. We can perceive speech sounds from a wide range of language communities, but we can accurately decode only sounds that have become familiar through long exposure and use. Human sensory deprivation experiments provide insight into the early needs for information necessary for the organization of a wide range of information processing and generating capabilities, as well as for their continued maintenance (Bruner, 1959, 1961; Denenberg, 1967; Fiske, 1961; Schultz, 1965; Thompson & Schaefer, 1961). It would seem that, once the brain has been programmed to operate upon a specific kind of information, deprivation of this information results in disorganization of the underlying brain functions in much the same way that we have come to recognize atrophy of other physical systems of the body when they are unused for long periods of time.

Allometric Development of Brain Structure and the Ontogeny of Behavior

Differentiation of cells proceeds at different rates for different cortical areas. Myelination of nerve fibers in the human cerebral cortex also proceeds at different rates in different regions. At birth, myelination is most advanced in the primary sensory areas and the motor cortex, and least advanced in frontal and posterior parietal association areas, where myelination of nerve fibers continues well into the fourth decade of life. The areas of association cortex that undergo the slowest course of cellular differentiation and myelination are pyhlogenetically new cortical areas that have undergone tremendous expansion in the human brain. These areas play an important role in the mediation of language behavior and the organization of affective and motivational behaviors.

Differential growth of different parts of the nervous system results in differential sensitivity to specific experiences at different times, which, in turn, affects brain structure. The result is a finely balanced dialogue between the nervous system and the environment. Appreciation of these facts allows insight into the process by which brain structure comes to reflect, in part, the structure of the environment. The entire process of sequential interactions between the environment and the nervous system is, in large part, under genetic control, for it is the genetic program that determines the broad limits of allometric growth of nervous system structures. This, in combination with the genetically determined biases of the sensory-perceptual operations of the brain, imposes major constraints on the types of experiences that can affect brain development and on the time periods during which specific modifications of brain structure can occur. In this way, genetically transmitted information influences not only the structural organization of individuals, but the patterns of interaction between individuals as well (Chance & Jolly, 1970).

Critical Periods in Development

A large number of observations show that animals are differently affected by similar experiences at different times in the course of development. Terms such as "critical period," "sensitive period," and "imprinting" have been used to refer to certain aspects of the different behavioral implications of experiences as functions of differences in age or level of development (Ambrose, 1963; Bateson, 1966; Bronson, 1965; Dubos, 1969; Fox, 1966; Gray, 1958; Hess, 1958; Hinde, 1962a, 1962b; Scott, 1962, 1968; Thorpe, 1961, 1965). Efforts have been made to understand particular patterns of allometric growth in the nervous system against the background of adaptive requirements of the organism at a given stage in development. Anokhin (1964) and his colleagues have studied the ontogenetic development of neural structures in man that are related to sucking and grasping. They report that cell groups of the facial nerve in the medulla that are related to movements of the mouth develop more rapidly than cell groups related to movements of the forehead, and that nerve fibers going to the mouth myelinate earlier and establish contact with muscle earlier in ontogenesis than is the case for any other branch of the facial nerve. A similar pattern of accelerated maturation of nerves mediating the grasp reflex was observed. This analysis included observations on differential patterns of maturation of motor cells in the spinal cord at different levels. Anokhin notes that the morphological substrate for functions that are vital to the survival of the term infant shows development far in advance of that which obtains for neighboring areas of the nervous system that support less crucial functions.

The study of critical periods in development was given considerable impetus by the demonstration that particular behaviors could be effectively established only during extremely narrow time periods, in some instances, periods of hours or days. Experiments have shown that ducklings allowed to follow moving objects other than the mother duck during the first day of life continued to follow the object to which they were first exposed. The term imprinting has been used to describe this phenomenon (Hess, 1958, 1962).

Specific types of learning other than the formation of primary social bonds have also been found to be possible only during rigidly bounded time periods. Under normal conditions of rearing, the young passerine bird demonstrates adult vocalization behavior by the end of the first year of life (Lanyon, 1960). If the young bird remains isolated from experienced adults until the summer of its first adult year, however, and is then exposed to the normal adult song patterns, it is not able to profit from this experience by adding appropriate fine modifications to its imperfect repertoire. The ability to modify song patterns during the first year, however, is considerable. If young birds are reared together, but still isolated from experienced adults, they develop more complex songs than are demonstrated by the bird that is reared alone. In addition, during the first year, the chaffinch reared in a normal way can add to his song repertoire as many as six different songs imitated from birds living in adjacent territories. Hand-rearing birds in isolation from their own species, but with early exposure to the song patterns of another species, may result in exclusive acquisition of the song patterns of the other species. Once incorporated into a bird's vocalization repertoire, these song patterns show no modification beyond the spring of the first year.

Environmental Deprivation

In the preceding discussion, we concentrated primarily on the effects of experiences at critical periods in development on future behavior. What of the case in which the critical period passes without the occurrence of appropriate experience during that time, or with the occurrence of inappropriate experience? First, let us consider the case in which appropriate experience has been withheld.

An infant monkey reared in isolation for three months shows a delayed ability to interact with other infant monkeys, but after six months of exposure to other infant monkeys normal social behavior patterns develop. If the monkey is isolated for the first six to twelve months of life, however, serious emotional disturbances result. After months of exposure to other infants these monkeys remain extremely withdrawn and show no evidence of social or exploratory behavior. They huddle in a corner in response to social or physical stimulation (Harlow, 1959, 1964). Other studies demonstrate that lesser degrees of social isolation, such as housing infant monkeys in cages that only allow them to watch and hear other monkeys, result in less extreme patterns of withdrawal. However, these monkeys frequently show stereotyped motor patterns and self-directed aggressive behavior. The isolation of infant monkeys from their mothers is associated with impaired patterns of social behavior, including inadequate sexual behavior, and aberrant patterns of mothering. To some extent association with peers compensates for the lack of exposure to the mother.

Studies with institutionalized human infants suggest that isolation from the mother or mother substitute can be endured for the first three months of life without producing irreversible impairment of intellectual and social behavioral development. However, if institutionalization, without provision for a substitute mother, is extended beyond three months, there is progressive impairment of emotional and intellectual development of a more permanent type (Casler, 1961; Goldfarb, 1945; Gray, 1958). It is reported that infants removed from institutions and placed in foster homes before six months may be expected to show normal patterns of behavioral development. Separation of human infants from mothers during the second half of the first year of life, however, is associated with depression, withdrawal, and failure to thrive (Casler, 1961; Goldfarb, 1945; Gray, 1958).

In all of these areas of work, most of the experiments have been undertaken with very young animals. This might well give rise to the impression that critical periods in development are restricted to early childhood. Such a conclusion would be premature. Studies on the development of ethical values demonstrate a progression of stages that continues through the second decade (Havighurst, 1964).

The Ontogeny of Behavior and Information Flow Between Organism and Environment

Even for the simple, stereotyped behavior patterns characteristic of the young of a species, close examination of the differentiation of the behavior reveals the shaping influences of environmental structure. In the case of the sea-gull chick, a pecking motion is directed at the bill of the parent bird in preparation for feeding. Just after hatching, the chick demonstrates far less accuracy in this movement than he shows one week later. However, this acquisition of accuracy is impaired by rearing in the dark. In addition, laughing gull chicks do not initially discriminate between models of their own parents and models of adult herring gulls. The laughing gull has a black head with a red bill; the herring gull, a white head and a yellow bill with a red spot on the lower mandible. The laughing gull chicks respond to the red spot. By one week of age, the same chicks are able to discriminate between these models and respond selectively to the models of their own parents. The intervening experience of being rewarded by food in association with pecking at the beaks of their own parents may well contribute significantly to the increasingly selective relationship between stimulus and response (Hailman, 1969). In this case we find an organism that has been prepared, largely through genetic influence, to respond with a pecking movement at physical stimuli in the environment that possess certain properties of shape, color, and motion.

During early stages in development the young organism may not be competent to organize its relationships with the environment in a manner that will support life. Under such circumstances, survival is dependent on the mediation of large classes of interaction with the environment by a competent organism, usually a parent. We find in such animals early demonstration of behaviors that serve to elicit from a parent the nutritional, protective, and supportive behaviors necessary for survival. Thus, the duckling shows the following response; the infant monkey, a grasp response; and the human infant, smiling and grasping. The formation of primary social bonds represents a crucial aspect of early development (Casler, 1961; Scott, 1962). Through this bond the parent comes to mediate the entire spectrum of information exchange operations between organism and environment. Disturbance of this relationship or formation of this relationship with an incompetent parent would be expected to have profound implications for all subsequent development.

Prosthetic Environments

We judge behavior to be incompetent in terms of specific dysfunctional relationships between organisms and environments. Then, in our role as therapists, we concentrate our efforts on modifying the behavior of the organism in a manner intended to reduce the degree of dysfunction. However, we could quite as logically modify aspects of the environment instead in order to accomplish the same objectives. If a child has difficulty gaining access to or making use of information that is necessary for normal behavioral development, then the environment of that child may be reorganized in a manner that makes the same information available in usable form.

A blind child is deprived of visual information about the physical environment. Guidance devices and reading devices developed for blind individuals have been designed to make information ordinarily presented to the visual system available to the auditory or somesthetic systems (Bliss, 1970; Kay, 1970). They provide an interface between an environment that is rich in visual information and an organism that cannot use visual information. Guidance devices provide patterns of sound or tactile stimulation that give information about the physical environment, and reading devices operate according to similar principles. These devices do represent a type of environmental design. However, it is possible to extend the process of environmental modification much farther so that existing environmental structures actually emit information that can be used by a blind individual without providing an electrical or electromechanical transform operation at the interface between the organism and the environment. It is possible to design an environment for preschool blind children that will afford maximum opportunity to make use of residual visual function as well as provide increased information about visual structures to the auditory and somesthetic systems.

Similar arguments can be made in the case of the deaf child. The opportunities that such a child has for developing speech depend directly on the kind and amount of residual hearing, the exposure to speech sound structure in the environment, and the time period during which such information is made available. Many congenitally deaf children realize a tremendous advantage in acquiring speech through the use of hearing aids during the first few years of life. It is just as logical to consider the design of environments for preschool deaf children in which all sounds are amplified as they are introduced into the environment. In this case, the teacher with normal hearing might wear earphones utilized to attenuate the sounds in the environment. When more is learned about the specific auditory information-processing deficits produced by early-acquired lesions of the central nervous system, some of the information-processing operations normally undertaken by components of the auditory nervous system could be undertaken by electronic devices before sounds are presented to the child.

Prosthetic environments can be envisioned not only for the child with sensory disabilities but also for the child with disabling patterns of gross behavioral development. It has been observed repeatedly that autistic children demonstrate little or no verbal behavior in ordinary social group situations. It has also been observed repeatedly that autistic children commonly become absorbed with the manipulation of machines and other physical structures. Instead of exerting pressure toward communication in traditional interpersonal settings, why not build machines that can allow the autistic child to use the language competence he has acquired and to expand that competence? The "talking typewriter" is a machine that permits programming of a standard electric typewriter keyboard in a variety of ways. Each time the child strikes a key or sequence of keys, he may be allowed to hear the sounds of letters or words. It has been found that many autistic children enjoy "playing" with this machine, and their spontaneous typing reveals the development of language competence that often surprises those who know them well, exceeding by a wide margin the level of language competence demonstrated in spontaneous speech (Goodwin & Goodwin, 1969).

In some instances our failures in environmental design are based on inaccurate conclusions concerning behavioral capabilities and needs. Many children are thought to be divergent in *most* of their behavior because they are so conspicuously divergent in *some* aspects of their behavior. Autistic children show, from early infancy, a marked disturbance in affective responsivity to other human beings. This represents a behavioral deficit that can serve to extinguish much of the repertoire of supportive teaching behaviors of the mother. The result can be superposition of some degree of maternal deprivation on top of the primary behavioral deficit. The same sequence is observed when these children grow older and move among other children and adults. Their characteristic failure to use speech voluntarily results in the extinction of verbal behaviors directed toward them, with consequent loss of learning opportunities. It is often assumed that these children have severe language disturbances and cannot profit from being spoken to. However, closer inspection invariably shows these children to be quite competent, if not precocious, in many aspects of language development. The inference that language capabilities are deficient is often incorrect, and withdrawal of verbal communication from the environment of such a child results in a secondary, and unnecessary, deprivation of learning opportunities. Similar types of reasoning have resulted in severe restrictions of early experience in the case of deaf children and blind children. In all of these instances, the result is unnecessary retardation of learning.

Would it not be more constructive to build new environments, designed on the basis of realistic appraisals of behavioral abilities and deficits? Such environments could provide support of potential adaptive behavioral growth and would not make demands that clearly cannot possibly be met. The design of environments that are modifiable and responsive not only to individual patterns of behavioral competence, but also to individual styles of behavioral expression, provides excellent opportunities to support available behavioral competence and to learn with greater precision just what an individual is and is not capable of (Cohen, 1967; Cohen, Filipczak, & Bis, 1967; Craik, 1970; Gewirtz, 1968; Lindsley, 1964).

Exploratory and Play Behaviors as Sources of Information

Exploration and play characterize much of the early behavior of many animals (Lowenfeld, 1967; Maddi, 1961; Welker, 1961). It has been observed that animals with simpler and more stereotyped behavioral repertoires demonstrate less exploratory and play behavior than animals showing longer periods of socialization and greater plasticity with respect to the effects of early experience on behavioral development.

Studies with primates demonstrate marked evidences of curiosity and exploratory behavior (Butler, 1965; Welker, 1961). Visual discrimination learning in the monkey can be sustained with rewards consisting solely of the opportunity to observe other monkeys or to watch people working in a laboratory. When monkeys are allowed choices of projected scenes, they select clearly focused images instead of blurred ones, and series of projected images or motion picture films rather than single, stationary frames. The monkeys view longer when motion pictures are projected brightly rather than dimly, at normal rather than at slow speeds, in color rather than in black and white, and right side up rather than upside down (Butler, 1965).

The extended period of time during which exploratory and play behaviors are dominant in the behavioral repertoires of children represents an extended opportunity for enlarging the range and competence of behaviors. The realization of this opportunity is contingent on the extent to which the environment is rich in relevant information. The child with a normal nervous system, growing up in an environment that is wanting in information, may be expected to show some of the same patterns of behavioral incompetence that we have come to expect of the child with early damage to the brain that interferes with the process of learning.

Learning and Education

Observation of the spontaneous behavior of animals attests to the curiosity and interest aroused by the behavior of other animals. This aspect of exploratory behavior offers great promise of supporting effective learning if appropriate experiences are allowed. In experiments on two-choice visual discrimination learning for food rewards, an observer monkey was noted to profit more from trials in which the performing monkey made mistakes than from trials that were rewarded with food (Darby & Riopelle, 1959). This fact made it clear that the observer monkey was correlating the performing monkey's responses with their consequences rather than simply imitating the responses.

A conditioned avoidance response has been learned more rapidly and more accurately by cats allowed simply to observe the behavior of experienced cats than by cats taught the same response by administering a shock after failure to jump over a hurdle when a buzzer sounded (John, Chesler, Bartlett, & Victor, 1968).

The apparent efficacy of observation learning suggests possible advantages from structuring the educational environment to allow broader exposure of naive students to experienced ones. This strategy is central to all apprenticeship relationships. However, the rigid segregation of school children by age makes observation learning less available than it might otherwise be. Perhaps it would be advantageous to allow even very young students to spend part of their time functioning as teachers of younger children. The opportunities for observation learning would thereby be greatly increased, and the young teachers might also realize significant learning advantages from the execution of their new teaching responsibilities.

Lack of clear definition regarding the aims of education has exempted the designers of educational programs and materials from critical scrutiny of their work. If objectives are not clarified, there is no possible way of measuring success in any enterprise. Once objectives have been clarified, it is possible to design educational materials that allow efficient and comprehensive acquisition of the new capabilities one wishes to attain, analysis of the behavioral capabilities already present, and construction of an orderly sequence of experiences designed to build from pertinent existing capabilities toward new ones. The suitability of specific experiences to such an objective is constantly monitored, and the materials out of which experiences are built are modified in accordance with empirical observation.

Let us take a very simple example of such an approach: the teaching of writing. Writing requires the learning of a finite set of visual structures and the relationships between these visual structures and the acoustic structures of the language. The choice of which visual forms to use is completely arbitrary, and different language communities have exercised radically different options in this matter. However, once a language community makes a decision, efficient use of the language requires conformity with the shared conventions. It makes little difference whether one writes from right to left or from left to right, but it makes a great deal of difference that one conforms in these practices with the conventions of his own language community. It is clear that a young child must be able to understand the difference between progressions of hand movement moving from right to left and progressions of hand movement in the opposite direction. In addition, he must learn to produce and perceive the visual pattern structures of a writing system in a discriminative manner. These elemental capabilities really have nothing to do with language *per se,* but they are necessary in order to learn efficient interconversions of the visual representations of language (reading and writing) with the auditory representations (speech). It seems sensible, therefore, to make sure that simple visual discrimination capabilities are taught before proceeding with the teaching of the recognition of words or even of letters. It also seems sensible to teach a child to replicate simple shapes and orientations before proceeding with the teaching of written language. Once begun, the teaching of reading and writing should proceed in just such a methodical way, from simpler to more complex, but related, behavioral operations.

Many of the features of such a teaching program have been incorporated into the writing program designed by Professor B. F. Skinner (Skinner & Krakower, 1968). A typical exercise early in the program may require that a child reproduce lines oriented in different ways. The model line is shown in one of a pair of boxes on a printed page. The child replicates the model by connecting dots in an appropriate manner in the adjacent box. The paper is chemically treated so that lines drawn with a yellow felt-tip pen in acceptable target regions become black, and lines drawn outside of these regions remain yellow. Similar principles are used as the program moves from the teaching of simple discriminations and replications of patterns and orientation of patterns to the teaching of printed letters, combinations of printed letters, and, finally, cursive script. In addition to providing a well-designed sequence of responses, the writing program demonstrates two other important design principles: the student is given immediate information about whether his responses are correct or incorrect, and correct responses are reinforced by the color change of the chemically treated paper.

Isolation of formal learning environments from the larger environments within which a child learns tends to diminish the contribution that even well-designed teaching materials make to the behavioral development of the child. The physical and social isolation of schools from the rest of the environment of the child serves to encumber his interest in learning and his parents' understanding of the importance of learning experiences in behavioral development. This tradition of isolation has resulted in a frequent dichotomization of learning in which the school is charged with the responsibility for teaching skills that will be needed at some later time and in some way that is almost always shrouded in vagueness. Learning about one's self, one's fellows, and the immediate human and physical environment, on the other hand, is left to the chance encounters of everyday life. Basic dimensions of human experience—affection and joy, love, fear, loneliness, compassion, aging, infirmity, sickness, death, discovery and invention, creativity, aggression and destructiveness, communication—are minimally represented in the main core of our educational experience.

These and other critical lacunae in the structure of early educational experience must be identified and filled. If early experience is impoverished, later behavior will be impoverished as well, and our richest opportunities for behavioral growth will have passed.

Environmental Biology

We are witnessing a growing concern about abuses of the physical environment that are endangering many forms of plant and animal life, including human life. Various subspecialties within biology and engineering are contributing to the current efforts to redefine our responsibilities concerning the utilization of natural resources and other aspects of the physical environment. We are less well equipped, however, when it comes to determining our responsibilities for structuring the environment in ways that accommodate particular structures of experience. There is nothing self-evident about the specific interrelationships between environmental structure and the structure of behavior. These interrelationships must be meticulously studied and inventoried, and this effort defines a new and vital area for applied behavioral science (Barker, 1965; Esser, 1971; Proshansky, Ittelson, & Rivlin, 1970; Studer & Stea, 1966).

Comprehensive study of the effects of the total environment, physical and experiential, on human life and behavior provides an unprecedented opportunity for medicine and biology to assume a close relationship to the social sciences. We might call this new area of concern and scientific work "environmental biology." It is not at all clear just what boundaries this new science should have, and we could only suffer from too rigid and too early a definition of boundaries. However, it is quite clear that broad study of the biological implications of man's environment will require new research strategies and new images of professional responsibility and concern that can be only dimly envisioned at present.

The fulfillment of creative work and the stimulation and opportunities for growth provided by education will, in some measure, be displaced into the behaviors that make use of leisure. When this is done, however, fundamental redefinitions of the boundaries of work, play and education will have been brought about. At the present time, one of the major deterrents to the effectiveness of formal education is the extent to which formal learning is isolated from the aspects of immediate experience in which we are most interested. As boundaries between classes of behavior become redefined, we can anticipate corresponding redefinition of the uses of physical space.

Environmental Design and Human Behavior Potential

Perhaps the most exciting dimension of the new science of environmental biology is the opportunity it provides us to learn more about man and the limits of human capabilities (Dubos, 1965). So much of the environment is restrictive and inflexible and functions in support of behaviors that become ritualized and stereotyped that one wonders whether we have not become accustomed to settling for very few of the experiences of which we are really capable. What, at the present time, can we say about the far reaches of human behavioral potential? In part, we must reply that most of the understanding we require to provide a meaningful answer has not yet been achieved. And, just as in the case of plant growth and development, we will not know the potential for the development of human thought and creative expression until we have deliberately studied the effects of the human environment on the unfolding of human behavior. In addition, we will have no idea of the extent to which every one of us has suffered preventable behavioral retardation because of specific environmental deficits until the interrelationships between environment and behavior are made clear by observation and bold new forms of experimentation.

REFERENCES

Ambrose, J. A. The concept of a critical period for the development of social responsiveness in early human infancy. In B. M. Foss (Ed.), *Determinants of infant behavior II*. New York: Wiley, 1963. Pp. 201–225.

Anokhin, P. K. Systemogenesis as a general regulator of brain development. In W. A. Himwich & H. E. Himwich (Eds.), *Progress in brain research*. Vol. 9. London: Elsevier, 1964. Pp. 54–86.

Barker, R. Explorations in ecological psychology. *American Psychologist,* 1965, **20,** 1–14.

Bateson, P. P. G. The characteristics and context of imprinting. *Biological Reviews of the Cambridge Philosophical Society,* 1966, **41,** 177–220.

Bennett, E. L., Diamond, M. C., Rosenzweig, M. R., & Krech, D. Chemical and anatomical plasticity of the brain. *Science,* 1964, **146,** 610–619.

Bliss, J. C. (Ed.) *IEEE Transactions on Man-Machine Systems,* 1970, **11,** 1–122.

Brattgård, S. O. The importance of adequate stimulation for the chemical composition of retinal ganglion cells during early post-natal development. *Acta Radiologica,* 1952 (Suppl. No. 96).

Bronson, G. The hierarchical organization of the central nervous system: Implications for learning processes and critical periods in early development. *Behavioral Science,* 1965, **10,** 7–25.

Bruner, J. S. The cognitive consequences of early sensory deprivation. *Psychosomatic Medicine,* 1959, **21,** 89–95.

Bruner, J. S. The cognitive consequences of early sensory deprivation. In P. Solomon, P. E. Kubzansky, P. H. Leiderman, J. H. Mendelson, R. Trumbull, & D. Wexler (Eds.), *Sensory deprivation.* Cambridge, Mass.: Harvard University Press, 1961. Pp. 195–207.

Butler, R. A. Investigative behavior. In A. M. Schrier, H. F. Harlow, & F. Stollnitz (Eds.), *Behavior of nonhuman primates.* Vol. II. New York: Academic Press, 1965. Pp. 463–493.

Casler, L. Maternal deprivation. *Monographs of the Society for Research in Child Development,* 1961, **26,** 1–64.

Chance, M., & Jolly, C. *Social groups of monkeys, apes and men.* New York: E. P. Dutton, 1970.

Cohen, H. L. Educational therapy. *Arena,* 1967, **82,** 220–225.

Cohen, H. L., Filipczak, J., & Bis, J. S. *Case I: An initial study of contingencies applicable to special education.* Silver Spring, Md.: Institute for Behavioral Research, 1967.

Craik, K. H. Environmental psychology. In *New directions in psychology.* New York: Holt, Rinehart & Winston, 1970. Pp. 1–121.

Darby, C. L., & Riopelle, A. J. Observational learning in the rhesus monkey. *Journal of Comparative and Physiological Psychology,* 1959, **52,** 94–98.

Denenberg, V. H. Stimulation in infancy, emotional reactivity and exploratory behavior. In D. C. Glass (Ed.), *Neurophysiology and emotion.* New York: The Rockefeller University Press & Russell Sage Foundation, 1967. Pp. 161–190.

Dubos, R. *Man adapting.* New Haven: Yale University Press, 1965.

Dubos, R. Lasting biological effects of early influences. *Perspectives in Biology and Medicine,* 1969, **12,** 479–491.

Esser, A. *Behavior and environment: The use of space by animals and men.* New York: Plenum Publishing Corp., 1971.

Fantz, R. L. Ontogeny of perception. In A. M. Schrier, H. F. Harlow, & F. Stollnitz (Eds.), *Behavior of nonhuman primates.* Vol. II. New York: Academic Press, 1965. Pp. 365–403.

Fiske, D. W. Effects of monotonous and restricted stimulation. In D. W. Fiske & S. R. Maddi (Eds.), *Functions of varied experience.* Homewood, Ill.: Dorsey Press, 1961. Pp. 106–144.

Fox, M. W. Neuro-behavioral ontogeny. A synthesis of ethological and neuro-psychological concepts. *Brain Research,* 1966, **2,** 3–20.

Gewirtz, J. L. On designing the functional environment of the child to facilitate behavioral development. In L. L. Dittmann (Ed.), *Early child care: The new perspectives.* New York: Atherton Press, 1968. Pp. 169–213.

Goldfarb, W. Effects of psychological deprivation in infancy and subsequent stimulation. *American Journal of Psychiatry,* 1945, **102,** 18–33.

Goodwin, M. S., & Goodwin, T. C. In a dark mirror. *Mental Hygiene,* 1969, **53,** 550–563.

Gray, P. H. Theory and evidence of imprinting in human infants. *Journal of Psychology,* 1958, **46,** 155–166.

Hailman, J. P. How an instinct is learned. *Scientific American,* 1969, **221** (6), 98–106.

Harlow, H. F. Love in infant monkeys. *Scientific American,* 1959, **200** (6), 68–74.

Harlow, H. F. Early social deprivation and later behavior in the monkey. In A. Abrams, H. H. Garner, & J. E. P. Toman (Eds.), *Unfinished tasks in the behavioral sciences.* Baltimore: Williams & Wilkins, 1964. Pp. 154–173.

Havighurst, R. J. Developing moral character. In A. Crow & L. D. Crow (Eds.), *Vital issues in American education.* New York: Bantam Books, 1964. Pp. 239–244.

Hess, E. "Imprinting" in animals. *Scientific American,* 1958, **198** (3), 81–90.

Hess, E. Imprinting and the "critical period" concept. In E. L. Bliss (Ed.), *Roots of behavior.* New York: Harper, 1962. Pp. 254–263.

Hinde, R. A. Sensitive periods and the development of behaviour. In S. A. Barnett (Ed.), *Lessons from animal behaviour for the clinician.* London: National Spastics Society Study Group & Heinemann Medical Books, Ltd., 1962. Pp. 25–36. (a)

Hinde, R. A. Some aspects of the imprinting problem. In *Imprinting and early learning, 1961.* London: Symposia of the Zoological Society of London, 1962. Pp. 129–138. (b)

John, E. R., Chesler, P., Bartlett, F., & Victor, I. Observation learning in cats. *Science,* 1968, **159,** 1489–1491.

Kay, L. A preliminary report on ultrasonic spectacles for the blind. In *AFB Research Bulletin,* No. 21. New York: American Foundation for the Blind, 1970. Pp. 91–100.

Lanyon, W. E. The ontogeny of vocalization in birds. In W. E. Lanyon & W. N. Tavolga (Eds.), *Animal sounds and communication.* Washington, D. C.: American Institute of Biological Sciences, 1960. Pp. 321–347.

Lindsley, O. R. Geriatric behavioral prosthetics. In R. Kastenbaum (Ed.), *New thoughts on old age.* New York: Springer, 1964. Pp. 41–60.

Lowenfeld, M. *Play in childhood.* New York: Wiley, 1967.

Maddi, S. R. Exploratory behavior and variation-seeking in man. In D. W. Fiske & S. R. Maddi (Eds.), *Functions of varied experience.* Homewood, Ill.: Dorsey Press, 1961. Pp. 253–277.

Melzack, R. Effects of early experience on behavior: Experimental and conceptual considerations. In P. H. Hoch & J. Zubin (Eds.), *Psychopathology of perception.* New York: Grune & Stratton, 1965. Pp. 271–299.

Melzack, R., & Burns, S. K. Neurophysiological effects of early sensory restriction. *Experimental Neurology,* 1965, **13,** 163–175.

Proshansky, H. M., Ittelson, W. H., & Rivlin, L. G. (Eds.) *Environmental psychology; man and his physical setting.* New York: Holt, Rinehart & Winston, 1970.

Riesen, A. H. Stimulation as a requirement for growth and function in behavioral development. In D. W. Fiske & S. R. Maddi (Eds.), *Functions of varied experience.* Homewood, Ill.: Dorsey Press, 1961. Pp. 57–80.

Riesen, A. H. Sensory deprivation. In E. Stellar & J. M. Sprague (Eds.), *Progress in physiological psychology.* New York: Academic Press, 1966. Pp. 117–147.

Rosenzweig, M. R., Krech, D., Bennett, E. L., & Diamond, M. C. Modifying brain chemistry and anatomy by enrichment or impoverishment of experience. In G. Newton & S. Levine (Eds.), *Early experience and behavior.* Springfield, Ill.: Charles C Thomas, 1968. Pp. 258–298.

Schultz, D. P. *Sensory restriction.* New York: Academic Press, 1965.

Scott, J. P. Critical periods in behavioral development. *Science,* 1962, **138,** 949–958.

Scott, J. P. Critical periods in behavioral development. In N. S. Engler, L. R. Boulter, & H. Osser (Eds.), *Contemporary issues in developmental psychology.* New York: Holt, Rinehart & Winston, 1968. Pp. 181–197.

Skinner, B. F., & Krakower, S. A. *Handwriting with write and see.* Chicago: Lyons and Carnahan, 1968.

Studer, R. G., & Stea, D. Architectural programming, environmental design, and human behavior. *Journal of Social Issues,* 1966, **22,** 127–136.

Thompson, W. R., & Schaefer, T., Jr. Early environmental stimulation. In D. W. Fiske & S. R. Maddi (Eds.), *Functions of varied experience.* Homewood, Ill.: Dorsey Press, 1961. Pp. 81–105.

Thorpe, W. H. Sensitive periods in the learning of animals and men: A study of imprinting with special reference to the induction of cyclic behavior. In W. H. Thorpe & O. L. Zangwill (Eds.), *Current problems in animal behaviour.* London: Cambridge University Press, 1961. Pp. 194–224.

Thorpe, W. H. The ontogeny of behavior. In J. A. Moore (Ed.), *Ideas in modern biology.* New York: The Natural History Press, 1965. Pp. 484–518.

Walk, R. D., & Gibson, E. J. A comparative and analytical study of visual depth perception. *Psychological Monographs,* 1961, **75,** 1–44.

Welker, W. I. An analysis of exploratory and play behavior in animals. In D. W. Fiske & S. R. Maddi (Eds.), *Functions of varied experience.* Homewood, Ill.: Dorsey Press, 1961. Pp. 175–226.

Wiesel, T. N., & Hubel, D. H. Effects of visual deprivation on morphology and physiology of cells in the cat's lateral geniculate body. *Journal of Neurophysiology,* 1963, **26,** 978–993.

Psychophysiology and Psychophysics

In psychophysics and emergently in psychophysiology, precision of measurement has been a dominant concern. It is not surprising, therefore, that some workers in these fields have adapted their tools to the precise measurement of abnormal function. Some of them have been interested in collecting base-line data; some, in analyzing the implications of the manifold clinical and phenomenological observations such as perceptual distortion, slowness of response, and many other phenomena of psychopathology. Still others have been interested in obtaining the facts from which to fashion etiological theories. The chapters in Part Three reflect these differences of purpose.

Here, as in other parts of the book, the lines between disciplines blur. Although all contributors in this part are psychologists whose primary area of competence is the study of behavior, each of them demonstrates in a different way the influence of physiology. Both Venables and Clausen are concerned with the possibility of integrating data, although in quite different areas—psychopathology and mental retardation, respectively—under a concept of altered arousal function. In neither case is it found possible to approach this task simply; a number of other concepts must be brought into play. In Chapter 14 Venables is concerned with the various mechanisms involved in the transmission, registration, and storage of sensory input—selective attention and orienting—and the ways in which these may be disturbed in schizophrenia. Clausen, in Chapter 15, surveys the evidence for and against arousal impairment in mental defectives and notes that the findings are too complex and contradictory to fit a simple form of arousal theory. He suggests that a modified and differentiated conceptualization of arousal may hold some promise for a theory of mental deficiency. This is necessitated not only by the lack of homogeneity among mental defectives, but also by the apparent lack of consistency among the many peripheral and central measures of arousal.

In contrast to most forms of psychopathology and mental deficiency—for which there is insufficient evidence for organic etiology—the behavioral deviations Benton deals with in Chapter 12 are known to have an organic cause—brain damage. His review of the data with respect to somesthetic function leads to the conclusion that the concept of cerebral dominance can be neither wholly accepted nor wholly rejected. The subtle investigation of this question supports hemispheric asymmetry in the sense that lesions on the left and right side have different behavioral implications, but conflicts with asymmetry in that lesions judged on neurological evidence to be unilateral are associated with bilateral behavioral defects.

Here, as elsewhere in human pathology, the diagnostic problem is inescapable and is encountered in many different ways. Benton's conclusion makes it difficult to use the subject as his own control in diagnosing unilateral brain lesions. Clausen comments on the vast heterogeneity of those classified as mentally defective and notes that, while many are underaroused, others are overaroused. Venables finds it necessary to separate in terms of his theory acute and/or paranoid schizophrenic patients from chronic or regressed schizophrenic patients. In Chapter 10 Sutton suggests that the *a priori* classification of patients as to diagnostic category be treated as only the first step in a series of successive approximations. In his iterative strategy, he proposes that the psychophysiological differences obtained may also in turn be used as independent variables in order to discover the psychiatric characteristics shared by patients who are similar in their psychophysiological functions. The next iterative steps would be to select patients in terms of these psychiatric traits and to attempt a broader-ranged psychophysiological description of these patients. (Gurland, in Part Five of this volume, discusses several examples of iterative strategy.)

On the whole, the chapters in this part belong to a "second phase" of theory making. The first blush of promise has worn off, and the simpler forms of the theories have been found wanting. We are now in a retrenchment phase, beginning with an attempt to survey progress to date. More complex versions of the theories are beginning to emerge. This re-evaluation means different things to different researchers. Sutton has suggested that because of methodological difficulties much of the research available cannot be interpreted rigorously and its meaning remains ambiguous. Venables has undertaken the painstaking integration of data collected under a number of different conceptual headings. Clausen has compared, and found contradictory, the results of many studies relating to the arousal concept in mental deficiency.

By contrast, Chapter 13 by King may be considered phase one theory. He surveys the area of memory for temporal duration and proposes that investigations in this area might shed light on developmental processes and on memory impairments in aging, as well as in neurological and psychiatric diseases. Particularly in psychopathology, studies of this kind might contribute to an understanding of such psychological states as perplexity, feelings of unaccountable strangeness or familiarity, disorientation of time and place, and, less directly, possibly even of person. It is of interest to note that Joseph Zubin (Zubin, J., & Barrera, S. E. Effect of electric convulsive therapy on memory. *Proceedings of the Society for Experimental Biology and Medicine,* 1941, **48**, 596–597) did one of the pioneer studies on the disassociation between memory as recognition and memory as the sense of familiarity when he reported on these two aspects of memory following electroshock therapy.

Although in a somewhat different direction, Chapter 11 by Kugelmass is a phase two kind of review. He surveys the evidence for differences in autonomic response as a function of social group membership, and forces us to realize that here is yet another set of variables which need to be controlled in our evaluation of autonomic function in psychopathology. The autonomic measurements that would classify a member of one group as psychopathological may be normal for a member of another group. That measurements are physiological does not guarantee that they are culture free.

CHAPTER 10

Fact and Artifact in the Psychology of Schizophrenia

SAMUEL SUTTON

In 1956, Horwitt recounted a rather sorry history of various assertions, based on research data, of biochemical differences between schizophrenic patients and normal individuals which have proved to be artifacts of differences in diet, differences in psychological state, or differences that arose from comparing institutionalized patients with noninstitutionalized normals. Two of the differences that had been reported turned out to arise from differences in the quantities of orange juice and coffee used by the two populations being compared (Kety, 1959a, 1959b).

A comparable consideration is long overdue for differences between patients and normals in objective psychological measures. Here the primary sources of artifact are probably not diet or institution-wide infections, but rather a number of psychological states associated either with the illness or with the effects on personality of the institutional environment. In the last several decades, thousands of reports have appeared asserting sensory, perceptual, conceptual, or psychomotor differences between psychiatric patients and normals. Although it is conceivable that patients are different from normals in all of these functions, one's suspicions are aroused when the general finding is that the patient performs more poorly than the normal, whatever the measure used. The patient's reaction time is slower; his sensory threshold is less sensitive; his perceptual and conceptual performance is less adequate. Are these all, in fact, truly psychomotor, sensory, perceptual, or conceptual differences, or are they secondary side effects of the fact that patients are less motivated, less cooperative, or less attentive than normals during the testing session? Certainly such factors would tend to reduce the efficiency of patient performance on any function tested. Additionally, a number of attitudinal states are associated with various illnesses. Thus the conservativeness and rigidity of the depressive patient or the suspiciousness and need for certainty of the paranoid patient may interact dramatically with threshold measurements in which the degree of conservatism versus risk taking will influence the sensitivity of the measure obtained. Similarly, in size constancy experiments such attitudes would give results in the direction of overconstancy (Raush, 1952). The kinds of questions and doubts I am raising are not logically different from the kinds of criticisms made in the last two decades about the many reports of biochemical differences between psychotic patients and normals.

For certain purposes, the problem is not serious; it is useful to know that reaction time speeds up with clinical improvement (King, 1969), and such objective measures may prove valuable as additional indicators of the state of the patient. However, when we wish to use our measures to infer that the nervous system of patients is somehow different from that of normals, that is, *when we wish to use our psychological data to develop inferences about an organic, as opposed to a functional, basis of some mental illness,* we must know whether flicker fusion thresholds are in fact poorer, or that reaction times are in fact slower, and so on. For this purpose we need to know the source of the poorer performance and should not interpret as a sensory defect what is, in fact, a secondary by-product of the overall motivational state of the patient. Similarly, it would be incorrect to interpret as a sensory defect behavior that arises from the patient's preoccupation with his hallucinations.

The issues raised here may have implications beyond the problem of controlling for artifact. In fact, it may be that for the illness under study poor performance on all tasks implicates in some fundamental way a general state variable such as increased or decreased arousal level, increased neural noise, or reduced neural inhibitory control. There are a large number of such hypotheses which, if found to be true, could account for a generalized decrement of performance and increase in intraindividual variability. The problem, however, is how to design experiments so as to support one of these hypotheses as opposed to the others, as well as to rule out trivial explanations of the findings.

Still another issue requires clarification. As scientists are materialists, in one sense every performance reflects the state of the nervous system. However, what is meant here by central nervous system differences or organic etiology requires explanation. The issue is best illustrated with a physiological measure. If a particular group of patients shows a lower percentage of alpha in their electroencephalograms (EEGs)—if the record is dominated by low-voltage fast activity—it may mean one of several things. If this is a manic group in a high state of excitement, the predominance of low-voltage fact activity may simply be reflecting this state, since low-voltage fast EEG activity is known to be correlated with focused attention and mental activity. If this is what the finding means, I would argue that it does not add significantly to our knowledge about physiological etiology in mental illness. On the other hand, if we could show that the low-voltage fast activity were primary—arising perhaps from an excess or deficiency of some brain metabolite—then we would have the kind of information that would be relevant to establishing a physiological dysfunction as an etiological agent in the illness. The heightened psychological activity might then be a reflection, rather than the cause, of the kind of EEG we are recording. Of course, in this hypothetical example, further steps would be necessary to establish the source of the deviant metabolite. If it were a result of deviant psychological processes, we would be back in the same bind.

The key to the search for a physiological source or etiological agent for mental illness is temporal sequence. One might think of general paresis as a model. Although many of the symptoms of the illness may be dependent on psychological and cultural conditions, the disease does not develop without prior invasion of the brain by the spirochete. In this example, if some individuals were infected and did not develop general paresis, the spirochete would not be eliminated as an etiological agent; it would then be a necessary but not sufficient condition, and such a finding would necessitate the specification of other required conditions. However, the inverse would be more damaging to the hypothesis. If one could ever get general paresis without the presence of the spirochete, this would weaken the hypothesis that the spirochete is the key etiological agent. In this case, the spirochete might be a sufficient but not a necessary cause.

The problem is very similar to the ones involved in the evaluation of the effects of drugs. To the extent that we wish to use objective psychological measures to evaluate the impact of a drug on the nervous system, it serves no purpose to interpret the poorer flicker fusion thresholds or slower reaction times found under the drug condition as a primary alteration of the sensory, perceptual, or motor systems, if, in fact, they are the result of sleepiness or mood alteration. Thus any solutions that are worked out for more valid comparisons between patients and normals in regard to basic psychological functions should have implications and perhaps direct application to the evaluation of the effects of drugs.

Unfortunately the present status of our knowledge with respect to comparisons of patients and normals on objective measures can be summarized by saying that it is sadly deficient with respect to these problems. It is certainly true that when chronic schizophrenics are tested they give slower reaction times than normals do, but at present we are unable to interpret the meaning of such a finding. It is unfortunate that the majority of studies reporting differences in performance between patients and normals cannot be given precise and specific interpretation. The purpose of this chapter is to examine what strategies may be adopted which would begin to meet the test of the criticisms that I have indicated thus far. I intend, not to undertake a critical review of available findings, but rather to try to summarize the available strategies in psychological research for obtaining findings that could constitute the early steps in the search for a physiological etiology in mental illness.

OBJECTIVITY VERSUS VALIDITY

One direction of solution must be dismissed at the outset. Objectivity in the classical Watsonian sense, for example, the use of reaction time as opposed to a verbal response, does not get us much nearer to our goal. The problem I have posed is one of validity—what is it that is being measured? What do obtained differences mean? If our problem in interpreting findings with patients is due to motivational or attentional variables, then reaction time is at least as susceptible to influence by these variables as any verbal response—perhaps more so. A similar caveat must be entered with respect to physiological measures such as the EEG, the galvanic skin response, the electromyogram, and the heart rate. All of these measurements are strongly influenced by the psychological state of the subject. In a recent critique of human evoked potential research (Sutton, 1969), I have been led by the findings to assert that the most significant source of variability in evoked potential data arises from failure to exert adequate experimental control over the psychological state of the subject, to which, the evidence shows, the evoked potential is enormously sensitive.

Actually, in threshold situations, verbal or choice responses are often much better than a measure such as reaction time. The former at least permit accuracy indicators, as one can not only ask a subject whether a light is flickering but also inquire which of several lights is flickering. When the question is in the yes-no form, one must accept the subject's response on faith. Of course, reliability and variability measures can be used to add some conviction to the obtained value, but one is in a much better position with the addition of an accuracy indicator. This makes it possible to correct for responses such as a statement that the subject perceives flicker, but identifies the wrong stimulus as flickering. As Dember has phrased it, it is the difference between asking a child whether he knows how much two and two is, and asking him for the answer.

As will be developed later, it is not my intent to dismiss objective measures such as reaction time or physiological measures. Rather I will attempt to specify what strategies are necessary to make such responses yield valid data for our purposes.

DETECTION AND FORCED-CHOICE TECHNIQUES IN THRESHOLD WORK

Detection theory has formalized the distinction between sensory and criterion measures (Swets, 1964). In traditional psychophysics, except for the use of catch trials, the experimenter is at the mercy of the subject's degree of caution in making a psychophysical judgment. In the method of limits, if the subject feels that he must be quite sure before he is willing to say that he detects the stimulus, thresholds will be quite high. On the other hand, if he is willing to take risks, thresholds will be lower. One would like to obtain an estimate of the subject's threshold performance that is independent of such criterion factors. This would obviously be of service in research on psychopathology, where anxiety and rigidity are among the attitudinal sources of artifact that we would like to overcome. Detection theorists have worked out the rationale and calculations that permit the obtaining of a separate measure for the sensory factor (d') and for the criterion factor (β). They have shown that under certain conditions d' can be constant despite experimental manipulation of β (the degree of cautiousness of the subject).

In the detection theory yes-no procedure, the stimulus in each trial is either present or absent, and the subject must say whether it is present or absent. The temporal forced-choice procedure may be even more useful for work in psychopathology. Here every trial consists of three (or more) observation intervals, and the stimulus is present in only one of them. Whether the stimulus is in the first, second, or third interval is random. The subject's task is to identify at the end of each trial whether the stimulus occurred in the first, second, or third interval of the trial. While the detection procedure can give a measure of the sensory factor that is independent of the subject's criterion, the temporal forced-choice procedure does not permit varying degrees of caution. This arises from the fact that the subject must in effect say "present" once for every trial, and there is nothing about the first, second, or third interval that makes choosing it a more or less cautious response. (Of course, if the subject shows a consistent preference for one of the intervals, the argument is weakened. But such position biases can be easily tested for.)

There is another sense in which the role of criterion is minimized in the forced-choice technique. In the detection method, the subject must maintain some memory of the stimulus across the testing session; when the perception matches this memory he can say "present," and when it does not he can say "absent." In the temporal forced-choice technique, each trial is independent in this sense, since the subject is simply identifying which of the intervals is most different. He knows that the positive stimulus occurs in only one interval of every trial and that any perceptual difference may be used to identify the correct interval. Consequently, he is always making a comparison. Nothing in the structure of the task requires him to exercise some criterion in order to decide how much of a difference is necessary before he can say "present." Finally, the temporal forced-choice technique shares with the detection technique the presence of an accuracy indicator. This permits the experimenter to detect and to correct for chance or bizarre performance.

One of the first applications of the power of the forced-choice technique to research in psychopathology was made by Clark, Brown, and Rutschmann (1967). Using a method of limits, they were able to replicate the often-reported finding of poorer flicker fusion thresholds in schizophrenic patients. However, when the forced-choice technique was used on the same subjects, these differences evaporated—schizophrenic patients performed as well as normals. This strongly suggests that the findings of poorer flicker fusion on the part of schizophrenic patients with the method of limits is due to their conservative bias, that is, their desire for greater certainty. It is such results that bring into serious question so many of the reported differences between schizophrenics and normals.

MULTIPLE VALUES OF A VARIABLE

An approach that has generality for a wider range of studies than those involving thresholds is to compare patients and normals at several values on some variable rather than at some arbitrary isolated point. This approach, which is becoming more widely used, is very desirable because it provides additional information and reduces the likelihood of misinterpreting the findings. Thus differences between patients and normal persons on a two-choice reaction time procedure may lead to interpretations that the patients' slower reaction time is due to the choice, to deficient information processing, or to difficulty in discrimination. However, Venables (1958) used a range of conditions from no choice (simple reaction time) to eight choices. He found that the curve for the schizophrenic patients exactly parallels that for the normals; it is simply displaced by a constant. The interpretation, therefore, is that an information-processing deficit is not supported by these data; rather, the deficit, whatever its source, is constant at all information levels.

The measuring of more than one point or of a complete function permits one to detect differences between groups in the slope of some part of the curve. This would be an interesting finding, but the interpretation is not straightforward. For example, reduced motivation or attention might hamper the difficult portion of the task disproportionately more than the easy portion. The result would be a difference in slope whose meaning is trivial.

Optimally, it is desirable to construct experiments so that the aspects which are to be compared are not salient or even evident to the subject. Otherwise positive findings may arise from differential attitudes between patients and normals toward some part of the task. Consequently, when we studied the effect of shift of sensory modality on reaction time in consecutive trials, the stimuli were presented at random and the subject made the identical finger-lift response to both light and sound stimuli. There was nothing in the task or the instructions to alert the subject that our interest was in reaction time as a function of sequence or in modality shift.

One aspect of the problem of comparing patients and normals which is highlighted in reaction time research is what may be called the level problem. Since Kraepelin we have known that reaction time is slower in schizophrenic patients than in normals. When we use reaction time to test some new hypothesis and obtain positive results, can we therefore assume that the new hypothesis has actually been supported? Or are the positive findings trivial in that they arise secondarily out of the fact of slower reaction time in the patients?

Another aspect of the level problem is known under the law of initial value (Lacey, 1956). This has been of particular concern in physiological measures. If one group's initial level is closer to the ceiling of the range for that variable, then the application of a treatment or experimental variable that moves the response toward the ceiling may result in smaller effects for the group that is closer to the ceiling to begin with. For example, is the smaller contraction of the pupil of a schizophrenic in response to light (Lidsky, Hakerem, & Sutton, 1971) due to the fact that the pupils of these patients are more contracted to begin with?

There are several approaches to the solution of the level problem. In our modality shift research, schizophrenics respond more slowly than normals both when the sequence is in the same sensory modality and when the sequence involves a shift in sensory modality (Kriegel, Sutton, & Kerr, in press). Our first impulse is to use difference scores—by subtracting ipsimodal reaction time from crossmodal reaction time, we can see whether the residual is greater for the schizophrenics. However, many statistical arguments have been marshalled against such difference scores. We have generally used covariance analysis, which can be viewed as a method of statistically equating the groups on the initial variable (ipsimodal reaction time) in order to assess whether the increment in the experimental variable (crossmodal reaction time) significantly discriminates between groups.

Fleiss and Tanur (Chapter 28) of our Biometrics Unit have made a systematic critique of the use of covariance analysis in these situations. Among their arguments is that the covariance technique involves extrapolation to values that are typically beyond the ranges of either group. Such extrapolations would require that linearity hold over values not observed in the actual samples. Instead of covariance analysis, they propose that several groups (including schizophrenics and normals) be tested. The relationship between ipsimodal reaction time and crossmodal reaction time can be plotted for all groups. The schizophrenic point on the curve can then be tested to see whether it deviates significantly from the general trend.

An excellent, but rarely feasible, alternative approach to the level problem is to select and match subjects on the basis of the initial variable (e.g., ipsimodal reaction time), and for only these matched subjects make the comparison between groups in crossmodal reaction time. This approach has been used occasionally (Zahn, Rosenthal, & Shakow, 1961), but we have not found it very practical. The attrition in sample size is generally too severe to permit the use of this method. Additionally, such selection may introduce a bias. The fastest schizophrenics and the slowest normals may be atypical for their groups. As a complementary approach this may be very valuable, but using it by itself would be quite risky.

IMPROVING PATIENT PERFORMANCE

In contrast to the foregoing, one need not always accept the differences in level between groups. One may use the strategy of attempting to bring patient performance up to the level of normal individuals. This may be considered a negative strategy, as its main purpose is not so much to find differences between patients and normals, but rather to avoid artifactual differences. It has been shown that by manipulating the motivational situation reaction time differences between schizophrenics and normals disappear (Rosenbaum, MacKavey, & Grissel, 1957), suggesting that the source of the difference between the groups is not the motor or information processing system. Rather, the difference appears to be motivational —under ordinary conditions normals perform optimally, whereas patients do not.

This approach becomes less of a negative strategy when the experimenter then turns to the question of examining exactly what has to be altered in order to improve patient performance (e.g., positive versus negative reinforcement) or of investigating the causes of the poor motivation in the patients (e.g., the nature of the institutional experience). By indicating what variables have been effective in improving patient performance, this approach may become a powerful source of hypotheses as to the origin and treatment of the illness. It is the approach that has been favored by researchers oriented toward learning theory.

SUPERIOR PATIENT PERFORMANCE

Since the problems with which we are trying to cope are ordinarily associated with poorer performance by patients on all measures, it would add powerfully to one's degree of conviction in regard to group differences if measures could be devised in which patients perform better than normals. Such a result could hardly be a trivial by-product of poor attention or motivation in the patients. We have been working for the last several years to develop such measures, and on one of these we have now obtained sufficient data. This measure is based on the well-known Bunsen-Roscoe or Bloch's law of time-intensity reciprocity for stimuli shorter than some duration known as the critical duration. The law states that below critical duration the determinant of the response is the total energy; it does not matter how the energy is distributed in time. Thus a 4-msec pulse of light of 5 intensity units is equivalent to a 2-msec pulse of light of 10 intensity units. The product, 20, is the same for both, and both of these pulses will yield a constant response: there will be the same reaction time, or they cannot be discriminated from each other, and so on. If, however, either pulse or both of them exceed critical duration, then this equivalence of response for equal-energy stimuli breaks down.

Several years ago, I proposed the possibility that schizophrenic patients would have shorter critical durations than normals. We tested and found that at fairly dim intensity levels normals gave the same reaction time to a 4- and a 2-msec light pulse which were equal in energy, whereas our schizophrenic patients gave a slightly longer reaction time to the 4-msec than to the 2-msec pulse. This would be consistent with an interpretation that the patients had a critical duration shorter than 4 msec and therefore were not completely utilizing the full 4 msec of the light stimulus in generating the speed of the reaction time response.

The group differences were quite small, however, and we were not completely satisfied with the precision and reliability of our control over the intensity of the light flashes. Therefore we temporarily abandoned this venture and awaited the completion of several years of systematic work with normals on time-intensity reciprocity by Mitchell Kietzman of our laboratory. Last year we felt ready to resume the patient work, and Patrick Collins did so, using the design shown in Figure 1. The square waves at the bottom of the figure show the stimuli. We used a 2-msec light pulse at an intensity about one log unit above detection threshold. The second

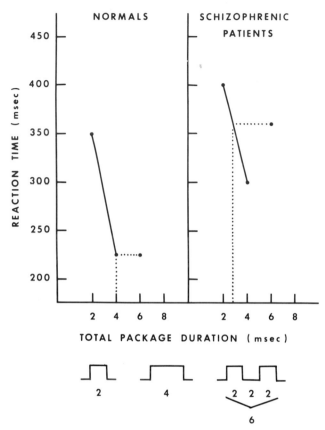

Figure 1. Hypothetical relationship between reaction time and duration of light pulse package for schizophrenics and normals. The 2- and 4-msec packages are single pulse, while the 6-msec package is double pulse. The dotted line shows the projected duration of a single pulse that would yield the same reaction time as the 6-msec double-pulse package. The projection assumes full integration of the 6-msec package for the normals and less than full integration for the schizophrenics.

pulse is at the same intensity but has a duration of 4 msec. It might be useful to think of this as two 2-msec pulses with a zero interval. The third stimulus is two 2-msec pulses of light separated by a 2-msec interval of darkness. These three stimuli are presented in random order, and the subject is instructed to lift his finger as rapidly as possible at the occurrence of each stimulus. (Though there are three stimuli, it is not a choice re-action.) On the left is a hypothetical curve for normals, based on our knowledge that at this intensity the critical duration for a reaction time response is about 10 msec. The reaction time response is more rapid to the 4-msec pulse than to the 2-msec pulse since it contains more energy. However, the 2 on—2 off—2 on stimulus, which has the same energy as the 4-msec pulse, yields the same reaction time; they contain the same energy.

In passing, I should note that in psychophysical studies with normals using verbal reports these equal-energy stimuli cannot be discriminated from each other. The right side of Figure 1 shows the predicted performance for schizophrenic patients if they have critical durations shorter than 6 msec. First, as is well known, reaction time is slower for the schizophrenic patients. However, note that, since we predict that the critical duration is less than 6 msec for the patients, the reaction time is slower to the 2–2–2 package than to the 4-msec package. This would arise from the fact that not all the energy of the second pulse of the 2–2–2 package is integrated, and therefore the patient is reacting as if this package contained less energy than the 4-msec package. This is shown by projecting the 2–2–2 reaction time onto the time axis to obtain an estimate of the duration of a single pulse whose energy is equal to the amount of energy of the 2–2–2 package that has been utilized.

Note that in the predicted result for the patient we have, despite his slower reaction time, better discrimination. With his *motor* response, he would be making a discrimination that the normal person cannot make, either with reaction time or as a psychophysical discrimination. We suspect (and we are now in the process of checking this) that the patient also cannot discriminate these stimuli psychophysically.

One other issue should be clarified. The reaction time of the patient is slower than that of the normal. Furthermore, the patient reacts more slowly to the 2–2–2 than to the 4-msec package. How could one call such a finding better performance? The answer is that we know of no way, either by instruction or by any experimental manipulation, to get the normal to produce different reaction times to the two packages. In fact, we know of no response that the normal can use to distinguish these packages.

The other nice feature of this design is that it requires a positive difference for the schizophrenic patient and no difference in the normal. The implication of this requirement, under the conditions of this experiment where (1) the response is the same for all stimuli—finger lift, (2) the stimuli are presented in random sequence, and (3) the differences between stimuli are probably not available to awareness, is that poorly motivated performance would tend to lead to greater variability and to reduction of the likelihood of obtaining significant differences between the 4-msec package and the 2–2–2 package. In other words, a patient's not performing the task optimally would make him appear more like a normal—not responding differentially to the stimuli. This feature, therefore, would increase our confidence in the validity of positive findings.

The actual findings (Collins, 1972) were in accord with the predictions. All of the 10 normals tested give essentially equal reaction times to the two equal-energy packages. Of the 10 schizophrenics tested, 7 were significantly outside the limits of normal variability for equal reaction time for the two equal-energy packages. They gave longer reaction time to the 2–2–2 than to the 4-msec package—the finding that would be predicted by the hypothesis of shorter critical duration. By contrast, none of a third group, who consisted of hospitalized nonschizophrenic patients, gave significantly longer reaction times to the 2–2–2 package.

It should be noted that all of the patients were under phenothiazine treatment, thus suggesting that the finding in the schizophrenic group is not a drug effect. We are currently looking at which phenothiazine was administered, as well as the various dosages used. Several other controls with respect to drugs are also in process.

THE ITERATIVE METHOD

The iterative method is not new in science or new to research in psychopathology. The purpose of giving it a name and developing it explicitly is to enter a plea for a more extensive use of iterative approaches. The problem to which we are addressing the iterative method arises from the diagnostic imprecision and the overlap among diagnoses that now exists in psychopathology. The investigator attempting to use precise and objective research measures must deal with the problem of specifying the diagnostic group in which he expects his measures to detect differences. If a measure results in average differences between schizophrenics and normals, but there is a high degree of overlap between the groups—is this so because the measure is not very good, or because, even with the most careful diagnosis, schizophrenia consists of several diagnostic entities and normality conceals many undetected pathologies? Furthermore, the researcher may often ask himself whether his measures may be of use for improving diagnostic precision. These questions can be approached via the iterative method. In essence the method involves successive alternating in the specification of which is the dependent and which is the independent variable.

In our study of critical duration 3 of the 10 schizophrenic patients did not show a significant difference between the equal-energy packages. We first examined whether the reason was that these 3 patients had more variable reaction times, that is, were they the patients who performed least optimally? As it turned out, this was not so. Alternatively, were these, perhaps, the patients who were less ill, or, more importantly, was it possible that these patients constituted a different subgroup of schizophrenics? In this study all the subjects had been given a structured interview (the Current and Past Psychopathology Scale—CAPPS—developed in our Biometrics Unit) which produces ratings on 30 symptom scales (Spitzer & Endicott, 1969). We compared the two groups of schizophrenic patients, the 7 with significant differences on the equal-energy stimuli and the 3 who did not show significant differences. On 28 of the 30 scales the ratings of the two groups were essentially the same, varying only at random. However, on a scale entitled Speech Disorganization, patients who had a high rating were the ones who showed significant differences on the equal-energy packages, while those who had a low rating did not show significant differences. The other scale, Auditory Hallucinations, showed a similar but somewhat weaker difference between the two schizophrenic groups. Now 2 out of 30 comparisons may turn up by chance, but here is the strength of the iterative method. We can now undertake a new study in which subjects are selected in terms of their ratings on these scales and see whether the critical duration differences hold up. Our hypothesis now is that only those who have high ratings on these symptoms will show the reduced critical duration.

It should be noted that the Speech Disorganization scale of the CAPPS is probably misnamed. Our probing of the rating criteria used suggests that the scale taps what is normally called thought disorder or the degree to which sequential utterances are relevant to each other or appear to flow logically.

If the first iterative step is successful, other iterative steps can be followed. What I mean by the first iterative step is that, having found (without a prior prediction based in theory) that only the schizophrenic patients with shorter critical duration were rated as high on thought disorder, we would then select a sample based on the best measures of thought disorder currently available, and test for critical duration in this sample as compared with other subjects. If our results are replicated, we can subsequently use critical duration as an independent criterion for cases of thought disorder and begin to refine the initial measures of thought disorder in order to form a clearer diagnostic cluster with respect to which we may then begin to discover other physiological and psychological characteristics. For example, are the patients with shorter critical duration and thought disorder also those who show familial incidence of psychopathology; do they show differences on physiological and biochemical measures; do they respond differently to drugs; will their time-intensity reciprocity in other sensory modalities also be different; what other psychological measures characterize this group? By proceeding along such paths, it may become possible for the objective investigator to contribute to the problem of diagnosis in psychiatry as well as to move in the direction of developing good etiological hypotheses.

We have not yet taken the first iterative step in our critical duration study. Our first venture using the iterative procedure was carried out in the context of our studies of the ease or difficulty of shifting sensory modality in sequential reaction time trials (Kriegel et al., in press). In that study, Kriegel began with patients specified as schizophrenic by hospital diagnosis and with normals obtained from the usual sources—hospital attendants, students, and so on. The two samples chosen in this way showed a significant difference—the schizophrenic patients were disproportionately retarded in their reaction time by shift of sensory modality. However, Kriegel et al. also used an objective structured diagnostic interview. According to the interview results, only half of the schizophrenic sample received a diagnosis of schizophrenia and only half of the normal sample received a diagnosis of normality. When the two purified groups were compared—the "interview" schizophrenics with the "interview" normals —the modality shift differences between groups were heightened. Furthermore, despite the reduction of each original sample by half, the interindividual reaction time variability in the "purified" groups was significantly reduced. In this instance, the first step in the iterative procedure added conviction both to the structured interview diagnosis and to the modality shift measure as being associated with schizophrenia.

Still other applications of an iterative approach are cited by Gurland in Chapter 22 of this book.

CONSTRUCT VALIDATION

The iterative method is a special case of the general approach of construct validation. The iterative method is most useful in the special situation where one variable is difficult to specify precisely (diagnosis) while the variable that can be defined precisely (objective measure) depends for its relevance on its association with the imprecisely defined variable. The construct validation approach, however, is more general. It involves the use of converging operations—the process of making and testing additional inferences in order to interpret a finding properly. For our critical duration experiment, the use of a two-pulse package of light may lead some to attempt to interpret our finding as having to do with temporal resolution and not with temporal integration. However, such an interpretation is in conflict with our earlier finding of longer reaction time for the schizophrenic patients to a 4-msec light flash than to a 2-msec light flash which was equal in energy (by being more intense).

The study in the same patients of temporal processing in other sensory modalities, as well as the use of physiological measures such as the evoked potential and the pupillary response, will permit still further delineation of the exact nature of the differences. Furthermore, such converging operations may permit the specification of the physiological basis of the findings.

A number of other properties of temporal integration can be used to further validate our inference. For example, beyond critical duration there is a region of partial integration in which duration is still relevant but is no longer equivalent to intensity. Finally, there is a duration usually referred to as utilization time beyond which only the intensity of the stimulus is relevant. We can therefore investigate whether partial integration and utilization time are also altered in patients who display a shorter critical duration. Furthermore, we are repeating these studies with a verbal report discrimination rather than reaction time. In normals, we know that critical duration and utilization time are longer for verbal report than for reaction time. We can thus check whether for the schizophrenic patients shorter critical duration and utilization time will be obtained for verbal report as well. All of these characteristics of temporal integration could provide additional means of testing whether schizophrenics are indeed different from normals in the way in which they process energy over time.

SUMMARY

I have tried to review the available strategies for designing experiments in psychopathology which permit meaningful and valid interpretations. I have been particularly concerned with the kinds of psychological experiments that may contribute to organic etiological formulations. Six topics have been considered:

1. The use of threshold procedures that eliminate or control criterion variables and permit an estimate of true sensory sensitivity.
2. The measurement of complete parametric functions and the initial level problem.
3. Bringing patient performance up to the level of the normals in cases where motivational and attitudinal factors are at fault.
4. Finding measures on which patients perform better than normals.
5. The iterative approach to the problem of diagnostic imprecision.
6. The role of construct validation in the interpretation of findings.

Most of these are not so much alternative as complementary approaches.

ACKNOWLEDGMENTS

I am indebted to Patrick Collins, Jean Endicott, Barry Gurland, Mitchell Grossberg, Gad Hakerem, Muriel Hammer, Mitchell Kietzman, Jewell Kriegel, Joseph Fleiss, Karen Olson, and Robert Spitzer for assistance with various aspects of this work. The research was supported under Grants MH-11688 and MH-07776 from the National Institute of Mental Health, United States Public Health Service.

REFERENCES

Clark, C., Brown, I., & Rutschmann, J. Flicker sensitivity and response bias in psychiatric patients and normal subjects. *Journal of Abnormal Psychology,* 1967, **72**, 35–42.

Collins, P. Reaction time measures of visual temporal integration in schizophrenic patients, other psychiatric patients, and normal subjects. Unpublished doctoral dissertation, Columbia University, 1972.

Kety, S. S. Biochemical theories of schizophrenia. Part I. *Science,* 1959, **129**, 1528–1532. (a)

Kety, S. S. Biochemical theories of schizophrenia. Part II. *Science,* 1959, **129**, 1590–1596. (b)

King, H. E. Psychomotility: A dimension of behavior disorder. In J. Zubin & C. Shagass (Eds.), *Neurobiological aspects of psychopathology.* New York: Grune & Stratton, 1969. Pp. 99–128.

Kriegel, J., Sutton, S., & Kerr, J. Effect of modality shift on reaction time in schizophrenia. In M. L. Kietzman, S. Sutton, & J. Zubin (Eds.), *Experimental approaches to psychopathology.* New York: Academic Press, 1972, in press.

Lacey, J. I. The evaluation of autonomic responses: Toward a general solution. *Annals of the New York Academy of Sciences,* 1956, **67**, 123–164.

Lidsky, A., Hakerem, G., & Sutton, S. Pupillary reactions to single light pulses in psychiatric patients and normals. *The Journal of Nervous and Mental Disease,* 1971, **153**, 286–291.

Raush, H. L. Perceptual constancy in schizophrenia. I. Size constancy. *Journal of Personality,* 1952, **21**, 176–187.

Rosenbaum, G., MacKavey, W. R., & Grissel, J. L. Effects of biological and social motivation on schizophrenic reaction time. *Journal of Abnormal and Social Psychology,* 1957, **54**, 364–388.

Spitzer R. L., & Endicott, J. DIAGNO II: Further developments in a computer program for psychiatric diagnosis. Supplement to the *American Journal of Psychiatry,* 1969, **125** (7), 12–21.

Sutton, S. The specification of psychological variables in an average evoked potential experiment. In E. Donchin, & D. B. Lindsley (Eds.), *Average evoked potentials—methods, results, and evaluations.* NASA SP-191, 1969. Pp. 237–262.

Swets, J. A. *Signal detection and recognition by human observers.* New York: Wiley, 1964.

Venables, P. H. Stimulus complexity as a determinant of the reaction time of schizophrenics. *Canadian Journal of Psychology,* 1958, **12,** 187–190.

Zahn, T. P., Rosenthal, D., & Shakow, D. Reaction time in schizophrenic and normal subjects in relation to the sequence of a series of regular preparatory intervals. *Journal of Abnormal and Social Psychology,* 1961, **63,** 161–168.

CHAPTER 11

Psychophysiological Indices in Psychopathological and Cross-Cultural Research

In a recent evaluation of the scope and methods of cross-cultural research Frijda and Jahoda (1966) suggested that psychophysiological techniques might be expected to make an important contribution. These techniques would appear to be specifically relevant to a number of cross-cultural issues of current interest. In addition their application might bring about closer integration between the growing body of cross-cultural research and developments in other areas of psychology.

Actually, a sprinkling of articles reporting on this kind of research has appeared during the past few years. Systematic differences in skin conductance between races have been reported by Bernstein (1965), Johnson and Landon (1965), and Malmo (1965). Investigations concerned with phasic short-term psychophysiological reactions have also been carried out (Kugelmass & Lieblich, 1968; Lazarus, Tomita, Opton, & Kodama, 1966; Tursky & Sternbach, 1967). In all of these studies the basic research paradigm involves a comparison of psychophysiological responses between two or more groups of individuals differing in racial, ethnic, or cultural backgrounds.

Psychophysiological studies utilizing such a research strategy have probably taken place most frequently in the investigation of psychopathology. Textbooks on abnormal psychology are already drawing heavily on this growing body of research which relates to the implications of psychophysiological functioning in psychosis, neurosis, psychopathy, and mental deficiency (Buss, 1966; Lynn, 1966; Maher, 1966). Given the close similarity in research paradigms, it would appear worth while for future investigators of cross-cultural psychophysiological studies to consider this body of research experience. On the other hand, a similar consideration should be of importance to those who are interested in pushing into cross-national studies of psychopathology (Zubin, 1969b).

A recent review of psychophysiological studies in psychopathology suggests that many of the original findings should be re-evaluated (Stern & McDonald, 1965). There would appear to be a high degree of inconsistency in the results of different studies of the same or very similar aspects of psychophysiological activation. More thought must be given, therefore, to the reasons for such a situation with the hope that it will be possible to guide future research in normal/abnormal comparisons more effectively as well as to avoid similar pitfalls in cross-cultural research.

INDIVIDUAL VARIATION

Close systematic examination of the autonomic response research data indicates a very large order of individual differences in almost any group studied up to the present. One of the major findings in this field has been the remarkable range of different individual patterns of autonomic responsivity when several indices are measured simultaneously, a phenomenon that has been called autonomic response stereotypy. Even within single-channel indices there appear to be different basic patterns of response reactivity (Unger, 1964). There also appears to be quite a degree of difference among individuals in the relative degree of stability or reliability of these patterns. A recent unpublished study in this laboratory using normal subjects suggests that there may be large individual differences in the stability of single autonomic indices which may not be apparent if reliability is tested through an analysis of group data. A somewhat similar observation was made by Acker (1964), who studied tranquilized mental patients. Wenger, Clemens, Coleman, Cullen, and Engel (1961) have also specifically warned about this in regard to multichannel patterns.

Given this situation of striking intra- and interindividual differences, it is readily apparent that a closer examination of the individual data within each group might be worth while. Perhaps it would be appropriate to examine the possibility of meaningful subgroupings of individuals within the sample. This would, of course, require more adequate detailed presentation of individual data. Although the Russian workers in psychophysiology have been very sensitive to the need for a fractionation of psychiatric diagnostic groups, they provide research reports that are sadly lacking in data presentation. Western research, on the other hand, has been stressing group averages. If the psychopathological or even the normal groups are really heterogeneous in psychophysiological types, it does not appear strange that small samples of the so-called same populations turn up some conflicting results.

A number of encouraging findings have indicated that psychopsysiological responses could be more systematically related to subdivisions of psychiatric diagnostic or prognostic categories (Hare, 1968; Stern, Surphlis, & Koff, 1965; Venables & Wing, 1962). In this connection Bernstein (1967) has shown that the use of carefully rated reactivity to the environment may be a significant factor in distinguishing even further within the chronic schizophrenic population.

This problem is most acute when there is a possibility that the particular sample drawn may be biased in a way that is related to autonomic functioning. Subjects may be eliminated from conditioning experiments if they do not meet certain criteria of responsivity. Only certain kinds of quiet patients may be permitted to remain off tranquilizers and thus be more likely to be selected for research, or highly excitable patients may be eliminated as unsuitable for testing.

CULTURAL VARIATION

The above would suggest that in cross-cultural testing of psychophysiological differences serious consideration should be given to carrying out the finest subgroup analysis possible within any groups tested. Contradictory findings have already appeared in that Lazarus et al. (1966) suggest *higher* skin conductance in Japanese than in Americans, whereas Malmo (1965) and Wenger in Johnson and Landon (1965) suggest that Orientals have *lower* skin conductance than Caucasians. It would seem best to avoid such broad categories as Caucasians or Orientals if possible. A specific demonstration in support of the need to go to a much finer level of group analysis may be seen in the finding of Tursky and Sternbach (1967) that American housewives of Irish ancestry showed consistently lower palmar skin resistance than white American housewives of other ethnic backgrounds. Data from this laboratory also support the need to consider ethnic and racial subgroupings within a small nation. Systematic differences in relevant GSR (galvanic skin response) reactivity were found to exist between groups of Jewish subjects of different ethnic backgrounds (Kugelmass & Lieblich, 1968). Similar results were also obtained in a sample of Israeli psychiatric clinic patients (Lerner, 1969). Examination of Israeli Bedouin tribesmen indicated even more extensive psychopyhsiological differences. A comparison of Israeli Jewish subjects with samples from two different Bedouin tribes indicated that the Israeli Bedouin tribesmen tended to have higher basic skin conductance. During contact with the Bedouin it was noted that some tribesmen appeared to be of Negro origin. Following the findings of Bernstein (1965) and of Johnson and Landon (1965), which indicate lower skin conductance in American Negro subjects, a sample of Negroid Bedouin was drawn from a third tribe (Abu Blal). The basic skin conductance of this group not only turned out to be lower than that of the other two Bedouin samples, but appeared to be even lower than the conductance of the Israeli Jewish groups previously mentioned (Kugelmass, 1969). Thus even within Israeli Negev Bedouin, whose total population is about sixteen thousand, there appear to be psychophysiologically different subgroups.

VARIATION AMONG AUTONOMIC INDICES

Another potential source of the apparently contradictory results may lie in the use of many different indices purported to be measuring psychophysiological activation (not to mention differences in apparatus, scoring criteria, etc.). After struggling so long with attempts to relate psychophysiological changes to complex differentiated theories of "emotion," it is understandable why psychologists were inclined to opt for an attempt to work according to the conceptually more parsimonious model of activation or arousal. Evidence soon began to accumulate, however, of the very low correlations among different autonomic measures, all of which should be theoretically related to the same construct of activation. To some extent these low correlation findings among indices across subjects were countered by the more reassuring higher intraindividual correlations of these same measures. On the other hand, research findings from several areas suggests that the different measures may be reflecting somewhat different functional mechanisms: autonomic conditioning (Purohit, 1966); stress film reactions (Goldstein, Jones, Clemens, Flagg, & Alexander, 1965); experimental lie detection (Thackray & Orne, 1968); and sleep research (Johnson & Lubin, 1966).

Lacey (1967) recently marshalled a large amount of this evidence and has gone on to propose a revision of activation theory that includes the specification of dissociable mechanisms specifically related to different indices. Whether or not the specific proposals stand up to thorough experimental testing (see Germana & Klein, 1968), this new approach probably marks a trend toward more careful analysis of different aspects of autonomic activation. Not only has it become apparent that there may be dissociable components of autonomic activation which differ functionally from physiological subsystem to subsystem (e.g., cardiovasular system vs.

sweat glands), but this also seems possible within a subsystem (Edelberg & Wright, 1964; Martin & Venables, 1966). A remarkable amount of dissociation among different indices of electrodermal activity previously thought to be closely related to arousal and activation has been demonstrated in sleep studies by Johnson and Lubin (1966).

IMPLICATIONS

All of the foregoing would suggest that one must carefully consider the theoretical meaning and, in particular, the generality of any psychophysiological difference appearing in psychopathological or cross-cultural comparisons. Aside from the usual need for replication, it seems important to check such a finding against related indices of activation. Just this was done by Hare (1968) in an extensive survey of the psychophysiological findings in research of psychopaths. He then concluded that "these studies suggest that whatever evidence exists for differences in resting level of autonomic functioning appears to be confined to some aspect of electrodermal activity [p. 3]." This will properly restrict any theoretical formulation of autonomic functioning in the psychopath.

An even more complex situation may occur in which different indices of activation appear to be negatively related in a group comparison. Research in this laboratory uncovered such a pattern of cross-cultural differences in basic activation measures. Different samples of Israeli Bedouin tribesmen (El Houzarel tribe; Abu Rhabiah tribe) tend to have both a *higher* level of skin conductance and a *lower* mean pulse rate than the Israeli Jewish subjects tested. From a descriptive point of view it is possible to view this as a consistent pattern of group differences in autonomic functioning which could be termed ethnic-group response stereotypy in analogy to a description of individual differences in pattern of responses. A more fundamental contribution, of course, would be an explanation of the apparent differentiation in the two indices of autonomic arousal. It is possible that these findings might be "explained" by correction for individual differences in the range of activation within each index (Hare, 1968; Lykken, Rose, Luther, & Maley, 1966). Another reason for evaluating any psychophysiological finding in regard to other channels of activation is the possible interaction of different functional systems. It has been shown, for example, that changes in pulse rate measures may be secondary to changes in rate of respiration (Wood & Obrist, 1965).

From a theoretical point of view further consideration is needed to the relation of different activation response indices within a given autonomic channel. This is particularly important in regard to proposed psychopathological or cross-cultural differences in conditioning. The conceptualization of autonomic conditioning includes a hierarchy of more basic processes. These range from multiple-response indexed processes such as sensitization and habituation to single-trial measured processes termed initial reactivity. Studies dealing with the basic issue of autonomic conditioning have been forced to utilize an increasingly sophisticated methodology in order to analyze the separate roles of these subprocesses. After a recent extensive review of the literature, Thompson (1967) was forced to conclude that "it would seem that conditioned alpha blocking resembles sensitization more closely than it resembles conditioning [p. 518]." Only very recently has there been reassurance that GSR conditioning as such, above and beyond sensitization, could be demonstrated (Gale & Stern, 1967; McDonald & Johnson, 1965). More specifically related to this issue in group comparisons is a factor analytic study of GSR conditioning carried out by Prescott (1966), which presents "further evidence that reactivity and not learning has been the subject of measurement in aversive autonomic conditioning studies, and that behavioral theories based upon such studies have questionable support [p. 10]."

In line with Prescott's warning, Mednick and Schulsinger (1968) have reported findings that encourage serious reconsideration of Mednick's influential learning model of the development of schizophrenia. After comparing a schizophrenia-prone group to a control group, they suggest that there was probably no real difference in GSR conditionability between the groups, and that the observed difference was more likely to be due to the greater overall responsiveness and the relative failure of habituation in a high-risk group.

Any theoretical exploitation of a cross-cultural or psychopathological group difference in psychophysiology will thus have to consider the testing paradigm used. Before the difference is ascribed to a higher-order construct, that is, conditioning, the basic principle of parsimony requires examination of the possibility that such a difference is a reflection of a lower-order construct such as sensitization or even more basically is due to an initial difference in reactivity. Closer examination of the testing paradigms may be useful even when no differences in the higher-order function are found. In a recent study of differential GSR conditioning as a function of age no significant differences in conditioning were found among three groups (Morrow, Boring, Keough, & Haesly, 1969). Nevertheless, these groups "differed significantly from each other in the manner that differential conditioning was achieved [p. 299]."

In this laboratory we have been studying psychophysiological functioning in different ethnic groups, using a paradigm derived from experimental lie detection. The GSR reactions to a series of stimuli are recorded. Through the operations of the paradigm one of the stimuli has been given distinctive relevance ("hot" card) in contrast to the other stimuli. In studies of several different samples of Israeli Jewish subjects it was found that those of Near Eastern origin had significantly lower GSR reactivity to the relevant card than those of Western origin. On the other hand, these two Jewish subgroups did not differ significantly in their GSR reactions to the other card stimuli. The results thus suggest an ethnic difference in differential GSR reactivity. Subsequent similar testing of Bedouin tribesmen produced the predicted results of very low GSR reactivity to the relevant stimulus. In the case of the Bedouin, however, reservation in regard to a difference in differential GSR reactivity is needed, since the GSR responses to all stimuli tended to be lower, even if less distinctly so, than the response to the relevant stimulus. In this case it would be more cautious to first consider the possibility of an ethnic difference in general GSR reactivity. A finer analysis of additional relevant data would be necessary to clarify whether an ethnic difference in differential GSR reactivity above and beyond the general GSR reactivity difference actually exists.

The present discussion has attempted to focus on a number of issues relevant to the use of psychophysiological response indices in both cross-cultural and normal/pathological group comparisons. In attempting to mount a systematic biometric attack on psychopathology, Zubin (1969a) constructed a Mendelejeff-like table of different classes of responses elicited under different stimulus conditions. He then formulated six different models to be considered in an investigation of the etiology of mental disorders. In order to test hypotheses derived from these models it was proposed that appropriate techniques be drawn from certain of the categories specified in the table mentioned above. One set of hypothesized deviant behaviors related to a group of the models (genetic, internal environment, and brain-function) would seem to require the development of culture-free techniques. One likely source of such techniques would be the psychophysiological indices presently under consideration.

Zubin's attempt to develop culture-free measures of patient's behavior has concentrated on "the responses of patients to controlled stimulation during the first 1000 milliseconds following stimulation, under the assumption that the response follows so quickly after the stimulus that culture cannot directly modulate it [1969a, p. 302]." He has noted that this is obviously arbitrary, and is hopeful that a sophisticated methodology such as was developed to cope with the problems of psychophysical research will be able to handle culture-free measurement. Some research findings, including psychophysiological indices, are already being considered within this approach.

Some of the data already reviewed suggest that one needs to be very cautious in assuming that psychophysiological measures are culture free.

Indeed, much of the preceding discussion underlines the dangers of premature generalization in connection with these indices. One of the specific base-line indices mentioned in the Mendelejeff-like table which has been of strong interest in normal/pathological comparisons is basal skin conductance (Zubin, 1969a). Several different studies have already indicated systematic national, ethnic, or racial differences in level of skin conductance. To be sure, a final evaluation of the possible cultural as well as biological (including genetic) factors underlying these differences remains to be undertaken. It is certainly not permissible, under these circumstances, to consider basal skin conductance as a culture-free measure. There is also some suggestion that the phasic GSR index may be directly subject to cultural influences beyond the influence of the base-line level of skin conductance.

On the other hand, it would not be prudent to conclude that cultural influences are necessarily significant in connection with all psychophysiological indices. Quite probably certain indices are relatively more culture-free than others. In view of the growing awareness of dissociation among the different indices of activation it is clear that we require further systematic research on this issue.

From a theoretical point of view, it may be possible to predict that certain response indices would be more subject to cultural influences than others. This may be true even within a single physiological subsystem, where one response component appears to be related to the physical properties of the stimulus and another may be more closely tied to the broader "meaning" of the stimulus. It would appear that cultural influences would be more likely to influence the second component. Two specific examples may be suggested. The dilation component of the pupillary response appears to relate to a broad range of psychological variables (Kahneman & Beatty, 1966; Kugelmass, Hakerem, & Mantgiaris, 1969), but the mechanism underlying the constriction component may be entirely limited to the physical properties of light (Young, 1965). Much recent interest has focused on the possibility of two components in the evoked cortical potential, where there appears to be an early negative component that responds primarily to the physical aspect of the stimulus and a later positive component that reflects a higher congitive function (Sutton, Tueting, Zubin, & John, 1967).

SUMMARY

More fruitful application of psychophysiological indices to psychopathology and cross-cultural research would seem to require additional consideration of a number of basic methodological issues. It was suggested that further attention be directed toward (1) a more refined analysis of the groups under comparison, which may include psychophysiologically different subgroups; (2) a more critical approach to activation theory, which must cope with increasing evidence of dissociation among different indices of autonomic activation; and (3) a more sophisticated consideration of the particular testing paradigm utilized to provide for theoretical parsimony. Some consideration was given to the use of psychophysiological indices as culture-free measures.

ACKNOWLEDGMENTS

The research reported in this paper has been sponsored by the Air Force Office of Scientific Research, through the European Office, Aerospace Research, United States Air Force, under Contract AF 61(052)–839.

REFERENCES

Acker, C. W. An investigation of the variability in repeated psychophysiological measurements in tranquilized mental patients. *Psychophysiology,* 1964, **1,** 119–126.

Bernstein, A. S. Race and examiner as significant influences on basal skin impedance. *Journal of Personality and Social Psychology,* 1965, **1,** 346–349.

Bernstein, A. S. Electrodermal base level, tonic arousal, and adaptation in "chronic schizophrenics." *Journal of Abnormal Psychology,* 1967, **72,** 221–232.

Buss, A. H. *Psychopathology.* New York: Wiley, 1966.

Edelberg, R., & Wright, D. J. Two galvanic skin response affector organs and their stimulus specificity. *Psychophysiology,* 1964, **1,** 39–47.

Frijda, N., & Jahoda, G. On the scope and methods of cross-cultural research. *International Journal of Psychology,* 1966, **1,** 110–127.

Gale, E. N., & Stern, J. A. Conditioning of the electrodermal orienting response. *Psychophysiology,* 1967, **3,** 291–301.

Germana, J., & Klein, S. B. The cardiac component of the orienting response. *Psychophysiology,* 1968, **4,** 324–328.

Goldstein, M. J., Jones, R. B., Clemens, T. L., Flagg, G. W., & Alexander, F. G. Coping style as a factor in psychophysiological responses to a tension arousing film. *Journal of Personality and Social Psychology,* 1965, **1,** 290–302.

Hare, R. D. Psychopathy, autonomic functioning, and the orienting response. *Journal of Abnormal Psychology,* 1968, **73** (Monogr. Suppl. No. 3), Part 2, 1–24.

Johnson, L. C., & Landon, M. M. Eccrine sweat gland activity and racial differences in resting skin conductance. *Psychophysiology,* 1965, **1,** 322–329.

Johnson, L. C., & Lubin, A. Spontaneous and orienting response during sleep *Psychophysiology,* 1966, **3,** 8–17.

Kahneman, D., & Beatty, J. Pupil diameter and load on memory. *Science,* 1966, **154,** 1583–1585.

Kugelmass, S. Scientific Report, Contract AF 61(052)–839, Nov. 1, 1969.

Kugelmass, S., Hakerem, G., & Mantgiaris, L. A paradoxical conditioning effect in the human pupil. *Journal of General Psychology,* 1969, **80,** 115–127.

Kugelmass, S., & Lieblich, I. Relation between ethnic origin and GSR reactivity in psychophysiological detection. *Journal of Applied Psychology,* 1968, **52,** 158–162.

Lacey, J. I. Somatic response patterning and stress: Some revisions of activation theory. In M. H. Appley & R. Trumbull (Eds.), *Psychological stress.* New York: Appleton-Century-Crofts, 1967. Pp. 14–37.

Lazarus, R. S., Tomita M., Opton, E., & Kodama, M. A cross-cultural study of stress-reaction patterns in Japan. *Journal of Personality and Social Psychology,* 1966, **4,** 622–633.

Lerner, J. Department of Psychiatry, Hadassah University Hospital, Jerusalem, Israel. Personal communication, 1969.

Lykken, D. T., Rose, R., Luther, B., & Maley, M. Correcting psychophysiological measures for individual differences in range. *Psychological Bulletin,* 1966, **66,** 481–484.

Lynn, R. *Attention, arousal and the orientation reaction.* London: Pergamon Press, 1966.

McDonald, D. G., & Johnson, L. C. A re-analysis of GSR conditioning. *Psychophysiology,* 1965, **1,** 291–295.

Maher, B. A. *Principles of psychopathology.* New York: McGraw-Hill, 1966.

Malmo, R. B. Finger-sweat prints in the differentiation of low and high incentive. *Psychophysiology,* 1965, **1,** 231–240.

Martin, I., & Venables, P. H. Mechanisms of palmar skin resistance and skin potential. *Psychological Bulletin,* 1966, **65,** 347–357.

Mednick, S. A., & Schulsinger, F. Some premorbid characteristics related to breakdown in children with schizophrenic mothers. In D. Rosenthal & S. S. Kety (Eds.), *The transmission of schizophrenia.* Oxford: Pergamon Press, 1968. Pp. 267–292.

Morrow, M. C., Boring, F. W., Keough, T. E., III, & Haesly, R. R. Differential GSR conditioning as a function of age. *Developmental Psychology,* 1969, **1,** 299–302.

Prescott, J. W. Critical issues in conditioning theory and research. Paper presented at the IV World Congress of Psychiatry, Madrid, 1966.

Purohit, A. P. Personality variables, sex difference, GSR responsiveness, and GSR conditioning. *Journal of Experimental Research in Personality,* 1966, **1,** 166–173.

Stern, J. A., & McDonald, D. G. Physiological correlates of mental disease. *Annual Review of Psychology*, 1965, **16**, 225–264.

Stern, J. A., Surphlis, W., & Koff, E. Electrodermal responsiveness as related to psychiatric diagnosis and prognosis. *Psychophysiology*, 1965, **2**, 51–61.

Sutton S., Tueting, P., Zubin, J., & John, E. R. Information delivery and the sensory evoked potential. *Science*, 1967, **155**, 1436–1439.

Thackray, R. I., & Orne, M. T. A comparison of physiological indices in detection of deception. *Psychophysiology*, 1968, **4**, 329–339.

Thompson, R. F. *Foundations of physiological psychology*. New York: Harper & Row, 1967.

Tursky, B., & Sternbach, R. A. Further physiological correlates of ethnic differences in responses to shock. *Psychophysiology*, 1967, **4**, 67–73.

Unger, S. M. Habituation of the vasoconstrictive orienting reaction. *Journal of Experimental Psychology*, 1964, **67**, 11–18.

Venables, P. H., & Wing, J. K. Level of arousal and the sub-classification of schizophrenia. *Archives of General Psychiatry*, 1962, **7**, 114–119.

Wenger, M. A., Clemens, T. L., Coleman, D. R., Cullen, T. D., & Engel, B.T. Autonomic response specificity. *Psychosomatic Medicine*, 1961, **23**, 185–193.

Wood, D. M., & Obrist, P. A. Effects of controlled and uncontrolled respiration on the conditioned heart rate in humans. *Journal of Experimental Psychology*, 1965, **68**, 221–229.

Young, F. A. Classical conditioning of autonomic functions. In W. F. Prokasy (Ed.), *Classical conditioning, a symposium*. New York. Appleton-Century-Crofts, 1965. Pp. 358–377.

Zubin, J. The biometric approach to psychopathology—revisited. In J. Zubin & C. Shagass (Eds.), *Neurobiological aspects of psychopathology*. New York: Grune & Stratton, 1969. Pp. 281–309. (a)

Zubin, J. Cross-national study of diagnosis of the mental disorders: Methodology and planning. Supplement to the *American Journal of Psychiatry*, 1969, **125** (10), 12–20. (b)

CHAPTER 12

Hemispheric Cerebral Dominance and Somesthesis

ARTHUR L. BENTON

THE CONCEPT OF HEMISPHERIC CEREBRAL DOMINANCE

The historical development of the concept of hemispheric cerebral dominance has been characterized, since its inception about 100 years ago, by both increasing breadth and increasing differentiation. As everyone knows, the concept was "born" in the 1860s with the discovery by Broca of a specific association between motor aphasia and disease of the left frontal lobe. Broca's observation was quickly confirmed. Further clinical study showed that other areas of the left hemisphere played an equally crucial role in the production of aphasic disorders, and the doctrine of the dominance of the left hemisphere for language in right-handed individuals became firmly established, at least from a pragmatic standpoint.

For a number of decades the concept of left-hemisphere dominance was applied only to the language functions. Extension of the concept to cover other aspects of human mentation and behavior began in the early years of the twentieth century, with the work of Liepmann (1900, 1908) establishing "apraxia" as a distinctive category of behavioral deficit shown by patients with cerebral disease. In addition to his analysis of these higher-level psychomotor disorders, Liepmann was able to show that at least one type, so-called ideomotor apraxia, resulted from lesions of the left hemisphere, a correlation that has since been fully confirmed. In the 1920s, Gerstmann (1924, 1927, 1930), having described the peculiar deficit of "finger agnosia," related it and other disabilities (such as right-left disorientation) to disease of the parieto-occipital region of the left hemisphere. Subsequent study has shown that, although Gerstmann's localization was rather too precise, its general import was basically valid in the sense that finger agnosia and associated disabilities are associated far more frequently with disease of the left hemisphere than of the right (Benton, 1959, 1961; Heimburger, DeMyer, & Reitan, 1964; McFie & Zangwill, 1960). During the same period, there was a strong tendency on the part of such theorists as Head (1926) and Goldstein (1924) to emphasize the defects in abstract reasoning and conceptual thinking associated with aphasic disorders (and therefore, by inference, with disease of the left hemisphere).

These observations extended the concept of dominance of the left hemisphere to cover higher-level praxis, aspects of the body schema, and conceptual thinking, as well as language. At the same time, they fostered the idea that the left hemisphere was the "major" hemisphere insofar as the mediation of human conduct was concerned. Conversely, the right hemisphere was regarded as the "minor" or "subordinate" hemisphere, and indeed large regions of it were sometimes designated as "silent" areas with no obvious functional significance.

However, from the very birth of the concept in the 1860s, there were those who were skeptical of these claims for an exclusive dominance of the left hemisphere and who insisted that the right hemisphere also played a significant role in the mediation of language and other symbolic activities. Hughlings Jackson (1874), for example, placed emotive and automatic speech in the right hemisphere, and there were others who suggested that this hemisphere mediated "musical language," as reflected both in musical performance and in the recognition of melodies. Jackson (1876) was also the first to intimate that the right hemisphere had other distinctive functions, stating his belief that the parieto-occipital region of this hemisphere was particularly crucial for visual recognition and memory.

A later development of a conceptual nature was also of importance in raising the question of right-hemisphere "dominance" for certain functions. In a monograph that appeared in 1909, Rieger postulated the existence of two distinct and separately localized "apparatuses" (as he called them) in the brain, one subserving verbal-conceptual functions and the other subserving spatial-practical functions. Pursuing this idea, Reichardt (1923) surmised on the basis of clinicopathological study that the spatial "apparatus" was located primarily in the posterior right hemisphere, while the verbal "apparatus" was, of course, located in the left hemisphere. There followed a series of studies in the 1940s and early 1950s which provided strong, if not compelling, evidence that such deficits as impairment in visual space perception, constructional apraxia, so-called apraxia for dressing, and unilateral visual inattention occurred with considerably higher frequency in patients with lesions of the right hemisphere than in those with left-hemisphere disease. Thus a new dimension was added to the concept of hemispheric cerebral dominance: it was no longer concerned with a single hemisphere (i.e., the left) but rather was involved with the distinctive functions of each of the hemispheres.

Since that time, investigative work in the field of hemispheric cerebral dominance has been concerned primarily with the problem of identifying and defining the types of performance that appear to possess a differential association with the functioning of one or the other hemisphere. This work, which for the most part has dealt with linguistic, visual, and auditory performances, has generated a substantial body of knowledge about the role of each hemisphere in the processing of visual and auditory information of various types. Moreover, in recent years the attention of some investigators has turned to the question of whether hemispheric asymmetry in function is also demonstrable in the field of somesthesis. It is this question that is the specific topic of the present chapter.

THE DOCTRINE OF CONTRALATERAL INNERVATION

As is well known, the sensory examination is based on the doctrine of contralateral innervation, namely, that the sensory and motor functions of one side of the body are mediated by (or "represented in") the opposite cerebral hemisphere. This doctrine has a long and interesting history. The clinical facts that suggested it were known as early as 400 B.C., and the first explicit statement of the doctrine was made as early as A.D. 200 by Aretaeus of Cappodocia (Adams, 1856). However, for 1500 years thereafter, the theory was a controversial issue, many physicians preferring other explanations for the observation that a wound on one side of the brain leads to sensorimotor impairment on the other side of the body (cf. Giannitrapani, 1967). However, in the eighteenth century, the experimental demonstrations of Pourfour du Petit (1710) and the clinicopathologic correlations of Morgagni (1769) established the validity of the doctrine beyond any reasonable doubt. Its diagnostic value was then demonstrated by nineteenth-century clinicians, and it became the basis for the sensory examination in neurological diagnosis.

Nevertheless, despite the universal acceptance of the doctrine (which was, of course, fully warranted), exceptional cases that apparently did not follow the rule of contralateral innervation were reported from time to time. Oppenheim (1906), Foix (1922), and Goldstein (1927) described patients with lesions apparently confined to the left hemisphere who showed *bilateral* disturbances in stereognosis. Guillain, Alajouanine, and Garcin (1925) described a left-handed patient with a lesion of the right hemisphere who showed astereognosis and loss of position sense on the *right* side, in the absence of disturbances of sensitivity to touch and pin prick on that side.

Some of these early observers advanced the concept that, although simple sensory performances followed the rule of contralateral innervation, the left hemisphere played a special role in mediating higher-level performances (such as stereognosis and position sense) on *both* sides of the body. Thus, for example, Foix (1922) regarded the ipsilateral defects that he had observed in patients with left-hemisphere lesions as being disturbances of recognition which were of the same order as those seen in visual agnosia, rather than as elementary sensory deficits.

However, in the 1930s other observers (Bychowsky & Eidinow, 1934; Körner, 1938) reported studies of patients with unilateral lesions who showed bilateral disturbances of sensitivity to touch, pressure, pain, and vibration. Moreover, the majority of these patients had lesions of the right hemisphere (thus weakening the concept of a special role of the left hemisphere in the mediation of tactile performances on both sides of the body). The conclusion drawn by these observers was that tactile sensitivity on each side of the body is actually represented in both cerebral hemispheres rather than in only the contralateral hemisphere, as assumed by the traditional conception.

All these reports added up to a mere handful of cases and could scarcely be considered to offer a serious challenge to traditional concepts. However, it should be borne in mind that the apparent paucity of observations of bilateral or ipsilateral tactile deficit in patients with unilateral lesions may have been due to a methodological bias in the sensory examination. This bias consists in utilization of the procedure of comparing sensitivity on the side of the body suspected of being affected with that on the assumedly healthy side, and adopting the findings on the assumedly healthy side as the normative basis for judgments of the presence or absence of deficit on other side. Thus, in the conventional procedure, each patient serves as his own control and a clinical judgment is made without regard to the absolute level of performance on the assumedly healthy side, which may in fact deviate significantly from the group norm. It may be taken for granted that, in practice, gross deviations from normality on the assumedly healthy side would be noted by the examiner, in which case he would conclude that there were in fact bilateral disturbances in tactile sensitivity. But it is equally evident that relatively moderate deviations from normality on the assumedly healthy side might be missed or ignored, particularly in view of the rather crude assessment procedures employed in the typical sensory examination. In these circumstances, a decided difference in level of sensitivity between the two sides of the body would lead to the conclusion of ipsilateral sensory defect when in fact the patient suffered from bilateral disturbances of different degrees of severity on the two sides.

In his classic studies, Head (1920) did not describe bilateral sensory disturbances in any of the patients with unilateral lesions whom he discussed in such great detail. His judgments were made on the basis of a comparison of sensory performances on the two sides of the body. Yet, as Carmon (1969) has pointed out, examination of Head's data shows that, on occasion, thresholds for touch and pin prick which were classified as pathological when they were found on the hand contralateral to the lesion were considered to be normal when they occurred on the ipsilateral hand.

Thus these exceptional cases may not have been so exceptional after all. At the same time, these early observations failed to come to grips with a basic problem in this area, namely, to define tactile impairment explicitly in terms of a quantitative deviation from the expectations based on the performances of normal subjects.

RECENT STUDIES

So much for what may be called the prehistory of this topic. A new era was ushered in by the publication in 1960 of the comprehensive study by Semmes, Weinstein, Ghent, and Teuber of tactile performances in large samples of patients with unilateral lesions as well as in a group of control patients with peripheral nerve injuries involving the lower extremities. Utilizing objective assessment procedures, they examined war veterans with penetrating brain wounds involving either the left or the right hemisphere. The patients were given four somatosensory tests, namely, threshold for light pressure, two-point discrimination, point localization, and threshold for passive movement. The tactile tests were applied to the palm and the proprioceptive test to the middle finger of each hand. Since the two hands were tested independently, the sensitivity of each in the brain-lesioned group could be compared with that of the control group. On the basis of normative observations on the control group impairment was defined empirically as a performance level so poor that it could be expected to occur in the control group only 1% of the time.

Five specific findings in this major study are of particular interest:

1. Many patients with unilateral lesions showed somatosensory disturbance in the *ipsilateral* hand.
2. Ipsilateral defects occurred more frequently in patients with left-hemisphere lesions than in those with lesions of the right hemisphere.
3. In the patients with left-hemisphere lesions, tactile impairment of the contralateral hand appeared to be specifically associated with lesions of the left sensorimotor and posterior parietal areas, that is, it occurred more frequently with lesions of these areas than with lesions of other areas of

the left hemisphere. In contrast, no such association was found for the left hand, that is, the observed frequency of tactile impairment in the left hand was not significantly different for lesions in various parts of the right hemisphere. Moreover, this difference in hemispheric relationships held for the ipsilateral, as well as the contralateral, hand.

4. However, this differential relationship which was found for the tactile tests did not hold for the passive movement threshold. In the case of the proprioceptive test, there was a specific association between frequency of deficit and lesions in the sensorimotor area of both hemispheres.

5. On the right hand, the scores on the three tactile tests were positively and significantly intercorrelated. In contrast, the intercorrelations of the three scores on the left hand were lower and not always significant.

These results led Semmes et al. (1960; Semmes, 1968) to draw a number of conclusions.

1. Ipsilateral and bilateral somatosensory impairment can occur as a consequence of unilateral cerebral disease and is, in fact, not rare.

2. These ipsilateral and bilateral defects occur more frequently as a consequence of lesions of the left hemisphere than of the right hemisphere.

3. The representation of sensation in the left hand is more diffuse in the right hemisphere than is the corresponding representation for the right hand in the left hemisphere.

4. The patterns or combinations of tactile disturbances are different in the two hands. Specifically, dissociated impairment is more likely to be found in the left hand than in the right.

These findings of a relatively frequent occurrence of bilateral sensory deficits in patients with ostensibly unilateral lesions and their particularly high frequency in patients with left hemisphere damage were rather unexpected. It is natural to try to explain them first in a parsimonious way on the basis of some general disability such as aphasia or disturbances in attention. However, analyses of the relationship of aphasia, general mental impairment, and epileptic disorder to the sensory findings failed to disclose any significant associations between these factors and the occurrence of bilateral sensory deficit.

Since the publication of the study of Semmes et al. (1960), a number of investigations bearing directly or indirectly on its findings and conclusions have appeared. The information provided by these investigations may be considered in terms of the major conclusions of the original study. First, in regard to the question of the occurrence of bilateral or ipsilateral somatosensory defects in patients with unilateral disease, there is clear support for the generalization that such defects may be shown by patients with ostensibly unilateral disease. In this respect the relevant studies are as follows.

Vaughan and Costa (1962) found bilateral impairment of two-point discrimination in patients with both left- and right-hemisphere disease; bilateral impairment in pressure sensitivity was found only in the patients with left-hemisphere lesions.

Corkin, Milner, and Rasmussen (1964) found defects in pressure sensitivity, two-point discrimination, and point localization in patients who had undergone unilateral cortical excisions; the frequency of ipsilateral defects in point localization was particularly high.

Wyke (1966) reported that postural arm drift in the absence of vision, which is presumably determined, at least in part, by proprioceptive control, is bilaterally augmented in some patients with left-hemisphere lesions but not in those with right-hemisphere lesions.

Milner, Taylor, and Corkin (1967) found only contralateral deficit of tactile form recognition in patients with unilateral lesions.

Carmon and Benton (1969b) found bilateral impairment in the perception of the direction of punctate stimuli applied to the skin surface in patients with lesions of the right hemisphere but not in those with left-hemisphere lesions; they did not find ipsilateral deficits in the perception of the number of punctate tactile stimuli in either group of patients.

Carmon (1969) found ipsilateral impairment in two-point discrimination and in the absolute pressure threshold (but not in the differential pressure threshold) in patients with unilateral lesions.

These results are summarized in Table 1. Taken in their totality, they indicate that ipsilateral tactile and proprioceptive defects occur in patients with unilateral lesions. The specific nature of the sensory or perceptual performance appears to be a factor in the occurrence of ipsilateral deficit. Thus it is possible that two-point discrimination and point localization will prove to be the deficits most frequently observed. However, it is curious that the tactile perception of number, which would seem to be a similar task, does not show an impressive frequency of ipsilateral deficit.

With respect to the question of left-hemisphere "dominance" for the occurrence of ipsilateral somatosensory defects, inspection of Table 1 indicates that the results are less clear cut. The findings of Corkin et al. (1964) appear to be completely negative in this respect. Ipsilateral defects in pressure sensitivity, two-point discrimination, and point localization occurred with essentially equal frequency in patients with excisions in one or the other hemisphere. The findings of Carmon (1969) were also negative with respect to this question; he did find ipsilateral impairment in pressure sensitivity and two-point discrimination, but the two hemispheric groups did not differ in respect to the relative frequency of such impairment.

However, the studies of Vaughan and Costa (1962) and of Wyke

Table 1. Occurrence of Ipsilateral Defects in Patients with Unilateral Lesions

L = left-hemisphere lesions; R = right-hemisphere lesions; + = ipsilateral defect;
++ = particularly high frequency of ipsilateral defect; − = no ipsilateral defect.

	Semmes et al. (1960)	Vaughan & Costa (1962)	Corkin et al. (1964)	Wyke (1966)	Carmon & Benton (1969b)	Milner et al. (1967)	Carmon (1969)
Absolute pressure threshold	++(L) +(R)	+(L) −(R)	+(L) +(R)				+(L) +(R)
Differential pressure threshold							−
Two-point threshold	++(L) +(R)	+(L) +(R)	+(L) +(R)				+(L) +(R)
Point localization	++(L) +(R)		++(L) ++(R)				
Passive movement threshold	++(L) +(R)						
Postural arm drift				+(L) −(R)			
Perception of direction					−(L) +(R)		
Perception of number					−		
Form recognition						−	

(1966) support the indications of left-hemisphere "dominance" reported by Semmes et al. (1960). Vaughan and Costa found ipsilateral defects in pressure sensitivity in patients with left-hemisphere lesions but not in those with lesions of the right hemisphere. Both groups showed ipsilateral defects in two-point discrimination. Wyke found excessive drift of the contralateral arm in both groups of patients. However, excessive drift of the ipsilateral arm was shown only by the patients with left-hemisphere lesions.

Thus far the question of hemispheric "dominance" in respect to tactile functions has been considered only with respect to a special role of the left hemisphere. However, the study by Carmon and Benton (1969b) has raised the question of whether some tactile performances may not reflect a relative "dominance" of the right hemisphere. In this study, the tactile perception of direction and number in patients with unilateral lesions was investigated. The experimental procedure consisted in stimulating the palms of each hand with one to three small tactile stimuli presented in nine different combinations of direction and number (Figure 1). The patients were required to identify the presented tactile stimulus on a visual display showing all the combinations, either by pointing to it or by calling a number that was placed at the top of each square. Two types of errors were scored in evaluating performance: responses involving the incorrect identification of number, and responses involving the incorrect identification of the direction of the tactile stimulation. Thus, with the exception of the single-point stimulus, each stimulation could be scored simultaneously for these two aspects of response.

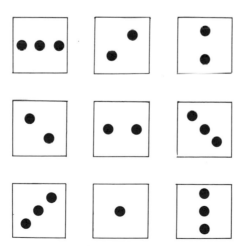

Figure 1. Visual display on which patient identified experienced pattern of tactile stimulation. (From Carmon & Benton, 1969b)

The mean error scores in the tactile perception of number and direction made by patients with left and with right hemispheric lesions are shown in Figure 2. The number of patients in each group (N's $= 30$) who made defective performances (defined as a number of errors greater than that made by the poorest control patient) is shown in Figure 3. Inspection of the figures indicates clearly that impairment in perceiving the number of tactile stimuli applied to the palms was confined to the contralateral hand in both groups of patients. However, there are hemispheric differences with respect to the tactile perception of direction. In the patients with lesions of the left hemisphere, the errors were confined to the contralateral hand. In contrast, a high proportion of patients with lesions of the right hemisphere showed defective tactile perception of direction on the ipsilateral, as well as the contralateral, hand.

Carmon and Benton (1969b) view their results as indicating that patients with lesions of the right hemisphere demonstrate the same spatial disability in this tactile performance that they are likely to show in visuoperceptive and visuoconstructive tasks. This interpretation is supported by the findings of the study by Dee (1970) that inferior performance on a test of tactile form perception was closely associated with the occurrence of visuoperceptive impairment and constructional apraxia in patients with cerebral disease.

The conclusion of Semmes and her coworkers that tactile functions are represented focally in the left hemisphere but more diffusely in the right hemisphere has not been subjected to searching empirical test. However, such work as has been reported has not provided confirmation of this generalization. Thus Corkin et al. (1964) found that severe somatosensory defect was associated only with lesions of the postcentral gyrus, and this was true of patients with lesions of either hemisphere. Similarly, Carmon and

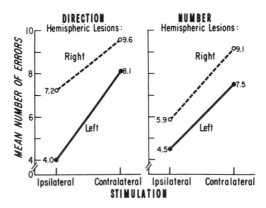

Figure 2. Mean error scores in the tactile perception of direction and number in patients with unilateral cerebral lesions. (From Carmon & Benton, 1969b)

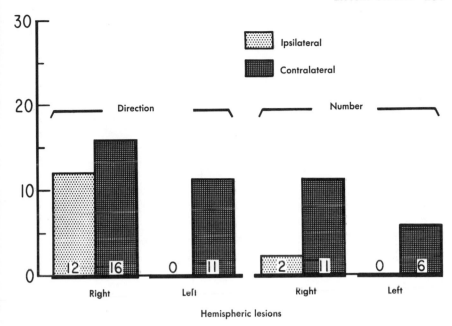

Figure 3. Frequency of defective performance in tactile perception of direction and number. (From Carmon & Benton, 1969b)

Benton (1969a) were unable to detect any difference in the effect of intrahemispheric locus of lesion on the frequency of tactile defects shown by patients with right- and with left-hemisphere lesions.

The further conclusion that tactile deficits are more closely intercorrelated on the right hand than on the left hand also has not been confirmed by subsequent work. Vaughan and Costa (1962) found a correlation coefficient of .52 between pressure sensitivity and two-point discrimination for the contralateral (right) hand in their patients with left-hemisphere disease, a value indicative of a substantial positive relation. However, they reported an even higher correlation coefficient (.87) for the contralateral (left) hand of their patients with disease of the right hemisphere. On their part, Carmon and Benton (1969a) did not find any impressive differences in the strength of the associations among various tactile performances in patients with left- and right-hemisphere lesions. Inspection of their results (Table 2) indicates clearly that the correlation coefficients among levels of tactile sensitivity on the contralateral hand were not higher in patients with left-hemisphere lesions than in those with lesions of the right hemisphere. The same holds for the interrelationships of the three measures of tactile sensitivity for the ipsilateral hand.

Table 2. Correlations among Tactile Performances in Patients with Unilateral Cerebral Lesions[a]

	Patients with Hemispheric Lesions			
	Right		Left	
Performance	Ipsi-lateral Hand	Contra-lateral Hand	Ipsi-lateral Hand	Contra-lateral Hand
Absolute and differential threshold	.41*	.65**	.16	.37*
Absolute threshold and two-point discrimination	.48**	.50**	.30	.45**
Differential threshold and two-point discrimination	.36*	.56**	.45**	.62**

[a] Carmon and Benton (1969a).
  * $p < .05$.
  ** $p < .01$.

CONCLUSIONS

This analysis of recent studies, beginning with that of Semmes et al. (1960), makes it abundantly clear that bilateral and ipsilateral somatosensory defects may be shown by patients with ostensibly unilateral disease, at least under the conditions of examination employed in the several studies. The question arises as to whether this circumstance does not merely reflect some more general mental impairment unrelated to sensory status, for example, fluctuations in attention, slowness in judgment, or aphasia. In this case, we would be dealing with a familiar phenomenon of no great theoretical or practical importance.

Although this possibility still cannot be completely excluded, the weight of evidence is against it. As has been pointed out, the analyses of Semmes et al. (1960) were negative in this respect. The findings of bilateral defect by Corkin et al. (1964) are particularly telling because their patients had rather limited cortical lesions and, from a general intellectual standpoint, were quite intact. Carmon and Benton (1969b) have also observed bilateral deficit in the tactile perception of direction in patients without the slightest evidence of general mental impairment or aphasia. Hence, even if the general explanation applies to some cases, it cannot be made to fit all of them.

Thus it is reasonable to conclude that at least some somatosensory performances on each side of the body are mediated by both the contralateral and ipsilateral hemispheres and not merely by the contralateral. As Semmes (1968) has pointed out, a substantial amount of physiological data is consonant with this concept of bilateral cerebral representation of somatosensory processes. No doubt the contribution of the ipsilateral hemisphere is generally smaller than that of the contralateral. However, it is possible that there is considerable individual variation in this respect. The implication of this conclusion for the clinical sensory examination is that the time-honored method of comparing sensitivity on the two sides of the body and using the patient as his own control has serious limitations and that the sensitivity of each side of the body should be assessed independently with reference to established normative standards.

In regard to the focal problem of whether there are differences between the two hemispheres in respect to the occurrence of bilateral or ipsilateral somesthetic defects, it seems that present findings tend to favor this possibility and yet are not sufficiently consistent to dictate a positive answer. As has been shown, some results suggest a relative dominance of the left hemisphere for certain performances, most notably for tactile pressure sensitivity and for postural arm control. However, other data do not support this trend. A crucial question here is why different investigators have obtained discrepant results. Until the reasons for these discrepancies are clarified, the hypothesis of a stronger ipsilateral representation of certain somatosensory processes in the left hemisphere must be considered rather questionable.

The other aspect of the problem is the one represented by the study of Carmon and Benton (1969b), indicating that the right hemisphere plays a particularly important role in the tactile perception of direction. The results of Corkin's (1965) study of tactile maze learning, in which she found that patients with lesions of the right hemisphere were consistently inferior to those with left lesions, support these indications of a relative dominance of the right hemisphere in the mediation of tactile performances involving a spatial component. This conclusion is not difficult to accept because it accords so well with the now widely accepted concept of a special role of the right hemisphere in the mediation of the spatial aspects of behavior. However, before accepting these findings at face value, one would like to see whether further studies, involving particularly a strict control of extent and type of lesion, will confirm them.

In conclusion, investigative work during the past decade has indicated the strong probability that bilateral and ipsilateral sensory defects are a frequent consequence of unilateral cerebral disease in man and the distinct possibility that lesions in each hemisphere have significantly different consequences in this respect. There are a number of unsettled questions which future research can be expected to answer. But the work to date has been more than sufficient to show that traditional conceptions of the somatosensory consequences of cerebral disease require considerable revision.

ACKNOWLEDGMENTS

The personal investigations cited in this chapter were supported by Research Grant NS–00616 and Program-Project Grant NS–03354 from the National Institute of Neurological Diseases and Stroke.

REFERENCES

Adams, F. *The extant works of Aretaeus the Cappodocian.* London: Sydenham Society, 1856.

Benton, A. L. *Right-left discrimination and finger localization: Development and pathology.* New York: Hoeber Medical Division, Harper & Row, 1959.

Benton, A. L. The fiction of the "Gerstmann syndrome." *Journal of Neurology, Neurosurgery, and Psychiatry,* 1961, **24,** 176–181.

Bychowsky, G., & Eidinow, M. Doppelseitige Sensibilitätsstorungen bei einseitigen Gehirnherden. *Nervenarzt,* 1934, **7,** 498–506.

Carmon, A. *Contralateral and ipsilateral tactile sensitivity in patients with unilateral cerebral lesions.* (Doctoral dissertation, University of Iowa) Ann Arbor, Mich.: University Microfilms, 1969. No. 69–13, 136.

Carmon, A., & Benton, A. L. Patterns of impaired tactile sensitivity in unilateral cerebral disease. *Harefuah,* 1969, **77,** 287–290 (Hebrew, with English summary). (a)

Carmon, A., & Benton, A. L. Tactile perception of direction and number in patients with unilateral cerebral disease. *Neurology,* 1969, **19,** 525–532. (b)

Corkin, S. Tactually guided maze learning in man: Effects of unilateral cortical excisions and bilateral hippocampal lesions. *Neuropsychologia,* 1965, **3,** 339–351.

Corkin, S., Milner, B., & Rasmussen, T. Effects of different cortical excisions on sensory thresholds in man. *Transactions of the American Neurological Association,* 1964, **89,** 112–116.

Dee, H. L. Visuoperceptive and visuoconstructive deficits in patients with unilateral cerebral lesions. *Neuropsychologia,* 1970, **8,** 305–314.

Foix, C. Sur une varieté de troubles bilatéraux de la sensibilité par lésion unilaterale du cerveau. *Revue Neurologique,* 1922, **29,** 322–331.

Gerstmann, J. Fingeragnosie: eine umschriebene Störung der Orientierung am eigenen Körper. *Wiener Klinische Wochenschrift,* 1924, **37,** 1010–1012.

Gerstmann, J. Fingeragnosie und isolierte Agraphie: Ein neues Syndrom.

Zeitschrift für die Gesamte Neurologie und Psychiatrie, 1927, **108**, 152–177.

Gerstmann, J. Zur Symptomatologie der Hirnläsionen im Übergangsgebiet der unteren Parietal- und mittleren Occipitalwindung. *Nervenarzt*, 1930, **3**, 691–695.

Giannitrapani, D. Developing concepts of lateralisation of cerebral functions. *Cortex*, 1967, **3**, 353–370.

Goldstein, K. Das Wesen der amnestischen Aphasie. *Schweizer Archiv für Neurologie und Psychiatrie*, 1924, **15**, 163–175.

Goldstein, K. Die Lokalisation in der Grosshirnrinde. In A. Bethe, G. Bergmann, G. Embden, & A. Ellinger (Eds.), *Handbuch der normalen und pathologischen Physiologie*. Berlin: Springer, 1927.

Guillain, G., Alajouanine, T., & Garcin, R. Un cas d'apraxie idéomotrice bilatérale coïncidant avec une aphasie et une hémiparésie gauche chez une gauchère. Troubles bilatéraux de la sensibilité profonde. *Revue Neurologique*, 1925, **2**, 116–124.

Head, H. *Studies in neurology*. London: Hodder & Stoughton, 1920.

Head, H. *Aphasia and kindred disorders of speech*. Cambridge: Cambridge University Press, 1926.

Heimburger, R., DeMyer, W., & Reitan, R. M. Implications of Gerstmann's syndrome. *Journal of Neurology, Neurosurgery, and Psychiatry*, 1964, **27**, 52–57.

Jackson, H. On the nature of the duality of the brain. *Medical Press & Circular*, 1874, **1**, 19.

Jackson, H. Case of large cerebral tumour without optic neuritis and with left hemiplegia and imperception. *Royal London Ophthalmic Hospital Reports*, 1876, **8**, 434–444.

Körner, S. C. Die Beeinflussbarkeit der Sensibilität an symmetrischen Hautgebieten bei einseitiger Hirnschädigang und bei Gesunden. *Deutsche Zeitschrift für Nervenheilkunde*, 1938, **145**, 116–130.

Liepmann, H. *Das Krankheitsbild der Apraxie ("Motorischen Asymbolie")*. Berlin: Karger, 1900.

Liepmann, H. *Drei Aufsätze aus dem Apraxiegebiet*. Berlin: Karger, 1908.

McFie, J., & Zangwill, O. L. Visual-constructive disabilities associated with lesions of the left cerebral hemisphere. *Brain*, 1960, **83**, 243–260.

Milner, B., Taylor, L., & Corkin, S. Tactual pattern recognition after different unilateral cortical excisions. Paper presented at the 38th Annual Meeting of the Eastern Psychological Association, Boston, 1967.

Morgagni, G. B. *The seats and causes of disease investigated by anatomy*. Translated by Alexander. London, 1769.

Oppenheim, H. Über einen bemerkenswerten Fall von Tumor cerebri. *Berliner Klinische Wochenschrift*, 1906, **13**, 1001–1004.

Pourfour du Petit, F. *Lettres d'un médecin des hôpitaux du roy à un autre médecin de ses amis*. Namur: Charles Gérard Albert, 1710.

Reichardt, M. *Allegemeine und spezielle Psychiatrie: ein Lehrbuch für Studierende und Arzte*. (3rd ed.) Jena: Fischer, 1923.

Rieger, C. Über Apparate in dem Hirn. *Arbeiten aus der Psychiatrischen Klinik zu Würzburg,* 1909, **5,** 1–197.

Semmes, J. Hemispheric specialization: A possible clue to mechanism. *Neuropsychologia,* 1968, **6,** 11–26.

Semmes, J., Weinstein, S., Ghent, L., & Teuber, H.-L. *Somatosensory changes after penetrating brain wounds in man.* Cambridge, Mass.: Harvard University Press, 1960.

Vaughan, H. G., Jr., & Costa, L. D. Performance of patients with lateralized cerebral lesions. *Journal of Nervous and Mental Disease,* 1962, **134,** 237–243.

Wyke, M. Postural arm drift associated with brain lesions in man. *Archives of Neurology,* 1966, **15,** 329–334.

CHAPTER 13

Sensory Retaining and the Problem of Human Memory

H. E. KING

The main findings from a recent series of experiments on human ability to retain sensory impressions over long periods of delay seem pertinent to the study of memory, on at least two counts. First, the experimental approach itself holds value, as a different way of looking at memory functioning than is usual, since most work on this subject has used verbal test material and has embraced a verbal learning approach to the study of human memory process. Second, the data generated by a sensory-retaining procedure—although systematic and reliable enough—prove to be not at all what we might expect if our ideas about the workings of memory were based only on methods strongly dependent on verbal skills and the use of symbolic language.

The method is simple and objective and consists of joining the techniques of sensory psychophysics with the goals of memory study in a more traditional sense. In essence, a particular sensory stimulus (the *standard*) is presented to an experimental subject (just once) followed by a period of preselected delay. The subject's task is to adjust a second, *variable* stimulus to match his "memory" of the original sensory impression:

Standard stimulus → Delay → Match (adjusted variable stimulus).

The elements of this sequence can then be varied by the investigator to extend his observation of the subject's ability to "register" and to "hold" specific sensory impressions through time. Different kinds of simple sensory materials can be used, of course, and the mode or strength of the stimuli may be varied independently. The key variable of *delay* is open to systematic and quantitative analysis. Other pertinent variables can also be exam-

243

ined, separately and conveniently, within the same experimental structure: any "interference," for example, caused by introducing new stimuli during delay, or constant errors that may depend on changes made in the psychophysical procedure. An overview of what has been learned thus far about human sensory-retaining ability, making variations of just this kind in the central paradigm, will form the substance of this chapter.

Before presenting a review of the experimental findings it may be useful to comment briefly on the particular value to be gained from a sensory-retaining approach to human memory study. We live in an era of renewed effort to solve the ancient puzzles posed by memory phenomena, and each day brings reports of an experimental attack on one facet of the problem or another. This resurgence of interest has many sources, but it is evident that primary among them have been (1) the analogies that can now be made between the operating principles of man-made computers and memory functioning; (2) the promise extended by discovery of the principles of DNA formation, as a possible physiological substrate for remembering; and (3) the state of development of learning theory, which currently demands a better grasp of just *what* elements of experience must be stored to provide the basis for all higher cognitive processes. All of this has served to redirect attention to one aspect of the mind-brain problem, in the form of the root question for physiological psychology: How does an event "experienced" become a part of the "structure" of an organism, so that it continues to influence subsequent related behavior?

It is a prosaic fact that much of what we know about memory, and about learned behavior generally, has been influenced strongly by the choice of experimental subject matter, that is, whether animal or man. Those who elect to observe animals, for the convenience they allow in experimentation, find a need for concepts such as "reward" and "reinforcement" or "punishment" to account for their data (despite the problems regularly met in trying to define the exact nature of these abstractions). Those who center their observation on human learning and memory, on the other hand, find little real need for these formulations, but discover instead that they must speak about "association" or "detection" or "insight" or "meaning" and "probability" to account for the obvious power of human subjects to learn and to remember. We can take one step further and ask, What are the guiding principles that have been identified as governing the operation of specifically *human* memory? To this question we receive a reply based heavily—if not exclusively—on the species-specific characteristic of speech (or the use of "internalized language"). Historically, experimental inquiry into human memory has made extensive use of verbal test materials, both meaningful and nonsensical, and has given greatest consideration to behaviors that can be either represented or expressed in words or numbers.

There can be no question, of course, about the importance of language for an understanding of human behavior in general and of memory in particular, since so much of what is important experience for man arrives in a verbal form or can be so represented. The awe-inspiring power of verbalization as a determinant of human behavior is not in question here. We stand well reminded, however, that infrahumans share no such facile means for the control of behavior—and yet they learn (and are said, by the visible nature of their learned acts, to "remember"). Man himself, in fact, begins life without speech and is entirely dependent on the senses for his experience of the world about him. The substrate for all learned or adapative behavior appears to rest on sense impressions that are directly apprehended. Rudimentary generalizations in behavior, based on events occurring in the environment or their sequence, may then—and only then—begin to arise. For this reason it is important to know far more than we now do about just how well sensory phenomena outlast the physical stimuli that give rise to them. Our attack on the problem will make use of a method old in the history of psychology, modified only slightly to yield information pertinent to human long-term sensory retention.

SENSORY RETAINING AS AN EXPERIMENTAL METHOD

Everyday experience makes it clear that certain sense impressions can be retained through time, at least for a while, although they may have been experienced only once, often in a not very dramatic or intense way. A certain color, for example, or taste or even a sound may have been "registered" only once, and yet can result in a positive "recognition" of the same sensation at a later moment. The evidence that the original impression is in some way still "borne in mind" may at times take a negative form and be expressed by rejecting other similar but not identical stimuli ("No, not this one, nor this . . . it was more like that one over there"). This commonplace observation, which in everyday life usually combines several different stimulus properties (e.g., the shape, color, and texture of an object), can also be demonstrated readily in the laboratory, where the sensory quality to be registered and retained can be reduced to a single sensory dimension. The method of successive comparison, in psychophysics, calls for judgments of exactly this kind. The quantitative approach that it makes possible to questions of sensory memory has been utilized in all of the experiments to be summarized here. It provides a sample of a kind of "retaining" behavior that is basic and that allows precise and convenient study in the laboratory, without a loss of semblance to behavior typical of everyday life. Also, it has been found that the task is accepted easily by experimental subjects, who seem untroubled by the fact that neither names nor words are needed to make this kind of delayed recognition of a sensory stimulus, as, for example, in judging the loudness of successive sounds. The instantaneous nature of comparing a delayed stimulus with another like it that has gone before in time seems nearly as direct and uncluttered, in fact, as was the apprehension of the original sensory experience.

Successive comparison had an early vogue in psychophysical research, being much used in the first part of this century. The method was later displaced by other techniques when it became obvious that, for certain kinds of matching, a greater precision was made possible by the simultaneous comparison of sensory stimuli (such as the brightness of two halves of a bisected disk), and because puzzling constant errors sometimes emerged when using certain forms of the delayed-matching procedure. Although these constant errors might be either positive or negative in sign, they were most often found to be negative by the favored procedure of the day (Woodworth, 1938, p. 439). They were unhappily named the "time errors" and were attributed to a "decay of the memory trace" through time. We shall have more to say about these "time errors" when enough data have been presented to make it clear that these effects were not well understood and were wrongly named (see also King, 1965, 1966b, 1969a, 1970; Plutchik & Schwartz, 1968). For the moment, however, it is more useful to point out that, even though the so-called time errors were attributed explicitly to the "decay of the trace through time" (Woodworth, 1938, p. 440; Woodworth & Schlosberg, 1954, p. 226), this conclusion did not give rise to much in the way of experimental variation of the interstimulus delay interval in a formal test of the hypothesis. Nor was there a systematic variation of the sensory modes under study, or a detailed evaluation of the procedures used to test for "recognition"—which we now know can influence memory-test data of all kinds (Adams, 1967). It was these omissions, so easily obvious in retrospect, that gave rise to the sensory-retaining experiments we will describe here.

Of the several possible variants of successive comparison procedure, the technique reported in this chapter is always an "adjustment" method (see Osgood, 1953, p. 44; Woodworth & Schlosberg, 1954, p. 199). Following a single exposure to a *standard* stimulus and a period of delay, the subject adjusts a *variable* stimulus from a value notably different from the standard until he judges it to be equated with his impression of the foregoing *standard*. Only one such match was contributed by each subject to a data pool, and performance by independent subject groups has been used to evaluate the influence of delay length on the accuracy of successive matching. Visual and auditory sensations have been the ones most often explored in this way, with separate experiments directed toward evaluating the stimulus parameters of intensity, frequency, and duration within each mode. The sense of touch has also been employed, although to a lesser degree, and current work centers on vibrotactile and pain sensation. The apparatus must be held under strict calibration over the entire observation period, of course, and any intercomparison of the data for different sensory systems must give full regard to their psychophysiological differences and individual units of measurement. The experiments have been carried forward together more to explore a *kind* of ability, on a broad empirical base, than to afford material intended for detailed intersensory comparison. All of the standard stimuli used were selected from the middle range, approaching neither the threshold of detection nor that of discomfort. In most experiments the subject was allowed five seconds of exposure to the standard, to attend to and to "register" the stimulus in question.

OVERVIEW OF THE DATA

It has been found, by exploring delay intervals that vary from only seconds in duration to prolonged lapses of days or weeks, that ordinary human subjects can make delayed sensory matchings of this kind with surprising accuracy (King, 1963a, 1963d, 1965, 1969a). They are able to reproduce, with only minimal error, the physical values of standard stimuli to which they have been exposed but once, and then only briefly. Delayed matches made to the *brightness* of a test light (Figure 1*a*) or to the *loudness* of a sound (Figure 1*b*) will serve to illustrate this consistently demonstrated ability. Moreover, the same sort of overall efficiency has also been observed to typify delayed sensory matches made to the *frequency* and the *duration* characteristics of both visual and auditory sample stimuli (King, 1963b, 1963c, 1965). If the experimental situation is turned around a bit, and delay is held constant while the value of the standard stimulus is varied, another form of the same clear and systematic relationship emerges. The exactness of delayed matching, by independent subject groups, to a wide range of variation in visual and auditory standard stimuli is illustrated in Figure 2. Essentially the same finding has been reported to typify delayed matches made in other sensory modes as well, when probed by other investigators. Canestrari (1967a) has explored the long-term retaining of light-touch sensation; Paul (1967) has examined perceived roughness; and several investigators have reported on the accuracy of delayed color matching (Christal, 1958; Collins, 1932; Hamwi & Landis, 1955; Hanawalt & Post, 1942).

Surprised by the demonstrated tenacity of what would appear to be rather weak and trivial sensory impressions, several investigators have un-

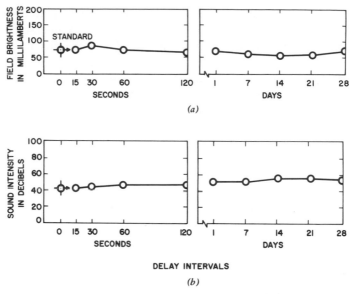

Figure 1. Brightness and loudness of the standard stimuli and mean adjusted matches of the variable stimuli after delay. Each open circle represents performance by an independent subject group. (After King, 1963a, 1965)

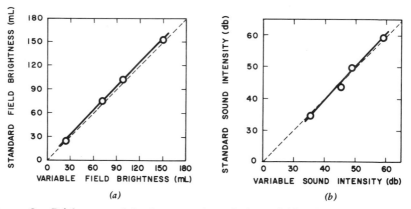

Figure 2. Brightness and loudness matches of the variable stimuli as a function of variation of the standard stimuli. One-minute delay; the open circles represent the means of independent subject groups. (After King, 1966a)

248

dertaken to interfere with the "trace" deliberately, as an alternative test of its vigor. Canestrari, for example, interposed other light-touch stimuli (to be "disregarded") during the delay interval, without significantly affecting the accuracy of long-delayed matches made to *standard* light-touch stimuli (1967b). On a different experimental tack, Lake (1967) attempted to distract the subject during registration of the standard stimulus by presenting uncomfortable levels of stimulation (via other sensory modes) at the same moment. Simultaneous exposure to mild pain (pressure on the skin; bright light in the eyes) did not serve, however, to reduce in any way the accuracy of delayed matches made to *standard* auditory stimuli eight days later. It seems likely that these extraneous stimuli, although intended to be "interfering," were in fact too different from the *standard* stimulus to become confused with it. When additional auditory stimuli were interposed, during delay-to-matching, that fell closer to the qualitative and quantitative value of a *standard* auditory stimulus, they were indeed found to influence the accuracy of delayed matching to some degree (King, 1966b). And, of course, the stimuli the most likely of all to commingle with or become confused with the *standard* are those alternate values in the same sensory dimension through which the subject must necessarily search in an effort to match the *standard*, that is to say, all of the other values of the adjusted *variable* stimulus that he must unavoidably see, hear, or otherwise experience during memory test. We shall return to this important point later.

It has also been learned along the way that the ability to recognize singly experienced sensory stimuli is well developed in quite young experimental subjects, 5–9 years old, and is not significantly diminished among normally aging subjects, 60–75 years of age. Neither incomplete development, from other points of view, nor the decline sometimes attributed to normal physiological aging appears to influence appreciably the precision of delayed matches made to touch (Canestrari, 1967a) or to sound stimuli (Hill, 1966).

These brief data summaries are necessarily incomplete. Obviously the specially interested reader must turn to the original experiments for the details of the experimental procedure or the analysis of results. Their primary finding—a relative invariance of single sensory impressions over long delay—is, nonetheless, clear and direct. It is the implication of this central phenomenon for a more general understanding of human memory that is in focus here. What has been sought is more systematic information on the way in which sensory experience relates to subsequent behavior, derived in a manner which permits the subjective nature of that experience to be tied to objectively measurable physical systems. Experience and learning, it can be argued, do not so much begin with words and numbers as end with them. The basic elements for accumulated experience are more likely to be sights and sounds, tastes and smells, touches, movements, aches and pains —as the philosophers have long suggested. The sensory-retaining experiment was devised to honor this psychobiologic substrate.* It is not supposed, of course, that the essence of experience is thereby measured or understood. Human beings, like other animals, live in a world of sensory flux that provides a continuing flow of signals to which they must gear all adaptive behavior. It is logical to assume that, if the animate organism is to accumulate experience—beyond a momentary biologic reactivity—and begin to arrive at the generalizations of experience that are called learning, there must exist ways in which sense messages can outlast the physical energies that give rise to them. We can go beyond this logical assumption, fortunately, and test the matter out by actual observation in the laboratory. This is the basic question posed in the sensory-retaining experiment. The answer forthcoming has been clear in its general outline and is not a little surprising.

SENSORY RETAINING IN RELATION TO HUMAN MEMORY

These single exposures to uncomplicated *standard* stimuli might seem, at first blush, to provide a most minimal "experience," giving rise to only a flimsy "trace," one that might be expected to wash out easily in the continuing flood of sensory signals to which the subject is exposed in the course of everyday life. A continuing background of sense information of varied kinds is vital to the organization of all adaptive response, however, as we soon discover when some part of it is blocked experimentally or pathologically. Its normal ebb and flow seems biologically important, especially to the higher animals, as an underlay for the processes of identification and orientation and the forming of behavior sequences of all kinds. Calling the attention of the human subject to some specific fragment of this flow (to what we have called the *standard* stimulus) seems to be enough to allow him to find that particular value again, after delay, in spite of its seemingly trivial nature and the fact that it is unnamed and is not repeated or otherwise "reinforced." Obviously, this ability must falter sooner or later. It was with the intent to capture and record this evanescence, in fact, that these experiments were originally devised. The obtrusive finding, however, is just the opposite. The seemingly momentary sensory "trace" has proved itself to be clear and long lasting. It is also interesting to note, in passing, that virtually no subject probed the full range of variable stimuli available to him, or gave any indication that he needed to search out the limits (highest

* Self-awareness or "consciousness" is not implied.

and lowest *variable* stimulus values) before attempting his reapproximation of the *standard*. Delayed matching to a "trace" resembled, rather, the adjusting of one of two stimuli simultaneously present, as one might adjust the brightness of a lamp to match the luminance of another next to it.

Certainly errors in matching occur, as they do for any other measure of behavioral response, owing to natural variation in the organism and to imperfections in our methods of measurement. They can be informative, therefore, about recurrent tendencies in the organism or can point to systematic faults in our methods of observation. Where constant errors have appeared among long-delayed matches, they were most often found to fall "above" the physical value of the original stimulus. That is to say, a matching value was chosen (after delay) that was louder, faster, higher, or rougher than the standard stimulus itself. It would be premature to conclude, however, that this type of error will always be found, for it has not always appeared among the forms of delayed matching already investigated (not for *brightness*, for example, or for *duration*). It is quite possible that these "positive" errors may result, in part, from some uncontrolled influence of procedure on performance, for example, a search begun more often or from a greater distance (disparity) "above" than "below" the standard value. Augmented matches of the kind have been found even when the "distance" and "direction" of search have been carefully controlled, however, and the positive constant errors noted have been observed to increase gradually over time (see again Figure 1b; loudness matches over delays ranging from 15 seconds to 28 days).

This progressive increment is difficult to understand if a positive constant error is held to arise only from some unidentified aspect of the procedure used for memory test. Although the tendency to augment the value of a sought standard over time is a much less clear and regular trend in the data than is the essential stability of the recaptured "trace," it does occur. Moreover, it seems likely that "rises" in the value of delayed matches, rather than "weakenings," occur as a function of delay. Because this finding seems opposite to what common sense might predict (how can something gain in value or energy through time?), it must be observed more closely in future work and must show itself able to resist changes deliberately made in procedure (the wording of instructions, e.g., with alternate subjects being asked to find sounds "as loud as" and "as soft as" the *standard*, etc.) before it is accepted. The data now existing make it quite clear, however, that a gradual dissipation or "fading of the trace" is not at all characteristic of the matches offered to long-held sensory experience and that, if anything, the reverse or a slight "positive" rise in matched value takes place as a function of delay.

One other general trend notable has been the relative ineffectiveness of efforts to "interfere" deliberately with the experimental sensory "trace." The most effective "interfering traces," as has been mentioned, appear to be those based on stimuli that most closely resemble the standard being sought. This is logical and is easily understood. It should be noted that both practical and theoretical implications follow from this statement. Just such stimuli are introduced into the sensory-retaining experiment, for the first time, at the moment of memory test in the form of the alternate values provided by adjustments made in the *variable* stimulus. The initial value presented by the experimenter as a starting point (from which the variable is adjusted to parity with the remembered standard), and all of the intermediate values of the *variable* stimulus passed through by the subject in his search for a match to the *standard*, may thus serve as potential sources of sensory "trace" interference. Starting-position errors in successive matching, such as those commonly found when the method of limits is used to determine sensory thresholds, are usually averaged out in the statistical analysis of the pooled data of groups, since the starting positions are typically randomized by the experimental design, as is the degree of disparity between the starting position and the standard stimulus value being sought. In looking back over the accumulated data on sensory retaining, however, it can be seen that the tendency for individual judgments of equivalence to be displaced in the direction from which search for a match to the *standard* was begun (see King, 1963c, p. 304; 1965, p. 111) may furnish the best clue extant on the effects of a true "trace interference," which may be likened to the action of proactive inhibition, well known from experiments on verbal learning.

Future investigation will be able to attack this question directly. With delay at first kept brief and held constant, the influence of variations in procedure on successive-comparison performance can be evaluated in detail. Once a satisfactory (nonbiasing) procedure has been chosen, the variable of delay can then be explored in purer form. The existing data suggest that interference inherent in features of the memory test procedure itself (i.e., starting point direction and distance) can exert an influence of as much as 15% on judged equivalence, that it can be a phenomenon altogether independent of delay, or that it may interact with the effects of delay for certain forms of sensory experience. The inescapable introduction of new sensory material at the moment of memory test thus provides us with a source of identifiable experimental artifact and a method for analyzing with some subtlety the possible interacting of mixable sensory "traces" over long delay.

The significance of these sensory-retaining explorations for the broad problem posed by human memory appears to rest mainly on two fundamentals: the different view that they permit of "registration" and of "retention," which is implicit in the use of unlearned nonverbal sensory material for memory study; and the principal finding of an accurate, long-term retaining resulting from a limited registration, which is not at all what one might predict from what is known about the retaining of learned verbal test material. What reflections can be offered at this time on the meaning of these findings for a general theory of memory? Probably the most basic observation that can be made is that the very form of the technique used in all of this work—a single stimulus presentation, under maximal attention, with no interference likely to enter before memory test—may contribute as much to the accuracy and persistence of the "sensory trace" under study as does the unlearned, nonverbal nature of the material to be retained. If we were to present only a single nonsense syllable to a subject, rather than the usual long lists to be mastered, and if this single presentation was followed by a delay containing no other similar syllables that might become confused (interfere) with it, would we not expect a rather accurate recognition of the original after the lapse of a day or a week? It would seem so. The sensory-retaining data as such do not permit a further test of this proposition, but they clearly suggest an analogue that can be examined using appropriate verbal memory materials. Sufficient evidence is now at hand (Adams, 1964, 1967; King, 1963a, 1963b, 1963c, 1963d, 1965, 1966a, 1966b, 1969a; Talland, 1965, 1968) to indicate that the retention of what has been "registered" by verbal learning, by motor learning, and by sensory retaining may not be governed by identical neuropsychological processes—in fact, probably is not. It seems likely, furthermore, that certain of the differences in performance currently held to characterize retention in these differing domains may rest partly on features of the procedures used for their study (see also Asch, 1969; Gibson, 1963, 1967; Tulving & Madigan, 1970). Great care is obviously needed in specifying the psychological dimensions of just what is presented to the subject for "registration" and the conditions under which we ask him to indicate any continuing influence of this original "experience" at a later moment.

Possibly the fact that much of what human beings find useful to retain is acquired only gradually (and often with difficulty) has overimpressed us with the notion that only the experience so gained (gradually learned) can be "retained." There must exist a substrate for the accumulation of the simplest kinds of experience, however, and some way in which the very first impression or association or stimulus relation can be carried forward in time, to combine with later experience to provide the basis for generalization and all subsequent higher learning. A neurophysiologic beginning has been made, in fact, toward probing for the existence of this hypothetical substrate (Starr & Livingston, 1963). Experiments have been shaped to investigate the temporal noncorrespondence between physical stimuli in the environment and their sensory-neural consequences, monitored systematically at different points within the central nervous system. A simple sound (click) can be followed, for example, from its origin in the physical environment to and through the ear and along the auditory conduction pathways to an ultimate projection on the auditory cortex. The definite delays recorded between discontinuation of the physical sound source and the subsequent neural events monitored along this peripheral-to-central system have been interpreted in terms of "active neural mechanisms resisting change"; and the hope has been expressed that "an analysis of the effects of prolonged stimulation may provide experimental access to some of the mechanisms underlying memory, learning and other phenomena relating to sensory experiences [Starr & Livingston, 1963, p. 430]." The recent work of Gol'dburt (1964), on judging the simultaneity or successiveness of paired tones, also emphasizes the likelihood that persistent neural excitation may underlie the judged simultaneity of what are, in physical fact, successive signals. "Our experiments provide fresh proof that the activity of the nervous system may persist much longer than the sensory stimulus producing it. I am inclined to regard the physiological basis of this persistence as consisting of Vvedenski's stable excitation and the 'persistent potentials' of Bishop [1956] and Grundfest [1959] [Gol'dburt, 1964, p. T1209]."

Although the findings of the inquiries into human sensory retaining surveyed here may relate in only the most general way to these neurophysiological data, something of the same functional end effect of resistance to change appears to typify the rudimentary sensory experiences that have been observed. It seems improbable that every experience once "registered" continues to live on in the neural life of the organism, although such speculation has long been entertained, by Henri Bergson, Eugen Bleuler, Sigmund Freud, William James, and Wilder Penfield, among others. By means of direct electrical stimulation of a subregion of the temporal cortex of the brain, Penfield (1954, 1959) has produced the experiential phenomena of a conscious reliving of some past episode or series of experiences as though one were playing back a "physiologic recording" of sense impressions from the distant past. (Interpretive phenomena have also been produced, such as recognition, *déja vu*, sadness, or fear.) That these evoked trains of experience differ from the sensory-retaining phenomena summarized here, we may be certain. The unexpectedly long-lived character of the phenomena found in both of these experimental situations indicates, however, that the biologically important substrate for "awareness" may be less ephemeral than the evidence of subjective consciousness would at first suggest.

SENSORIAL SUBSTRATE OF HIGHER PSYCHOLOGICAL FUNCTION

In any effort to think about the kinds of "experience" available to a human (or animal) subject in an experimental situation, we are prone to miss the most complex elements (e.g., the social) and also some of the simplest (e.g., the postural). Only recently has the sheer *quantity* of sensory input, via the reticular activating system, begun to be recognized as a matter of fundamental biologic significance. It is reasonable to suppose that some kinds of low-level *quality* of sensory input may also be basic—to form the necessary neural background for the maintenance of orientation in place, time, or position. Some way of relating the experience of the moment to other experience like it that has gone before, at greater or lesser intervals, is patently at work in an ununderstood but efficient way.

K. S. Lashley charged us with the need to ponder such matters in two of his final papers: "In Search of the Engram" (1950) and "The Problem of Serial Order in Behavior" (1951). As the result of his lifelong search for the paths or locations within the central nervous system for "learned acts," he came to hold that: "It is highly probable that immediate memory is maintained by some sort of after-discharge of the originally excited neurons," and also that "the stimulus is not only the object which the experimenter designates . . . but a whole background of other objects constituting the situation [Lashley, 1950, p. 473]." The memory trace, as he saw it, was always tied in with the apprehension of external spatial coordinates and with the animal's postural-reference system. Each memory was dated in a way that served to tie it to a series of related experiences (from the past), as well as to whatever relations were established among other stimulus elements simultaneously present. "The engram of a new association, far from consisting of a single bond or neural connection, is probably a reorganization of a vast system of associations involving the interrelations of hundreds of thousands or millions of neurons [p. 475]." Lashley also notes, "The trace of any activity is not an isolated connection between sensory and motor elements. It is tied in with the whole complex of spatial and temporal axes of nervous activity which forms a constant substratum of behavior [p. 478]."

Psychobiological investigators (Fletcher, 1964, 1965; Konorski, 1967; Livingston, 1967; Pribram, 1969; Somjen, 1967; Walshe, 1969) have found this view obviously fruitful, but it has yet to influence markedly either the theory or the experiments of most students of human verbal learning and memory. The most explicit ideas on the possible contribution of multiple internalized "traces" for the building of learned generalizations are those described by Adams as "closed-loop theory" (Adams, 1967,

1968). Drawing heavily on experimental data from verbal-learning retention, but apparently influenced by his long-standing interest in motor learning as well, Adams has hypothesized the action of more than one kind of
experiential "trace." His system calls for the internalization of both sensory
(and perceptual) traces for purposes of stimulus identification, and, in
addition, an internal mechanism for response recognition. Discrepancies
between these reference systems permit "the detection of error in a response sequence that can lead to error nulling [Adams, 1968, p. 493]."
The convergence of this view with Anokhin's "acceptor of action" (based
on the totality of afferent sensations), Mowrer's "conditioned sensations or
images," and the TOTE (test-operate-test-exit) circuits hypothesized by
Miller, Galanter, and Pribram, by which an animal continues to respond
until response error reaches zero, gives rise to optimism that the hitherto
largely separate data banks of animal learning and human memory study
may have begun to find a common interface. Each of these systems is complex in theory and cannot be discussed adequately in a few words. Nor is
it suggested that our artificially prepared stimulus-retaining laboratory situation represents accurately the natural manner in which complex organisms
receive and store complicated sensory information from the environment.
It can be stated, however, that human (and presumably infrahuman)
ability to receive, hold, and act upon seemingly fleeting and fragile sensory
impressions can readily be demonstrated; and that searching for a trace
and matching a response to it (Eimas & Zeaman, 1963), which is essentially
what Adams calls "response recognition [Adams, 1967, p. 299]," has come
under investigation on an independent line of inquiry. By an extension of
psychophysics into the realm of memory study, a body of data has been
generated that appears to fit rather closely some of the theoretical requirements for mechanisms needed to explain human verbal retention and animal
learning.

Those ancient problems of psychopathology posed by states of perplexity,
by feelings of unaccounted strangeness or familiarity, and by disorientation
for place and time suggest some flaw in the basic mechanisms by which the
organism keeps track of its fundamental position on the spatial and temporal axes of existence. Higher mental functions, such as intelligence or
learning ability and verbal memory for specific events, are often curiously
unaffected in the face of these deeply disturbed conditions. It is possible
that this is so because they *are* "higher psychologic functions," acquired and
organized in a way that permits compensation for errors in function by
means of a redundancy provided by the multiple neural registration of
acquired experience. In contrast, the integrity of the lowest-order sensory
systems may prove the more vulnerable to physiologic or pathologic change
just because they are rooted so intimately in the basic (unlearned) biologic

organization of the individual. A parallel for this exists in the way errors can be detected in suboptimal states of the organism at the simplest levels of psychomotor effector action, although no obvious deviations may be observed at higher or more integrated levels of perceptuomotor response (King, 1969b). It is premature, however, to go beyond conjecture at this point. It would press the data of sensory retaining entirely too far to imagine that the behavior sampled thereby is necessarily akin to this hypothesized sensorial substrate for other and more complex behaviors. Thinking about the demonstrated action of the one, however, may help us to speculate about the possible operation of the unseen other. The effortless precision by which sensory impressions selected from the continuous flow of human experience can be found again, by simple instruction, suggests the possibility of a continuous identification of all sorts of incoming sensory information, exactly "registered" and carried forward in time. This continuous background flow of low-level sensory qualitative information may serve both to maintain the orientation of the organism in space and time, and to provide a sort of necessary sensorial substrate (a carrier wave) for the exchange of other, more complex information with the environment. It is known, for example, that postural set contributes heavily to success in the delayed-response performance of animal subjects (Fletcher, 1964; 1965); indeed, Berlyne once defined the essence of animal learning as a "set that lasts for more than 24 hours"! These very general thoughts can be fruitful, of course, only as they lead to specific and testable hypotheses. It is conceivable, at least, that, even as the events of the last 20 years have brought a recognition of the animate organism's need for a certain *amount* of sensory input as a basic quantitative substrate for higher-order behavior (i.e., "activation" or "arousal"), we may now be entering a period in which a certain minimum of continuous qualitative sensory input will also be recognized as vital to the formation of all more complex forms of behavior patterning.

REFERENCES

Adams, J. Motor skills. *Annual Review of Psychology,* 1964, **15,** 181–202.

Adams, J. *Human memory.* New York: McGraw-Hill, 1967.

Adams, J. Response feedback and learning. *Psychological Bulletin,* 1968, **70,** 486–504.

Asch, S. A reformulation of the problem of associations. *American Psychologist,* 1969, **24,** 92–102.

Canestrari, S. The retention of tactile stimulation with young and elderly adults. Unpublished master's thesis, Department of Psychology, University of Richmond, 1967. (a)

Canestrari, S. The effect of interference on the retention of tactile stimulation. Unpublished study, Department of Psychology, Graduate College, University of Richmond, 1967. (b)

Christal, R. Factor analytic study of visual memory. *Psychological Monographs,* 1958, **72** (13, Whole No. 466).

Collins, M. Some observations on immediate colour memory. *British Journal of Psychology,* 1932, **22,** 344–352.

Eimas, P., & Zeaman, D. Response speed changes in an Estes' paired-associate "miniature" experiment. *Journal of Verbal Learning and Verbal Behavior,* 1963, **1,** 384–388.

Fletcher, H. Activity during delay interval and delayed response errors in monkeys. *Psychological Reports,* 1964, **14,** 685–686.

Fletcher, H. The delayed-response problem. In A. Schrier, H. Harlow, & F. Stollnitz (Eds.), *Behavior of nonhuman primates.* Vol. 1. New York: Academic Press, 1965. Pp. 129–165.

Gibson, J. The useful dimensions of sensitivity. *American Psychologist,* 1963, **18,** 1–15.

Gibson, J. On the proper meaning of the term stimulus. *Psychological Review,* 1967, **74,** 533–534.

Gol'dburt, S. N. *Federation Proceedings Translation Supplement,* 1964, **23,** T1206–T1210.

Hamwi, V., and Landis, C. Memory for color. *Journal of Psychology,* 1955, **39,** 183–194.

Hanawalt, N., and Post, B. Memory trace for color. *Journal of Experimental Psychology,* 1942, **30,** 216–227.

Hill, C. L. A developmental study in the retention of sensory experience. Unpublished manuscript, 1966.

King, H. E. The retention of sensory experience. I. Intensity. *Journal of Psychology,* 1963, **56,** 283–290. (a)

King, H. E. The retention of sensory experience. II. Frequency. *Journal of Psychology,* 1963, **56,** 291–298. (b)

King, H. E. The retention of sensory experience. III. Duration. *Journal of Psychology,* 1963, **56,** 299–306. (c)

King, H. E. Sensory storage in the human. *Federation Proceedings,* 1963, 515. (d)

King, H. E. The retention of sensory experience. IV. Short-delay versus long-delay intervals. *Journal of Psychology,* 1965, **60,** 103–115.

King, H. E. The retention of sensory experience. V. Variation of the standard stimuli. *Journal of Psychology,* 1966, **62,** 15–22. (a)

King, H. E. The retention of sensory experience. VI. Stimulus repetition and interference effects. *Journal of Psychology,* 1966, **64,** 59–61. (b)

King, H. E. Sensory retaining in the human. *Federation Proceedings,* 1969, **28,** 396. (a)

King, H. E. Psychomotility: A dimension of behavior disorder. In J. Zubin & C. Shagass (Eds.), *Neurophysiological aspects of psychopathology.* New York: Grune & Stratton, 1969. Pp. 99–128. (b)

King, H. E. A reconsideration of the "time-error" in successive-comparison. Unpublished manuscript, 1970.

Konorski, J. *Integrative activity of the brain.* Chicago: University of Chicago Press, 1967.

Lake, K. L. Long term memory retention of sound as a function of visual and tactile interference. Unpublished manuscript, 1967.

Lashley, K. In search of the engram. In *Symposia of the Society for Experimental Biology. IV, Physiological mechanisms in animal behavior.* New York: Academic Press, 1950. Pp. 454–482.

Lashley, K. S. The problem of serial order in behavior. In L. Jeffress (Ed.), *Cerebral mechanisms in behavior*: The Hixon Symposium. New York: Wiley, 1951. Pp. 112–136.

Livingston, R. Brain mechanisms in conditioning and learning. In F. Schmitt, T. Melnechuk, G. Quarton, & G. Adelman (Eds.), *Neurosciences research symposium summaries.* Vol. 2. Cambridge, Mass.: M.I.T. Press, 1967. Pp. 91–201.

Osgood, C. *Method and theory in experimental psychology.* New York: Oxford University Press, 1953.

Paul, L. The scaling and retention of sensations of roughness. Unpublished manuscript, 1967.

Penfield, W. The permanent record of the stream of consciousness. *Proceedings of the XIV International Congress of Psychology,* 1954, pp. 47–69.

Penfield, W. The interpretive cortex. *Science,* 1959, **129,** 1719–1725.

Plutchik, R., & Schwartz, A. Critical analysis of the problem of time-error. *Perceptual and Motor Skills,* 1968, **27,** 79–82.

Pribram, K. The physiology of remembering. In S. Bogoch (Ed.), *The future of the brain sciences.* New York: Plenum, 1969. Pp. 66–88.

Somjen, G. Sensory coding. *Science,* 1967, **158,** 399–405.

Starr, A., & Livingston, R. Long-lasting nervous system responses to prolonged sound stimulation in waking cats. *Journal of Neurophysiology,* 1963, **26,** 416–431.

Talland, G. *Deranged memory.* New York: Academic Press, 1965.

Talland, G. *Disorders of memory and learning.* London: Penguin, 1968.

Tulving, E., & Madigan, S. Memory and verbal learning. *Annual Review of Psychology,* 1970, **21,** 437–484.

Walshe, F. M. R. Some reflections upon memory and a "memory trace." In S. Locke (Ed.), *Modern Neurology.* Boston: Little, Brown, 1969. Pp. 321–332.

Woodworth, R. S. *Experimental psychology.* New York: Holt, 1938.

Woodworth, R., & Schlosberg, H. *Experimental psychology.* (Rev. Ed.) New York: Holt, Rinehart & Winston, 1954.

CHAPTER 14

Input Regulation and Psychopathology

PETER H. VENABLES

If psychopathology can be seen to have its roots in general psychology, then it is likely that theories, concepts, and findings from this parent source will have potential application in the abnormal field.

Many aspects of mental disease are capable of interpretation as disorders of selective attention. A large amount of work using this concept has been undertaken by experimental psychologists, but studies have been carried out by two rather separate groups of workers. It is unfortunate that the transmission of ideas between these groups has been limited, and with some notable exceptions (e.g., Callaway & Stone, 1960; Teichner, 1968) there have been few attempts to promote any cross fertilization.

One set of ideas has developed around the notion of the organism as an information-processing system, including such features as initial sensory input channels, short- and long-term storage systems, and central serial processing systems of limited capacity (e.g., Broadbent, 1958; Egeth, 1967; Norman, 1968; Treisman, 1969). An attempt to apply some of these ideas in the field of psychopathology was made by Venables (in press). Other approaches have been more concerned with individual differences in the extent to which aspects of the external world are perceived, and with the underlying physiological state relating to the perceptual selectivity exhibited by the subject. From this latter work dichotomies have developed (e.g., broadness versus narrowness of attention, augmentation versus reduction, repression versus sensitization) which may be collectively called aspects of "cognitive style." It is not surprising that in the field of psychopathology, in which characteristic differences between patients and normal subjects are sought, it is this approach that has been more used, in contrast to models developed around information-processing ideas (e.g., Silverman, 1967; Venables, 1964). A third group of studies with possibly potential value and applicability in the field of psychopathology is concerned with orientation. Many views on orientation would require the interaction of perceptual and memory processes in the comparison of received information with a stored "neural model," and thus provide direct comparison with the information-processing models of selective attention. These latter models have tended to be aphysiological, whereas orienting response ideas are centered around a physiological approach.

ORIENTATION AND ATTENTION

As an example the (at least superficial) closeness of the ideas of workers on orientation and on information-processing notions of attention may be seen in a comparison of the work of Sokolov (1960) and Norman (1968). In Sokolov's ideas of the orientation process, incoming stimuli reaching the cortex are compared to "neuronal models," which are stored traces of past stimulation. If the stimulus sample does not match the stored model, the reticular formation is activated and an orientation reaction is commenced. Norman's model is one of attention, and not orientation, and hence is organized to explain the processes involved in deciding to what stimuli the organism attends. In a similar way to Sokolov, Norman says, "Sensory inputs (after a number of stages of processing) activate their representation in storage . . . . This activation is the first step in interpreting the inputs [1968, p. 526]." Inputs are selected on the basis of several properties of cues that are essentially nonsensory, and to account for this Norman adds the variable of "pertinence," which he considers to be based on the "expectations of future inputs and the properties of the presently attended channel of information [1968, p. 527]." According to Norman pertinence must be determined before, or as, the input is being analyzed and selected; it cannot be determined after the selection has taken place. His model, thus, would appear to be similar in some characteristics to the Sokolov model, the main one being the comparison of sensory input to a stored model, this comparison proceeding before the organism's awareness of the process of perception and of the existence of the stimulus that gave rise to it. It is worth noting that Sokolov (1960) suggested that the mechanisms involved in his "neuronal models" and those involved in Pavlovian "dynamic stereotypes" (or perhaps what Hull, 1943, would call "habit family hierarchies") produced by conditioning processes are the same.

It might be suggested that orientation is not attention or selection of input; however, the original formulation of Pavlov (1927) shows the closeness of the two ideas. He describes the orientation reaction as "the reflex which brings about the immediate response in man and animals to the slightest changes in the world around them, so that they immediately orientate their appropriate receptor organ in accordance with the perceptible quality in the agent bringing about the change, making full investigation of it [p. 12]." The main superficial difference between orientation and attention ideas would appear to be that the stimuli to which the organism orients are primarily those which are novel, whereas those to which the organism attends are those which are important or, in Norman's terms, "pertinent." The experiment of Moray (1959), showing that a subject's attention may be captured by the sound of his own name, would appear to provide the greatest contrast between orientation and attention, as nothing could, perhaps, be less novel to a person than his own name. If, however, novelty is seen in an informational context, the presentation of a person's name in a context that provides low transitional probability of occurrence is, by definition, novel. Lovibond (1969) has provided data which support Sokolov's (1960) suggestion that an information theory analysis of orientation processes may be appropriate by showing that the rate of habituation of the skin conductance response closely fits the degree of uncertainty in the stimulus series.

ORIENTATION AND "GATING"

The other experimental approach that enables a possible interconnection between the ideas of attention and orientation is concerned with "environmental intake" and physiological response (e.g., Darrow, 1929; Dykman, Reese, Galbrecht, Ackerman, & Sunderman, 1968; Lacey, Kagan, Lacey, & Moss, 1963). Workers in this area have suggested that stimuli may be of two kinds. The first type requires sustained attentiveness or environmental intake and elicits heart rate deceleration and an increase in skin conductance. Stimuli of the second type, which demand a rejection of the environment and the setting in train of central processing operations, are accompanied by heart rate acceleration and an increase in skin conductance. The features of a former "intake" response are closely similar to those generally thought of as characterizing the orientation response in man, whereas those of the "rejection" response may possibly be similar to the defense reaction.

The necessary physiological and psychological consequence of the onset of the orientation response is its habituation. The organism is continually bombarded with stimuli, and if there were an orientation to, and close attention to, each one, disorganization would quickly follow. Jasper (1958) has said:

"The function of the reticular system in normal adaptive or integrative behavior may be more in the nature of a prevention of general arousal reaction to all stimuli, with a control of selective responsiveness to significant stimuli. Indiscriminate arousal reactions to all stimuli could only result in chaotic behavior, as may be the case in certain mental disorders [p. 321]."

Sokolov (1960), too, sees the reticular formation as involved in habituation and suggests that "habituation is the elaboration of an inhibitory conditional reflex regulating the transmission of impulses to the reticular formation [p. 211]." While inability to selectively attend to stimuli may be the feature of some psychopathological groups, inability to attend to a wide enough range of stimuli may be a feature of others. This may be seen as a deficiency in the orientation reaction.

In view of the fact that orientation and attention involve the mechanisms of transmission of sensory input, registration and storage of that input, comparison of input with items in storage, cortical-subcortical interaction to elicit or prevent orientation, and apparent subsequent elaboration of input into perception, the possibilities for malfunction in psychopathological states are legion. Therefore it is feasible to do no more than suggest directions in which further investigation can reasonably be pursued.

MECHANISMS, THEORIES, AND MODELS OF ORIENTATION

The Orienting Reflex: Introduction

The orienting reflex (OR) may be regarded as part of a generalized response system that has effects on learning and perceptual processes. Other forms of response that are elicited by stimuli, and that must be compared to the OR, are the adaptive and defensive reflexes (Sokolov, 1963). The "OR is a system of unconditioned, motor, autonomic and central responses elicited by any change in stimulation independent of stimulus quality [Graham & Clifton, 1966 p. 306]." At first presentation, heat or cold evokes an OR, but on repeated presentation it evokes a characteristic adaptive reaction with, for instance, vasodilation or vasoconstriction of peripheral blood vessels serving an appropriate function in maintaining the equilibrium of the organism.

The OR may be distinguished from the defensive reflex by certain evidence:

"(a) An OR is elicited by stimuli of low or moderate intensity while defense responses occur when the stimulus intensity is relatively high.

(b) With the OR there should be associated reciprocal responses of peripheral vasoconstriction and cephalic vasodilation. With the defense response there are concomitant responses of constriction in both head and periphery.

(c) An OR has the same response pattern to both onset and offset of a stimulus since both are changes in stimulation. This is not true of either defense or adaptation responses.

(d) Unlike adaptation and defense responses, which tend to be intensified by stimulus repetition, the OR diminishes rapidly (habituates) when a stimulus is repeated [Graham & Clifton, 1966, p. 306]."

Davis (1957) also provides data for distinguishing several patterns of autonomic response to stimuli. His P response pattern would seem to have the same characteristics as the OR, and his C and N response patterns to have characteristics similar to the adaptive reactions outlined above.

The Orienting Reflex and Heart Rate Change as a "Gating" Phenomenon

Sokolov (1963) provides evidence to suggest that autonomic activity occurring as part of the orienting reflex plays a part in the control of receptor sensitivity. In general it can be said that increased sympathetic activity which is accompanied by increased cortical activation is part of the OR. A possible exception to this overall position involves the role of heart rate (HR) and blood pressure. Although there is an implication in the Russian literature that HR acceleration is part of the OR, the work of the Laceys (e.g., as summarized in Lacey, 1967) suggests that HR deceleration is more correctly an aspect of the OR and is instrumental in bringing about enhanced attention to the environment. Heart rate acceleration, however, it is suggested, facilitates rejection of the environment.

This differentiation of the functions of HR increase and decrease had been recognized much earlier by Darrow (1929) in distinguishing "sensory" from "ideational" responses. Darrow, in turn, referred to the work of Lehmann in 1899, who described a quickening of the pulse during the concentration of attention and a slowing of the pulse after sudden sensory stimuli, and also mentioned the work of Zoneff and Meumann, who in 1902 showed "a tendency for all pleasant stimuli, whether ideational or sensory, to retard, and for all unpleasant stimuli to accelerate the pulse [pp. 186–187]." This introduction of the "feeling tone" elicited by the stimuli is a source of some confusion but appears to have been resolved by Edwards and Alsip (1969a), who show a HR deceleration to both pleasant and unpleasant pictures, and in line with the general position that HR acceleration involves rejection of the environment demonstrate HR increases on the presentation of tasks requiring manipulation of data.

A further factor that it is necessary to bear in mind is that HR changes *per se* are not sufficient correlates of perceptual sensitivity. Edwards and Alsip (1969b) showed that stimuli presented in periods of naturally occurring low and high HR were not differentially detected. The authors suggested that greater "elicited" changes may be required to show the gating effect.

The position of "heart rate change as a component of the orienting response [p. 305]" is extensively reviewed by Graham and Clifton (1966). One of the main considerations which they discuss in attempting to unravel the findings in the literature is the division of responses into "phasic" and "tonic," following Sharpless and Jasper (1956). The latter authors have stated that the phasic response is of short duration and appears with short latency; it habituates slowly and appears to be controlled by the diffuse thalamic portion of the reticular formation. In contrast, the tonic response has longer duration, habituates rapidly, and is controlled by the brain-stem reticular formation. Data reviewed by Graham and Clifton (1966) suggest that the acceleration phase of the HR response may be the phasic aspect of response, while the deceleratory phase has the characteristics of the tonic response. Thus the phasic aspects might be considered defensive, whereas the tonic aspect is orienting. They conclude that when "studies using simple nonsignal stimuli were examined in the light of Sokolov's criteria for identifying an OR, strong evidence was found that *HR deceleration is a major component of orientation* [p. 316]." The Laceys' hypothesis of HR acceleration as a response involved when the organism rejects the environment was considered to be akin to the defensive reflex described by Sokolov as "limiting" stimulus action, having, in other words, a negative feedback function with intense stimuli. Graham and Clifton (1966) conclude by suggesting that the data which they review show that "autonomic changes are important in the control of sensitivity to stimulation," and that "change in HR may be a particularly useful response in psychological investigations [p. 317]."

Although later work has been in agreement with the Laceys' position, some studies have produced conflicting results. The presence of verbalization has been shown to be of importance in the direction of HR change. If the task requires that the subject make a verbal response to the stimuli display, then even displays requiring maximum "intake" tend to produce an HR acceleration; if, however, the same display does not require a verbal response, HR deceleration is observed (Campos & Johnson, 1967). It seems likely that the respiratory changes required in anticipation of a verbal response may be responsible for the substitution of HR acceleration for deceleration (Clynes, 1960; Obrist, Wood, & Perez-Reyes, 1965; Wood & Obrist, 1964.

The Orienting Reflex and Skin Conductance Response as Indices of "Registration"

The emphasis in these studies has been on the heart rate component of the OR, which has, it is suggested, a "gating" function in permitting the intake of environmental stimuli or in causing its rejection. The skin conductance response (SCR) as an accompaniment of the HR change has not, in this context, received the same amount of attention, although Lacey (1959), following work by Darrow, Jost, Solomon, and Mergener (1942), suggested that "skin conductance increase is excitatory, whereas increase in cardiac rate is inhibitory of this simple transaction of the organism with the environment [p. 205]." Some work (e.g., Darrow, 1933; Edelberg, 1961; Martin & Edelberg, 1963) has suggested that the SCR has the function of increasing tactile sensitivity. This may be a rather peripheral and relatively minor aspect, however, and the real importance of the SCR may be that it is an index of subcortical activity.

The work by Pribram and his colleagues (Bagshaw & Benzies, 1968; Bagshaw, Kimble, & Pribram, 1965; Kimble, Bagshaw, & Pribram, 1965; Koepke & Pribram, 1966) provides evidence for this point of view and for the importance of the SCR as a component in the Sokolov model of the orienting reflex. In distinction to the gating function of HR, Pribram and his colleagues emphasize that the SCR—that is, the GSR (galvanic skin response)—appears to indicate registration of signals in the "neuronal store." They state:

"We had assumed the GSR and behavioral indices of orienting and habituation to run parallel. Our data make this unlikely. An alternative suggestion is that the GSR component of the orienting reaction signifies some process other than orienting. Tentatively the hypothesis may be entertained that the GSR is involved not in the production of orienting (or 'attention') directly, but in its *registration*. Only when such registration has occurred can the nervous system perform its normal 'tuning' or 'coding' function and so allow the representations or neuronal models of experienced inputs to accrue [Bagshaw et al., 1965, p. 118]."

This statement is the result of consideration of a study of skin conductance responding in groups of monkeys with ablation of the amygdala, hippocampus, or inferotemporal cortex. Only amygdalectomy produced a decreased skin conductance responsivity to the tone stimuli used. This result was unexpected in view of the well-established finding of high behavioral orienting and lack of habituation in most work on amygdalectomy (Goddard, 1964b) and, previously, after ablations of the temporal lobe (Klüver & Bucy, 1939). Thus Bagshaw and her colleagues (1965) suggest that a lack of behavioral habituation following amygdalectomy could be explained by the animal responding to every stimulus as if it were novel. It could appear as novel if previous presentation of the identical stimulus were not "registered" and there was no build-up of a neuronal model. Further work by Bagshaw and Benzies (1968) provides additional support for this position by examining it more directly and showing that, although amygdalectomy produces failure to demonstrate the SCR, HR, and respiratory rate components of the OR, EEG activation and ear-movement-orienting responses remain substantially intact.

The role of the amygdala in producing skin potential responses (close equivalents of SCR's: Martin & Venables, 1966) has been shown by Lang, Juovinen, and Vallsala (1964). These workers investigated the effect of stimulation of the amygdala and showed that weak stimuli produced a phasic response, whereas more intense stimuli, provoking after discharge of the amygdala, brought about a tonic response. They suggest that the brainstem reticular formation is a necessary transmitting structure in the elicitation of electrodermal activity from the amygdala. The role of the SCR as an indicator of "registration" and its association with the function of the amygdala have close but not identical parallels in the result of a study by Goddard (1964a), where low-intensity stimulation of the amygdala "acting as a functional lesion by scrambling the otherwise orderly traffic of impulses [p. 28]" was said to "disrupt the consolidation of the association of a stimulus with a noxious event [p. 23]."

The Role of Spontaneous Fluctuations

The relation between orientation, registration, and spontaneous fluctuations in skin conductance, introduced by Kimble et al. (1965) and Koepke and Pribram (1966), is not capable of easy interpretation. Kimble and his colleagues (1965) show that bilateral lesions in the lateral frontal cortex depress the SCR component of the orienting response; they note also that their unoperated groups of animals include those that can be classed as "stabile" (i.e., giving few spontaneous SCRs) and "labile" (i.e., giving many spontanous SCRs). They show that, although the "habituated" parts of the SCR records were similar for the stabile normal and the lateral frontal animals, the stabile animals oriented to a novel stimuli whereas the lateral frontal animals did not. It can be suggested, therefore, that the process of SCR orientation as such and the process of habituation (pre-sumably brought about by the process of successful registration of stimuli) can be considered separately.

In a study of SCR orientation Koepke and Pribram (1966) show that, in man also, labile subjects habituate less readily than stabile ones; although continuing to advance the suggestion presented above, that the SCR indi-cates registration, these workers also suggest that "the orienting reaction could be considered one type of attention response in that it prepares and focuses the organism for optimal perception. This should facilitate percep-tion of both the stimulus complex which aroused the orienting reaction and whatever situational change might follow [p. 447]." Thus orienting should be important in classical conditioning, and there is accord with the findings reported by Martin (1960) and Stern, Stewart, and Winokur (1961) that show better classical conditioning in labile subjects. Although Koepke and Pribram are discussing at this point the orientation reaction as a whole, they are doing so in the context of a study of GSR responding, and it is worth emphasizing here the proposition that it may be the HR change that indicates the "gating" response, while the SCR in Pribram's work, if correct, indicates registration.

The position is clearly not simple; a more indirect argument appears to be required to give a satisfactory explanation of the findings. One possibility is that spontaneous, non-stimulus-related SCRs are in a different class from stimulus-induced SCRs in the same way as spontaneous blocking or cortical rhythms may not be related to performance in the manner that induced responses are (Lansing, Schwartz, & Lindsley, 1959). The suggestion would be that an increase in spontaneous SCRs indicates only an increased general nervous system excitability or "arousal" (Silverman, Cohen, & Shmavonian, 1959). On the other hand, spontaneous SCRs might be thought of as indicating the operation of a cortical-subcortical regulatory system having the function of maintenance of *optimal* cortical excitation (Venables, 1967). Both these proposals suggest that spontaneous SCRs indicate something other than the operation of a registration of a stimulus in a neuronal model or long-term memory store.

A further, possibly more tendentious argument would suggest that spon-taneous SCRs do indeed indicate registration of stimuli but that, if these SCRs are not induced by a relevant external stimulus, they will involve the registration of what are strictly irrelevant or interfering stimuli. This will prevent the build-up of an uncontaminated trace in the store and hence will maintain the process of orientation by what are effectively "old" stimuli appearing "novel" in comparison to a model which is an imperfect representation of the "old" stimulus configuration.

Memory, Registration, Skin Conductance Responses, and Arousal

Another group of studies that has affinities with those just discussed, particularly in relation to the SCR as an index of registration, is concerned with the relation between arousal and consolidation of the memory trace (e.g., Batten, 1967; Berlyne, Borsa, Hamacher, & Koenig, 1966; Kleinsmith & Kaplan, 1963, 1964; MacLean, 1969; Walker & Tarte, 1963). These studies show in general that, if the subject exhibits "a state of high arousal" when material is presented for subsequent recall, the material appears to be less available to immediate memory (two minutes after presentation) than material presented under low-arousal conditions. On the other hand, under conditions of later recall (e.g., one hour or more) material presented under high-arousal conditions is recalled more effectively, whereas low-arousal material appears to have undergone a process of rapid deterioration.

One theory advanced to explain these findings involves the mechanism of reverberating neural circuits to suggest the relation between arousal and consolidation:

"Under conditions of low arousal, relatively little nonspecific neural activity will be available to support the reverberating trace, resulting in little consolidation and poor long-term retention. On the other hand, under conditions of high arousal the increased nonspecific neural activity will result in more reverberation, and thus retention should be better.

While reverberation is taking place, however, one might expect the trace to be relatively unavailable to the organism,* resulting in poor recall of the consolidating material during this interval [Kleinsmith & Kaplan, 1963, p. 190]."

This theory, originating from a suggestion by Walker (1958), thus provides not only for the better retention, but also for the immediate unavailability, of high-arousal items. Earlier, in describing these studies the words "a state of high arousal" were placed in parentheses. This was done not only because at this time it seems no longer correct to talk in an unqualified way about "arousal," but also because in these studies the use of the term arousal was rather specific. In their 1963 study Kleinsmith and Kaplan used paired-associate word-number pairs where the nature of the words used could be thought of as generating the high arousal and as

---

* Dr. Kaplan's current theoretical position is that the relative unavailability is a result of reverberation-generated neural fatigue rather than of reverberation *per se*. A statement of this position is to be found in Pomerantz, Kaplan, and Kaplan (1969).

being possibly memorable for other than the reasons suggested by the theory. In their next study, however, the same pattern of results was achieved with the use of nonsense syllable-number pairs, and the skin conductance changes occurring on presentation were used to define high- and low-arousal items. In Berlyne's studies (e.g., Berlyne et al., 1966) arousal during presentation was achieved by the use of white noise, and in MacLean's (1969) work the effectiveness of this technique in producing arousal was checked by concomitant SCR recording.

In some ways, therefore, there would seem to be parallels between these studies and those on orienting, where a stimulus typically produces a SCR response. In the former a high "arousal" response indicated by a large SCR is taken to parallel a high degree of reverberation in the "neural circuits" involved in the *consolidation* of recent, vulnerable memory traces. On the other hand, if Pribram and his colleagues are correct, the SCR is an index of *registration*.

One of the difficulties in reconciling the two approaches stems from consideration of the timing of the processes involved, particularly the time for which the high-arousal trace appears to be inaccessible. Examination of the studies cited suggests that the superiority of high-arousal over low-arousal items in recall is achieved after a minimum time of 20 minutes. In a very relative way, therefore, the trace of the high-arousal item is inaccessible for a comparatively long time, much longer indeed than the interstimulus interval of around one minute used in a number of experiments on orienting. A simple view that would identify Pribram's "registration" process with the "reverberation increasing" process of Kleinsmith and Kaplan would not appear tenable, as on this basis habituation would appear to be possible only if stimuli were presented with long intervals between them.

An experiment by Berlyne and Carey (1968) provides a possibility of solution. In this study the paired associates were Turkish (S) and English (R) words. White noise was coupled either with the presentation of the S word for two seconds or with the presentation of the S + R items together for two seconds, or for four seconds over the S and S + R presentation. Superiority of recall one day later was shown for both the two-second S and the two-second S + R white noise presentation over the four-second S and S + R presentation. These conditions involved, respectively, "termination and onset of white noise at the precise moment when the response term was revealed [Berlyne & Carey, 1968, p. 104]." Thus it is possible that, when the timing of incidental stimuli is such as to produce a phasic arousal response optimally placed in relation to the stimulus to be learned, there may not be subsequent inaccessibility of the trace. This view is supported by a statement by Berlyne and Carey: "It does not seem that higher arousal during learning invariably makes for better long-term recall but worse short-term recall. . . . It seems, rather, that there is an optimal, intermediate degree of arousal for learning."

Orientation and Memory

A further point of interdigitation between orientation and memory experiments is centered around the methods employed in the latter. In the majority of studies items were presented without the subject being specifically instructed to remember them; in this instance learning may be denoted as incidental. It is in these circumstances that the effect of item-accompanying arousal is most evident. When instructions are given, the effect of the accompanying "arousal" response is either absent or weak. Possibly the reason why the arousal effect is clearly shown only in the incidental learning situation is that it is only in this condition that the subject may or may not orient to the stimulus, and hence registration signaled by the SCR may be involved. In the intentional learning case the registration of stimuli may be programmed by other cortical events, and peripheral signaling by SCRs may be epiphenomenal.

The Role of the Hippocampus

It would be inappropriate to conclude an examination of work on orientation without referring to studies on the role of the hippocampus, particularly as Douglas (1967) has pointed out that this structure is ultrasensitive to many factors which influence brain functioning and Mednick (Chapter 18 of this book) has implicated hippocampal damage as a contributing factor in the development of schizophrenia. Studies on hippocampal lesions in man (e.g., Penfield & Milner, 1958) typically report anterograde amnesia. Work on animals, however, suggests, not a learning deficit, but rather an inability to show normal behavioral variability following hippocampal lesions (Douglas, 1967; Kimble, 1968). "The behavior of rats with hippocampal lesions . . . can be interpreted as an example of behavior of organisms relatively devoid of the neural machinery necessary for the production of stimulus-induced internal inhibition and the normal decrement in response which presumably results from that internal inhibition [Kimble, 1968, p. 291]." Thus hippocampal lesions may be expected to result in a deficiency of habituation of the orienting response to novel stimuli (Leaton, 1965). Hendrickson, Kimble, & Kimble (1969), however, point to a further interference with orienting brought about by hippocampal lesions and show that "orienting was absent or deficient when either a motivationally relevant stimulus or a novel neutral stimulus had previously captured the attention of hippocampally lesioned rats [p. 225]."

Thus the hippocampus appears to play a critical role in shifting attention.

The involvement of this structure in attentional processes is the subject of two slightly different interpretations. Kimble (Hendrickson et al., 1969) suggests that the "neural output from this structure in response to the occurrence of novelty or mismatch may act to inhibit certain excitatory systems . . . and reduce their effectiveness, thus allowing the animal to disengage its attentional processes and facilitate an attention shift to the novel or unexpected event [p. 225]." On the other hand, in the Douglas-Pribram attentional model (Douglas, 1967; Douglas & Pribram, 1966) "the hippocampus is postulated to exclude stimulus patterns from attention through a process of efferent control of sensory reception known as gating [Douglas, 1967, p. 435]." Two forms of gating are distinguished:

1. "Non-specific gating [which] results in the . . . exclusion of irrelevent stimuli during the process of the concentration of attention."
2. "Specific gating [which] acts to inhibit reception of specific stimuli . . . associated with nonreinforcement [pp. 435-436]."

Hendrickson et al. (1969) suggest that the gating hypothesis is untenable because it would suggest that hippocampally lesioned animals would be more distractible, whereas their experiments indicate the reverse. In spite of these differences in interpretation, there is agreement about the inhibitory function of the hippocampus, and this is reinforced by Redding (1967), who suggests an "antagonistic interaction between the hippocampus and the brain-stem reticular formation [p. 81]." This antagonistic interaction "is partially opposed by a facilitatory effect on the nonspecific thalamic systems [p. 82]." Hence it may be said "that the hippocampal stimulation alters in different ways the tonic and the phasic components of the arousal mechanism [p. 82]." The hippocampus may thus be involved in the heart rate component of the orienting response. If HR deceleration is the tonic component of the response, it should habituate more readily by inhibitory action of the hippocampus, while the accelerative component should, as the phasic component, be augmented. Graham and Clifton (1966) review evidence which suggests that this is the case.

Both Douglas (1967) and Kimble (1968) suggest that the hippocampus may have a role in the consolidation of memory. Thus Douglas suggests that that nonspecific gating has the function of protecting memory traces from interference. Kimble, employing the suggestion of the inhibitory role of the hippocampus, more directly invokes the "action decrement" theory of Walker (1958), mentioned earlier in connection with the work of Kleinsmith and Kaplan (1963). Walker suggests that the lowered capacity for rearousal following stimulation protects the perseverative consolidation process responsible for rendering memory traces permanent. The lowered capacity for rearousal spoken of here may be identified with the development of internal inhibition, which is the function of the hippocampus. It is this process that Douglas and Kimble suggest is involved in the memory defects shown as a consequence of hippocampal damage to man. Memory loss as a by-product of interference in human, but not in animal, studies may be explained as a function of the limitations of the testing situation with animals, while man with the presence of language has the possibility of generating many incorrect and interfering responses.

An Attempt at Synthesis

The integration of this analysis with that of the work on memory consolidation and arousal reviewed earlier is not wholly direct. Kleinsmith and Kaplan (1963), for instance, suggest that the better retention of items accompanied by an SCR occurs because the 'arousal' indicated by this response is productive of more reverberation. This increased reverberation brings in its train the action decrement or internal inhibition which is responsible for protection of the reverberation.

Douglas (1967) suggests that the "amygdaloid system makes stimuli more figural, while the hippocampal system converts figure into ground [p. 436]." We may interpret this in the present context as suggesting that the SCR in animals having an intact amygdala allows a stimulus to be registered as a "figure," while the intact hippocampus allows inhibition to develop to protect this process and turn the "figure into ground" as far as immediate recall processes are concerned. It is worth noting in this context that, although Bagshaw et al. (1965) showed that amygdalectomy produced an elimination of SCRs, hippocampal lesions had no effect on skin conductance responding.

No discussion was introduced earlier to outline the mechanism by which HR changes might produce the gating function described by Lacey (1967). Lacey has suggested that HR decreases bring about a decrease in blood pressure; this lowers the pressure on the carotid sinus receptors, thus bringing about in *increase* in cortical activation. The work of Bonvallet, Dell, and Hiebel (1954) is cited in support of this position. Work by Obrist (1963) showing lack of blood pressure changes accompanying "open" and "closed" gating behavior suggests, however, that the mechanism suggested by Lacey may not be relevant. Further doubt must also be felt in that arousal of the cortex would not *necessarily* be thought of as a preprequisite for intake of information, and the converse for internal manipulation of that information. Possible alternative mechanisms may be suggested that have the advantage of greater integration with the work described so far.

Under various experimental conditions the hippocampus displays a characteristic theta rhythm of 4–7 Hz (Green & Arduini, 1954). In reporting experimental studies of orienting behavior in relation to the presence of this theta rhythm, Grastyán, Karmos, Vereczkey, and Kellényi (1966) report that the "tonic orientation reaction was regularly accompanied by marked and continuous hippocampal theta activity," and furthermore that "the conclusion seemed warranted that in the presence of theta activity the hippocampus was in a predominantly inactive state [p. 48]." In the presence of theta activity, therefore, the inhibitory effect exerted by the hippocampus on the reticular formation is decreased and cortical arousal may result. The septal area appears to be of crucial importance in pacing the hippo-campal theta rhythm and may be considered as a convergent area for a variety of sensory input systems (Votaw, 1960). A number of studies (e.g., Bromley & Holdstock, 1969; Malmo, 1961) show that septal stimula-tion results in HR deceleration. It seems possible, therefore, that HR deceleration accompanies cortical desynchrony, as required by Lacey (1967), but that HR deceleration may be an epiphenomenon rather than a critical part of a visceral-cortical link and may be an accompaniment of a more critical limbic system gating-registration process. However, insofar as most physiological interactions are overdetermined and involve interlocking redundant pathways, the operation of the carotid-sinus cortical control system should not be dismissed.

PSYCHOPATHOLOGICAL IMPLICATIONS

The point of departure for the work reviewed above is the recognition that to consider at least some aspects of mental disease as disorders of attentional processes was not unreasonable. This might apply particularly in the case of schizophrenia (e.g., McGhie, 1969; Silverman, 1967; Venables, 1964). In suggesting an affinity between work on attention and work on orientation, the extent of reference to psychopathology has been widened in two main directions. First, it is worth while to examine studies on orientation in patient groups; second, insofar as the work reviewed has suggested the involvement of limbic structures in orientation, registration, consolidation, and selective gating, an examination of the possible role of these structures in disease processes is required. In view of the necessity to restrict the scope of this part of the chapter, attention will be directed to work on schizophrenia.

Orientation and Attention in Schizophrenia

Clinical reports such as those of McGhie and Chapman (1961) suggest that in the acute phase the schizophrenic is constantly aware of a wide range of stimuli other than those which should strictly be in the forefront of his attention, and that orientation to these "irrelevant" stimuli does not appear to habituate and forms an impairment to efficient performance.

This feature is inherent in the ideas of Shakow (1962) on "segmental set" and "inability to maintain a set to respond," and it is clearly evident in the findings of Callaway, Jones, and Layne (1965), who showed that in schizophrenics there was maintenance of a difference between the evoked responses to tones where the difference carried no information. The work of Milstein, Stevens, and Sachdev also (1969) provides some supporting evidence. They showed that the EEG alpha response to photic stimuli had a shorter latency and persisted longer in acute schizophrenics than in chronic patients and controls. In chronic patients the latency of alpha blocking was apparently greater than that in controls. A study by Hein, Green, and Wilson (1962), however, found no difference in alpha-blocking latency between chronic patients and controls, while work by Cromwell and Held (1969) on schizophrenic patients, whose chronicity status was uncertain as they had a mean hospital stay of 19 months, showed a shorter alpha-blocking latency than normal controls.

Zahn, Rosenthal, and Lawlor (1968) described work on the skin conductance and heart rate response to a 72-db tone and a faint light. Their patient group consisted of chronic schizophrenics. It was shown that these patients showed a higher skin conductance responsivity, which habituated less quickly than that of normal controls. When the performance of sub-diagnostic categories of patients within the total group was examined separately, it was found that responsivity was highest in paranoid patients and lower than normal among hebephrenics. There was no significant difference in habituation rate among subgroups of patients. The HR response showed a larger acceleration in patients than in normal individuals, and the rate of habituation was not significantly different between the two groups. The conjunction of HR acceleration with SCR is suggestive of an "environmental rejection" or "closed gate" type of response (Lacey, 1967).

This finding is in accord with data from Dykman et al. (1968), who examined skin resistance, heart rate, respiration rate, and muscle action potential responses to a series of tones in a patient group and were able to compare the results to findings from a similar type of study on student subjects. These workers defined three types of response pattern: "open," with a fall in resistance of more than 800 ohms and a HR deceleration; "closed," with negligible change in skin resistance; and "alerting," with skin resistance response of more than 800 ohms and a HR acceleration. It is to be noted that these patterns of response are defined in a rather different way from the usage of Lacey and other workers. All subjects exhibited a larger number of "alerting" responses than other patterns, but patients diagnosed as "nonaffect" schizophrenics showed a larger proportion of "closed" than " open" responses, the reverse of the pattern observed in the normal student subject. The schizophrenic patients who were of chronic status appeared to show a slower rate of skin resistance response habituation than the normal subjects, while their HR response habituated quickly. As the tone stimuli used were of 60-db intensity, this was a study in which an orientation response might be expected.

In contrast, in a study by Venables (1960) in which a 90-db tone and a 900-ft-lambert visual stimulus were used, and the response expected might be categorized as defensive, there was no difference in habituation rate of skin potential responses between normals and chronic schizophrenics. In contrast to the work of Zahn et al. (1968), Bernstein (1964), using a very similar situation and a population of chronic schizophrenic patients, showed a faster habituation of SCR in patients than in normals, with the most seriously ill patients showing the highest rate of habituation. No differences between the Zahn and Bernstein studies appear to account for the differences observed, except for the possibility that more of Bernstein's patients were like Zahn's hebephrenics, who seemed to be less responsive than normals.

A possibility that appears to emerge from these studies is that there is a tendency for acute and/or paranoid patients to be responsive to their environment and to show less habituation than normals, whereas the chronic or regressed patient tends to be slow in response and to show fewer and smaller responses. A 1958 study by Gamburg, quoted by Lynn (1963), is in accord with this summary: few of Gamburg's patients gave normal orientation reactions; patients diagnosed as simple schizophrenics tended to show no reaction at all, while the paranoids tended to give defensive reactions. It was also found that, when a patient gave a reaction, the autonomic disturbance continued for a longer time than normal. A much more extensive review of this field is to be found in Stern and McDonald (1965), but consideration of pertinent studies suggests little more than that a deficit in the mechanisms of orientation reviewed in this chapter appears possible. Venables (1967) suggested that some factors of dysfunction in schizophrenic performance might be explained as a partial failure of a homeostatic mechanism by which the level of cortical activity was controlled by inhibitory feedback from the reticular system. Work by MacKinnon (1969) provides experimental support for this view. Although ascending inhibition from the brain-stem reticular formation has been demonstrated by, for instance, Demetrescu and Demetrescu (1962), in the light of the present review a defect of the inhibitory function of the hippocampus might also by invoked as an explanatory mechanism of greater subtlety.

Hendrikson et al. (1969) have suggested that animals with hippocampal ablations show an inability to switch attention from one aspect of the field to another. Work by Sutton, Hakerem, Zubin, and Portnoy (1961) and Kristofferson (1967), showing that schizophrenics have more difficulty than normals in switching attention between modalities, provides an additional suggestion that a deficit of hippocampal functioning may be involved.

Schizophrenia and Hippocampal Dysfunction

Although it would be unwise and even bold to implicate the hippocampus too closely as the brain structure most closely associated with the appearance of schizophrenia, certain intriguing possibilities present themselves. The hippocampus is particularly vulnerable to disturbance (MacLean, 1968). It has been shown to be easily injured by anoxia (Spector, 1965), to readily retain corticosterone (McEwen, Weiss, & Schwartz, 1968), and hence to be capable of being disturbed by stress. High concentrations of serotonin (Paasonen, MacLean, & Giarman, 1957) and nonepinephrine (Fuxe, 1965) are found in the hippocampus, and several tranquilizing agents appear to act on hippocampal function (Killam, Killam, & Shaw, 1957; MacLean, Flanigan, Flynn, Kim, & Stevens, 1955–56). There has also been shown to be a large uptake of methionine by the hippocampus (Flanigan, Gabrieli, & MacLean, 1957), and this finding takes on particular importance in the light of work by Pollin, Cardon, and Kety (1961), who reported a worsening of symptoms when methionine was given to schizophrenics.

Finally, there are the studies reviewed, for instance, by Slater and Beard (1963) and Flor-Henry (1969), which show an association of temporal lobe epilepsy with psychosis. It is interesting to note that epilepsy in the dominant temporal lobe is associated with schizophrenia, and in the nondominant lobe with manic-depressive psychosis. If the neuronal model of Sokolov can be compared to the short-term memory process, in which storage may be in a verbal, auditory, or articulatory mode, then disturbance of the hemisphere responsible for speech would appear to bring about the greatest amount of dysfunction. Clearly there is not major structural dysfunction of the temporal lobes in all schizophrenics, but in patients with tumors involving the hippocampus symptoms that produce a disease picture undistinguishable from that of schizophrenia have been reported (e.g., by Malamud, 1967). We may thus be led to the conclusion that schizophrenia is an epiphenomenal disease which may (at least in some patients) be produced as a consequence of disturbance of function of the temporal lobes by a wide variety of causes.

REFERENCES

Bagshaw, M. H., & Benzies, S. Multiple measures of the orienting reaction and their dissociation after amygdalectomy in monkeys. *Experimental Neurology,* 1968, **20,** 175–187.

Bagshaw, M. H., Kimble, D. P., & Pribram, K. H. The GSR of monkeys during orienting and habituation and after ablation of the amygdala, hippocampus and infrotemporal cortex. *Neuropsychologia,* 1965, **3,** 111–119.

Batten, D. E. Recall of paired associates as a function of arousal and recall interval. *Perceptual and Motor Skills,* 1967, **24,** 1055–1058.

Berlyne, D. E., Borsa, A., Hamacher, J., & Koenig, I. D. V. Paired associate learning and the timing of arousal. *Journal of Experimental Psychology,* 1966, **72,** 1–6.

Berlyne, D. E., & Carey, S. T. Incidental learning and the timing of arousal. *Psychonomic Science,* 1968, **13,** 103–104.

Bernstein, A. S. The galvanic skin response orienting reflex among chronic schizophrenics. *Psychonomic Science,* 1964, **1,** 391–392.

Bonvallet, M., Dell, P., & Hiebel, G. Tonus sympathique et activité électrique corticale. *Electroencephalography and Clinical Neurophysiology,* 1954, **6,** 119–144.

Broadbent, D. E. *Perception and communication.* New York: Pergamon Press, 1958.

Bromley, D. V., & Holdstock, T. L. Effects of septal stimulation on heart rate in vagatomized rats. *Physiology and Behavior,* 1969, **4,** 399–401.

Callaway, E., Jones, R. T., & Layne, R. S. Evoked responses and segmental set of schizophrenia. *Archives of General Psychiatry,* 1965, **12,** 83–89.

Callaway, E., & Stone, G. Re-evaluating the focus of attention. In L. Uhr & J. G. Miller (Eds.), *Drugs and behavior.* New York: Wiley,1960. Pp. 393–398.

Campos, J. J., & Johnson, H. T. Affect, verbalization and directional fractionation of autonomic responses. *Psychophysiology,* 1967, **3,** 285–290.

Clynes, M. Computer analysis of reflex control and organization: Respiratory sinus arrhythmia. *Science,* 1960, **131,** 300–302.

Cromwell, R. L., & Held, J. M. Alpha blocking latency and reaction time in schizophrenics and normals. *Perceptual and Motor Skills,* 1969, **29,** 195–201.

Darrow, C. W. Differences in the physiological reactions to sensory and ideational stimuli. *Psychological Bulletin,* 1929, **26,** 185–200.

Darrow, C. W. The functional significance of the galvanic skin reflex and perspiration on the backs and palms of the hands. *Psychological Bulletin,* 1933, **30,** 712.

Darrow, C. W., Jost, H., Solomon, A. P., & Mergener, J. C. Autonomic indications of excitatory and homeostatic effects on the electroencephalogram. *Journal of Psychology,* 1942, **14,** 115–130.

Davis, R. C. Response patterns. *Transactions of the New York Academy of Sciences,* 1957, **19,** 721–739.

Demetrescu, M., & Demetrescu, M. Ascending inhibition and activation from the lower brain stem: The influence of pontine reticular stimulation on thalamocortical evoked potentials in cat. *Electroencephalography and Clinical Neurophysiology,* 1962, **14,** 602–620.

Douglas, R. J. The hippocampus and behavior. *Psychological Bulletin,* 1967, **67,** 416–442.

Douglas, R. J., & Pribram, K. H. Learning and limbic lesions. *Neuropsychologia*, 1966, **4**, 197–200.

Dykman, R. A., Reese, W. G., Galbrecht, C. R., Ackerman, P. T., & Sunderman, R. S. Autonomic responses in psychiatric patients. *Annals of the New York Academy of Sciences*, 1968, **147**, 237–303.

Edelberg, R. The relationship between the galvanic skin response, vasoconstriction and tactile sensitivity. *Journal of Experimental Psychology*, 1961, **62**, 187–195.

Edwards, D. C., & Alsip, J. E. Intake-rejection, verbalization, and affect: Effects on heart rate and skin conductance. *Psychophysiology*, 1969, **6**, 6–12. (a)

Edwards, D. C., & Alsip, J. E. Stimulus detection during periods of high and low heart rate. *Psychophysiology*, 1969, **5**, 431–434. (b)

Egeth, H. Selective attention. *Psychological Bulletin*, 1967, **67**, 41–57.

Flanigan, S., Gabrieli, E. R., & MacLean, P. P. Cerebral changes revealed by radioantography with S^{35}-labeled 1-methionine. *Archives of Neurology and Psychiatry*, 1957, **77**, 588–594.

Flor-Henry, P. Psychosis and temporal lobe epilepsy: A controlled investigation. *Epilepsia*, 1969, **10**, 363–395.

Fuxe, K. Evidence for the existence of monoamine neurons in the central nervous system. IV. Distribution of monoamine nerve terminals in the central nervous system. *Acta Physiologica Scandinavica*, 1965, **64**, 37–84.

Goddard, G. V. Amygdaloid stimulation and learning in the rat. *Journal of Comparative and Physiological Psychology*, 1964, **58**, 23–30. (a)

Goddard, G. V. Functions of the amygdala. *Psychological Bulletin*, 1964, **62**, 89–109. (b)

Graham, F. K., & Clifton, R. K. Heart rate change as a component of the orienting response. *Psychological Bulletin*, 1966, **65**, 305–320.

Grastyán, E., Karmos, G., Vereczkey, L., & Kellényi, E. E. The hippocampal electrical correlates of the homeostatic regulation of motivation. *Electroencephalography and Clinical Neurophysiology*, 1966, **21**, 34–53.

Green, J. D., & Arduini, A. A. Hippocampal electrical activity in arousal. *Journal of Neurophysiology*, 1954, **17**, 533–557.

Hein, P. L., Green, R. L., & Wilson, W. P. Latency and duration of photically elicited arousal responses in the electroencephalograms of patients with chronic regressive schizophrenia. *Journal of Nervous and Mental Disease*, 1962, **135**, 361–364.

Hendrickson, C. W., Kimble, R. J., & Kimble, D. P. Hippocampal lesions and the orienting response. *Journal of Comparative and Physiological Psychology*, 1969, **67**, 220–227.

Hull, C. L. *Principles of behavior*. New York: Appleton-Century-Crofts, 1943.

Jasper, H. H. Recent advances in our understanding of the ascending activities of the reticular system. In H. H. Jasper, L. D. Proctor, R. S. Knighton, W. C. Noshay, & R. T. Costello (Eds.), *Reticular formation of the brain*. Boston: Little, Brown, 1958. Pp. 319–331.

Killam, E. K., Killam, K. F., & Shaw, T. The effects of psychotherapeutic compounds on central afferent and limbic pathways. *Annals of the New York Academy of Sciences*, 1957, **64**, 784–805.

Kimble, D. P. Hippocampus and internal inhibition. *Psychological Bulletin*, 1968, **70**, 285–295.

Kimble, D. P., Bagshaw, M. H., & Pribram, K. H. The GSR of monkeys during orienting and habituation after selective partial ablations of the cingulate and frontal cortex. *Neuropsychologia*, 1965, **3**, 121–128.

Kleinsmith, L. J., & Kaplan, S. Paired associate learning as a function of arousal and interpolated interval. *Journal of Experimental Psychology*, 1963, **65**, 190–193.

Kleinsmith, L. J., & Kaplan, S. Interaction of arousal and recall interval in nonsense syllable paired-associate learning. *Journal of Experimental Psychology*, 1964, **67**, 124–126.

Klüver, H., & Bucy, P. C. Preliminary analysis of the functions of the temporal lobes in monkeys. *Archives of Neurology and Psychiatry*, 1939, **42**, 979–1000.

Koepke, J. E., & Pribram, K. H. Habituation of GSR as a function of stimulus duration and spontaneous activity. *Journal of Comparative and Physiological Psychology*, 1966, **61,**, 42–448.

Kristofferson, M. W. Shifting attention between modalities: A comparison of schizophrenics and normals. *Journal of Abnormal Psychology*, 1967, **72**, 388–394.

Lacey, J. I. Psychophysiological approaches to the evaluation of psychotherapeutic process and outcome. In E. A. Rubenstein & M. B. Parloff (Eds.), *Research in psychotherapy.* Washington: National Publishing, 1959. Pp. 160–208.

Lacey, J. I. Somatic response patterning and stress: Some revisions of activation theory. In M. H. Appley & R. Trumbull (Eds.), *Psychological stress.* New York: Appleton-Century-Crofts, 1967. Pp. 14–37.

Lacey, J. I., Kagan, J., Lacey, B. C., & Moss, H. A. The visceral level: Situational determinants and behavioral correlates of autonomic response patterns. In P. H. Knapp (Ed.), *Expression of the emotions in man.* New York: International Universities, 1963. Pp. 161–196.

Lang, H., Juovinen, T., & Vallsala, P. Amygdaloid after discharge and galvanic skin response. *Electroencephalography and Clinical Neurophysiology*, 1964, **16**, 366–374.

Lansing, R. W., Schwartz, E., & Lindsley, D. B. Reaction time and EEG activation under alerted and non-alerted conditions. *Journal of Experimental Psychology*, 1959, **58**, 1–7.

Leaton, R. M. Exploratory behavior in rats with hippocampal lesions. *Journal of Comparative and Physiological Psychology*, 1965, **59**, 325–330.

Lovibond, S. H. Habituation of the orienting response to multiple stimulus sequences. *Psychophysiology*, 1969, **5**, 435–439.

Lynn, R. Russian theory and research in schizophrenia. *Psychological Bulletin*, 1963, **60**, 486–498.

McEwen, B. S., Weiss, J. M., & Schwartz, L. S. Selective retention of corticosterone by limbic structures in rat brain. *Nature*, 1968, **220**, 911–912.

McGhie, A. *Pathology of attention.* Harmondsworth: Penguin, 1969.

McGhie, A., & Chapman, J. Disorders of attention and perception in early schizophrenia. *British Journal of Medical Psychology*, 1961, **34**, 103–116.

MacKinnon, P. C. B. The palmar anhidrotic response to stress in schizophrenic patients and in control groups. *Journal of Psychiatric Research*, 1969, **7**, 1–8.

MacLean, P. D. Ammon's Horn: A continuing dilemma. Foreward to S. R. y Cajal. *The structure of Ammon's Horn*. Translated by L. M. Kraft, Springfield, Ill.: Charles C Thomas, 1968. Pp. v-xix.

MacLean, P. D. Induced arousal and time of recall as determinants of paired associate recall. *British Journal of Psychology*, 1969, **60**, 57–62.

MacLean, P. D., Flanigan, S., Flynn, J. P., Kim, C., & Stevens, J. R. Hippocampal functions: Tentative correlations of conditioning, EEG, drug and radioautographic studies. *Yale Journal of Biology and Medicine*, 1955–56, **28**, 380–395.

Malamud, N. Psychiatric disorders with intracranial tumors of the limbic system. *Archives of Neurology*, 1967, **17**, 113–123.

Malmo, R. B. Slowing of heart rate after septal self-stimulation in rats. *Science*, 1961, **133**, 1128–1130.

Martin, I. Variations in skin resistance and their relationship to GSR conditioning. *Journal of Mental Science*, 1960, **106**, 281–287.

Martin, I., & Venables, P. H. Mechanisms of palmar skin resistance and skin potential. *Psychological Bulletin*, 1966, **65**, 347–357.

Martin, R. D., & Edelberg, R. The relationship of skin resistance changes to receptivity. *Journal of Psychosomatic Research*, 1963, **7**, 173–179.

Milstein, V., Stevens, J., & Sachdev, K. Habituation of the alpha attenuation response in children and adults with psychiatric disorders. *Electroencephalography and Clinical Neurophysiology*, 1969, **26**, 12–18.

Moray, N. Attention in dichotic listening: Affective cues and the influence of instructions. *Quarterly Journal of Experimental Psychology*, 1959, **9**, 56–60.

Norman, D. A. Toward a theory of memory and attention. *Psychological Review*, 1968, **75**, 522–536.

Obrist, P. A. Cardiovascular differentiation of sensory stimuli. *Psychosomatic Medicine*, 1963, **25**, 450–458.

Obrist, P. A., Wood, D. M., & Perez-Reyes, M. Heart rate during conditioning in humans: Effects of UCS intensity, vagal blockade, and adrenergic block of vasomotor activity. *Journal of Experimental Psychology*, 1965, **70**, 32–42.

Paasonen, M. K., MacLean, P. D., & Giarman, N. J. 5-Hydroxytryptamine (serotonin, enteramine) content of structures of the limbic system. *Journal of Neurochemistry*, 1957, **1**, 326–333.

Pavlov, I. P. *Conditioned reflexes, an investigation of the physiological activity of the cerebral cortex*. Translated and edited by G. V. Anrep. London: Oxford University Press, 1927.

Penfield, W., & Milner, B. Memory deficit produced by bilateral lesions in the hippocampal zone. *Archives of Neurology and Psychiatry,* 1958, **79,** 475–497.

Pollin, W., Cardon, P. V., & Kety, S. S. Effect of amino acid feedings in schizophrenic patients treated with iproniazid. *Science,* 1961, **133,** 104–105.

Pomerantz, J. R., Kaplan, S., & Kaplan, R. Satiation effects in the perception of single letters. *Perception and Psychophysics,* 1969, **6,** 129–132.

Redding, F. K. Modification of sensory cortical evoked potentials by hippocampal stimulation. *Electroencephalography and Clinical Neurophysiology,* 1967, **22,** 74–83.

Shakow, D. Segmental set: A theory of the formal deficit in schizophrenia. *Archives of General Psychiatry,* 1962, **6,** 1–17.

Sharpless, S., & Jasper, H. Habituation of the arousal reaction. *Brain,* 1956, **79,** 655–680.

Silverman, A. J., Cohen, S. I., & Shmavonian, B. M. Investigation of psychophysiologic relationships with skin resistance measures. *Journal of Psychosomatic Research,* 1959, **4,** 65–87.

Silverman, J. Variations in cognitive control and psychophysiological defense in the schizophrenias. *Psychosomatic Medicine,* 1967, **29,** 225–251.

Slater, E., & Beard, A. W. The schizophrenia-like psychoses of epilepsy. 1. Psychiatric aspects. *British Journal of Psychiatry,* 1963, **109,** 95–150.

Sokolov, E. N. Neuronal models and the orienting reflex. In M. A. B. Brazier (Ed.), *The central nervous system and behavior.* New York: Josiah Macy, Jr., Foundation, 1960. Pp. 187–276.

Sokolov, E. N. *Perception and the conditioned reflex.* New York: Macmillan, 1963.

Spector, R. G. Enzyme chemistry of anoxic brain injury. In C. W. M. Adams (Ed.), *Neurohistochemistry.* New York: Elsevier, 1965. Pp. 547–557.

Stern, J. A., & McDonald, D. G. Physiological correlates of mental disease. *Annual Review of Psychology,* 1965, **16,** 225–264.

Stern, J. A., Stewart, M. A., & Winokur, G. An investigation of some relationships between various measures of galvanic skin response. *Journal of Psychosomatic Research,* 1961, **5,** 215–223.

Sutton, S., Hakerem, G., Zubin, J., & Portnoy, M. The effect of shift of sensory modality on serial reaction time: A comparison of schizophrenics and normals. *American Journal of Psychology,* 1961, **74,** 224–232.

Teichner, W. H. Interaction of behavioral and physiological stress reactions. *Psychological Review,* 1968, **75,** 271–291.

Treisman, A. M. Strategies and models of selective attention. *Psychological Review,* 1969, **76,** 282–299.

Venables, P. H. The effect of auditory and visual stimulation on the skin potential response of schizophrenics. *Brain,* 1960, **83,** 77–92.

Venables, P. H. Input dysfunction in schizophrenia. In B. Maher (Ed.), *Progress in experimental personality research.* Vol. 1. New York: Academic Press, 1964. Pp. 1–47.

Venables, P. H. Partial failure of cortical-subcortical integration as a factor underlying schizophrenic behaviour. In J. Romano (Ed.), *The origins of schizophrenia*. Amsterdam: Excerpta Medica, 1967. Pp. 42–53.

Venables, P. H. Signals, noise, refractoriness and storage: Some concepts of value to psychopathology? In M. L. Kietzman, S. Sutton, & J. Zubin (Eds.), *Experimental approaches to psychopathology*. New York: Academic Press, in press.

Votaw, C. L. Study of septal stimulation and ablation in the macaque monkey. *Neurology*, 1960, **10**, 202–209.

Walker, E. L. Action decrement and its relation to learning. *Psychological Review*, 1958, **65**, 129–142.

Walker, E. L., & Tarte, R. D. Memory storage as a function of time with homogeneous and heterogeneous lists. *Journal of Verbal Learning and Verbal Behavior*, 1963, **2**, 113–119.

Wood, D. M., & Obrist, P. A. Effects of controlled and uncontrolled respiration on the conditioned heart rate response in humans. *Journal of Experimental Psychology*, 1964, **68**, 221–229.

Zahn, T. P., Rosenthal, D., & Lawlor, W. G. Electrodermal and heart rate orienting reactions in chronic schizophrenia. *Journal of Psychiatric Research*, 1968, **6**, 117–134.

CHAPTER 15

Arousal Theory in Mental Deficiency

JOHS. CLAUSEN

Mental deficiency is a condition resulting from many different causes and may consequently involve considerable heterogeneity, with respect to both identifying characteristics and degree of impairment. It is not surprising, therefore, that the field has suffered from a lack of unifying theoretical concepts. There seems to be a general assumption that the various etiological categories have their specific behavioral characteristics, although there are very few data to support this assumption. Research in mental deficiency has largely ignored etiological classification; data from normal individuals have been compared with those from mental defectives in general, or at best with those from gross groupings such as the dichotomies organic/familial, high grade/low grade, endogenous/exogenous, or trainable/educable.*

General theoretical contributions in Ellis' *Handbook of Mental Deficiency* (1963b) included Ellis' theory of short-term memory (now in the process of revision), Spitz's Gestalt psychology theory of brain modifiability, and Zeaman's theory of attention in the discrimination learning of retardates. In recent mental deficiency literature, an increasing number of articles have discussed experimental data in terms of impairment of the arousal mechanism or in closely similar terms. Since Moruzzi and Magoun's pioneering work (1949), there has been a steady increase of interest in the ascending reticular activating system (ARAS) as a possible neurological substrate for the arousal mechanism. In a field in search of a theory it is

* The dichotomy educable/trainable is frequently used by special education teachers. The terms serve to distinguish those who are capable of some degree of achievement in academic subjects from those who are not. The dividing line between the two categories is placed at IQ of 50 (Heber, 1959).

285

not surprising that the arousal theory has been considered for mental deficiency.

Arousal in Mental Deficiency

Most authors who have discussed arousal theory have stopped short of a definition. In the present chapter "arousal" refers to the general response or response readiness of an individual, modifiable by stimulation and measurable in terms of performance level or psychophysiological activity.

Several authors have commented on the relationship between arousal and the brain-stem reticular formation. French (1960) stated:

"It now appears likely that the brain-stem reticular formation represents one of the more important integrating structures if not, indeed, the master control mechanism in the central nervous system . . . . First, it is known to be implicated in the arousal response and wakefulness. Second, it exerts a critical degree of influence over motor functions concerned in phasic and tonic muscular control. Third, the central brain stem is capable of modifying the reception, conduction, and integration of all sensory signals to the degree that some will be perceived and others rejected by the nervous system [p. 1281]."

Berlyne (1960) also stated that the function of the ARAS is to keep the organism mobilized and receptive to incoming information. From the French quotation and from descriptions of behavior in animals with experimental lesions of the reticular system, such as those of Lindsley (1960): "slows performance rate and retards learning in the cat [p. 1566]," and Hernández-Péon, Brust-Carmona, Eckhaus, Lopez-Mendoza and Alcocer-Cuaron (1956): "learning seems to require the functional integrity of the brain stem reticular formation [p. 91]," it seems justifiable to conclude that animals with reticular formation lesions exhibit behaviors reminiscent of those characteristic of mental deficiency in humans. It seems also to be a reasonable assumption that humans with reticular formation impairment will show signs of mental deficiency.

The question is now to what extent we can turn this proposition around and assume reticular formation impairment in mental deficiency. This is such a bold venture that we have to make proper reservations. First of all we can only indirectly assume a relationship between central nervous system functioning and mental deficiency. We are assuming the validity of Samuels' (1959) conclusions in her review of the relationship between reticular mechanisms and behavior, as quoted: "Constructs such as attention, perception, motivation, drive, reward, and punishment possess a common factor of non-specific reticular activation in addition to their specific properties [p. 20]." She also notes that "they [the cortical connections] provide a means whereby the cortex can control the activating mechanism of the brain stem and thus influence its own level of arousal [p. 15]." It is the arousal behavior that is directly observable in the mentally defective, but it is the suggested relationship between arousal and reticular formation that makes the arousal theory particularly fascinating, allowing psychophysiological measures to be regarded as indicators of arousal.

One other reservation must be made. It would be an obvious mistake to assume that all mentally defective subjects show less arousal than normals. Some defective subjects seem to be so easily aroused as to be excessively distractable and hyperactive. It may be, therefore, that we would have to regard hyper- as well as hypofunctions of arousal in relation to mental deficiency. This is consistent with the fact that the relationship between arousal and quality of performance describes an inverted U (e.g., Hebb, 1955; Sternbach, 1966, p. 72). Most recent studies of defectives that have discussed arousal or have used measures that may be considered arousal indicators have been concerned with low arousal levels. An exception is Tizard's two articles (1968a, 1968b), one of which considered habituation of EEG (electroencephalogram) and skin potential responses to auditory stimuli, and the other sleep patterns in hyperactive, mentally defective children. The fact that arousal impairment in the present chapter seems synonymous with low arousal level reflects only the fact that few investigators have studied hyperactive subjects.

Also, observation of defective subjects, particularly high-grade ones, indicates that some do not show overt signs of lack of alertness and responsivity. Rather, they seem characterized by lack of concentration or by impairment of endurance. Whether this is a quantitative difference or a difference in mechanism remains a question, but these observations should make us cautious of too rigid a concept of arousal impairment in defectives.

Studies of Behavioral Arousal

In the last 10 years, several investigators in mental deficiency have invoked the arousal concept. A common feature of these investigators' studies is that an erudite discussion of the definition of arousal has been avoided. Although this is understandable in view of the global nature of the concept, the result is that the significance and the extent of arousal impairment in the mentally deficient are difficult to assess with any degree of exactitude. The main purpose of the following review is, therefore, to show the increasing concern with the arousal function in mental deficiency and the variety of behavioral variables involved in these studies.

In 1961, Berkson reviewed studies that concerned various aspects of responsiveness in the mentally defective, such as the patellar reflex, EEG frequency and amplitude, alpha blocking, GSR (galvanic skin response), and startle reflex. He discussed these findings in relationship to the prevalent theoretical formulations in mental deficiency. Priority was given to Lindsley's 1957 observation that mental deficiency may reflect impairment of the ARAS.

Baumeister and Ellis (1963), in a study of delayed response capacity in mental defectives, found that performance improved in the presence of distraction. Without using the word arousal, they discussed their findings in rather similar terms: "Perhaps the distractor may have maintained alertness which might have been low during the delay intervals in the test environment [p. 721]."

Semmel (1965) compared mentally defective and normal children on a vigilance task, on the assumption that vigilance performance is ". . . a sensitive behavioral index of the ability of organisms to maintain 'base level arousal states' [p. 44]." In accordance with prediction, the mentally defective subjects had lower overall vigilance scores, poorer performance at each temporal point during the task, and an earlier and more rapid vigilance decrement than the normal subjects. Interpolated rest and/or novelty conditions, however, had no significant effects on vigilance performance.

In an article entitled "Theories of Arousal and Retardation Potential," Horowitz (1965) presented the view that mental deficiency is a function of stimulation offered by the environment as it interacts with the arousal characteristics of the infant. Horowitz saw adjustment of environmental stimulation as a means of preventing or reducing retardation.

Holden (1965) determined reaction time to visual, auditory, and cutaneous stimuli presented in three different ways: (a) each stimulus singly, (b) the three stimuli randomized over successive trials, and (c) the three stimuli simultaneously. His finding of no difference between the trimodal random and unimodal stimulus groups was regarded as support of a subnormal prestimulus arousal hypothesis.

In discussing their extensive review of reaction time in mental deficiency, Baumeister and Kellas (1968) stated, "Enough evidence has been presented to lead to the tentative conclusion that retardates suffer a prestimulus arousal deficiency or attention lag [p. 188]." They related this deficiency to impairment of the ARAS.

Crosby (in press; article in preparation) compared normals and defectives on the Continuous Performance Test (CPT) developed by Rosvold, Mirsky, Sarason, Bransome, and Beck (1956). Crosby considered CPT performance to be primarily a measure of attention and found indeed that the retardates displayed more lapses of attention, but were no more affected by distraction, than the nonretardates. With reference to Jasper's emphasis on attention as differentiated or focused arousal, Crosby interpreted the findings as consistent with arousal deficiency in the patient groups.

Stereotyped movements in severely defective patients were viewed as a mechanism for arousal maintenance by Karrer (1966).

In the Ability Structure Project (Clausen, 1966), an attempt was made to define subgroups in mental deficiency on the basis of constellations of impaired and intact functions. The possibility was explored that the ability structure or profile of abilities was related to the etiology of mental deficiency. For this purpose a battery of 32 tests, including sensory, motor, perceptual, and complex mental functions, was administered to 276 mentally defective and 112 normal subjects. Rather than supporting the notion of different ability structures, the data indicated that the defectives did not clearly differ from each other in a qualitative aspect, but rather that they constituted a semihomogeneous mass, with most functions impaired. In spite of greater-than-normal across-trait variability, they tended to a certain fuzzy kind of similarity, regardless of etiology. Particularly impressive were the findings of poor performance for pure tone threshold, a relatively dull task, coexisting with nearly normal performance for the more interesting speech threshold, and of relatively better performance on complex motor tasks than on simple ones. It seemed as if a central mechanism that permeated practically all the functions tapped by the battery, but to differential degrees, was impaired. In view of the contemporary concern with the relationship of the arousal mechanism to the ARAS, arousal theory seemed to constitute a reasonable model. Specifically, it was indicated that defectives do not control their own level of arousal to the same extent that normals do and that they do not anticipate events. They lack the normal person's readiness to respond to outside stimuli and are not able to focus attention on a task for a sustained period of time. They cannot muster arousal in preparation for critical moments and are therefore more highly dependent on the arousal characteristics of the stimuli than are normals. Another aspect is the limitation of retardates in the integration of cues that exceed a certain degree of complexity.

Predicting Behavior Deficits from Arousal Impairment

From their general concept of the behavioral consequences of reticular formation impairment, several authors have assumed such impairment in the mentally defective. Well known is Lindsley's 1957 statement: "The process of 'differentiation,' which seems to be necessary to perception and the formation of habits and also in the intellectual application of these, may be a process which is lacking or improperly timed in the mentally deficient person. It is conceivable that some innate property of organization of the

ARAS is lacking in such persons . . . [pp. 79–80]." Hernández-Péon (1966) related increased latencies in averaged scalp potentials in retardates to slow and unstable mechanism of attention. Rosvold (1967) observed: "Such results as these suggest that at least some types of mental retardation may be due to dysfunctions in the activating pattern of the brain. Early in the life of the organism this could so attenuate the effectiveness of environmental stimuli as to lead to retardation in mental development [p. 181]."

Although an element of circular reasoning is involved, let us assume arousal impairment in the majority of the mentally defective, and see what deductions can be made with respect to behavior in mental deficiency. In some cases there are data in the literature which have bearing on the prediction; in others, suggestions will be offered for further experiments that need to be done. It is always easier, of course, to make predictions about relationships that other investigators have already considered and put to experimental tests.

A person with impaired arousal would (by definition) be less responsive to his environment than would normal individuals. This could be reflected in a wide variety of functions, such as sensory threshold determination, motor reactivity and speed, or any other task which would rely on attention, particularly the sustained attention fundamental to vigilance tasks. As a direct consequence, perceptual functions, as well as cognitive functions such as memory, problem solving, and concept formation, would seem to be impaired, if for no other reason than that the individual would not be able to mobilize whatever resources he possessed.

A large body of literature indicates differences between normals and defectives in all of these areas. Relatively recent reviews of such results are to be found in Ellis (1963), Stevens and Heber (1964), and Clausen (1966), and in Ellis' series of International Reviews (1966–1971).

In defectives—in contrast to normals—stimulus expectancy would produce relatively little arousal, and sensory input would have correspondingly greater significance for arousal level. Accordingly, one would expect that background stimulation and presignal stimulation would have greater effects for sensory detection or motor response in defectives than in normals. For sensory stimulation, one would expect in defectives greater advantage of bilateral over unilateral stimulation, and bimodal over unimodal stimulation, as compared with normals. The difference between normals and defectives should be a function of stimulus intensity with greatest difference at low intensity. Recent studies of Baumeister and coworkers (Baumeister & Kellas, 1968, pp. 170–171) indicated that for reaction time tasks defectives are differentially slow (in comparison to normals) at lower stimulus intensities. In his 1965 study, Holden found that educable defectives had shorter reaction time to trimodal simultaneous stimuli than to trimodal random or to unimodal stimuli. Unfortunately, however, Holden's study did not allow for a comparison between normals and defectives, as data were obtained from defectives only.

From the relationship between level of performance and task complexity found in the Ability Structure Project (Clausen, 1966), it may be predicted that, over a wide range of motor tasks, defectives, as compared to normals, would describe an inverted U-shaped curve. They would do poorly on simple tasks that rely heavily on arousal and also on complex tasks where inferior muscular coordination would impair their performance. In an intermediate range of complexity, they would do relatively better because the arousal value of the task would be reflected in the performance. Since they cannot control their own level of arousal, they are more dependent on the stimulating property of the signal or the task.

Consistent with arousal theory is Zeaman and House's (1963) finding that it is the period before learning starts which is prolonged in defectives. Once learning starts, the slope of the curve is the same as for normals. The prelearning phase may be considered a period in which the arousal level is building up to a functional level.

The Russian school of mental deficiency (or oligophrenia, as they prefer to call the condition) has emphasized impairment of the orienting response in such patients (e.g., Luria, 1961; Sokolov, 1960). The orienting response, as measured by cortical desynchronization and autonomic variables—for example, blood volume changes, GSR, heart rate, and respiration—is found to dissipate much faster in defectives than in normals. Since the physiological variables that have been included in the criterion of the orienting reflex are similar to those that have been used to indicate heightened arousal in animals, the impaired orienting reflex may be considered a special case of arousal deficit. Not surprisingly, Razran (1961) reported that Anokhin and Sokolov discussed the orienting reflex in terms of reticular formation activity.

Psychophysiology of Arousal in Mental Defectives

The assumption of the ARAS as a neurophysiological substrate for arousal has already been made (Berlyne, 1960; French, 1960; Hernández-Péon et al., 1956; Lindsley, 1957, 1960; Samuels, 1959). In animal studies, arousal has been identified by desynchronized alpha frequency and increased sympathetic activity. It would appear, therefore, that the investigation of psychophysiological functions would be particularly relevant to arousal theory. If mental defectives suffer arousal decrement, this may be reflected in a higher percentage of alpha; less sympathetic activity (lower blood pressure, slower heart rate, slower respiration rate, and higher GSR) during rest, as well as in response to stimuli; faster habituation to a series of stimuli;

faster recovery; and longer latencies, and perhaps smaller amplitudes, of evoked potentials. In defectives with increased arousal, the manifestations would be the opposite.

Neurophysiological and psychophysiological data in mental deficiency are sparse. Publications dealing with EEG's are regularly clinical rather than experimental in orientation, and percentage of alpha is generally not reported. Gibbs and Gibbs (1965) have stated that the EEG is normal in the majority of defectives and that the abnormalities which do occur (i.e., seizure activity) are not specific for the condition.

Berkson (1961), in his review of studies of responsiveness in mental defectives, found that the defective person had faster recovery from alpha blocking, lower GSR (Down's syndrome patients excepted), less GSR reactivity, and longer reaction time. He concluded as follows: "Although the speed of physiological responses does not seem to differentiate normals from defectives, it consistently has been shown that the speed of voluntary responses is slower in mentally deficient groups [p. 284]." As previously mentioned, among the possible underlying mechanisms for these conditions, Berkson discussed Lindsley's suggestion of ARAS impairment.

In a more recent and more extensive survey, Karrer (1966) reviewed studies of autonomic variables (blood pressure, blood volume changes, heart rate, heart rate variability, GSR, and respiration) with respect to resting level, spontaneous fluctuations during rest, reactivity to stimulation, and habituation to repeated stimulation. Although the data are incomplete, Karrer listed seven trends that emerged from the available information. Among the autonomic characteristics he found for the defectives were (1) markedly lower than normal basal GSR (although some etiological groups have higher resistance); (2) fewer spontaneous fluctuations in GSR and acceleratory heart rate activity; (3) diminished responsivity, at least to weak and brief stimuli; (4) faster recovery from brief stimuli and shorter GSR response latencies; and (5) a possible generalized patterning of functions.

If arousal is considered a general state of neuronal excitation, one might expect that arousal decrement would result in faster poststimulus recovery and longer latencies. As mentioned by Berkson's and Karrer's reviews, several studies in the literature suggest faster recovery for defectives. Berkson's (1961) finding of faster recovery of alpha blocking in response to light flashes, however, was not confirmed by Wolfensberger and O'Connor (1965, 1967). Vogel (1961) reported faster recovery for GSR, pulse rate, finger volume, breathing rate, and blood pressure in response to cold pressor test. Clausen and Karrer (1961) found a gradual increase of electrical phosphene thresholds in successive determinations in normal subjects, but not in defectives—in spite of the higher thresholds of the latter. In a later publication Clausen, Alterman, and Karrer (1965) reported that prolonged, rather intense stimuli produced significant increases of phosphene threshold in normals but not in defectives, and in a recent study Clausen and Karrer (1969) found longer recovery time for GSR among nonorganic patients, in comparison to organic patients and normal controls. One defect in some of these studies is the fact that response amplitude was not properly considered. Consequently, in some instances the shorter recovery may simply reflect smaller response amplitudes. Although the data on recovery time in general are consistent with the expectation, the support is not especially strong.

The problem of response latencies seems to be even more controversial, and there is some doubt whether Karrer's summary statement of shorter GSR latency accurately reflects the situation. Although Kodman, Fein, and Mixon (1959) and Grings, Lockhart, and Dameron (1962) reported shorter GSR latencies, this was not confirmed by Wolfensberger and O'Connor (1965, 1967). Clausen and Karrer (1969) also failed to find differences in latencies for GSR and for blood volume changes for the forehead and finger. There seems to be mounting evidence, however, that defectives have prolonged latencies of evoked cortical potentials (Ellingson, 1970; Galbraith, Gliddon, & Busk, 1970; Hernández-Péon, 1966). Additional information is needed, but at this point we cannot regard the evidence as inconsistent with the expectation.

Previous discussions of autonomic balance (Eppinger & Hess, 1915; Wenger, 1941, 1943) have emphasized that sympathetic dominance may result from either increased sympathetic activity or from decreased parasympathetic functions. No report has been found in the literature on autonomic balance in defectives. It would indeed be interesting to know whether the reported higher level of sympathetic activity (for specific variables) during rest is accompanied by parasympathetic increase or decrease. The corresponding relationship in autonomic reactivity would also be of interest. Particularly relevant are the functions that are exclusively or predominantly controlled by one or the other branch of the autonomic nervous system: for example, pupillary contraction, salivation, and stomach and pancreas secretion (parasympathetic activity), as well as sweat secretion and piloerection (sympathetic activity). A decrease in parasympathetic activity would indicate a lack of inhibition of sympathetic activity. Sersen (1970) reviewed studies of classical conditioning in mental deficiency and concluded that defectives are impaired in their ability to inhibit response. The independence of the various autonomic variables and the functional differentiation between resting stage and reactivity, however, should remind us that the problem of inhibition may be complex indeed.

Sternbach (1966) observed, "As a general rule of thumb, the ANS [autonomic nervous system] produces faster, adjustive responses to stressful stimuli, but these are short-acting; then the endocrines' hormonal secretion comes into the picture, and their effects last longer [p. 18]." Increased sympathetic activity during rest would then imply excessive activity within the adrenergic system. Our observation of the independence of autonomic variables, however, would not be consistent with such an interpretation. Neurophysiological mechanisms may more readily explain the patterns which have been found, since some sort of differentiation, and perhaps localization, is involved. In the anatomical complexity of the brain-stem reticular formation and the diffuse thalamocortical projection system, various types of dysfunctioning may occur. It would be futile, however, to speculate on specific mechanisms until we have more systematic information about the manifestation of impairment.

Since sleep represents minimum arousal, and since Hernández-Péon (1965) and Akert (1965) stressed the close relationship between arousal and sleep systems, it becomes a point of interest to record patterns of sleep stages in mental defectives. Whether the resting level and the reactivity aspect of autonomic activity correspond to the tonic and phasic activities described for sleep is an open question. If, however, autonomic reactivity and REM (rapid eye movement) sleep both represent the phasic aspect, defectives should have less REM than normals. Expectations about differences in sleep patterns between normals and psychopathological populations should be tempered by the relative lack of differences found by Hartman (1967) between psychotics and normals.

There is some support, however, for characteristic sleep patterns in retardates. Petre-Quadens and Jouvet (1966) found increased phasic and decreased tonic activity in defectives and a significant reduction in REM sleep. In a later study, the same authors (1967) found a normal REM percentage in cases diagnosed as Down's syndrome and typus amstallodamensis, but decreased REM in patients with cystinuria, PKU (phenylketonuria), and unknown etiology. Feinberg, Braun, and Shulman (1969) reported low amounts of REM sleep in Down's syndrome cases, a similar trend in PKU cases, normal amounts in brain-damaged subjects, and widely varying amounts in undifferentiated patients. All groups of mental defectives had a paucity of sleep spindles and atypical K complexes. Schmidt, Kaelbling, and Alexander (1968) also reported less REM time for Down's syndrome cases, and Castaldo (1969) found that in such patients severity of deficiency was related to diminished REM time.

If mental defectives have impaired arousal, one might expect a lessened ability to anticipate stimulation. This might be reflected in recordings of CNV (contingent negative variation) and in evoked potentials to absent stimuli (Sutton, Braren, Zubin, & John, 1965), which probably depend on expectancy. Unfortunately, the literature does not seem to include any reports on CNV in defectives, nor has anybody used Sutton's procedure with defectives.

A promising approach is also described by Karrer (personal communication, 1969). He reports that a negative shift in dc potential is associated with arousal, whereas a positive shift occurs when the subject drifts into a drowsy state after having responded to a stimulus. The dc potentials in defective subjects obviously deserve closer investigation.

Relationship Between Psychophysiological Measures

Several experimental findings, some of them well documented, clearly are not consistent with a simple arousal theory. The EEG pattern (percentage of alpha as an index of desynchronization) has already been mentioned, although clinical material may not be adequate for the problem. Another consideration is that autonomic responses cannot be regarded as constituting a general response pattern, with uniform activity of all autonomic variables. Comments on the independence of autonomic variables have been made in several studies. Karrer and Clausen (1964) found higher resting levels (increased sympathetic-like activity), lower GSR, higher blood pressure, and greater finger volume changes, although only the result for GSR reached statistical significance. Heart rate and heart rate variability, however, remained at or below the levels of the normal subjects. In a study on the orienting response, Clausen and Karrer (1968) found a differential change in the number of responses when recordings for two sessions were compared. The normals showed a decrease in the number of responses for blood pressure, blood volume changes in the forehead, and orienting, whereas the defectives showed an increase in these measures. The normals showed practically no change for GSR responses, while the defectives showed a clear decrease. These findings were viewed as indications of the independence of cardiovascular measures and GSR. The same data, when analyzed for temporal factors (Clausen & Karrer, 1969), indicated the independence of the variables in the low correlations between them, and in the different trends in three of the variables (GSR, blood volume changes of the head, and blood volume changes of the finger) across eight successive stimuli. In a repeated study of resting levels, Clausen and Karrer (1970) found higher blood pressure, faster heart rate, and lower skin resistance—indicating increased sympathetic-like activity—with unchanged blood volume of the finger, respiration amplitude, and respiration period. A further manifestation of the independence of autonomic variables is the frequent finding in defectives of an absence of response in some variables, coexisting with responses in others. The variables showing response or nonresponse may vary from subject to subject. These observations are consistent with the principle of symptom specificity of Malmo, Shagass, and Davis (1950) and with the principle of autonomic response stereotypy of Lacey and Lacey (1958).

The autonomic independence is clearly demonstrated in a current study (Clausen & Sersen, article in preparation), in which seven autonomic variables were recorded in normal subjects during the various sleep stages throughout the night. With but few exceptions, the intercorrelations among the autonomic variables in the same subject during a night approached zero.

The indications of independent autonomic variables would suggest that the traditional concept of equivalence within the autonomic nervous system needs to be de-emphasized, and that the relationship between the various autonomic variables should be scrutinized more closely. Such revisions may lead to a more differentiated concept of arousal. Perhaps Wenger's (1941, 1942) factor analytical approach to autonomic functions should be re-activated. Wenger was particularly concerned with autonomic balance and found that a two-factor solution described the data: an autonomic factor and a muscle tension factor. His findings are not really relevant to our present problem, however, in that we would be particularly interested in the components of his autonomic factor.

A theory of impaired arousal in mental defectives would predict decreased sympathetic activity during rest. Most studies, however, have found increased rather than decreased resting activity in relation to normals (Berkson, Hermelin, & O'Connor, 1961; Clausen & Karrer, 1970; Karrer & Clausen, 1964; O'Connor & Venables, 1956; Pryer & Ellis, 1959) but decreased responsiveness to stimuli (Berkson et al., 1961; Clausen & Karrer, 1970; Grings et al., 1962; Karrer & Clausen, 1964; Vogel, 1961). The increased sympathetic activity during rest is consistent with Sternbach's (1966, p. 39) observation that any abnormality investigated is likely to show strong apparent sympathetic dominance during the resting state.

An increase in sympathetic resting level with a simultaneous decrease in sympathetic responsivity has several conceptual consequences. As suggested by Claridge (1967), resting level and reactivity may represent separate tonic and phasic dimensions, similar to the tonic and phasic epochs assumed for sleep (e.g., Jouvet, 1965). Mental defectives may alternatively be considered as having continuous nonspecific activity from internal (or external) sources, which would appear as increased arousal while attentuating attention to external stimuli, that is, low signal-to-noise ratio.

Animal Studies and Arousal Theory

If mental deficiency is to be conclusively related to ARAS impairment, it will be necessary to record directly from this region. Since such recording is not possible with patients, the answer must be sought in animal studies.

Kaplan, in our laboratories, has initiated a series of studies in which the type of organic decrement often found in the severely mentally defective is inflicted upon animals. The task is then to determine, by behavioral methods, whether a condition equivalent to "mental deficiency" exists. If this phase of the project is successful, the next step will be direct recording from the ARAS in these animals. We should also study any autonomic changes that may occur.

Massive impairment of the ARAS renders animals extremely unresponsive to their surroundings, a condition similar at least in some aspects to what one may see in severely retarded individuals. Is it possible to administer less severe impairment, leaving overt behavior relatively intact but with consequences for the subtle and complex processes, such as learning?

Lack of Specificity in Arousal Theory

Any attempt to bring the varied aspects of mental deficiency under a single theoretical construct is a hazardous venture. It has not been made easier by the unfortunate move of the American Association for Mental Deficiency in adopting a definition that includes individuals who have an IQ more than one standard deviation below the mean, and who demonstrate impairment in adaptive behavior (Heber, 1959), the criteria for which are extremely dubious.

Another difficulty with a unitary theoretical approach is reflected in Karrer's (1966) discussion of his review of autonomic nervous system functions in defectives. He found that two of the principal characteristics —lessened reactivity and the greater effect of longer and more intense stimuli—are consistent with Spitz's (1963) satiation theory and with Ellis' (1963a) short-term memory theory, as well as with arousal theory. Shorter recovery time and faster extinction (Luria, 1963) in defectives are consistent with short-term memory and arousal theories, but not with satiation theory. Since Karrer's review there have been several reports (Ellingson, 1970; Galbraith et al., 1970; Hernández-Péon, 1966) on longer latency for evoked potentials in defectives, which would support satiation and arousal theories more than short-term memory theory. But the precision of these theories leaves much to be desired. If they all can predict events equally well, either they are confined to generalities that are not relevant for the verification of the theory, or they represent different ways of saying the same thing.

Another indication of the limitation of the arousal theory is its non-differential applicability to other psychopathological conditions. Rimland (1964) has concluded that autistic children suffer from arousal impairment. Similarly, Claridge (1967) has accounted for behavioral characteristics in neurosis and psychosis by the theory that central nervous arousal depends on two interacting mechanisms, tonic arousal and arousal modulation. Although these concepts have superficial similarity to tonic and phasic autonomic activity, as mentioned earlier, there are also distinct differences. One is left with the conclusion that a theory so general that it applies to four main categories of psychopathology is not serving any category very well. It is conceivable, of course, that abnormal arousal is characteristic for all types of psychopathology. If so, the question is whether manifestation of arousal abnormality in relationship to patterns of psychophysiological functions varies with the type of psychopathology, or whether other distinguishing characteristics must be sought.

Any general theory of mental deficiency will center around a relationship between behavior deficit and some sort of central nervous system impairment. Any of a number of central nervous system functions may be considered as being impaired and can be used to predict the behavioral deficit that would result. The deficiencies predicted are very likely to be found, because the behavior deficit in mental deficiency is so general. The problem is to get beyond the general statements and into specific relationships.

The Promise of Arousal Theory

One virtue of arousal theory (or any similar theory) is that it is not difficult to conceive that level of arousal may result from neurophysiological impairment, as well as from lack of practice or exercise, or may be related to attitude and habit. This would parallel the observation that mental deficiency may have many different etiologies, probably including deprivation of psychological stimulation.

In that arousal theory considers a relationship between neurophysiology and the behavior of an organism, it holds considerable fascination for psychophysiology. As this chapter has shown, the theory in its simple form, as referring to general central nervous system excitation or overall alertness of an individual, is not tenable for mental deficiency. The relationship is much more complex, and it is this complexity with which we must come to grips.

One avenue of approach (and possibly the best one) would be to obtain a solid foundation of information about psychophysiological mechanisms in defectives and to relate these findings to some behavioral indices of arousal. An outline of such a program for psychophysiological variables would include investigation (and perhaps confirmation) of (1) independence between autonomic variables, including individual patterns of autonomic nervous system variables and autonomic balance; (2) relationship between autonomic resting level and reactivity; (3) relationship to etiology; (4) relationship between autonomic functions and cortical activity such as evoked potentials and percentage of alpha; (5) recording of the contingent negative variation; (6) recording of dc potentials; and (7) study of sleep patterns in mental defectives. The behavioral variables would focus on vigilance tasks or on a particular version of the continuous performance task, perhaps supplemented with some motor functions, and on modification of responsivity through stimulus intensity manipulation or operant conditioning procedures. An independent but related program would consist of the animal studies discussed above.

ACKNOWLEDGMENTS

The author would like to express his gratitude to Dr. Eugene Sersen and Dr. Arnold Lidsky for their constructive critical comments on the manuscript.

REFERENCES

Akert, K. The anatomical substrate of sleep. In K. Akert, C. Bally, & J. P. Schadé (Eds.), *Sleep mechanisms.* New York: Elsevier, 1965. Pp. 9–19.

Baumeister, A. A., & Ellis, N. R. Delayed response performance of retardates. *American Journal of Mental Deficiency,* 1963, **67,** 714–722.

Baumeister, A. A., & Kellas, G. Reaction time and mental retardation. In N. R. Ellis (Ed.), *International review of research in mental retardation.* Vol. 3. New York: Academic Press, 1968. Pp. 163–193.

Berkson, G. Responsiveness of the mentally deficient. *American Journal of Mental Deficiency,* 1961, **66,** 277–286.

Berkson, G., Hermelin, B., & O'Connor, N. Physiological responses of normals and institutionalized mental defectives to repeated stimuli. *Journal of Mental Deficiency Research,* 1961, **5,** 30–39.

Berlyne, D. E. *Conflict, arousal and curiosity.* New York: McGraw-Hill, 1960.

Castaldo, V. Down's syndrome: A study of sleep patterns related to level of mental retardation. *American Journal of Mental Deficiency,* 1969, **74,** 187–190.

Claridge, G. S. *Personality and arousal.* New York: Pergamon Press, 1967.

Clausen, J. *Ability structure and subgroups in mental retardation.* Washington, D. C.: Spartan Books, 1966.

Clausen, J., Alterman, A., & Karrer, R. Further comparison of electrical sensitivity of the eye in mentally retarded and normal children. *American Journal of Mental Deficiency,* 1965, **69,** 474–481.

Clausen, J., & Karrer, R. Electrical sensitivity of the eye in the mentally retarded. *Training School Bulletin,* 1961, **58,** 3–13.

Clausen, J., & Karrer, R. Orienting response—frequency of occurrence and relationship to other autonomic variables. *American Journal of Mental Deficiency,* 1968, **73,** 455–464.

Clausen, J., & Karrer, R. Temporal factors in autonomic responses for normal and mentally defective subjects. *American Journal of Mental Deficiency,* 1969, **74,** 80–85.

Clausen, J., & Karrer, R. Autonomic activity during rest in normal and mentally deficient subjects. *American Journal of Mental Deficiency,* 1970, **75,** 361–370.

Clausen, J., & Sersen, E. Autonomic activity during various stages of sleep. Article in preparation.

Crosby, K. G. Attention and distractibility in mentally retarded and average children. *American Journal of Mental Deficiency,* in press.

Crosby, K. G. Response latency and accuracy of retardates on the continuous performance test. Article in preparation.

Ellingson, R. J. Neurophysiology. In J. Wortis (Ed.), *Mental retardation—an annual review.* Vol. 1. New York: Grune & Stratton, 1970. Pp. 164–177.

Ellis, N. R. The stimulus trace and behavioral inadequacy. In N. R. Ellis (Ed.), *Handbook of mental deficiency.* New York: McGraw-Hill, 1963. Pp. 134–158. (a)

Ellis, N. R. (Ed.) *Handbook of mental deficiency.* New York: McGraw-Hill, 1963. (b)

Ellis, N. R. (Ed.) *International review of research in mental retardation.* New York: Academic Press, 1966–71. 5 vols.

Eppinger, H., & Hess, L. Vagotonia. A clinical study in vegetative neurology. *Nervous and Mental Disease Monograph Series,* No. 20. Translated by W. M. Kraus & S. E. Jelliffe. New York: The Nervous and Mental Disease Publishing Co., 1915.

Feinberg, I., Braun, M., & Shulman, E. EEG sleep patterns in mental retardation. *Electroencephalography and Clinical Neurophysiology,* 1969, **27,** 128–141.

French, J. D. The reticular formation. In J. Field, H. W. Magoun, & V. E. Hall (Eds.), *Handbook of physiology.* Section 1. *Neurophysiology.* Vol. 2. Washington, D. C.: American Physiological Society, 1960. Pp. 1281–1305.

Galbraith, G. C., Gliddon, J. B., & Busk, J. Visual evoked responses in non-retarded and mentally retarded subjects. *American Journal of Mental Deficiency,* 1970, **75,** 341–348.

Gibbs, F. A., & Gibbs, E. L. The electroencephalogram in mental retardation. In C. H. Carter (Ed.), *Medical aspects of mental retardation.* Springfield, Ill.: Charles C Thomas, 1965. Pp. 112–135.

Grings, W. W., Lockhart, R. A., & Dameron, L. E. Conditioning autonomic responses of mentally subnormal individuals. *Psychological Monographs,* 1962, **76** (39, Whole No. 558).

Hartmann, E. *The biology of dreaming.* Springfield, Ill.: Charles C Thomas, 1967.

Hebb, D. O. Drive and the C.N.S. (conceptual nervous system). *Psychological Review,* 1955, **62,** 243–254.

Heber, R. A manual on terminology and classification in mental retardation. *American Journal of Mental Deficiency,* 1959, **64** (Monogr. Suppl. No. 2).

Hernández-Péon, R. Central neuro-humoral transmission in sleep and wakefulness. In K. Akert, C. Bally, & J. P. Schadé (Eds.), *Sleep mechanisms.* New York: Elsevier, 1965. Pp. 96–117.

Hernández-Péon, R. Physiological mechanisms in attention. In R. W. Russel (Ed.), *Frontiers in physiological psychology.* New York: Academic Press, 1966. Pp. 121–147.

Hernández-Péon, R., Brust-Carmona, H., Eckhaus, E., Lopez-Mendoza, E., & Alcocer-Cuaron, C. Functional role of brain stem reticular system in salivary conditioned response. *Federation Proceedings,* 1956, **15**, 91. (Abstract)

Holden, E. A. Reaction time during unimodal and trimodal stimulation in educable retardates. *Journal of Mental Deficiency Research,* 1965, **9**, 183–190.

Horowitz, F. D. Theories of arousal and retardation potential. *Mental Retardation,* 1965, **3**, 20–23.

Jouvet, M. Paradoxical sleep. In K. Akert, C. Bally, &. J. P. Schadé (Eds.), *Sleep mechanisms.* New York: Elsevier, 1965. Pp. 20–57.

Karrer, R. Autonomic nervous system functions and behavior. In N. R. Ellis (Ed.), *International review of research in mental retardation.* Vol. 2. New York: Academic Press, 1966. Pp. 57–83.

Karrer, R. Personal communication, 1969.

Karrer, R., & Clausen, J. A comparison of mentally deficient and normal individuals upon four dimensions of autonomic activity. *Journal of Mental Deficiency Research,* 1964, **8**, 149–163.

Kodman, F., Fein, A., & Mixon, A. Psychogalvanic skin response audiometry with severe mentally retarded children. *American Journal of Mental Deficiency,* 1959, **64**, 131–136.

Lacey, J. I., & Lacey, B. C. Verification and extension of the principle of autonomic response-stereotypy. *American Journal of Psychology,* 1958, **71**, 50–73.

Lindsley, D. B. Psychophysiology and motivation. In M. R. Jones (Ed.), *Nebraska symposium on motivation.* Lincoln: University of Nebraska Press, 1957. Pp. 44–105.

Lindsley, D. B. Attention, consciousness, sleep and wakefulness. In J. Field, H. W. Magoun, & V. E. Hall (Eds.), *Handbook of physiology.* Section 1. *Neurophysiology.* Vol. 3. Washington, D. C.: American Physiological Society, 1960. Pp. 1553–1593.

Luria, A. R. An objective approach to the study of the abnormal child. *American Journal of Orthopsychiatry,* 1961, **3**, 1–16.

Luria, A. R. *The mentally retarded child. Essays based on a study of the peculiarities of the higher nervous functions.* New York: Macmillan, 1963.

Malmo, R. B., Shagass, C., & Davis, F. H. Specificity of bodily reactions under stress. *Research Publications of the Association for Research in Nervous and Mental Disease,* 1950, **29**, 231–261.

Moruzzi, G., & Magoun, H. W. Brain stem reticular formation and activation of the EEG. *Electroencephalography and Clinical Neurophysiology*, 1949, **1**, 455–473.

O'Connor, N., & Venables, P. H. A note on the basal level of skin conductance and Binet IQ. *British Journal of Psychology*, 1956, **42**, 148–149.

Petre-Quadens, O., & Jouvet, M. Paradoxical sleep and dreaming in the mentally retarded. *Journal of Neurological Science*, 1966, **3**, 608–612.

Petre-Quadens, O., & Jouvet, M. Sleep in the mentally retarded. *Journal of Neurological Science*, 1967, **4**, 354–357.

Pryer, R. S., & Ellis, N. R. Skin conductance and autonomic lability as a function of intelligence in mental defectives. *American Journal of Mental Deficiency*, 1959, **63**, 835–838.

Razran, G. The observable unconscious and the inferable conscious in current Soviet psychophysiology. *Psychological Review*, 1961, **68**, 81–147.

Rimland, B. *Infantile autism: The syndrome and its implication for a neural theory of behavior.* New York: Appleton-Century-Crofts, 1964.

Rosvold, H. E. Some neuropsychological studies relevant to mental retardation. In G. A. Jervis (Ed.), *Mental retardation: A symposium.* Springfield, Ill.: Charles C Thomas, 1967. Pp. 167–185.

Rosvold, H. E., Mirsky, A. F., Sarason, I., Bransome, S. D., Jr., & Beck, L. H. A continuous performance test of brain damage. *Journal of Consulting Psychology*, 1956, **20**, 343–350.

Samuels, I. Reticular mechanisms and behavior. *Psychological Bulletin*, 1959, **56**, 1–25.

Schmidt, H. S., Kaelbling, R., & Alexander, J. Sleep patterns in mental retardates: Mongoloids and monozygotic twins. *Psychophysiology*, 1968, **5**, 212.

Semmel, M. I. Arousal theory and vigilance behavior of educable mentally retarded and average children. *American Journal of Mental Deficiency*, 1965, **70**, 38–47.

Sersen, E. A. Conditioning and learning. In J. Wortis (Ed.), *Mental retardation —an annual review.* Vol. 1. New York: Grune & Stratton, 1970. Pp. 28–41.

Sokolov, E. N. Neuronal models and the orienting reflex. In M. A. B. Brazier (Ed.), *The central nervous system and behavior.* New York: Josiah Macy, Jr., Foundation, 1960. Pp. 187–276.

Spitz, H. H. Field theory in mental deficiency. In N. R. Ellis (Ed.), *Handbook of mental deficiency.* New York: McGraw-Hill, 1963. Pp. 11–40.

Sternbach, R. A. *Principles of psychophysiology.* New York: Academic Press, 1966.

Stevens, H. A., & Heber, R. *Mental retardation.* Chicago: University of Chicago Press, 1964.

Sutton, S., Braren, M., Zubin, J., & John, E. R. Evoked-potential correlates of stimulus uncertainty. *Science*, 1965, **150**, 1187–1188.

Tizard, B. A controlled study of all-night sleep in overactive imbecile children. *American Journal of Mental Deficiency*, 1968, **73**, 209–213. (a)

Tizard, B. Habituation of EEG and skin potential changes in normal and severely subnormal children. *American Journal of Mental Deficiency,* 1968, **73,** 34–40. (b)

Vogel, W. The relationship of age and intelligence to autonomic functioning. *Journal of Comparative and Physiological Psychology,* 1961, **54,** 133–138.

Wenger, M. A. The measurement of individual differences in autonomic balance. *Psychosomatic Medicine,* 1941, **3,** 427–434.

Wenger, M. A. The stability of measurement of autonomic balance. *Psychosomatic Medicine,* 1942, **4,** 94–95.

Wenger, M. A. The measurement of autonomic balance in children: Method and normative data. *Psychosomatic Medicine,* 1943, **5,** 241–253.

Wolfensberger, W., & O'Connor, N. Physiological responsiveness and habituation of normals and institutionalized retardates as function of stimulus intensity and duration. *American Journal of Mental Deficiency,* 1965, **70,** 21–37.

Wolfensberger, W., & O'Connor, N. Relative effectiveness of galvanic skin response latency, amplitude and duration scores as measures of arousal and habituation in normal and retarded adults. *Psychophysiology,* 1967, **3,** 345–350.

Zeaman, D., & House, B. J. The role of attention in retardate discrimination learning. In N. R. Ellis (Ed.), *Handbook of mental deficiency,* New York: McGraw-Hill, 1963. Pp. 159–223.

PART FOUR

The Internal Milieu

One can sketch out three general alternatives with respect to the relevance of the internal milieu to the etiology of any specific psychiatric disorder. The "Ur-cause" may be internal, it may be in the external environment, or it may involve an interaction between the internal and the external milieu. Although these alternatives can be stated clearly, it is doubtful that they are clearly separable in practice. When the end product is as complex a phenomenon as a psychiatric disorder, we must always consider factors at several levels. Thus, for example, the secondary complications of hospitalism—the response of the patient to the restrictive and dependency-producing environment of the hospital—must be dealt with on their own level. Even with a physiological Ur-cause, such behaviors are not automatically eliminated by the treatment of the physiological system involved.

Even when we take as our model the role of the spirochete in general paresis, isolation of the spirochete as the cause has only a limited meaning. It means essentially two things: (1) that in the absence of the spirochete there would be no general paresis; and (2) that environmental modification of behavior without halting the attack of the spirochete on the central nervous system would be inadequate. However, it can hardly be the spirochete that produces the delusions of grandeur characterizing the illness. These must obviously arise out of the interaction of the disordered brain and the cultural milieu. Social factors may also be involved in the predisposition of some portion of the population to a disease such as syphilis, as an indirect result of cultural norms regarding, for example, methods of birth control.

On the other hand, even where the Ur-cause is environmental, internal processes cannot be ignored. As John points out, the brain must process aberrant as well as normal information, and knowledge of these modes of processing may be important in understanding and treating the illness. Furthermore, the hormonal secretions and their interactions surely condition such emotional states as anxiety and anger, and drugs may change a subject's psychological state even when it arises from his interaction with the social environment. It is instructive that in research with monkeys, ulcers can be brought about by direct stimulation of the hypothalamus (French, J. D., Porter, R. W., Cavanaugh, E. B., & Longmire, R. L. Experimental gastroduodenal lesions induced by stimulation of the brain. *Psychosomatic Medicine,* 1957, **19**, 209–220), as well as by psychological pressures of "executive" decision making (Brady, J. V., Porter, R. W., Conrad, D. G., & Mason, J. W. Avoidance behavior and the development of gastroduodenal ulcers. *Journal of the Experimental Analysis of Behavior,* 1958, **1**, 69–72). It is also worth noting that in human beings both psychological and physiological treatment can be used to bring relief from ulcers, whatever the cause of the illness.

Explicitly interactional hypotheses in psychopathology present an even more complex case. Thus environmentally produced anxiety may cause a permanent change in the physiological substrate, which in turn may become a source of psychological disturbance. Psychosomatic illness is the area in which interactional hypotheses have been most prevalent.

Converging from different fields and with different approaches, the chapters in Part Four try to deal with the internal causes, correlates, or consequences of altered psychological states. The hypotheses of Mednick and Schulsinger (Chapter 18) directly implicate causes at several levels: a genetic predisposition interacts with prenatal or birth complications which affect the hippocampus of the brain. In the authors' formulation, this in turn produces a predisposition to the learning of avoidance responses, out of which subsequent psychiatric disturbance is seen to arise.

In contrast to Mednick and Schulsinger, who begin with individuals at high risk for schizophrenia, John starts with an analysis of normal processes. In Chapter 17, he marshalls impressive data of electrophysiology in order to explore the processes by which sensory stimuli are coded in the brain and by which the sequence of stimuli is represented and stored, and the mechanisms by which the representations of experience can be released in an orderly sequence. He emphasizes that orderly spatiotemporal patterns of activity in extensive neuronal ensembles are essential to coherent mental activity. Such conceptualizations lead to specific suggestions as to how to look for electrophysiological sources, or representations, of aberrant activity.

Beginning with the known effects of injected antibodies in causing changes in the electrical activity of the brain as well as in behavior, Rapport proposes in Chapter 16 the systematic study of immunoneurology as a promising tool in relation to psychopathology. His survey of the present status of the field indicates that a number of methodological problems must be resolved before a viable science of immunoneurology can begin to make significant advances.

Two of the chapters deal with the effects of drugs on behavior, but from very different perspectives. In Chapter 19, Jarvik reviews the major classes of psychotropic drugs with respect to their efficacy, as well as the particular light they cast on the possible role of biological factors in the psychoses. Lehmann, on the other hand, is concerned in Chapter 20 with the methodological sources of error in drug research, as well as with the epistemological issues that arise when trying to comprehend the subjective effects of psychotropic drugs within the framework of a materialistic science. The mind/body problem, he argues, has not been and cannot be laid to rest.

It is of interest that no author in Part Four takes the explicit position that the cause of psychopathology lies exclusively in the internal milieu. Rather, to the extent that these chapters take a position on this issue, it is in the direction of multiple or interactional causation.

CHAPTER 16

Can Immunoneurology Develop into a Viable Discipline?

MAURICE M. RAPPORT

THE IMMUNONEUROLOGICAL SCENE

It has long been recognized that the brain is a complex organ, that its parts have separate and distinguishable functions, and that more or less complete analysis of these parts is a first step in attempting to understand the structure and operation of the whole organ. Each discipline is able to make a unique contribution to analysis of the parts, and within recent years an increasing number of investigators have been tempted to apply immunological methods to study the brain, recognizing the inherent potential of these methods for sensitivity and specificity. In some cases their efforts have been remarkably productive. There is, of course, a facet of immunology that makes this discipline especially interesting: since antibodies are able to damage cells, antibodies can cause lesions in the brain. Immunological methods should be useful, therefore, for examining brain function and its pathological disturbance, and it is thought that these methods can perhaps be tuned more finely than others capable of inducing experimental alterations in behavior, such as those based on electrolytic lesions or the action of drugs.

The term immunoneurology is of relatively recent vintage. Although it might justifiably have been introduced almost a century ago in connection with cases of encephalitis following vaccination for rabies, the first use of the term actually occurred within the decade and has been credited to F. O. Schmitt. The initial experiments in this new discipline were reported by

Mihailovic and Jankovic (1961). These investigators prepared in rabbits antibodies against brain tissue of cats and found that, when these antibodies were then injected into the central nervous system of cats, they caused a change in the EEG pattern. The actual experiments were somewhat more complicated. The antisera were prepared against a homogenate of a specific region, either caudate nucleus or hippocampus, and immunoglobulin fractions from the antisera (rather than purified antibodies) were injected through a cannula into the lateral ventricle. Three to four injections were given daily for four successive days. A progressive decrease in electrical activity (EEG), which was confined to the caudate nucleus, was observed with antibodies against caudate nucleus but not with either antibodies to hippocampus or normal rabbit globulin. Profound behavioral changes, such as depressive and catatonic states, were also seen.

Because this elaborate experiment provoked considerable interest, there was corresponding concern, ranging from doubt to disbelief, when repeated efforts to reproduce it were unproductive. To my knowledge no published account confirming this study has yet appeared, nor have the authors suggested, in their subsequent publications, a reason for the difficulty. They have, nevertheless, extended these studies to include monkeys trained to perform tasks of delayed alternation and visual discrimination (Mihailovic, Divac, Mitrovic, Milosevic, & Jankovic, 1969). Animals injected with anti-caudate globulin showed profound impairment in ability to perform a delayed alternation test, whereas performance of a visual discrimination task was little affected. In contrast, animals receiving antihippocampus globulin exhibited impairment in the delayed alternation test that was limited to the days during which the protein was injected, whereas animals receiving normal globulin showed no impairment.

The most recent advance by these Yugoslavian investigators is a still more complex experiment (Jankovic, Rakic, Veskov, & Horvet, 1968) showing that antibody to brain protein alters defensive conditioned reflexes in cats. For this experiment antibodies were prepared in rabbits against a protein fraction from whole cat brain, obtained by saline extraction and precipitation with ethanol. The total globulin fraction (containing the antibodies) was injected into the lateral ventricle of cats that had been trained previously to discriminate between an aversive stimulus (800-Hz tone, 3-second duration), detected by leg flexion and activation of an electromyographic response, and a negative stimulus (700-Hz tone, 3-second duration). The cats that received a single injection of 15 mg of the globulin from antisera against cat brain protein either showed inadequate responses to the conditioned stimulus or lost the ability to discriminate between positive and negative tones. No effects were detected in control animals injected with the globulin fraction, either from antisera against liver proteins or from normal rabbit serum.

There are also a number of reports that antibodies can alter the function of various nervous structures. These include the effects of antibody to giant squid axon on the electrical activity of this nerve (Huneeus-Cox & Fernandez, 1967), the effect of antiserum to nerve-ending membranes of cat cerebral cortex on the ultrastructure of isolated nerve endings (DeRobertis, Lapetina, Pecci Saavedra, & Soto, 1966) and on the electrical activity of single mollusk neurones (of the land snail, *Cryptomphallus aspersa*) (DeRobertis, Lapetina, & Wald, 1968), and changes in the electrical activity of cockroach brain induced by antibody to lobster brain (Jankovic, Rakic, & Sestovic, 1969). It is well documented that antibody to nerve growth factor can affect sympathetic ganglia to produce a condition called immunosympathectomy, thereby providing a reasonably solid foundation for these various observations. Many of the studies have been reviewed by Cerf (1968).

Immunopsychiatry?

The behavioral studies, which seem destined to remain controversial until they are adequately confirmed, are closely related in scientific objective to another area of investigation that may be of considerable practical importance and is perhaps even more controversial for this reason. I refer to the works of Heath (1970) and his collaborators, which have been advanced to support his hypothesis that schizophrenia is caused by an autoimmune process directed to the septal region of the brain. In these studies, which have been in progress for more than 20 years, it is claimed that a labile psychotomimetic protein (taraxein) is present in the serum of schizophrenic patients, and that symptoms in monkeys similar to those shown by patients with schizophrenia (catatonia) can be produced by injection of antibody to the septal region (Heath & Krupp, 1967). The antibody is thought to induce alterations in membrane permeability and neural transmission in this region. In view of our current ignorance concerning the etiology of schizophrenia, such hypotheses cannot be considered lightly, and it is not irrelevant, therefore, to ask what needs to be done either to acquire additional evidence in their support or to reduce significantly the probability of their validity.

Reproducibility, the Goal; Antibody, the Obstacle

It would not be unfair to state that the very small number of published reports involving experiments in which antibodies are injected into a living brain, as well as the skeptical attitudes of many members of the scientific and medical communities toward them, is indicative of some bizarre quality. These behavioral experiments are complex in design and expensive in effort, and one would not expect other investigators to repeat them unless they had some conviction that the results not only were reproducible but also could be extended. A change in status is clearly dependent on increasing the volume of such work, and two advances will be essential if studies of this kind are to be brought out of the shadows of the suspect. They must be made reproducible, and they must be made convenient enough to attract a larger number of investigators.

Probably the major problem involves reproducibility, particularly of antibody. When antigenic mixtures are used to induce the formation of antibodies, the mixture of antibodies that is produced may be (and frequently is) quite variable. Even antibodies formed against pure antigens may be heterogeneous, and considerable variation in both the quantity of antibody (titer) and its reactivity with antigen (avidity) may be detected in the responses elicited in different animals. Rapid developments in studies of antibody structure within the past decade have shown that antibodies fall into different molecular categories and that these have widely different potentials for reaction. Since we must contend not only with this kind of variability but also with that arising as a result of differences among the immunogenic capacities of different antigens (i.e., their competition for the antibody-producing apparatus), it is not difficult to appreciate why reproducibility represents such an enormous obstacle. How can one solve this problem? There seems to be no way to avoid biometrics. The initial attack should probably involve the study of a number of individual antisera, a number sufficient to judge the frequency with which the observed bioelectric or behavioral effect can be reproduced. These results must be reported with candor, a rather unusual requirement. It is indeed rare that such evaluations are made or at least reported in the field of immunology, and investigators have grown so accustomed to putting their best foot forward in scientific reports that they compromise the value of such reports when the observations are difficult to repeat.

There is an important practical consideration in this connection. The amount of antiserum that can be harvested from laboratory animals is limited. The rabbit, which is the most convenient, provides about 50–60 ml of antiserum under optimal conditions. If larger quantities of antibody are needed to complete a series of experiments, the investigator has two alternatives. He can either pool the antisera from a number of laboratory animals, or he can arrange to raise the antiserum in large animals, such as sheep or horses. Since both alternatives have limitations, neither will eliminate the resistance to obtaining information on reproducibility that stems from added inconvenience, effort, and expense. The use of antibodies prepared in large animals seriously limits the number of investigators who will be capable of repeating the experiment, because most of those interested probably do not have access to the required facilities. Furthermore, the availability to a single investigator of a large quantity of antiserum from one animal minimizes his inclination to study antisera from a significant number of animals. One of the major advantages of preparing antisera in laboratory animals is that the experiment becomes more accessible to other laboratories. The major disadvantage is that the pooling of antisera to acquire a sufficient quantity may very well dilute a potent antiserum with an ineffective one, or reduce the specificity of the response. The best resolution of this dilemma is to develop a test system that permits the screening of antisera before they are pooled or that permits some selected phase of the study to be completed with the antiserum from a single animal.

Cues in a Model from the Past

This plea for a series of experiments large enough to permit an honest evaluation of the reproducibility and for greater candor in the reporting of results will not in itself confer scientific vitality on this field. What it *will* do, if successful, is provide a soil that may be fertile enough to permit the acomplishment of the next step: the chemical isolation of the antigen or antigens against which the effective antibodies are directed. Until this step is completed, it is doubtful whether the field will be productive enough to sustain the interest of investigative groups that will offer both competence and objectivity.

The elements in this effort are not unlike those faced by an earlier scientific generation in a similar area. Almost 50 years ago, immunologists, having become aware of the specificity of serological reactions, used them to detect differences between cancer tissue and normal tissues. Although the experimental procedures were sound, the results were not decisive, and after 10–15 years of sustained effort the work was abandoned and the field remained almost dormant for a period of 20 years. Its resurrection has been exceedingly slow despite some substantial progress (Rapport & Graf, 1969). It may be of some interest to review this historical episode briefly, since it is obvious that much of my orientation toward the needs of the discipline of "immunoneurology" comes from analogies drawn from the conceptually simpler field of tissue-specific antigens.

By the mid-twenties, it was realized that some antigens are specific for certain cells and tissues, and attempts were made to explore these differences in order to establish a rational approach to either the diagnosis or the treatment of cancer. Numerous reports were published showing that an antiserum to cancer tissue reacted more strongly with various extracts of the cancer tissue than with similar extracts of "normal" tissue. These differences were more readily found when alcoholic extracts were used. The serological technique was complement fixation because of its sensitivity and because it could be used with water-insoluble substances that were abundantly present in the alcoholic extracts. After more than 15 years of work, these studies were virtually abandoned. Probably this must be attributed to a number of factors, but especially to the feeling that despite the wealth of data there were too many complexities inherent in the studies to allow decisive interpretation of the findings and their further development. Some of these complexities must have been (1) awareness that the immunizing antigen, the material used to prepare the antisera, was a complex mixture of antigens; (2) knowledge that antisera must certainly contain antibodies against many different substances; (3) realization that the serological technique was a method that gave the sum of the contributions of many individual immunological systems, and therefore differences could not be interpreted with precision; (4) recognition that differences between tissues are not an adequate measure of differences between cells, and that since tissues are composed of heterogeneous cell types in varying amounts, a "normal control" for malignant tissue was usually not accessible; (5) discovery that the alcoholic extracts, which were most useful for demonstrating the largest differences, contained mainly lipids, a class of substances for which the laboratory technology for definitive separation of different components was still underdeveloped and inadequate for the quantities of material available. Added to these factors was the problem of experimental design and selection of results: since more extensive comparisons of the reactivity of antisera with various normal and pathological tissues reduced the apparent specificity, the potential of the experimental findings could be preserved only by narrowly limiting, either consciously or subconsciously, the comparisons that were made. For example, one might find that antiserum to kidney carcinoma reacted with extracts of this tissue, but not with extracts of normal kidney, liver, or heart. But if normal spleen were included, the differences might be much smaller, and this tissue was usually not examined.

In the early 1950s my colleagues and I undertook to re-examine this problem, mainly for the reason that the chemical basis for immunological activity of lipids was a virtually unexplored field, having lagged far behind similar studies of polysaccharides and proteins. We developed methods for fractionating complex lipids by chromatography on silicic acid, we devised a scheme for simplifying the interpretation of enormous quantities of serological data, and we then committed ourselves to establishing the chemical nature of serologically active lipids. After several years of single-minded perseverance with a transplantable animal tumor, we returned to studies of human tumors and were able, through some very good fortune, to show that antibodies against a single lipid could account for the reactivity of antisera prepared against many different kinds of human tumors. This lipid was a relatively simple substance, cytolipin H, whose chemical structure could be precisely determined. It proved to be a glycosphingolipid, a substance of characteristic molecular design localized in cell membranes. Once this pure substance was available for study, it caused a drastic alteration both in the course and in the goals of studies in this area. The original objective of detecting chemical differences between normal cells and malignantly transformed cells was now broadened to include the immunological detection and measurement of specific membrane markers in all cells. Particular emphasis was directed to the nervous system, where glycosphingolipids have had a traditional importance ever since Thudichum, in some of the earliest explorations of animal biochemistry, established that such compounds were present in large amounts in the brain. The transformation of goals that follows a single decisive contribution to a field overburdened by complexity constitutes an interesting story in itself, but we must rather ask what can be learned from this model that will provide some nurture for the field of "immunoneurology."

We may consider that the neurological and behavioral phenomena of immunoneurology are analogous to the serological measurements in the model. Then what is called for initially is some decisive identification of the nature of at least one brain antigen that can be related to these phenomena produced by heterologous antibodies. Such a result would make it possible to determine the underlying basis for the specificity of the observations, whether they were due to differences in the composition of different brain areas such as septum, caudate nucleus, and hippocampus, or whether they resulted primarily from differences in the accessibility of different areas to the injected antibody.

The Way to Go: Neuroimmunology versus Immunoneurology

There are three ways of attacking this problem. The classical one is to purify the active component or components from the antigenic mixtures that have been observed to produce the antibodies causing the interesting biological effects.

The second method of attack is to determine the effects of each kind of antiserum that can be prepared against a pure brain antigen. A number of these antigens are now available—for example, basic protein of myelin, S-100 protein, 14-3-2 protein, α-albumin, and various enzymes, among the proteins; and galactocerebroside and gangliosides, among the glycosphingolipids. The number of these reagents is still quite limited, and therefore the probability of finding the interesting neurological and behavioral effects may be quite small. There are, after all, many thousands of macromolecular components in brain that may be responsible for or contribute to such effects.

The third method of attack is based on the assumption that the behavioral effects of antibody are attributable mainly to disruption of membrane functions, since it is well known that antibodies do not normally penetrate a membrane barrier, and there is no reason to believe that antibodies injected intracerebrally are an exception. One would then systematically attempt to determine the nature of membrane antigens and to examine the effects of antibodies prepared against them.

To some degree each of these approaches is presently being undertaken, simply as a consequence of the limited range of experimental attacks on such a complex problem as behavior. These kinds of studies may be thought of as constituting a subdiscipline of "neuroimmunology" in which the major emphasis is on exploring the immunochemistry of nervous tissue components, in contrast to "immunoneurology," where the major emphasis is on neurological and behavioral events and immunology simply provides some of the tools and techniques. The development of a strong foundation in "neuroimmunology" is the surest method of creating a viable "immunoneurology." Although the road ahead may be long, it is one that promises considerable novelty. Progress will undoubtedly require intimate cooperation by biochemist, immunologist, neurophysiologist, and physiological psychologist. To achieve this kind of interdisciplinary cooperation is as challenging as the biological problem involved.

REFERENCES

Cerf, J. A. Données récentes en immuno-neurologie. Effets electrophysiologiques d'anticorps dirigés contre le système nerveux. *Actualités Neurophysiologique,* 1968, **8,** 316–339.

DeRobertis, E., Lapetina, E., Pecci Saavedra, J., & Soto, E. F. *In vivo* and *in vitro* action of antisera against isolated nerve endings of brain cortex. *Life Sciences,* 1966, **5,** 1979–1989.

DeRobertis, E., Lapetina, E. F., & Wald, F. The effect of antiserum against nerve-ending membranes from cat cerebral cortex on the ultrastructure of isolated nerve endings and mollusc neurons. *Experimental Neurology,* 1968, **21,** 322–335.

Heath, R. G. Perspectives in biological psychiatry. *Biological Psychiatry,* 1970, **2,** 81–88.

Heath, R. G., & Krupp, I. M. Catatonia induced in monkeys by anti-brain antibody. *American Journal of Psychiatry,* 1967, **123,** 1499–1504.

Huneeus-Cox, F., & Fernandez, H. L. Effect of specific antibodies on the excitability of internally perfused squid axons. *Journal of General Physiology,* 1967, **50,** 2407–2419.

Jankovic, B. D., Rakic, L., & Sestovic, M. Changes in electrical activity of the cockroach *Blatta orientalis* brain induced by anti-lobster brain antibody. *Experientia,* 1969, **25,** 1049–1050.

Jankovic, B. D., Rakic, L., Veskov, R., & Horvat, J. Effect of intraventricular injection of anti-brain antibody on defensive conditioned reflexes. *Nature,* 1968, **218,** 270–271.

Mihailovic, L., Divac, I., Mitrovic, K., Milosevic, D., & Jankovic, B. D. Effects of intraventricularly injected anti-brain antibodies on delayed alternation and visual discrimination tests performance in rhesus monkeys. *Experimental Neurology,* 1969, **24,** 325–336.

Mihailovic, L., & Jankovic, B. D. Effects of intraventricularly injected anti-nucleus caudatus antibody on the electrical activity of the cat brain. *Nature,* 1961, **192,** 1665–1666.

Rapport, M. M., & Graf, L. Immunological reactions of lipids. *Progress in Allergy,* 1969, **13,** 273–331.

CHAPTER 17

Where Is Fancy Bred?

E. ROY JOHN

The basic question with which neuropsychology must ultimately grapple is how mental phenomena arise. Contemporary psychology effectively sustains a mind-brain dualism in which, no matter how assiduously we pay lip service to the general proposition that mental phenomena are produced by the brain, we carefully avoid suggesting that particular neurophysiological or neuropsychological observations might be related to subjective experience. A good part of current neuropsychology and neurophysiology involves detailed analysis of how information is transformed from the peripheral receptors into activity in the pathways of the specific sensory systems and is coded, stored, and retrieved. A certain amount of progress has been made in achieving insight into the mechanisms by which information processing is mediated. Analyzing the responses of cells that respond to various stimuli, we are seldom reminded and we seldom bear in mind that in some fashion the firing of such cells must be responsible for generating the subjective experience which is caused by the impact of these stimuli upon the organism. In the enormous volume of material published in the last decade about sensory mechanisms, about sensory coding, about information processing in the nervous system, only a miniscule amount has attempted to deal with the problem of how subjective experience such as sensation, let alone perception, arises from those sensory mechanisms. In some unknown fashion, conscious experience is generated from the unitary cellular events that represent the molecular level of response to afferent stimuli. This chapter will begin with an attempt to discuss what we know about the neuronal events reflecting the arrival of information about sensory stimuli in the brain, and I will then attempt to discuss the ways in which conscious experience might arise from the processes that have been described.

319

However, conscious experience has many dimensions. A report of extero-ceptive stimulation, the awareness of sensation, represents that part of ex-perience which is stimulus bound. This is perhaps the least interesting of the categories of mental phenomena which we must ultimately explain. Al-though subjective awareness of stimulus-bound experience is certainly im-portant to understand, we must also turn our attention to thinking, to imagination, even to fantasy. These mental processes represent departures from rigidly stimulus-bound experience and reflect some of the degrees of freedom of operation of the machinery of the brain. Understanding stimulus-bound experience ought to be particularly useful, as it provides an initial vantage point from which to examine these other processes. Thought and imagination and fantasy consist, to a large extent, of releasing a reflection of awareness of stimuli in their absence, of relating events into combinations different from those that are conventionally experienced, of distorting stimuli from the forms in which they normally impinge upon us. Almost 150 years ago, intense intellectual controversy raged about the concept of "imageless thought." Psychologists debated the extent to which our thought processes were composed of a stream of memories and stimulus representa-tions that constituted essential ingredients in the thought process. One effect of the enthusiastic adoption of "operational" philosophies by psychology, in its eagerness to join the more accepted sciences, has been to create an intellectual climate in which concern with such questions has been re-nounced by respectable scientists. Yet, for the first time, psychology has methods that make it possible to consider these problems from a biological viewpoint.

We believe that some psychiatric disorders represent defects in the pro-cesses discussed above: defects in the way that experience past and present is perceived; defects in the way that thought is constructed from a sequence of released memories or images of past, present, or future experience; de-fects in the process of imagination in which the fluctuating content of con-sciousness deviates from whatever rules normally govern it, consistently leading to particular content representing an aspect in the life of the indi-vidual that has assumed a larger amount of threat or a greater potential value than is usually the case for the content in question; defects in fantasy so that memories of past experience and stimulus-bound representations are combined in a fashion which consistently causes distress for the individual, eliciting anxiety, fear, or sadness.

Clearly, the use of "defects" in this series of descriptions of psychiatric disorder implies a belief that it is meaningful to speak about "normal" thought, "normal" imagination, "normal" fantasy. This belief is expressed on two levels. First, I believe that the mechanisms of the brain operate in basically the same fashion from individual to individual—memories are stored and released, and stimuli represented or distorted in a way which is determined largely by the characteristics of the machinery that has been developed in man to perform these functions. The implication, therefore, is that there is a range of probable performance of that machinery when it comes to constructing sequences of released memories and represented experiences—a range in which certain kinds of sequences are more probable than others, in which the emotional consequences of certain kinds of sequences serve to make them more probable or less probable, in which the content of mental experience, although unknown and unpredictable in its fine detail, fluctuates within certain expected limits that are undoubtedly extremely broad.

From this follows the belief that there is a class of disordered thought process which reflects a disruption of that machinery, such that the combinations which arise in the stream of thought, the structure of imagination, the content of fantasy, are not only extremely improbable, but also consistently so. Such disorders might be metabolic, or they might arise from traumatic injury to the brain. Certain parts of the machinery might either become hyperexcitable or function at a lower level than would normally be the case, biasing the content of thought, of imagination, or of fantasy in a direction that reflected over- or underactivation of certain regions, or failing to exercise feedback mechanisms in which the content of mental experience was somewhat regulated by the emotional consequences elicited by that mental content.

One can also envisage a second class of disorder arising, not from malfunction of the machinery of the brain, but from the fact that the stimuli and memories that had been accumulated by an individual, constituting the blocks of imagery available to be released from storage to comprise the content of thought processes, were themselves abnormal, arising from situations so traumatic, so unpleasant, so emotion-laden and unusual as to be beyond the bounds of what we consider as normal experience. An individual who has accumulated a warehouse stocked with abnormal building blocks must also build abnormal structures.

Thus we can discern two classes of potential disorder: abnormal mental processes arising from malfunction of the machinery of a brain processing normal material, and abnormalities arising from proper functioning of the machinery of a brain processing abnormal material. In either case, it would seem central to an understanding of these mental processes to understand the fundamental mechanisms by which sensory stimuli are coded in the brain, by which the *sequence* of stimuli that constitute an experience is represented and stored, and the mechanisms by which the representations of that experience can be released in an orderly sequence. We must seek, in our detailed analysis of those mechanisms, for an explanation of how the subjective experience of the sensation or the intrusion of the released memory into consciousness is accomplished. We must be adamant that there is a physical process by which that transform occurs, that there is some aspect of the neurophysiological processes which we study, as we study storage and release of information in the brain, which explains how conscious experience arises. We must insist that the content of our studies in neurophysiology and neuropsychology is not only about brain processes but is also the stuff from which we will construct an understanding of how the mental concomitant of these brain processes is produced. I want to express the conviction that conscious experience is a consequence of the neurophysiological processes which we presently have the tools to analyze, and to take issue with the belief that mental phenomena and the content of subjective processes are not yet and may never be within our purview. As we come to understand the mind-brain transform, we will find insights into physiological sources of the various kinds of distortion of experience which are propaedeutic to disorders of thought, of imagination, and of fantasy, a large part of the problems we have set ourselves to solve.

MECHANISMS OF MIND-BRAIN

This section of the chapter has been entitled "Mechanisms of Mind-Brain" to emphasize that the kinds of phenomena and processes which will be discussed herein reflect the particular brain mechanisms that I consider most likely to be involved in the mind-brain transform.

Representational Systems

A body of data which has been summarized elsewhere (John, 1967) indicates that, as different parts of the brain are simultaneously stimulated, during the period of time in which an experience takes place, interactions between these different brain regions create a common mode of activity which can persist in these regions for some time after the stimulus is terminated. When a common mode of activity persists for sufficiently long, certain changes are assumed to take place, such that the probability of the associated set of structures displaying that mode of activity in the future is substantially enhanced. I have defined this associated group of structures as a "representational system," responsible for storing the information about the experience that is represented by the common mode activity. Central to the idea of the representational system is the prediction that, if a portion of the system subsequently enters that characteristic mode of activity, the system as a whole will enter the same mode and thereby will recreate the stored representation of the original experience. Various kinds of evidence support this formulation. The salient features of this evidence will be discussed in what follows.

The first observation which will be cited is that, during learning, regions of the brain which initially display very different kinds of electrical response to a stimulus gradually acquire a strikingly similar mode of activity. This phenomenon was reported first in our own laboratories and has subsequently been confirmed by a large number of other investigators (Dumenko, 1967; Galambos & Sheatz, 1962; Glivenko, Korol'Kova, & Kuznetsova, 1962; John & Killam, 1959; John, Ruchkin, & Villegas, 1963, 1964; Knipst, 1967; Korol'Kova & Shvetz, 1967; Livanov, 1962, 1965; Yoshii, Pruvot, & Gastaut, 1957).

EVOLUTION OF VISUAL EVOKED RESPONSE

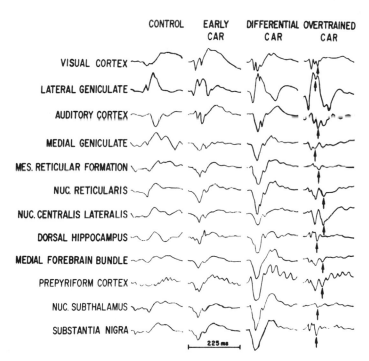

Figure 1. Average response wave shapes recorded from various structures in cat brain in response to a flickering light. The columns are as follows: CONTROL —wave forms from a naive animal; EARLY CAR—flicker is the cue for an avoidance response; DIFFERENTIAL CAR—the animal has learned a frequency discrimination. Wave shapes shown are obtained when the animal gives an avoidance response; OVERTRAINED CAR—the result of extreme overtraining in the differential CAR. Arrows indicate a late component that is usually absent in trials failing to elicit a conditioned response.

An example of this evolution of similarity can be seen in Figure 1, where each column presents the average evoked responses recorded from the listed structures as a flickering light is presented to a cat. The left column of data illustrates the average evoked response elicited by the stimulus from a naive animal. The second column shows the change in the evoked responses after the animal learned to perform an avoidance response with flicker as the cue. Note that the general shape of the evoked response has more similar features from structure to structure than were apparent at the control stage. The third column of data shows the change in the evoked response after differential training, in which the animal was taught to attend not only to the presence of the stimulus but also to its quality. A frequency discrimination has been established between flickering light at this frequency and flickering light at a different frequency that was the cue for an approach response. The similarity between different regions has now become extremely marked. The fourth column shows the result of extreme overtraining in this differentiation. The marked similarity seen in the third column has been diminished. A number of regions no longer display an adherence to the common pattern, although some anatomical structures continue to show closely similar features of electrical response. In numerous animals, these qualitative observations have been quantitatively confirmed by the computation of intercorrelation matrices (John et al., 1964; John, 1967). These data show that, when the brain of the cat is processing information about a familiar event, many regions of the brain enter a mode of electrical activity which is shared by a large number of structures.

A comparable phenomenon seems to occur in man. Figure 2 presents results obtained by Livanov (1962). At the upper left (a), we see the outline of a head on which a large number of electrodes have been placed. The correlation coefficient between each electrode and every other electrode has been calculated. The electrodes for which a significant intercorrelation was observed are marked in black with a line connecting them. The man from whom these recordings were taken was sitting at rest. At the upper right (b), the intercorrelations are seen 15 seconds after the subject was given a task in mental arithmetic. Widespread synchronization of activity has occurred, with the activity of many regions of the cortex closely coupled, as shown by the widespread distribution of dark circles indicating regions highly intercorrelated with other regions. At the lower left (c), the figure shows that this state continues for 30 seconds after the mental task was imposed. At the lower right (d), the figure illustrates the return to the original resting state, after the solution to the problem in mental arithmetic was correctly provided by the subject. These data show that in normal man during mental tasks a wide part of the surface of the brain enters a shared state in which a common mode of activity is displayed.

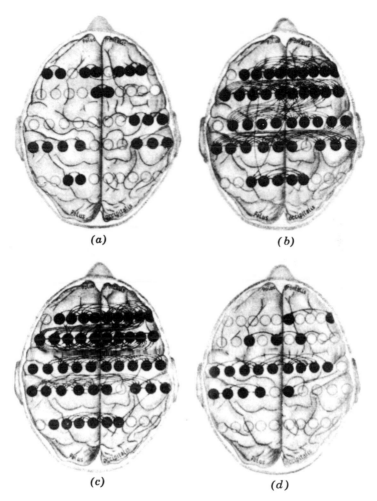

(a) (b)

(c) (d)

Figure 2. Pair synchronization of biopotentials of human brain cortex during mental work. Circles on the brain cortex map indicate electrode placement. Arrows connect the areas of high-degree synchronization. (a) Before the arithmetical problem; (b) 15 seconds after the problem was given (c) 30 seconds after the problem was given (d) after the solving of the problem. (From Livanov, 1962)

In Figure 3, we see comparable data recorded from a patient with "obsessive neurosis" (Aslanov, 1970). It is striking that in this individual the frontal regions display closely coordinated activity when the subject is at rest. Instead of the differentiated picture seen in Figure 2a, in which regions of the brain are relatively uncoupled, this individual at rest seems to be undergoing intense mental activity.

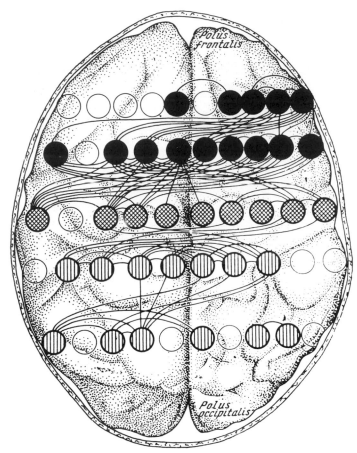

Figure 3. As in Figure 2, for a patient with "obsessive neurosis." (From Aslanov, 1970)

Figure 4*b* shows the distribution of correlation coefficients in a schizophrenic patient at rest; Figure 4*c*, the change in this distribution during the solving of a mental arithmetic problem (Gavrilova, 1970). Note that the frontal regions are coupled while this patient is at rest, and that these regions are not integrated with the activity in the remainder of the cortex during the performance of a mental task. These findings differ greatly from those for the normal subject, seen in Figure 2 and in Figure 4*a*.

These data suggest that the establishment of coherence is an essential feature of mental activity in a normal man, that the obsessive neurotic and the paranoid schizophrenic give indications of being involved in intense mental activity when we would expect them to be at rest, and that the

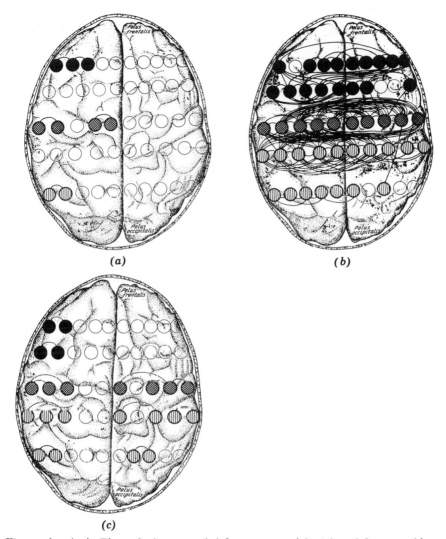

Figure 4.   As in Figure 2, data recorded from a normal in (*a*) and from a schizo-phrenic in (*b*) and (*c*). (From Gavrilova, 1970)

schizophrenic does not integrate the activity of frontal regions of the cortex with more posterior regions under circumstances which normally accomplish this.

Release of Activity Patterns in Generalization

In animal studies (Bartlett & John, 1970; John, Ruchkin, Leiman, Sachs, & Ahn, 1965; John, Shimokochi, & Bartlett, 1969; Ruchkin & John, 1966), it has been shown that part of the similarity observed between different brain regions when an animal is presented with a familiar stimulus is not actually caused by the stimulus, but rather reflects activity patterns released from storage by activation of the representational system.

One demonstration of this phenomenon can be seen in Figure 5 (Ruchkin & John, 1966). The upper (*a*) row of data shows the average evoked response in the lateral geniculate nucleus (left) and the nucleus reticularis (right) as a trained animal responds correctly upon the presentation of the 10-Hz flicker CS which was used during training. The bottom (*c*) row of

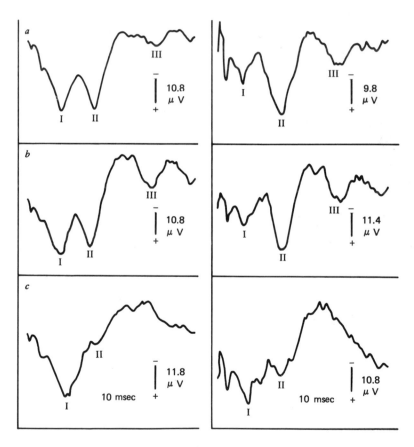

Figure 5. Generalization (b) and no-response (c) averages are based on 42 evoked potentials, and conditioned-response (a) averages on 100 evoked potentials. Averages are from lateral geniculate nucleus (left) and nucleus reticularis (right). Analysis epoch is 90 msec. (From Ruchkin & John, 1966)

data shows the evoked potential wave shape caused by presentation of a 7.7-Hz test stimulus, with which the animal had no previous experience and to which no behavioral response was made. The second (b) row shows the average evoked response caused when the 7.7-Hz stimulus was presented *and* elicited behavioral generalization, in which the animal performed the conditioned response initially established to the 10-Hz CS. Note the difference between the second and third rows of data. The second row clearly resembles the first row, although the stimuli were different. Components II and III are small or absent in the third row but present in the second row. These components cannot be attributed to the physical stimulus, which was identical in both cases. We interpreted this phenomenon as evidence that under certain circumstances presentation of a novel stimulus could lead to the activation of a representational system and the release of a memory (as shown by the behavior), which was reflected in electrical activity as if a familiar stimulus had occurred.

Similar phenomena obtained on the single-neuron level (John & Morgades, 1969a) indicate that during generalization the temporal pattern of firing of neuronal ensembles actually reproduces the normal firing pattern displayed by such ensembles during the presentation of the familiar conditioned stimulus. These results are illustrated in Figure 6.

It was possible, of course, that these phenomena reflected the actions of nonspecific factors, such as arousal or attention or movement or level of motivation. A variety of controls were carried out to provide reassurance that such was not the case. The most convincing controls, indicating that these released wave shapes were related to activation of the memory of a specific stimulus and its meaning rather than to such unspecific factors, were experiments on what we called differential generalization (John, Shimokochi, & Bartlett, 1969). In these experiments, cats were trained to perform one behavior (CR1) upon presentation of a flicker (V1) or a click (A1) at one frequency and to perform a different behavior (CR2) upon presentation of a flicker (V2) or a click (A2) at a different frequency. [In some animals, CR1 was an approach response and CR2 an avoidance response (CAR). In other animals, the two responses were both CARs which required the depression of levers on opposite sides of a work panel. In a third group, the responses were both approach responses to get food but were performed by different manipulanda.]

After these behaviors were thoroughly established and well overtrained, the procedure referred to as differential generalization was introduced. In this procedure, trials with a neutral stimulus (V3 or A3), the frequency of which was located midway between the two conditioned stimuli, were occasionally interspersed in random sequences of the two conditioned stimuli which had been used during differential training. On some occasions,

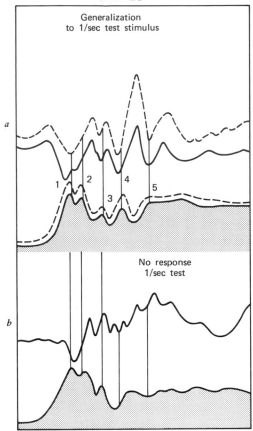

CATI LG

Generalization
to 1/sec test stimulus

a

1 2 3 4 5

No response
1/sec test

b

Figure 6. Average evoked response and poststimulus histogram wave shapes simultaneously recorded from a chronically implanted microelectrode. (*a*) *Upper dotted curve*: usual wave shape of average evoked response to a 2/second flicker CS in trials resulting in correct performance of a conditioned lever press for a food reward. *Lower dotted curve*: the poststimulus histogram, which shows the probability of unit firing as a function of time after presentation of the 2/second CS. *Upper solid curve*: average evoked response wave shape elicited by 1/second test stimulus in trials resulting in generalization, in which the conditioned response was performed to this neutral stimulus. *Lower solid curve*: the shaded area under this curve shows the probability of discharge in the neuronal ensemble as a function of time after presentation of the 1/second test stimulus in trials resulting in generalization. Note the close similarity between the wave shapes of evoked responses and poststimulus histograms elicited by the CS and the test stimulus when generalization occurs. (*b*) Average evoked response (*upper curve*) and poststimulus histogram (*lower curve, shaded*) elicited by the 1/second test stimulus in trials when generalization fails to occur. Note the differences in components 4 and 5 under these circumstances.
All computations based on 200 representations of the stimulus spanning 10–20 behavioral trials. Analysis epoch is 125 msec. (From John & Morgades, 1969a)

the animal treated $V3$ as if it were functionally equivalent to $V1$ and performed CR1 in response to $V3$ presentation ($V3$ CR1). On other occasions, the animal treated $V3$ as if it were equivalent to $V2$ and performed the opposite behavior ($V3$ CR2). The $V3$ presentations leading to these two different outcomes were analyzed separately. Typical results are shown in Figure 7.

Figure 7 illustrates data obtained from a cat in which CR1 consisted of a lever press for food (CR) while CR2 consisted of a lever press to avoid electric shock (CAR). The upper wave shape in Figure 7 illustrates the evoked potential normally observed in the lateral geniculate body of this cat upon presentation of $V1$, when CR was correctly performed ($V1$ CR). The bottom wave shape illustrates the potential typically elicited in this structure upon presentation of $V2$, when the conditioned avoidance response was correctly performed ($V2$ CAR). The other wave shapes in the figure illustrate the average evoked responses observed when $V3$ elicited performance of the CR (illustrated in the second wave shape—$V3$

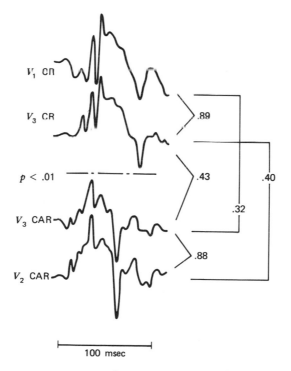

100 msec

Figure 7. Average response wave shapes recorded at left lateral geniculate body to the CR and the CAR. V_1, V_2, and V_3 are different flicker frequencies. Numbers at right give correlations between wave forms. (From John, Shimokochi, & Bartlett, 1969)

CR) and when $V3$ resulted in the performance of the CAR (illustrated in the third wave shape—$V3$ CAR). The intermittent line between the second and third average evoked responses indicates the portions of the analysis epoch in $V3$ CR and $V3$ CAR that were significantly different at better than the 0.01 level. These results have now been replicated in 14 animals.

Since $V3$ presentation occurred in a random sequence of $V1$ and $V2$, it occurred as frequently after $V1$ as it did after $V2$. The correct responses to $V1$ and $V2$ were performed on opposite sides of the apparatus. Thus $V3$ trials occurring after a $V1$ presentation found the animal on one side of the apparatus, facing in the opposite direction from his orientation when $V3$ trials occurred after a $V2$ presentation. The $V3$ trials presented in different orientations were analyzed separately, and no evidence of an influence of orientation on the average evoked response wave shape was observed.

Perhaps the most convincing control for possible artifact due to position or movement which was carried out involved the training of a cat to perform a left-lever press for food (CR-L) on presentation of a steady tone ($T1$) and a right-lever press for food (CR-R) upon presentation of a different steady tone ($T2$). After the establishment of this differential response, $V3$ was presented paired with $T1$ on some trials and paired with $T2$ on other trials. In these trials $V3$ had no cue value, being a passive concomitant of the conditioned stimulus presentations. Average evoked responses to $V3$ were computed separately when it had been paired with $T1$, resulting in performance of CR-L, and when it had been paired with $T2$, resulting in performance of CR-R. Only slight differences were observed between these wave shapes.

Evidence of this sort led us to conclude that the released activity observed under such circumstances was not of nonspecific origin but was related to the activation of a specific memory. We call this released activity the readout component. Examination of the correlation coefficients seen at the right side of Figure 7 shows that the readout component really recapitulates the effect of the usual conditioned stimulus. Thus $V3$ CR correlates highly with $V1$ CR, while $V3$ CAR correlates highly with $V2$ CAR. It is clear, therefore, that a representational system is built in the brain by experience which, upon subsequent stimulation by an appropriate novel stimulus, has the capability of releasing an accurate facsimile of the electrical effects of this past experience.

Readout components with closely similar shapes have been observed in a wide variety of structures under these circumstances. We have found them in 65 out of 96 electrode placements that we have studied, distributed among 26 different anatomical regions. Readout wave shapes appear almost simultaneously in a variety of regions, suggesting that the representational system is activated in a unitary fashion.

It seems reasonable to suggest that the mechanism whose action can be seen in the release of the readout component is involved when memories are activated during the thought process, during imagination, and during fantasy. Similar phenomena have been observed in man, as shown by a study in which some of us participated with Dr. Zubin some years ago (Sutton, Tueting, Zubin, & John, 1967).

Figure 8 shows a result from that study. Subjects were presented with single or double clicks, which could be either loud or soft. In some sessions the subject was asked to guess whether the stimuli would be loud or soft, whereas in other sessions he was instructed to guess whether the stimuli would be single or double. Figure 8 shows that, when intensity was the relevant dimension, the evoked potential wave shape showed a marked deflection from the first click and little or no response to the second stimulus, even when the second click was present. Conversely, when singleness versus doubleness was the relevant dimension, all evoked responses contained a clear second deflection at the time when the second click was present or *ought* to have occurred. In the case of the single clicks, the two upper pairs of tracings in the figure, the clear responses seen in the latter part of the wave shape were caused by the absence of an expected click. Barlow, Morrell, and Morrell (1967) have similarly demonstrated the production of evoked potential by man when an expected event fails to occurr.

Another example of this is shown in Figure 9. These data were reported by Klinke, Fruhstorfer, and Finkenzeller (1968). The upper wave shape in this figure shows the average evoked response elicited by 80 repetitions of triplets of clicks. The second wave shape shows the average evoked response elicited by presentations of "triplets" from which the middle click had been deleted. The response to the absent click is unequivocally clear. The third and fourth lines of the figure illustrate the repetition of this experiment with a different subject.

The examples given above indicate that a man can produce an evoked response at the time that a stimulus is expected. In other work (John, Herrington, & Sutton, 1967), we have shown that the wave shape of an evoked response depends on the geometric form of the visual stimulus. In that work, we showed that stimuli having the same form but differing with respect to physical size and stimulus energy elicited evoked responses of markedly similar wave shape. We suggested at that time that this similarity of wave shape, caused by stimuli of similar meaning but different energy, indicated that the brain was computing an invariant which reflected stimulus *significance*. The ability to perform this computation suggested

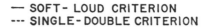

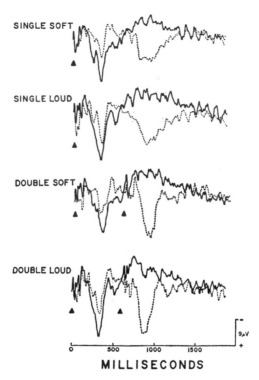

Figure 8. Average response wave forms obtained to four types of clicks for one subject. Triangles indicate points at which clicks were delivered. (From Sutton, Tueting, Zubin, & John, 1967)

that experience with a geometric form built a representational system capable of releasing the wave shape typical for this form, upon appropriate stimulation.

It was decided to seek for direct evidence that such was the case. Herrington and Schneidau (1968) recorded the responses of subjects to the presentation of squares and circles. When the evoked response wave shape typically elicited by a geometric form had been determined for a subject, the patterned stimuli were terminated. The subject was then asked to look at the screen and *imagine* that he saw a square or a circle appear before him whenever a blank flash was presented. The responses evoked by the blank flashes were averaged.

In some instances, as seen in Figure 10, it was possible to tell the sub-

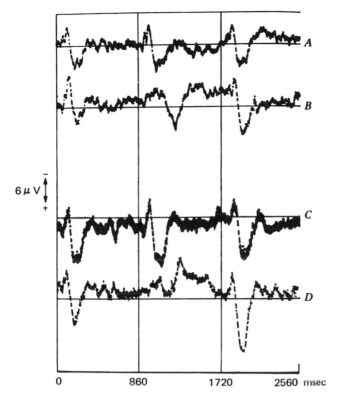

6 μ V

0   860   1720   2560 msec

Figure 9. Typical responses from two subjects (curves *A* and *B* from RK, curves *C* and *D* from HF). The sweep starts with the onset of a stimulus. Each curve represents 80 summations. *A* and *C* are average responses to triplets of clicks; in *B* and *D* the middle click has been deleted. (From Klinke, Fruhstorfer, & Finkenzeller, 1968)

ject which form he had imagined in his visual field. There was sufficient similarity between the wave shape of the average evoked response elicited by actual presentation of the stimulus and that released from imagination during presentation of a blank flash. These data show that the readout phenomenon which we have discussed has its counterpart in man, that indeed the representational system built during experience can be activated, and that during the process of thought or imagination the representational system literally re-creates the electrical activity caused by the past experience, which is retrieved into consciousness.

Our first answer, then, to the question, "Where is fancy bred?" is that not only does it originate, as Warren McCulloch stoutly maintained, in the head (1951) but, furthermore, it arises in the anatomically extended representational systems whose electrical activity we have been describing.

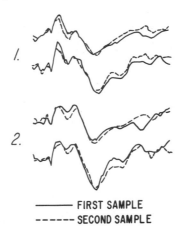

——— FIRST SAMPLE
------ SECOND SAMPLE

Figure 10. Evoked potentials recorded from vertex of scalp of a human subject. *1. Top*: while the subject attempts to visualize a *square* in his visual field each time that it is illuminated by a blank flash. *Bottom*: as before, but while subject thinks of a *circle. 2. Top*: during presentation of a *square* in the visual field. *Bottom*: as before, but during presentation of a *circle* of equal area. In each case, the solid wave shape represents the first average response computation, and the dotted wave shape represents a replication. Each computation is based on 100 repetitions. The analysis epoch was 500 msec. (From Herrington & Schneidau, 1968)

We have not as yet talked about the detailed neuronal mechanisms responsible for these processes. The evoked potentials that we have described are a reflection of underlying neuronal events. Unfortunately, because of limitations of space, these data cannot be presented here. Essentially, however, they amplify the conclusion that the correlates of specific experiences are widespread throughout the brain. Thus we have shown that, just as with the wave forms of slow activity recorded with a gross electrode, the firing pattern of individual neurons evoked by two differentially conditioned stimuli are distinctly different from each other and are constant across large regions of the brain (John & Morgades, 1969a, b). In still other experiments, we have shown that the invariance in firing patterns of neurons does not arise from synchronization in the activity of adjacent subgroups of neurons; rather, it is statistical in nature (Morrell, Nord, & John, unpublished data). At any instant, different cells fire and this firing varies greatly from one presentation of the stimulus to another. Yet the statistical pattern that emerges is invariant, both in the temporal pattern obtained for a particular stimulus, and over wide regions of the brain.

It is clear that information about a stimulus is represented in the brain, not by the firing of specific cells which stand for this event, but rather by the appearance of characteristic temporal patterns of coherence in the activity of huge neuronal ensembles distributed extensively throughout a variety of anatomical regions. This evidence argues for diffuse distribution of information and its representation by a statistical spatiotemporal process, rather than by deterministic firing of specific localized cells in a unique and invariant response. If this is the case, then there can be no "pontifical" cell that receives the report of the reporters; the information that impinges on the brain must be integrated statistically, assessing coherent spatiotemporal patterns in the activity of diffuse ensembles of many cells.

This conclusion supports our intuitive feeling that the richness of sensory experience cannot be mediated by a particular neuron but must arise in some fashion from the activity of large numbers of cells responsive to a wide variety of stimulation. "Awareness" of the many different but coexistent facets of each moment, which we can define as *information about the information*, must also demand the appearance of coherent processes in populations of cells. There seems to be no logical reason to differentiate between the statistical processes necessary to represent the information about sensation in the brain and those which represent the information about the information. We postulate, therefore, that subjective experience is the concomitant of orderly activity in neuronal ensembles. The content of the mind, we argue, is the sum of those coherent, spatiotemporal processes in neuronal populations of which the momentary activity of the brain is composed.

This whole, the existence of conscious experience, is not to be deduced from the sum of the parts of which brain activity is composed, the firing of single cells. There are other examples in nature in which the whole is greater than the sum of its parts and in which the characteristics of the whole cannot be inferred from an examination of the parts. There is no mystery in this, nor need we now insist upon a deductive explanation of how mental experience arises. Logically, this proposal is no more objectionable than the postulates of quantum mechanics, themselves rather arbitrary. We postulate that mind arises in brain as a consequence of the appearance of orderly spatiotemporal patterns of activity, in extensive neuronal ensembles. These coherent or statistically nonrandom events not only represent information in the brain but also constitute a process with the concomitant of subjective experience. We regard that postulate, not as a metaphysical utterance, but as a scientific, working hypothesis. Presumably, future research will shed further light upon the mechanisms of this process.

POSSIBLE CAUSES OF PSYCHIATRIC DISORDER

We distinguished earlier between two possible types of psychiatric disorder—one which arose from normal processing of experiences that social norms would define as abnormal, and another which arose from malfunction of the brain mechanisms necessary for processing, storing, and retrieving information and therefore essential to the processes of thinking, imagination, and fantasy. For the conceptual scheme which has been proposed in this paper, the first kind of abnormality provides little theoretical difficulty. Past traumatic experiences, stored by representational systems constructed as described, must be expected inevitably to arise in consciousness, to influence the content of thought, to be the subject of fantasy, to direct the imagination. To understand these disorders and to deal with them, it would seem essential to identify the traumatic experience and to make its effects explicit to the individual. Psychological and pharmacological techniques must be utilized to dull or perhaps even obliterate the effect that such experience has had on the representational systems of the brain.

The second kind of psychiatric disorder, which has its origin in malfunctions of brain mechanisms, would seem to have a number of possible causes. It might arise from changes in the metabolic characteristics of the system, resulting in an alteration of the signal-to-noise ratio, so that the coherence levels necessary for information to be stored and retrieved, reflecting the ease of access and the probability of access to memories, have been either drastically raised or lowered. There has been, as it were, a change in the confidence level which the system requires to accept data. Some suggestion that this might be the case can be found in the work of Callaway, Jones, and Layne on segmental set in schizophrenia (1965).

Similarly, one can conceive of a representational system which has a bias due to the pathological excess of activity in certain regions, perhaps arising from metabolic disorders or from prolonged, intense stimulation. The studies of the recovery cycle by Shagass and Schwartz (1964) provide support for the suggestion that in many psychiatric disorders the aftereffects of excitation are abnormal. Inhibitory processes may not be as effective as in the normal individual. Under such circumstances, the representational system might remain relatively close to the level of excitation required for it to become activated as a whole because of the tonic bombardment of the system by the activity of some abnormal region. We have provided evidence that a representational system can be activated by the occurrence of activity in one of its parts. One can conceive of changes in the levels of tonic activation of different recollections such that the memories or actions represented by particular systems will play an abnormally frequent role in imagination, will compel fantasy, and will occupy thought more than one might consider normal. This kind of activity might be illustrated by the pattern seen for the obsessive psychotic in the work of Livanov, cited earlier. Conversely, defects in the activity of certain regions might cause failure to participate in the formation of representational systems, as suggested by the reported failure of frontal regions of psychotic patients to become integrated with other parts of the brain during mental activity. These deficits in activity might influence thought, imagination, and fantasy, either because certain affective or cognitive components that normally constitute a portion of such recollections are absent, or because the feedback mechanisms that normally control the emergence of such content into consciousness are functioning inadequately.

In order to evaluate such notions, one must measure the signal-to-noise ratio in the central nervous system of individuals suffering from psychiatric disorders. It is essential to devise measures of neural integrative function to determine whether various brain regions participate appropriately in the establishment of representational systems and whether the relative involvement of various functional systems of the brain in the representation of experience is properly balanced. Measures of reactivity must be devised to establish whether different types of information have appropriate impact and contribute to the dynamic construction of representational systems in a fashion accurately reflecting their contribution to an experience.

The same fundamental mechanisms must be responsible for the storage, retrieval, and representation of information in the brain, whether it be incorporated into realistically perceived sensations and experiences, normal thought images, plausible imagination, and enriched fantasy, or into misperceived experience, bizarre content of consciousness, distorted imagination, and distressing fantasies that dominate consciousness to an extent harmful to the individual. Recent experiments provide insight into the statistical nature of the mechanisms by which information is represented in the brain. It seems logically parsimonious to assume that the mechanism of subjective experience, the processing of information about information, is similarly statistical. Although it will undoubtedly be difficult to devise the appropriate functional measures, useful insights into the nature of psychiatric disorder might be obtained from this theoretical viewpoint.

REFERENCES

Aslanov, A. S. Correlation between cortical potentials in patients with obsessive neuroses. In V. S. Rusinov (Ed.), *Electrophysiology of the central nervous system.* New York: Plenum, 1970. Pp. 39–47.

Barlow, J. S., Morrell, L., & Morrell, F. Some observations on evoked responses in relation to temporal conditioning to paired stimuli in man. *Proceedings of the International Colloquium on Mechanisms of Orienting Reactions in Man,* Bratislava-Smolenice, Czechoslovakia, 1967.

Bartlett, F., & John, E. R. Means and variances of average-response wave forms. *Science,* 1970, **169,** 304–305.

Burns, B. D., & Smith, G. K. Transmission of information in the unanesthetized cat's isolated forebrain. *Journal of Physiology,* 1962, **164,** 238–251.

Callaway, E., Jones, R. T., & Layne, R. S. Evoked responses and segmental set of schizophrenia. *Archives of General Psychiatry,* 1965, **12,** 83–89.

Chow, K. L., Lindsley, D. F., & Gollender, M. Modification of response patterns of lateral geniculate neurons after paired stimulation of contralateral and ipsilateral eyes. *Journal of Neurophysiology,* 1968, **31,** 729–739.

Dumenko, V. N. The electrographic study of relationships between various cortical areas in dogs during the elaboration of a conditioned reflex stereotype. In I. N. Knipst (Ed.), *Contemporary problems of electrophysiology of the central nervous system.* Moscow: Academy of Science, 1967. Pp. 104–111.

Galambos, R., & Sheatz, G. C. An electroencephalograph study of classical conditioning. *American Journal of Physiology,* 1962, **203,** 173–184.

Gavrilova, N. A. Spatial synchronization of cortical potentials in patients with disturbances of association. In V. S. Rusinov (Ed.), *Electrophysiology of the central nervous system.* New York: Plenum, 1970. Pp. 129–143.

Gerstein, G. L. Detection and interpretation of interactions between neurons. Paper presented at the 3rd International Biophysics Congress, Cambridge, Mass., 1969.

Glivenko, E. V., Korol'Kova, T. A., & Kuznetsova, G. D. Investigation of the spatial correlation between the cortical potentials of the rabbit during formation of a conditioned defensive reflex. *Fiziolgicheskii Zhurnal SSSR imeni I. M. Sechenova,* 1962, **48,** 1026.

Herrington, R. N., & Schneidau, P. Effects of imagery on waveshape of visual evoked response. *Experientia,* 1968, **24,** 1136–1137.

Hubel, D. H., & Wiesel, T. N. Receptive fields, binocular interaction and functional architecture in the cat's visual cortex. *Journal of Physiology,* 1962, **160,** 106–154.

John, E. R. *Mechanisms of memory.* New York: Academic Press, 1967.

John, E. R., Herrington, R. N., & Sutton, S. Effects of visual form on the evoked response. *Science,* 1967, **155,** 1439–1442.

John, E. R., & Killam, K. F. Electrophysiological correlates of avoidance conditioning in the cat. *Journal of Pharmacology and Experimental Therapeutics,* 1959, **125,** 252.

John, E. R., & Morgades, P. P. Neural correlates of conditioned responses studied with multiple chronically implanted moving microelectrodes. *Experimental Neurology,* 1969, **23,** 412–425. (a)

John, E. R., & Morgades, P. P. Patterns and anatomical distribution of evoked potentials and multiple unit activity by conditioned stimuli in trained cats. *Communications in Behavioral Biology,* 1969, **3,** 181–207. (b)

John, E. R., Ruchkin, D. S., Leiman, A., Sachs, R., & Ahn, H. Electrophysiological studies of generalization using both peripheral and central conditioned stimuli. *Proceedings of the 23rd International Congress of Physiology,* Tokyo, 1965, **4,** 618–627.

John, E. R., Ruchkin, D. S., & Villegas, J. Signal analysis of evoked potentials recorded from cats during conditioning. *Science,* 1963, **141,** 429–431.

John, E. R., Ruchkin, D. S., & Villegas, J. Signal analysis and behavioral correlates of evoked potential configurations in cats. *Annals of the New York Academy of Sciences,* 1964, **112,** 362–420.

John, E. R., Shimokochi, M., & Bartlett, F. Neural readout from memory during generalization. *Science,* 1969, **164,** 1519.

Klinke, R., Fruhstorfer, H., & Finkenzeller, P. Evoked responses as a function of external and stored information. *Electroencephalography and Clinical Neurophysiology,* 1968, **25,** 119.

Knipst, I. N. Spatial synchronization of bioelectrical activity in the cortex and some subcortical structures in rabbit's brain during conditioning. In I. N. Knipst (Ed.), *Contemporary problems of electrophysiology of the central nervous system.* Moscow: Academy of Science, 1967. Pp. 127–137.

Korol'Kova, T. A., & Shvets, T. B. Interrelation between distant synchronization and steady potential shifts in the cerebral cortex. In I. N. Knipst (Ed.), *Contemporary problems of electrophysiology of the central nervous system.* Moscow: Academy of Science, 1967. Pp. 160–167.

Lettvin, J. Y., Maturana, H. R., McCulloch, W. S., & Pitts, W. What the frog's eye tells the frog's brain. *Proceedings of the Institute of Radio Engineers,* 1959, **47,** 1940.

Livanov, M. N. Information processing in the nervous system. In *Proceedings of the 22nd International Congress of Physiological Science,* Leiden Amsterdam: Excerpta Medica Foundation, 1962, P. 899.

Livanov, M. N. The role of distant synchronization of cortical biopotentials in realization of temporary connections. In *Proceedings of the 23rd International Congress of Physiological Science,* Tokyo. Amsterdam: Excerpta Medica Foundation, 1965. P. 600.

McCulloch, W. S. Why the mind is in the head. In L. A. Jeffress (Ed.), *Cerebral mechanisms in behavior.* New York: Wiley, 1951. Pp. 42–111.

Morrell, F., Engel, J., & Bouris, W. The effect of visual experience on the firing pattern of visual cortical neurons. *Electroencephalography and Clinical Neurophysiology,* 1967, **23,** 89.

Ruchkin, D. S., & John, E. R. Evoked potential correlates of generalization. *Science,* 1966, **153,** 209–211.

Shagass, C., & Schwartz, M. Recovery functions of somatosensory peripheral nerve and cerebral evoked responses in man. *Electroencephalography and Clinical Neurophysiology,* 1964, **17,** 126–135.

Spinelli, D. N., Pribram, K. H., & Weingarten, M. Visual receptive field modification induced by non-visual stimuli. *Federation Proceedings,* 1966, **25,** 574. (Abstract)

Sutton, S., Tueting, P., Zubin, J., & John, E. R. Information delivery and the sensory evoked potential. *Science,* 1967, **155,** 1436–1439.

Yoshii, N., Pruvot, P., & Gastaut, H. Electroencephalographic activity of the mesencephalic reticular formation during conditioning in the cat. *Electroencephalography and Clinical Neurophysiology,* 1957, **9,** 595.

CHAPTER 18

A Learning Theory of Schizophrenia: Thirteen Years Later

SARNOFF A. MEDNICK and FINI SCHULSINGER

In 1958, one of us suggested a theory (Mednick, 1958) that considered schizophrenia to be a pattern of well-learned avoidance responses. The theory proposed a number of specific, measurable physiological characteristics that would predispose to, or, better, give an aptitude for learning, avoidance responses. It was suggested that this aptitude functions in the same manner as perfect pitch and nimble fingers might predispose one to learning to play the violin. Given the aptitude, many interacting variables would help to determine whether the pattern would or would not be learned. The theory had the peculiar advantages of testability and flexibility. It was precise enough to be testable and, when shown to be wrong, was young enough to be flexible.

Properties of the theory tended to orient research work and thinking in certain directions. If the behavior pattern in schizophrenia was taken as a complex set of avoidance responses, this had certain consequences for what might be the most promising approach to dealing with the disorder, because such well-learned, avoidance responses are automatically self reinforcing and are extremely difficult to extinguish or to replace.

In animal research an avoidance response (typically a gross act) can be extinguished by physically preventing the response from occurring in the presence of the avoidance stimulus and not delivering the punishment. In terms of the theory, however, the bulk of the schizophrenic's avoidance responses are thoughts. These are, at this time, beyond our technical capacity to prevent or control. Thus, once well learned, these avoidance responses are for all practical purposes beyond our control. No, in terms of treatment, it would be better to deal with the individual before these avoidance responses were learned. This rationale was an important reason that led us to concentrate our efforts in directions leading to research and theory on *primary prevention*. We were also attracted to research on prevention since by its nature this approach would open the opportunity for experimental-manipulative designs rather than the mire of correlative designs in which workers in the field have, until now, been struggling.

Research on prevention that acknowledges the likelihood of genetic and childhood etiology must by its nature be long term, arduous, and expensive. Much is at stake in the choice of the modes of intervention to be evaluated. A single investigator's or team of investigators' lifetime might with great luck and longevity be sufficient for two such studies. Combing the field of schizophrenia research did not yield many reliable suggestions regarding interventive techniques. Almost all such research had been completed on individuals already quite schizophrenic. It seemed possible that the results of these studies might reflect only the ravaging effects of schizophrenia rather than any factor (relating to etiology) that might have given hints as to possible interventive techniques (see Mednick & McNeil, 1968). For these reasons, we turned to the study of populations currently not mentally ill but at high risk for schizophrenia.

A LONGITUDINAL PROJECT

In 1962 in Copenhagen, Denmark, we intensively examined 207 "normally functioning" children of chronic and severely schizophrenic mothers. We also examined 104 controls. The study is prospective and longitudinal. We intend to follow these 311 subjects for 20–25 years. During the course of these years we estimate that approximately 100 of the high-risk children will succumb to some form of mental illness; 25–30 should become schizophrenic.

The high-risk design can be conceptualized as developing at three levels. At the first level we can study the distinguishing characteristics of children with schizophrenic mothers in comparison with children with no familial psychiatric background. At the second level we can estimate that about 50% of the high-risk children will become seriously socially deviant. Rather good controls for these deviants are the children with schizophrenic mothers who do not become deviant. At the third level we can estimate that perhaps 15% of the high-risk subjects will be diagnosed as schizophrenic. The remaining 35% of high-risk deviants can be considered appropriate controls for these schizophrenics, as may the nondeviant, high-risk children and the low-risk children.

Such a study may not be readily or at least easily replicated. Others using even the same design may not be attracted to the same variables. In view of this fact a form of replication can be built into the design. At the second level, the eventually deviant individuals may be conceived of as suffering breakdown in waves. Thus there are potential replications of the first data analysis. (It should be mentioned that the precision of the replication might be attenuated if the waves differ in age of breakdown or diagnosis.) At the third level the schizophrenics may be conceived of as suffering breakdown in two waves.

There are certain advantages in the study of such high-risk populations:

1. They have not yet experienced many aspects of the schizophrenic life, such as hospitalizations and drugs. Therefore these factors do not yet color their reactions.

2. The researchers, relatives, teachers, and the subject himself do not know that he will become schizophrenic, thus relieving the data of a certain part of the burden of bias. The bias is certainly not greater for the future schizophrenic than for other high-risk subjects who do not succumb.

3. The information we gather is current, not retrospective. That part of our inquiry that is retrospective is less so than it would be if the subjects were adults.

4. The data are uniformly and systematically obtained. This is in contrast to retrospective studies that make use of childhood and school records concerning adult schizophrenics.

Since 1962, 20 of our high-risk children have suffered severe psychiatric breakdown. We will briefly summarize the 1962 premorbid characteristics that distinctly differentiated these 20 sick children from controls. The major part of our remarks will consist of some speculations concerning the etiology of schizophrenia in the light of these and related research findings.

Method

The high- and low-risk samples were matched, individual for individual for certain variables (Table 1).

As may be seen, the average age of the sample was 15.1 years (the range was 9–20 years). There would have been some advantage in testing a younger group. However, it will take 20–25 years for the present sample to pass through the major risk period for schizophrenia. The subjects' mean age was selected so as to maximize the probability that the investigators would still be alive at the conclusion of this risk period. Studies of 3-year old and 11-year old high-risk samples are also being undertaken.

Table 1. Characteristics of the Experimental and Control Samples

	Control	Experimental
Number of cases	104	207
Number of boys	59	121
Number of girls	45	86
Mean age[a]	15.1	15.1
Mean social class[b]	2.3	2.2
Mean years of education	7.3	7.0
Percentage of group in children's homes (5 years or more)[c]	14	16
Mean number of years in children's homes (5 years or more)[c]	8.5	9.4
Percentage of group with rural residence[d]	22	26

[a] Defined as age to the nearest whole year.

[b] The scale runs from 0 (low) to 6 (high) and was adapted from Svalastoga (1959).

[c] We considered only experience in children's homes of 5 years' or greater duration. Many of the children in the experimental sample had been in children's homes for brief periods while their mothers were hospitalized. Such experience was regarded as quite different from that of children who actually had to make a children's home their home until they could go out and earn their own living.

[d] "Rural residence" was defined as living in a town with a population of 2500 persons or fewer.

Procedures

In addition to weight and height the following measures were taken in the intensive 1962 examinations:

1. Psychophysiological conditioning and extinction testing.
2. Wechsler Intelligence Scale for Children (Danish adaptation).
3. Personality Inventory.
4. Word Association Test.
5. Continuous Association Test.
6. Adjective Check List.
7. Psychiatric interview, yielding level of adjustment rating.
8. Parent interview.
9. School report.
10. Midwife's report on pregnancy and delivery.

More detailed statements of methodology can be found in Mednick and Schulsinger (1965a, 1965b, 1968).

Results

As of 1970, the first wave of 20 breakdowns (which we call the Sick Group) had been identified. (For their clinical status see Mednick & Schulsinger, 1968.) Of these, 13 have been admitted to psychiatric hospitals with many diagnoses, including schizophrenia. The 7 not admitted include some who are clearly schizophrenic. The clinical status of these individuals was ascertained by our follow-up procedures. To each of these 20 we matched another high-risk subject (Well Group) of the same age, sex, social class, and institutional rearing status. In addition we matched these subjects for the psychiatrist's 1962 level of adjustment rating. We tried as much as possible to select for the Well Group individuals who, since 1962, had shown some improvement in level of adjustment. Also 20 individuals selected from the low-risk group constituted a Control Group for comparison purposes.

This matching yielded two groups of high-risk subjects. In 1962, both were judged to be equal in level of adjustment. Yet since then one group has improved in level of mental health; the other group has suffered severe psychiatric breakdown. Why? Part of the answer could lie with the predisposing characteristics measured in 1962 at the time of the intensive examination.

The most important characteristics distinguishing the Sick Group from the Well and Control Groups were the following:

1. Those in the Sick Group lost their schizophrenic mothers to psychiatric hospitalization much earlier in their lives than did the other two groups. These early-hospitalized mothers were also more severely schizophrenic. Individuals in the Well Group lost their mothers at approximately the same time as did the Control Group. In view of the greater severity of illness of the mothers who left their homes early, these data may be interpreted in relatively genetic or environmental terms.

2. The teachers' reports indicated that the subjects in the Sick Group tended to be disturbing to the class. They were disciplinary problems and tended to be domineering and aggressive. They created conflicts and disrupted the class with their talking. This was true of 53% of the Sick Group, 18% of the Well Group, and 11% of the Control Group.

3. On the Continual Association Test, where the subject is asked to give, in one minute, as many single-word associations as he can to a stimulus word, the Sick Group showed two distinctive patterns. These individuals had a strong tendency to rattle off a whole series of words that were interrelated but, contextually, relatively irrelevant. Their associations also tended to "drift" away from the stimulus word. Contrary to instructions and cautions they might begin responding to their own responses; for example, to

the stimulus word "table" they might respond "chair, top, leg, girl, pretty, sky. . . ." Those in the Sick Group who do not show drifting can apparently manage to avoid this only by restricting themselves to one or two responses per stimulus word for the entire one-minute period.

4. Some of the variables most sharply differentiating the Sick Group from the Well and Control Groups were the electrodermal measures (galvanic skin response, GSR) taken during the psychophysiological testing. These measures largely reflect the functioning of the body's stress mobilization mechanisms.

(a) The latency of the GSR was substantially shorter for the Sick Group than for either of the other two groups.

(b) The GSR latency for the Sick Group did not show any signs of habituation. This was especially marked in the responses to the UCS (unconditioned stimulus) stress stimulus trials. The Control and Well Groups' rapid habituation of latency was seen in the progressive increase of their response latencies from the first to the last of the stress trials. The latencies of the Sick Group, on the other hand, progressively decreased, suggesting a negative habituation or even increasing irritability. From the first to the last UCS trial, 69% of the Well Group exhibited a slowing of response latency (habituation); 75% of the Sick Group actually *increased* the speed of their response.

(c) A well-documented characteristic of conditioned GSR behavior is the rapidity with which it demonstrates experimental extinction. In both the Well and the Control Groups electrodermal responsiveness was already dropping off by the end of the stress stimulus trials. After these stress trials we presented a series of nine nonreinforced test trials for generalization and speed of extinction of the conditioned response. The Well and Control Groups displayed very rapid extinction, that is, they responded to only one or two of the extinction test trials. The Sick Group, however, exhibited great resistance to extinction in many cases, responding with tenacity until the very end of the extinction series.

(d) The Sick Group showed a remarkably fast rate of recovery from momentary states of automatic imbalance. Once a GSR was made, we measured the rate at which recovery to basal level proceeded. On some trials rate of recovery almost perfectly separated the Sick and Control Groups. The pooled Sick and Well Groups' distributions for rate of recovery typically found 70% of the Sick and 30% of the Well Group above the median.

The above material is discussed in greater detail in Mednick and Schulsinger (1968).

5. In a previous report on the differences between the Sick, Well and Control Groups we pointed out that, although in our analyses of data on birth complications "there was a slight general tendency for the Sick Group

to have had a more difficult birth, none of the differences reached statistical significance [Mednick & Schulsinger, 1968, pp. 280–281]." Subsequent, more careful, examination of these data revealed, however, that although it was true that no single complication significantly differentiated the groups, 70% of the members of the Sick Group had suffered one or more serious pregnancy or birth complications (PBC). This contrasted with 15% of the Well Group and 33% of the Control Group. The PBCs included anoxia, prematurity, prolonged labor, placental difficulty, umbilical cord complications, mother's illness during pregnancy, multiple births, and breech presentations. Careful perusal of these data brought out an additional striking relationship within the Sick Group (and the entire high-risk group): there was a marked correspondence between PBCs and the anomalous electrodermal behavior reported above. All the GSR differences between the Sick and Well Groups could be explained by the PBCs in the Sick Group. In the Control Group and low-risk group the PBCs were not as strongly associated with these extreme GSR effects. This suggests that the PBCs trigger some characteristics that may be genetically predisposed. The PBCs seem to damage the modulatory control of the body's stress-response mechanisms; they are associated with rapid response onset, poor habituation of the response, poor extinction of the conditioned electrodermal response, and very rapid recovery from the response. In terms of the theoretical orientation guiding this project this pattern of poor ANS (autonomic nervous system) modulation may be viewed as an important etiological factor in the development of mental illness, especially schizophrenia.

These findings were quite intriguing. We have attempted to interpret them, and to make some small tests of these interpretations, and we have begun new research exploring hypotheses raised by these results.

The finding that immediately raised fertile questions was the high frequency of PBCs in the Sick Group. What damage might these PBCs have done and where? We first sought for inklings of brain sites particularly sensitive to being damaged by PBCs. We then examined animal studies in which analogous damage had been inflicted by surgical lesion to these same particularly sensitive brain sites. The reports of the behavior of animals suffering surgically inflicted lesions to these same areas were then searched for instances of behavior similar to those that we observed in our PBC-Sick Group subjects. We hoped in this manner to generate hypotheses regarding specific sites of brain lesions in our PBC subjects.

BRAIN SITES OF SELECTIVE VULNERABILITY

Future difficulties for the fetus result from PBCs chiefly because of the great sensitivity of neural tissue to anoxia. (Mechanical damage probably plays a less significant role, although through vascular obstruction it can also lead to anoxia.) Researchers have singled out particular brain structures as being "selectively vulnerable" to the effects of anoxia. These areas include, most prominently, the hippocampus, the amygdala, and the Purkinje cells of the cerebellum. Of these areas, Spector (1965) singles out the hippocampus as being the most vulnerable. He evaluates the effects of anoxia by studying "biochemical lesions," that is, "the initial chemical changes in tissues following the application of harmful agents and preceding anatomical evidence of damage [p. 552]." The chemical changes he has studied as a function of anoxia have been losses in certain enzymes which precede "histological evidence of cell injury by approximately 10h [hours]. It is noteworthy that chemical changes appeared in the hippocampus immediately after anoxia, whilst the other areas showed earliest loss of enzymes after 1–6 h [p. 552]."

Friede (1966) also indicates that the hippocampus (Ammon's Horn) represents one of "the most striking examples of selective vulnerability in the brain and in particular Sommer's Sector, H 1, is known to be a characteristic site for anoxic damage [p. 12]." (Friede links this vulnerability of H 1 to relatively low levels of lactate dehydrogenase in Sommer's Sector.)

ANIMAL ABLATION LITERATURE

Therefore, with the hippocampus as our chief suspect and the amygdala and the cerebellum (Purkinje cells) as additional suspects, we turned next to the animal ablation literature. The strategy here was to see if we could find any similarity between the behavior of members of our Sick Groups with PBCs and the behavior of animals with circumscribed lesions to each of these suspect areas. Conditioning and extinction behaviors are frequent dependent variables in animal ablation studies. This facilitated comparisons with our data since our subjects had gone through a conditioning and extinction session.

Briefly stated, our findings showed that the behavior of hippocampal animals was in some surprising ways like that of our PBC-Sick Group subjects. At this point we must sound a strong note of caution: below we will be relating rat-instrumental and human-classical conditioning data. To draw analogies across two species and two types of conditioning is doubtless a questionable procedure. In this case, however, it has proved of great value for hypothesis formation. It must be emphasized that these ideas are presented in this spirit.

Several aspects of the behavior of hippocampal rate that are of interest to us in the present context should be briefly stated.

1. Rats with hippocampal lesions manifest relatively fast response latency (Kimble, 1969; Rabe & Haddad, 1969; Silveira, 1967).

2. Rats with hippocampal lesions display very poor habituation of the latency of their responses. Whereas normal and cortically damaged control groups exhibit habituation by responding with increasing latencies across a series of test trials, the response latencies of the hippocampal rats do not slow down. These rats continue to respond as though they were experiencing the stimulus for the first time (Kimble, 1968).

3. Rats with hippocampal lesions show great resistance to the experimental extinction of conditioned behavior (Isaacson, Douglas, & Moore, 1961; Niki, 1965).

4. Rats with hippocampal lesions are hyperactive (Kimble, 1963; Roberts, Dember, & Brodwick, 1962).

5. Rats with hippocampal lesions acquire a conditioned avoidance response in a shuttle box more quickly than control or cortically damaged rats (Isaacson, Douglas, & Moore, 1961; Kimble & Gostnell, 1968; Rabe & Haddad, 1969).

In comparing these characteristics with the characteristics described above for the Sick Group we can detect considerable similarity. Both the Sick Group subjects with PBCs and the hippocampal rats manifest fast response latency, very poor habituation, and poor extinction of a conditioned response. We can also tentatively link the hyperactivity of the hippocampal rats to the unruly classroom behavior of our Sick Group subjects. The two points that do not immediately relate to each other are the fast avoidance conditioning of the hippocampal rats and the fast GSR recovery of the Sick Group with PBCs. In terms of some of the components of a theory of schizophrenia advanced earlier (Mednick, 1966; Mednick & Schulsinger, 1968), however, these seemingly independent points may actually be closely related. Thus, if we assume that the fast GSR recovery of the Sick Group with PBCs is also characteristic of the hippocampal rats, we can postulate some basis for the puzzling and consistent finding of unusually fast avoidance learning on the part of the hippocampal rats. Whether one takes a reinforcement or contiguity position, one crucial variable influencing the speed of avoidance conditioning in a shuttle box is the rapidity and amount of fear reduction following a successful avoidance response. After the avoidance response has been made, the speed and the amount of reinforcement depend, in large part, on the speed of fear reduction and hence on the rate of recovery from the stress response (Zeaman & Wegner, 1954). Any rat that recovers unusually rapidly from a stress response will receive a correspondingly rapid reward of fear reduction when he leaps from the electrified grid floor of the shuttle box into the safe compartment. His reinforcement will be greater than that of a rat with normal or slow recovery rate. Thus this fast recovery could be considered an aptitude for avoidance learning. If it does constitute such an aptitude, one would expect that the subjects in the Sick and Well Groups who manifested a fast rate of recovery would also show fast avoidance learning or have learned a large number of avoidance responses. Mednick, Schulsinger, and Lampasso (1971) correlated average rate of GSR recovery with a score for avoidant associates that had been devised by Diderichsen (1967). In the Sick and Well Groups the two scores correlated positively ($r = 0.48$, 23 d.f., $p < .05$). For the Sick, Well, and Control Groups the correlation was also significant ($r = 0.41$, 40 d.f., $p < .01$). In this sample those who had a faster rate of recovery tended to have shown more avoidant associates.

If such fast recovery were *directly* demonstrated, the similarity of hippocampal rats to our PBC-Sick Group subjects would be striking. In the light of the sensitivity of the human hippocampus to the anoxic effects of PBCs, this similarity would suggest the hypothesis that in our high-risk children the PBCs have resulted in damage to the hippocampus. What is further suggested is the possibility that the resultant behavioral anomalies are in some way predispositional to psychiatric breakdown and schizophrenia in individuals with schizophrenic mothers.

In summary, we can say:

1. The most likely site of brain damage resulting from PBCs seems to be the hippocampus, especially Sommer's Sector, H 1.

2. High-risk children who have suffered PBCs exhibit a specific and unique pattern of conditioning, habituation, extinction, and GSR behavior. (This pattern is also exhibited by low-risk children with PBCs but at a diminished level.)

3. This pattern is strikingly similar to the conditioning, habituation, and extinction behavior of rats that have experienced surgical lesions to the hippocampus. These surgical lesions encompass what in the human being would be Sommer's Sector, H 1 (Kimble, 1969).

Another important aspect of behavior that is characteristic of hippocampal rats has been observed in infants who may have suffered anoxia and hence hippocampal damage at birth. Kimble (1968) indicates that "damage to the hippocampus should impair the process of habituation to novel stimuli, as has been reported [Leaton, 1965, p. 291]." This same failure of habituation to novel stimuli has been reported for infants at the ages of 2 days, 5 days, and 30 days in cases where the mother had undergone heavy anesthesia during delivery. The controls were infants of the same age whose mothers had undergone mild or no anesthesia (Conway & Brackbill, 1969). Maternal heavy anesthesia during delivery can affect the fetus, producing retarded respiration and anoxia (Moya & Thorndike, 1963). In the context of this general discussion it is tempting to postulate that in this study anesthesia-induced anoxia produced some hippocampal damage in these children which, in turn, resulted in the behavioral manifestation of a failure of habituation.

Joffe (1969) subjected a group of pregnant rats to repeated, severe, inescapable electric shocks. The resultant pups were tested for response latency and avoidance conditioning in a shuttle box. In comparison to controls, the gestational-stressed pups demonstrated a significantly faster response latency and made significantly more avoidance responses. It is possible to conjecture that the gestational stress produced anoxia (via arterial contractions?), which damaged the vulnerable hippocampus and resulted in the characteristic fast latency and superior avoidance conditioning, a pattern quite similar to that of our perinatally stressed Sick Group. In this context it is important to report a study by B. Mednick (1969), who (working with the records of the mothers of the Sick and Well Groups subjects) found that the pregnancies of the Sick Group subjects' mothers had been marked by far more stress and social upset than the pregnancies of the mothers of Well Group subjects. The psychological shock may be as effective as electric shock during pregnancy.

We are suggesting the existence of a relationship between a pattern of observed habituation-conditioning-extinction findings in our PBC-Sick Group and hypothesized hippocampal damage. Some biochemical-neurophysiological mechanisms may be very tentatively related to this discussion.

Knigge (1963, 1966) has demonstrated that the hippocampus exerts an inhibitory effect over ACTH (adrenocorticotrophic hormone) release from the pituitary gland. Weiss, McEwen, and De Silva (1969) have evidence that this inhibitory influence is called into play only during states of stress reaction. During such stress states a damaged hippocampus could provide a weakened inhibitory influence on the pituitary gland and result in oversecretion of ACTH. Interestingly enough, such ACTH oversecretion may be expected to prolong the extinction of a conditioned response (De Weid, 1965, 1966; De Weid & Bohus, 1966). Such prolonged extinction effects were of course observed in our PBC-Sick Group subjects and hippocampal rats. It may be suggested that one basis for this failure of extinction was a superabundance of circulating ACTH due to the failure of a damaged hippocampus to sufficiently inhibit ACTH-pituitary secretion during the stressful psychophysiology session.

This failure to inhibit ACTH secretion because of hippocampal inadequacy may also partially explain the state of hyperarousal that seems characteristic of the schizophrenic (Ax, Beckett, Cohen, Frohman, Tourney, & Gottlieb, 1962; Goldstein, Sugerman, & Stolberg, 1965; Malmo, Shagass,

& Smith, 1951; Mirsky, 1969; Ray, 1963; Venables, 1964, 1966; Venables and Wing, 1962; Zahn, 1964). Biochemically this could be due to the lack of adequate hippocampal inhibition of ACTH secretion during stress periods. The explanation of the state of hyperarousal may also follow a relatively nonbiochemical, neurophysiological route. On the basis of a series of studies observing cortically evoked potentials to visual and auditory stimuli, while concurrently stimulating the hippocampus, Redding (1967) concluded that the hippocampus exerts an inhibitory influence on the brain-stem reticular formation. Therefore an inadequate hippocampus exerting a less than normal inhibitory influence on the reticular formation could contribute to the existence of a chronic state of hyperarousal. Mechanisms by means of which this hyperarousal and hyperlability could translate themselves into the clinical symptoms and life condition of schizophrenia have been elaborated in detail in earlier publications (Mednick, 1958, 1962, 1966; Mednick & Schulsinger, 1968) and will not be repeated here.

We are now, perhaps, at a point where we can hypothesize that PBC factors lead to defective hippocampal functioning, which in combination with genetic and environmental factors could conceivably play a vital predispositional role in some forms of schizophrenia. This linking of hippocampal functioning and schizophrenia is not an entirely new idea. Necrosis of neural tissue in Sommer's Sector of the hippocampus has been very regularly found in neuropathological studies of the epileptic (Blackwood, McMenemey, Meyer, Norman, & Russell, 1967). Chapman (1966) and Slater, Beard, and Glithero (1965), among others, have pointed to the great similarity of epileptic states of consciousness, especially psychomotor epilepsy, to the disturbances of consciousness in the schizophrenic. Roberts (1966) conceptualized schizophrenia "as a disordering of an entire brain system . . . correlated with malfunction in the dorsal hippocampal limbic system [p. 279]." There has also been a considerable amount of research linking PBCs with serious behavioral disturbances and schizophrenia in children (Knobloch & Pasamanick, 1962; Pasamanick, Rogers, & Lilienfeld, 1956; Pollack & Woerner, 1966; Taft & Goldfarb, 1964) and adults (Lane & Albee, 1966; Stabenau & Pollin, 1967). Perhaps the earliest statement of the possible role of PBCs in the etiology of schizophrenia can be credited to Rosanoff (1938).

There are studies that have demonstrated "typical" hippocampal lesion behavior in the schizophrenic. Milstein, Stevens, and Sachdev (1969) showed very poor habituation and very fast latency of the alpha attenuation response for chronic adult schizophrenics. As early as 1937, Cohen and Patterson reported poor habituation of the cardiac response in schizophrenics. Zahn (1964) observed poor habituation of the GSR in chronic schizophrenics. Vinogradova (1962) demonstrated that chronic schizophrenics take an unusually large number of trials to extinguish a conditioned plethysmograph response.

Recently Ax attempted to replicate the crucial fast-recovery finding on schizophrenic populations by re-examining old data stored on magnetic tape. He obtained results completely in line with the findings reported above. Schizophrenics recovered from GSR at a significantly faster rate than did controls (Ax & Banford, 1970). Gruzelier and Venables (1970), in two separate studies, observed that schizophrenics recover from GSR at a faster rate than controls, show poor or no habituation, and manifest a faster latency of GSR. Lidsky, Hakerem, and Sutton (1967) observed unusually fast recovery from contraction (redilation) of the pupils of a subgroup of their psychiatric patient population in comparison to controls.

The adjective chronic has been used above to modify the noun schizophrenia. It may well be that hippocampal dysfunction is an important contributing predispositional factor in only some types of schizophrenia, perhaps the more typical process, chronic, or poor premorbid types. Our Sick Group subjects tend to be "early onset" cases, suggesting that many of them may have a relatively poor prognosis. It is also possible that degree of hippocampal dysfunction will be found to relate to degree of seriousness of illness.

The emphasis on neurophysiological, biochemical, and traumatic variables and materials in this chapter should not be interpreted as a denigration of the capability of genetic forces to produce identical hippocampal insufficiency or a disregard for the necessity of an appropriate environment to cultivate the learning of schizophrenic modes of behavior and thought. The emphasis on PBCs should not be read as denying the possibility that postnatal injury or high fever could also produce similar brain damage. Finally, we have dealt exclusively with the possible impact of hippocampal injury. We could have also brought the septum, the amygdala, and other limbic areas into the discussion. Indeed, the functioning of the entire temporal lobe is not irrelevant in this area. However, for reasons that were made evident above, the hippocampus seems the best candidate for our attention.

IMPLICATIONS FOR FUTURE STUDY

In terms of the theoretical orientation of the authors, the condition of schizophrenia (predisposed by a variety of conditions and circumstances) is a pattern of well-learned avoidance responses. In terms of treatment, such well-learned avoidance responses are difficult to extinguish. Every time an avoidance response is successfully made, it is automatically and immediately reinforced. In animal research a shuttle-box avoidance response can be extinguished by physically preventing the rat or dog from performing the avoidance response in the presence of the avoidance stimulus and not delivering the punishment. However, most avoidance responses in schizophrenics are thoughts. These are difficult, if not truly impossible, to prevent or control. Thus, for theoretical as well as practical and humane reasons, our research thinking centers on primary prevention rather than treatment. In view of our findings, one potentially useful field of intervention that suggests itself is the pregnancy and birth process. *If* a sound hippocampus is a prerequisite for sound mental health and *if* we can avoid PBCs in high-risk populations, we may be able to avert hippocampal damage and hence reduce the probability of mental illness. Second, in view of the possible involvement of poorly modulated hormonal secretions, research on psychopharmacological intervention at an early premorbid age seems indicated. Such a study is now in its early stages. We are also beginning an additional longitudinal prospective study on the long-term consequences of PBCs in children with schizophrenic parents.

SUMMARY

1.   We have observed a distinctive premorbid pattern of behavior in a group of adolescents who suffered psychiatric breakdown.

2.   This distinctive pattern of behavior is closely associated with pregnancy and birth complications in these breakdown subjects.

3.   The pregnancy and birth complications could have produced anoxic states in the neonate, which in turn would be likely to damage certain "selectively vulnerable" areas of the brain. The most "selectively vulnerable" area is the hippocampus.

4.   The adolescents who suffered pregnancy and birth complications and who later displayed psychiatric breakdown exhibit a pattern of conditioning habituation, extinction, and GSR behavior that is strikingly analogous to the behavior of rats with surgically inflicted hippocampal lesions.

5.   When mothers have undergone heavy anesthesia during delivery (possibly resulting in anoxia and, hence, hippocampal damage in the fetus), the neonate exhibits a pattern of habituation typical for hippocampally lesioned rats.

6.   Certain aspects of the behavior of schizophrenics in GSR, conditioning, and extinction studies closely resemble the behavior of hippocampal rats.

7.   Neurophysiological and biochemical mechanisms are described that could mediate the hypothesized relationship between a damaged or weakened hippocampus and the pattern of behavior of the breakdown group.

8. Reference is made to earlier papers that offer an explanation as to how the behavioral anomalies of the breakdown group could translate themselves into the clinical symptoms and life condition of schizophrenia.

ACKNOWLEDGMENTS

This research is supported by a grant from the Schizophrenia Research Program of the Scottish Rite Committee and by Public Health Service Research Grant 1 RO1 MH-19225-01A1 from the National Institute of Mental Health.

REFERENCES

Ax, A. F., & Banford, J. L. The GSR recovery limb in chronic schizophrenics. *Psychophysiology,* 1970, **7**, 145–147.

Ax, A. F., Beckett, P. G. S., Cohen, B. D., Frohman, C. E., Tourney, G., & Gottlieb, J. S. Psychophysiological patterns in chronic schizophrenia. In J. Wortis (Ed.), *Recent advances in biological psychiatry.* Vol. IV. New York: Plenum, 1962. Pp. 218–233.

Blackwood, W., McMenemey, W. H., Meyer, A., Norman, R. M., & Russell, D. S. *Greenfield's neuropathology.* Baltimore: Williams & Wilkins, 1967.

Chapman, J. The early symptoms of schizophrenia. *British Journal of Psychiatry,* 1966, **112**, 225–251.

Cohen, L. H., & Patterson, M. Effect of pain on the heart rate of normal and schizophrenic individuals. *Journal of General Psychology,* 1937, **17**, 273–289.

Conn, J. W. Aldosteronism in man. *Journal of the American Medical Association,* 1963, **183**, 775–781.

Conway, R., & Brackbill, Y. Effects of obstetrical medication on infant sensorimotor behavior. Paper presented at the meeting of the Society for Research in Child Development, Santa Monica, Calif., 1969.

De Weid, D. The influence of the posterior and intermediate lobe of the pituitary and pituitary peptides on the maintenance of a conditioned avoidance response in rats. *International Journal of Neuropharmacology,* 1965, **4**, 157–167.

De Weid, D. Inhibitory effect of ACTH and related peptides on extinction of conditioned avoidance behavior in rats. *Proceedings of the Society of Experimental Biological Medicine,* 1966, **122**, 28–32.

De Weid, D., & Bohus, B. Long term and short term effects of retention of a conditioned avoidance response in rats by treatment with long acting pitressin and MSH. *Nature,* 1966, **212**, 1484–1486.

Diderichsen, B. Formelle Karakteristika ved Associations—forløbet hos en gruppe børn med høj risiko for schizophrenia. Københavns Universitet, 1967.

Friede, R. The histochemical architecture of Ammon's Horn as related to its selective vulnerability. *Acta Neuropathologica,* 1966, **6,** 1–13.

Ganong, W. F., Biglieri, E. G., & Mulrow, P. J. Mechanisms regulating adreno-cortical secretion of aldosterone and glucocorticoids. *Recent Progress in Hormone Research,* 1966, **22,** 381–430.

Goldstein, L., Sugerman, A. A., & Stolberg, H. Electro-cerebral activity in schizophrenic and non-psychotic subjects: Quantitative EEG amplitude analysis. *Electroencephalography and Clinical Neurophysiology,* 1965, **19,** 350–361.

Gruzelier, J., & Venables, P. H. Personal communication, 1970.

Isaacson, R. L., Douglas, R. J., & Moore, R. Y. The effect of radical hippo-campal ablation on acquisition of avoidance response. *Journal of Comparative and Physiological Psychology,* 1961, **54,** 625–628.

Joffe, J. M. *Prenatal determinants of behaviour.* New York: Pergamon Press, 1969.

Kimble, D. P. The effects of bilateral hippocampal lesions in rats. *Journal of Comparative and Physiological Psychology,* 1963, **56,** 273–283.

Kimble, D. P. Hippocampus and internal inhibition. *Psychological Bulletin,* 1968, **70,** 285–295.

Kimble, D. P. Personal communication, 1969.

Kimble, D. P., & Gostnell, D. Role of the cingulate cortex in shock avoidance behavior of rats. *Journal of Comparative and Physiological Psychology,* 1968, **65,** 290–294.

Knigge, K. M. Feedback mechanisms in neural control of adrenohypophyseal function: Effect of steroids implanted in amygdala and hippocampus. *2nd International Congress on Hormonal Steroids,* Milan, 1966, p. 208. (Abstract No. 361)

Knigge, K. M., & Hays, M. Evidence of inhibitive role of hippocampus in neural regulation of ACTH release. *Proceedings of the Society for Experimental Biological Medicine,* 1963, **114,** 67–69.

Knobloch, H., & Pasamanick, B. Etiological factors in early infantile autism and childhood schizophrenia. Paper presented at the International Congress of Pediatrics, Lisbon, Portugal, 1962.

Lane, E., & Albee, G. W. Comparative birth weights of schizophrenics and their siblings. *Journal of Psychology,* 1966, **64,** 227–231.

Leaton, R. N. Exploratory behavior in rats with hippocampal lesions. *Journal of Comparative and Physiological Psychology,* 1965, **59,** 325–330.

Lidsky, A., Hakerem, G., & Sutton, S. Psychopathological patterns of pupillary response to single light pulses. Paper presented at the 5th Colloquium on the Pupil, University of Pennsylvania, Philadelphia, 1967.

Malmo, R. B., Shagass, C., & Smith, A. A. Responsiveness in chronic schizophrenia. *Journal of Personality,* 1951, **19,** 359–375.

McEwen, B. S., Weiss, J. M., & Schwartz, L. S. Selective retention of corticosterone by limbic structures in rat brain. *Nature,* 1968, **220,** 911–912.

Mednick, B. Unpublished study, 1969.

Mednick, S. A. A learning theory approach to research in schizophrenia. *Psychological Bulletin,* 1958, **55,** 316–327.

Mednick, S. A. Schizophrenia: A learned thought disorder. In G. Nielsen (Ed.), *Clinical psychology: Proceedings of the XIV International Congress of Applied Psychology.* Copenhagen: Munksgaard, 1962. Pp. 167–178.

Mednick, S. A. A longitudinal study of children with a high risk for schizophrenia. *Mental Hygiene,* 1966, **50,** 522–535.

Mednick, S. A., & McNeil, T. F. Current methodology in research on the etiology of schizophrenia. *Psychological Bulletin,* 1968, **70,** 681–693.

Mednick, S. A., & Schulsinger, F. Children of schizophrenic mothers. *Bulletin of the International Association of Applied Psychology,* 1965, **14,** 11–27. (a)

Mednick, S. A., & Schulsinger, F. A longitudinal study of children with a high-risk for schizophrenia: A preliminary report. In S. Vandenberg (Ed.), *Methods and goals in human behavior genetics.* New York: Academic Press, 1965. Pp. 255–295. (b)

Mednick, S. A., & Schulsinger, F. Some premorbid characteristics related to breakdown in children with schizophrenic mothers. *Journal of Psychiatric Research,* 1968, **6,** 267–291 (Suppl. No. 1).

Mednick, S. A., Schulsinger, F., & Lampasso, A. Unpublished study, 1971.

Milstein, V., Stevens, J., & Sachdev, K. Habituation of the alpha attenuation response in children and adults with psychiatric disorders. *Electroencephalography and Clinical Neurophysiology,* 1969, **26,** 12–18.

Mirsky, A. F. Neuropsychological bases of schizophrenia. *Annual Review of Psychology,* 1969, **20,** 321–348.

Moya, F., & Thorndike, V. The effects of drugs used in labor on the fetus and newborn. *Clinical Pharmacology and Therapeutics,* 1963, **4,** 628–638.

Mulrow, P. J. Metabolic effects of adrenal mineralocorticoid hormones. In A. B. Eisenstein (Ed.), *The adrenal cortex.* Boston: Little, Brown, 1967. Pp. 293–313.

Niki, H. The effects of hippocampal ablation on the inhibitory control of operant behavior in the rat. *Japanese Psychological Research,* 1965, **7,** 126–137.

Pasamanick, B., Rogers, M., & Lilienfeld, A. M. Pregnancy experience and the development of childhood behavior disorder. *American Journal of Psychiatry,* 1956, **112,** 614–618.

Pollack, M., & Woerner, M. G. Pre- and perinatal complication and "childhood schizophrenia": A comparison of 5 controlled studies. *Journal of Child Psychology and Psychiatry,* 1966, **7,** 235–242.

Rabe, A., & Haddad, R. K. Acquisition of 2-way shuttle box avoidance after selective hippocampal lesions. *Physiology and Behavior,* 1969, **4,** 319–323.

Ray, T. S. Electrodermal indications of levels of psychological disturbance in chronic schizophrenics. *American Psychologist,* 1963, **18,** 393.

Redding, F. K. Modification of sensory cortical evoked potentials by hippocampal stimulation. *Electroencephalography and Clinical Neurophysiology,* 1967, **22,** 74–83.

Roberts, D. R. Functional organization of the limbic systems. *International Journal of Neuropsychiatry*, 1966, **2**, 279–292.

Roberts, D. R., Dember, W. N., & Brodwick, M. Alternation and exploration in rats with hippocampal lesions. *Journal of Comparative and Physiological Psychology*, 1962, **55**, 695–700.

Rosanoff, A. J. *Manual of psychiatry*. New York: Wiley, 1938.

Silveira, J. M. The deficit in the disinhibition of attention after bilateral hippocampal lesions: Brightness discrimination and reversal in the hippocampectomized rat. Unpublished master's thesis, University of Oregon, 1967.

Slater, E., Beard, A. W., & Glithero, E. Schizophrenia-like psychoses of epilepsy. *International Journal of Psychiatry*, 1965, **1**, 6–30.

Spector, R. G. Enzyme chemistry of anoxic brain injury. In C. W. M. Adams (Ed.), *Neurohistochemistry*. New York: Elsevier, 1965. Pp. 547–557.

Stabenau, J. R., & Pollin, W. Early characteristics of monozygotic twins discordant for schizophrenia. *Archives of General Psychiatry*, 1967, **17**, 723–734.

Svalastoga, K. *Prestige, class and mobility*. Copenhagen: Gyldendal, 1959.

Taft, L., & Goldfarb, W. Prenatal and perinatal factors in childhood schizophrenia. *Developmental Medicine and Child Neurology*, 1964, **6**, 32–43.

Venables, P. H. Input dysfunction in schizophrenia. *Progress in Experimental Personality Research*, 1964, **1**, 1–47.

Venables, P. H. Psychophysiological aspects of schizophrenia. *British Journal of Medical Psychology*, 1966, **39**, 289–297.

Venables, P. H. Personal communication, 1969.

Venables, P. H., & Wing, J. K. Level of arousal and the subclassification of schizophrenia. *Archives of General Psychiatry*, 1962, **7**, 114–119.

Vinogradova, N. V. Protective and "stagnant" inhibition in schizophrenics. *Zhurnal Vysshei Nervnoi Deaietelnostni, Imeni L. P. Pavlova*, 1962, **12** (3), 426–431.

Weiss, J. M., McEwen, B. S., & De Silva, T. Personal communication, 1969.

Zahn, T. P. Autonomic reactivity and behavior in schizophrenia. *Psychiatric Research Reports*, 1964, **19**, 156–171.

Zeaman, D., & Wegner, N. The role of drive reduction in the classical conditioning of an autonomically mediated response. *Journal of Experimental Psychology*, 1954, **48**, 349–354.

CHAPTER 19

The Influence of Drugs on Psychopathological Processes

MURRAY E. JARVIK

Today everyone is aware that pharmacological agents are being widely used in the treatment of mental disease. What is less well known are the reasons why such chemicals are being used, how much good they do, and how much harm they cause. Mental disease has always been an enigma. Diagnosis is based on abstract interpersonal relationships, and for the functional disorders there is no concrete referent which can be put into a bottle, weighed, or examined under the microscope—at least not yet. It is not surprising, therefore, that drug treatment for mental disease is administered like other forms of magic previously prevalent in medical practice.

The belief that drugs can cure disease and improve the quality of life goes back to primitive times. The pain-easing and pleasure-giving properties of wine, opium, and cannabis have been known since the dawn of history. To this day, however, the mechanism of action of these drugs has not been revealed. Primitive peoples have used medicinal herbs and other natural products in the treatment of somatic disorders as well. For example, cinchona bark, the source of quinine, was used very successfully by South American Indians in the treatment of malaria. However, not many other examples of successful primitive somatic therapy, which, of course, had to be empirical in nature, come to mind. Indeed, rational pharmacotherapy, whereby drugs are designed for a purpose, is both recent and rare. If one leafs through a current textbook of pharmacology, it is surprising to see how many drugs were discovered through trial and error. Even the most important drug of the twentieth century, penicillin, was discovered by accident.

The important difference between witches' brews, asafetida bags, and organic food, on the one hand, and psychopharmacological agents, on the other, is that attempts have been made and are being made to evaluate scientifically the efficacy of this latter group of drugs. Unfortunately, well-controlled evaluations are rare.

In 1957, Virginia Staudt and Joseph Zubin, in their review "A Biometric Evaluation of the Somatotherapies in Schizophrenia," anticipated the large-scale evaluation of drug therapy to be conducted by the National Institute of Mental Health and the Veterans Administration. Drug therapy, which was not included in this Staudt and Zubin study, is a form of somatother-apy; in fact, it is the form that has almost replaced all the other major treatments considered, including insulin, pentylenetetrazol, electroshock, and psychosurgery (lobotomy). Unlike the somatotherapies prevalent in 1957, pharmacotherapy is repeated almost daily and may persist almost indefinitely, whereas shock therapy is usually given for only a short course of time and psychosurgery, of course, is performed only once. Staudt and Zubin's findings were that the somatotherapies taken as a whole seemed to have short-term advantages but that the ultimate recovery rate was about the same for treated and untreated individuals. It must be noted at the outset that such disappointing results are essentially similar to those achieved with psychopharmacology.

The psychopharmacological revolution has pushed other therapies into the background. This is not to say that convulsive shock therapy or brain surgery is no longer used or useful. Indeed, there is even evidence that for certain conditions such as depression drug therapy has unfairly dis-placed shock therapy, which is generally more effective. Brain surgery no longer has many vigorous proponents; the possibility of irreversible mu-tilations is greater from the knife than from the pill. There is no question that pharmacotherapy has "cornered the market" in hospital psychiatry today.

Moreover, drug therapy has provided psychiatry with its greatest op-portunity for scientific evaluation of a form of therapy. In order to make a totally scientific investigation of any problem it is necessary to measure and isolate the relevant variables. Psychotherapy, which has traditionally been the favored treatment method of psychiatrists, is, generally speaking, very difficult to characterize, whereas a drug is easy to describe. You can hold it in your hand, and you can weigh it. Two patients, each receiving 500 mg of chlorpromazine, are receiving the same thing. Two patients receiving psychotherapy are probably receiving two different things. Some type of standardization is necessary, and pharmacotherapy of psychiatric illness provides a model for evaluating other types of therapy.

Drugs have a distinct advantage over other methods of psychiatric treatment in that one can more readily do double-blind control studies. Furthermore, dose response curves can be obtained. If a larger amount of treatment produces a greater effect, we know that there is a functional relationship. Presumably, similar studies could be done with psychotherapy, with the amounts of psychotherapy measurable along a linear scale like the grams of a drug. Of course, in any type of therapy, one can make comparisons between untreated and treated patients; however, it is necessary to have large numbers of patients given the same type of treatment, and psychotherapists vary considerably in their abilities and approaches. Furthermore, withholding treatment from patients may be more difficult to justify, especially if they are management problems. This constitutes a very serious difficulty in psychiatric research.

The assessment of psychotherapeutic methods in man, the problem to which Staudt and Zubin addressed themselves, is apparently extremely difficult. The questions are the same whether the treatment is psychological, physical, or chemical. The difficulty is in determining the degree of mental illness. Rating scales are the favorite method and may well be the best. However, raters vary in competence, and one might expect more reliable and valid results from trained than from naive observers. Although for years investigators have sought more objective criteria such as specific hormonal change or the presence of some chemical in the urine, none has been forthcoming, and investigators of psychopathology always return to rating scales. Some of the most popular scales include those devised by Burdock, by Wittenborn, and by Lorr, although there are many others. Modifications of the Minnesota Multiphasic Personality Inventory and a variety of depression scales are also used. How does one determine the validity of these scales? It is very hard to avoid some circularity even if the ratings of psychiatrists are taken as criteria, for, indeed, psychiatrists probably run through the same items in their mind as are contained in the scales.

HOW DRUGS WORK

Increasing knowledge of body biochemistry makes it abundantly clear that drugs operate through their resemblance to substances within the body and their ability to compete with or replace these substances. All of life seems to be a remarkable transformation of chaos into order, and this seems to come about by a fitting into place of molecules. The way in which nucleic acids work to trap constituents from their environment into chains of other nucleic acids or proteins seems to be a model of the way in which life works. In essence, this is an apparent refutation of the second law of thermodynamics with entropy decreasing, at least temporarily. It appears to come about because very complicated things fit together. The great elaboration of this principle of complementarity finds itself in the economy of the body, where every substance, of course, traces itself back to DNA. The lock and key arrangement can be seen quite clearly in the workings of hormones and enzymes. Enzymes act on their substrates by matching a configuration in some ways and accelerating certain chemical reactions. Hormones may influence reactions by fitting into a portion of the enzyme involved.

Certain diseases may be characterized by imbalance or absence of substances in the body. These may be treated by drugs that simulate the missing substances or stimulate their production. For example, diabetes mellitus can be treated with insulin or oral hypoglycemic agents. Replacement is a very rational method of treatment. In Parkinsonism, there is frequently a deficiency of dopamine in the brain and giving patients L-dopa can alleviate this lack.

BIOLOGICAL BASIS OF PSYCHOSIS

Psychiatric nosology still tends to be descriptive rather than etiological. The official classification scheme of the American Psychiatric Association in 1968 still distinguished between psychoses associated with organic brain syndromes and those not attributable to physical conditions. Unfortunately the latter category—the functional disorders—includes schizophrenia, manic-depressive illnesses, and neuroses.

The neurotic disorders have been characterized mainly by anxiety, plus exaggerated reactions to people and the environment. These are the disorders upon which psychotherapy thrives, whether validly or not. On the other hand, the psychotic disorders have generally been considered refractory to psychotherapy. At least, psychotherapists don't like to handle psychotics, and several studies (Grinspoon, Ewalt, & Shader, 1968; May, 1968) have indicated that psychotherapy is ineffective whereas phenothiazine drugs are effective. Drugs for the treatment of anxiety have been very popular since the middle 1950s. The most successful of these are sedative-hypnotic drugs resembling ethyl alcohol in many ways. Even less can be said about the validity of their use and the mechanism of action. Unfortunately it is difficult to compare this group of drugs with psychotherapy in the control of anxiety because neurotic patients are not found in captive conditions like psychotics.

No clear-cut disturbance in chemistry has yet been demonstrated in mental disorders. Nevertheless, the efficacy of drugs that work must be related to some chemical action. There have been numerous reports of substances in the blood, tissues, spinal fluid, and urine of mental patients that are supposedly characteristic of the disease. To this date (1971), no substance which is characteristic of a neurosis or psychosis has been convincingly demonstrated. However, there is one extremely strong piece of evidence that the major psychoses have an organic basis. This is the work of Kallmann (1953), who showed that the concordance rate of schizophrenia and manic-depressive psychosis varied directly with the genetic relationship between individuals. If there is indeed a genetic cause of psychosis, it must be biochemical, since DNA is a chemical responsible for carrying genetic information.

It may be that the affective disorders are due to a disturbance in the metabolism or the synthesis of neurotransmitters such as norepinephrine or dopamine. In the more serious psychotic disorders such as schizophrenia, Himwich, Narasimachari, Heller, Spaide, Haškovec, Fujimori, and Tabushi (1970) and Mandell, Buckingham, and Segal (1971) have suggested that the substance involved might be dimethyl tryptamine or a related indole compound. If a simple test were available to determine the presence of such an abnormal compound, diagnosis would be greatly simplified and, of course, validation of rating scales would then be possible.

Even the purely psychological theories of mental illness could be better understood by uncovering underlying neurological and chemical factors. The "instinctive" urges and the repressive tendencies must reside somewhere. Work in physiological psychology on animals has told us a great deal about the relationship between motivation and emotion, and parts of the brain such as the limbic system (Thompson, 1967). Mental conflicts and psychic tension must produce their effects not only in the body but also in the brain. The chemical changes associated with learning (of unpleasant experiences) have not yet been identified, but undoubtedly will be.

Diseases such as diabetes and tuberculosis, though genetically determined in part, are treatable, and so should schizophrenia be. The fact that genetic determinants appear to be important in the etiology of psychotic disorders does not mean that environmental interactions, such as those provided by psychotherapy, should be ignored. In fact, talking to a patient and giving a drug are two ways of getting at his brain. That psychotherapy is less effective is not a necessary consequence of genetic determination.

Drug therapy has two advantages over psychotherapy for both psychotic and neurotic disorders. First, the efficacy of drug therapy has been demonstrated statistically in controlled experimental situations. The same cannot be said for psychotherapy, even for neuroses. Furthermore, drugs are much easier to administer since special training is not required, and a single therapist can simultaneously administer treatment to hundreds of patients. Nevertheless, patients with mental problems frequently demand or desire psychotherapy, or their families seek it for them.

ANIMAL MODELS OF MENTAL DISEASE

Animal psychology offers a great deal of promise for psychopharmacology. Not only can one study different types of drugs in animals but one can also examine the effects of the drugs on the brain by combining pharmacological with surgical, electrophysiological, and histological methodology. The great missing link in comparing animal with human psychopharmacology is the nature of mental disease in man. Are the psychoses unique to man, or do analogous mental abnormalities exist in animals? Are the experimental neuroses of Pavlov related to anything seen in man? To make a meaningful comparison, it is necessary to have a common reference point. Certainly the basic physiological processes of lower mammals are more similar to those of man than are psychological processes. Verbal behavior simply does not exist in subhuman species, and this is just the kind of behavior on which internal conflict, anxiety, and depression depend to reveal themselves. To be sure, nonverbal types of behavior also manifest themselves in these diseases, including disturbances of sleep, of eating, of sexual behavior, and of attitude, demeanor, and facial expression, but they are by no means specific. And the hallmarks of psychosis are hallucinations and delusions, which can be revealed only through verbal behavior. Also, disordered thinking and inappropriate affect, such as laughing and crying at the wrong time, are characteristically human and cannot be reproduced in lower animals. There are, however, primitive analogies to these conditions that could be investigated (Darwin, 1872).

There are compelling reasons for research in psychopathology in animals. We are all part of an evolutionary chain, and it is unlikely that there is a discrete appearance of any function in human beings which does not exist, at least in some rudimentary form, in lower animals. Also, certain experiments can be conducted in animals which would be morally or ethically wrong to carry out on human subjects.

CLASSIFICATION OF PSYCHOPHARMACEUTICALS

Today several different classes of drugs are used in psychiatry. The most widely used are the *antianxiety* drugs. The *antipsychotic* drugs are the mainstay of mental hospitals. Two groups of drugs are available for the affective disorders: the *antidepressants* and the *antimanic* agents. Then, of course, there exists a wide variety of drugs that are self-administered, for pleasure. These include agents that carry stringent legal penalties against their use and dissemination.

Psychopharmacological agents can be classified by their chemistry, their physiological effects, their mode of action, or their use. A chemical classification is not adequate because, although progress is being made in this direction, the relationship between structure and functions is not yet fully elucidated. For example, it is still not known why compounds are apparently different as the butyrophenones and the antipsychotic phenothiazines have such similar actions, while slight changes in the phenothiazine structure can produce major functional differences. Classification by physiological effects can be confusing to the clinician, who, after all, is primarily responsible for the use of most of these drugs, because many side effects are not essential to the main action of the agents. Classification by mechanism of action would be the most desirable but unfortunately is not possible for any of the drugs currently in use. When the pathological physiology of mental disease is known, particularly at a cellular and a molecular level, and when the actions at these same levels can be identified, this classification will be the only one acceptable.

This leaves us with classification by use. Although arbitrary and in many ways unsatisfactory, it is probably the best we have. It should be made clear, however, that the use of a drug for a given purpose, even by highly respected physicians, does not mean that the drug actually accomplishes the purpose. Nowhere must this distinction be kept clearer than in psychopharmacology, where the therapeutic effect of a drug is anything but obvious (Jarvik, 1970).

Antipsychotic Drugs

The drugs used in the treatment of psychoses include the phenothiazines, the butyrophenones, reserpine, and a number of others. As a class phenothiazines, especially chlorpromazine, are the most commonly used of the antipsychotic drugs and also rank very high in the list of drugs prescribed in medicine generally. Chlorpromazine (CPZ) was first used in France as a potentiating agent for preanesthetic medication; in the early 1950s it was found to be very helpful in the treatment of psychotic patients, and its success gave rise to the era of psychopharmacology. Although various congeners have been introduced, none of them seems to show a significant or distinct advantage over CPZ as a therapeutic agent. Two of the larger studies that have been conducted are one by the National Institute of Mental Health (1964) and another by the Veterans Administration (see Casey, Bennett, Lindley, Hollister, Gordon, & Springer 1960).

Today CPZ is by all measures the most important antipsychotic agent. It was the first and remains the most successful. Its congeners, which are other phenothiazines, differ in various properties from it; but, as mentioned above, their ability to ameliorate the signs and symptoms of the various psychotic states is not noticeably superior. Is there something about the chemical structure of the antipsychotic phenothiazines that gives us a clue to the mechanism of action? We know that all the phenothiazines used in psychiatry have a three-carbon bridge between the three-ring structure and the side-chain nitrogen. Other phenothiazines are ineffective in the treatment of psychoses. It is generally thought that the adrenergic blocking properties arc the most important properties of the antipsychotic phenothiazines. If this is true, one would expect some relationship between their structures and the structure of norepinephrine.

The behavioral effects of CPZ and the other phenothiazines may give some hint as to their antipsychotic actions. They all produce sedation to a greater or lesser extent in animals. Though the sedative effect perhaps contributes to the antipsychotic action of CPZ, it is not essential for it. Tolerance develops rather rapidly to sedation, but not to the beneficial effect on psychotic behavior. Furthermore, the piperazine phenothiazines appear to have relatively less sedative effect.

Conditioned responses in animals of certain types are impaired by the phenothiazines and indeed have been used as a screening procedure for such drugs. Some workers believe that the blocking action of these substances upon catecholamines and particularly dopamine is responsible for this effect. All of the antipsychotic phenothiazines possess the ability to produce an extrapyramidal syndrome characterized in man by Parkinsonism. It would be very useful to both clinicians and investigators if all of the actions of CPZ could be explained through some type of specific action upon a catecholamine such as dopamine. Perhaps, however, a mixture of blocking actions upon various amines, such as dopamine, norepinephrine, and 5-hydroxytryptamine, accounts for the action of this drug. Certainly, centrally acting adrenergic blocking agents such as phenoxybenzamine or propanolol do not appear to mimic the actions of CPZ.

The distribution of the biogenic amines in the central nervous system is not uniform. For one thing, they appear to originate in cells of the midbrain. However, they are distributed via the processes of these midbrain cells to various other parts of the brain, thus accounting for the nonuniform distribution therein. The action in the central nervous system of CPZ, for example, has really not been localized to the cortex, thalamus, limbic systems, or basal ganglia. Indeed, its actions at the brain-stem level, particularly on the reticular activating system and chemoreceptor trigger zone, have been stressed by a number of investigators.

Although the phenothiazines are effective in the treatment of psychosis, they are not remarkable in this respect (Klein & Davis, 1969). In other words, many patients are not benefited by the phenothiazine drugs. Many attempts have been made to determine whether there are different varieties of psychosis which could be helped by different drugs, but no definitive results have been obtained as yet.

Nonphenothiazine Antipsychotics

A number of nonphenothiazine antipsychotic drugs have been tried; some have been discarded, and others are still being used. The rauwolfia alkaloids are the most interesting but are hardly used anymore. They have been abandoned even in the face of studies that showed them to be effective. The death of a treatment such as this is an interesting phenomenon, probably explained by the availability of better, more easily handled agents (the phenothiazines) and by the fact that mental depression is a fairly common side effect of rauwolfia. The rauwolfia alkaloids are still used in the treatment of hypertension, however, and seem to be fairly effective.

Another group that resembles the phenothiazines and seems to have some comparable effectiveness against psychosis consists of the thioxanthenes. It is unlikely that they will replace the phenothiazines because they have not demonstrated any particular superiority.

The third group, which is currently in use, is the butyrophenones. This group is favored in certain countries, particularly Belgium, France, and other parts of western Europe. The butyrophenones seem to be comparable to the very potent phenothiazines and produce many of the same toxic effects, including extrapyramidal syndromes.

Antidepressant Drugs

Two classes of antidepressant drugs have been used in psychiatry. The first was the monoamine oxidase inhibitors, which seem to have suffered the same fate as the rauwolfia alkaloids. Both of these abandoned groups of drugs are extremely interesting because of their biochemical action and particularly their interaction with biogenic amines. They provided much fuel for the fire of catecholamine theories of mental illness. The rauwolfia drugs release such amines as norepinephrine and hydroxytryptamine from storage within the cells. The monoamine oxidase inhibitors prevent the intracellular destruction of these amines. The effects of other drugs upon amines are not so evident.

The second class of antidepressants was derived from the phenothiazines. This was the group of tricyclic antidepressants, of which the first member was imipramine. This drug and its congeners, although they share properties with chlorpromazine, also have different effects that might be considered stimulating. In some ways they resemble cocaine, and one theory of how they act rests on the general assumption that they interfere with the re-uptake of norepinephrine into the cells. Thus the effective levels of biogenic amines are raised and so, thereby, is the mood. Again, although these drugs have been shown to be effective, they are really not a great deal better than a placebo and appear to be less beneficial than electro-convulsive shock therapy.

Indeed, many depressed patients simply are not helped by antidepressant drugs. These drug-refractory patients constitute a real problem for those interested in the mechanism of action of antidepressants on the psychopathology of disease.

Antimanic Drugs

The latest drug to be officially added to the armamentarium of psychopharmacological agents used in affective disorders is lithium. Although this ion has been studied for its usefulness in mania for decades, it was only recently approved by the Food and Drug Administration. It does indeed appear to be effective in quieting manic patients. The phenothiazines are also used for the same purpose, but of course they have a variety of side effects, including extrapyramidal syndromes, which are not desirable. Lithium lacks these but has its own dangers, and blood levels must be carefully monitored. It is a simple ion and seems to work, at least in part, by displacing potassium from inside the cell. Whether it also has a specific action on catecholamines, as many investigators feel, is a question that has not been definitinely answered.

Antianxiety Drugs

The other group of drugs that has been widely used in psychiatry consists of the antianxiety agents. There are two distinct classes of these drugs, but they share properties in common. The first is meprobamate (e.g., miltown or equanil), and the second is chlordiazepoxide (librium) and its congeners. These drugs bear a striking resemblance in many respects to the older, well-known sedative-hypnotics, such as alcohol, the barbiturates, bromides, and general anesthetics.

The drugs prescribed in the treatment of anxiety certainly constitute the most popular group of psychopharmaceuticals in use today. There is a good deal of cross tolerance between these agents, and they are all pleasant, well liked, and prone to be habit forming. It is a moot point whether the tendency to produce addiction is greater with the propanedoles and the benzodiazepines than with alcohol or barbiturates. There have even been some legal battles over this issue, but one gets the general impression that individuals using the antianxiety drugs are less likely to increase the dose to the point where they develop severe physical dependence.

In regard to theorizing concerning the mode of action, we are in a much worse position with the antianxiety drugs than with the antipsychotic or mood-elevating drugs. No one has suggested that the antianxiety drugs operate through biogenic amines. Indeed, they resemble the sedative-hypnotics very closely, and a good mechanism of action has not yet been suggested for these. Perhaps they work in the same way as the general anesthetics and influence membrane permeability, because of their fat solubility or their ability to form clathrates.

The pleasure of being intoxicated undoubtedly contributes to the popularity of this group. Not only are they valuable as antianxiety agents; they also can substitute for alcohol and are useful hypnotics. Alcoholics like them and will tend to take them particularly when they want to avoid detection by legal alcohol determination. There is a strong suggestion that anxiety is state dependent, and any change to another state can provide relief—perhaps this is how they work. On the other hand, if the individual is anxious when sober, then when he is drunk with any of these drugs, the chances are he will not function as well in the intellectual or motor sphere. This impairment of performance may be less important to an individual, however, than the extreme unpleasantness that accompanies the anxiety he feels while performing well.

Specificity

Another problem in regard to psychopharmaceuticals involves the question of specificity of these agents. Some rather disturbing studies have indicated that, contrary to expectation, phenothiazines are useful in the treatment of depression, and antidepressants in the treatments of psychosis. Of course, a very clear description of the psychiatric syndrome susceptible to each drug may throw some light on this paradox. However, such findings pose a problem for the catecholamine theory of affective disorder.

DRUGS USED FOR PLEASURE

All of the other drugs that we will touch upon are either illegal or capable of being used illicitly. The stimulants include such legal drugs as xanthines, including caffeine, and theobromine, stimulants to which people undoubtedly become strongly habituated. Nicotine, which is found in tobacco, in another habit-forming stimulant. The sympathomimetic amines, particularly dextroamphetamine, are also stimulants upon which people become strongly dependent. Incidentally, animals also will self-administer these drugs. It has been shown that the amphetamines when taken in very large doses will produce a psychotic syndrome strongly resembling that seen in naturally occurring psychoses, such as schizophrenia. Not only are there disturbances in mood and thinking, but auditory hallucinations also occur. This type of hallucinatory activity is different from what one sees with the usual hallucinogenic drugs, which produce primarily visual effects.

The hallucinogenic drugs include the indole-containing ones, such as LSD, mescaline, psilocybin, and also the cannabis derivatives (e.g., marijuana and THC). In addition, there are the anticholinergic hallucinogens such as ditran and scopolamine. Then there is a miscellaneous group of drugs such as phencyclidine. During the past 15 years, considerable research on hallucinogenic drugs has resulted in a fair knowledge of what they do to psychological functions acutely, but chronic effects are in much greater doubt. Although a tremendous amount has been written on the subject, particularly in the lay press, it is difficult to say yet how good or how bad these drugs are. Certainly they have become amazingly popular, perhaps because of the change in state they induce. Why do people want to take a "trip"? The reason may be curiosity or a desire to escape from the unpleasantness of reality. These drugs have been proposed from time to time as possible psychotherapeutic agents; however, controlled studies either have not been performed on a particular drug or have shown it to be lacking in efficacy.

The hallucinogen which has created more controversy than any other is marijuana. The discrepancy between the existence of severe laws and their lax observance is a real threat to the American legal system. Law enforcement officers tend to press for even stricter laws, whereas many of the more highly educated members of the legal profession feel that the laws should be changed to conform with reality. One cannot legislate properties into a drug (such as dangerous toxicity), but one can certainly make it illegal. The evidence today is that marijuana, as it is generally smoked, is a relatively innocuous substance. However, it is capable of producing an acute psychotic state characterized by disturbances in mood and perception. Individuals under its influence may be considered intoxicated and less rational and responsible than in the normal state. The possibility that this drug may induce permanent psychiatric disorders has been considered and even reported in the literature. Nevertheless, very large populations of intelligent individuals apparently do not take the warning of the dangers of this drug too seriously. If they are misguided, there is an epidemic of ignorance.

With all hallucinogens, such as LSD, there is a strong possibility that use in critical amounts may push a prepsychotic individual into a psychotic state. Retrospective studies give us an inkling that such may be the case.

Moreover, it would appear that psychotic persons have a greater than normal tendency to use hallucinogenic drugs, even though they may be the population at risk. This kind of vicious cycle compounds the problem and makes rational analysis difficult.

The hallucinogenic drugs have also been termed psychotogenic (Jarvik, 1970). One of their possible virtues is the ability to produce a model psychosis in the laboratory, thus affording investigators the possibility of comparing psychotic behavior with normal behavior in the same individual both before and after the drug experience. Such behavior can also be compared to that of spontaneously occurring psychosis. Furthermore, at least in the past, investigators have had the opportunity of experiencing the psychotic state for themselves, for whatever this was worth. Today, of course, the laws are extremely stringent and human research is rather difficult to undertake.

The somewhat tolerant view of marijuana usage expressed by many members of the intelligentsia is not extended to the potent analgesic drugs, particularly heroin. This difference in attitude occurs because the highly addictive properties of heroin and the opiates have been so widely publicized. However, the degree of impairment of function produced by heroin appears to be considerably less than that produced by sedative hypnotic drugs such as alcohol or by the hallucinogenic drugs. There are two main problems with heroin: It produces strong physiological dependence, and it is illegal. The combination of these two factors make the heroin addict extremely susceptible to crime, and this constitutes a very serious social problem to our nation.

The fact that alcohol is legal presents a logical dilemma because the law is inconsistent and somewhat arbitrary. The mere fact that alcohol has been legal since 1933 does not make it safe or desirable. On the other hand, the experience of prohibition indicated that outlawing the sale of alcohol encouraged the crime of bootlegging and attendant racketeering and gangsterism. Advocates of the legalization of marijuana point out that crime could be reduced by making the use of this drug legal. On the other hand, legalization would probably result in a greatly increased use of the drug, just as it has with alcohol, and cause a general increase in the incidence of toxic reactions. The question of whether people should be allowed to endanger their health and that of others is a debatable moral and ethical issue.

SUMMARY

Since 1955 the practice of psychiatry has been changed remarkably by the large-scale introduction of pharmacotherapy. Drugs presently in use include antipsychotic phenothiazines and butyrophenones; antidepressant tricyclic compounds; lithium salts, which are prescribed in the treatment of mania; and drugs effective against anxiety, which are closely related to or include the sedative-hypnotics. The investigator and the clinician are both concerned with questions of the relative efficacy versus the dangers of these classes of drugs. By and large, they are considered relatively safe and effective, but a quantitative statement concerning these parameters is both needed and yet difficult to obtain. The mechanism of action of these drugs, including their therapeutic effects, is still a matter of conjecture, although a great deal of information has been gathered during the past two decades. Current views favor the idea that brain amines are involved in the action of the antipsychotic and antidepressant drugs. There is greater divergence of opinion concerning lithium, and the sedative-hypnotic drugs remain as great a mystery as they were at the beginning of the century. Another class of drugs which have a strong influence on psychopathological processes has come into prominence in recent years because of the widespread social and legal effects. These are the hallucinogenic or psychotogenic drugs, which are taken for pleasurable purposes but may produce harmful effects.

The psychotherapeutic drugs have contributed something toward the understanding of psychopathology. The fact that some of them are effective for certain diseases does not prove, as some advocates have claimed, that the diseases are organically caused. However, it does prove that an organic link exists; otherwise the drugs would be without effect. Analysis of this link is our greatest hope for understanding mental disease of all kinds. As long as drugs were without effect, as seemed to be the case until the middle 1950s, biological psychiatrists had less evidence that even a physiological link was involved in mental disease. On the other hand, if the hallucinogenic drugs can actually cause psychoses that are indistinguishable from endogenous psychoses, this is very strong evidence that such diseases do not have to be caused by unfortunate environmental interaction. Although there is still the possibility that alternative etiological factors may be involved, the induction of clinical psychotic states by drugs certainly lends strong weight to the idea that organic factors are involved. What remains now, of course, is to identify the parts of the brain and the chemical structures which underlie such psychotic states.

REFERENCES

American Psychiatric Association, Committee no Nomenclature and Statistics. *Diagnostic and statistical manual of mental disorders.* (2nd ed.) Washington, D.C.: APA, Mental Hospital Service, 1968.

Casey, J. F., Bennett, I. F., Lindley, C. J., Hollister, L. E., Gordon, M. H., & Springer, N. N. Drug therapy in schizophrenia. A controlled study of the relative effectiveness of chlorpromazine, promazine, phenobarbital and placebo. *Archives of General Psychiatry*, 1960, **2**, 210–220.

Darwin, C. *The expression of the emotions in man and animals.* London: Murray, 1872.

Grinspoon, L., Ewalt, J. R., & Shader, R. Psychotherapy and pharmacotherapy in chronic schizophrenia. *American Journal of Psychiatry*, Part 2, 1968, **124**, 1645–1652.

Himwich, H. E., Narasimachari, N., Heller, B., Spaide, J., Haškovec, L., Fujimori, M., & Tabushi, K. Comparative behavioral and urinary studies on schizophrenics and normal controls. In R. E. Bowman & S. P. Datta (Eds.), *Biochemistry of brain and behavior.* New York: Plenum, 1970. Pp. 207–221.

Jarvik, M. E. Drugs used in the treatment of psychiatric disorders. In L. S. Goodman & A. Gilman (Eds.), *The pharmacological basis of therapeutics.* (4th ed.) New York: Macmillan, 1970. Pp. 151–203.

Kallmann, F. J. *Heredity in health and mental disorder: Principles of psychiatric genetics in the light of comparative twin studies.* New York: W. W. Norton, 1953.

Klein, D. F., & Davis, J. M. *Diagnosis and drug treatment of psychiatric disorders.* Baltimore: Williams & Wilkins, 1969.

Mandell, A. J., Buckingham, B., & Segal, D. Behavioral, metabolic and enzymatic studies of the brain indole-ethyl-amine N-methylating system. In B. T. Ho & W. M. McIsaac (Eds.), *Brain chemistry and mental disease.* New York: Plenum, 1971. Pp. 37–60.

May, P. H. *Treatment of schizophrenia: A comparative study of five treatment methods.* New York: Science House, 1968.

National Institute of Mental Health, Psychopharmacology Service Center Collaborative Study Group. Phenothiazine treatment in acute schizophrenia. *Archives of General Psychiatry*, 1964, **10**, 246–261.

Staudt, V., & Zubin, J. A biometric evaluation of the somatotherapies in schizophrenia. *Psychological Bulletin*, 1957, **54**, 171–196.

Thompson, R. F. *Foundations of physiological psychology.* New York: Harper & Row, 1967.

CHAPTER 20

Psychopharmacology— Rationale and Mystique

Psychotropic drugs have been important factors in the third revolution in psychiatry. The first was a *moral* one which changed cultural attitudes toward mental illness. It was started by Pinel, at the time of the French Revolution, when he removed the chains from the oppressed inmates in asylums for the insane, thus establishing for patients who suffer from mental disorders the right to require the same respect, compassion, and professional interest as any other patient under the care of a physician.

The second psychiatric revolution occurred around the turn of the last century. It was characterized by Freud's *theoretical* and systematic attack on psychopathology and psychodynamics, two fields that until then had remained closed to scientific inquiry.

The third revolution started just before World War II with the *therapeutic* breakthrough of two unspecific, physical therapies—induced hypoglycemic and convulsive shock treatments—followed by a rapid development of new social techniques in the therapeutic management of the mentally ill and, in the early 1950s, by the discovery of the antipsychotic, antidepressant, and new psychotomimetic drugs.

The impact of these psychotropic drugs was explosive, not only upon the clinical scene, but also upon the *Zeitgeist* and many other social aspects of Western civilization. The new drugs have been responsible, among other things, for an economic boom in the pharmaceutical industry and for the development of a new scientific discipline, that is, psychopharmacology. In addition, they have contributed to the world-wide problem of nonmedical drug abuse with all its accompanying medical, social, and legal complexities and complications.

TWO ROOTS OF PSYCHOPHARMACOLOGY

Psychopharmacology, the science of psychotropic drugs that influence objective behavior and subjective experience through their effects on the central nervous system, is rooted in both psychology and pharmacology. Being thus a hybrid science, it has inherited two very different, fundamental dimensions or epistemological orientations:

1. An objective, scientific approach which is focused entirely on observationally given data.
2. A subjective, introspective, or value-directed, clinical approach.

The first dimension is expected to yield rational explanations of cause and effect relationships, as well as quantifiable predictions, while the second dimension clearly invites personal bias and mystique.

The scientific approach to psychopharmacological phenomena has a long and well-respected tradition in the two parent sciences of pharmacology and experimental as well as clinical psychology. Modern methods of biochemistry and biophysics, ultramodern instrumentation and laboratory techniques, well-standardized psychometric methods, carefully established behavior-rating scales and structured interview inventories are all available to produce data for statistical evaluations so sophisticated that they could hardly be imagined 20 years ago, before the advent of the recent generation of computers.

SOURCES OF SYSTEMATIC AND PERSONAL ERRORS

There is no need to dwell on the rational methods and techniques and what they can achieve, because a great body of excellent literature on this subject is already in existence. However, it may be appropriate here to emphasize the fact that at least five sources of error are associated with the collection of data on psychotropic drug action:

1. Well-known, simple observational or instrumental errors in the comparatively rare instances when distinct pointer-readings can be registered as responses to psychotropic drugs (e.g., as tapping speed, reaction time, averaged evoked potential, etc.).
2. Unrecognized or uncontrollable interference phenomena due to the interaction of multiple, complex, or unknown intervening variables (e.g., anxiety, attention, motivation, etc.).
3. Faulty, imprecise, or ambiguous observations due to lack of perceptual or cognitive competence or experience (e.g., in the recording of

clinical behavior-rating scores by an inadequately trained rater or an observer who lacks certain basic, individual requirements, such as empathy).

4. Impersonal bias due to inferences and interpretations that are the result of indoctrination with certain principles of a specific school of thought (e.g., psychoanalysis or learning theory).

5. Personal rater and subject bias due to specific attitudes, psychological sets, and expectations that are idiosyncratically determined.

Errors of type 1 can be avoided and corrected simply by devoting greater care to observations and instrumentation; errors of type 3 may be reduced through better and longer training methods; errors of type 4 could probably be eliminated through more systematic selection of raters, and errors of type 5 through the use of double-blind experimental designs. But errors of type 2, and also in part of type 3, are by their very nature often uncontrollable. There is little an investigator can do about lack of motivation in his subject or lack of empathy in himself, particularly if these defects are not measurable or he is not aware of them.

COGNITIVE AMBIGUITIES

Even if due consideration is given to all these possible errors, and adequate measures are taken to reduce them to a minimum, there still remains another half-open, methodological back door through which ambiguities or misinterpretations of results may slip into the results of the best-controlled experiments. Problems of this type may arise because of the lack of cognitive sharpness of such "sophisticated" concepts as bound versus free substances, negative feedback, biphasic action, and false transmitters.

A certain drug effect may, for instance, be explained either as the direct manifestation of its *excitatory* action on specific receptors or, conversely, as the indirect effect of its *blocking* action on the receptors, the observed excitation then being the effect of the ensuing increased production of analogous excitatory substances, which may have occurred as the result of negative feedback within the central nervous system. As another example, an apparent *stimulant* effect on behavior might be produced secondarily by a drug that primarily *inhibits* higher inhibitory centers, thus releasing disinhibited behavior. In general, such elasticity or "softness" of explanatory mechanisms has, until recently, been outside the realm of basic science and has been thought of more as the prerogative of theories that are based mainly on hypothetical constructs, for example, psychoanalysis.*

* The lack of rigor that characterizes the acceptance of much psychopharmaco-

Furthermore, several psychophysiological concepts, which until very recently served as hard cognitive currency and thus provided some of the anchoring points or building blocks for the constructing and testing of hypotheses in psychopharmacology, have today acquired a somewhat floating quality. For example, the important concept "arousal" has become so global in its meaning that in the light of recent experimental findings it no longer fits psychophysiological facts accurately (Ax, in press), and a single, operational definition can no longer be given for it.

"Arousal" may be defined behaviorally in terms of psychomotor phenomena (e.g., motor activity or vigilance), introspectively in terms of experienced tension, or physiologically in terms of autonomic functioning as well as patterns of electroencephalographic activity. These different operational aspects are by no means always highly correlated with each other, and even in the single field of autonomic activity the different functions (e.g., cardiovascular, respiratory, GSR, etc.) manifest a remarkable degree of dissociation (Lacey, 1967).

Sleep is another of the apparently timeless concepts that in recent years has shown a great deal of semantic wear and tear. How is a state of sleep to be determined? By observing the gross behavior of a person? As everyone knows, such judgments would be utterly unreliable since sleepwalking and simple sleep resemblance could not be recognized in this manner with any degree of accuracy. If one takes the presence or absence of awareness as the criterion of sleep, he runs into the epistemological difficulty that the determination of awareness is dependent on introspective short-term recall (whether or not the subject was aware of the administration of a stimulus at a given time), and there are conditions which are not sleep but in which short-term recall is disordered (e.g., in a fugue state or Korsakoff's syndrome). The EEG pattern has long been assumed to provide objective evidence of sleep. But with increased knowledge of EEG dynamics during sleep, it is no longer possible to distinguish with absolute certainty the "aroused" electrocerebral activity occurring during "paradoxical sleep" from certain nonsleep activities reflected in the EEG.

Although it may be argued that problems of this kind affect all of the behavioral sciences and not just psychopharmacology, the latter should bring these uncertainties into sharper focus for three reasons:

1. Psychopharmacology has introduced a new "microscopic" research

logical research today has been pointed out repeatedly. In this connection I should like to quote from one of my publications: "If such loose associations between membrane effects, storage sites and receptor organs have to be involved without any clearcut causal sequence being suggested, we do not really have to resort to neuropharmacology to speculate but can remain in the realm of psychological theorizing [Lehmann, 1967, pp. 310–311]."

tool that permits quantitative study of behavior with previously unobtainable precision and thus requires also much higher precision in the definition and determination of fundamental conditions and dynamics.

2. Psychopharmacology has to deal with phenomena for which there are no adequate methodological precedents, for example, the psychedelic experiences.

3. Psychopharmacology reaches out into the pragmatic, clinical approach and reasonable theoretical formulations, but has to insist on the utmost possible precision, since a person's health and even life might depend on it.

Yet, since it is painful for an investigator—in psychopharmacology, as in any other science—to have to accept the fact that his data are of questionable origin or doubtful validity, he may well at this point make certain assumptions without having all the necessary rigorous, rational evidence—and thus resort to mystique.

DEFINITION OF "MYSTIQUE"

For the purpose of this discussion I shall define "mystique" as an assumption that (1) is not based on primary rational evidence; (2) has an emotional appeal for the person making the assumption; (3) serves the purpose of either short-circuiting the need for complex and difficult research or of concealing certain deep-seated inconsistencies or contradictions in a set of established facts; and (4) is—for all practical purposes—treated as though it were as valid as rationally established evidence.

Obviously, this definition of mystique describes some of the characteristic properties of any theory or even of a mathematical formulation. Like mystique, theory or mathematics does not constitute primary evidence; both may serve the purpose of short-circuiting the need for more research or of reconciling apparent inconsistencies in the observed facts. Also, a theory or a mathematical formulation often has emotional appeal for the person applying it and may even be treated as though it constituted valid evidence.

But mystique is more prominently determined by emotional factors than a theory or a mathematical rationale, and is more frequently accepted uncritically in the place of primary evidence than either theory or mathematical formulation. The latter can and must be validated, for example, by observation of their predicted results, by systematic experimental testing, or by a rigorous analysis of their rational components. Mystique, on the other hand, is consistently (almost anxiously) "protected" against such searching examination, because the scientist resorting to mystique depends in turn on its rationalizing protection against the uneasiness that would trouble him if he became aware of the ambiguities he would otherwise have to face. In psychodynamic parlance one may say that mystique, in the sense it is used here, refers to an epistemological "defense mechanism," brought into operation for the purpose of avoiding the anxiety that would result from an individual's surpassing of his ambiguity tolerance.

For the psychopharmacologist who is dealing with human subjects, this kind of "defense" offers itself quite naturally, because cultural and other social influences, rather than observational evidence or rational argument, will have to determine, at least partly, the answers to some of his most important questions (e.g., What is mental pathology? What is therapeutic effect?).

In blunt terms, the provocative thesis I am trying to defend in this chapter is that psychopharmacologists and, in fact, all behavioral scientists who mainly follow an objective scientific approach today have a low tolerance for ambiguity. Physicists found themselves in a similar predicament around the turn of the century with the advent of quantum mechanics, but —after considerable struggle—they have now adjusted to it, at the level of a newly found epistemological maturity that is characterized by a greatly increased tolerance for ambiguity.

MORE METHODOLOGICAL PROBLEMS

Impossibility of Direct Experimental Verification

The different mechanisms of action that have been proposed to account for psychotropic drug effects present serious methodological and epistemological problems. As an example, the hypothesis that the therapeutic effects of antidepressant drugs are due to an increase of available catecholamines or to an altered balance of biogenic amines in the brain (Schildkraut, Davis, & Klerman, 1968) seems to resist any attempt to test it directly within the central nervous system. Although there are reliable methods to assess the presence and quantity of biogenic amines and their metabolites in body fluids, it has until now been impossible to ascertain whether the relevant substances found in the blood, urine, or spinal fluid reflect peripheral or central conditions. This is equally true for the claims that certain drugs compensate for the effects of disordered enzyme functions in the brain, for example, niacin in schizophrenia (Ban & Lehmann, 1970), or alter the permeability of cellular membranes and the balance of intracellular and extracellular electrolytes—an action mechanism that is currently being proposed for the therapeutic effects of lithium (Schou, 1968). It is not possible, for obvious reasons, to make a chemical analysis of living human brain tissue, even though this may occasionally be approximated, to a very limited degree, through the use of implanted electrodes in human subjects. Nor is it valid in psychopharmacology to extrapolate directly from animal experiments, as we are used to doing in the case of physiological phenomena (e.g., metabolic or endocrine processes), because the contents of human ideas and affective states are not reproducible in animals (e.g., paranoid delusions or guilt feelings).

For similar reasons, there seems to be no way to confirm or refute directly the neurophysiological theories that implicate synaptic inhibition as the principal mechanism of psychotropic drug action, as has, for example, been proposed for LSD (Marrazzi, Meisch, Pew, & Bieter, 1967).

Impossibility of Achieving Truly Comparable Conditions

Most behavioral scientists hold the theoretical assumption that identical physical input—in the form of drugs or physical stimuli—into the central nervous system, under identical conditions, will produce identical effects. This concept of invariant transduction is really part of a mystique, since it is impossible to ever achieve identical conditions in two different individuals at any one time, or in the same individual on different occasions. And making this point is more than splitting hairs, because it is well established that such factors as having been once exposed to certain drugs or experiences may permanently change a subject's reactions, on both the physiological and the behavioral level, when he is re-exposed to the same experience or drug.*

We know enough about learning or practice effects and drug tolerance to make allowance for their interference with our experiments. However, there are so many other extraneous and internal factors that may powerfully influence a subject's experiential, behavioral, and physiological responses and that may be difficult or impossible to know—from suggestion to play acting, from mood to motivation, from periodic to unpredictable metabolic and physiological fluctuations—that we have every reason to remain extremely humble and modest about our ability to control the pertinent factors when we set up sophisticated experiments in the behavioral sciences, including psychopharmacology and psychophysiology.

---

* For instance, the familiar observation that marijuana has only slight effects on most subjects when smoked for the first time, but much stronger effects the second and third time, may reflect the induction of specific enzymes by the first smoking. These enzymes, in turn, may produce metabolites of marijuana which, once formed, may exert stronger psychoactive effects than the original material (Mechoulam, 1970).

Unlimited Complexity of Psychological Substrate

Psychophysiological theories involving conditioning phenomena (Ban, 1964) are beset by still another type of difficulty. The trouble here is that the central nervous system of man is much more complex than that of any other animal—more specifically, that man's levels of abstraction potential and symbolic representation are higher by several orders of magnitude than the corresponding levels of his nearest relatives, the primates. Because of his extraordinary ability to abstract—or, in conditioning terms, to generalize as well as differentiate—man can unpredictably alter or inhibit responses to which he has been conditioned. He may do so through introspection or insight-directed learning, and the almost unlimited and sometimes highly idiosyncratic equivalence of different stimuli (Klüver, 1936) which is available to man reduces the reliability and validity of psychophysiological methods from the lawfulness of a one-to-one cause/effect relationship to mere statistical probability.

THE MIND/BODY PROBLEM

These difficulties are to be expected in a field which, like psychopharmacology, straddles the different universes of discourse that are related to the ancient mind/body conundrum. Notwithstanding all persuasive efforts of modern philosophy to reduce this time-honored problem to a meaningless pseudo existence, the methodological problems associated with it still relate to four universes of discourse, which are represented by the concepts of psychological versus somatic nature and the phenomena of private experience versus public performance. Epistemologically, the psychopharmacologist always has to make decisions about whether he will apply a rational-logical and empirical-observational or a phenomenological (and sometimes esoteric) approach to his data. As a rule, the scientific (i.e., the objective, logical, or observational) approach is chosen in preference to the phenomenological method, which would give at least equal weight to subjective reporting of individual private experiences. But in making this scientific choice, an investigator deliberately sacrifices potential validity for demonstrable reliability. This may satisfy his need for established certainty but cannot be defended on the grounds that such an approach is inherently more valid.*

* The challenge has been raised that, in practical terms, it is meaningless to speak of high validity and low reliability. Yet certain psychological procedures (e.g., unstructured interviews or projective tests) may at times establish data of surprisingly high validity, although it may not be possible to replicate these results with other experimenters using the same instruments, or even with the same experimenter at other times.

BASIC ASSUMPTIONS IN BEHAVIORAL AND NATURAL SCIENCES

For the sake of conceptual tidiness and the avoidance of ambiguity, behavioral scientists—and thus investigators of psychotropic drug effects —have adopted certain basic assumptions which to them have the "self-evident" nature of axioms. Axioms have long enjoyed unquestioned scientific respectability and immunity. But now there is evidence that such time-honored axioms have been tested, found wanting, and rejected by the natural sciences, such as physics. If, under these circumstances, little effort still is being made to question all axiomatic assumptions in the behavioral sciences, then such axioms seem to acquire the qualities of a mystique, because the persistence of these axioms is determined principally by the need of the behavioral scientists for certainty and by their lack of sympathy for relativity and ambiguity of concepts.

At the risk of being tediously speculative by analogy, I should like to review very briefly some of the concepts of modern physics, in order to see what they may have to teach us in the behavioral sciences. Elkes (1962), a psychopharmacologist, has written that "the chief merit of behavior may perhaps lie in its intolerance to facile analogies borrowed from other branches of science [p. 87]." But this certainly does not absolve behavioral sciences from the obligation of seriously considering important epistemological precedents in other sciences.

The physicist Niels Bohr introduced the term complementarity to de-

How can one explain, then, the fact that clinicians continue to use such procedures with considerable overall success? How can they possibly know when these measures will yield valuable findings and when not? There are two possible answers. In the first place, the clinician, before using an investigative procedure of low reliability, usually makes the accurate judgment that he will have time and opportunity to treat his data as tentative until he has been able to validate them on some other level. Thus at worst he risks hardly more than the loss of a short period of time, while at best he gains all the benefits of a most productive shortcut. Second, the clinician may immediately "sense" when his procedure will yield valid data and when it should not be used. He does so, not by the same mechanism by which a superstitious gambler "knows" when he is "hot" and when the dice will roll for him, but rather because he has learned from experience that a certain number of inner and outer conditions have to be fulfilled for the procedure to produce valid results, and he is able to sense (even if he cannot make the reason explicit) when the ensemble of these conditions exists. On the other hand, systematic reliability testing of the same procedure may have explicitly controlled an insufficient number of factors and thus have shown erroneously that the procedure can produce only inconsistent results. Summarizing the state of affairs, one can say that the use of psychological procedures of proven low reliability is not necessarily a waste of effort and time. Furthermore, statements about the low reliability of certain procedures should not be accepted too rapidly.

scribe the strange and apparently paradoxical duplicity of the electromagnetic force, which can be demonstrated to exist either as a diffuse field or as discrete particles, that is, photons. Similarly, electrons manifest themselves in certain experiments as discrete particles and in other experiments as wave packets. Might behavioral science not consider a similar concept of complementarity by clearly acknowledging the essential difference between the two classes of psychological and somatic phenomena and by accepting that one or the other class of phenomena will appear, according to the experiment that is being performed? Instead, much energy is being expended in efforts to argue away the double aspects of the mind/body problem as semantic phoniness.

Heisenberg's uncertainty principle asserts that it is impossible to obtain precise information simultaneously on both the position and the speed of an electron, since every gain of information about one of the two factors must invariably lead to a loss of information about the other. In the behavioral sciences, we are faced with a similar problem of exchanging any increase of information about subjective experience with a loss of information about its objective, physical substrate, since it is impossible to intensify the exploration of one source of information without interfering quantitatively with the other, or, at least, with information about the relationship between the two.* However, we prefer to stress the exclusive

* Perhaps this claim requires some substantiation. Let us assume that an individual, wired to the most sophisticated telemetering equipment we can imagine, serves as the subject of a psychological experiment, and that we wish to obtain the most detailed information possible on his personal experiences as well as on his physical (and behavioral) reactions during the experimental situation. We can obtain information about the subject's personal experiences only through his introspective report, and about his physical reactions only through the registration of our telemetering instruments, which may include numerous implanted cerebral electrodes. Now, if we want an authentic and complete introspective report of the subject's experiences—which may involve solving a cognitive problem, performing the sexual act, listening to a Bach fugue, or piloting a jet plane—we must not interrupt with any stimuli that are extraneous to these experiences. We may simultaneously obtain our detailed and objective instrument recording of the subject's physical reactions, but we will never be able to relate it meaningfully to his personal experiences unless we introduce time markers into the experimental situation. Either these would have to be perceptual stimuli, which the subject could later recall as having occurred simultaneously with certain specific experiences (feelings, thoughts, images), or the subject would have to interrupt the train of his experiences at frequent intervals to give us segments of his introspective report.

In either case we would have to accept a considerable loss of subjective information, which can be valid and complete only if it is the result of an unbroken experience. And yet, if we do not intrude with perceptual time markers or periodic reports into the subject's personal experience, we will inevitably be losing much of the meaning of any psychophysiological information we may have obtained.

validity of only one class of information—the subjective or the objective, depending on our particular philosophical orientation—rather than to accept both as being equally valid, with the understanding that information about one of the two must always be more precise than information about the other.

Strict determinism no longer exists in the conceptual framework of modern quantum physics. One second before emitting beta radiation, a radioactive atom cannot be distinguished from neighboring atoms that may manifest beta decay an hour later or 50 years later. Although accurate statistical information is available about the number of atoms that, in a given period of time, will emit radiation, there is—in the absence of causal antecedents for weak interaction (radioactivity)—no way of identifying future radioactive atoms individually. The internal dynamics of particles within the nucleus of an atom are now characterized by internal degrees of freedom, which assert "that the positions and momenta of particles may not always be sufficient for their complete dynamical description [de-Shalit, 1966, p. 1065]." However, in the behavioral sciences we still tend to adhere to the axiom of strict determinism, and most behavioral scientists would be appalled by a methodological concept of "spontaneous emergence" of thoughts or impulses without determining antecedents that could, at least in principle, be described in known conceptual terms.

Modern cosmology even accepts the possibility that "matter is injected (by some as yet unknown law of physics) into the visible universe at the centers of galaxies [de Vaucouleurs, 1970, p. 1211]," perhaps coming from some "entirely extraneous, spatial dimension [Jeans, 1928, p. 352]." But could a behavioral scientist today seriously consider the possibility that there is not "a twisted molecule for every twisted thought"—or, expressed differently, that there are things in the mind which are not in the brain, that things may get into the mind "by some as yet unknown law"? Lashley refers to the mind as an "intricate web of dependent processes [Klüver, 1952, p. xxii]." However, Sherrington (1941), rather bemused about the problem, cannot see that the brain is "a converter of energy into mind or vice-versa [p. 318]."

It is true that physicists have been enjoying some compensation for conceding the loss of strict determinism by their gratifying success in predicting events at the macroscopic level and by their fine and detailed mathematical understanding of the statistical intricacies at the particle level. However, Newtonian physics had already attained considerable capability for predicting events by employing statistical laws—as in thermodynamics—without having had to sacrifice determinism as a principle. To surrender this fundamental principle was a feat that modern physics did not accomplish without a hard conceptual struggle, and the fact that some physicists today calmly consider the possibility that some presently not fully explainable phenomena may be the manifestations of new and unknown laws is, in my opinion, proof of an epistemological openness that we as behavioral scientists have not yet reached—perhaps, because we do not aspire to it. At any rate, we might do well to ponder the possibility that we might achieve certain gains, if we released our clinging hold on strict determinism—gains not only in terms of a wider cognitive horizon but perhaps also in therapeutic results and predictability, for example, through a phenomenological-existential approach, which would not have to be unscientific although definitely nondeterministic.

Glancing back once more at modern physics, we note that this science has recently relinquished several of its most cherished assumptions, such as the conservation of parity and the invariance of time reversal, the latter having been one of the conceptual strongholds of physics for a very long time, since the laws of mechanics and electromagnetism require it (McMillan, 1966). Other invariant concepts (e.g., the conservation of lepton number, baryon number, electric charge, and energy) are still maintained, but physicists are prepared to relinquish any of these assumptions, if new evidence or a better theory should make this necessary or advisable.

In contrast, we in the behavioral sciences cling to many assumptions with such emotional fervor that even experimental work along certain lines may be strongly inhibited. For example, the general assumption that all extraneous information must be received through sensory channels discourages serious research work in parapsychology.

INFORMATION EXCHANGE BETWEEN THE INNER AND OUTER OBSERVER

The widely, though not universally, held assumption that only public performance can be considered a legitimate source of scientific data in the behavioral sciences, places unwarranted restrictions on the evaluation of certain phenomena, such as the effects of psychotomimetic drugs on man. These substances often produce in the consumer such a rapid and intense flux of perceptions, ideas, and emotions that their effects cannot be expressed adequately by the individual, either verbally or nonverbally, at the time. Nevertheless it is by no means meaningless to ask what went on inside the subject, because he frequently retains a clear recollection of the experience and may later, in retrospect, provide important information on the immediate effects of the drug involved.

In an attempt to give mathematical expression to the circumstances under which such special conditions might prevail, let us borrow one of the most famous mathematical formulations of Newtonian physics:

$$X_r = \frac{2kM}{v^2},$$

the equation* that relates the relevant factors in gravitational attraction to each other, and apply it to the human situation of internal/external information exchange under the effects of a psychotomimetic drug like LSD. We might transpose this formulation into

$$E = \frac{kI}{v^2},$$

where E stands for a subject's expressive (verbal or nonverbal) behavior potential; k, for an arousal constant, that is, a measure of arousal produced by a unit of stimulation; I, for the intensity of internal stimulation; and v, for the density of awareness quanta per time unit, if it is assumed that awareness is not a continuous process but is "quantized" into discrete "moments" of varying length according to metabolic or other determining conditions within the individual (Lehmann, 1965).

If we then replace the left side of this formulation by Tuller's (1949) term for the quantity of information transmitted in time T, that is,

$$FT \cdot \log\left(1 + \frac{a}{n}\right),$$

where F is the bandwidth of the channel; a, the amplitude of the information-carrying signal; and n, the noise in the channel, we obtain:

$$FT \cdot \log\left(1 + \frac{a}{n}\right) = \frac{kI}{v^2}.$$

At a very high rate of awareness flux (as under the influence of LSD) v may become so large that the left side of the equation may approximate zero, and at this point an outside observer may no longer be able to obtain any information about what is going on inside the subject.

---

* Here r is the distance of a body from the center of the mass, M; k is Newton's gravitational constant, that is, the force that two particles exert on each other over a unit distance; and v is the escape velocity of a body (11.2 km/sec for a rocket on the surface of the earth).

MATHEMATICS OR MYSTIQUE?

It is interesting that during the first 30 years of the twentieth century modern physics had to partially *destroy* the philosophy that had served it so well for some centuries—the safe and monolithic constructs of Newtonian physics with its fully determined causality, its unbroken continuity of measurement, and its unequivocally established identity of all phenomena, whereas modern behavioral science is still striving hard to *create* such a Newtonian system and to overcome all the existing inconsistencies and dichotomies which—in contrast to the situation in the natural sciences—have never ceased to haunt it.

Perhaps, today's physicists can live with their conceptual anomalies without feeling alienated, because they can reconcile them, at least to some extent, with mathematical symbols. But only the mystique of a personal belief in the simple, unitarian nature of all basic phenomena can make analogous anomalies acceptable in the behavioral sciences. Does it follow, then, that mathematics is playing the role of mystique in physics, and mystique is playing the role of mathematics in the behavioral sciences?

REFERENCES

Ax, A. F. The psychophysiology of schizophrenia. In M. L. Kietzman, S. Sutton, & J. Zubin (Eds.), *Experimental approaches to psychopathology*. New York: Academic Press, in press.

Ban, T. A. *Conditioning and psychiatry*. Chicago: Aldine, 1964.

Ban, T. A., & Lehmann, H. E. Nicotinic acid in the treatment of schizophrenias. CMHA Progress Report No. 1, 1970.

De-Shalit, A. Remarks on nuclear structure. *Science,* 1966, **153,** 1063–1067.

De Vaucouleurs, G. The case for a hierarchical cosmology. *Science,* 1970, **167,** 1203–1213.

Elkes, J. Subjective and objective observation in psychiatry. In *The Harvey lectures,* Series 57. New York: Academic Press, 1962. Pp. 63–92.

Jeans, J. *Astronomy and cosmogony*. Cambridge: Cambridge University Press, 1928.

Klüver, H. The study of personality and the method of equivalent and non-equivalent stimuli. *Character and Personality,* 1936, **5,** 91–112.

Klüver, H. Introduction. In F. Hayek, *The sensory order*. Chicago: University of Chicago Press, 1952. Pp. xv–xxii.

Lacey, J. I. Somatic response patterning and stress: Some revisions of activation theory. In M. H. Appley & R. Trumbull (Eds.), *Psychological stress*. New York: Appleton-Century-Crofts, 1967. Pp. 14–37.

Lehmann, H. E. Discussion: Neurophysiology of perception. In P. H. Hoch &

J. Zubin (Eds.), *Psychopathology of perception*. New York: Grune & Stratton, 1965. Pp. 104–110.

Lehmann, H. E. Psychopharmacology is a hybrid science. Critical evaluation of: Clinical pharmacology of imipramine and related antidepressant compounds. By G. L. Klerman & J. O. Cole. *International Journal of Psychiatry*, 1967, **3**, 309–313.

McMillan, E. M. Current problems in particle physics. *Science*, 1966, **152**, 1210–1215.

Marrazzi, A. S., Meisch, R. A., Pew, W. L., & Bieter, T. G. Quantified LSD effects on ego strength. In J. Wortis (Ed.), *Recent advances in biological psychiatry*. New York: Plenum, 1967. Pp. 197–207.

Mechoulam, R. Marihuana chemistry. *Science*, 1970, **168**, 1159–1166.

Schildkraut, J. J., Davis, J. M., & Klerman, G. L. Biochemistry of depressions. In D. H. Efron, J. O. Cole, J. Levine, & J. R. Wittenborn (Eds.), *Psychopharmacology: A review of progress 1957–1967*. Washington, D. C.: U. S. Government Printing Office, 1968. Pp. 625–648.

Schou, M. Lithium in psychiatry therapy and prophylaxis. *Journal of Psychiatric Research*, 1968, **6**, 67–95.

Sherrington, C. *Man on his nature*. Cambridge, England: University Press, 1941.

Tuller, W. G. Theoretical limits on the rate of transmission of information. *Proceedings of the Institute of Radio Engineers*, 1949, **37**, 468–478.

PART FIVE

Problems of Psychiatric Classification

All science classifies, for only in this way can it begin to find the regularities that are the foundation of its laws. Classification in psychopathology has been done primarily in terms of medical diagnosis, which traditionally involves skill aided by some of the basic sciences.

The medical concept of diagnosis ideally requires knowledge of etiology, ability to predict the course of the abnormality, and ability to evaluate the effectiveness of various treatments. Unfortunately the enumeration of these aspects of diagnosis constitutes a list of unknowns for most psychiatric maladies. One possible reason for the state of classification, which Joseph Zubin (Classification of the behavior disorders. *Annual Review of Psychology*, 1967, **18**, 373–406) has characterized as chaotic, is the basic model used. The medical model has not incorporated within itself enough of the significant variables (e.g., those dealing with social, cultural, and behavioral factors), and for those that it has incorporated there is not yet enough hard information to serve as an adequate basis for classification.

A number of the chapters in other parts of this book have implications for classification on other bases, independent of the medical model. Thus classification in terms of physiological measures, sociocultural groupings, drug responses, and behavioral analysis are mentioned or explicitly discussed in other chapters, along with statistical approaches applicable to many kinds of empirical data. Throughout the field of psychopathology, considerable dissatisfaction with traditional modes of clinical classification has been expressed, and a number of alternatives are being explored.

We must not allow this dissatisfaction with particular systems of classification to obscure the fact that agreement does exist among researchers on the need for effective classification. Both clincal practice and objective research in psychopathology make an implicit classificatory decision—

393

normal versus abnormal—and require further subdivisions of these categories. Thus classification is significant both for research and for clinical practice, and concern with this subject is reflected in many of the chapters in this volume.

In Part Five, an essentially medical framework is retained as the basis of the approach to classification, and various modifications of current diagnostic procedures are proposed to improve the collection and interpretation of potentially classificatory data. The four chapters of this part have tried to view the problem of classification in a broad way, exploring both methodological and substantive aspects of the process. In Chapter 21 Spitzer and Endicott deal with ways of making more precise the categories of behavior already in use. They show that computers may be utilized, not only as a direct aid to the practicing diagnostician, but also as an aid to clarification of the relevant information, since the rules of combination and the degrees of stress on particular factors must be made explicit. Making the rules explicit allows them to be manipulated, thus revealing what is involved in having the computer arrive fairly reliably at the same diagnosis as a psychiatrist.

Gurland emphasizes in Chapter 22 the need for a flexibility that allows the choice of the system of classification most useful for each particular purpose. He points out that there is no reason to expect a single all-purpose "best" method of classification, and that what is called for primarily is an explicit coordination between the goal and the method of classification. Furthermore, classification should not be seen as static. By taking account of findings imperfectly associated with a given basis of classification, the criteria of classification may themselves be improved, then retested, and so on, as many times as seems profitable. Nevertheless Gurland agrees with the argument made by international health associations that have been trying to cope with the chaos resulting from lack of standardization. Each country (and sometimes each section of a country) has been insistent on using its own idiosyncratic way of classifying patients. The result of the ensuing chaos has been that we do not know enough about the distribution of the various types of disorders. Gurland would hold the obtaining of such distributional information to be one purpose for which a practical standardized classification is appropriate, however inappropriate it may be for many other purposes. No classification technique, including the imprecise technique of psychiatric diagnosis, ought to be expected to serve all purposes at the same time.

In Chapter 23 Burdock and Hardesty employ a structured clinical interview that gives rise to numerical measures based on the behavior of the patient being observed. It is thus intended to improve the chances of obtaining a measure of high reliability. Taking the problem of classification to the next step—namely, of fine-grained examination of the implications of the categories obtained—their chapter utilizes this standardized observational measure to analyze the relationship of psychopathology to intelligence. Their findings contradict the simplistic assumption of an inverse relationship between intelligence and severity of psychopathology, for they find almost all their correlations to be very close to zero. They go on to explore what is clearly a much more complicated relationship between intelligence and psychopathology than can be attributed in any direct way to the severity of disorder. Their study is also of interest as an example of the fruitfulness of an objective approach in reopening a problem that many clinicians had thought to be resolved.

Finally, in Chapter 24 Hunt examines still another important classificatory technique used in clinical practice: the personality inventory. He investigates the problem of detecting the person who is trying to deceive the tester by appearing sicker or less sick than he actually is. Detection of the individual who dissimulates or malingers is not a simple task; nor is the effect of such attempts to impress the tester simply a linear one, influencing single variables only. Although some factors are especially sensitive to various kinds of impression making, Hunt shows us that the interrelationship among factors constituting the personality profile also changes. The reader may wish to compare Hunt's treatment of impression management to that of Salzinger and Salzinger in Part Two of this volume; the latter authors stress its importance in behavioral terms for all patient observations.

In summary, Part Five shows that even classification, traditionally a foundation for the study of the psychiatric patient, is undergoing change in the direction of greater conceptual clarification and more precise measurement.

CHAPTER 21

The Value of the Interview for the Evaluation of Psychopathology

ROBERT L. SPITZER and JEAN ENDICOTT

The study of psychopathology—its phenomenology, etiology, course, and response to treatment—requires techniques for evaluating the aspects of human behavior that are judged to be relevant to the construct of psychopathology. For hundreds of years, the primary methods of obtaining relevant data about psychiatric patients were naturalistic observation and the interview. For the purposes of this chapter, "interview" refers to a situation in which a trained person gathers a body of information about a subject by asking him questions and making observations and evaluations of his responses. It differs from naturalistic observation or ordinary conversation in that the interviewer exerts some control over the interaction for the purpose of obtaining the desired information.

The interview as a procedure for obtaining information came under attack with the advent of the scientific method and the realization of the need for reliable measurement techniques. First of all, the reliability of data collected during the interview was often shown to be disappointingly low because of variability among interviewers in regard to the topics covered and the manner in which questions were phrased. In addition, an interviewer often varies his interviewing procedure on subsequent occasions. Second, this variability was shown to result to a large degree from the interaction between the interviewing style of the interviewer and the characteristics of the patient. For example, interviewers whose style is to challenge patients aggressively are more likely to elicit data suggesting patient hostility.

These and other limitations of evaluations based on the interview procedure led many researchers to reject or disparage it as a data-gathering technique and to turn to other methods that seemed to offer more methodological rigor, such as self-report questionnaires or strictly observational procedures in naturalistic or experimental settings. We believe that investigators who have rejected the interview have often been forced to ignore completely or to evaluate inadequately, several important dimensions of psychopathology. This chapter discusses some of the areas of psychopathology which we think can be reliably and validly evaluated using an interview.

At this point, it is necessary to clarify the boundaries of what is, in our opinion, a useful way of conceptualizing psychopathology. First of all, psychopathology is concerned with behavior and/or functioning of individuals. To us, this includes not only that which can be directly observed, but also private experiences, such as thoughts, feelings, and perception. One quality (perhaps the only quality) that all psychopathological behavior or functioning shares is that it is judged to be undesirable in some fashion. It may be undesirable to the individual who is exhibiting or experiencing it, for example, a painful mood. It may be undesirable to other people with whom the individual interacts, for example, belligerence. And, finally, it may be undesirable to society in general, for example, the compulsive setting of fires. Merely deviant, that is, statistically unusual behavior, which is not considered undesirable by someone is not included as psychopathology; for example, genius is not psychopathology, but its converse, mental retardation, is.

Although all psychopathology is considered undesirable by someone, undesirable behavior that is consistent with and apparently reinforced by subgroup norms often is not considered psychopathology. Examples are some varieties of criminal behavior and some of the expected behaviors of soldiers in combat. We would argue, with others, that these forms of behavior can also be considered to be in the domain of psychopathology and therefore to be worthy of study.

Undesirable behavior or disordered functioning, when due to organic defects or processes, is sometimes, but not always, considered psychopathological. For example, *grand mal* seizures are generally not regarded as psychopathology, unless associated with some disturbance of personality or "ego" functioning.

Some behavior, which is undesirable from the perspective of the person experiencing it, may not be considered psychopathology if it is regarded as appropriate to the situation in which it occurs. Examples are a grief reaction to the death of a loved one and an anxiety reaction during combat.

With the above qualifications in mind, we use the term psychopathology to include subjective distress, impaired thought processes, impaired relations with other people, abnormal motor behavior, inappropriate behavior or affect, impaired ability to carry out goal-directed activities, and impaired ability to adequately test reality.

We will now discuss the value of the interview as a data-gathering procedure for each of these broad areas.

The Interview as a Data-Gathering Procedure

By "subjective distress" we mean unpleasant thoughts about oneself or painful inner states, such as feelings of guilt, depression, or anxiety. The reason that simple observation is often not an adequate procedure for evaluating these conditions is that many individuals experience these painful inner states without visible alteration in their appearance or motor behavior. Conversely, facial expression and bodily posture are often poor guides to the identification of specific inner experiences. On the other hand, there is considerable evidence that it is possible to construct self-report questionnaires which permit cooperative subjects to accurately report the presence and intensity of different inner states. However, for many subjects, self-report procedures are not useful because the individuals are too disturbed to complete the task, cannot read or understand the intent of the questions, or are motivated in some way to falsify their responses. Although the same problems can interfere with the ability of an interviewer to obtain information about these inner states, the interviewer can often lessen their effect through his interaction with the subject. For example, he may calm the disturbed patient sufficiently so that he can answer questions. He can clarify the meaning of questions and responses. He can often detect the intent to falsify or the tendency to under- or over-report and can make efforts to get the subject to give accurate information. Another procedure for evaluating subjective distress is to make a content analysis of a segment of a subject's verbal productions in response to a standard neutral stimulus, such as "Talk for five minutes." This has proved to be a useful procedure, but it would seem to have the limitation of not permitting clarification of the subject's responses and of being dependent on his spontaneous report of material relevant to an assessment of subjective distress.

Impairment in a subject's thought processes can be demonstrated in many different ways. The subject's speech may be so disorganized as to render it unintelligible to others. Milder impairment may be revealed by the juxtaposition of statements, each of which is intelligible, but which lack a logical connection or inherent relationship. In milder impairment, there may only be a tendency to give excessive and unnecessary details or to proceed indirectly to a goal idea with many parenthetical and irrelevant additions. There are also instances in which impaired thought processes are revealed, not by an analysis of the formal properties of a subject's speech (as in previous examples), but by analyzing the logic by which a subject reaches conclusions. At times the impairment in thought processes is evident only to the subject himself, as, for example, an inability to concentrate or a feeling that his thoughts are racing. Self-report measures are severely limited in their ability to evaluate this dimension of psychopathology. Many subjects, although they can acknowledge difficulties in concentration or other subjectively experienced difficulty with their thinking on a self-report measure, are not aware of the difficulty that others have in understanding their speech or their thinking. Procedures that depend on naturalistic observation of spontaneously elicited speech are likely to miss or underestimate the presence of impaired thought processes because such procedures do not permit questioning the subject to determine the underlying logic of his statements. In addition, impaired thought processes may not be revealed unless a subject is directed to discuss certain selected topics or is put under some stress.

The dimension "impaired relations with people" has several components. It includes the subjective element of negative attitudes toward people, as well as manifest behavior that interferes with satisfactory relationships with others. Although self-report measures can tap some aspects of negative attitudes toward people, many subjects are reluctant to acknowledge to themselves or others that they have such attitudes as suspiciousness, resentment, or prejudice. Frequently these attitudes can be observed directly in the interaction of an interview or detected when a subject describes how he behaves in various situations. Self-report measures can also be used to obtain information about manifest behavior, but frequently subjects are unaware of behavior that they exhibit which impairs their relationships with other people. Often it is necessary to obtain detailed information through probing to clarify whether the difficulty in an interpersonal relationship is caused by the subject's psychopathology or the behavior of the other person involved. Naturalistic observation would seem to offer an ideal method for evaluating manifest disturbance in interpersonal relations. However, even in a highly structured setting such as a psychiatric ward, the samples of behavior that are available for observation are only a small part of the universe of the subject's total interaction with others. The advantage of the interview, of course, is that the subject can be questioned about the entire gamut of possible interactions that may have occurred with other people.

Information on abnormal motor behavior such as psychomotor excitement or retardation, or posturing, can best be obtained by observation. This can be done during an interview, but the time period may represent a poor sampling of the subject's ongoing behavior. Self-report measures of this dimension are unreliable and often reflect the subject's feelings of "restlessness" or being "slowed down," rather than actual motor behavior.

By "inappropriate behavior" we mean behavior that is odd, eccentric, or not in keeping with the situation. "Inappropriate affect" refers to affect that is not appropriate for the situation or is incongruous with the content of the subject's speech. It is very difficult to obtain measures of these by self-report alone, since generally the subject is not aware of the inappropriateness of his behavior or affect. Naturalistic observation would seem to be the best source of information for inappropriate behavior. To determine inappropriate affect, however, it is often necessary to encourage the subject to talk about specific situations or topics that would be expected to have strong emotional meaning for him.

In the evaluation of impaired ability to carry out goal-directed activities, both the interviewer and self-report measures must rely on what the subject is able and willing to communicate about his difficulties. However, the interviewer can probe to clarify circumstances and can try to overcome attempts to conceal impairment. Observational techniques can reveal difficulties of which the subject may be unaware. However, it is difficult to observe subjects at work or while engaged in leisure-time activities.

Of all the dimensions of psychopathology, impairment in reality testing is the one most difficult to evaluate without the use of the interview. Such manifestations of impaired reality testing as hallucinations or delusions, require a judgment on the part of a trained person that what the subject perceives or believes is at variance with reality. Attempts to tap this dimension by such self-report items as "Do you see things that other people do not see?" or "Do you have ideas that people do not understand?" have only limited success. Some subjects answer the first question affirmatively, although they do not have visual hallucinations, because they misinterpret the meaning of the question and think it refers to their attentiveness or sensitivity to detail. The interview, on the other hand, permits probing for a full description of the perceptual experience as well as for information regarding the setting in which it occurs, so that the interviewer can judge whether the experience was a true perception, an illusion, or a hallucination. Similarly, a subject may answer affirmatively to the second question and be referring only to political or religious beliefs to which he ascribes. By skillful interviewing, however, it is often possible to determine the nature of a subject's personal beliefs, the manner in which he arrived at them, and the likelihood that they are at variance with reality. The use of observation alone to measure reality testing has limited validity because the subject's behavior may reveal very little about his beliefs or his perceptions.

The foregoing discussion should indicate the unique role of the interview as a means of obtaining data relevant to psychopathology: the interview is the only procedure that permits access to data relevant to *all* of the dimensions of psychopathology discussed earlier. In view of its great potential as a source of data, can it be improved to meet some of the criticisms mentioned in the beginning of this chapter?

The Structured Interview

During the past few years, attempts have been made by us (Spitzer, Fleiss, Burdock, & Hardesty, 1964; Spitzer, Endicott, & Fleiss, 1967; Spitzer, Endicott, Fleiss, & Cohen, 1970), and others (Wing, Birley, Cooper, Graham, & Issacs, 1967) to improve the research value of the data collected during a psychiatric interview by standardizing the interview procedure, so that variability associated with differences in interviewing techniques and coverage is reduced. Interview schedules are developed in order to combine the advantages of flexibility and rapport that are inherent in clinical interviews with the advantages of completeness of coverage and comparability of method of eliciting information. The interview schedules consist of a series of statements and questions that the interviewer uses to obtain the information from the subject. The schedules are organized in such a manner that when skillfully administered they have the feel of a clinical interview. They can be used to elicit information either on small units of behavior (e.g., insomnia) or for rather broad dimensions (e.g., depressive syndrome).

Many of the questions in interview schedules can be open ended so as to stimulate the subject to discuss an area (e.g., "How do you feel about yourself?") and to avoid creating a set in which the subject merely says "yes" or "no" to a list of symptoms provided by the interviewer. Some areas can be more specifically explored with direct close-ended questions (e.g., "Do you need a drink to get through the day or to feel well?"). Supplementary questions and alternative phraseology can be provided to clarify or probe areas when the interviewer wishes more information. The interviewer can be urged to use general probes for more information or for clarification (e.g., "Describe what actually happens," or "What do you mean?").

The initial reaction of many clinicians to the use of an interview schedule is generally negative. A more positive attitude almost invariably results, however, either from watching an experienced interviewer use an interview schedule, or from the clinician himself becoming experienced in its use. Two opposing tendencies can interfere with the effective use of an interview schedule. The first is to adhere so rigidly to the schedule that transitions from topic to topic are awkward, previous information is ignored, and no modifications in the questions are made for the specific circumstances of the subject. The second is to use the interview schedule as if it were only an outline of suggested coverage from which the interviewer creates his own specific questions, thus reducing comparability with the results of other interviewers.

Interview schedules increase the reliability of the data elicited during an evaluation interview. However, interview-elicited data cannot be scored directly, but generally are dependent on the clinician's recording of his evaluation of the material elicited. Furthermore, some of the criticisms of the interview as a procedure for assessing psychopathology have been directed at the use of clinical judgments, rather than at the means of obtaining the information.

Procedures for standardizing clinical judgments antedate procedures for standardizing the interview by several decades. A great variety of rating scales and inventories describing and defining psychopathological behavior have been available to research investigators (Lorr, Klett, McNair, & Lasky, 1966; Overall & Gorham, 1962; Wittenborn, 1955). These rating scales have generally been used in a setting where the data upon which the judgments are based are obtained by an unstructured clinical interview. Well-constructed rating scales, in which careful attention is given to defining terms, giving examples, and providing instructional material, have been used with high interrater agreement provided that the raters have access to the same interview data.

Procedures that combine an interview schedule with an inventory of carefully defined relevant items or rating scales descriptive of psychopathology reduce sources of error variance present in both the procedure for eliciting the data and that for recording the clinical judgments based on the material. With our colleagues we have developed four procedures of this type: the Mental Status Schedule, the Psychiatric Status Schedule, the Psychiatric Evaluation Form, and the Current and Past Psychopathology Scales. Figure 1 shows a portion of the Mental Status Schedule, which was the first such instrument developed.

In terms of interrater agreement, these procedures have been found to be highly reliable, with coefficients generally higher than those based on unstructured clinical interviews (Spitzer, Endicott, Fleiss, & Cohen, 1970; Spitzer, Fleiss, Endicott, & Cohen, 1967). In addition, their application in a variety of research studies has yielded considerable information supporting the usefulness of evaluations based on a structured clinical interview for a number of research purposes.

Groups known to differ in the amount of psychopathology, such as normal persons, outpatients, and inpatients, are differentiated at a high level. Similarly, different diagnostic groups and subtypes are clearly differentiated (Figure 2). These procedures have been of value in evaluating

Interviewer should identify himself, offer to shake hands, and explain the purpose of the interview.

   (Please tell me your full name.) (How old are you?) (Are you married?) (Any children?) (What [is, was] your work or occupation?)

ORIGINAL COMPLAINT

How long has it been since you came to the [hospital, clinic]?

Now I would like to hear about your problems or difficulties and how they led to your coming to the [hospital, clinic]. *If patient fails to specify event or behavior which precipitated admission:*

   (But what actually happened that made it necessary for you to go to the [hospital, clinic]?)

   (How did you happen to come to this [hospital, clinic]?)

   PROBLEM

What problems or difficulties do you have now?

   MOOD

What kinds of moods have you been in recently?

   WORRIES

What kinds of things do you worry about?

If patient admits worries:

   (How much do you worry?)

   FEARS

What kind of fears do you have?

Some people have fears they know don't

1 Refuses to shake hands.

2 Perspires profusely or his hand is either wet or clammy when shaken.

   ORIGINAL COMPLAINT

3*Gives a description of his behavior which is inadequate or insufficient to account for admission (e.g., just says he got "nervous" or "depressed").

   MOOD

4 Says he has felt elated or "high."

5 Says he feels nothing, has no feelings, or feels dead.

   WORRIES

6 Says he has no worries or that nothing bothers him.

7 Mentions he worries a lot or that he can't stop worrying.

   FEARS

8 Admits to three or more different fears or says that he keeps feeling afraid of different things.

9 Mentions a fear of being abandoned or left all alone.

10 Indicates he is fearful of losing his mind or losing control of his emotions.

11 Indicates a morbid fear that something terrible will happen to him.

12 Indicates he has an irrational fear of

Figure 1. Page 1 of the Mental Status Schedule.

This section should be used only with patients who have been in a psychiatric ward or clinic; it may be omitted in repeated testing.

make sense—like crowds or certain activities.
What kind of fears do you have like this?

If patient indicates a fear:
  (Does this fear of .... prevent you from doing something you want to do?)
  ANXIETY
How often do you feel anxious or tense?
  (How much of the time do you feel this way?)

  RESTLESSNESS
What about feeling restless?

  DEPRESSION
How often do you feel depressed or blue?
  (How much of the time do you feel this way?)
  CRYING
When was the last time you felt like crying?
  SELF-APPRAISAL
How do you feel about yourself?
Do you like yourself?
  (When you compare yourself with other people, how do you come out?)

  RESPONSE TO CRITICISM
How do you feel when people criticize you?

a particular object or situation (e.g., crowds, heights) [*phobia*].
13 Says he gets attacks of sudden fear or panic.
14 Indicates his fear prevents him from participating in some activity.

  ANXIETY
15 Admits that he is bothered by feelings of anxiety.
16 Admits he feels anxious practically all the time.
  RESTLESSNESS
17 Says he has felt restless or unable to stay still.
  DEPRESSION
18 Admits he is bothered by feelings of sadness or depression
19 Admits he feels depressed practically all the time.
  CRYING
20 Admits he feels like crying.

  SELF-APPRAISAL
21 Mentions he loves himself or that he thinks he is perfect.
22 Accuses himself of being unworthy, sinful, or evil.
23 Indicates he is bothered by feelings of inadequacy or says he doesn't like himself.
24 Indicates he is bothered by feelings of guilt.
  RESPONSE TO CRITICISM
25 Indicates he feels hurt or overwhelmed when criticized.

Figure 1.   (Continued)

response to treatment (Gottschalk, Gleser, Gleghorn, Stone, & Winget, 1970) and have proved useful also in determining the relative efficacy of different treatment modalities (Herz, Endicott, Spitzer, & Mesnikoff, 1971).

In addition to the above uses, computer programs have been written that take as input the data collected with these procedures and, using a decision tree model, yield a psychiatric diagnosis (Spitzer & Endicott, 1968, 1969).

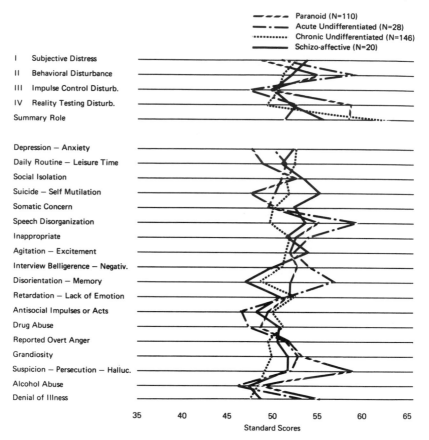

Figure 2. Mean Psychiatric Status Schedule scores of four schizophrenic subtypes.

The computer-derived diagnoses show substantial agreement with diagnoses provided by a heterogeneous group of well-trained clinicians; in one study almost perfect agreement was found between the computer diagnoses of schizophrenia and those made by two clinicians screening a group of maternity patients for the presence or absence of this disorder (Schachter, 1970).

The purpose of this chapter has been to show the potential value of the interview and the hazards of failing to use it as an evaluation procedure. This is not to minimize the value of noninterview procedures, which are superior as measures of some specific aspects of psychopathology. However, in any broad assessment of psychopathology, the interview will continue to be indispensable for a long time to come.

REFERENCES

Gottschalk, L. A., Gleser, G. C., Gleghorn, J. M., Stone, W. N., & Winget, C. N. Prediction of changes in severity of schizophrenic syndrome with discontinuation and administration of phenothiazines in chronic schizophrenic patients: Language as a predictor and measure of change in schizophrenia. *Comprehensive Psychiatry,* 1970, **11,** 123–140.

Herz, M. I., Endicott, J., Spitzer, R. L., & Mesnikoff, A. Day versus inpatient hospitalization: A controlled study. *American Journal of Psychiatry,* 1971, **127,** 1371–1382.

Lorr, M., Klett, C. J., McNair, D. M., & Lasky, J. J. *Inpatient multi-dimensional psychiatric scale manual.* Palo Alto, Calif.: Consulting Psychologists Press, 1966.

Overall, J. E., & Gorham, D. The brief psychiatric rating scale. *Psychological Reports,* 1962, **10,** 799–812.

Schachter, J. Development of a screening questionnaire for schizophrenia. *Archives of General Psychiatry,* 1970, **23,** 30–34.

Spitzer, R. L., & Endicott, J. DIAGNO: A computer program for psychiatric diagnosis utilizing the differential diagnostic procedure. *Archives of General Psychiatry,* 1968, **18,** 746–756.

Spitzer, R. L., & Endicott, J. DIAGNO II: Further developments in a computer program for psychiatric diagnosis. Supplement to the *American Journal of Psychiatry,* 1969, **125** (7), 12–21.

Spitzer, R. L., Endicott, J., & Fleiss, J. L. Instruments and recording forms for evaluating psychiatric status and history: Rationale, method of development and description. *Comprehensive Psychiatry,* 1967, **8,** 321–343.

Spitzer, R. L., Endicott, J., Fleiss, J. L., & Cohen, J. The psychiatric status schedule: A technique for evaluating psychopathology and impairment in role functioning. *Archives of General Psychiatry,* 1970, **23,** 41–55.

Spitzer, R. L., Fleiss, J. L., Burdock, E. I., & Hardesty, A. S. The mental status schedule: Rationale, reliability and validity. *Comprehensive Psychiatry,* 1964, **5,** 384–395.

Spitzer, R. L., Fleiss, J. L., Endicott, J., & Cohen, J. Mental status schedule: Properties of factor-analytically derived scales. *Archives of General Psychiatry,* 1967, **16,** 479–493.

Wing, J. K., Birley, J. L. T., Cooper, J. E., Graham, P., & Isaacs, A. D. Reliability of a procedure for measuring and classifying "present psychiatric state." *British Journal of Psychiatry,* 1967, **113,** 499–515.

Wittenborn, J. R. *Psychiatric rating scales.* New York: Psychological Corp., 1955.

(PSS) Psychiatric Status Schedule (Subject Form, 2nd Ed.), Robert L. Spitzer, M.D., Jean Endicott, Ph.D., and George M. Cohen, M. S., Evaluation Section, Biometrics Research, New York State Department of Mental Hygiene, 722 W.168 Street, New York 10032, October, 1968.

(MSS) Mental Status Schedule, Robert L. Spitzer, M.D., Eugene I. Burdock, Ph.D., and Anne S. Hardesty, M.S., Evaluation Section, Biometrics Research, New York State Department of Mental Hygiene, 722 W.168 Street, New York 10032, 1964.

(CAPPS) Current and Past Psychopathology Scales, Robert L. Spitzer, M. D., and Jean Endicott, Ph.D., Evaluation Section, Biometrics Research, New York State Department of Mental Hygiene, 722 W.168 Street, New York 10032, November, 1968.

(PEF) Psychiatric Evaluation Form (Form R2), Robert L. Spitzer, M.D., Jean Endicott, Ph.D., Alvin Mesnikoff, M.D., and George M. Cohen, M.S., Evaluation Section, Biometrics Research, New York State Department of Mental Hygiene, 722 W.168 Street, New York 10032, January, 1968.

CHAPTER 22

A Flexible Approach to Psychiatric Classification

BARRY GURLAND

Systems of classification are somewhat like maps of incompletely explored territories; prettiness and popularity may be all we have to go by in making a choice, yet these qualities are no proof of accuracy. For a similar reason the choice between competing classifications in psychiatry is not easy; none has established a clear superiority in usefulness over all others. There exist few standards for recognizing and avoiding classifications that will lead the research worker to go around in circles or will strand the clinician in a desert of false predictions.

"The present status of the classification of behavior disorders is, to say the least, chaotic. There are at least 50 different types of classifications in varying degrees of use throughout the world ranging from those which deny the existence of behavior disorders as entities to those [which] regard all behavioral disorders as manifestations of a single underlying dimension —inability to cope with life's vicissitudes—to those [which imply] that there are differentiable entities in the field of behavior disorders just as there are entities in the field of physical disorders [Zubin, 1967, pp. 375–376]."

It is scarcely surprising that there is a bewildering range of choices in psychiatric classification, since for each purpose (and there are many) a different type of classification may be required. Determination of etiology, prediction of outcome, and selection of treatment are only three of the important aims of psychiatric classification. Furthermore, even when the focus is kept on one purpose alone, such as the detection of etiology, there is little to guide us as to which theoretical model we should adopt as a basis for a system of classification. Zubin (1968) has conceptualized no

409

fewer than six classes of scientific models that could be hypothetically applied to psychiatric etiology alone. Finally, cutting across the purposive and conceptual frameworks for systems of classification, there is a spectrum of assessment methods, from the intuitive to the statistical, for fitting subjects into a given framework.

In this aura of uncertainty the most graceful position for the clinician's mind is to be open, though, in the words of G. K. Chesterton, "the object of opening the mind as of opening the mouth is to shut it again on something solid." Hence the views expressed in this chapter will be tempered with a spirit of flexibility.

A few examples of the available classifications in the area of the mental or behavioral disorders will be reviewed, and their respective merits and demerits will be highlighted in order to demonstrate the value of moving freely from one classification to another as the purpose of the occasion demands. In addition, it will be shown that comparing and contrasting different classifications can lead to each being reciprocally illuminated and sharpened.

To simplify the examples used in this review, the first part of the chapter will emphasize the use of classifications in which the main purpose is to guide the management of the patient, and the data for classification are restricted to descriptive psychopathology. The second part of the chapter will deal with classification in which the main purpose is research into the etiology of psychiatric disorder, and the data include primarily descriptive psychopathology and neurophysiological responses. In the rest of the chapter the discussion will range a little more widely.

Throughout, a pragmatic view will be taken as to the usefulness of classifying psychiatric patients or their disorders. No absolute allegiance is given any conceptual model, whether of the social-cultural, developmental, learning theory, genetic, internal environment, or neurophysiological type (Zubin, 1967).

THE APPLICATIONS OF CLINICAL, COMPUTERIZED, AND STATISTICAL CLASSIFICATIONS OF DESCRIPTIVE PSYCHOPATHOLOGY; AND THE USEFULNESS OF COMPARING THESE METHODS OF CLASSIFICATION

Clinical Method

Clinical diagnosis in psychiatry has been increasingly under attack, partly on the alleged grounds that it is unreliable (Kreitman, Sainsbury, Morrissey, Towers, & Scrivener, 1961; Ward, Beck, Mendelson, Mock, & Erbaugh, 1962). By "clinical diagnosis" is meant the pithy label or short set of terms assigned to a patient by a clinician "so as to convey to himself and others as much as possible about etiology, the immediate manifestations, and the prognosis of the patient's condition [Shepard, Brooke, Cooper, & Lin, 1968, p. 13]."

Unreliability of diagnosis may arise for several reasons: the judgments upon which diagnosis is based are often highly subjective; the style of interview may differ between clinicians (Fiedler, 1950); the perception of psychopathology may depend on the training of the interviewer (Sharpe, Gurland, Fisher, & Fleiss, 1969); the vocabulary used to describe a patient's symptoms generally lacks universally accepted definitions (Sharpe et al., 1969); labels may be drawn from different diagnostic systems; and the criteria for placing a patient in a given diagnostic category may differ between psychiatrists from different training backgrounds (Kendell, Sharpe, Cooper, Gurland, Gourlay, & Copeland, 1971). These weaknesses of clinical diagnosis—despite its widespread usage—have until recently militated against its being the optimal method of classification for any purpose.

However, the method of clinical diagnosis has recently been vastly improved. The introduction of structured interviewing (Spitzer, Fleiss, Burdock, & Hardesty, 1964; Wing, Birley, Cooper, Graham, & Isaac, 1967) encourages consistency of interview style; inventories of items for rating behavior ensure coverage of a wide range of symptoms, ratings of discrete behaviors allow the separation of hard from soft data; and definitions of each item of behavior provide a common descriptive vocabulary. Capitalizing on these refinements of diagnostic method, Wing et al. (1967) showed that two clinicians could completely agree in 83.7% of cases on a provisional diagnosis based on the present psychiatric state of the patient. In addition, there is increasing usage of the International Classification of Diseases—the ICD (now the official diagnostic system of many countries, including the United States and the United Kingdom)—and the World Health Organization is working toward a common description of each label in the ICD. Hence clinical diagnosis need not be removed on grounds of unreliability from the repertoire of classificatory methods.

Aside from the issue of reliability, another reason advanced for doubting the value of clinical diagnosis is that heterogeneity and lack of specificity are evident in the symptoms shown by patients in a diagnostic group (Wittenborn, Holzberg, & Simon, 1953; Zigler & Phillips, 1961). However, this criticism may again be more a comment on the practice than on the potential of diagnosis. The relationship between the psychopathology shown by patients and the diagnoses made on them by public mental hospital psychiatrists has been shown to be far stronger in London than in New York (Gurland, Fleiss, Cooper, Sharpe, Kendell, & Roberts, 1970).

Where diagnosis is used to predict response to treatment or long-term prognosis, it is likely that the more homogeneous are the groups with respect to psychopathology the more accurate will be the prediction. In fact, the definition of clinical diagnosis given at the beginning of this section is consistent with diagnosis based on mutually exclusive categories of descriptive psychopathology. Even then, this value of diagnosis should not stand or fall on whether it is the only determinant of treatment or the only predictor of outcome. There is no doubt "that variables other than diagnosis may be as important as, or more important than, diagnosis in predicating choice of treatment [Bannister, Salmon, & Lieberman, 1964, p. 731]." It is enough that a diagnosis summarizes a large body of information relevant to treatment and prognosis.

Given reliability, there is good evidence that clinical diagnoses can be useful. Organic states have quite different prognoses from affective disorders (Post, 1962; Roth, 1955); phobic neurosis responds less well to deconditioning if there is an admixture of obsessional neurosis (Gelder, Marks, Wolff, & Clarke, 1967); schizophrenics recover sooner and more fully with phenothiazines than with psychotherapy alone (May, 1968), but the same is unlikely to be true with personality disorders of the schizoid type; depressive states benefit from antidepressants (Pare, 1968), and manic states from lithium (Fieve, 1968; Gershon, 1968). These instances only touch on the list of useful predictions to be made from clinical diagnosis.

Whatever the usefulness of diagnosis, some clinicians would feel that conventional diagnosis carries with it certain connotations of an unacceptable nature. The use of the term schizophrenia may be taken to mean that the clinician believes the patient to be suffering from a biological disease and that the proper treatment is one of the somatic therapies. However, the flexible clinician is more pragmatic than theoretic in his approach to classification.

Computerized Method

Computer-programmed diagnoses (Glueck, 1965; Spitzer & Endicott, 1968), of either the logical decision tree or the probability model, have the signal advantage of rigid consistency in the criteria of the categories they can offer (although these criteria are by no means universally agreed upon, and two computer programs might give quite different diagnoses to the same patient). The decision tree method is somewhat more flexible than the probability model since "it does not require knowledge or estimates of the base rate of occurrence of symptoms or signs for each diagnosis (which is likely to vary from population to population) [Spitzer & Endicott, 1968, p. 746]." However, observations on or by the patient form the raw material with which the computer must work, and these observations are not necessarily equally valid for all patients. Patients may relate their symptoms more or less accurately, depending on their education, language difficulty or proficiency, attitudes toward the hospital or toward middle-class psychiatrists, or level of psychiatric sophistication (Dohrenwend & Chin-Shong, 1967). Furthermore, florid symptoms such as auditory hallucinations may not have their usual morbid connotation in cultures with a strong mystical flavor (Kiev, 1964). There is no reason why computer programs should not take these reservations into account (other than the complexity of the task), but so far none of the programs available do so.

Clinical versus Computerized Method

Computer diagnoses are likely to be most useful when large samples of patients are to be compared between divergent psychiatric settings, but with the patients coming from much the same sociocultural background. On the other hand, clinical diagnosis might be preferred when the assignment of the individual patient to a category is important. When an atypical or unusual clinical picture is observed, it may be necessary to pursue a more refined exploration of the paradoxical symptoms in order to assess the weight of confidence to be placed in them.

"In the interpretations of observations, both wisdom and judgment play an essential part [and] of preeminent importance is judgment; judgment of the integrity of a patient, of his intelligence and the consequent weight to be placed on his statements, of the relative importance of different pieces of evidence; judgment of the value of instrumental and other technical procedures, and of no small moment, judgment of the specialists who carry out these procedures [Cohen, 1943, p. 19]."

Even more important than choosing between computer and clinical diagnosis is the possibility of fruitful interaction between them. Even in settings where individuals must be speedily categorized for clinical *triage* and reliance is therefore placed on clinical diagnosis, it is valuable to subsample the patients also with computer diagnoses. In this way, the comparability of diagnoses between clinicians and over time can be checked and discrepancies examined more closely. Conversely, when computer diagnoses are appropriate, a quality control can be kept by subsampling with clinical diagnosis, so that the programming of the computer can be modified if a particular diagnostic group is being inaccurately represented.

Glueck and Stroebel (1969) suggest that a close partnership between the clinician and the computer may lead to the best classification of a patient. After experienced clinicians have assigned patients to groups that they expect to be distinctive, multiple discriminant analysis is used to calculate an optimal set of weights for subsequent classification. The probability of a clinically valid assignment is then determined on a further sample of patients. "Those patients who do not have high probability of membership in any of the available groups require further clinical scrutiny to determine if these are exceptional, uncommon, or highly deviant cases, or if new group categories should be created to accommodate them in the future [p. 5]."

Statistical Method

The application of statistical approaches to the organizing of psychiatric symptoms can enable a system of categories to be derived that are relatively free of traditional diagnostic prejudice. Discriminant function (or canonical variate) analyses can be used to classify patients, for instance, in terms of their response to treatment, while clustering or typological procedures (Lorr, 1966) provide syndromes of psychiatric symptoms that might not have been previously recognized. Both discriminant function and clustering analyses are based on discrete items covering the patient's symptoms and signs and can thus be independent of clinical diagnosis—although, when a clinician provides the discrete observations, a bias may be introduced toward finding clusters of symptoms or patients in accordance with his diagnostic expectations (Kendell, 1968).

In selecting treatment and predicting outcome for patients, discriminant function analysis may or may not be more accurate than other methods of classification (Meehl, 1954). Discriminant function can, after a trial of treatment, determine the features that best distinguish the treatment responders from the nonresponders. However, there is no way of assuring that the results obtained on one sample of patients will apply to other patients who differ in clinical or sociocultural features. Therefore, this statistical approach is most useful when the treatment repertoire is relatively stable and patients are more or less homogeneous.

As mentioned above, typologies derived by factorial analyses and clustering techniques (Moran, 1966; Pilowsky, Levine, & Boulton, 1969) may define groups of patients or disorders already recognizable within the traditional clinical framework or may point to new groups. The argument in favor of adopting such a new classification may rest on proof that a new group has, for instance, a characteristic etiology or treatment response that is more predictable than the one for the old group. Such proof, if forthcoming, should clearly swing the clinician in favor of using the new groupings. However, a quite different line of reasoning may be advanced to press the adoption of statistical typologies, namely, that they represent discrete syndromes occurring in nature rather than in the clinician's mind. The latter line of reasoning is not convincing. There are many technical weaknesses in numerical taxonomies (Fleiss & Zubin, 1969), not the least of which is the need for a great number of cases gathered without selective bias from a widely representative population and examined with great care by reliable instruments covering a universe of items important to psychopathology. These conditions are rarely fulfilled. In addition, there is no general agreement about the proper statistical treatment of the data and consequently differing typologies may be derived from the same data.

Statistical versus Clinical Method

It is important for the clinician to be able to make independent decisions about treatment in addition to having the benefit of the discriminant function or typological analysis on a patient. One reason for this statement has already been mentioned, namely, that for some patients who are poor communicators the data derived from discrete items of information may be misleading. Another reason is that clinical judgments, in the present state of technology, may be the quickest method of reaching clinical decisions, particularly if the statistical approach requires feeding data into a computer. Also, in an era of spiraling medical costs it should not be forgotten that computers may be more expensive than clinicians. Above all, it is critical for the clinician to retain his skills in predicting and evaluating treatment in order to be able to detect an unexpected and thought-provoking outcome of treatment.

Many advances in the treatment of psychiatric illness appear to have occurred in such an unexpected manner that it is difficult to imagine how the strict system of observations necessary for statistical techniques could have substituted for the serendipity of the pioneering clinicians. Shrewd observations by clinicians led to the application of electroshock therapy in depressive disorders, the use of phenothiazines in schizophrenia, and the detection of the dangerous effects of cheese ingestion in patients who were taking monoamine oxidase inhibitors (Blackwell, Price, & Taylor, 1967). Iproniazid was a treatment for tuberculosis before it was noted to cause euphoria and was thus tried as an antidepressive agent (Crane, 1956). Imipramine was first tried in schizophrenia but found instead to help depressed patients (Kuhn, 1958).

Another factor making dependence on a rigid and strict system of observations undesirable is that the universe of items relevant to the description of a condition may change over time. The clinician is best situated to note and react to such a change. Ödegård (1967) has described the disappearance of mutism, posturing, and extreme incoherence from the characteristic picture of schizophrenia and has pointed to the emergence of subtle abnormalities in place of the previously gross symptoms.

Granted that clinical diagnosis and statistical approaches to classification can coexist, that in itself is not enough. Integration is a higher ideal. The clinician can sharpen his own powers of discrimination by learning to recognize in the consulting room the behaviors and constellations of behaviors of the patient which have proved statistically to be most distinctive for prognosis or treatment response. When the identification of statistically derived types of patients appears useful, the clinician may improve his ability to identify these types by checking his own attempts against the statistical analysis based on a patient's discrete data.

Nathan, Robertson, and Andberg (1969) examined the degree to which traditional judgments about the diagnostic significance of psychopathology were matched by the actual behavior of patients in various diagnostic categories. After nineteen common symptoms of affective psychopathology had been evaluated, several unexpected findings emerged. For instance, anxiety did "not reflect sensitive differences in psychopathological conditions, a conclusion which goes directly against traditional psychiatric teaching which emphasizes the utility of anxiety as a prime indicator of the psycho-neuroses [p. 241]." Furthermore, the symptoms of depersonalization reflected "acute turmoil and an impending psychotic episode" rather than schizophrenia. On the other hand, elevated mood was a "sensitive measure of a restricted number of psychopathological conditions [p. 241]." The implication of these findings is that traditional diagnostic thinking must be reformulated so as to accord with the facts.

RESEARCH INTO ETIOLOGY: THE APPLICATIONS OF CLASSIFICATIONS BASED ON PSYCHOPATHOLOGY AND ON PHYSIOLOGY AND THE USEFULNESS OF COMPARING THESE TYPES OF CLASSIFICATION

Psychopathological System

The psychopathology shown by a patient is the very stuff that forms the conventional definitions of psychiatric disorder. Thus a classification of psychiatric disorder based on psychopathology might be expected to be useful in the sphere of clinical practice. This expectation is partially fulfilled, for instance, in that psychopathology is a useful prognostic indicator and a determinant of appropriate treatment (Gurland, Fleiss, Sharpe, Simon, Barrett, Copeland, Cooper, & Kendell, 1972).

However, confidence in the validity and potential usefulness of a psycho-pathological classification would be increased were there more certainty about the relationship between psychopathology and physiology. Different emotions may give rise to the same physiological state. Thus Gelder and Matthews (1968) found it impossible to distinguish between the arousal of a subject (as measured by forearm blood flow) occasioned by performing an annoying task of mental arithmetic and that arising from fearful visual-izations of a phobic situation. Furthermore, the same clinical state may result from quite different physical causes, as is seen in the schizophreniform syndromes occurring in disseminate lupus erythematosus, temporal lobe epilepsy, and myxoedema. Conversely, in our ignorance, we must assume that different clinical syndromes may arise from the same underlying physical process. As Hudson (1965) pointed out in the case of *Treponema pallidum,* the manifestations of disease produced by a single physical agent may vary dramatically between cultural groups.

Physiological System

Physiological behavior could constitute an objective, precise, and rational basis for classifying psychiatric patients or their disorders. To achieve this end, the abnormality of the physiological behavior chosen for testing must either be related closely to the mechanisms underlying psychopathological behavior, or occur exclusively within a class of psychiatric disorders de-fined on, for instance, clinical grounds. Nothing so pure is yet available for either alternative. Thus, although physiological tests have potential value as diagnostic tools (Zubin, 1966) and as predictors of a patient's response to treatment (Shagass, Naiman, & Mihalik, 1956), in actual clinical practice they are hardly ever used in these ways.

Psychopathological versus Physiological Systems

Important consequences would flow from the achievement of a perfect relationship between a physiological abnormality and a distinct type of psychopathology. There would be a high likelihood of a causal relationship between that physiopathology and psychopathology; the former could be used as an objective measure of the latter; and there would be good reason to expect that type of psychopathology to have a characteristic etiology, natural history, and response to treatment.

Unfortunately, such a perfect relationship has not yet been found in such psychiatric disorders as neuroses and the functional psychoses; therefore we must start with imperfect relationships and try to make them more perfect. One way of doing this follows the lines of an iterative technique (Sutton, 1970; see also Chapter 10, this volume). The iterative technique starts by an examination of the relationship between different classifications (e.g., physiological and psychopathological) on a given group of subjects. Each classification is then progressively modified so as to improve the relationship on successive groups of subjects.

The initial step in the iterative process might be the choice of a psychopathological classification that is reasonably expected to reduce variance among groups of patients for the physiological behavior under examination. Separation of subjects into schizophrenics and "normals" might constitute such a classification, with reaction time as the relevant index of physiological behavior. Reaction time has been extensively tested in these groups (Huston, Shakow, & Riggs, 1937; Sutton, Hakerem, Zubin, & Portnoy, 1961; Zubin & Sutton, 1970). A noniterative approach would end by assessing the significant differences between the two groups in reaction time (e.g., concurrent validation). The iterative technique goes further and reviews the psychopathological classification scheme in the light of the reaction time results. If there was (as is generally found) considerable overlap between the reaction times of schizophrenics and normals, then both of these groups would be refined with the hope of reducing the overlap. Of course, the success of this venture would have to be tested on new samples of subjects.

Refinement of the clinical classification could proceed by *a priori* reasoning. Either group may contain patients who have been mislabeled; in that event, consensus diagnoses between clinicians of different persuasion or between psychiatrist and computer may isolate a purer group of schizophrenics or normal individuals (Kriegel, 1967). Alternatively the schizophrenics may be sorted into subgroups within which behavior is relatively homogeneous; for instance, if specific symptoms such as affect might determine the reaction time results, the schizophrenics with blunting of affect might be separated from those with depression; or if certain syndromes are regarded as crucial, then perhaps patients with blunting of affect, thought disorder, and delusions of control might be grouped together. There are many variations on this theme, such as separating patients with process and with reactive schizophrenia, those with and without family history, or those in active and in quiescent phases.

Refinement of the clinical classification would also proceed in a more empirical manner than that outlined above. Schizophrenics can be divided into classes in terms of their reaction times, and a search may be instituted for the clinical characteristics that might also distinguish these classes. The search can be imaginatively clinical or mathematically disciplined (e.g., multiple regression analyses). Insights into relevant clinical groups can facilitate the selection of additional cases for the reaction time experiments. In this way, by successive approximations, groups of patients can be defined with increased chances of having a common etiology, natural history, and treatment response. Thus the iterative process may lead by gradual stages to the discovery of a valid and useful psychiatric classification.

An outstanding example of the iterative technique may be found in the work of Satterfield (1969). He subdivided a sample of depressed patients into three groups on the basis of the recovery functions of their auditory evoked responses. The two extreme groups (hyper- and hyporecovery) differed also on other aspects of their evoked potentials, suggesting "a basic neurophysiological difference" between these groups. Satterfield further examined their responses to electroconvulsive therapy and their family histories of depressive disorder. These features again distinguished the groups, "lending weight to the validity of the notion that these may indeed be two different kinds of depressive disorder [p. 25]." Following up this notion, Satterfield explicates a rationale for expecting the hyper-recovery group to respond best to psychic energizers and the hyporecovery group to respond best to tranquillizers, and promises a replication study followed by a comparative trial of the effectiveness of the drugs mentioned above.

The iterative technique could also be usefully applied to the controversy about whether there is continuity or discontinuity between certain diagnostic categories. This is particularly relevant to classification of the affective disorders. Clinical approaches alone have not settled this issue, and statistical treatment of clinical ratings has failed to provide a definitive solution. An iterative approach linking clinical with biochemical and psychological measures might provide evidence for or against the continuum hypothesis of neurotic and psychotic depression.

Court (1968) builds on such an approach in urging that mania may be a severer form of the psychotic process underlying depression. He presents equivocal clinical evidence of a continuum (e.g., depression may sometimes shift to mania without an intervening period of normality; additional stress may sometimes provoke mania in a depressed patient; electroconvulsive therapy and lithium may be effective in both conditions). To support this clinical evidence he quotes Coppen (1965), who states that "manics show the same shift in residual sodium as do depressives but with a more extreme departure from normality [p. 1138]." Court derives similar support from simple reaction time experiments, both his own and those of Lundholm (1922). He moves to the clearly iterative technique when he indicates that only some types of depressive disorders may lie on this continuum. The clues he presents for differentiating these depressive disorders are the response to lithium and the level of urinary 17-hydroxy-corticosteroids (Bunney & Mason, 1965). This interplay of concept, clinical observation, treatment response, and physiological or psychological measures lies at the heart of the iterative process.

A wide-ranging strategy for the initial steps in the iterative process has been adopted by Ralph Gerard and his coworkers (Gerard, 1964). This multidisciplinary group of researchers carried out a seven-year program entitled The Schizophrenia and Psychopharmacology Joint Research Project. They examined 208 male patients at the Ypsilanti State Hospital, about half these patients being independently diagnosed as schizophrenic by three psychiatrists. The patients were given approximately 400 separate measures, including psychiatric rating forms, ward behavior inventories, psychological test batteries, and physiological and biochemical tests. Patients were divided into five subgroups by *clinical* means. Gerard reports:

"At least two kinds of schizophrenia (paranoid and non-paranoid) that had been separated on the basis of clinical criteria were also separated by our tests. It was very satisfying to find that in many respects our results do fit in with clinical subgroups, while differing in *useful* ways [1964, p. 331]."

However, these workers did not stop here. By successive factorial screening of the schizophrenic sample, and using measures only from the areas of psychology, physiology, and biochemistry (i.e., excluding psychiatric data), seven subgroups of patients were derived. According to a psychiatrist with this project (H. von Brauchitsch) "the seven groups . . . appeared to present well defined and easily recognizable clinical entities [p. 332]." Gerard concludes that after seven years of study, by a team that included at its peak more than 40 scientists, there emerge from the amassed data "seven clear subgroups" of schizophrenia, and "anyone who does research or theorizing in the future . . . can advance from this base [1964, p. 333]."

OTHER ASPECTS OF FLEXIBILITY IN CLASSIFICATION

There are times when change may be required, not in the way of classifying patients but in the labels given to the various classes. A diagnostic label may have connotations that reflect past usage rather than current knowledge. For instance, as late as the 1920s in the United States, "schizophrenia" was extensively used only for patients with a poor prognosis (Lewis, 1966). Although there is wide recognition today that schizophrenia has improved in prognosis since the introduction of the term [mainly with the advent of somatotherapy around 1934 and of pharmacotherapy around 1955 (Ödegård, 1967)], it is still possible that a patient with a benign form of schizophrenia might be handicapped in obtaining early release from hospital because a pessimistic attitude, based on the earlier views of schizophrenia, pervades the staff. Moreover, the expectation that schizophrenia will follow a slow course of only partial recovery may lead to a self-fulfilling prophesy. As Szasz (1966) persistently warns us, psychiatric diagnoses may be "swung as semantic blackjacks [p. 148]." In these circumstances a change in the name of his disorder may be beneficial to the patient.

When Not to Adopt a Flexible Approach to Classification

Up to now, this chapter has proposed a flexible approach to classification and one that is open to change. There are advantages, however, to setting limits to such flexibility. Longitudinal studies on the prevalence of psychiatric disorders cannot be pursued if diagnostic criteria change over time. Also, communication between psychiatrists, either within or between countries, is made more difficult by an unstable system of classification. For certain purposes, therefore, it may be necessary to adhere to a rigid and arbitrary diagnostic system.

When Not to Classify Patients

Finally, it is willingly acknowledged that there are aspects of psychiatric treatment that clearly do not hinge upon gross classification of the patient. When one treatment mode, such as psychoanalysis, is favored above all others, there is less need to resort to gross classification. The same holds true when all disorders are held to be maintained by the same mechanism or to arise from the same etiology, such as conditioned maladaptive responses. "What is the new look of diagnosis?" asks Salzinger (1970). "The new look says to look where the behavior is! . . . There are only three basic concepts to be learned and they are discriminative stimulus, response class, and consequence of the response (that is, reinforcement) [p. 26–27]." In these instances it is more pertinent to elicit and classify at a discrete level the unique features of the patient's life history that enable application to his condition of psychoanalytic or learning theory methods, as the case may be.

Some behavioral analysts, such as Kanfer and Saslow (1969), argue that each patient must be treated in the light of his unique experiences. Categorization of the patient, by conventional diagnoses or symptom classification, is of little help in predicting the outcome of treatment.

"Therapeutic intervention can be based on a comprehensive knowledge of two sets of variables which maintain problematic behaviors: those inferred from the patient's history, and those in his current situation. . . . This approach sacrifices the taxonomic features of the usual diagnostic enterprise for greater specificity and heavier contributions of the obtained observations toward direct use in the therapeutic intervention [Kanfer & Saslow, 1969, p. 443]."

Yet Cooper, Gelder, and Marks (1965) have shown, and Gelder et al. (1967) have confirmed, that isolated phobias respond better than agoraphobias to treatments based on learning principles. The response to desensitization may depend as much upon the type of disorder treated as upon the particular method (of desensitization) employed (Gelder & Marks, 1966). Furthermore, parts of the assessment technique suggested by Kanfer and Saslow might be misleading if given to a patient during an affective disorder. For instance, one step in assessment, the motivational analysis, deals with how a patient ranks "various incentives in their importance to him [Kanfer & Saslow, 1969, p. 426]." This ranking, whether made by the patient or by independent observers, would seem to require cautious interpretation if the patient is affectively disordered. Finally, it seems premature to assume that a classification based on symptoms cannot be a useful initial guide to treatment, especially of the pharmacological variety. Nevertheless, it is well to bear in mind that the determination of treatment requires more than classification of the patient. Flexibility in the choice of classification extends to opting to minimize classification of the patient in certain circumstances where treatment is better approached from a unitary viewpoint.

SUMMARY AND CONCLUSIONS

This chapter is based on the premise that, for the present, the most useful approach to psychiatric classification is to be flexible. Flexibility means choosing one or more classificatory *methods* (e.g., clinical, computerized, or statistical) or *systems* (e.g., psychopathological or physiological) that suit the purpose of the moment (e.g., prognosis, selection of treatment, or detection of etiology), and making a different choice for other purposes at other moments.

Flexibility also means a willingness to modify classifications so as to improve their usefulness. In this chapter a way is described of highlighting the aspects of a classification that need refinement by contrasting one method or system of classification with another. One example given is that computer diagnoses can reveal inconsistent criteria in clinical diagnoses; conversely, clinical diagnoses can detect inappropriate grouping of patients by the computer. A more elaborate process for sequentially contrasting and modifying classifications ("the iterative process") is also described.

Finally, in pursuing the theme of flexibility in classifying psychiatric disorders, this chapter paradoxically mentions occasions that call for a rigid approach to classification, such as when studying changes over time in the prevalence of psychiatric conditions. Also mentioned are occasions that require minimizing classification in order to treat each patient according to his unique characteristics.

REFERENCES

Ax, A. F. The physiological differentiation between fear and anger in humans. *Psychosomatic Medicine*, 1953, **15**, 433–442.

Bannister, D., Salmon, P., & Lieberman, D. M. Diagnosis-treatment relationships in psychiatry: A statistical analysis. *British Journal of Psychiatry*, 1964, **110**, 726–732.

Blackwell, B., Price, J., & Taylor, D. Hypertensive interactions between monoamine oxidase inhibitors and foodstuffs. *British Journal of Psychiatry*, 1967, **113**, 349.

Bunney, W. E., & Mason, J. W. Study of a patient with 48-hour manic-depressive cycles. II. Strong positive correlation between endocrine factors and manic defense patterns. *Archives of General Psychiatry*, 1965, **12**, 619–625.

Cohen, H. *The nature, method and purpose of diagnosis.* Cambridge, England: University Press, 1943.

Cooper, J. E., Gelder, M. G., & Marks, I. M. The results of behavior therapy in 77 psychiatric patients. *British Medical Journal*, 1965, **1**, 1222–1225.

Coppen, A. Mineral metabolism in affective disorders. *British Journal of Psychiatry*, 1965, **111**, 1133–1142.

Court, J. H. Manic-depressive psychosis. *British Journal of Psychiatry*, 1968, **114**, 1523–1530.

Crane, G. E. The psychiatric side effects of iproniazid. *American Journal of Psychiatry*, 1956, **112**, 494.

Dohrenwend, B., & Chin-Shong, E. Social status and attitude towards psychological disorder: The problem of tolerance of deviance. *American Sociological Review*, 1967, **32**, 417–433.

Fiedler, F. E. A comparison of therapeutic relationships in psychoanalytic, non-directive and Adlerian therapy. *Journal of Consulting Psychology*, 1950, **14**, 436–445.

Fieve, R. R., Platman, S. R., & Plutchik, R. R. The use of lithium in affective disorders. I and II. *American Journal of Psychiatry*, 1968, **125**, 487–498.

Fleiss, J. L., & Zubin, J. On the methods and theory of clustering. *Multivariate Behavioral Research*, 1969, **4**, 235–250.

Gelder, M. G., & Marks, I. M. Severe agoraphobia: A controlled perspective trial of behavior therapy. *British Journal of Psychiatry*, 1966, **112**, 309–320.

Gelder, M. G., Marks, I. M., Wolff, H. H., & Clarke, M. Desensitisation and psychotherapy in the treatment of phobic state. A controlled inquiry. *British Journal of Psychiatry*, 1967, **113**, 53–73.

Gelder, M. G., & Matthews, A. M. Forearm bloodflow and phobic anxiety. *British Journal of Psychiatry*, 1968, **114**, 1371–1376.

Gerard, R. W. Nosology of schizophrenia: A cooperative study. *Behavioral Science,* 1964, **9,** 311–333.

Gershon S. Use of lithium salts in psychiatric disorders. *Diseases of the Nervous System,* 1968, **29,** 51–55.

Glueck, B. C., Jr. Computers in psychiatry. *American Journal of Psychiatry,* 1965, **122,** 325–326.

Glueck, B. C., Jr., & Stroebel, C. F. The computer and the clinical decision process: II. Supplement to the *American Journal of Psychiatry,* 1969, **125** (7), 2–7.

Gurland, B. J., Fleiss, J. L., Sharpe, L., Simon, R., Barrett, J. E., Jr., Copeland, J., Cooper, J. E. & Kendell, R. E. The mislabeling of depressed patients in New York State hospitals. In J. Zubin & F. A. Freyhan (Eds.), *Disorders of mood.* Baltimore: Johns Hopkins Press, 1972. Pp. 17–31.

Gurland, B. J., Fleiss, J. L. Cooper, J. E., Kendell, R. E., & Simon, R. Cross-national study of diagnosis of the mental disorders: Some comparisons of diagnostic criteria from the first investigation. Supplement to the *American Journal of Psychiatry,* 1969, **125** (10), 30–39.

Gurland, B. J., Fleiss, J. L., Cooper, J. E., Sharpe, L., Kendell, R. E., & Roberts, P. Cross-national study of diagnosis of mental disorders: Hospital diagnoses and hospital patients in New York and London. *Comprehensive Psychiatry* 1970, **11** (1), 18–25.

Hudson, E. H. Treponemotosus and man's social evolution. *American Anthropologist,* 1965, **67** (4), 885–901.

Huston, P. E., Shakow, D., & Riggs, L. A. Studies on motor function in schizophrenia. II. Reaction time. *Journal of General Psychology,* 1937, **16,** 39–82.

Kanfer, F. H., & Saslow, G. Behavioral diagnosis. In C. M. Franks (Ed.), *Behavior therapy: appraisal and status.* New York: McGraw-Hill, 1969. Pp. 417–444.

Kendell, R. E. An important source of bias affecting ratings made by psychiatrists. *Journal of Psychiatric Research,* 1968, **6,** 135–141.

Kendell, R. E., Sharpe, L., Cooper, J. E., Gurland, B. J., Gourlay, J., & Copeland, J. R. M. The diagnostic criteria of American and British psychiatrists. *Archives of General Psychiatry,* 1971, **25,** 123–130.

Kiev, A. *Hallucinations in mystical cultures. Magic, faith and healing.* New York: Collier Macmillan, 1964.

Kramer, M. Some problems for international research suggested by observations on differences in first admission rates to mental hospitals of England and Wales and of the United States. In *Proceedings of the Third World Congress of Psychiatry.* Vol. 3. Montreal: McGill University Press, 1961. Pp. 153–160.

Kreitman, N., Sainsbury, P., Morrissey, J., Towers, J., & Scrivener, J. The reliability of psychiatric assessment: An analysis. *Journal of Mental Science,* 1961, **107,** 887–898.

Kriegel, J. *Reaction time in schizophrenics and normals as a function of stimulus uncertainty, guessing, and modality shift.* (Doctoral dissertation, Columbia University) Ann Arbor, Mich.: University Microfilms, 1967. No. 67–15,496.

Kuhn, R. Treatment of depressive states with G-22355 (imipramine and hydrochloride). *American Journal of Psychiatry,* 1958, **115,** 459.

Lewis, N. D. C. History of the nosology and the evolution of the concepts of schizophrenia. In P. H. Hoch & J. Zubin (Eds.), *Psychopathology of schizophrenia.* New York: Grune & Stratton, 1966. Pp. 1–18.

Lorr, M. Classification of the behavior disorders. *Annual Review of Psychology,* 1961, **12,** 195–216.

Lorr, M. (Ed.) *Explorations in typing psychotics.* Oxford: Pergamon Press, 1966.

Lundholm, H. Reaction time as an indicator of emotional disturbances in manic-depressive psychosis. *Journal of Abnormal and Social Psychology,* 1922–23, **17,** 293.

May, P. R. A. *Treatment of schizophrenia: A comparative study of five treatment methods.* New York: Science House, 1968.

Meehl, P. E. *Clinical versus statistical prediction.* Minneapolis: University of Minnesota Press, 1954.

Moran, P. A. P. The establishment of a psychiatric syndrome. *British Journal of Psychiatry,* 1966, **112,** 1165–1171.

Nathan, P. E., Robertson, P., & Andberg, M. M. A systems analytic model of diagnosis. IV. The diagnostic validity of abnormal affective behavior. *Journal of Clinical Psychology,* 1969, **25** (3), 235–242.

Ödegård, Ö. Changes in the prognosis of functional psychoses since the days of Kraepelin. *British Journal of Psychiatry,* 1967, **113,** 813–822.

Pare, C. M. B. Recent advances in the treatment of depression. In A. Coppen & A. Walk (Eds.), *Recent developments in affective disorders. A symposium.* Ashford, Kent: Headley, 1968. Pp. 137–150. (*British Journal of Psychiatry,* Spec. Publ. No. 2.)

Pilowsky, I., Levine, S., & Boulton, D. M. The classification of depression by numerical taxonomy. *British Journal of Psychiatry,* 1969, **115,** 937–945.

Post, F. The significance of affective symptoms in old age. *Maudsley monograph,* No. 10. London: Oxford University Press, 1962.

Roth, M. The natural history of mental disorder in old age. *Journal of Mental Science,* 1955, **101,** 281.

Salzinger, K. Diagnosis: Who needs it? *Journal of Clinical Issues in Psychology,* 1970, **1** (2), 25–27.

Satterfield, J. H. Auditory evoked cortical response studies in depressed patients and normal control subjects. Paper presented in part at the National Institute of Mental Health Workshop on the Psychobiology of the Depressive Illnesses, College of William and Mary, Williamsburg, Va., 1969.

Shagass, C., Naiman, J., & Mihalik, J. An objective test which differentiates between neurotic and psychotic depression. *Archives of Neurology and Psychiatry,* 1956, **75,** 461–471.

Sharpe, L., Gurland, B., Fisher, B., & Fleiss, J. L. The accuracy of trans-Atlantic communication in psychiatry. Paper presented at the meeting of the American Psychological Association, Miami Beach, 1969.

Shepherd, M., Brooke, E. M., Cooper, J. E., & Lin, T. An experimental approach to psychiatric diagnosis. *Acta Psychiatrica Scandinavica,* 1968, **44,** 7–89 (Suppl. No. 201).

Spitzer, R. L., & Endicott, J. DIAGNO: A computer program for psychiatric diagnosis utilizing the differential diagnostic procedure. *Archives of General Psychiatry,* 1968, **18,** 746–756.

Spitzer, R. L., Fleiss, J. L., Burdock, E. I., & Hardesty, A. S. The Mental Status Schedule: Rationale, reliability and validity. *Comprehensive Psychiatry,* 1964, **5,** 384–395.

Sutton, S. Personal communication, 1970.

Sutton, S., Hakerem, G., Zubin, J., & Portnoy, M. The effect of shift of sensory modality on serial reaction time: A comparison of schizophrenics and normals. *American Journal of Psychology,* 1961, **74,** 224–232.

Szasz, T. S. The psychiatric classification of behavior. A strategy of personal constraint. In L. D. Eron (Ed.), *The classification of behavior disorders.* Chicago: Aldine, 1966. Pp. 123–170.

Ward, C. H., Beck, A. T., Mendelson, M., Mock, J. E., & Erbaugh, J. K. The psychiatric nomenclature: Reasons for diagnostic disagreement. *Archives of General Psychiatry,* 1962, **7,** 198–205.

Wing, J. K., Birley, J. L., Cooper, J. E., Graham, P., & Issac, A. D. Reliability of a procedure for measuring and classifying "Present Psychiatric State." *British Journal of Psychiatry,* 1967, **113,** 499–515.

Wittenborn, J., Holzberg, J., & Simon, B. Symptom correlates for descriptive diagnosis. *Genetic Psychology Monographs,* 1953, **47,** 237–301.

Zigler, E., & Phillips, L. Psychiatric diagnosis and symptomatology. *Journal of Abnormal and Social Psychology,* 1961, **63,** 69–75

Zubin, J. A cross-cultural approach to psychopathology and its implications for diagnostic classification. In L. D. Eron (Ed.), *The classification of behavior disorders.* Chicago: Aldine, 1966. Pp. 45–85.

Zubin, J. Classification of the behavior disorders. *Annual Review of Psychology,* 1967, **18,** 373–406.

Zubin, J. Classification of human behavior. Paper presented at the meeting of the Canadian Psychological Association, Calgary, Alberta, Canada, 1968.

Zubin, J., & Sutton, S. Assessment of physiological, sensory, perceptual, psychomotor and conceptual functioning in schizophrenic patients. *Acta Psychiatrica Scandinavica,* 1970, **46,** 247–263 (Suppl. No. 219).

CHAPTER 23

A Multivariate Analysis of the Relations Between Intelligence and Psychopathology

EUGENE I. BURDOCK and **ANNE S. HARDESTY**

Since the 1960s two developments have occurred that are facilitative for investigations of the relations between intelligence and psychopathology. One is the burgeoning use of computers with the consequent possibility of submitting massive amounts of numerical data to multivariate analysis. The second is the increasing amount of systematic quantitative information on the differences between maladaptive behaviors of "normals" (community subjects without psychiatric history) and of mental patients.

Intelligence as a scientific concept was introduced by Herbert Spencer and Francis Galton, both of whom believed in the existence of "an ability super-ordinate to and distinct from special abilities [Butcher, 1968, p. 15]." "Intelligence," as Butcher points out (p. 22), is a noun, and because nouns often refer to attributes, we are inclined to think of intelligence as a thing organisms have, although it is really a description of how they behave. It may be argued that the concept has outlived its usefulness in some respects, that the idea of some general cognitive capacity present in varying amounts in all human activities is not as plausible as the reductionist notion of separate skills or singular accomplishments in increasingly narrower areas. Nonetheless, Terman's studies confirm "general intelligence, measured by conventional tests, as the most important psychological variable that can at present be assessed, and (despite large individual changes in IQ) the most stable and predictive over the life span [Butcher, 1968, p. 274]." As an independent or classifying variable it has proved crucial in many psychologically meaningful investigations. This evidence that IQ excels other personality traits is the "hard fact" demanded by Zubin (1965).

Echoing through a half century of the literature on psychopathology and psychodiagnostics is a recurring theme of the effect of mental illness on intelligence, or at least on the functional use of intelligence. Rabin and Guertin (1951; Rabin, 1965) published comprehensive and critical reviews of research related to this theme in the period from 1914 to 1963. Essentially two concepts appear to be central to most investigations of the relation between intelligence and psychopathology: that patterning and scatter on intelligence tests possess diagnostic significance (see, e.g., Pressey & Cole, 1918; Rapaport, Gill, & Schafer, 1945; Wechsler, 1939, 1946); and that mental patients are characterized by a·lower premorbid IQ than their peers or their siblings (Lane & Albee, 1970) or by lowered intellectual efficiency during the morbid state (Rabin & Guertin, 1951; Yates, 1966, p. 131). Wechsler (1939) has asserted that "differences between verbal and performance test scores . . . have a special interest for the clinician because such discrepancies are frequently associated with certain types of mental pathology [p. 146]." It has been further maintained that the intellectual defect of the mental patient affects various mental functions in a hierarchical order, what Rabin (1965) calls "the hypothesis of selective impairment [p. 481]."

The introduction of the Wechsler Bellevue Intelligence Test (Wechsler Adult Intelligence Scale, WAIS, in its current revised version) allowed for better studies in adults with or without pathology because its standardization among adults was superior to that of the Stanford-Binet. Rabin (1965) in his own earlier study found a mean Wechsler IQ of 91.4 for a two-year cohort of unselected mental hospital admissions, with nonpsychotics functioning best and schizophrenics least well.

There has been much argument in the last two decades about the psychodiagnostic significance of scatter, many clinicians clinging doggedly to their beliefs in systems or assumptions that either have not been amenable to quantitative investigation or have not proved valid in research. Harris and Shakow (1937) were critical of the scatter studies, centering their objections around the failure of investigators to employ normal control groups and citing their own findings that, when mental age was held constant, differences in scatter among groups of delinquents as well as among schizophrenics tended to disappear. Zubin, Burdock, Sutton, and Cheek (1959) have proposed that studies aimed at demonstrating the prognostic power of psychological tests include specification of the patient population, objective criteria of outcome, homogeneous conditions, and results amenable to statistical evaluation. But few studies have been found that meet these requirements. Payne (1961), reviewing studies of cognitive dysfunction, criticized the "unfortunate tendency" of psychologists to relate test results to psychiatric diagnostic categories that "do not have the status of scientific concepts [p. 196]."

The purpose of the present study is to compare the multivariate and univariate techniques for investigating those questions raised in the literature. The multivariate technique of canonical correlation was applied to examine the relations between an individually administered intelligence test (WAIS) and an individually administered test for psychopathology (Structured Clinical Interview, SCI) from scores of a sample of psychiatric inpatients. The normative data for both the intelligence test and the test of psychopathology are based on scores of subjects who are at large in the community and who are without apparent psychiatric impairment.

SUBJECTS AND INSTRUMENTS

Over a period of several years every patient newly admitted to the New York State Psychiatric Institute was examined on the SCI within three days of admission. Some of these patients also received a battery of psychological tests administered by the clinical psychology unit, usually at the request of the admitting psychiatrist. Of the 310 patients examined with the SCI during an 18-month period 148 (47.7%) were found to have current WAIS profiles in their case records. These 148 patients comprise the sample in the current study. There were 65 men and 83 women; the age range was from 18 to 72; and six diagnostic groups were represented, over 60% of the patients being labeled as schizophrenic.

The Wechsler Adult Intelligence Scale (Wechsler, 1955) is an individually administered test standardized on a representative sample of 1700 adult subjects, aged 16–65, of different occupations and from different geographic areas in the United States. It consists of 11 rationally derived subtests, each focused on a different area of intellectual functioning, and each correlating significantly with the others. The subtests are classified according to the nature of the tasks into one of two major groups: a verbal group, in which the required responses consist of words or numbers, and a performance group, in which pictures or objects must be manipulated, with the accompanying verbal exchange less important. The W-B has been translated into and standardized in several other languages (e.g., in German by Wechsler, Hardesty, & Lauber, 1956), and the reports of its reliability and validity in other language communities are similar to those for the United States. A number of factor analyses have been performed (Cohen, 1955). The division of the WAIS into its two major dimensions seems to be vindicated in the factor studies.

The Structured Clinical Interview (Burdock & Hardesty, 1968, 1969b) is a standardized psychological method for the evaluation of psychopathology comparable to the standardized psychological methods used for the individual evaluation of intelligence. The evaluation is based on the display of behaviors and attitudes described as critical in the clinical literature that can be reliably assessed in an individual testing session, that are discriminating, and that are amenable to quantitative treatment. The norms are based on community subjects with no history of psychopathology. Although SCI scores and profiles may serve as adjuncts to diagnosis, it must be emphasized that the SCI is a psychological, not a psychiatric, technique; it involves a carefully controlled stimulus situation, not a free inquiry; it is ahistorical; it focuses on manifest behavior; and it is not couched in psychiatric terminology.

The SCI consists of both an interview protocol and an inventory of 179 behavioral items. The examiner records his judgments of the psychological significance of the subject's responses by checking "yes" or "no" for each item as the interview progresses. The interview usually takes about 20 minutes. Since the examiner records his judgments during the interview, no additional time is required for completion of the schedule after the subject has departed. The SCI is intended both for screening and for determining changes in psychopathology.

The inventory part of the technique was constructed by identifying in the psychological and psychiatric literature areas of psychopathology generally recognized as having symptom significance. From each of these areas were drawn representative verbalizations, attitudes, and actions significant of psychopathology. These behaviors were then broken down into discrete items. The interview in turn was constructed so as to provide a uniform stimulus context in which to direct the subject's attention toward these areas of adaptation and to give him an opportunity to exhibit ideation and behavior from which the psychologist can judge the presence or absence of psychopathology. The approach to areas of potential pathology is oblique rather than direct, the interviewer's inquiries being so phrased as to offer the subject the opportunity to invest them with his own meanings. Such direct questions as are necessary are cast in a form to preclude simple "yes" or "no" responses. Although the stimuli are ambiguous, the responses are evaluated with explicit reference to the preselected behavioral items of the inventory.

The inventory is molecular, with items so worded that a judgment of "yes" by the examiner indicates the presence of an element of maladaptive behavior.

The items of the SCI have been clustered into 10 nonoverlapping subtests:

1. Anger-Hostility (reflected either in verbalization or in behavior).

2. Conceptual Dysfunction (disturbances of concept formation, concept retention, or concept evocation that interfere with cognitive functioning, and that express themselves in defects of communication, orientation, memory, attention, and concentration).

3. Fear-Worry (reports or displays of apprehensiveness, nervousness, or anxiousness).

4. Incongruous Behavior (modes of expression that seem contradictory to one another or that represent anomalous and unusual ways of doing usual things).

5. Incongruous Ideation (contradictory emotions, strange or bizarre notions incompatible with reality, outright delusions, or ideas that are uncoupled from the socially expected emotional toning, i.e., ideation with inappropriate affect or without affect).

6. Lethargy-Dejection (reflected in physical as well as in emotional expression).

7. Perceptual Dysfunction (hallucinatory experiences).

8. Physical Complaints (reports of somatic problems).

9. Self-Depreciation (feelings of guilt, inferiority, or worthlessness).

10. Sexual Problems (difficulties stemming from sexual attitudes or behavior).

The norms for the SCI are derived from three samples of subjects: (1) 48 subjects between 18 and 31 years of age who were either sales clerks, secretaries, or college students; (2) 95 community subjects between 18 and 56 years of age who were seeking vocational advice; (3) 49 16- or 17-year-old students from various Manhattan high schools. The German edition of the manual, which is still in preparation, has been standardized on a group of 232 subjects drawn from a broad range of occupations. The norms compare reasonably well with those of the American samples.

Several selected groups of nonpsychiatric subjects have shown patterns of scores approximating those of the community subjects used for standardization. For example, two small groups of subjects under exceptional stress (10 patients on their first visit to a cancer clinic, and 7 tested the day before surgery for intractable pain) both showed a greater number of signs of psychopathology than the norm group, but remained within one standard deviation of the mean level of the norm. This may be taken as some evidence that the SCI does not confound psychopathology with reaction to stress.

Details of the mathematical and statistical procedures used in the standardization of the SCI are presented in the manual. It suffices to say here that the raw scores of the 10 subtests have been transformed so as to smooth the distribution and then converted to standard form. The characteristic profiles of groups of in- and outpatient psychiatric subjects will be found in the SCI manual (pp. 21-22). These data represent more than 1000 inpatients and 100 outpatients. Applications of the SCI in studies of changes induced by drugs are reported elsewhere (Burdock & Hardesty, 1968, 1969a; Gershon, Hekimian, Burdock, Park, & Floyd, 1970; Hekimian, Gershon, & Floyd, 1970; Johnson, Gershon, Burdock, Floyd, & Hekimian, 1971).

STATISTICAL METHODOLOGY

A comparison of WAIS IQs with SCI level of psychopathology scores was obtained by means of the Pearson product moment correlation. However, in order to assess the relations between the 10 subtests of the WAIS (vocabulary was omitted for this study) and the 10 subtests of the SCI, Hotelling's (1936) multivariate method for determining the relations between two set of variates was applied. This method involves transforming the two sets of scores into two new sets which have unit variances and zero means and in which each variate is independent of the others in its group. A series of successive uncorrelated linear combinations of the two sets (canonical variates) are then sought which yield the maximum (the canonical) correlations obtainable from the data. They emerge from the analysis in hierarchical order so that the amount of common variance accounted for in the first canonical correlation represents the maximum obtainable from that particular configuration. Similarly, the second and any subsequent canonical correlations represent the amount of residual common variance exclusive of the prior canonical correlations. Each canonical correlation reflects a particular weighting of the original variates. It is thus possible by inspection to observe the relative contributions of elements of the two sets of variates to the particular canonical correlation in question.

RESULTS

All the subjects of this study were psychiatric patients who were functioning with sufficient maladaptiveness to be hospitalized for their psychiatric handicaps. The distribution of WAIS scores in Figure 1, though slightly skewed to the left, shows a higher mean IQ (104.3) and a higher standard deviation (17.6) than the WAIS standardization sample. There is no evidence, therefore, of lower than average intelligence for the group as a whole, although their premorbid mean may, of course, have been still higher. Figure 2 shows the frequency distribution of scores for level of

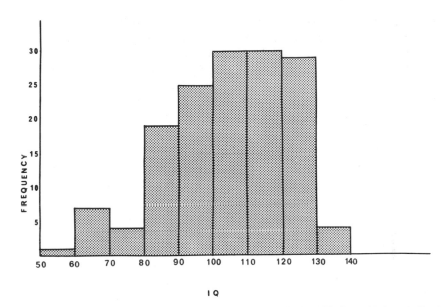

Figure 1. Frequency distribution of IQ scores on the WAIS for 148 hospitalized patients.

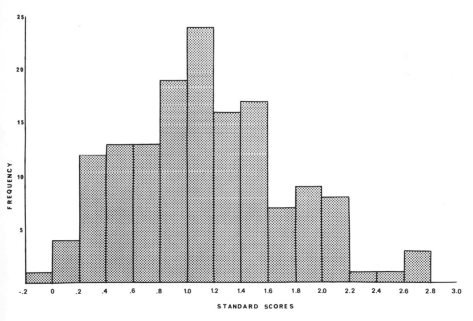

Figure 2. Frequency distribution of SCI scores for level of psychopathology of 148 hospitalized psychiatric patients.

433

psychopathology on the SCI. The higher the score, the more pathology was observed. The distribution is similar to that shown by 870 hospitalized mental patients (Burdock & Hardesty, 1969b, p. 21). It has a mean value of 1.125, and a standard deviation of 0.589. Thus the sample is higher in global intelligence than the average standardization population on the WAIS, yet displays as much psychopathology as the average hospitalized patient group, as illustrated in Figure 3. For this sample, as is shown in Table 1, the correlations of SCI level of pathology score with WAIS full-scale IQ, with WAIS verbal quotient, with WAIS performance quotient, and with WAIS verbal-minus-performance quotient are all in the neighborhood of zero.

Table 2 features the bivariate correlations between weighted scores on the WAIS and SCI that are statistically significant. The Conceptual Dysfunction subtest of the SCI has significant negative correlations with 6 of the 10 WAIS scales; the Physical Complaints subtest is accompanied by poor scores on 3 of the performance subtests. Both of these results seem quite credible. The other correlations are not so easy to rationalize: the Lethargy-Dejection subtest correlates negatively with performance on Digit Symbol; the subtest of Self-Depreciation correlates positively with 3 of the WAIS verbal scales and with Similarities; but the subtest for Sex Problems correlates significantly with all 5 of the performance scales as well as with 2 of the verbal subtests.

The multivariate model reveals a different picture. Table 3 shows the results of canonical correlation of the 10 WAIS scales with the 10 subtests of the SCI. The first canonical correlation of .55 is significant at $p < .025$. No additional canonical combination was of significance. The contributions of the two sets of variables to the canonical correlation are proportional to the weights listed in Table 3. Thus, for the WAIS, Similarities suffers most, or is least functionally available, when the pattern of pathology on the SCI is most pronounced, but Object Assembly and Picture Arrangement are positively associated with high scores in psychopathology. For the SCI the most important contribution to the canonical correlation is made by Conceptual Dysfunction. Perhaps this reflects an impairment of the ability to communicate or, as Cameron (1939) has suggested in regard to schizophrenia, an incongruity of conceptual performance rather than a loss of conceptual ability. The scores on Sexual Problems vary positively with intellectual proficiency, as was also true in the bivariate correlations of Table 2. Physical Complaints and Lethargy-Dejection also retain the negative relation to intellectual function that these two subtests display in Table 2.

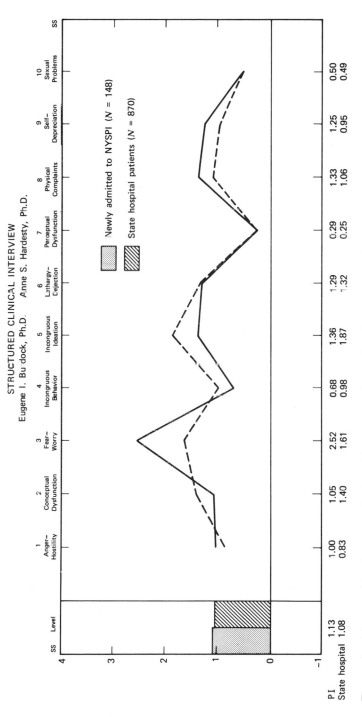

Figure 3. Mean profiles of psychopathology of two groups of mental patients.

Table 1. Correlation of WAIS IQ with SCI Level of Pathology[a]

WAIS IQ	Correlation
Full scale	.03
Verbal scale	.04
Performance scale	.01
Verbal-performance discrepancy	
Verbal — performance	.06
Absolute difference between verbal and performance	.06

[a] SCI level score is mean elevation of the 10 subtests.

SUMMARY

This study was intended to illustrate a technique by which certain clinical assumptions can be tested against empirical data. In this sample of patients some relationships predicated in the clinical literature are not confirmed: (1) lower IQs for mental patients; (2) correlation between intellectual level and severity of mental illness; (3) diagnostic significance of differences between verbal and performance scores.

The bivariate correlations between the SCI subtests and the subtests of the WAIS suggest that conceptual impairment has a negative influence on intellectual achievement, that higher WAIS scores are accompanied by a greater propensity to engage in self-depreciation and to verbalize sexual problems, and that physical complaints depress scores on the performance subtests of the WAIS. Canonical correlation reveals a significant overall association between psychopathology and intellectual efficiency. Conceptual impairment is confirmed as the primary source of interference with the expression of intelligence. Lethargy-Dejection, which appeared relatively unimportant in the bivariate analysis, emerges as a large contributor in the multivariate analysis of the influence of psychopathology on intelligence, next in importance to Physical Complaints. The multivariate method discloses that the WAIS component most seriously impaired by psychopathology is the Similiarities subtest, which has been described (Wechsler, 1944) as throwing light on "the logical character of the subject's thinking processes [p. 86]."

Table 2. Bivariate Correlations between Subtests of the SCI and Subtests of the WAIS[a]

SCI	Information	Compre-hension	Arith-metic	Simi-larities	Digit Span	Digit Symbol	Picture Comple-tion	Block Design	Picture Arrange-ment	Object Assembly
Anger-Hostility	—	—	—	—	—	—	—	—	—	—
Conceptual Dysfunction	—	-.20*	—	-.17*	—	-.26**	-.21*	—	-.26**	-.18*
Fear-Worry	—	—	—	—	—	—	—	—	—	—
Incongruous Behavior	—	—	—	—	—	—	—	—	—	—
Incongruous Ideation	—	—	—	—	—	—	—	—	—	—
Lethargy-Dejection	—	—	—	—	—	-.17*	—	—	—	—
Perceptual Dysfunction	—	—	—	—	—	—	—	—	—	—
Physical Complaints	—	—	—	—	—	—	—	-.20*	-.23**	-.23**
Self-Depreciation	.18*	.18*	.18*	—	—	—	—	—	.18*	—
Sexual Problems	.29**	—	.26*	—	—	.18*	.20*	.21*	.19*	.17*

[a] — indicates $|r| < .17$; $p > .05$.
* $p < .05$.
** $p < .01$.

Table 3. Results of Canonical Correlation of Ten SCI Subtests with Ten WAIS Subtests[a]

SCI Weights		WAIS Weights	
Anger-Hostility	—.04	Information	.28
Conceptual Dysfunction	—.51	Comprehension	.20
Fear-Worry	—.15	Arithmetic	.27
Incongruous Behavior	.22	Similarities	—1.09
Incongruous Ideation	.02	Digit Span	— .08
Lethargy-Dejection	—.37	Digit Symbol	.36
Perceptual Dysfunction	.28	Picture Completion	.34
Physical Complaints	—.44	Block Design	— .14
Self-Depreciation	.20	Picture Arrangement	.79
Sexual Problems	.47	Object Assembly	.80

[a] $R_c = .55, \Lambda = .38, \chi^2_{100} = 134, p < .025.$

REFERENCES

Burdock, E. I., & Hardesty, A. S. A psychological test for psychopathology. *Journal of Abnormal Psychology,* 1968, **73,** 62–69.

Burdock, E. I., & Hardesty, A. S. A research tactic for evaluation of drug specificity in schizophrenia. In D. V. Siva Sankar (Ed.), *Schizophrenia: Current concepts and research.* Hicksville, N.Y.: P. J. D. Publications, 1969. Pp. 174–181. (a)

Burdock, E. I., & Hardesty, A. S. *A structured clinical interview: SCI manual.* New York: Springer, 1969. (b)

Butcher, H. J. *Human intelligence.* New York: Barnes & Noble, 1968.

Cameron, N. Schizophrenic thinking in a problem-solving situation. *Journal of Mental Science,* 1939, **85,** 1012–1034.

Cohen, J. The efficacy of diagnostic pattern analysis with the WB. *Journal of Consulting Psychology,* 1955, **19,** 303–306.

Gershon, S., Hekimian, L. J., Burdock, E. I., Park, S., & Floyd, A. Relative efficacy of butaperazine and chlorpromazine in acute schizophrenia. *Current Therapeutic Research,* 1970, **12,** 810–818.

Harris, A. J., & Shakow, D. The clinical significance of numerical measures of scatter on the Stanford-Binet. *Psychological Bulletin,* 1937, **34,** 134–150.

Hekimian, L. J., Gershon, S., & Floyd, A. A clinical evaluation of four proposed antidepressants—relationship to their animal pharmacology. *International Pharmacopsychiatry,* 1970, **3,** 65–76.

Hotelling, H. Relations between two sets of variates. *Biometrika,* 1936, **28,** 321–377.

Johnson, G., Gershon, S., Burdock, E. I., Floyd, A., & Hekimian, L. J. Comparative effects of lithium and chlorpromazine in the treatment of acute manic states. *British Journal of Psychiatry,* 1971, **119,** 267–276.

Lane, E. A., & Albee, G. W. Intellectual antecedents of schizophrenia. In M. Roff & D. F. Ricks (Eds.), *Life history research in psychopathology.* Minneapolis: University of Minnesota Press, 1970. Pp. 189–207.

Payne, R. W. Cognitive abnormalities. In H. J. Eysenck (Ed.), *Handbook of abnormal psychology.* New York: Basic Books 1961. Pp. 193–261.

Pressey, S. L., & Cole, L. W. Irregularity in a psychological examination as a measure of mental deterioration. *Journal of Abnormal Psychology,* 1918, **13,** 285–294.

Rabin, A. I. Diagnostic use of intelligence tests. In B. B. Wolman (Ed.), *Handbook of clinical psychology.* New York: McGraw-Hill, 1965. Pp. 477–497.

Rabin, A. I., & Guertin, W. H. Research with the Wechsler-Bellevue Test: 1945–1950. *Psychological Bulletin,* 1951, **48,** 211–248.

Rapaport, D., Gill, M., & Schafer, R. *Diagnostic psychological testing.* Vol. 1. Chicago: Year Book Medical Publishers, 1945–46.

Wechsler, D. *The measurement of adult intelligence.* (1st ed.) Baltimore: Williams & Wilkins, 1939.

Wechsler, D. *The measurement of adult intelligence.* (3rd ed.) Baltimore: Williams & Wilkins, 1944.

Wechsler, D. *Wechsler-Bellevue Intelligence Scale.* Form 2. New York: Psychological Corp., 1946.

Wechsler, D. *Wechsler Adult Intelligence Scale manual.* New York: Psychological Corp., 1955.

Wechsler, D., Hardesty, A. S., & Lauber, H. *Die Messung der Intelligenz Erwachsener.* Berne, Switzerland: Hans Huber Verlag, 1956.

Yates, A. J. Psychological deficit. *Annual Review of Psychology,* 1966, **17,** 111–144.

Zubin, J. Psychopathology and the social sciences. In O. Klineberg & R. Christie (Eds.), *Perspectives in social psychology.* New York: Holt, Rinehart & Winston, 1965. Pp. 189–208.

Zubin, J., Burdock, E. I., Sutton, S., & Cheek, F. Epidemiological aspects of prognosis in mental illness. In B. Pasamanick (Ed.), *Epidemiology of mental disorder.* Washington, D. C.: American Association for the Advancement of Science, 1959. Pp. 119–142.

CHAPTER 24

The Differentiation of Malingering, Dissimulation, and Pathology

HOWARD F. HUNT

Most diagnostic and screening methods in psychiatry presuppose, in one way or another, that the patient is cooperative and truthful—that the symptoms and disabilities he claims accurately reflect his condition as he perceives it, and that his responses on examination do not consciously and deliberately attempt to conceal anything of note. Unfortunately, this presupposition does not always hold: some subjects *malinger*—pretend to diseases and symptoms they do not have; others *dissemble*—hide such of their abnormalities as they perceive, in a conscious attempt to appear normal and healthy.

Although one could argue that no one is as sick as the healthy person who feigns illness, the illness that such a person has is not the one implied by the symptoms he claims. Here his malingering is the significant diagnostic symptom and must be detected if corrective action is to be undertaken. Similarly, a person who deliberately conceals illness does himself a dangerous disservice, but again the dissimulation must be detected. More practically, pressing and understandable economic motives can encourage both malingering (e.g., to secure such benefits as discharge from military service or compensation for injury) and dissimulation (e.g., to obtain insurance or to pass psychiatric and psychological screening to qualify for a desired position). As our society becomes more tightly organized—more managed, as it were—and as people become more sophisticated, the pressures, and thus the problem of malingering and dissimulation, may be expected to increase. In fact, Whyte (1957), writing only half in jest, supplied specific rules for cheating on psychological screening tests. By following these rules, a subject presumably could dissemble his idiosyncrasies and present the appearance of an "all-American boy" on the tests, to win the coveted appointment to the vacant vice-presidency.

The space available in this book is too brief to permit a comprehensive review of the defenses that professional workers have erected against malingering and dissimulation. The obvious approach—to identify persons who are generally dishonest and to discount appropriately whatever they report —is not feasible. The classical studies of Hartshorne and May (1928) early indicated that honesty and dishonesty, as such, are not general traits. Rather, they are distressingly specific to the situation, so that a person may be meticulously truthful in one context but quite undependable in another. Therefore whether or not a subject is attempting deception with respect to matters of diagnostic concern must be determined in that context. Nor have attempts to develop deception-proof tests been notably successful (Anastasi, 1961). Performance on most psychological tests can be distorted significantly by conscious attempts to "fake" results, though not always to the subject's practical advantage (Benton & Spreen, 1961; Carp & Shavzin, 1950; Cofer, Chance, & Judson, 1949; Grayson & Olinger, 1957; Hunt, 1946; Hunt & Older, 1943; Shaw, 1962).

VALIDITY INDICATORS

The most widely employed and promising approach to the problem of deliberate deception has been to include validity indicators in the tests so that a determination of the dependability of each record can be made from performance on the test itself. The Minnesota Multiphasic Personality Inventory (MMPI), an objective, self-report personality test, was one of the first to exploit this technique substantially by supplementing the primarily clinical scales with the validity scales "?", L, F, and ultimately K (Hathaway & McKinley, 1951; McKinley, Hathaway, & Meehl, 1948). This feature of the test led to considerable research during and after World War II on the effects of malingering and dissimulation on MMPI performance. Some of the findings, unlike many others in the personality field, have held up well on cross validation (Cofer et al., 1949; Gough, 1950; Hunt, 1948).

The MMPI consists of 566 statements describing symptoms, attitudes, and matters of personal history and custom to which the subject responds by indicating whether each is generally true or generally false, as applied to him, on an answer sheet or by sorting cards. Those that he cannot answer or that do not apply he classifies as "Cannot Say" or "?"; a count of "?"

items is kept to determine whether enough items have been answered definitely to permit interpretation of the clinical scales.

The *F* scale consists of 64 statements that normal people (and most patients, as well) answer predominantly in one direction only—statements about family, religion, and bizarre symptoms that about 9 out of 10 subjects agree on in denying or affirming (e.g., "I loved my mother. I am not afraid to handle money. I believe I am being plotted against. I believe there is a god."). Persons who answer carelessly or who are unable to understand the test would be expected, by chance alone, to answer a number of these items in an atypical direction and thus receive high *F* scores. These would invalidate the record or indicate that the subject's performance was atypical and required special interpretation.

The *L* (or Lie) scale grew out of a strategem employed by Hartshorne and May. It consists of 15 items all referring to obvious, highly sanctioned virtues which, unfortunately, characterize almost none of us (e.g., "I would rather win than lose in a game. I get angry sometimes. I do not always tell the truth. My table manners are not quite as good at home as when I am out in company. Once in a while I laugh at a dirty joke."). A person claiming more than a very few of the virtues suggested would get a high *L* score, implying lack of candor and an attempt to create an unduly favorable impression in accordance with prevailing "official" standards.

The *K* scale of 30 items is a complex and highly sophisticated later addition to the MMPI (Meehl & Hathaway, 1946). It is designed to provide an indicator of and a correction for a "test-taking" attitude—a defensive optimism that would conceal pathology and weakness, at one extreme, and a tendency toward exhibitionistic display of personal troubles and defects, at the other. Although such test-taking attitudes are "part of the pathology" in a case, their effect is to modify answers to items throughout the test so as to alter scores on the clinical scales and thus influence interpretation. A person getting a high *K* score tends to deny personal inadequacies, as well as difficulties in mentation and self-control, and avoids criticism of others; a low *K* score implies the opposite and is achieved by admitting a large number of personal difficulties and faults and by excessive self-criticism (e.g., "At times I feel like smashing things. I certainly feel useless at times. I have very few quarrels with people in my family. I worry over money and business. I think nearly anyone would tell a lie to keep out of trouble.") Scores on this scale not only can be interpreted in their own right (as can *F* and *L* scores under some circumstances), but also supply a numerical correction to be added to or subtracted from the scores of some of the clinical scales, as appropriate, to overcome the systematic bias introduced into the subject's responses by his general test-taking attitude.

The major clinical scales, which do not directly concern us here, include Hypochondriasis, Depression, Hysteria, Psychopathic Deviate, Masculinity-Femininity, Paranoia, Psychasthenia, Schizophrenia, and Hypomania; others have been developed for specific purposes by various investigators (see Dahlstrom & Welsh, 1960; Welsh & Dahlstrom, 1956). Originally, it was hoped that a peak score on a specific scale would index the appropriate clinical diagnosis, but clinical use quickly showed that this was not the case. Rather, the entire profile of scores has to be considered; and the proper application of the MMPI in clinical diagnosis has turned out to be as complex, subtle, and demanding as the use of projective devices.

EXPERIMENTAL MALINGERING AND DISSIMULATION

In an initial attempt during World War II to investigate the effect of deliberate deception on the MMPI, I gave the group form to 109 ASTP (Army Specialized Training Program) students in psychology, at the close of a testing course given as part of their training for army personnel work. Of this group, 56 took the test under instructions to *malinger* sufficiently severe personality abnormality to ensure a neuropsychiatric discharge or psychiatric disqualification from military service. The remaining 53 took the test under instructions to conceal their personality abnormalities as much as possible—to *dissimulate*—so that they would be certain *not* to be excluded from induction or discharged from the service on psychiatric grounds. Both groups were cautioned to falsify in such a way as to avoid detection. All subjects also took the MMPI honestly, about half before and half after the experimental testing.

About a year later, I was able to subject 74 U. S. Navy general-court-martial prisoners to essentially the same procedure. All were volunteer subjects who took the test anonymously, with knowledge of honestly obtained results as the incentive, under all three conditions: honestly and under instructions to *malinger* and to *dissimulate*. The order of the experimental conditions varied here, as well, with about half malingering first and half malingering last and all taking the test honestly in between. The specific instructions for each condition were the same as before, except that restoration to active duty status was added to the goals or reference conditions for dissimulation to make the task more meaningful for the prisoners. Each profile generated by each subject under each condition was transcribed into a separate profile form, with all identifying marks as to subject and condition removed, to permit judgments as to the status of the profile to be made "blind"—on the basis of profile characteristics alone, uncontaminated by knowledge of the criterion conditions.

All subjects in both experiments were males in late adolescence or early adulthood. The ASTP subjects had been selected carefully for special training and had had at least two or three years of high school; a number had attended college for several years. All of the prisoners were literate and had finished at least the fifth grade. None had been to college, though a number had had several years of high school; a substantial portion had left school as early as the law allowed. All had been screened for feeblemindedness by the professional staff, and, though some of the prisoners exhibited minor degrees of psychopathy, none showed sufficient clinical deviation to be disqualified officially for military service.

The *malingered* profiles of both the ASTP and prisoner subjects clearly differed from the corresponding *honest* profiles. With large elevations on the Hypochondriasis, Depression, Hysteria, Psychasthenia, and Schizophrenia scales, plus excessively high *F* scores, the profiles resembled those produced by professional mental health workers instructed to imitate paranoid schizophrenia and severe psychoneurosis, as reported by Gough (1947), and the profiles produced by college students instructed to answer pathologically enough to avoid being drafted, as reported by Cofer et al. (1949).

The effect of *dissimulation* was less clear cut and uniform. The *dissimulated* profiles differed from the corresponding *honest* profiles in a much more variable way, particularly among the prisoners, and showed no characteristic stigmata beyond generally lower scores on the clinical scales and the *F* scale and a fairly uniform increase in *K*. Only a few showed elevations in the *L* (or Lie) scale sufficiently high to excite suspicion. As in the Cofer study, most dissimulated records looked honest and were essentially within normal limits, among the ASTP cases, or normal to borderline, among the prisoners. Not only did the *L* scale fail to detect dissimulation, but also the *K* correction of the clinical scales, though in the proper direction, was insufficiently strong to overcome the effects either of malingering or of dissimulation to an appreciable or statistically significant degree (see also Grayson & Olinger, 1957).

I had developed a tentative scale for malingering and dissimulation from item analysis of part of the prisoner data, before publication of *K*. This scale contained a number of *F* items and a great many that eventually appeared in *K*. The item overlap with *K*, plus Gough's finding (1947) that *F* minus *K* separated his simulated from his authentic pathological profiles, suggested that the *F raw score* minus the *K raw score* might be useful as a general deception indicator to identify both malingerers and dissimulators.

Accordingly, tentative cutting scores for $F - K$ were set in advance, quite arbitrarily, from an inspection of MMPI profiles from various sources (including a few from the ASTP group) and from rough estimates of the probable frequencies of various $F - K$ values for honestly performing subjects under various circumstances. Then this indicator was cross-validated on the prisoner sample by "blind" mechanical sorting of the 222 profiles that these subjects had produced in taking the MMPI three times.

The cutting scores and major results appear in Figure 1, which shows the percentages of all the records called "malingered," "honest," or "dissimulated" from $F - K$ that actually had been produced under these instructions. Thus 82% of the profiles called "malingered" by the $F - K$ index had been malingered in fact; 78% of those called "dissimulated" were produced under instructions to dissimulate; and 61% of those called "honest" by $F - K$ were honest.

The favorable outcome of this cross validation is easy to understand, given the nature of the F and K scales. High F scores arise when a subject answers a lot of the F items in the atypical direction, and generally the atypical answer implies an unusual attitude or bizarre symptom of obvious pathological significance. Similarly, self-criticism and self-blame and a parading of one's problems and difficulties produce a low K score. Malingerers, therefore, *should* get high positive $F - K$ scores. By the same reasoning, a person dissimulating—denying—whatever pathology he thinks he has should get negative $F - K$ scores from minimizing his admission of atypical symptoms and attitudes (reducing F) and from concealing personal inadequacies and difficulties under a cloud of optimism about himself (increasing K).

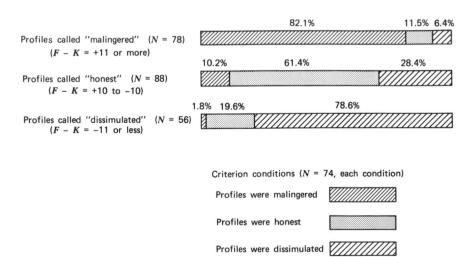

Figure 1. Accuracy of discrimination of malingered, dissimulated, and honest profiles on the MMPI by $F - K$ index (74 U. S. Navy court-martial prisoners).

Table 1. $F — K$ Values for Malingered, Honest, and Dissimulated Profiles on MMPI (74 U.S. Navy court-martial prisoners) (N each cell in parentheses)

	Conditions of Testing		
$F — K$ "Diagnosis"	Malingered	Honest	Dissimulated
$F — K$ in "malingered" range (+11 and over)	87% (64)	12% (9)	7% (5)
$F — K$ in "honest" range (+10 to —10)	12% (9)	73% (54)	34% (25)
$F — K$ in "dissimulated" range (—11 and below)	1% (1)	15% (11)	59% (44)
	100% (74)	100% (74)	100% (74)

Table 1 presents these results in a more definitive form by showing the percentages of actually malingered, honest, and dissimulated profiles correctly identified by $F — K$, using these cutting scores (87% of the malingered, 73% of the honest, and 59% of the dissimulated profiles were correctly identified). The index worked fairly well in detecting malingering but showed a large margin of error with respect to dissimulation, and misclassified about one-third of dissimulated profiles as honest.

The ASTP profiles were not included in this analysis because some of them had contributed indirectly to the derivation of K. However, a classification of these MMPI records according to the cutting scores given above confirmed the ability of the index to detect malingering (88% of the malingered but only 2% of the honest profiles showed $F — K$ of +11 or above); but $F — K$ of —11 or below failed utterly to discriminate dissimulated from honest profiles. The overlap between the honest and dissimulated $F — K$ distributions for the ASTP sample was almost complete, indicating that the difficulty was too serious to be overcome simply by adjusting the cutting score up or down. Indeed, this confirmed the suggestion of Cofer et al. (1949) that for college students to dissimulate on the MMPI meant essentially that they took the test honestly. (The research described above is covered in greater detail in Hunt, 1948.)

The effect of clinical psychiatric pathology on the index was essentially unknown, particularly for men in the peculiar motivational situation of military personnel; therefore a series of normative comparisons was made to determine "false positive" rates for the index for various nominally honest populations. These data appear in Figure 2, with the rates for honest, but anonymous, prisoner profiles presented in the first bar for comparison. The second bar shows the false positive rates on the index for 173 male patients given the MMPI routinely on admission to a Veterans Administration neuropsychiatric hospital in 1946. Of these patients, 12% got $F - K$ scores suggesting malingering (the same incidence of such scores that appeared among the honest prisoner profiles); the incidence of values suggesting dissimulation, however, rose to 32%, as compared with 15% in the prisoner sample. In view of the prevailing motivational situation inferred for this population at that time, when veterans with adjustive difficulties being admitted to a psychiatric hospital seemed to be more concerned with getting in than with staying out, the rate for $F - K$ scores in the dissimulation range may underestimate the corresponding rate for the usual population of psychiatric patients. Also, the malingering rate is probably too high. This speculation is supported by the higher incidence of $F - K$ values in the dissimulation range (and the lower incidence in the malingering range) among Perlman's sample (1950) of psychiatrically abnormal male and female cases drawn at random from the MMPI norm files at the University of Minnesota.

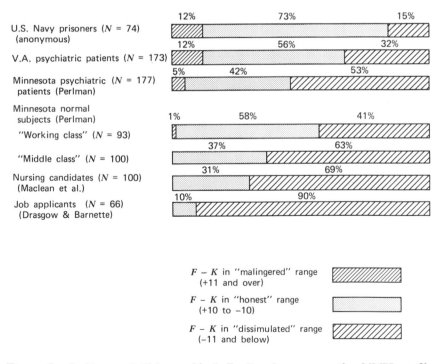

Figure 2. Incidence of "false positive" $F - K$ values among the MMPI profiles produced by various populations of nominally "honest" subjects.

INTERPRETATION

Perlman was inquiring into the contribution of social class membership or status to test-taking attitude, on the assumption that the positive relationship that had been found between educational level and K score (Meehl & Hathaway, 1946) might actually be a reflection of social status. His data are of interest here because, although the $F - K$ indication for dissimulation was worthless for the ASTP college students (presumably largely middle class), it had some discriminative value for the prisoners, who were predominantly from the working class. Perhaps some correction for social class, such as Gough's status scale for the MMPI (1948), would improve the index.

Perlman drew random samples of both normal and abnormal cases from the MMPI norm files, classified them as middle or working class by occupation (Warner, et al., 1949), and, among other things, compared $F - K$ distributions for the two classes. Although there were no substantial or consistent class differences for the abnormal cases (combined in bar 3 of Figure 2), pronounced differences appeared for the normal cases. As indicated in bars 4 and 5, middle class normal persons tended to have larger negative $F - K$ scores and differed from working class normals in the same way that dissimulated and honest MMPI profiles differed among the prisoners! (This was confirmed by Nelson, 1952.) The incidence of index values in the dissimulation range, however, was so high in the working class sample that correction for social status does not seem worthwhile on a practical basis. Also, the absence of a social class effect among the abnormal cases—precisely those whose dissimulation would be of greatest importance—indicates that a correction for status probably would be gratuitous.

As Figure 2 shows, $F - K$ values in the malingering range are comparatively rare in nominally honest samples, but they are predominant in experimentally induced malingering. The index appears to have practical values, therefore, in detecting deliberate attempts to feign psychiatric illness. Gough, in a summary article on $F - K$ (1950), has presented normative data calculated from a number of studies to show that the index dependably detects such malingering, using cutting scores in the $+9$ to $+11$ range and above as the diagnostic sign, in confirmation of the data presented here. The accuracy of detection is far from absolute, of course. Rather, high positive values of the index should be considered only as identifying cases requiring special study and attention because of the substantial probability that they are feigning psychiatric illness.

Data from other personality tests (Hunt, 1946) and item analysis of the MMPI records indicate that the malingerer "overdoes it," that is, claims to have pathological symptoms that persons with authentic psychiatric illnesses generally deny (Gough, 1954), in keeping with lay misconceptions as to psychological abnormality. This distortion permits $F - K$ to detect malingering and is the basis for a special "dissimulation" (malingering) scale developed by Gough. The tendency to overemphasize pathology is not restricted to malingering in the personality sphere but appears also in malingered mental defect (Hunt & Older, 1943) and, more recently, has been reported in malingered organic intellectual deterioration (Benton & Spreen, 1961; see also Fromm, Sawyer, & Rosenthal, 1964).

However, $F - K$ values in the dissimulation range are so common among nominally honest subjects (around 50% in the basic MMPI norm group: Gough, 1950) that the index is of little or no practical value in detecting deliberate attempts to conceal pathology. Even so, the data in Figure 2 (bars 6 and 7) on nursing candidates and job applicants indicate that some group of items akin to $F - K$ might work—the effort has not been entirely misdirected, by any means. The MacLean, Tait, and Catterall (1953) data came from a random sample of applicants for nursing training and suggest that the frequency of $F - K$ values in the dissimulation range rises under selection conditions that encourage a person to make a favorable appearance. The Drasgow and Barnette data (1957), obtained from a well-motivated sample of male job applicants, demonstrate the same effect even more strikingly. These men, who were applying for jobs at a variety of occupational levels, knew that they were taking the test under industrial selection conditions in which the results would contribute to acceptance or rejection. Ninety per cent had $F - K$ scores of -11 or beyond, a substantial increase over the usual incidence among either normal or pathological cases. Even more noteworthy, a correlation of .61 in the appropriate direction was found between $F - K$ and number of dependents (a powerful motivation)! This would appear to clinch the argument that $F - K$ is indeed responsive to practical motivation toward making a favorable impression. The difficulty is that we simply do not have, at present, sensitive methods to distinguish outright dissimulation from the more subtle defensiveness that is so much a part of the civilized facade a person presents to the world, and even to himself.

Powerful response sets or response biases (Edwards, 1953, Rorer, 1965) did result from instructions to malinger or dissimulate, leading the subject to slant his responses systematically to admit to or to deny psychopathic symptoms and other socially undesirable attributes. Indeed, a large number of the test items are quite transparent with respect to their social desirability/undesirability. As Figure 2 indicates, the MMPI would appear to be open to response bias effects under normal selection conditions. Edwards and Heathers (1962; Edwards, 1964) and others have suggested that the high correlation between desirability ratings and the primary factor loading of the MMPI makes its scores less a measure of adjustment level than an artifact of social desirability.

This is too severe an indictment, however, of the test as ordinarily used (see Kleinmuntz, 1967; Lanyon & Goodstein, 1971). For example, Block (1965) modified the regular MMPI scales to produce scales free of social desirability influence. A series of factor analyses of these modified scales produced factor structures essentially the same as those obtained by factor analysis of the standard MMPI; a social desirability set did not appear to account for significant response variability on the MMPI in his study. Cardinet and Hunt (1955), in a factor analysis of the MMPI data produced by the prisoners, found that the factorial composition of the test remained surprisingly stable across the three conditions. A large first factor, "psychiatric hypochondriasis," appeared under all conditions, with K as the purest measure. A "neurosis" factor appeared almost as consistently, with loadings on Hs, D, and Hy that converged under dissimulation to appear as a common group factor. Two other factors, "psychosis" and "psychopathic deviate," appeared under both honest and malingered conditions, but collapsed into one factor under dissimulation. The effect of malingering versus honest conditions appeared largely in raising or lowering of the scales, but dissimulation did change the pattern of intercorrelation among the scales, disrupting the pattern of the profiles as well as influencing the elevation of the scores. Thus a response set to dissimulate not only is harder to detect by $F - K$, but also changes the differential diagnostic implications of the test by altering the profile substantially.

How important is it, in practical terms, to distinguish between outright dissimulation and the subtle defensiveness of normal persons, and will really psychopathic cases be missed in large quantity under conditions of attempted dissimulation? To determine whether a normal, middle class subject is dissimulating at all, regardless of the effect, is very difficult. In a clinical setting, however, the determination may be unimportant if the MMPI is used simply for the identification of cases with psychiatric problems requiring further study. The presence of genuine, clinically significant psychiatric illness impairs the ability to simulate normality successfully.

For example, 19 (36%) of the 53 ASTP subjects in the dissimulation sample described above had abnormal or borderline profiles under the honest condition (at least one clinical scale score above $T = 70$). Of these, 16 (84%) successfully produced normal profiles when dissimulating (no T score above 69). In contrast, 68 (92%) of the 74 U. S. Navy prisoners had abnormal or borderline honest profiles, but only 23 (34%) of these were able successfully to simulate normal profiles. The ASTP and prisoner groups differed considerably in their titre of psychopathy, as indicated by their life statuses, and the prisoners, who were more pathological, showed a statistically significantly lower frequency of successful dissimulation. As indicated earlier, $F - K$ was useless in separating honest from dissimulation ASTP profiles because of the complete overlap between the groups in distribution of this score. For the prisoners, however, an $F - K$ cutting score of -11 correctly identified 22 of the 23 *successful* dissimulators, at a maximum cost of misidentifying only 11 honest profiles, normal or abnormal.

Similarly, Grayson and Olinger (1957), in a study of the ability of 45 diagnosed psychiatric inpatients to simulate normality on the MMPI, found that only 11% achieved profiles within conventional normal limits. Seventy-three per cent showed "improvement" (defined by a lowering of the scores on the clinical scales), but 62% exhibited no change in the diagnostic category implied by the test, though some showed a "softening" or reduction in the deviancy of the personality pattern. The remaining 11% underwent a shift to another diagnostic category, sometimes of a type suggesting a "reaction formation" against their most bizarre and salient (to them) symptoms (e.g., a depressed, obsessive-compulsive psychoneurotic shifted to a pattern suggestive of hypomania or an acting-out disorder). Finally, the patients able to simulate the greater improvement tended, to a statistically significant degree, to be those released earlier for a trial visit or discharge.

In short, efforts to dissimulate psychopathy, to the extent that they are successful, may reflect a person's ability to discriminate and then to control or eliminate his most bizarre and socially undesirable symptoms, to cope adaptively with the institution and then with the outside world. Persons with more severe disabilities have correspondingly less success in their efforts at dissimulation, perhaps because of their impaired social discrimination, and may only distort their profiles rather than make them normal.

Do elevated K and low F scores have any clinical implications apart from dissimulative distortion? Several converging lines of evidence suggest that they do. Improvement in psychotherapy usually produces an elevation in K (Schofield, 1950, 1953). Hersher (1956) also found increases in K between pre- and posttherapy testings to be related to improvement as judged by acquaintances and therapists. If only self-rating had been involved, this relationship between K and improvement could have been attributed to some sort of unconscious self-deception, but the relationship with improved overt behavior over a period of several months after therapy indicates that something more fundamental had taken place. A series of clinical interviews with improved and unimproved patients, posttherapy, revealed that the improved patients had acquired an understanding of the importance of using self-control techniques, especially those of avoiding introspection and the circumstances which, they had learned, aroused emotional disturbance. On the MMPI, this led to the denial, as present problems, of symptoms and difficulties that the patients had affirmed before therapy, and thus to an increase in K. Also, the improved patients retained elevated scores on the "subtle" (nonsomatic) items of the Hy scale, but showed substantial decreases in the "obvious" symptomatic items of Hy and the other clinical scales (Wiener, 1948). The subtle Hy items deal largely with the propensity to use denial as a defense and are more resistant to "faking" than the obvious items. In general, the improved patient would appear to have become more defensive, but in a constructive way that implied enhancement of ego functioning and decreased subjective distress, plus effective behavioral control.

Ruch and Ruch (1967) have suggested, in quite a different context, that self-inventories such as the MMPI may work in predicting success in selling *because* they can be faked, not in spite of it. Here the subject's capacity for "sensible deception," for giving the answers the employer or customer wants, is an indicator of the subject's appreciation of and response to the demands of the job. These authors reasoned that successful salesmen will be more likely to "give the right answers," and that the "right answers" for salesmen will produce high K scores on the MMPI. (The Ruchs point out that the description by Dahlstrom and Welsh, 1960, of the high K normal could easily be a description of the successful salesman.) If so, K should be a reasonably good predictor of success in selling, and uncorrected MMPI scales should predict better than the same scales corrected for K. This turned out to be the case, and correcting the scales for K reduced their predictive value for this task almost to zero. We argued above that the data of Drasgow and Barnette on job applicants indicated that $F - K$ was indeed responsive to practical motivation toward making a favorable impression; it may also prove to be an indicator of a person's ability to do so—an important skill in many aspects of social functioning.

REFERENCES

Anastasi, A. *Psychological testing.* (2nd ed.) New York: Macmillan, 1961.

Benton, A. L., & Spreen, O. L. Visual memory test: The simulation of mental incompetence. *Archives of General Psychiatry,* 1961, **4,** 79–83.

Block, J. *The challenge of response sets.* New York: Appleton-Century-Crofts, 1965.

Cardinet, J., & Hunt, H. F. L'influence de l'attitude des sujets sur la composition factorielle du MMPI. *Revue de Psychologie Appliquée,* 1955, **48,** 305–310.

Carp, A. L., & Shavzin, A. R. The susceptibility to falsification of the Rorschach psychodiagnostic technique. *Journal of Consulting Psychology,* 1950, **14,** 230–233.

Cofer, C. N., Chance, J., & Judson, A. J. A study of malingering on the MMPI. *Journal of Psychology,* 1949, **27,** 491–499.

Dahlstrom, W. C., & Welsh, G. S. *An MMPI handbook.* Minneapolis: University of Minnesota Press, 1960.

Drasgow, J., & Barnette, W. L., Jr. *F − K* in a motivated group. *Journal of Consulting Psychology,* 1957, **21,** 399–401.

Edwards, A. L. The relationship between judged desirability of a trait and the probability that the trait will be endorsed. *Journal of Applied Psychology,* 1953, **37,** 90–93.

Edwards, A. L. Social desirability and performance on the MMPI. *Psychometrika,* 1964, **29,** 295–308.

Edwards, A. L., & Heathers, L. B. The first factor of the MMPI: Social desirability or ego strength. *Journal of Consulting Psychology,* 1962, **26,** 99–100.

Fromm, E., Sawyer, J., & Rosenthal, V. Hypnotic simulation of organic brain damage. *Journal of Abnormal and Social Psychology,* 1964, **69,** 482–492.

Gough, H. G. Simulated patterns on the MMPI. *Journal of Abnormal and Social Psychology,* 1947, **42,** 215–225.

Gough, H. G. A new dimension of status. I. Development of a personality scale. *American Sociological Review,* 1948, **13,** 401–409.

Gough, H. G. The *F − K* dissimulation index for the MMPI. *Journal of Consulting Psychology,* 1950, **14,** 408–413.

Gough, H. G. Some common misconceptions about neuroticism. *Journal of Consulting Psychology,* 1954, **18,** 287–292.

Grayson, H. M., & Olinger, L. B. Simulation of "normalcy" by psychiatric patients on the MMPI. *Journal of Consulting Psychology,* 1957, **21,** 73–77.

Hartshorne, H., & May, M. A. *Studies in the nature of character.* I. *Studies in deceit.* New York: Macmillan, 1928.

Hathaway, S. R., & McKinley, J. C. *The Minnesota Multiphasic Personality Inventory.* New York: Psychological Corp., 1951.

Hersher, L. Openness to experience and client-centered theory. Unpublished doctoral dissertation, University of Chicago, 1956.

Hunt, H. F. The effects of deliberate deception on MMPI performance. *Journal of Consulting Psychology,* 1948, **12,** 396–402.

Hunt, W. A. The detection of malingering: A further study. *U. S. Naval Medical Bulletin,* 1946, **46,** 249–254.

Hunt, W. A., & Older, H. J. Detection of malingering through psychometric tests. *U. S. Naval Medical Bulletin,* 1943, **41,** 1318–1323.

Kleinmuntz, B. *Personality measurement.* Homewood, Ill.: Dorsey Press, 1967.

Lanyon, R. I., & Goodstein, L. D. *Personality assessment.* New York: Wiley, 1971.

McKinley, J. C., Hathaway, S. R., & Meehl, P. E. The MMPI. VI. The *K* scale. *Journal of Consulting Psychology,* 1948, **12,** 20–31.

MacLean, A. G., Tait, A. T., & Catterall, C. D. The *F* minus *K* index on the MMPI. *Journal of Applied Psychology,* 1953, **37,** 315–316.

Meehl, P. E., & Hathaway, S. R. The *K* factor as a suppressor variable in the MMPI. *Journal of Applied Psychology,* 1946, **30,** 525–564.

Nelson, S. E. The development of an indirect, objective measure of social status and its relationship to certain psychiatric syndromes. Unpublished doctoral dissertation, University of Minnesota, 1952.

Perlman, M. Social class membership and test-taking attitude. Unpublished M. A. thesis, University of Chicago, 1950.

Rorer, L. G. The great response style myth. *Psychological Bulletin,* 1965, **63,** 129–156.

Ruch, F. L., & Ruch, W. W. The *K* factor as a (validity) suppressor variable in predicting success in selling. *Journal of Applied Psychology,* 1967, **51,** 201–204.

Schofield, W. Changes in responses to the MMPI following certain therapies. *Psychological Monographs,* 1950, **64** (5, Whole No. 311).

Schofield, W. A further study of the effects of therapy on MMPI responses. *Journal of Abnormal and Social Psychology,* 1953, **48,** 67–77.

Shaw, M. E. The effectiveness of Whyte's rules: How to cheat on personality tests. *Journal of Applied Psychology,* 1962, **46,** 21–25.

Warner, W. L., Meeker, M., & Eells, K. *Social class in America.* Chicago: Science Research Associates, 1949.

Welsh, G. S., & Dahlstrom, W. G. *Basic readings on the MMPI in psychology and medicine* Minneapolis: University of Minnesota Press, 1956.

Whyte, W. H., Jr. *The organization man.* Garden City, N. Y.: Doubleday, 1957.

Wiener, D. N. Subtle and obvious keys for the MMPI. *Journal of Consulting Psychology,* 1948, **12,** 164–170.

PART SIX

Mathematical Description

Mathematics has been the dominant source of scientific metatheory through-out the several hundred years of modern science, as well as an indispensable research tool. Today its role in psychopathology is still largely limited to the utilization of statistical techniques to help in the interpretation of data. Al-though this is an essential role, it fails to tap the potential contributions of mathematics to generating new theory, extending the inferences one may draw from existing theory, or guiding the total research conception so that existing or possible mathematical tools can be used more effectively.

Current concepts in psychopathology lack the clarity necessary for op-timal use of mathematical formulations. For that very reason, however, it may be quite profitable to make the attempt. Precise definitions of meaning-ful concepts in this field may turn out to be "erroneous" but have the ad-vantage that one at least knows exactly what it is that is not so; and, in the process of discovering this, one must have worked out a set of explicit stan-dards by which to judge the definitions erroneous.

The implications for psychopathology of the papers in Part Six include highly abstract model building, systematization of methods for collecting theoretically relevant data, and approaches to analyzing data in theoretically relevant ways. In Chapter 29 Rapoport examines one set of problems in game theory that have structural characteristics one might expect to be formally relevant for defining conditions generative of some types of pathol-ogy. The most immediate value of working with such a model would be the setting up of a systematic set of dimensions entailed by the model, and the clear delineation of the aspects of psychopathology entailed by these di-mensions. As an indication of the clarifying questions arising from such a procedure, let us consider Bateson's double-bind hypothesis (Bateson, G., Jackson, D. D., Haley, J., & Weakland, J. Toward a theory of schizophrenia. *Behavioral Science*, 1956, **1**, 251-264) in terms of Rapoport's model. Ac-cording to the double-bind hypothesis (which tries to explain the genesis of schizophrenia), the preschizophrenic child is exposed to an inescapable environment, the schizophrenogenic mother, who punishes him for doing what she requires him to do—and if he does not do it, she punishes him for not doing it. It is obvious that the "victim" of the double bind is in a "game" (in Rapoport's sense) with minus values for either of his two possible choices; but it becomes immediately apparent that we do not know what values to assign the victimizer, or what total sum to assign the game. Since these questions seem relevant to the double-bind hypothesis—and not merely to this game theory model of it—the attempt to answer them should strengthen (and probably modify) the hypothesis.

A quite different approach to aiming one's procedures at better utilization of mathematical aid is illustrated by Lazarsfeld in Chapter 25. One of the most pervasive problems in making inferences in any aspect of psychopathology is the great difficulty in separating causal connection from other kinds of association between any two (or more) variables. Lazarsfeld, using data from a substantive domain outside of psychopathology, outlines a procedure that should be applicable to many issues in psychopathology—for example, the old but still unresolved problem of interpreting the quantitative association between social class and prevalence of psychopathology. Lazarsfeld's procedure, the panel technique, requires information on both variables from the same population at two points in time: the distribution of cases changing on one variable but not on both is potentially the most revealing aspect of such data for causal inferences.

Chapter 26, in which Guttman presents an analysis of projective techniques in terms of a partial-order scalogram, has more general implications, both substantively and methodologically. First, it raises a number of questions about projective techniques—of the several thousand possible combinations of the characteristics used in this analysis, only a handful actually exist as projective tests. To what extent is this so because of historical accident? To what extent does it reflect an underlying but unspecified structure of the relevant universe? Is it the nature of what is being tested or of the test designers that has produced the high degree of ordering found among the existing tests? These and a number of other related questions arise as a direct outgrowth of Guttman's analysis. A second, more general implication of this chapter is that this technique of analysis is applicable to any body of material to which sets of ordered characteristics can be assigned (syndromes, persons, populations, etc.) and can reveal aspects of the structure of the material, thus yielding significant new questions. Any body of data which can be highly ordered by the Guttman technique must have a large number of combinations of characteristics that are actually nonexistent though logically possible.

Many sets of data cannot be ordered by the Guttman technique. Different approaches to organizing data are discussed in the chapters by Solomon and by Fleiss and Tanur. In Chapter 27 Solomon, dealing with a problem that has long held Joseph Zubin's attention (see, most recently, Fleiss, J. L., & Zubin, J. On the methods and theory of clustering. *Multivariate Behavioral Research,* 1969, **4**, 235–250), namely, clustering, describes some new methods of arriving at groups of variables or groups of individuals based exclusively on the data collected and independent of *a priori* logical considerations. Part Five of this volume, "Problems of Psychiatric Classification," discussed some of the ways in which the field of psychopathology is involved in developing empirical diagnostic groupings. Solomon presents new procedures for accomplishing this task. The groupings empirically arrived at can then be related, as Solomon shows for aphasic individuals, to clinical criteria for validation. They can also be related to the theoretical considerations that go into diagnostic classification and thus can be used to shed light on formal aspects of diagnosis. Finally, they can be related to outcome of illness, premorbid history, and responsiveness to different treatments, and thus constitute a general research tool.

Fleiss and Tanur, in contrast to Solomon, who seeks new groups, wrestle in Chapter 28 with the statistical problem of the comparison of intact groups whose existence is already accepted according to some criteria. In psychopathology this problem is especially pervasive, since the typical research paradigm consists of the examination of the functioning of abnormal groups relative to each other and relative to normal groups. Experimental designs can deal with confounding variables by the random assignment of individuals to groups; in contrast, the constitution of psychopathological groups is predefined and therefore is not under the control of the researcher. Fleiss and Tanur present the argument that the common use of the analysis of covariance to exclude the confounding variables is based on the unacceptable premise that statistical manipulation can somehow undo the real but uninteresting differences between groups that exist along with the differences that are of significance to the investigators. They conclude their chapter by presenting a method that contributes toward the solution of the group-comparison problem without having to make unacceptable assumptions.

Part Six presents some precise methods of analysis and should also provide many workers in the field of psychopathology with bases for new ways of conceptualizing and of doing research.

CHAPTER 25

Mutual Relations Over Time of Two Attributes: A Review and Integration of Various Approaches

PAUL F. LAZARSFELD

THE PROBLEM OF MUTUAL EFFECT

Over the last 40 years an increasing number of publications have dealt with the problem of how to make causal inferences from nonexperimental data. This literature has helped to clarify the vague notion of cause and has at the same time provided a variety of useful statistical techniques. The present chapter deals with only one specific approach, the so-called panel technique; its main feature is repeated observations on the same people. The discussion will cover its history and its rationale and will contribute some new ideas to its execution. Other types of causal analysis will only be mentioned inasmuch as they are related to the problem on hand. No comparison of merits will be attempted, and certainly no claim of superiority for the panel technique is implied.

The basic issue will be demonstrated by a set of data that is easily accessible. Rosenberg (1957) interviewed Cornell sophomores to ascertain their occupational choices and what he called their occupational values. He divided the occupational choices into those that were people oriented (PO) —for instance, teaching and medicine—and those that were not people oriented (NPO)—for instance, engineering and business. The occupational values were divided in the same ways: for example, rendering a service versus getting rich. The details of this classification are irrelevant here; we shall accept the two dichotomies as they appear in Rosenberg's book.

Table 1. Cross-sectional Relation between Occupational Choice and Occupational Value, 1950

		Value		
		PO	NPO	Total
Choice	PO	226	89	315
	NPO	166	231	397
	Total	392	320	712

The topic of the present chapter begins with a cross tabulation of the replies given by Cornell sophomores. The interrelation between their occupational choices and values is given in Table 1. It is clear that choices and values are positively associated. But the table does not permit a causal interpretation. It might be that peoples' choices are caused by their values; it might also be, however, that, once a choice has been made for whatever reason, the student acquires the appropriate values—and of course there can be a continuous feedback between the two items; finally, third factors might play a decisive role—for instance, people from certain types of families might develop PO choices as well as PO values.

In the late 1930s the present author suggested that the unraveling of the causal process involved might be facilitated by obtaining the same information from the same people a second time. This procedure, the panel study, was applied in a study of the 1940 election. The data then obtained and the way in which they are treated were reported in *The People's Choice,* especially in the introduction to the third edition, where a more detailed account is given (Lazarsfeld, 1968).

An "index of mutual interaction" was developed to describe the influence of two factors upon each other. We shall come back to this index presently. At the moment what matters is to see what kind of information is obtained by repeated interviews. We stay with Rosenberg's material: Table 2 is a so-called 16-fold table, which resulted when he reinterviewed the same students two years later as seniors. Since the appearance of *The People's Choice* this type of 16-fold table has been subjected to a variety of treatments. In addition to the original development of the index of mutual interaction two main trends can be distinguished. Coleman (1964) and Boudon (1968) accepted the use of dichotomies and developed more refined types of analysis. Campbell (1963) and Pelz and Andrews (1964) proposed to apply the panel technique to quantitative variables, which led them to use traditional correlation analysis. Their approach was then converted into the use of path analysis, especially by Duncan (1966) and Heise (1969).

Table 2. "People-Oriented" Occupational Values and Occupational Choices in 1950 and 1952—Full Cross Tabulation

Occupational Values and Choices, 1950	Occupational Values and Choices, 1952				
	PO Choice-PO Value	PO Choice-NPO Value	NPO Choice-PO Value	NPO Choice-NPO Value	Total
PO choice-PO value	163	15	30	18	226
PO choice-NPO value	21	29	8	31	89
NPO choice-PO value	36	8	73	49	166
NPO choice-NPO value	6	14	43	168	231
Total	226	66	154	266	712

It is the contention of the present chapter that all these authors made valuable contributions. But the relation between their procedures and approaches to the original analysis has never been brought out. These connections will be explored now with one proviso: the whole discussion will be in terms of dichotomies. This makes the structure of the problem much clearer. Once the main results are obtained, it is quite easy to translate some of them into the language of regression or path analysis. The inverse is not possible. The statistics of dichotomies lead to results that cannot be covered by the algebra of linear equations.

The algebraic treatment of a system of interconnected dichotomies has received only scant attention in the literature. It can be greatly simplified by using a specific symbolism. Although this author has already presented the symbolism on various occasions, it will be helpful to introduce here a brief summary.

A SYMBOLISM FOR THE ANALYSIS OF DICHOTOMOUS SYSTEMS

1. Dichotomies are numbered arbitrarily, and "responses" are arbitrarily designated as positive $(+)$ or negative $(-)$. A "response pattern" to four items might be, for example, $(+ + - +)$; this could refer to four objects and to a person who owns all but the third, or it could refer to a test in which all but the third question are answered correctly.

2. The proportion of people showing a specific response pattern is given by p_s, where s, the *signature*, is a sequence of indices corresponding to the list number of the dichotomies. Thus $p_{1\bar{2}\bar{3}4}$ would be the proportion of people

giving the response pattern mentioned in (1). A bar over an index means a negative response for the item thus numbered.

3.   If an item is listed but not considered in a specific count, it does not appear in the signature. Thus $p_{2\bar{3}4}$ is the proportion of people having the response pattern $(+ - +)$ for the last three items, irrespective of their response to item 1. Obviously $p_{2\bar{3}4} = p_{12\bar{3}4} + p_{\bar{1}2\bar{3}4}$ and also $p_{2\bar{3}4} = p_{24} - p_{234}$.

4.   In the present context attributes can be ordered in a sequence according to the time at which they were observed. It is often important to know what difference an earlier attribute makes on the frequency of a later one. This "effect" of item 1 on item 2 may then be measured by

$$f_{12} = \frac{p_{12}}{p_1} - \frac{p_{\bar{1}2}}{p_{\bar{1}}} = \frac{(1 - p_1)p_{12} - p_{\bar{1}2}p_1}{p_1 p_{\bar{1}}}$$

$$= \frac{p_{12} - p_1(p_{12} + p_{\bar{1}2})}{p_1 p_{\bar{1}}} = \frac{p_{12} - p_1 p_2}{p_1 p_{\bar{1}}}.$$

Thus f_{12} is the difference between the conditional probability that item 2 is $+$, given that item 1 is $+$, and the conditional probability that item 2 is $+$, given that item 1 is $-$.

5.   In the preceding formula $p_1 p_{\bar{1}} = c_1$ can be considered a measure of the symmetry in the cut of the item; $c_1 = 0.25$ when $p_1 = p_{\bar{1}}$ and decreases as $|p_1 - p_{\bar{1}}|$ increases. In a formal way one can construct

$$f_{21} = \frac{p_{12} - p_1 p_2}{p_2 p_{\bar{2}}} = \frac{f_{12} c_1}{c_2}.$$

It is easily shown that $f_{12} \cdot f_{21}$ equals the square of the traditional phi coefficient between the two items.

6.   The numerator in f_{12} can be put into the form of a determinant:

$$p_{12} - p_1 p_2 = \begin{vmatrix} p_{12} & p_1 \\ p_2 & 1 \end{vmatrix} = \begin{vmatrix} p_{12} & p_{1\bar{2}} \\ p_{\bar{1}2} & p_{\bar{1}\bar{2}} \end{vmatrix}.$$

This determinant will be symbolized by [12] and called the *cross product*. Any two dichotomous items form a fourfold table; their cross product [*ik*] will turn out to be a very fundamental computing device. It vanishes if the relative frequency of k is the same in the two subsets created by item i.

7.   Conditional probabilities within subsets are symbolized by Greek letters. Thus, for example,

$$\frac{p_{12}}{p_1} = \pi_{2,1} \quad \text{and} \quad \frac{p_{1\bar{2}3}}{p_{1\bar{2}}} = \pi_{3,1\bar{2}},$$

or, more generally,

$$\frac{p_{si}}{p_s} = \pi_{i,s},$$

where s stands for any signature, and i for the item on which we focus.

8. If a sample is stratified by the response to an item, say item 3, *contingent* cross products may be computed for the two ensuing subsets. They would be symbolized thus:

$$[12;3] = \begin{vmatrix} p_{123} & p_{13} \\ p_{23} & p_3 \end{vmatrix} \quad \text{and} \quad [12;\bar{3}] = \begin{vmatrix} p_{12\bar{3}} & p_{1\bar{3}} \\ p_{2\bar{3}} & p_{\bar{3}} \end{vmatrix}.$$

Actually we shall mainly use the conditional effect coefficients, to wit:

$$f_{12;3} = \frac{[12;3]}{p_{13}p_{\bar{1}3}} \quad \text{and} \quad f_{12;\bar{3}} = \frac{[12;\bar{3}]}{p_{1\bar{3}}p_{\bar{1}\bar{3}}}.$$

9. Joint relative frequencies will be classified according to their *level* of stratification, that is, by the number of indices that appear in the signature. When cross products are formed, we speak of their order, to stay with the traditional terminology of correlation analysis. Thus $[12; 34]$ is a cross product of second order; its highest entry is p_{1234}, a relative frequency of fourth level.

10. To obtain an easier flow we shall talk interchangeably of dichotomies, attributes, or items. Also interchangeable will be the terms proportions, probabilities, and (relative) frequencies. When we want to stress numbers in their unadjusted form, we shall always talk of raw frequencies.

THE FORMULATION OF THE PROBLEM

We now return to the question of how a 16-fold table can be fully analyzed. It is assumed that two attributes under study interact and that their interaction is clarified by repeated interviews. In the emerging tables, as in Table 2, the cases where the position on both dichotomies remains unchanged can be found in the main diagonal of the 16-fold table. Cases in the minor diagonal have changed on both attributes, and their number is usually small. In the other eight cells we find the cases that changed on one attribute only; for reasons to be explained later we shall call these the "critical" cells.

Assuming that we are dealing with a process of interaction between two attributes, we can raise the question as to which of the two is stronger. This is a vague term that covers a variety of possibilities: one attribute might affect the other, it might make the other change, it might drag the other along when it itself changes, etc. Each of these ideas can be translated into a combination of cells, and the possible variations are very numerous indeed. The problem is to bring some order into the way in which a 16-fold table can be analyzed. The following four principles will be applied to facilitate this task:

1. We shall concentrate on the relative strengths of the two attributes. All indices are developed with the purpose of *comparing* the two factors with each other; no statement about each one separately is intended.

2. Therefore all the processes to be considered will be symmetrical; this means that in any formula describing some kind of mutual influences the signatures pertaining to the two attributes will appear in the same algebraic form. If they are interchanged, the index will only change its sign.

3. Terms like "relative strength," "influence," and "effect" are used interchangeably; they are supposed to evoke an intuitive imagery. Their precise meaning derives from the algebraic procedures by which corresponding indices are derived. The algebra can lead in turn to finer distinctions within the originating imagery.

4. The level of stratification will be the guiding principle of organization. Each index to be developed will be classified according to whether the highest joint frequency in it is of the second, third, or fourth level.*

The Coleman-Boudon Model (Second-Level Analysis)

If we restrict ourselves to second-level joint frequencies, we can just determine which attribute observed the first time predicts better the other one at the second observation. In this situation the f coefficient is the best indicator, and so our final criterion will be the difference between f_{14} and f_{23}. In our concrete example the two figures are 0.31 and 0.35, respectively, and therefore in these terms "value" is somewhat stronger than "choice" in their mutual interaction. This, incidentally, is the approach that Campbell (1963) took in his original comments. (Because he discussed quantitative variables, he, of course, compared correlation coefficients and not f coefficients.)

---

* The main example in the following pages will be Table 2. For the convenience of the reader the symbols linking the algebra with the table can be summarized as follows:

1 = PO choice time 1	3 = PO choice time 2
$\bar{1}$ = NPO choice time 1	$\bar{3}$ = NPO choice time 2
2 = PO value time 1	4 = PO value time 2
$\bar{2}$ = NPO value time 1	$\bar{4}$ = NPO value time 2

After some reflection one will notice that this approach neglects an important point. An item might appear to be stronger because the other item that it predicts is more unstable. The literature, therefore, soon abandoned this elementary form of using the cross-lagged correlation approach. The idea that has been pursued explicitly or implicitly by all authors concerned is best represented by the following scheme:

Odd item: ("choice")

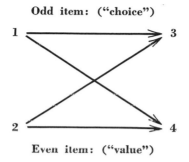

Even item: ("value")

For quantitative variables this imagery is easily translated into a set of linear equations. For dichotomies, however, a different way, first introduced by Coleman and later simplified by Boudon, proved necessary.

Let us focus on the proportion of students who, the second time, make a people-oriented choice of occupation. Their relative frequency p_3 can be divided into four subsets according to choices and values expressed the first time. For each of these four subsets, we can compute separate conditional probabilities that the second choice will be people-oriented. The same can be done for the second expression of values. Our main example then produces the conditional probabilities shown in Table 3.

Now assume that these proportions observed at the second interview come from three sources: the persistence of an earlier position; the influence of the two factors on each other, as it is exercised over time; and finally

Table 3. Conditional Probabilities of Expressing PO Choices and PO Values for Subgroups Formed by First Choice and First Value

Pattern of First Choice and Value	Signature s	Row Totals	Relative Row Frequencies	
			$\pi_{3,s}$	$\pi_{4,s}$
+ +	1 2	226	0.79	0.85
+ −	1 $\bar{2}$	89	.56	.33
− +	$\bar{1}$ 2	166	.27	.66
− −	$\bar{1}$ $\bar{2}$	231	.09	.21
		712		

changes that cannot be accounted for by just considering the two factors and their mutual effect. This idea can be succinctly summarized in the model of

Schema I

Pattern Frequencies at First Observation		At Second Observation	
(1)	(2)	% p_3: $\pi_{3,s}$	% p_4: $\pi_{4,s}$
$+\ +$	p_{12}	$a_{13} + a_{23} + e_3$	$a_{14} + a_{24} + e_4$
$+\ -$	$p_{1\bar{2}}$	$a_{13}\ \ \ \ + e_3$	$a_{14}\ \ \ \ + e_4$
$-\ +$	$p_{\bar{1}2}$	$a_{23} + e_3$	$a_{24} + e_4$
$-\ -$	$p_{\bar{1}\bar{2}}$	e_3	e_4

Schema I. The first two columns classify respondents according to the choices (1) and the values (2) which they express at the first interview. The other two columns refer to the proportions of respondents who at the second interview express, respectively, people-oriented choices and people-oriented values. These conditional probabilities are decomposed into three parts. The letters a_{13} and a_{24} pertain, respectively, to the contribution that the first observation makes to the second observation on the same item. The letters a_{14} and a_{23} symbolize the contribution that the first item makes to the other item the second time. The letters e_3 and e_4 give the proportion of people with PO choices and PO values who had neither of these people-oriented responses the first time. The top line of these conditional frequencies in Schema I implies clearly an assumption; the contributions of the two observations the first time are the same for one attribute irrespective of whether the other attribute was people oriented before. We shall come back to this assumption in the next section. For the moment the task is to analyze this model in more detail.

Any model imposes restrictions on the empirical data it is supposed to represent. If in the schema of the model we subtract the second line from the first, we get a_{23} and a_{24} in the first and second columns, respectively. But the same results are obtained if we subtract the fourth line from the third. This means that in the case where the data fit the model exactly we would have to find that

$$\pi_{3,12} - \pi_{3,1\bar{2}} = \pi_{3,\bar{1}2} - \pi_{3,\bar{1}\bar{2}}.$$

This condition can be put into the form

$$f_{23\,;1} = f_{23\,;\bar{1}}. \tag{1a}$$

This means that the stability of choice is the same for students with and without people-oriented values.

By repeating the same operation, beginning with lines 1 and 3, we obtain the equivalent restriction

$$f_{13;2} = f_{13;\bar{2}}.$$ (1b)

By applying the same operations to the even item (last column of the model) we obtain

$$f_{14;2} = f_{14;\bar{2}} \quad \text{and} \quad f_{24;1} = f_{24;\bar{1}}.$$ (1c)

Empirical data have to satisfy these conditions at least approximately in order that they can be represented by the model of Schema I. This result deserves the name of *Theorem A*.

What equations exist between the parameters of the model and empirical data that would fit it perfectly? We shall derive the answer for the "odd" attributes only; the result for the "even" attribute is established by replacing index 3 by index 4. Schema I can be rewritten so that it pertains to simple proportions and not to ratios, as shown in Schema II.

Schema II

$$p_{123} = p_{12}(a_{13} + a_{23} + e_3)$$
$$p_{1\bar{2}3} = p_{1\bar{2}}(a_{13} \qquad + e_3)$$
$$p_{\bar{1}23} = p_{\bar{1}2}(\qquad a_{23} + e_3)$$
$$p_{\bar{1}\bar{2}3} = p_{\bar{1}\bar{2}}(\qquad e_3)$$

An inspection of Schema II permits us to derive the following set of equations:

$$p_3 = a_{13}p_1 + a_{23}p_2 + e_3,$$ (2a)

$$p_{13} = p_1(a_{13} + e_3) + p_{12}a_{23},$$ (2b)

$$p_{23} = p_{12}a_{13} + p_2(a_{23} + e_3).$$ (2c)

These three equations in turn can be combined to form cross products. As a result we now have a new set of equations wherein the parameters of the Coleman-Boudon model are the coefficients in a series of linear equations:

$$[13] = p_{13} - p_1 p_3 = a_{13}p_1\bar{p_1} + a_{23}[12],$$ (3a)

$$[23] = p_{23} - p_2 p_3 = a_{23}p_2\bar{p_2} + a_{13}[12].$$ (3b)

If we now divide Equations 3a and 3b by $p_1\bar{p_1}$ and $p_2\bar{p_2}$ respectively, we obtain *Theorem B:*

$$f_{13} = a_{13} + f_{12}a_{23},$$ (4a)

$$f_{23} = a_{23} + f_{21}a_{13}.$$ (4b)

The f coefficients are empirical data. The a values can now be computed from Equations 4a and 4b. This links the latent parameters of the Coleman-

Table 4. The Parameters for the Model of Schema II Applied to Table 2

	Stability	Susceptibility	$e_3(e_4)$
Value	0.51 (a_{13})	0.20 (a_{23})	0.08
Choice	.48 (a_{24})	.16 (a_{14})	.21

Boudon model to manifest observations. As mentioned before, the equations for the even item emerge if in Equations 4 we replace index 3 by index 4.

It will be helpful to fix the terminology for the four main coefficients of the model. We call a_{13} and a_{24} the *stability* of each attribute; a_{23} and a_{14} will be called the *susceptibility* of each to the influence of the other. The main substantive result for the present example is that "values" are relatively more susceptible to the influence of "choice" and at the same time more stable. This can be seen from Table 4.

No estimation is needed in this case because Equations 4a and 4b and the corresponding equations for the even item have just the right number of unknowns to permit solution by Cramer's rule. However, as we shall see presently, various conventional significance tests can be applied if manifest higher-level frequencies are compared to those that would be derived from the Coleman-Boudon model.

If the linear model were to satisfy the whole process, we could compute the cross product between the two second observations. It can be shown in a variety of ways that the following equations would have to hold:*

$$[34] = [13]a_{14} + [23]a_{24}$$
$$= [14]a_{13} + [24]a_{23} = 0.07. \tag{5}$$

The values of p_3 and p_4 are not determined by the model and can therefore be taken from the empirical data. As can be seen, the values are $p_3 = 0.41$ and $p_4 = 0.53$. This permits computation of the model value of $p_{34} = p_3p_4 + [34]$, $p_{3\bar{4}} = p_3p_{\bar{4}} - [34]$, and so on.

Table 5 gives in the first line the data fitted to the model, and in the second line the actual data. It can be seen that the actual association is greater than would be accounted for by the parameters of Equation 5. Thus further analysis is needed.

---

* This is a special case of a general theorem that is proved elsewhere (Lazarsfeld, 1961). In the present case it is assumed that the association between items 3 and 4 is due solely to their connection with items 1 and 2 as established by equations of the type of Equation 4.

Table 5. Computed and Actual Joint Proportions

	P_{34}	$P_{3\bar{4}}$	$P_{\bar{3}4}$	$P_{\bar{3}\bar{4}}$
Computed	0.27	0.07	0.32	0.34
Actual	.32	.09	.22	.37

CAUSAL INTERPRETATION OF DIFFERENTIAL ASSOCIATIONS (THIRD-LEVEL ANALYSIS)

We saw that the Coleman-Boudon model implies a restrictive assumption. If attributes 1 and 2 affect attribute 3, their contributions are independent of each other. The consequence is that in a strict sense $f_{13;2} = f_{13;\bar{2}}$ and $f_{23;1} = f_{23;\bar{1}}$. If their joint contribution is larger than $a_{13} + a_{23}$, then an additional term has to be introduced into the first equation of Schema I:

$$\pi_{3,12} = a_{13} + a_{23} + d + e_3. \qquad (6)$$

The value of d is easily computed by substituting Equation 6 for the first line of Schema I. It can then be seen directly that

$$d = f_{13;2} - f_{13;\bar{2}} = f_{23;1} - f_{23;\bar{1}}. \qquad (7)$$

The parameter d is usually called the "interaction" between items 1 and 2. It is very important not to confuse this notion with the mutual effects of a pair of attributes. The statistical notion of interaction refers to two independent items observed at the same time. The mutual effect problem refers to the relation between the two items across time, where each is both dependent and independent. The fact that the terminology is confusing is regrettable, but it is too well established to permit change. At the moment the imagery for the two cases is distinct, and the algebra can make the matter perfectly clear.

To be concrete we exhibit in Table 6 the conditional relations of 2 and 4 if the sample is stratified by item 1 (the figures are taken, of course, from Table 2). For Table 6, the f coefficient on the left side, $f_{24;1}$, equals 0.52; on the right side, $f_{24;\bar{1}} = 0.44$. Therefore $d_4 = f_{24;1} - f_{24;\bar{1}} = 0.52 - 0.44 = 0.08$, which by Equation 7 equals $f_{14;2} - f_{14;\bar{2}}$. We have given d the index 4 to indicate that the "dependent" item here is the value system of the respondent.

It is not difficult to give a substantive interpretation to $f_{24;k}$. It measures the stability of the even attribute under the two conditions of the odd attribute being positive or negative the first time. Or, in terms of the concrete example, if students made a people-oriented occupational choice in 1950,

Table 6. Stratification by Choice in 1950

		PO (+) Value in 1952 (Item 4)			NPO (—) Value in 1952 (Item 4)		
		PO (+)	NPO (—)	Total	PO (+)	NPO (—)	Total
Value in 1950 (Item 2)	PO (+)	193	33	226	109	57	166
	NPO (—)	29	60	89	49	182	231
Total		222	93	315	158	239	397

they are less likely to change their value systems than if they made a non-PO choice.

It is obviously possible to compute the same index for the odd attribute. The figures can be taken directly from Table 2 and would have to be arranged as in Table 6, using item 1 instead of item 2, and item 3 instead of item 4. The computation shows that $d_3 = f_{13;2} - f_{13;\bar{2}} = f_{23;1} - f_{23;\bar{1}} = 0.05$, somewhat smaller than d_4. Forgetting significance problems, we can see that the odd attribute observed the first time predicts changes in the even attribute somewhat better than "the other way around."

Some authors have considered $d_4 - d_3$ as another index of mutual effect. The literature is reviewed by Rees (1971), who correctly raises an objection: In this approach we fail to take into account what happened to the "independent" item between the two observations. If we consider the change in one attribute and the first value of the other, we deal with prediction and not with interaction over time. The idea should be abandoned, therefore, just as the simple cross-lagged correlation idea was (Yee & Gage, 1968). Rees is right in saying that three observations would be needed: then one could compare changes in one item between the first two observations with changes in the other item between times 2 and 3. At the end of this chapter a solution for the case with only two observations available will be discussed.

Thus we conclude that the analysis of third-level data provides useful insights but no new index of mutual effect.

Two additional remarks should be helpful. First, $d_4 - d_3$ is a second-order difference for which various significance tests are available. In dichotomous algebra it corresponds to the third-level symmetric parameter — a generalization of the cross product. In the Coleman-Boudon model it vanishes because $d_3 - d_4 = 0$. In conventional correlation analysis it cannot be expressed at all, because it uses data which would correspond to a triple covariance Σxyz. Most certainly it should not be confused with partial correlations.

Second, a 16-fold table in terms of proportions has 15 degrees of freedom. We have so far consumed 11 of them. This leaves 4 more for discussion; they are obviously implied in the fourth-level data. The simplest way to put it is this: the four cross products in the four rows of 16-fold Table 2 are still free. How would we use them for mutual effect analysis on that level?

THE INDEX OF MUTUAL EFFECT (FOURTH-LEVEL ANALYSIS)

To build up an appropriate analysis we start with the students who at the first interview gave "inconsistent" responses—either "choice" or "value" was people oriented, but not both. Some of them had become consistent at the second round. In which direction did this harmonization come about? In terms of choice and value they were originally either $(+ \ -)$ or $(- \ +)$; at the second interview some of those students had become consonant, that is, either $(+ \ +)$ or $(- \ -)$. The four cells containing these dissonant to consonant cases have been marked by an asterisk $(*)$ in Schema III (for the moment the letters and triangles in the schema should be neglected).

Schema III. The eight "critical cells" containing the case where there is change on one but not on both attributes between two interviews.

		Time 2				
	O E	$+$ $+$	$+$ $-$	$-$ $+$	$-$ $-$	Row total
Time 1	$+ \ +$		Δ E_1	Δ O_1		p_{12}
	$+ \ -$	* O_2			* E_2	$p_{1\bar{2}}$
	$- \ +$	* E_3			* O_3	$p_{\bar{1}2}$
	$- \ -$		Δ O_4	Δ E_4		$p_{\bar{1}\bar{2}}$
	Column total	p_{34}	$p_{3\bar{4}}$	$p_{\bar{3}4}$	$p_{\bar{3}\bar{4}}$	1

Obviously, two extreme cases can happen: (a) all students who move from dissonant to consonant positions adjust their second choices to conform to their first values; or (b) they all end up with the values one would expect from their earlier choices. In the imagery of a harmonization process it will make intuitive sense to say: In the first case values dominate choices; in the second case choices are dominant.

To facilitate the following discussion we use the letters O_i and E_i as shown in Schema III instead of the dichotomous symbolism. Obviously $E_1 = p_{123\bar{4}}$, $O_3 = p_{\bar{1}23\bar{4}}$, and so on.

Most concrete cases will represent a mixture of the two extremes. In Schema III we have marked with O and E the proportions in those cells which indicate, respectively, the dominance of the odd item (the choice) or the even item (the value); the numerical subscript serves to indicate the row in which the cell can be found. (How the dominance can be explained in rows 1 and 4 will be detailed below.) Using the dichotomous symbolism, we can express the probability, for example, of $(- +)$ moving to $(+ +)$ as follows:

$$\frac{E_3}{p_{\bar{1}2}} = \frac{p_{\bar{1}234}}{p_{\bar{1}2}} = \pi_{34,\bar{1}2}.$$

The probability of a movement from $(+ -)$ to $(+ +)$ is of course $\pi_{34,1\bar{2}}$. If $\pi_{34,1\bar{2}} > \pi_{34,\bar{1}2}$, then in this respect the odd item dominates the even one. As usual, the difference can be put into a more symmetric form if, from Schema III, we introduce the determinant

$$\Delta_1 = \begin{vmatrix} O_2 & E_2 \\ E_3 & O_3 \end{vmatrix}.$$

Then

$$\pi_{34,1\bar{2}} - \pi_{34,\bar{1}2} = \frac{\Delta_1}{g_{1\bar{2}} \cdot g_{\bar{1}2}} = h_1,$$

where $g_{1\bar{2}} = O_2 + E_2$ and $g_{\bar{1}2} = E_3 + O_3$. We shall call h_1 the *index of relative concurrence* and justify the term presently. If h_1 is positive, the odd item is dominant on this level; if h_1 is negative, the even item is stronger.

But such an index would not yet properly describe the relative importance of the two factors in maintaining consistency, because the following consideration enters. Suppose we find that the value of h_1 indicates that choice (O) is stronger than value (E). The numerical result might still be due to the fact that values are less attached to a consonant pattern than choices, that they oscillate more, irrespective of the choice pattern. Index h_1 would then overrate the relative importance of choice.

How do we take this problem into account? Again attachment is a vague notion and needs to be specified in the present context. The appropriate way is to look at the first and the last rows of Schema III, which contain the students who at the first interview were consonant, either $(+ +)$ or

(— —). The cases in the two middle cells of the two rows are those that break away from the original consonance and end up dissonant at the second interview. These cells are marked by a triangle in Schema III.

The disruption of an initial consonance might be due to a variety of reasons: other factors impinge on the people outside the choice-value pattern; accidental factors that influence the answers enter at the time of the two interviews; technical errors affect the data processing. For the present purpose, however, the sources of the shift are irrelevant. The essence is that the four triangle cells permit us to define what we mean when we decide that one factor is less attached than the other. The less attached factor is the one where more cases break away from consonance. For each factor two such cells come into play to describe the "breakaway"; in regard to choice, for instance, it is the people who move from (+ +) to (— +) and those from (— —) to (+ —). In both cases the choice changes but not the value.

Now in the light of our preceding discussion we want to be sure that an item does not appear dominant just because it is more attached to the congruent pattern. In Schema III we have, therefore, marked as O_1 and O_4 the cells which *do not* support the relative influence of the even item; figuratively speaking, O_1 and O_4 are "good" for the odd item. A reasonable *index of relative attachment* is now based on these breakaway cases. By analogy it will use their determinant:

$$\Delta_2 = \begin{vmatrix} E_1 & O_1 \\ O_4 & E_4 \end{vmatrix}.$$

The index will be

$$h_2 = \frac{\Delta_2}{g_{12} \cdot g_{\overline{12}}},$$

where $g_{12} = E_1 + O_1$ and $g_{\overline{12}} = O_4 + E_4$. But h_2 should be weighed negatively when a total *index of mutual effect* is formed. Combining all these considerations, we find that such an index was originally proposed by the formula

$$I = h_1 - h_2,$$

and it still seems appropriate. Here I is positive if the odd item is stronger, and negative if the even item is stronger.*

---

* Actually Δ_1 and Δ_2 were standardized somewhat differently in the original study. But this has no bearing on the general discussion. The present way of dividing by g_k is more in keeping with the spirit of time direction, which suggests preference for the directional type of f indices. Also, h_k varies between -1 and $+1$, while the older standardization made for less fixed bounds.

Our basic example (Table 2) provides the following data:

$$\Delta_1 = \begin{vmatrix} 21 & 31 \\ 36 & 49 \end{vmatrix}, \quad \Delta_2 = \begin{vmatrix} 15 & 20 \\ 14 & 43 \end{vmatrix};$$

$$h_1 = -0.03, \qquad\qquad h_2 = 0.08;$$

and therefore

$$I = h_1 - h_2 = -0.11.$$

Thus to a small extent values affect choices relatively more than choices affect values, as far as an analysis of the fourth stratification level is concerned. It is important to compare this result with the findings in Table 4. There we found choices to be stronger than values in the sense that earlier choices contributed more to later values than the other way around. Now we are analyzing which of the two factors contributes more to a cohesive pattern; here the values are relatively dominant.

It obviously would not make any sense to raise the question of which finding is more important. Clearly the two results deal with different parts of the total process. The answer depends on the problem in hand. Suppose that our two items are children's exposure to television and their propensity to violence and that in an initial survey the two attributes were found to be positively associated. We would make a second set of interviews in order to see "what makes for what." The correct approach would be to analyze the resulting 16-fold table in terms of the Coleman-Boudon model to compare the two relative susceptibilities. But suppose we find marked positive associations within each row of the 16-fold table. This would show that an enduring pattern has acquired functional autonomy, so that we mainly want to know what, relatively, the two attributes contribute to pattern maintenance; then the index of mutual effect would be appropriate.

In both cases we try to approximate a controlled experiment to obtain leads for action. In the second case we might want to know how to break the pattern; in the first we might want to argue that television watching does not lead to violence—it is the other way around. In both cases, incidentally, we might go on to look for spurious third factors, but this is outside of the program we set for this chapter.*

It is algebraically clear that the results on the second and the fourth level

---

* Since the resurrection of path analysis several authors have applied it to the findings of *The People's Choice.* But most writers knew the material only from an early publication by D. Campbell, which did not discuss the full 16-fold tables. Thus they did not become aware that we wanted to study relative depth of attitudes— the second case. Path analysis is a parallel to the Coleman-Boudon model and cannot contribute anything to the analysis of fourth-level data.

of analysis can vary independently from each other. Helpful insights can be gained by constructing "custom-tailored" 16-fold tables with paradoxical combinations. A general procedure has been developed for such construction, but space does not permit its inclusion here.

Our analysis is not yet complete. As a result of introducing the two terms of the index of mutual effect, 13 degrees of freedom are now consumed. In what way should the 2 remaining ones be used?

It is obviously useful to know how many people altogether break away from or join the consistent pattern. This would mean adding the number of cases in all eight critical cells and computing this figure as a proportion of the total sum. In our original example this figure is 0.34. This is then proposed as an additional index because the index of mutual effect is of greater information value if the proportion that shifts on one item but not on both is large.

We are free and need to choose one more index. Intuition suggests filling one gap, alluded to in the discussion of third-level data: the simultaneous consideration of change in both attributes.

THE ANDERSON INDEX

If we don't have a third wave of interviews, we can make the simplifying assumption that the relation between the second and third observations would be the same as that between the first and the second. The only difference would be that the outcome of the first 16-fold table would be the initial stage of the second one. The original figures would be the transition probabilities if recomputed as proportions of each row (Anderson, 1951). We can use Schema III as background for our further discussion because we shall only use the probabilities of one step move at a time—but so that two steps lead to a complete reversal of the original pattern. Then E_i and O_i can be used as transition probabilities, provided they are considered divided by their respective row totals.

Then the relative roles of the two attributes could be described in terms of the time sequence of their changes: if a two-step full change comes about, we could have here a new index of relative importance: Which attribute "leads," that is, which changes first?

The change from $(+\ +)$ to $(-\ -)$, for instance could come about in two different ways. The odd item could change first: $(+\ +) \rightarrow (-\ +) \rightarrow (-\ -)$. In terms of Schema III the probability of this sequence is $O_1 O_3$. The alternative sequence, $(++) \rightarrow (+\ -) \rightarrow (-\ -)$, could also occur; it would have the probability $E_1 E_2$. The probability for a lead of the odd item is, therefore, $O_1 O_3 - E_1 E_2$. We have to consider three other changes: from

$(+-)$ to $(-+)$, from $(-+)$ to $(+-)$, and from $(--)$ to $(++)$. If the odd item is in the lead, then the probabilities for these three sequences are, respectively, E_2E_4, E_3E_1, and O_4O_2. A similar computation can be carried out for the three remaining cases, where the even item has the lead. The corresponding path probabilities are, respectively, O_2O_1, O_3O_4, and E_4E_3.

We then may use as the new index the difference between the probabilities that the odd item leads and the probabilities of the sequences that give the lead to the even item. After reordering terms this index turns out to be

$$A = (O_1 - O_4)(O_3 - O_2) + (E_1 - E_4)(E_3 - E_2).$$

If A is positive, then in terms of this imagery the odd item is "stronger" than the even; if A is negative, the even item is stronger. A possible intuitive interpretation of A would be as follows. Any probability of increasing the frequency of the odd attribute has a positive sign. A probability that a step decreases the total positive frequency of the odd item is counted as negative in index A. This can be seen by comparing the index formula with Schema III.

The Anderson index is not the only way of relating change to change. If observations at three time periods are available, one could apply the whole analysis of this chapter to a 16-fold table in which the basic units are two subsequent shifts in two attributes. However, this would exceed the program of the present discussion.

We can compute for our example of Table 2 the Anderson index A by dividing the numbers in the critical cell through their respective row totals. The value is $A = 0.01$. In a weak way the odd-item choice is leading in a process in which the original 16-fold table is seen as a Markov chain of interaction between the two attributes. It would be interesting to study the equilibrium state of this process and the manner in which it depends on the values of O_i and E_i. The problem is complex and could only be approached by computer simulation.

The index A uses the entries in the critical cells differently from I, the index of mutual effect. The two indices cannot be transformed into each other. Thus A consumes the last degree of freedom in the description of a 16-fold table.

CONCLUSIONS

The model delineated in this chapter applies to two complementary situations. On the one hand, it can be used merely to describe a 16-fold table in a concise and intuitively helpful way. The 15 parameters and indices introduced contain exactly the same amount of information as the 15 free cells of a 16-fold table. However, they facilitate decision making if one wants to condense the available information. One might, for instance, make simplifying assumptions, as in the case of the Coleman-Boudon model; or one might concentrate on the index of mutual effect and forget about additional information available on the fourth stratification level. Many other such simplifications can also be useful.

Instead, one can proceed in a reverse way. One might for systematic reasons be interested in certain structural problems. Then one would start with assumptions on the parameters and indices and would raise the question of what kind of 16-fold table would emerge from such assumptions. The answer would give leads to further interpretation.

From a more substantive point of view this chapter has had two purposes. One was related to the general problem of how to interpret empirical data. Authors are likely to use terms like "process" and "interaction" rather loosely. The analysis here has tried to show that, given a specific procedure (in this case panel analysis), such terms acquire more precise meaning or are shown to cover several meanings indiscriminately. The reader will certainly have sensed also a hidden claim to have contributed to the "chicken and egg" problem.

A second purpose was to eliminate some old misunderstandings and avoid some future ones. Thus, for instance, it has occasionally been intimated that there is a contradiction between what Campbell calls the "cross-lagged panel correlation" and this author's work on the index of mutual effect. The present treatment shows that they are compatible because the analyses refer to different stratification levels. Similar considerations come into play with a number of recent publications applying path analysis to panel data. By definition path analysis is concerned only with second-level data and neglects higher stratification levels. The content of a 16-fold table includes data on the third and fourth stratification levels, which path analysis in its present form cannot analyze; whether such data are empirically worth while or should be neglected is a different question.

The discussion here was restricted to the algebra of dichotomous systems. Some of the resulting formulas bear obvious parallels to equations emerging from regression and path analysis; others do not. An investigation of the parallels between the two algebraic approaches has not been attempted here. Excluded also has been the question of whether dichotomous data or quantitative variables are more subject to error. This can really be answered only after one has discussed the problem of how to deal with variates that are not directly accessible to empirical observation.

Finally a word about the organization of the chapter is in order. At first reading it may seem rather pedantic to make the distinction of stratification levels the guiding idea. But there are at least two grounds on which to defend this procedure. On the one hand, such organization seems the best way to interrelate the indices for panel analyses that have been proposed by various authors. And, second, the stratification levels seem to lead to conceptual distinctions that otherwise might be overlooked or clouded; this has been repeatedly emphasized in the preceding pages.

Much traditional statistical analysis uses data where normal distributions are assumed; this assumption makes the use of higher-level data unnecessary. In social research, however, these higher-level data are certainly indispensable, and how to deal with them succinctly and economically constitutes an urgent problem. The author does not want to prejudge whether the ideas discussed in this chapter could be helpful to the study of relations between continuous variates; on the other hand, he also does not want to conceal his optimism in this regard.

REFERENCES

Anderson, T. W. *Probability models for analyzing time changes in attitudes.* The Rand Corporation, 1951.

Boudon, R. A new look at correlation analysis. In H. M. Blalock & A. B. Blalock (Eds.), *Methodology in social research.* New York: McGraw-Hill, 1968. Pp. 199–235.

Campbell, D. T. From description to experimentation: Interpreting trends as quasi-experiments. In C. W. Harris (Ed.), *Problems in measuring change.* Madison: University of Wisconsin Press, 1963. Pp. 212–242.

Coleman, J. S. *Introduction to mathematical sociology.* Glencoe, Ill.: The Free Press, 1964.

Duncan, O. D. Path analysis: Sociological examples. *American Journal of Sociology,* 1966, **72** (1), 1–16.

Heise, D. R. A model for causal inference from panel data. Unpublished manuscript, University of Wisconsin, 1969.

Lazarsfeld, P. F. The algebra of dichotomous systems. In H. Solomon (Ed.), *Studies in item analysis and prediction.* Stanford: Stanford University Press, 1961. Pp. 111–157.

Lazarsfeld, P. F. *The people's choice.* (3rd ed.) New York: Columbia University Press, 1968.

Pelz, D. C., & Andrews, F. M. Detecting causal priorities in panel study data. *American Sociological Review,* 1964, **29,** 836–848.

Rees, M. B. A comparison of cross-lagged path, and multivariate causal inference techniques applied to interest, information, and aspiration among high-school students. Unpublished doctoral dissertation, Northwestern University, 1971.

Rosenberg, M. *Occupations and values.* Glencoe, Ill.: The Free Press, 1957.

Yee, A. H., & Gage, N. L. Techniques for estimating the source and direction of causal influence in panel data. *Psychological Bulletin,* 1968, **70,** 115–126.

CHAPTER 26

A Partial-Order Scalogram Classification of Projective Techniques

LOUIS GUTTMAN

Projective techniques have been classified according to various criteria by various authors, but no consensus seems to have been reached as to what may be the most fruitful way. For a review of the problem see Zubin, Eron, and Schumer (1965, esp. pp. 13–18). One of the most systematic approaches has been that of Gardner Lindzey (1959), who proposed a framework for defining the similarities and differences among eleven projective techniques. He used six kinds of criteria for classification, each kind consisting of one or more subcriteria. His conclusion was that a simple heuristic grouping of the eleven techniques into five subgroups was an optimal way of classification, and that "there seemed to be little basis for preferring the more cumbersome [multidimensional] method of classification [p. 168]."

Lindzey's work was done before the development of multidimensional scalogram analysis (MSA) (Guttman, 1966; Lingoes, 1968; see also examples in Bloombaum, 1968; Guttman, Lieblich, & Naftali, 1969; Shoham, Guttman, & Rahav, 1970; Wollstein, 1968). His use of crude measures of similarity in order to try to find "clusters" among the techniques may now be seen to account for his rather negative conclusions about the possibility of more systematic classification. We shall present here a reanalysis of Lindzey's system, and show how it leads to a rather neat partial ordering of all of the techniques in a two-dimensional scalogram space. The notion of clusters is not necessary or even very appropriate. One kind of technique may blend into the next, and new varieties can be devised to fill out the space.

While the present example may be the first application of partial-order scalogram analysis (POSA) in clinical psychology, more typical uses in the future will undoubtedly be for the partial ordering of *individuals* on the basis of their responses within projective and other techniques. This is one of the multidimensional solutions that scalogram theory offers for data which are not unidimensional (cf. Wollstein, 1968, for an MSA of clinical data). The need for multidimensional solutions in clinical psychology has long been recognized (Zubin et al., 1965, esp. pp. 571–573) Given systematic data on individuals, one could then go on to study the structure of the *empirical* relations among the projective techniques, along the lines used for attitude questionnaires (Elizur, 1970; Guttman, 1959; Jordan, 1969) and intelligence and achievement tests (Guttman, 1965b, 1970; Schlesinger & Guttman, 1969).

The present analysis deals with the structure of the universe of content of the projective techniques, which is a prerequisite for developing a theory for the structure of the empirical interrelations. This analysis is intended to be suggestive rather than definitive for the classification problem of projective techniques, though our results seem rather substantial in their own right.

Domain and Range of Items

A test item—whether of a projective technique, attitude questionnaire, intelligence or achievement test—consists of a stimulus and possible responses. The set of all stimuli we call the *domain* for the items; and the possible responses, their *range*. It is possible to distinguish attitudinal items from intelligence items by consideration of their ranges. An attitudinal item is one whose range is from positive to negative vis-à-vis a social object of its domain. An intelligence item is one whose range is from right to wrong in a logical sense of its domain (Guttman, 1965a). We have studied Lindzey's and other classifications in quest of a similarly common range for items of all projective techniques, but with no success as yet. Accordingly, we shall not attempt a faceted definition of projective techniques here. Instead, we shall accept Lindzey's list of eleven techniques as given—without formalizing what they have in common—and go on to ask only how the eleven differ among themselves. In terms of Lindzey's criteria, they differ both in their domain elements and in the ranges of their items.

In reviewing Lindzey's subcriteria, we find that they can be restated as four facets for the domain, two for the range, and two that seem to characterize both the domain and the range. One further criterion—"method of construction: rational or empirical"—refers to correlates and not just to definition, and so is not considered here. In addition, we shall not consider another of Lindzey's subcriteria, "sensory mode," since this also seems to be a correlate rather than a basic component of a definition of the projectiveness of a technique.

Four domain facets, with their elements or categories, are (maintaining Lindzey's terminology with slight modifications and with new notation) as follows:

A. Structure
  a_1. unstructured
  a_2. structured

B. Scope
  b_1. holistic
  b_2. holistic-dimensional
  b_3. dimensional

C. Purpose
  c_1. general personality
  c_2. general personality and
    specific traits
  c_3. specific traits

D. Administration
  d_1. individual
  d_2. group
  d_3. group or self

Two facets of the range, with their elements, are as follows:

E. Suggested responses
  e_1. free
  e_2. restricted

F. Mode of response
  f_1. expression
  f_2. construction
  f_3. associative
  f_4. completion
  f_5. choice or ordering

Two facets that may be considered common to both domain and range are as follows:

G. Content orientation
  g_1. high
  g_2. medium
  g_3. low

H. Formality of interpretation
  h_1. low
  h_2. high

The structuples (or profiles) of the eleven projective techniques over the eight facets *ABCDEFGH* are given in Table 1. The assignment of structuples in the table follows that of Lindzey, with slight modifications made by collapsing categories of some of his subcriteria. It is our intention here, not to discuss the correctness of the assignment of the structuples, but to accept them as given, and to go on to analysis of the structure generated by this assignment. Our results may be suggestive of clearer definitions and assignments of the concepts concerned, for future consideration.

Specification of Order of "Projectiveness" within Each Facet

The projective techniques are arranged in Table 1 according to the results of the partial ordering now to be discussed. As a preliminary to this

Table 1. The Eleven Projective Techniques and Their Structuples

Projective Technique	Domain $A\ B\ C\ D$	Range $E\ F$	Both $G\ H$
I. Psychodrama	$a_1 b_1 c_1 d_1$	$e_1 f_1$	$g_1 h_1$
II. Make-A-Picture Story test (MAPS)	$a_1 b_1 c_1 d_1$	$e_1 f_2$	$g_1 h_1$
III. Drawing and Painting	$a_1 b_2 c_1 d_1$	$e_1 f_1$	$g_2 h_2$
IV. TAT	$a_2 b_2 c_1 d_1$	$e_1 f_2$	$g_1 h_1$
V. Blacky	$a_2 b_3 c_3 d_1$	$e_1 f_2$	$g_1 h_1$
VI. Rorschach	$a_1 b_2 c_2 d_1$	$e_1 f_3$	$g_2 h_2$
VII. Word Association	$a_2 b_3 c_3 d_1$	$e_1 f_3$	$g_1 h_1$
VIII. Sentence Completion	$a_2 b_3 c_3 d_2$	$e_2 f_4$	$g_1 h_1$
IX. Picture Frustration study	$a_2 b_3 c_3 d_3$	$e_2 f_4$	$g_1 h_1$
X. Szondi	$a_2 b_3 c_2 d_1$	$e_2 f_5$	$g_3 h_2$
XI. Picture Arrangement	$a_2 b_3 c_3 d_3$	$e_2 f_5$	$g_3 h_2$

discussion, it may be helpful to inspect Table 1 to see some of its more obvious features.

Criteria A and B form a perfect scale between themselves: a_1 ("unstructured") goes only with b_1 and b_2, while a_2 ("structured") goes only with b_2 or b_3. Thus A and B generate a scale of four ranks: $a_1b_1 > a_1b_2 > a_2b_2 > a_2b_3$. It may be possible, of course, to think of constructing new projective techniques that will have "nonscalable" structuples involving a_2b_1 and a_1b_3. Nevertheless, the present behavior of constructors of projective techniques seems definitely oriented toward regarding A and B as having a common direction, with a_1 and b_1 going one way, while a_2 and b_3 go the opposite way.

Similarly, we find c_1 appearing only with d_1: "general personality" goes only with "individual administration." However, c_3—"specific traits"—goes with each form of administration, d_1, d_2, and d_3. Thus there also seems to be a common orientation for c_1 and d_1. This is shared by a_1b_1, since a_1b_1 goes only with c_1d_1 in Table 1.

Studying the other criteria in the same fashion shows a definite pattern of interlinking among them: e_1 goes only with d_1, f_1 only with e_1, g_1 only with h_1, and conversely, and so on.

The behavior of the authors of the eleven projective techniques, according to the pattern in Table 1, leads to a specification of which direction is "more projective" and which is "less projective" for each of the eight facets separately. If we accept, for example, that, for facet A, "unstructured" is more projective than "structured," then the consistency of empirical relationships among the facets may be taken as the basis for further specifying that, in facet B, "holistic" is more projective than "dimensional"; in facet C, the purpose of "general personality" is more projective than the purpose of "specific traits"; and so on for the remaining facets. In symbols, we shall accept as specifications, with respect to the concept of projectiveness of a test, that within each of the respective eight facets the following order relations hold:

$$a_1 > a_2 \qquad e_1 > e_2$$
$$b_1 > b_2 > b_3 \qquad f_1 > f_2 > f_3 > f_4 > f_5$$
$$c_1 > c_2 > c_3 \qquad g_1 > g_2 > g_3$$
$$d_1 > d_2 > d_3 \qquad h_1 > h_2$$

The Partial Order for the Cartesian Space

The above eight specifications of order within facets lead in turn to specification of a single partial order of "projectiveness" for the Cartesian space $ABCDEFGH$ as a whole. The most projective test of all the possibilities in this space is that with the structuple $a_1b_1c_1d_1e_1f_1g_1h_1$—it is the highest possible on all the facets of the space. The least projective test is that with the structuple $a_2b_3c_3d_3e_2f_5g_3h_2$—it is the lowest possible on all the facets of the space. All other tests are of intermediate degrees of projectivity, but in general need not be comparable to each other in their degrees.

Tests with the highest possible and lowest possible structuples actually occur among the eleven techniques of Table 1. They are Psychodrama and Picture Arrangement, respectively. All the remaining nine techniques are, accordingly, less projective than Psychodrama but more projective than Picture Arrangement.

Table 1 has been arranged to bring out the interesting fact that all eight techniques in the first column are actually comparable with each other. Their structuples form a perfect scale, or chain, in the partly ordered Cartesian space. For example, MAPS is less projective than Psychodrama because, although both are the same on the facets of $ABCDEGH$, MAPS is lower on F. Similarly, TAT is less projective than MAPS: both are the same on $CDEFGH$, but TAT is less than MAPS on A and B. And so on down the column. Symbolically, we may write, with respect to degree of projectiveness of these eight techniques, that

$$I > II > IV > V > VII > VIII > IX > XI,$$

where the Roman numerals are those assigned to the techniques in Table 1.

In the second column of Table 1 are listed three techniques that, although comparable to each other, are not comparable to any of the techniques in the first column, except for the highest and lowest (the latter are always comparable with all structuples in any partial order). Together with the two most extreme techniques, the second column forms another perfect scale, with the ordering

$$I > III > VI > X > XI.$$

A way of portraying the complete partial order of the eleven techniques simultaneously is shown in Figure 1. Tests I and XI are at the extremes of the diagram and are comparable to all other tests. Descending line segments connect comparable tests, the transitivity of comparability being indicated by the fact that any two comparable tests are connected by a sequence of descending line segments.

The relative heights of the tests in the two vertical arms or scales of Figure 1 were fixed by considering their relative scale ranks in departing from Psychodrama. A simple technical way of doing this is to assign scores —*joint* scores in the language of POSA—to the structuples by merely adding up the subscripts of their components. Thus Psychodrama gets a joint score of 8 (all its eight subscripts equal 1), MAPS a joint score of 9, Draw-

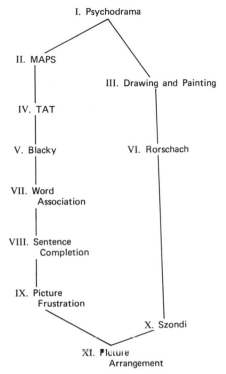

Figure 1.   The partial order of the eleven projective techniques.

ing and Painting a joint score of 11, and so on, down to Picture Arrangement with a joint score of 23. Such a scoring ensures a proper ranking
within any perfect scale of the partial order. There is nothing in the partial
order *per se,* however, that says this is a proper way for comparing *across*
scales. For this purpose, *lateral* scoring is needed, and there are not enough
structuples here (eleven is too few) for a stable multidimensional POSA
analysis.

We content ourselves here, then, with regarding Figure 1 as suggestive
of an appropriate portrayal of the similarities and differences among the
eleven projective techniques with respect to the partly ordered concept of
"projectiveness." As remarked before, Table 1 was arranged to correspond
to Figure 1.

Completing the Space of Projective Techniques

Although we started with a list of only eleven projective techniques, we
have wound up with a Cartesian space *ABCDEFGH* which has $2 \times 3 \times$

$3 \times 3 \times 2 \times 5 \times 3 \times 2 = 3240$ structuples (the product of the respective numbers of elements in all facets). Clever psychologists can undoubtedly devise further projective techniques, one for each of the remaining $3240 - 11 = 3229$ not listed by Lindzey. Indeed, even more than this should be possible, for more refined elements could be used for each of our eight facets, and further facets might be added. The universe of projective techniques should be rich indeed.

This returns us to the clustering hypothesis for the techniques proposed by Lindzey. On the basis of his own analysis of the equivalent of Table 1, he suggested five clusters:

Cluster 1: Sentence Completion, Picture Frustration
Cluster 2: MAPS, TAT, Blacky
Cluster 3: Psychodrama, Drawing and Painting, Rorschach
Cluster 4: Szondi, Picture Arrangement
Cluster 5: Word Association

If we compare these proposed clusters with the configuration in Figure 1, we see that each is but a contiguous segment of the partial order. The proposal does not take cognizance of the blending of one "cluster" into the next. Indeed, the "clustering" is more apparent than real; for a small set of data, especially with as few as eleven points, there is no reliable mechanical way of discussing the presence or absence of clustering. A theoretical framework, such as that of ordered facets, is needed for a stable analysis.

The theoretical framework presented in this chapter, along with the analysis of the eleven existing techniques, suggests that it may be more appropriate to regard the space of projective techniques as partly ordered, but uniformly filled out and not "clustered." The present empty positions in the space may be filled in with further projective techniques.

The next question is: Given the *definitional* interrelations among the techniques in partly ordered *ABCDEFGH,* what are their *empirical* interrelations? If all the tests were administered to the same population, what would the structure of the interrelations of the results be? Before one can begin to answer such a question, it would be necessary to specify what one meant by statistical interrelationships. Here the problem of the undefined common range for items arises. As pointed out in the first two sections of this paper, progress has been made on the structural theory of attitudes (Elizur, 1970; Guttman, 1959; Jordan, 1969) and of intelligence tests (Guttman, 1965a, 1965b, 1970; Schlesinger & Guttman, 1969) by virtue of the basis of a common range for each of these areas. The problem of range remains for projective techniques.

Let us close with a remark on the ordering (within the domain) of the elements of facet *F:* "mode of response." Lindzey suggested no notion of order here, although he essentially uses this facet for determining his five clusters. We ourselves did not specify the order $f_1 > f_2 > f_3 > f_4 > f_5$ in advance, although we had preliminary ideas about this. The order adopted here is a result of a preliminary multidimensional scalogram analysis (GL MSA-I), which requires no *a priori* specification of order, and which showed the present ordering of the elements of this facet to be optimal for POSA of the projective techniques. Ideally, the concept of "projectiveness" should have been defined clearly in advance, so that the orderings within facets would also be done *a priori*. That this was not the case again reflects the absence of a basic definition of what is meant by the class of projective techniques. In this chapter, we have classified but have not offered a basic definition for such techniques.

ACKNOWLEDGMENT

This research was supported in part by the National Science Foundation of the United States Government, Grant No. GS-929 to the University of Michigan.

REFERENCES

Bloombaum, M. The conditions underlying race riots as portrayed by multi-dimensional scalogram analysis: A reanalysis of Lieberson and Silverman's data. *American Sociological Review*, 1968, **33**, 76–91.

Elizur, D. *Adapting to innovation: A facet analysis of the case of the computer.* Jerusalem: Jerusalem Academic Press, 1970.

Guttman, L. A structural theory for intergroup beliefs and action. *American Sociological Review*, 1959, **24**, 318–328.

Guttman, L. A faceted definition of intelligence. *Studies in Psychology, Scripta Hierosolymitana* (Hebrew University, Jerusalem), 1965, **14**, 166–181. (a)

Guttman, L. The structure of interrelations among intelligence tests. In *Invitational conference on testing problems.* Princeton: Educational Testing Service, 1965. Pp. 25–36. (b)

Guttman, L. The nonmetric breakthrough for the behavioral sciences. In *Proceedings of the Second National Conference on Data Processing.* Information Processing Association of Israel, 1966. Pp. 495–510.

Guttman, L. Integration of test design and analysis. In *Invitational conference on testing problems.* Princeton: Educational Testing Service, 1970. Pp. 53–65.

Guttman, R., Lieblich, I., & Naftali, G. Variation in activity scores and sequences in two inbred mouse strains, their hybrids, and backcrosses. *Animal Behavior*, 1969, **17**, 374–385.

Jordan, J. *Attitudes toward education and physically disabled persons in eleven nations.* East Lansing: Latin American Studies Center, Michigan State University, 1969.

Lindzey, G. On the classification of projective techniques. *Psychological Bulletin,* 1959, **56,** 158–168.

Lingoes, J. The multivariate analysis of qualitative data. *Multivariate Behavioral Research,* 1968, **3,** 61–94.

Schlesinger, I. M., & Guttman, L. Smallest space analysis of intelligence and achievement tests. *Psychological Bulletin,* 1969, **71,** 95–100.

Shoham, S., Guttman, L., & Rahav, G. A two-dimensional space for classifying legal offenses. *Journal of Research in Crime and Delinquency,* 1970, **7,** 219–243. Also in S. Shoham (Ed.), *Israel studies in criminology.* Tel Aviv: Gome Publishing House, 1970. Pp. 36–76.

Wollstein, S. Postpartum psychosis, nonmetric-epidemiological study in psychopathology. Unpublished dissertation for the Master of Public Health degree, Hebrew University-Hadassah Medical School, Jerusalem, 1968 (also to be published in the *Israel Annals of Psychiatry and Related Disciplines*).

Zubin, J., Eron, L. D., & Schumer, F. *An experimental approach to projective techniques.* New York: Wiley, 1965.

CHAPTER 27

Clustering Procedures and Application

HERBERT SOLOMON

Data analysis has undergone a resurgence in the last two decades. In the main, this is due to the advent and development of the electronic computer and its extraordinary capacity to ingest data and spew out its product in accordance with instructions supplied by the appropriate algorithm. The eager and sometimes voluminous collection of data by investigators of the late nineteenth century and first half of this century was denied the additional analysis it merited by the lack of a computer technology.

Scientists and scholars have long been concerned with "sorting things into groups," and this is one important aspect of data analysis. Under numerical taxonomy, we can list two objectives: (1) establishing clusters in the data, and (2) classifying the data into groups. The latter can be viewed as a subset of the former. In the former category, we require the data to produce both the number of groupings or clusters and the assignment of each element or individual to these groupings. In the latter category, the number of groups or clusters is predetermined, each group is labeled, and rules are desired on the basis of which an assignment of each element is made to one of the fixed groups. Classification procedures may also be termed assignment procedures.

It is not prudent to convey a sharp distinction between clustering and classification in an operational sense. If a classification procedure is not producing meaningful groups through the assignments that are made, then changes are called for—namely, revising the predetermined groupings either in number or in shape or both on the basis of the new information. This sequential revision of groups on the basis of the data available at any one time suggests that one is indirectly engaging in clustering procedures. On the other hand, it is desirable to keep in mind the conceptual differences

just mentioned between attempts at clustering and attempts at classification.*

DATA SUMMARIZATION AND REPRESENTATIONS

An essential step in numerical taxonomy is the representation of the
associations among the variables on which data have been collected. Among
other important steps, there are the processes of developing numbers to
measure phenomena, making decisions on the employment of nominal,
ordinal, or continuous data, and subsequent coding of these data for
analysis. In this chapter we do not review these issues, but we are mindful
of their impact on the data analysis that will undergo investigation. Thus
we return quickly to clustering and classification techniques and the basic
summarizations of data for these purposes.

There are several ways to begin the data summarization. All give a picture
of data interrelationship, but each offers special advantages to an investigator. One representation is that of the scatter matrix. Here we portray the
total scatter or dispersion displayed by n individuals or elements, each
measured on p variables (n points in a p-dimensional space), by a matrix
with p rows and p columns, where an element in the ith row and jth
column, say t_{ij}, is the sum of the n cross products of measurements (taken
around the mean) on variable x_i with measurements (taken around the
mean) on variable x_j.

If each element in the scatter matrix T is divided by n, the resulting matrix is the covariance matrix with cell entries s_{ij}, and we label this K. Now,

---

* Almost 20 years ago, I joined the Columbia faculty as a mathematical statisti-
cian with responsibilities in statistical theory and applications of statistics to a number of areas in professional education. Among my duties over a 6-year period was
service as a statistical advisor for a number of doctoral dissertations in psychopathology. Some of the statistical theory available for these investigations seemed rather
sterile. At that point in time, multivariate normal models for classification had been
developed by Abraham Wald; these were followed a little later by models from
T. W. Anderson, R. Sitgreaves, and others. However, these models were either too
unrealistic or too tedious to employ. Moreover, they did not directly attack the
clustering problem.

It seemed apparent, then, that the time for multivariate data analysis was at hand,
though it had to await further development of the fledgling computer then coming
upon the scene. Just about that time, I began to discuss these issues with Joseph
Zubin. Zubin had for some years been pushing clustering methodology that was
directly attuned to the problem at hand and had already developed some techniques.
In this chapter, I trust there is some response to the problems he and I discussed
during the middle 1950s.

if we also divide each element, s_{ij}, in K by the standard deviations of x_i and x_j, the resulting element, $r_{ij} = s_{ij}/s_i s_j$, is the correlation coefficient between x_i and x_j, and the resulting matrix is now the correlation matrix, which we label R.

An important advantage of T is the manner in which it can be decomposed into two matrices that are specially pertinent in clustering and classification studies. In a classification study, the n elements will be assigned to k predetermined groups. Each group with, say, n_i elements can be viewed as a universe with its own scatter matrix formed as before and labeled W_i. If we sum all the W_i scatter matrices, we obtain $W = \overset{k}{\underset{i}{\Sigma}} W_i$ and let this represent the within scatter or homogeneity of the groupings. Likewise, if for each of the k groups we compute the group mean (a p-dimensional vector where the rth coordinate is the mean value based on the n_r observations for x_r) and then produce the $(p \times p)$ scatter matrix for these group mean values, each taken about the grand mean value (a p-dimensional vector where the rth coordinate is the mean value for x_r based on all n observations) and then multiplied by the size of the group, we obtain a $(p \times p)$ matrix that we label B, for it expresses a measure of the "betweenness" or heterogeneity of the k groups. The central point in this development is the existence of the fundamental matrix equation

$$T = W + B.$$

This result suggests immediately an index by which classification (predetermined number of groups) can be evaluated and, by extension, a way in which clustering can be terminated at some cluster size. For any given data set, T is fixed. Thus measures of "groupness" or "clusterness" as functions of W and B are thrust forth for examination. An interesting discussion and applications of these measures are given in Friedman and Rubin (1967).

Thus far we have discussed some summarization of multivariate data in matrix form, either T (scatter), K (covariance), or R (correlation), and the kinds of grouping criteria that are suggested by the T format. Intuitively we see that any grouping criterion is a function of homogeneity within groups and heterogeneity between groups, and indices such as $|T|/|W|$, log $(|T|/|W|)$, and trace $(W^{-1}B)$ are specific quantities embodying these notions. We shall discuss other indices as we proceed, but each will be a function of homogeneity within groups and heterogeneity between groups in which attempts will be made to minimize the former, maximize the latter, or do both. For the correlation coefficient index, large values indicate homogeneity; small values, heterogeneity.

DISTANCE MATRIX

Another method of summarizing the data that is more appropriate on occasion is to find the distance between each pair of the n points in p-dimensional space. This leads to a representation in matrix form of an $n \times n$ matrix where each element in the ith row and the jth column, say, d_{ij}, is the distance in the p-dimensional space between the ith element or individual and the jth element or individual. All the elements in the main diagonal are zero. The distance matrix is akin to the correlation matrix in that both may be viewed as similarity matrices—the jumping-off place for clustering and classification attempts.

The decision as to whether correlation matrices or distance matrices are to be employed is usually determined by the problem at hand. If n individuals or n elements are to be grouped on the basis of p measurements on each, then the $n \times n$ distance matrix is the natural summarization; if the p measurement variables are to be grouped on the basis of the measurements on n individuals or n elements, then the $p \times p$ correlation matrix is the natural summarization of the data. The latter matrix is the natural beginning point in factor analysis, where parsimony in the number of latent measurement variables is the desired goal. We will return to factor analysis and its place in clustering in subsequent sections. In some taxonomic situations the question of which measure of similarity to employ, whether it is of the association or the distance type, will require some thought. Although we will touch on these points, these inquiries will not be featured in this exposition.

There still remains some discussion of appropriate distance measures. Because we will normally think of our data bases as n points in a p-dimensional space for clustering individuals or elements, the distance measures usually appropriate and available are Euclidean distance and Mahalanobis distance. The Euclidean distance between individuals or elements with respect to all p measurement variables may be written in vector notation as

$$d_{ij}^2 = (P_i - P_j)'(P_i - P_j),$$

where d_{ij} is the Euclidean distance between individual i and individual j, and P_i and P_j are column vectors, each with p rows listing the p measurements on the ith and jth individuals, respectively. The product of the difference row vector $(P_i - P_j)'$ by its transpose is a scalar. This is the distance function with which most of us are familiar.

The Mahalanobis distance may be written, in the notation above, as

$$_M d_{ij}^2 = (P_i - P_j)'W^{-1}(P_i - P_j),$$

where W^{-1} is the inverse matrix of $W = \overset{k}{\underset{i}{\Sigma}} W_i$ and W_i is obtained for each of the $i = 1, 2, \ldots, k$ groups by

$$W_i = \sum_{m=1}^{n_i} (P_{mi} - C_i)\,(P_{mi} - C_i)'.$$

Here C_i is the vector of means for group i.

Note that a grouping of elements is necessary to compute W_i and W. Thus the Mahalanobis distance takes into account the associations or interrelationships in the measurement variables. If two measurement variables are highly correlated, the Euclidean distance can be misleading because of the equal weight it imposes inaccurately on each measurement variable; but this will not be the case with the Mahalanobis distance. The Mahalanobis distance is more tedious to compute and for a long time was avoided for this reason alone, but the computer has brought it within reach. Actually, if each of the correlations between the measurement variables is low, the error in employing the Euclidean distance is not damaging. As a rule of thumb, correlations as high as .5 will not produce Euclidean distances that lead to operational difficulties.

Other distance measures appear in the literature. The Minkowski distance is the name applied to all distance measures of the form

$$d(i, j) = \left(\sum_{m=1}^{p} |x_{im} - x_{jm}|^n \right)^{1/n}.$$

We have discussed the case of $n = 2$. When $n = 1$, the label "city-block" distance is sometimes employed, and this may be relevant for some distance situations.

DEVELOPMENT

The major thrust of this exposition will be the application to some specific data sets of the concepts discussed previously and the development of several simple-minded clustering procedures. Before we get to the data sets, let us examine several clustering procedures. Recall that we are dealing with n points in a p-dimensional space and are trying to group the n points, except when we are interested in grouping the p measurement variables. In the former situation, we begin with an $n \times n$ distance matrix; in the latter, the $p \times p$ correlation matrix is the basic summarization. Conceptually we can list all the possible clustering configurations achieved by dividing the n points (individuals or elements) into k clusters, each containing at least one element. If for each clustering configuration an appropriate index for grouping could be computed (some have already been mentioned and discussed), we could then list and rank all the configurations by this index and select the best one. Operationally we could do this for each value of k, as $k = 1, 2, \ldots, n$. For example, $k = 1$ means putting all elements in one cluster, and $k = n$ means considering each point as a cluster with one element. However, this is an impossible task even for a computer when n and p are only moderate in size.

A TOTAL ENUMERATION PROCEDURE

In a paper by Fortier and Solomon (1966) an attempt was made for one specific data set to look into total enumeration of all clustering partitions and then to select the best clustering by the use of an appropriate index. The data set consisted of 19 socioeconomic measurement variables for which responses were available from approximately 225 individuals. The initial investigators of this study, Kahl and Davis (1955), were interested in replacing the 19 variables by a set of fewer measurement variables and intended to accomplish this by a cluster analysis of the data, employing Tryon's (1939) technique. In this technique, clustering is begun by inspection of the correlation coefficients to achieve an initial clustering partition, and the process ends after a number of iterations of the initial partitioning. Each iteration, including the first, is examined by an index that is essentially the ratio of the heterogeneity between groups and the homogeneity within groups, and the clustering (or iterations) stops when no appreciable gain is registered by the index. Note that inspection looms very large in clustering, and this has ramifications for computer usage.

This technique was employed, and the partitioning resulted in placing the 19 variables into 8 clusters. These appear in Table 1.

If we were to examine all possible partitions of 19 variables into 8 clusters, we would soon give up the attempt, for there are 1,709,751,003,480 distinct partitions. In addition we should also look at the partitionings obtained when 19 variables are allocated to $k = 2, 3, \ldots, 7, 9, \ldots, 18$ clusters; these numbers also would be most formidable. Actually the number of distinct partitions of n elements into k groups, say, $P_{n,m}$, is a Sterling number of the second kind and obeys the recursion formula

$$P_{n,m} = mP_{n-1,m} + P_{n-1,m-1}.$$

This permits easy construction of a table, and one appears in Fortier and Solomon for $m = 2, 3, \ldots, 18, n = 3, 4, \ldots, 19$.

To overcome the large universes generated by total enumeration of

Table 1. Clustering of the 19 Variables in Kahl-Davis Data by Four Procedures

Cluster[a]	Tryon's Method Variables	Fortier-Solomon C* Method	King Stepwise Procedure	Two-Dimensional Representation
1	12. Area rating 14. House rating	The same variables	The same variables	The same variables merged with 11
2	15. Subject's father's education 9. Subject's mother's education	The same variables	The same variables	The same variables merged with 13, 19
3	2. Friend's occupation 17. Wife's education	The same variables	The same variables	The same variables merged with 3, 8
4	4. Subject's occupation, Census 1. Subject's occupation, Warner 10. Source of income	The same variables	The same variables merged with 3,8,5,7	The same variables
5	16. Wife's father's occupation, North-Hatt 6. Wife's father's occupation, Census	Not a cluster	Not a cluster	Not a cluster
6	11. Census tract 18. Income	Not a cluster	Not a cluster	Not a cluster
7	3. Subject's education 8. Subject's self-identification	The same variables	See cluster 4 above	See cluster 3 above
8	19. Subject's father's occupation, North-Hatt 13. Subject's father's occupation, Census	Not a cluster	Not a cluster	See cluster 2 above

[a] The clusters are ordered by decreasing values of Tryon's index.

497

clustering partitions, Fortier and Solomon tried random sampling. Using a computer, they obtained 10,000 clusterings by unrestricted random sampling for each fixed size of number of clusters, $k = 2, 3, \ldots, 18$ (170,000 clustering configurations in all). These results were disappointing. In fact, the specific Kahl and Davis clustering result of 19 variables in 8 clusters, obtained through Tryon's method of constructing clusters sequentially, had a value for their clustering index larger than the best value of that clustering index obtained from our 10,000 partitions for $k = 8$. The clustering index employed was essentially the Holzinger "coefficient of belongingness," an index that measures the ratio of heterogeneity between groups to homogeneity within groups by employing the ratio of the average correlation of all pairs of variables that are in a group (over all groups) to the average correlation of all pairs of variables not in a group.

Fortier and Solomon (1966) proposed a new clustering index, which was employed on the Kahl-Davis data. It is developed in the following way. Let two variables be clustered if the correlation coefficient, say, ρ, is greater than some preassigned constant ρ^*. The gain (positive or negative) incurred by taking an action a could be expressed by $G_{ij}(a)$. Suppose we let $\rho^{*2} = .50$ for purposes of exposition, since $\rho \geqslant .7$ signifies a close relationship. Then we may write

$$G_{ij}(a) = (\rho_{ij}^2 - .5)[g_{ij}(a)],$$

where

$$g_{ij}(a) = \begin{cases} +1 & \text{if the } i\text{th and } j\text{th variables are put in the same cluster,} \\ -1 & \text{otherwise.} \end{cases}$$

Now we sum over all pairs, once a clustering configuration is fixed, and obtain a value, call it C, where

$$C(A) = \sum_{i<j} G_{ij}(a_{ij}).$$

Here a_{ij} is the specific action taken for the pair (i, j), and A is the matrix of those a_{ij}'s. Observe that some a_{ij}'s depend on others. For instance, if the pair (X_2, X_3) is in the same cluster and this is so for the pair (X_3, X_4), then the pair (X_2, X_4) is also in the same cluster.

Let us now consider as foci of clusters only the pairs where $D_{ij} = (\rho_{ij}^2 - .5)$ is positive, or, in other words, the pair of variables are closely associated. In this way we can eliminate a large number of clustering partitions from evaluation—those that should not be examined because they never could produce optimal values of the clustering index C.

For the 19×19 correlation matrix, the resulting D matrix has 16 positive values. This suggests an examination of from 1 to 16 clusters. There may be fewer than 16 clusters, as we shall see soon, even if we choose to include all 16 pairs in the analysis. Before we do this, a closer examination of the index C shows

$$C(A) = 2 \sum_{(i,j \in 8)} D_{ij} - \sum_{i<j} D_{ij},$$

where S is the set of pairs of variables that belong to the same cluster. Thus the critical quantity is

$$C^* = \sum_{(i,j \in 8)} D_{ij}.$$

This is so because $\Sigma_{i<j} D_{ij}$ is a constant for any fixed data set. It is the sum of the elements of the lower half of the D matrix, and each element is fixed when ρ_{ij} and ρ^* are given.

We would like C^* to be as large as possible, and we hope to achieve this maximum value by a quick selection of positive D_{ij}'s. In general, the choice of, say, r of the D_{ij}'s leads to $k \leqslant r$ clusters and to $s \geqslant r$ elements in the summing evaluation of C^*. If $k < r$, then $s > r$, since at least two pairs (three or more variables) are grouped together, introducing one or more new D_{ij} values.

In mathematical terms one must maximize C^*, but choosing the appropriate partition of the n variables into k clusters is a matter of judicious selection by inspection procedures rather than by algebraic techniques. For the data, the set of partitions to be investigated consists of all r pairs out of the 16 positive D_{ij}'s. Each time, D_{ij}'s will be chosen implicitly, and these must be summed together with the r D_{ij}'s already chosen. There are $\binom{16}{r}$ possible combinations for each value of r, and these represent a heavy work load for all values of r from 2 to 15. Nevertheless, this was done for all the combinations associated with each value of r from the data, and the maximum C^* was obtained for each r.

If we plot the maximum C^* as a function of r, we find for the data that the optimal value of r is 6 and for this data set leads to five clusters. The curve depicting max C^* as a function of r rises sharply as r increases, reaches a plateau, and then decreases sharply. Where the plateau stage is reached is where the marginal gain due to clustering no longer increases with added clusters, and this is the value of r that is optimal. This feature is typical of clustering indices when the optimal value of the index for each cluster size is plotted against the number of clusters. Five out of the eight clusters obtained by employing the Tryon technique are reproduced in this way. There is a striking resemblance between the two listings—one obtained by expertise and iteration, the other by strict enumeration of an admissible set of partitions evaluated by an objective index based on the gain (or loss) incurred by an assignment action of variables to a cluster.

A STEPWISE CLUSTERING PROCEDURE

The data set of 19 measurement variables can serve as a base for the examination of other clustering techniques, and we continue along these lines before examining other data sets. A rapid clustering technique has been provided by King (1966). It does not guarantee optimal or sub-optimal clusterings but is done rather quickly on a computer. When King applied it to the data, it provided clusterings very similar to the one produced by Tryon's procedure and to the cluster listing obtained from the C^* method. This is a staggering development because the computer time involved is infinitesimal for the King procedure, as contrasted with the Fortier-Solomon technique.

The technique proposed by King is a stepwise clustering procedure. This is its principal asset because it leads to a simple and quick algorithm that involves $(n-1)$ scannings of a correlation matrix based on n variables. At each scanning or pass, the variables are sorted into a number of groups that is one less than at the previous pass. In this way, we obtain $(n-k)$ groups of variables at the kth scanning. The $(n \times n)$ matrix can also be a distance matrix. In that case, we sort individuals or elements into groups.

The procedure operates as follows. We will employ the correlation matrix as our similarity matrix for expository purposes, and bring in the distance matrix when appropriate to highlight differences.

As a start, we can view the n variables as n groups, one variable to each group. Now we scan the correlation matrix for the maximum cell entry (naturally without regard to sign). In a distance matrix we would seek the minimum-distance cell entry. We suppose that the maximum correlation is between variables X_i and X_j, and label it $r_{i'j'}$. We place X_i and X_j in the same group, and we now have $(n-1)$ groups: $X_1, X_2, \ldots, (X_i, X_j), \ldots,$ X_{n-1}, X_n. This produces an $(n-1) \times (n-1)$ correlation matrix, all pairs of correlation coefficients over the original $(n-2)$ variables plus the correlations obtained by pairing each of these with the concocted variable, $X_i + X_j = Y_{ij}$. Essentially, we are representing the group of two elements by its centroid.

On the second pass of what is now an $(n-1) \times (n-1)$ correlation matrix, a third variable may join the group of two variables formed on the first pass if the correlation between it and Y_{ij} is maximum, or the maximum correlation value in the reduced correlation matrix may again involve two individual variables. Thus we would get either one group of three variables and $(n-3)$ groups each containing one variable, or two groups each containing two variables and $(n-4)$ groups each containing one variable. In either situation we merge variables and revise the correlation matrix as on the first pass. In the former case the centroid of the group of three variables represents its group, and in the latter case each group with two variables is represented by its centroid. Recall that we do not have to divide the sum of the variables by the number of variables to obtain the centroid because the correlation coefficient is invariant when one variable of the pair is always multiplied by the same constant.

Thus, at each pass, the two groups with the highest correlations are merged and the total number of groups to that point is reduced by one. After a variable has joined a group of variables, it cannot be removed from that group. In this way it is possible to miss an optimal grouping. This is very similar to selection of predictors in stepwise linear regression. It should also be mentioned that a group can lose its identity by merging with another group on a later pass. By the time all the scanning is completed, we have produced successively $(n-1)$, $(n-2)$, $(n-3)$, ..., 3, 2 groupings.

The clustering index employed by King for measuring the worth of the grouping is that of minimum correlation (or maximal distance) between the group centroids when the scanning has placed the n variables into two groups. King employed this clustering index in examining the $(n-1)$ scannings of his stepwise clustering procedure on the Kahl-Davis data. He then compared his results with those obtained with Tryon's method and with the Fortier-Solomon C^* method. In his article, we note that on his sixth pass he obtained 13 clusters that reproduce exactly the Fortier Solomon results if we count the isolates in their results as clusters with one member.

TWO DIMENSIONAL REPRESENTATION

We will employ this clustering technique on other data sets. As mentioned previously, however, we continue first with other clustering techniques that we will apply to the 19 socioeconomic variables in the Kahl-Davis data. At this point we turn to an older technique originally proposed for quite another purpose. Factor analysis was developed in the early years of this century to provide a conceptual model for mental measurement; this was the intent of Spearman, Thomson, and the early workers in the field. However, the extensions by Thurstone, Kelley, and others into multiple common factor analysis brought the technique somewhat afield from the designs of the initiators. Their work in multiple linear common factor analysis, coupled with Hotelling's (1933a, 1933b) fundamental papers on principal component solutions and the computational algorithm to make that method feasible, has brought us to what we term factor analysis today. In effect, what we now have is a research tool for achieving parsimony by expressing the total variation found in n correlated variables in terms of

$m \leqslant n$ orthogonal variables with the added hope that m is much smaller than n. Thus by factor analysis we secure another representation of the data; and if this can be done economically, say by reducing the n oblique dimensions to two or three orthogonal dimensions, the grouping of data becomes easier.

The advent of the computer has made it possible to perform principal component factor analyses rather quickly. A computer program for this technique exists in many computation centers. Even if the number of orthogonal dimensions produced by principal components is more than two, we can employ the first two dimensions to represent the data and measure the error in doing this. Principal component factors are produced in the order of their contributions to the total variation in these data—the first is the largest, the second is the next largest, and so on. Moreover, the contribution that the ith factor makes to the total variation is equal to the ratio of the ith largest eigenvalue of the correlation matrix to n, the number of variables. Thus, if we employ only the first two principal components, we know how much of the total variation in the data is still unexplained when the representation of n correlated variables in two orthogonal dimensions is attempted.

The Kahl-Davis data were subjected to factor analysis. A principal component solution was not attempted because the data correlation matrix is not positive definite. It was possible, however, to do a Thurstone centroid solution; this was followed by a simple structure rotation. The reader is referred to Thurstone's (1947) text for an account of these techniques. It suffices here to say that, once this is accomplished, the first two factor loadings (coefficients of the linear form in the m factors) can serve to represent the 19 variables. These are plotted on a graph in Figure 1. By eye, the points (variables) are grouped as follows: (11, 12, 14), (9, 13, 15, 19), (1, 4, 10), (2, 3, 8, 17); 7, 16, and 18 remain as isolates or groups of one element. Naturally we can still assign these to one of the four groups.

In Table 1, this clustering is compared with the Kahl-Davis results, the Fortier-Solomon C^* results, and the King stepwise clustering procedure results. There is remarkable overlap in the products of the four procedures. A glance at Table 1 demonstrates this phenomenon. It will be recalled that these procedures run the gamut from total enumeration (Fortier & Solomon, 1966) to stepwise procedures (King, 1966) to two-dimensional representation of 19 variables (factor analysis) to expertise followed by sequential modification (Tryon, 1939). All this suggests that for exploratory purposes an investigator should try the simplest or most economical procedure, since in many cases this will give meaningful clusters. These can then be adjusted by expertise, other methods, or both.

We have omitted a host of other methods that employ expertise in the

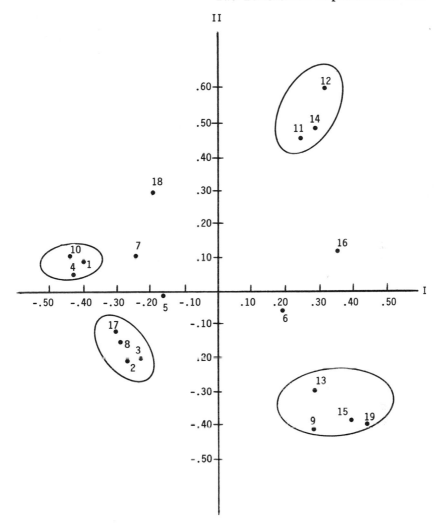

Figure 1. Two-dimensional representation of Kahl-Davis data.

clustering scheme. The methods that we have described in detail force the data to tell the clustering story. Thus we are captives of either the actual clustering configurations we are trying to assess from the data or the coarseness of the measurement variables, or both. Our exploratory clustering procedures can be viewed as providing an initial partitioning for those who then wish to employ their own knowledge or conjectures to modify the clustering configuration. There are several papers in the literature now available (and no doubt more will appear) that deal principally with sequential modification of a specific clustering partition. Each modification is checked by the value of the clustering index employed by the investigator, and naturally he seeks partitionings whose index values suggest that a good or optimal clustering has been achieved. As we mentioned earlier, we are not featuring any of these techniques in this chapter. For investigators who wish to begin with a partitioning and do not employ the techniques we have discussed in detail or do not attempt guesses, a random partitioning can serve as a beginning. Sequential modifications may take longer to achieve a desirable partitioning, but if several random starts lead in a majority of cases to the same or roughly the same clustering, one has more confidence in the results.

OTHER DATA SETS

Total enumeration (Fortier & Solomon, 1966), stepwise clustering (King, 1966), and factor analysis as a tool to achieve parsimony in data representation have been discussed in detail and applied to the Kahl-Davis data set of 19 socioeconomic variables. Each of these techniques relies only on the data to achieve a clustering partition, as contrasted with, say, the Tryon technique employed by Kahl and Davis, which employed sequential modification of an initial partitioning.

With the total enumeration results for the Kahl-Davis data set made available by Fortier and Solomon as a base, we noted that the King technique and the factor analysis approach gave very good results. This was also true for the Tryon procedure, but we emphasize the others because they rely only on the data and thus do not require any expertise except for the clustering algorithms.

Let us now examine two other data sets. In the spirit of exploratory analysis and because of limitations on space, we will report only on the employment of the King stepwise clustering procedure on these data sets. We will see how informative clusterings are obtained for each data set with a nominal amount of computer time, although the precomputer preparation effort may take some time, as it would, however, for any clustering procedure.

1. Eighty-two children under observation at the Aphasia Institute, Stanford School of Medicine, were placed in one of seven diagnostic categories by the staff. On the basis of 27 physiological, psychological, and biographical measurements of each child, the 82 children were clustered by King's stepwise procedure. In this case, the summarization was an 82×82 distance matrix. Each cell entry was the Mahalanobis distance in 27-dimensional space between a pair of children. From the clustering printout, it appears that there are two clusters of children. One contains those classified clinically

as 2, 3, and 6; the other cluster, those classified clinically as 1 and 7. The numbers of children in categories 4 and 5 are too small to give information. The seven categories are as follows:

Diagnosis	Number of Children
1. Mentally retarded	17
2. Severe hearing imparment	10
3. Neurologically handicapped/aphasic	30
4. Oral Apraxia	5
5. Dysarthric	4
6. Maturational lag	9
7. Autistic	7
	82

Thus it appears that the 24 children in categories 1 and 7 are alike, and the 49 children in categories 2, 3, and 6, are alike, a conclusion accepted subsequently by the staff as more in line with suggested treatment. This effort was aided in large measure by my colleague, Professor Jon Eisenson of the Stanford Medical School, who brought the data to my attention.

2. On the basis of 25 measurements each, 238 individuals convicted of first-degree murder in California over a recent 10-year period were studied to determine whether an association existed between the 25-dimensional description and the penalty decision that resulted in life imprisonment for 135 and capital punishment for 103. These 25 variables consisted of biographical information on the individual, description of the crime, and information on the defense counsel, the prosecution, and the judge. A King stepwise procedure was employed to cluster the 238 individuals and then to seek a substantive association, if any, between the characteristics of the individual, the characteristics of the crime, the judicial process, and the penalty decision. My thanks for the data under analysis go to several law review students at Stanford University, with whom I worked on this study. One of their major concerns was to see whether there was any association between the penalty decided upon by a jury, which under the law is given no instruction on the standards to be employed in reaching a decision, and the socioeconomic characteristics or the racial and ethnic background of the defendant. Either of these associations would be unconstitutional under the Fourteenth Amendment to the U.S. Constitution, a matter presently under review by the U.S. Supreme Court because of a petitioner who claims that standardless sentencing violates the Constitution. The clustering printout did not reveal any significant associations between the penalty and the background of the defendant—whether he was Black, Mexican-American, or White, or whether or not he was a blue-collar worker. At the 58th pass,

there was one significant group that contained 18 members all of whom had received the life penalty. As the number of passes increased, this group remained the principal group until the last few passes. At the 75th step the group contained 34 members, of whom 30 received life imprisonment. At the 100th step the group contained 42 life cases out of 62 members, and at the 125th step the group contained 63 life cases out of 102 members—a 62% to 38% composition that should be measured against the 55% to 45% mixture for all 238 cases. What we seem to be getting is clustering that indicates very little or no association of penalty with defendant and judicial characteristics. This also may have judicial implications, for it appears that a penalty jury is in effect tossing for each defendant a coin whose sides appear in a 55% to 45% mixture.

SUMMARY

Some of the theory and procedures of clustering either variables or individuals are developed and illustrated. Of the procedures presented, the stepwise method due to King seems to be the most preferable for exploratory analysis or for a first look at data. It does not guarantee an optimal clustering but has the decided advantage of requiring far less computer time than its competitors.

Its application to a problem in the clustering of variables (Kahl-Davis data) yielded clusters consistent with those provided by other procedures. Its application to a problem in the clustering of individuals (82 aphasic children) yielded two clusters that seemed to have clinical validity. Its application to another such problem (238 first-degree murderers) yielded clusters that indicated little if any association between a convict's racial, ethnic, or socioeconomic background or the characteristics of judge and opposing counsel, and the penalty decision arrived at by a jury.

ACKNOWLEDGMENT

This paper is a revised version of a talk given in Mamaia, Romania, in September, 1970, at the Anglo-Romanian Conference on Mathematics in the Archeological and Historical Sciences.

REFERENCES

Fortier, J. J., & Solomon, H. Clustering procedures. In P. R. Krishnaiah (Ed.), *Proceedings of the international symposium on multivariate analysis.* New York: Academic Press, 1966. Pp. 493–506.

Friedman, H. P., & Rubin, J. On some invariant criteria for grouping data. *Journal of the American Statistical Association,* 1967, **62,** 1159–1178.

Hotelling, H. Analysis of a complex of statistical variables into principal components. I. *Journal of Educational Psychology,* 1933, **24,** 417–441. (a)

Hotelling, H. Analysis of a complex of statistical variables into principal components. II. *Journal of Educational Psychology,* 1933, **24,** 498–520. (b)

Kahl, J. A., & Davis, J. A. A comparison of indexes of socio-economic status. *American Sociological Review,* 1955, **20,** 317–325.

King, B. F. Step-wise clustering procedures. *Journal of the American Statistical Association,* 1967, **62,** 86–101.

Thurstone, L. L. *Multiple-factor analysis.* Chicago: University of Chicago Press, 1947.

Tryon, R. C. *Cluster analysis.* Ann Arbor: Edwards Bros., 1939.

CHAPTER 28

The Analysis of Covariance in Psychopathology

JOSEPH L. FLEISS and JUDITH M. TANUR

Research in psychopathology must often, unavoidably, consist in the comparison of intact groups. For example, the only way known to compare schizophrenics with normal persons is to study a sample of available schizophrenics and to compare their data with those of a sample of available normals. No method yet exists for randomly assigning a given subject to one or the other of these two populations. Even if one did, the ethical implications of its use would be serious.

A recognized difficulty with the comparison of intact groups is that the samples invariably differ not only in group membership but also on many more factors that may be associated with the variable of interest. When a major confounding factor is quantitative, this variable is often used in an analysis of covariance ostensibly to determine, as McNemar (1962) puts it, ". . . what the result would be if the groups were made comparable with respect to the uncontrolled variable [p. 366]."

An Example

Consider, for example, the greater lengthening for schizophrenics than for normals of reaction time when a stimulus in one modality (light or sound) is preceded by a stimulus in the other. This phenomenon has interested investigators in the Biometrics Research laboratories for a number of years (Sutton, Hakerem, Zubin, & Portnoy, 1961; Sutton & Zubin, 1965; Kriegel, 1967).

In their later reports, these investigators have relied, often with the advice of the authors of this chapter, on analyses of covariance to compare schizophrenics with normals. The reasoning behind the use of this method of analysis is something like the following.

Define by ipsimodal reaction time the time that a subject takes to react to a stimulus which was preceded by a stimulus in the same modality, and by cross-modal reaction time the time that he takes to react to a stimulus which was preceded by a stimulus in another modality. For both individual normals and individual schizophrenics, a longer ipsimodal reaction time is associated with a greater lengthening of the difference between the cross-modal and ipsimodal reaction times. Schizophrenics have, on the average, larger cross-modal–ipsimodal differences than normals. But schizophrenics also have, on the average, longer ipsimodal reaction times than normals. The thought is that the analysis of covariance will succeed in determining whether the greater mean cross-modal–ipsimodal difference for schizophrenics is entirely a function of their longer mean ipsimodal reaction time.

Kriegel (1967) presents data on differences in reaction time between normals and schizophrenics for light and for sound stimuli. Here we consider data only for uncertain trials (those in which the subject was not told which stimulus to expect) and examine the cross-modal shift for light, that is, the difference between the reaction time to a light stimulus which was preceded by a sound stimulus and the reaction time to a light stimulus which was preceded by another light stimulus.

Nineteen hospitalized male patients diagnosed as schizophrenic by the hospital and 22 male control subjects presumed to be normal were studied. On the basis of information elicited during a standardized psychiatric interview, the sample of patients was divided into two groups, one consisting of 11 clear-cut schizophrenics and the second consisting of 8 patients who seemed not to be schizophrenic. The sample of presumed normals was likewise split into two groups, one consisting of 11 clear-cut normals and the other consisting of 11 subjects with some degree of psychiatric symptomatology. The summary data for the clear-cut normals and clear-cut schizophrenics are presented in Table 1.

The analysis of covariance table for the comparison of these two groups appears as Table 2. The algebra of the analysis of covariance is described in most textbooks treating statistics at the elementary or intermediate level (e.g., Dixon & Massey, 1957, Ch. 12; Edwards, 1966, Ch. 16; McNemar, 1962, Ch. 18; Maxwell, 1958, Ch. 8; Myers, 1966, Ch. 12; Snedecor, 1956, Ch. 13).

In brief, the analysis of covariance algorithm is as follows. Let Y represent the variable of experimental interest (also termed the dependent variable), and X the covariate or concomitant variable. In the example being considered, Y is the cross-modal–ipsimodal difference and X is the ipsimodal reaction time.

Table 1. Summary Data on Two Groups for Responses in Milliseconds to Light Stimuli during Uncertain Trials

Group	n	Cross-modal–Ipsimodal Difference (= Y)		Ipsimodal Reaction Time (= X)		Slope Within Group (= $b_{Y.X}$)
		Mean	Variance	Mean	Variance	
Clear-cut normals	11	4.91	84.6909	218.73	680.0182	0.0753
Clear-cut schizophrenics	11	32.09	1359.6909	274.91	3808.6909	0.0442

Table 2. Analysis of Covariance for Data of Table 1

Source of Variation	df	Sum of Squares — Y	Sum of Squares — X	Sum of Products — XY	Adjusted Sum of Squares — Y	df
Between groups	1	4,063.14	17,359.06	8,398.35		
Within groups	20	14,443.82	44,887.09	2,195.50	14,336.43	19
Total	21	18,506.96	62,246.15	10,593.85	16,703.96	20

$$F_{1,19} = \frac{(16,703.96 - 14,336.43)}{14,336.43/19} = \frac{2367.53}{754.55} = 3.14$$

1. Apply the full arithmetic of the analysis of variance to obtain sums of squares for Y. For example, since the overall mean for Y is 18.50, therefore the sum of squares between groups for Y is $11(4.91 - 18.50)^2 + 11(32.09 - 18.50)^2 = 4063.14$.

2. Apply the full arithmetic of the analysis of variance to obtain sums of squares for X. For example, since the overall mean for X is 246.82, therefore the sum of squares between groups for X is $11(218.73 - 246.82)^2 + 11(274.91 - 246.82)^2 = 17{,}359.06$.

3. For each source of variation specified in the analysis of variance table, calculate a sum of cross products using the formula for the corresponding sum of squares but, instead of squaring an indicated quantity, cross-multiply the indicated quantity in X and that in Y. Thus the sum of cross products between groups for X and Y is $11(4.91 - 18.50) \times (218.73 - 246.82) + 11(32.09 - 18.50) \times (274.91 - 246.82) = 8398.35$.

4. Identify the source of variation representing the hypothesis to be tested. Let H_{yy}, H_{xx}, and H_{xy} be the corresponding sum of squares for Y, sum of squares for X, and sum of cross products for X and Y, and let df_H denote the number of degrees of freedom in H_{yy}. In our example, these sums of squares and cross products are precisely the ones we just calculated, and $\mathrm{df}_H = 1$.

5. Identify the source of variation representing the error term for the hypothesis to be tested, that is, the row of the analysis of variance table providing the denominator of the F ratio for testing the hypothesis. Let E_{yy}, E_{xx}, and E_{xy} be the corresponding sums of squares and cross products, and let df_E denote the number of degrees of freedom in E_{yy}. In our example, the error terms are found in the row representing variability within groups. Thus $E_{yy} = 14{,}443.82$, $E_{xx} = 44{,}887.09$, $E_{xy} = 2195.50$, and $\mathrm{df}_E = 20$.

6. Using the quantities specified in step 5, calculate the adjusted sum of squares for error:

$$E'_{yy} = E_{yy} - \frac{E_{xy}{}^2}{E_{xx}}. \tag{1}$$

In our example,

$$E'_{yy} = 14{,}443.82 - \frac{2195.50^2}{44{,}887.09} = 14{,}336.43.$$

7. Using the quantities specified in steps 4–6, calculate the adjusted sum of squares for the hypothesis

$$H'_{yy} = (H_{yy} + E_{yy}) - \frac{(H_{xy} + E_{xy})^2}{H_{xx} + E_{xx}} - E'_{yy}. \tag{2}$$

In our example, the row representing total variability provides $H_{yy} + E_{yy}$, $H_{xx} + E_{xx}$, and $H_{xy} + E_{xy}$. Therefore

$$H'_{yy} = 18{,}506.96 - \frac{10{,}593.85^2}{62{,}246.15} - 14{,}336.43$$

$$= 16{,}703.96 - 14{,}336.43 = 2367.53.$$

8. Test the hypothesis by referring the quantity

$$F = \frac{H'_{yy}/\mathrm{df}_H}{E'_{yy}/\mathrm{df}'_E} \tag{3}$$

to tables of critical values of the F distribution with df_H and $\mathrm{df}'_E = \mathrm{df}_E - 1$ degrees of freedom, and reject the hypothesis if F exceeds F_α (df_H, df'_E), the critical value for a significance level of α. In our example, $\mathrm{df}'_E = 20 - 1 = 19$, and

$$F = \frac{2367.53/1}{14{,}336.43/19} = \frac{2367.53}{754.55} = 3.14.$$

The critical value for a significance level of 0.05 is 4.38 for 1 and 19 degrees of freedom. Since the calculated F ratio is less than the critical value, we cannot reject the hypothesis.

We have not yet specified just what the hypothesis was that was being tested. A frequent statement of the hypothesis is something like this: "The mean group differences on Y are zero when the group means on X are made equal." Another statement of the hypothesis is: "The group means on Y, after adjustment for mean differences on X, are equal." In the sequel we shall present criticisms of these and other statements of the hypothesis underlying the application of the analysis of covariance to the comparison of different intact groups. We shall show that, for what seems to be the only logical statement of the hypothesis in the context of research in psychopathology, a research strategy and a method of analysis quite different from those usually employed are necessary.

In the next section we shall review some of the uses of the analysis of covariance, and discuss some of the assumptions underlying its application. In the third section we shall consider in some detail the logic of attempting, by means of a statistical procedure such as the analysis of covariance, to undo the effects of the uncontrolled composition of different groups. We shall conclude that no amount of statistical manipulation can tell one what might have been had certain differences been nonexistent. In the final section, we shall present an alternative approach to the comparison of intact groups and shall illustrate its use on the example just given.

THE USES AND ASSUMPTIONS OF THE ANALYSIS OF COVARIANCE

The analysis of covariance was first introduced to statistical practitioners in general by R. A. Fisher (1932) and to statistical practitioners in psychopathology by Joseph Zubin (Garrett & Zubin, 1943). Since its introduction, several logically distinct uses of the analysis of covariance have become recognized. Its most frequent application in psychopathology is as an adjunct to experimental design. Randomization is employed to assign treatments to experimental units; the covariate is unaffected by treatments (this is most often assured by measuring X before the administration of treatment); and the analysis of covariance is employed to increase experimental precision by removing from the error term, E_{yy}, that part of the residual variability in Y linearly predictable from X. This use is described by Edwards (1966, Ch. 16) and Myers (1966, Ch. 12), among others.

Uses of the Analysis of Covariance

The use of the analysis of covariance in multivariate analysis to assess the significance of the added contribution of Y to the discriminant function defined by X is described by Rao (1966, especially the discussion of the hypothesis H_{02}). Its use in providing an unbiased analysis of the data from a design balanced except for a datum being missing is due to Bartlett (1937).

In this chapter, only the following frequent and controversial use of the analysis of covariance in psychopathology is discussed in any detail. Interest often resides in a comparison of the mean values of Y for different intact groups (e.g., normal children versus mental retardates, or normal subjects versus schizophrenics). Measurements are available on a variable X which is correlated with Y within each group and which varies in mean value across the different groups. The analysis of covariance is employed to determine whether the group differences on Y would diminish to insignificance if the group differences on X were statistically eliminated.

It is solely in the context of this use that McNemar (1962, Ch. 18) and Maxwell (1958, Ch. 8), for example, describe the analysis of covariance. McNemar even goes so far as to suggest: "But, if . . . there is only a small, chance difference between the groups on the uncontrolled variable [here denoted as X], the use of the covariance adjustment may not be worth the effort [p. 372]." This suggestion would rule out the first use outlined above, for in the case of treatments assigned randomly to experimental units any group differences on X would necessarily be a result only of chance. Since the first use has an unimpeachable logical basis (Cochran, 1957), Mc-Nemar's advice seems ill founded.

Assumptions Underlying the Analysis of Covariance

Before discussing the use of the analysis of covariance with intact groups, some comments seem in order concerning the assumptions underlying any application of the method. Most of the textbooks cited above mention the assumptions of independence of observations on different experimental units, of linear regression with the same slope for each group, and of equal variability within each group about the group's own regression line. Elsewhere in the literature, other assumptions are erroneously postulated for the analysis of covariance. Since these errors may result in misinterpretations of the results of an analysis of covariance, or in failure to apply the technique when it is indeed appropriate, we shall attempt to correct some of them.

Evans and Anastasio (1968) and Werts and Linn (1969), for example, state that the analysis of covariance is inapplicable whenever the slope of the straight line fitted to the pairs of group means,

$$b_H = \frac{H_{xy}}{H_{xx}}, \tag{4}$$

is different from the average slope of the straight lines fitted to pairs of individual values within groups,

$$b_E = \frac{E_{xy}}{E_{xx}}. \tag{5}$$

That this statement is invalid may be seen from an algebraic result presented by Smith (1957). He showed that the adjusted sum of squares for the hypothesis presented in Equation 2 is algebraically equivalent to

$$H'_{yy} = \left(H_{yy} - \frac{H^2_{xy}}{H_{xx}} \right) + \frac{H_{xx}E_{xx}}{H_{xx} + E_{xx}} (b_H - b_E)^2 \tag{6}$$

$$= T_1 + T_2,$$

say. The term T_1 measures the variability of the mean Y's about the straight line fitted to the group means. The term T_2 measures the difference between the two slopes.

Consider, now, the case of a number of individuals measured on X and randomly assigned to two groups, with each group then given a different treatment. In this case of only two groups, the term T_1 is identically zero, for two pairs of means determine a straight line perfectly. The only way for a significant difference between the two treatments to be declared is, then, for the term T_2 to be significant. But, if T_2 is significant, the authors just cited would declare the analysis of covariance invalid because of the failure of a presumed assumption. One is left with a paradox. If these authors are correct, then the only way for the analysis of covariance on two groups to be valid is for the treatments to be judged not to differ significantly. Therefore the analysis of covariance can never be used to detect a difference between two treatments.

A similar kind of paradox exists for more than two treatments, for the assumption that $b_H = b_E$ is equivalent to the assumption that a specifiable contrast in the treatment means must be zero, no matter what the treatments are. The source of the paradox is easily identified: the requirement that $b_H = b_E$ is not necessary for the validity of the analysis of covariance.

A second misconception reported in the literature will be cited. Winer (1962) states that "if the covariate is not affected by the treatments, it is reasonable to expect that the between-class regression will . . . be linear [p. 587]." If the between-class regression is found to be nonlinear, Winer contends that "interpretation of the adjusted treatment means becomes difficult [p. 588]."

If Winer is correct, then, even when all assumptions of the analysis of covariance are satisfied, and even when the treatments differ, the term T_1 in Equation 6, which measures the departures of the mean Y's from their own line, should be insignificant. But, if there are in general p treatments, T_1 accounts for fully $(p - 2)$ of the $(p - 1)$ degrees of freedom for comparing treatments. Thus, if Winer is correct, the only way for one to conclude that the treatments differ, without at the same time bringing into question the appropriateness of the analysis of covariance, is for T_2, but not T_1, to be significant. The unreasonableness of basing a comparison of p treatments on a term, T_2, with only a single degree of freedom (implying that a single contrast is sufficient to summarize all treatment differences) indicates that Winer's concern about the meaning of the significance of T_1 is unfounded.

THE ANALYSIS OF COVARIANCE IN COMPARING INTACT GROUPS

We now consider in some detail the use of the analysis of covariance in an attempt to undo built-in differences among intact groups.

Criticisms in the Literature

Caution against this use of the analysis of covariance has been counselled by many authors. Cochran (1957, p. 264) and Winer (1962, p. 580), for example, warn that the analysis of covariance may result in biased comparisons in that it may underestimate differences among groups.

The problem is that one usually knows only what the data show: that X and Y are correlated within each group, and that the groups differ in their mean levels of X as well as in their mean levels of Y. What the data cannot show is whether one's value of X precedes or follows, in a sequence of cause and effect, the group to which one belongs. If group membership causally influences one's value of X, and if one's value of X causally influences one's value of Y, then the analysis of covariance will indeed underestimate the effect of group membership on Y. Meehl (1969), by citing a number of examples, makes the point quite cogently that one must know (not merely believe) what the sequence of cause and effect is before using concomitant variables for so-called statistical control.

Kahneman (1965) has shown how unreliability in measuring the covariate may result in biased comparisons, with group differences being overestimated. Anderson and Bancroft warn throughout their chapter on the analysis of covariance (1952, Ch. 21), and Smith warns throughout his paper (1957), that the method is not to be applied to the comparison of intact groups whenever X is measured with error.

The problem is that the slope estimated from pairs of individual values within groups, b_E (see Equation 5), has its denominator but not its numerator systematically inflated by a multiple of the squared standard error of measurement of X. The slope estimated from the pairs of group means, b_H (see Equation 4), on the other hand, is relatively unaffected by errors in measuring X, because taking average values of X across the different subjects within the various groups reduces unreliability. The consequence is that the component T_2 of the adjusted sum of squares for groups (see Equation 6) is systematically too large, resulting in increased chances of falsely rejecting the null hypothesis.

Almost every variable studied in psychopathology, including observed overt behavior, intelligence, socioeconomic status, and reaction time, is measured with some degree of unreliability. The sources of unreliability are numerous and thus not easily controlled: there are inevitable errors of measurement, and, with respect to a subject's behavior, there is the phenomenon that the subject himself will vary from hour to hour and from day to day.

An unbiased large-sample procedure due to Lord (1960) may be employed when duplicate determinations are made on the covariate, but the procedure has been developed only for the case of two groups. No procedure seems yet to have been suggested for the case of only a few repeat measurements when more than two groups are being compared. Only when many repeat determinations have been taken, over many points in time, is the standard method of analysis, with the mean of these repeat determinations serving as the covariate, valid.

The overwhelming weight of logic is on the side of those who warn that neither the analysis of covariance nor any other statistical technique can undo systematic differences which were out of the investigator's control. Lord (1967, 1969) and Meehl (1969) elaborate on a simple statement of the problem by Anderson (1963): "One may well wonder what exactly it means to ask what the data would be like if they weren't what they are [p. 170]."

A Model for Which the Analysis of Covariance Is Valid: Collinearity

It would appear from the foregoing criticisms that it is the *method* of the analysis of covariance which is invalid for comparing intact groups. This is not necessarily so. Rather, it is the assumed model and the phrasing of the hypotheses and of the inferences which are usually invalid.

Let us, for later comparative purposes, consider first the case where randomization is possible. We will assume that each of p groups is assembled by assigning to it a random sample of n out of a total of np subjects. If X represents the value on the covariate, assumed to be measured before the imposition of treatment, and if Y represents the value on the dependent variable, then the model equation representing the effect of X on Y to be expected before any treatments are imposed is

$$Y_k = \mu + \beta(X_k - \overline{X}_.) + e_k; \quad k = 1, \ldots, np. \tag{7}$$

The parameter μ represents the grand mean of Y; β represents the slope of the line associating Y with X; $\overline{X}_.$ is the mean value of X; and e_k represents a residual random variable with mean 0, constant variance for all k, and all residual terms mutually independent.

In the presence of treatment effects, cognizance must be taken in the notation of the p treatments groups and of the n different subjects in each group. If we let the subscript i denote groups and the subscript j denote subjects, the model equation of the analysis of covariance is given by

$$Y_{ij} = \mu + \alpha_i + \beta(X_{ij} - \overline{X}_{..}) + e_{ij}; \quad i = 1, \ldots, p; j = 1, \ldots, n. \tag{8}$$

The parameters μ and β and the random variables $\{e_{ij}\}$ represent the same components as in Equation 7, $\overline{X}_{..}$ is the mean value of $X (= \overline{X}_.$ of Equation 7), and α_i represents the effect added to μ by the ith treatment.

The least squares estimate (also termed the adjusted estimate) of the mean response to the ith treatment is

$$(\widehat{\mu + \alpha_i}) = \overline{Y}_{i.} - b(\overline{X}_{i.} - \overline{X}_{..}). \tag{9}$$

Here $\overline{X}_{i.}$ and $\overline{Y}_{i.}$ are the mean values of X and Y for the ith treatment, and b is the slope estimated from the row of the analysis of covariance table representing variability within groups, that is, b is equal to b_E (see Equation 5). The hypothesis to be tested is that the treatments are equally effective, or equivalently that $\alpha_1 = \ldots = \alpha_p$. The statistic used for testing this hypothesis is the F ratio resulting from the analysis of covariance (see Equation 3).

Totally different from the development above is that for the case of p intact groups. With respect to the model equation, to begin with, all one can usually assume is that, within each of the p groups, Y is linearly associated with X by means of a slope which is constant across groups:

$$Y_{ij} = \mu_i + \beta(X_{ij} - \overline{X}_{i.}) + e_{ij}; \quad i = 1, \ldots, p; j = 1, \ldots, n. \tag{10}$$

The parameter μ_i represents the mean value of Y in the ith group, and β and $\{e_{ij}\}$ represent what they did above. The important distinction between Equations 8 and 10 is that in the former the effect of X on Y is properly represented as a function of how far any single value of X is from the overall mean of X, $\overline{X}_{..}$, whereas in the latter the effect of X on Y depends on how far an individual value of X is from the mean value of X for that particular group.

The least squares estimate of the assumed common slope is as before, but that of the mean for the ith group is merely

$$\mu_i = \overline{Y}_{i.}. \tag{11}$$

The so-called adjusted mean given by Equation 9 has absolutely no meaning in the context of p intact groups. Unlike the case for the first model, here the overall mean, $\overline{X}_{..}$, is a function of which groups were chosen for inclusion in the study. The vacuousness of estimating a given group's mean as a value depending on what the other $(p - 1)$ groups were is obvious.

The only hypothesis which may reasonably be tested in the context of the second model is that the group means are *collinear* with the regression lines within the groups, that is, that the group means on Y are linearly related to the group means on X with the same slope, β, as is assumed to apply to the regression line within each group. The formal statement of the hypothesis is

$$\mu_i - \mu_k = \beta(\overline{X}_{i.} - \overline{X}_{k.}) \quad \text{for all } i \text{ and } k. \tag{12}$$

The test of this hypothesis is provided by the F ratio given in Equation 3.

It is unfortunate in some respects that this test is identical to the test of the hypothesis for the first model, because the inferences and subsequent multiple comparisons are totally different. For example, failure to reject the hypothesis implies in the first model that the effects of p treatments might be the same, but implies in the second not at all that the p groups might be the same, but rather that all the data might be arrayed along the same straight line, with distinctions among groups not affecting the association between X and Y.

Rejection of the hypothesis might well be followed up in the first model by applications of the Scheffé multiple comparison procedure (Halperin & Greenhouse, 1958) to any and all contrasts suggested by the data. Rejection might well be followed up in the second model, on the other hand, by an attempt to determine for which groups the pair of means is not collinear with the pairs of values within groups. The Bonferroni method of analysis (Miller, 1966, pp. 67–70) would be preferable to the Scheffé method in the second model unless the number of groups was very large (Dunn, 1961).

The Bonferroni method is applied as follows. The difference for the ith group between the observed and predicted means is

$$D_i = (\overline{Y}_{i.} - \overline{Y}_{..}) - b(\overline{X}_{i.} - \overline{X}_{..}), \tag{13}$$

with an estimated squared standard error of

$$s_i^2 = MS'_e \left(\frac{p-1}{np} + \frac{(\overline{X}_{i.} - \overline{X}_{..})^2}{E_{xx}} \right). \tag{14}$$

The quantity E_{xx} is the sum of squares for X in the row for variability within groups of the analysis of covariance table, and MS'_e is the adjusted residual mean square for Y, with degrees of freedom $df'_E = p(n-1) - 1$.

The significance of the departure of the means of the ith group from collinearity is tested by referring the quantity

$$t_i = \frac{D_i}{s_i} \tag{15}$$

to the t distribution with df'_E degrees of freedom. If α is the desired overall significance level, however, the test of the significance of D_i is made at a level of α/p, that is, using as the critical value the quantity

$$B = t_{df'_E} (\alpha/p). \tag{16}$$

Here B is the tabulated critical value for a significance level equal to α divided by the number of groups being studied. For values of α/p not tabulated, the following approximation is usually adequate:

$$B \doteq z_{\alpha/p} + \frac{1}{4df'_E} z_{\alpha/p} (1 + z^2_{\alpha/p}), \tag{17}$$

where $z_{a/p}$ is the value cutting off the fractions $\alpha/2p$ from the upper tail and $\alpha/2p$ from the lower tail of the standard normal distribution.

Comments on Collinearity

The phenomenon of collinearity is an important one in the social sciences, for it must often be determined whether the regression line fitted to pairs of group means (the so-called ecological regression) is the same as the regression line fitted to data within groups (see Goodman, 1959). Social scientists are often interested in whether the ecological regression can be used for making inferences about the regression within groups, so that the model just given for the analysis of covariance may be a useful one. If collinearity has been established for a particular pair of variables, an investigator may well be justified in assuming collinearity for similar variables and thus in using an available regression line between groups to represent an unavailable regression line within groups.

Such usefulness does not seem to extend to psychopathology, however, where interest seems instead to lie in the problem of whether the differences among the p groups on X somehow explain their differences on Y. The belief underlying the application of the analysis of covariance to such a problem seems to be that the natural state of affairs is that group means are arrayed along the same regression line as are individual values within groups. Thus, when the group means are found by a significant result in the analysis of covariance not to be so arrayed, the belief is that something worthy of especial note has been discovered. The fallacy here is that the assumption of collinearity as representing the expected state of nature is unfounded. The fact that unreliability in measuring X biases the slope within groups relative to the slope among groups is sufficient reason why observed collinearity is exceptional in psychopathology; there is no reason to expect that collinearity is a natural rule.

In the example of reaction time differences between normal persons and schizophrenics, and indeed with almost all natural phenomena, no model appears to be available for predicting group differences from individual covariation. This does not mean that one cannot study statistically the performance of schizophrenics relative to normals. What it does mean is that the regression within groups (and hence the analysis of covariance) is not relevant for such study.

A STRATEGY ALTERNATIVE TO THE ANALYSIS OF COVARIANCE

A research strategy radically different from the kind so far employed is necessary for determining whether a group such as schizophrenics behaves in a manner contrary to what would be predicted. The basis for the strategy to be suggested here is that predictability is to be determined, not by the performance of *individual* subjects, but rather by the average performance of many differing *groups* of subjects. To illustrate the principle, we consider again the example of reaction times used at the beginning of the chapter. The only logical way that seems to exist for the greater lengthening in re- action time exhibited by schizophrenics to be declared unusual and thus worthy of further study is for there to be fitted a well-defined regression line to pairs of means for many different kinds of subjects (normals, neurotics, depressives, etc.), all having in common the fact that they are not schizo- phrenic, and only then to find that the observed mean lengthening of reaction time for the schizophrenics departs significantly from that predicted by the fitted line.

The necessity for assessing the deviance of the pair of means for a given sample relative to the line determined for other pairs of means, but not to the regression within groups, has been pointed out by Smith (1957, p. 285 and Section 8) in the context of agricultural research and by Ehrenberg (1968) in the context of anthropometric research. The required statistical calculations are as follows.

Let $(\overline{X}_0, \overline{Y}_0)$ denote the pair of means for the group which is of research interest, and let $(\overline{X}_i, \overline{Y}_i)$ denote the pair of means for the ith group used in fitting the prediction line, $i = 1, \ldots, p$. The equation of the line fitted by unweighted least squares (i.e., ignoring inequalities in variances and in sample sizes) is

$$\overline{Y}' = \overline{Y}_. + c(\overline{X} - \overline{X}_.),\tag{18}$$

where $\overline{X}$ is the mean value of X for a group whose mean value of Y is to be predicted, and where

$$\overline{Y}_. = \frac{1}{p}\sum_{i=1}^{p}\overline{Y}_i,\tag{19}$$

$$c = \frac{\sum_{i=1}^{p}(\overline{X}_i - \overline{X}_.)(\overline{Y}_i - \overline{Y}_.)}{\sum_{i=1}^{p}(\overline{X}_i - \overline{X}_.)^2},\tag{20}$$

and

$$\overline{X}_. = \frac{1}{p}\sum_{i=1}^{p}\overline{X}_i.\tag{21}$$

The variability of the p means about their own regression line is measured by

$$s^2 = \frac{1}{p-2} \left[\sum_{i=1}^{p} (\overline{Y}_i - \overline{Y}_\cdot)^2 - c^2 \sum_{i=1}^{p} (\overline{X}_i - \overline{X}_\cdot)^2 \right], \quad (22)$$

with $(p-2)$ degrees of freedom.

The predicted mean value of Y when the mean value of X equals $\overline{X}_0$ is

$$\overline{Y}'_0 = \overline{Y}_\cdot + c(\overline{X}_0 - \overline{X}_\cdot), \quad (23)$$

and the discrepancy between the observed and predicted mean values of Y is

$$d = \overline{Y}_0 - \overline{Y}'_0 = (\overline{Y}_0 - \overline{Y}_\cdot) - c(\overline{X}_0 - \overline{X}_\cdot). \quad (24)$$

The squared standard error of d is

$$s_d^2 = s^2 \left[1 + \frac{1}{p} + \frac{(\overline{X}_0 - \overline{X}_\cdot)^2}{\sum_{i=1}^{p} (\overline{X}_i - \overline{X}_\cdot)^2} \right]. \quad (25)$$

The hypothesis that the mean for the group of interest lies on the same straight line as do the means of all the other groups studied may then be tested by referring the quantity

$$t_{p-2} = \frac{d}{s_d} \quad (26)$$

to tables of the t distribution with $(p-2)$ degrees of freedom.

Example

We failed, in the example at the beginning of the chapter, to find a significant difference for uncertain light stimuli between the clear-cut schizophrenics and the clear-cut normals by an analysis of covariance, with the difference between the cross-modal and ipsimodal reaction times being the dependent variable (Y) and ipsimodal reaction time being the covariate (X). We now proceed to make use of the data for all four of the groups found: the clear-cut normals, the questionable normals, the clear-cut schizophrenics, and the questionable schizophrenics.

The approach outlined in the previous section consists of fitting a straight line to the pairs of means for the three groups of subjects who are not clear-cut schizophrenics, and then determining whether or not the pair of means for the clear-cut schizophrenics falls on that line. The straight line fitted by unweighted least squares to the three groups of subjects who are not clear-cut schizophrenics is shown in Figure 1. The equation of the line is

$$\overline{Y}' = 11.90 + 0.1959(\overline{X} - 254.09). \tag{27}$$

The fit is seen to be an excellent one, with the variability of the three points about their own line being measured by a variance of

$$s^2 = 0.0530, \tag{28}$$

with 1 degree of freedom. The mean value of X (ipsimodal light) for the clear-cut schizophrenics is 274.91, yielding a predicted mean value for Y (cross-modal–ipsimodal difference for light) of $\overline{Y}'_0 = 15.98$. Since the observed mean value of Y for the clear-cut schizophrenics is $\overline{Y}_0 = 32.09$, therefore $d = \overline{Y}_0 - \overline{Y}'_0 = 16.11$. The squared standard error of d is

$$s_d^2 = 0.0530 \left[1 + \frac{1}{3} + \frac{(274.91 - 254.09)^2}{2955.00} \right]$$
$$= 0.0784, \tag{29}$$

so that the standard error of d is $s_d = 0.28$.

The value of the t ratio for testing whether the pair of means for the clear-cut schizophrenics lies on the line fitted to the other pairs of means is

$$t_1 = \frac{16.11}{0.28} = 57.55. \tag{30}$$

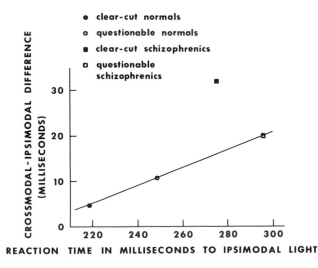

Figure 1. Straight line fitted to pairs of means for the three groups that were not clear-cut schizophrenics: $\overline{Y}' = 11.90 + 0.1959(\overline{X} - 254.09)$.

This t ratio, with but a single degree of freedom, is significant at the 0.05 level. The conclusion would be that the clear-cut schizophrenics have a mean cross-modal–ipsimodal difference in reaction time not predictable by their mean ipsimodal reaction time. The difference between the analysis of covariance performed at the beginning of the chapter, where significance was not found, and the regression analysis just performed, where significance was found, is that predictability in the former was determined by covariation within groups, whereas predictability in the latter was determined by covariation between groups.

SOME FINAL REMARKS

The analysis just described was haphazard: there was no original intention to have four groups to analyze rather than two, nor was any attempt made to have equal precision in estimating the mean values of Y. In the future, a more efficient approach would call for the identification of many of the factors that distinguish schizophrenics from normals: having a mental disorder, being hospitalized, having been treated with drugs some time in the past, and so on. Samples of subjects from groups defined in terms of various combinations of such factors would be drawn and studied. These samples would have one feature in common: they would all consist of subjects who are not schizophrenic.

After the variables were transformed so that a nearly linear relation could be fitted to all pairs of means (this is no mean task; some of the problems likely to be encountered are discussed by Ehrenberg, 1968), a sample of schizophrenics could be drawn and studied, and its pair of means examined in relation to the previously fitted line, as described above.

The validity of applying a t test to the ratio in Equation 26 is open to question. Strictly speaking, the procedure is valid only if the p groups used to set up the straight line are a random sample from some universe consisting of many potential groups. Since such a universe exists only hypothetically, the requirement of a random sample of groups can never really be met. Instead, one must be sure to select groups defined by the presence or absence of enough factors to assure that the variability of their mean responses is high.

Although the precisions of the mean values of Y do not enter explicitly into any of the calculations, it is desirable that they be equal. Otherwise, the estimates from unweighted least squares, although unbiased, are not as precise as possible. One way of assuring their near equality is to specify a desired standard error for each mean value of Y, say a, and then to continue sampling subjects from each group studied until the standard error of that group's mean, using the group's standard deviation in the numerator, becomes less than a. This sampling procedure introduces no bias in estimating the mean, since the sample mean and sample variance are independent for normally distributed variables.

The recalculation of the mean and standard deviation after a new subject is studied is simplified by the following identities. Let $\overline{Y}_{n-1}$ and s^2_{n-1} denote the mean and variance calculated for $(n-1)$ subjects, let $\overline{Y}_n$ and s^2_n denote the mean and variance calculated for n subjects, and let Y_n denote the value observed for the nth subject. Then

$$\overline{Y}_n = \frac{Y_n + (n-1)\overline{Y}_{n-1}}{n} \tag{31}$$

and

$$s^2_n = n(\overline{Y}_n - \overline{Y}_{n-1})^2 + \frac{n-2}{n-1} s^2_{n-1}. \tag{32}$$

ACKNOWLEDGMENT

This work was supported in part by grant MH 08534 from the National Institute of Mental Health.

REFERENCES

Anderson, N. H. Comparison of different populations: Resistance to extinction and transfer. *Psychological Review,* 1963, **70,** 162–179.

Anderson, R. L., & Bancroft, T. A. *Statistical theory in research.* New York: McGraw-Hill, 1952.

Bartlett, M. S. Some examples of statistical methods of research in agriculture and applied biology. Supplement to the *Journal of the Royal Statistical Society,* 1937, **4,** 137–169.

Cochran, W. G. Analysis of covariance: Its nature and uses. *Biometrics,* 1957, **13,** 261–281.

Dixon, W. J., & Massey, F. J. *Introduction to statistical analysis* (2nd ed.) New York: McGraw-Hill, 1957.

Dunn, O. J. Multiple comparisons among means. *Journal of the American Statistical Association,* 1961, **56,** 52–64.

Edwards, A. L. *Experimental design in psychological research.* New York: Holt, Rinehart & Winston, 1966.

Ehrenberg, A. S. C. The elements of lawlike relationships. *Journal of the Royal Statistical Society,* Series A, 1968, **131,** 280–302.

Evans, S. H., & Anastasio, E. J. Misuse of analysis of covariance when treatment effect and covariate are confounded. *Psychological Bulletin,* 1968, **69,** 225–234.

Fisher, R. A. *Statistical methods for research workers* (4th ed.) Edinburgh: Oliver and Boyd, 1932.

Garrett, H. E., & Zubin, J. The analysis of variance in psychological research. *Psychological Bulletin*, 1943, **40**, 233–267.

Goodman, L. A. Some alternatives to ecological correlation. *American Journal of Sociology*, 1959, **64**, 610–625.

Halperin, M., & Greenhouse, S. W. A note on multiple comparisons for adjusted means in the analysis of covariance. *Biometrika*, 1958, **45**, 256–259.

Kahneman, D. Control of spurious association and the reliability of the controlled variable. *Psychological Bulletin*, 1965, **64**, 326–329.

Kriegel, J. *Reaction time in schizophrenics and normals as a function of stimulus uncertainty, guessing, and modality shift.* (Doctoral dissertation, Columbia University) Ann Arbor, Mich.: University Microfilms, 1967. No. 67-15,496.

Lord, F. M. Large-sample covariance analysis when the control variable is fallible. *Journal of the American Statistical Association*, 1960, **55**, 307–321.

Lord, F. M. A paradox in the interpretation of group comparisons. *Psychological Bulletin*, 1967, **68**, 304–305.

Lord, F. M. Statistical adjustments when comparing preexisting groups. *Psychological Bulletin*, 1969, **72**, 336–337.

McNemar, Q. *Psychological statistics* (3rd ed.) New York: Wiley, 1962.

Maxwell, A. E. *Experimental design in psychology and the medical sciences.* London: Methuen, 1958.

Meehl, P. E. Nuisance variables and the ex post facto design. Report No. PR-69-4, Research Laboratories of the Department of Psychiatry, University of Minnesota, 1969.

Miller, R. G. *Simultaneous statistical inference.* New York: McGraw-Hill, 1966.

Myers, J. L. *Fundamentals of experimental design.* Boston: Allyn and Bacon, 1966.

Rao, C. R. Covariance adjustment and related problems in multivariate analysis. In P. R. Krishnaiah (Ed.), *Multivariate analysis.* New York: Academic Press, 1966. Pp. 87–103.

Smith, H. F. Interpretation of adusted treatment means and regressions in analysis of covariance. *Biometrics*, 1957, **13**, 282–308.

Snedecor, G. W. *Statistical methods.* (5th ed.) Ames: Iowa State College Press, 1956.

Sutton, S., Hakerem, G., Zubin, J., & Portnoy, M. The effect of shift of sensory modality on serial reaction time: A comparison of schizophrenics and normals. *American Journal of Psychology*, 1961, **74**, 224–232.

Sutton, S., & Zubin, J. Effect of sequence on reaction time in schizophrenia. In A. T. Welford & J. E. Birren (Eds.), *Behavior, aging and the nervous system.* Springfield, Ill.: Charles C Thomas, 1965. Pp. 562–597.

Werts, C. E., & Linn, R. L. Considerations when making inferences within the analysis of covariance model. Research Bulletin RB-69-28, Educational Testing Service, Princeton, 1969.

Winer, B. J. *Statistical principles in experimental design.* New York: McGraw-Hill, 1962.

CHAPTER 29

Games as Tools in the
Study of Choice Behavior

ANATOL RAPOPORT

Experiments on choice behavior typically lead to inferences concerning the subject's preferences. If his choices completely determine the outcomes, then the only information revealed is about the subject's preferences among the outcomes. The situation becomes more involved and psychologically more interesting if the outcomes are determined not only by the subject's choices but also by some other circumstances. If these other circumstances are chance events, the subject's choices may provide information about his estimation of the probabilities of the chance events, about the differences between his degrees of preference for the outcomes, or about his propensities for taking risks, and so on.

Of special interest are choice experiments in which the outcomes are determined partly by the choices of one subject and partly by those of another (or others). If the set of choices and the set of outcomes are exactly specified, and if how the choices of all concerned determine the outcomes is known in advance to all, the choice situation is called a game. The choosers are called players.

PROPERTIES OF GAMES

The simplest possible games are those with two players, each of whom chooses between two alternatives. The so-called 2×2 games can be schematized in matrix form as follows:

$$C_1 \qquad\qquad C_2$$

	C_1	C_2
R_1	a_2 a_1	b_2 b_1
R_2	c_2 c_1	d_2 d_1

The general 2×2 game.

The first player, called Row, chooses between the upper and lower rows of the matrix. The second player, called Column, chooses between the left-hand and the right-hand columns of the matrix. The result of the choices is one of four outcomes of the game, represented by the four entries in the matrix. For instance, if Row chooses the upper row and Column the right-hand column, the outcome is the entry in the upper right-hand corner of the matrix. The entry is a pair of numbers, the lower left representing Row's utility for the outcome, the upper right Column's utility. Utilities are the player's preferences for the outcomes represented on an interval scale. In game theory, it is usually assumed that preferences can be represented as utilities. The corresponding numbers are called payoffs.

It is important to keep in mind that, when a game is represented by a matrix, the choices (of row or column) by the players are assumed to be made simultaneously; or (which is the same thing) each player chooses in ignorance of the other's choice. In most "real" games (so-called parlor games) choices are made consecutively and are called the moves of the game. Nevertheless it is shown in game theory that a game with a finite number of moves can be "collapsed" into a matrix representation, where the rows and columns represent single independent choices of each player. These choices are then called strategies.

A strategy, then, is essentially a plan of action, chosen in advance, which allows for every contingency that may arise in the course of the game. In game theory a "rational player" is supposed to be able to foresee all of these contingencies. In short, all two-person games can be represented by strategy matrices. The 2×2 matrix is the simplest of these matrices.

Assume that the preferences of the players for the outcomes can be represented by numerical payoffs. If the sum of the two payoffs is the same in all the entries of the game matrix, the game is called a constant-sum game. We can easily see that, in a constant-sum game, the more one of the players gets, the less the other gets (or the more he loses). Hence in such a game the "interests" of the two players are diametrically opposed to each other; the players are in conflict. If the sum of the payoffs is not the same in all entries of the game matrix, the game is caller non-constant-sum. In such a game, the interests of the players may be partially coincident and partially in conflict. Such games are sometimes called mixed-motive games.

Game theory can be defined as a theory of rational choice in conflict situations. That is, game theory undertakes to answer the question of how a "rational" player should choose among alternatives if the outcomes are determined partly by his choices and partly by the choices of other players whose "interests" do not in general coincide with his own.

A "rational" player is defined as one who (1) has well-defined preferences among the outcomes, usually expressed in numbers on an interval scale; (2) is aware of the payoffs that will accrue to him as a result of the simultaneous choices of strategies made by all players; (3) chooses in a way that will maximize his own payoff (without regard for the payoffs of others) under the constraints of the situation.

If the game is a constant-sum game with two players, then it is shown in game theory that a "rational choice" can be designated for each of the players. This "rational choice" has the property that no other choice can get the player in question a larger payoff, assuming that his opponent (the player with diametrically opposed interests in this case) will also make the prescribed "rational choice."

Two cases are distinguished. In one, the rational choice is a choice of one of the proffered alternatives. In the other, such a simple rational choice cannot be singled out. In that case, the rational choice is a probabilistic mixture of choices, a so-called *mixed strategy*. A mixed strategy is essentially a choice determined by chance, where the probabilities of all the proffered alternatives have been assigned. The rational, or optimal, mixed strategy then amounts to assigning a certain probability to each of the available alternatives. This optimal assignment of probabilities has the property that the statistically expected payoff to the player will be the largest possible, assuming that the opponent chooses *his* optimal mixed strategy.

Constant-sum games can be used to test the rationality of the players under the assumption that the payoffs represent the utilities of the outcomes. The relative frequencies of choices in repeated plays of the same game can be interpreted as estimates of the probabilities with which the strategies are chosen. Systematic discrepancies between the observed frequencies and the probabilities prescribed by optimal mixtures can be interpreted either as departures from rationality or as a refutation of the assumption that the payoffs represent actual utilities. In the latter case, attempts can be made to identify the "true" utilities associated with the outcomes of the situation.

If the former interpretation is adopted, the psychologist might look for factors in the players' perceptions to which departures from rationality can be attributed.

In the case of preference-ordered alternatives, a "rational solution" is clearly the choice of the most preferred alternative. For "risky" alternatives, a "rational solution" can be defined as one that maximizes expected utility. In regard to the choices that a player is faced with in a game of chess or bridge or poker, finding the rational solution may require considerable reasoning ability, and the factors involved in the player's success or failure may be of psychological interest. Nevertheless, in all of these examples involving a single decision-maker or two decision-makers with diametrically opposed interests, the "rational solution" is always there and provides a level of reference against which the subject's performance is to be evaluated.

In the study of non-constant-sum games, there is no such level of reference. The concept of rationality becomes bifurcated into "individual" and "collective" rationality. The choices dictated by each of these rationality principles are in general not the same. It is this ambivalence that provides non-constant-sum games with their rich psychological content.

The best example of a game that illustrates the conceptual complexities of non-constant-sum games is a 2×2 game called Prisoner's Dilemma. Its structure is exemplified in Game 1.

	C_2	D_2
C_2	1 1	10 -10
D_1	-10 10	-1 -1

Game 1.

From the entries in the matrix, it is clear that Row's "rational" choice is the lower row, D_1, and Column's rational choice is the right-hand column, D_2, because either player gains more or loses less if he chooses D, regardless of how the other player chooses. Such a strategy is called a *dominating* strategy. Two "rational" players are assumed, by definition of "rational player," to choose the dominating strategies D in Game 1. The outcome of these choices, however, shown in the box D_1D_2, is worse for *both* players than the outcome shown in the box C_1C_2. The game simulates a situation in which each individual pursues his "obvious" interest and makes a "rational decision"; yet each could have obtained a larger payoff if both had made the opposite choice. Dilemmas of this sort are, of course, common in real life. Formulating a simple game model of such a situation provides an opportunity to study the situation experimentally and to analyze results quantitatively.

Thus, on the one hand, the game can simulate a situation that touches on psychological matters "deeper" than the physiology of sensations, organization of perception, span of memory, or rote learning. On the other hand, the data can remain hard and strictly quantifiable. In this way, a research tool is provided for bridging the gap between "scientific psychology," in which only "hard," preferably quantifiable data are accepted as evidence, and "interesting psychology," which is concerned with attitudes, beliefs, motivations, social interactions, and the like.

That such aspects of decision are tapped by the game just described can be seen by analyzing the pressures presumably acting in favor of one or the other of the two alternative choices.

TYPES OF GAMES

To fix ideas, suppose that two subjects are playing the Prisoner's Dilemma game repeatedly, the outcome of each player being known to both. Suppose, further, that the outcome of a particular play is C_1C_2. The play continues. Row must decide whether on the next play he should choose C or D. If he reasons about the situation, his thinking may be somewhat as follows.

"If we both play C, we are both better off than if we both play D. Perhaps Column also realizes this and is prepared to play C. In that case, I should 'cooperate' and play C also. On the other hand, if he plays C, I could take advantage of it by playing D, thus getting 10 units of payoff instead of 1 unit. Moreover, Column may be already contemplating the advantage of playing D. If he does defect (plays D), I shall be the sucker, losing 10 points just because I trusted him. Should I not beat him to the punch and play D myself so that I will lose only 1 unit instead of 10?

"On the other hand, continuing to play C is advantageous to both of us. We can continue to play C only if we trust each other not to defect to D. Am I justified in supposing that he trusts me, and, if so, am I not better off reinforcing that trust by continuing to cooperate (play C)?"

At times, Row will continue to play C following the outcome C_1C_2. At other times, he may defect to D. We now denote by x_1 the conditional probability that Row plays C following C_1C_2. In symbols, $x_1 = P(C_1|C_1C_2)$.

An estimate of x_1 is the relative frequency of C choices by Row following the C_1C_2 outcome in the entire protocol of plays.

Similarly, we define:

$$y_1 = P(C_1|C_1D_2), \quad z_1 = P(C_1|D_1C_2), \quad w_1 = P(C_1|D_1D_2).$$

Column's conditional probabilities are defined analogously. Thus $y_2 = P(C_2|D_1C_2)$, and so on. Since Prisoner's Dilemma is a *symmetric* game, one that looks the same to both players, $x, y, z,$ and w have the same meaning when referred to Row's or Column's conditional probabilities of choice.

Each of these conditional probabilities represents a propensity of a player to play C following the particular outcome. The complementary probabilities, $\bar{x}_1 = P(D_1|C_1C_2)$, and so on, are, of course, the propensities to do the opposite. Each of the propensities has a different psychological flavor.

For example, x has some aspect of "trustworthiness," that is, the propensity not to defect in the pursuit of self-interest *after* mutually beneficial cooperation has been established.

Also, y has some aspect of "martyrdom" or, perhaps, of "forgiveness," for y is the propensity to *continue* to play C (to seek cooperation) even after one has been "betrayed" by the other. Of course, y can also be interpreted as "a tendency to try to teach by example" or as "an attempt to communicate to the other that one is willing to give him another 'chance' " or even as plain foolishness. The labels given to the propensities are merely suggestive. In no instance are they meant to convey the impression that they capture the "essence" of "trustworthiness" or "forgiveness" or whatever.

To continue, z can be interpreted as "repentance," the propensity to return to cooperation after one has successfully double-crossed the other. The conditional probability w can be interpreted as a propensity to *initiate* cooperation or, perhaps, as "trust," for it makes sense to choose C after the outcome DD only if one believes that the other player, too, "has come to his senses" and is likely to cooperate.

All of these propensities are pure numbers and raise no problem of "scaling," such as is frequently encountered in attempts to measure attitudes or preferences. The values of probabilities are absolute and can be meaningfully compared with each other. Thus, given a large number of responses, we are able to examine the "profile" of a subject population, which may be a manifestation of interesting psychological traits.

Let us now examine another 2×2 game almost, though not quite, as simple as Prisoner's Dilemma. Its structure is shown as Game 2.

As in Prisoner's Dilemma, a dominating strategy is available to both players. Row stands to gain more (or lose less) if he chooses S, regardless of how Column chooses. Column also stands to gain more, regardless of

$$S_2 \qquad\qquad T_2$$

	S_2	T_2
S_1	8 −½	−½ 8
T_1	−1 −2	−2 −1

Game 2.

how Row chooses, if he chooses S. If each chooses his dominating strategy, the outcome S_1S_2 obtains. As a result, Column wins 8 points and Row loses ½ point.

Imagine what might happen if this game is played repeatedly without communication. Row continues to lose, and there is no way he can improve his situation if Column stands pat with his strategy S. Row can, however, "take revenge" on Column by switching to T, thus making Column lose 1 unit in outcome T_1S_2. If Row does this, he himself suffers a loss of 2 units. Therefore, from the point of view of maximizing his own utility, the "revolt" is not justified. It may, however, have a long-range effect that will enable Row to get more. Column may not be pleased with the repeated outcome T_1S_2 even though Row loses more than Column does in that outcome. Column can get out of that situation by switching to T_2, thus effecting the outcome T_1T_2, but here Column gains even less (−2), and the outcome T_1T_2 gives Row the opportunity to switch to S_1. If Column does not at the same time also switch to S_2, S_1T_2 will result, in which Row gets his largest payoff (+8). After S_1T_2, however, Column has the opportunity to restore the status quo by returning to S_2 (provided Row does not at the same time switch to T_1).

In Game 2 it seems worthwhile for Row to let the game go through the cycle $T_1S_2 \rightarrow T_1T_2 \rightarrow S_1T_2 \rightarrow S_1S_2$ (assuming Column switches immediately or at least not too long after T_1S_2 occurs) since the losses in T_1S_2 and T_1T_2 will be more than compensated by the gain in S_1T_2. But it will not pay Column to go through the cycle. Column may, therefore, forestall the cycle by switching to T_2 before Row "revolts," thus "treating" Row to a share of the gain. In fact, if Row "submits" to Column, that is, continues to choose S_1, never defecting to T_1, it is up to Column to share with Row any fraction of the gain he chooses. He can share 50% by simply alternating between S_2 and T_2, or any other fraction from 0% to 100%, as long as Row submits.

In short, Column has complete control of the fraction of the maximum payoff (+8) that Row will receive. He fixes that fraction by apportioning his choices between his "selfish" strategy, S_2, and his "thoughtful" strategy,

T_2. Row, on the other hand, has a "threat" strategy, T_1, available against Column, which he can resort to if he is not satisfied with the way Column treats him when he (Row) plays his "safe" strategy, S_1. If Row resorts to the threat strategy, the result is costly to both players, but the very existence of this strategy may exert pressure on Column to share a "fair" fraction of the maximum payoff. How much is a "fair" fraction (i.e., one that will forestall Row's use of the threat strategy), to what extent the use of the threat strategy will induce Column to share more, and other questions of this sort can be answered "statistically" by examining the protocols of repeated plays of many subjects.

Let us now examine the propensities in the Threat Game, analogous to those in Prisoner's Dilemma. Since the Threat Game is not symmetric, there are eight instead of four propensities to examine:

$x_1 = P(S_1|S_1S_2)$, that is, the probability that Row chooses S following S_1S_2.

$x_2 = P(S_2|S_1S_2)$, that is, the probability that Column chooses S_2 following S_1S_2.

And, similarly,

$$y_1 = P(S_1|S_1T_2).$$

$$y_2 = P(S_2|S_1T_2).$$

$$z_1 = P(S_1|T_1S_2).$$

$$z_2 = P(S_2|T_1S_2).$$

$$w_1 = P(S_1|T_1T_2).$$

$$w_2 = P(S_2|T_1T_2).$$

As in the case of Prisoner's Dilemma, we can make conjectures concerning the psychological pressures reflected in these propensities. In some cases it will be useful to examine the complementary conditional probabilities, for example, $\bar{x}_1 = 1 - x_1$, and so on.

Consider first $\bar{x}_1 = P(T_1|S_1S_2)$. Its magnitude may be interpreted as the degree of Row's dissatisfaction with the outcome S_1S_2, that is, his propensity to "revolt." On the other hand, $\bar{x}_2 = P(T_2|S_1S_2)$ may be interpreted as Column's willingness to share with Row a portion of the maximum payoff or, alternatively, as the extent to which Column "appeases" Row, forestalling the latter's use of the threat strategy.

Next, y_1 may be interpreted as Row's propensity to allow Column to establish the status quo following S_1T_2, where Row gets the largest payoff.

y_2 is the propensity of Column to re-establish the status quo.

$\bar{z}_1 = P(T_1|T_1S_2)$ is Row's propensity to *persist* in using the threat strategy if Column does not "yield."

z_2 is Column's propensity to *resist* Row's threat (not yielding by a switch to T).

w_1 is Row's propensity to take advantage of Column's "yielding" to threat $(T_1S_2 \to T_1T_2)$ and so of obtaining the maximum payoff.

$\bar{w}_2 = P(T_2|T_1T_2)$ is Column's propensity to allow Row to get his maximum payoff after yielding to threat.

Once again, the analysis of the structure of the game is richly suggestive psychologically. At the same time, the interpretations are linked in all instances to concrete, easily quantifiable data (frequencies of choices).

In view of the very different structures of the two games examined, the question naturally arises how many "different" 2×2 games there are. Clearly, if the payoffs are given on a continuous scale, the number of games with different payoff configurations is infinite. If, however, the payoffs are given only on an ordinal scale, the number of games is finite, since in that case only the preference order of the payoffs determines the structure of the game. Assume that each player's payoffs are strictly ordered, that is, a player is not indifferent between any pair of payoffs. Two games are called strategically equivalent if one matrix can be transformed into the other by simply relabeling the rows, the columns, or the players. It turns out that there are exactly 78 nonequivalent 2×2 games.

These 78 games can be classified according to some general structural criteria. In some games, for instance, a dominating strategy is available to each player, and so a "natural outcome" can be singled out: how the players should choose if their choices are governed by the principle of maximizing their individual payoffs. In other games, only one of the players has a dominating strategy. Here also a "natural outcome" can be singled out: the player who has a dominating strategy chooses it, while the other player, assuming that the first will choose his dominating strategy, chooses the strategy that will maximize his own payoff. In a third type of game, neither player has a dominating strategy, and the "natural outcome" must be defined in some other way.

Another way of classifying the games is according to the way the interests of the two players are related. In some games, the most preferred outcomes of the two players are in the same cell of the matrix. Clearly, in games of this sort, the interests of the two players coincide, so that, even in the absence of communication, two players maximizing their individual payoffs will simply choose the corresponding strategies.

In other games, the preferences of the players for the four outcomes are exactly opposed to each other. In these games, which are called games of complete opposition, classical game theory prescribes a "rational solution" for each player, and hence any departure from the solution can be interpreted as a deficiency of cognition rather than as a resultant of opposed psychological pressures.

Of the 78 games in the 2×2 category, 21 are "no conflict" games and 3 are games of complete opposition. The remaining games are "mixed-motive" games, in which the interests of the two players are partially opposed and partially coincident. For instance, in Prisoner's Dilemma, the interests of the players are in conflict in the sense that Row prefers the outcome D_1C_2, whereas Column prefers C_1D_2. However, their interests coincide in that both prefer the outcome C_1C_2 to D_1D_2. Again, in the Threat Game (Game 2), Row prefers S_1T_2 while Column prefers S_1S_2. But both players prefer either outcome in row S to either outcome in row T.

Of the 78 games, 12 are symmetric; that is to say, they look exactly alike to both players. For example, Prisoner's Dilemma is a symmetric game; the Threat Game is not.

Of the 12 symmetric games, 8 are "no conflict" games. The remaining four (including Prisoner's Dilemma) are psychologically interesting. These four games are shown as Games 3–6. The rows and columns of Prisoner's Dilemma ("Martyr") have been interchanged in order to display the "natural outcome" in the upper left-hand corner of all four matrices. The natural outcome is defined here as the outcome that results if each player avoids the choice whereby he *might* suffer the largest loss.

1	10		
1	−1		
−1	−10		
10	−10		

Game 3.   "Exploiter"

−1	10
−1	1
1	−10
10	−10

Game 4.   "Leader."

−1	1
−1	10
10	−10
1	−10

Game 5.   "Hero."

−1	−10
−1	10
10	1
−10	1

Game 6.   "Martyr."

We have designated the four games by nicknames derived from the result that obtains if one or the other player shifts away from the natural outcome while the other player stays with it. In Game 3 the player who shifts benefits himself and hurts the other; hence he is an "exploiter." In Game 4, the player who shifts benefits both himself and the other, but himself more than the other; he is a "leader." In Game 5 the player who shifts benefits both himself and the other, but the other more than himself; he is a "hero." Finally, in Game 6 (Prisoner's Dilemma) the player who shifts from the natural outcome hurts himself and benefits the other; he is a "martyr."

Note next that in the first three games both players have a motivation to shift since, if a player shifts alone, he gains more than in the natural outcome. Yet if both shift, both will suffer the largest loss. Thus there is also a counterpressure against shifting. "Exploiter" and "Leader" belong to a class of "pre-emption" games in which the player who shifts *alone* from the natural outcome can assure himself the largest payoff. Moreover, if he can somehow convince the other player that he is determined to choose the "defecting" strategy, the other has a choice of either submitting to the pre-emption or of not submitting and thus suffering the largest loss, with, perhaps, a partial consolation that in such case the would-be pre-emptor will also suffer the largest loss. In the "Exploiter" game, the player who submits to pre-emption gets a payoff smaller than that in the natural outcome. This game has also been called "Chicken" or "Brinkmanship." In experiments where explicit communication between players is not allowed, the pre-emptor communicates his "resolve" to obtain the largest payoff by playing the defecting strategy repeatedly regardless of whether or not the other submits. If the other does not submit, a "lock-in" on the outcome worst for both occurs, and repetitions of the game engender a battle of wills until one or the other "gives in," until the two come to their senses and return to the natural outcome, or until both go bankrupt.

"Hero" is interesting in that the pressure *not* to shift from the natural outcome (for fear of the result of a double shift) is coupled with another pressure in the same direction, deriving from the greater advantage of letting the *other* shift alone. "Let the other be the hero." Consequently, in repeated plays, the natural outcome may become "locked in" even though *both* players could get bigger payoffs if only one of them (the "hero") shifted. This game has also been called "Apology." When two people have quarreled, an apology by one of them may be of benefit to both. Yet often each would prefer the other to apologize, with the result that the quarrel is prolonged.

It is also interesting to note that, if both players try to be an "exploiter," a "leader," or a "hero," both suffer the largest loss. But if both assume the "martyr" role, both gain.

USES OF GAMES

Because of the way in which the structural analysis of these simple games suggests conceptualizations rooted in psychological and ethical terminology, psychologists have been understandably attracted to this experimental tool. A frequent procedure is to devise a game that simulates some situation of concern to psychologists. For example, a social psychologist may be interested to know what role "threats" play in situations with a conflict of interests. It may seem to him that the Threat Game described above simulates a situation of this sort. One way to proceed would be to use a programmed player to take the part of Row, the player with an available "threat strategy." By varying the extent to which the programmed player makes use of the threat strategy, and by examining the corresponding behavior of the bona fide Column player, the psychologist can hope to get some answers to his questions. Or the psychologist may want to know what conditions enhance or inhibit cooperation between people in a situation of partial conflict of interest. He may arrange for people to play Prisoner's Dilemma under various experimental conditions, for various stakes, and so on, and examine the corresponding frequencies of choosing the "cooperative" strategy, C, and the "uncooperative" strategy, D. Or a psychologist may want to know whether differences of personality will be reflected in the way in which people play games of pre-emption, where "resolve" is demonstrated by persistent choices of the "risky" strategy.

Promising as these approaches seem to be, they are fraught with certain dangers. Some of these dangers have been pointed out repeatedly, for example, the questionable justification of extrapolating from the results of a laboratory experiment to conclusions bearing on behavior or motivations in "real life." However, I have in mind here a different kind of danger. We have intuitive notions that we know what we are talking about when we use words like "threat," "cooperation," and "resolve." Actually these words reflect what we have abstracted from a great variety of situations or behavior patterns that our language community has traditionally subsumed under the same name. In effect, however, the psychological components of all those different situations and behavior patterns may be widely different, so that there is no reason whatsoever to suppose that a hypothesis such as "Threats tend to inhibit cooperation," "Threats tend to enhance cooperation," "Threats tend to be reciprocated," or "Threats tend to enhance the dominance of one part to a conflict over the other" has any meaning. Probably situations can be found in real life, all subsumed under the word threat, with very different effects on the people concerned. Similarly, if one psychologist simulates "threat" in the laboratory in one way, and another in a different way, they may obtain "inconsistent results" and engage in a polemic about how "threat ought to be properly defined" or simulated, or about how each other's experimental procedures should be improved.

The approach suggested here avoids this difficulty. The "psychological interpretations" that we have made of certain quantifiable aspects of choice behavior are no more than nicknames for the parameters—mnemonic devices, not to be mistaken for anything else. The experimental psychologist can study these variables or parameters as functions of experimental conditions or of the number of plays of the game or of the payoffs, or he can compare their distributions in different populations without worrying about what they "mean." *If* his attention is called to certain recurring regularities that are suggestive of a psychological hypothesis, *then* he can formulate a hypothesis derived from his results and can design experiments to test this hypothesis in other, preferably quite different situations.

The suggested experimental approach is thus offered as a hypothesis-generating approach, not as a procedure for testing psychological hypotheses already made, because psychological hypotheses often are formulated in terms of concepts that have not yet been sufficiently operationalized. On the other hand, the "propensities" and other variables, or parameters, suggested by the game experiments described here are completely operationalized, since they are defined in terms of observable, quantifiable variables. The problem of connecting these quantities to psychologically interesting concepts arises later, after a great deal has been learned about these quantities themselves.

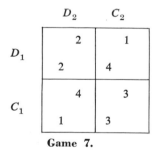

Game 7.

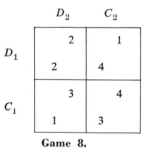

Game 8.

As an example, compare Games 7 and 8. We recognize Game 7 as a structural equivalent of Prisoner's Dilemma, while Game 8 has a somewhat different structure, although it resembles Prisoner's Dilemma in that the outcome C_1C_2 is preferred by both players to D_1D_2. However, unlike Prisoner's Dilemma, Game 8 gives one of the players (Row) the opportunity to *force* the outcome C_1C_2 by choosing C_1 repeatedly. This is so because, when Row chooses C_1, Column can get his largest payoff (4) by choosing C_2. Whether C_1C_2 continues as the outcome depends on whether Row is content with the second largest payoff in a situation where he has the opportunity to get the largest payoff in D_1C_2 by switching D_1. Thus the outcome C_1C_2 is not an equilibrium, but it can be kept going if Row "resists the temptation" of switching in pursuit of his largest payoff.

Observe that in Prisoner's Dilemma the "cooperative" outcome C_1C_2, which is also not an equilibrium, can be kept going only if *both* players resist the temptation of switching to D in pursuit of a larger payoff. We would expect more frequent defections in Game 7 than in Game 8.

The question naturally arises how much more frequent they would be. If we equilibrate the "temptations" in both games (the differences between the largest and the next-to-largest payoffs), then we can state a null hypothesis: the defections of the two players in Game 7 are independent events. According to this hypothesis, if the probability of defection in Game 7 is $\bar{x} = 1 - x$ (see above), then the probability of defection in Game 8 ought to be $1 - x^2 > 1 - x$. Almost certainly, however, the null hypothesis will be refuted, since the interaction between the players' choices in repeated plays is very strong. In addition to evidence for such interaction, we can also obtain a quantitative measure of the "degree of linkage" between the two players. We may also find that the distributions of x_1 in Game 8 in a population of players is different from that of $x_1 = x_2$ in (symmetric) Game 7, a result that also raises interesting psychological questions.

The point of these examples is that the strategic structures of the experimental games provide a firmer point of anchorage for developing a theory of choice behavior than do psychological concepts used as a point of departure in constructing the game. The strategic structure completely displays the *objective* features of the choice situation. It can be varied systematically, both qualitatively, in passing from one structure to another, and quantitatively, in changing the magnitudes of the payoffs or of the payoff differences within the same strategic structure. The latter variations are particularly helpful in "separating the pressures" presumably acting on the players.

In comparing Games 9, 10, 11, and 12, it is seen that Game 9 is again Prisoner's Dilemma. In this game, *two* pressures are acting on each player to induce him to defect from C to D: first, the desire of the larger gain $(11 > 10)$; second, the desire to minimize loss *should the other defect* $(-9 > -10)$. In Game 10, only one of these pressures is acting, namely, the first. If the other defects, C and D yield the same payoff (-10). Also in Game 11, only one pressure is acting, namely, the second: *only* if the other defects, is D preferable to C. Finally, in Game 12, neither pressure is acting. It makes no difference in either player's payoff whether he himself chooses C or D; only the *other* player's choice determines the difference

	C_2	D_2
C_1	10 10	11 -10
D_1	-10 11	-9 -9

Game 9.

	C_2	D_2
C_1	10 10	11 -10
D_1	-10 11	-10 -10

Game 10.

	C_2	D_2
C_1	10 10	10 -10
D_1	-10 10	-9 -9

Game 11.

	C_2	D_2
C_1	10 10	10 -10
D_1	-10 10	-10 -10

Game 12.

between a gain of 10 and a loss of 10. Here neither player has any control over his own payoffs, but each has complete control over the *other's* payoffs. Choices of D in this game can be attributed either to error or to a purely competitive motivation (a desire to maximize the difference between one's own and the other's payoff instead of the magnitude of one's own) or to sheer malevolence. It has also been pointed out that players might choose "irrationally" just to break the monotony of repeated choices in protracted runs. This factor might be estimated by varying the length of runs.

Games like 10, 11, and 12 are not included in our 78 strategically inequivalent games because, in these games, the magnitude of the payoffs are not strictly ordered. If such games are included, the number of strategically inequivalent games turns out to be 726. This is still a manageable number. However, the number of strategically inequivalent 3×3 games (two players with three strategies each) turns out to be about 1.8×10^9. It is, of course, out of the question to list all such games, let alone examine them experimentally one by one. One naturally looks to a *taxonomy* that would single out interesting classes of 3×3 games. A taxonomy of this sort would be a contribution to a *systematics* of conflict situations based on clear structural characteristics. At the same time it would be richly suggestive to the psychologist for generating concepts and hypotheses relevant to a theory of choice in a conflict situation.

Joseph Zubin—Bibliography

Pintner, R., Rinsland, H. D., & Zubin, J. The evaluation of self-administering spelling tests. *Journal of Educational Psychology*, 1929, **20**, 107–111.

Maller, J. B., & Zubin, J. The effect of motivation upon intelligence scores. *Journal of Genetic Psychology*, 1932, **41**, 136–151.

Zubin, J. *Some effects of incentives: A study of individual differences in rivalry.* New York: Teachers College, Columbia University, 1932.

Zubin, J. Vocational guidance and the American Jewish School. *Jewish Education*, 1932, **4**, 174–179.

Zubin, J. The chance element in matching tests. *Journal of Educational Psychology*, 1933, **24**, 674–681.

Zubin, J. Statistical report on data. In H. Carrington, An instrumental test of the independence of a "Spirit Control." *Bulletin of The American Psychical Institute*, 1933, **1**, 32–36.

Zubin, J. The method of internal consistency for selecting test items. *Journal of Educational Psychology*, 1934, **25**, 345–356.

Zubin, J. Note on the standard error of the difference between coefficients of variation of correlated variables. *Journal of Applied Psychology*, 1934, **18**, 491–492.

Landis, C., Katz, S. E., & Zubin, J. Empirical evaluation of three personality adjustment inventories. *Journal of Educational Psychology*, 1935, **26**, 321–330.

Zubin, J. Note on a transformation function for proportions and percentages. *Journal of Applied Psychology*, 1935, **19**, 213–220.

Zubin, J. Note on a graphic method for determining the significance of the difference between group frequencies. *Journal of Educational Psychology*, 1936, **27**, 431–444.

Zubin, J. *Choosing a life work.* Cincinnati: Union American Hebrew Congregations, 1937.

Zubin, J. The determination of response patterns in personality adjustment inventories. *Journal of Educational Psychology*, 1937, **28**, 401–413.

Zubin, J., & Gristle, M. An empirical scale for measuring militarism-pacifism. *Psychological Record*, 1937, **1**, 27–32.

Zubin, J. The mentally ill and mentally handicapped in institutions. Supplement No. 146 to the *Public Health Reports*, 1938.

Zubin, J. Regional differences in the care of mental defect and epilepsy. *Proceedings of the American Association of Mental Deficiency*, 1938, **43**, 167–178.

Zubin, J. Socio-biological types and methods for their isolation. *Psychiatry,* 1938, **1,** 237–247.

Zubin, J. The statistics of card guessing. *The Statistical Journal of the Statistical Association of the College of the City of New York,* 1938, **1,** 9–16.

Zubin, J. A technique for measuring like-mindedness. *Journal of Abnormal and Social Psychology,* 1938, **33,** 508–516.

Bolles, M. M., & Zubin, J. A graphic method for evaluating differences between frequencies. *Journal of Applied Psychology,* 1939, **23,** 440–449.

Zubin, J. Economic aspects of mental health: Formal discussion, summary and critique. In F. R. Moulton (Ed.), *Mental health.* Publication No. 9 of the American Association for the Advancement of Science. Lancaster, Pa.: The Science Press, 1939. Pp. 211–218.

Zubin, J. Nomographs for determining the significance of the difference between frequencies of events in two contrasted series or groups. *Journal of the American Statistical Association,* 1939, **34,** 539–544.

Zubin, J., & Scholz, G. C. Regional differences in the hospitalization and care of patients with mental diseases. Supplement No. 159 to the *Public Health Reports,* 1940.

Zubin, J. A psychometric approach to the evaluation of the Rorschach Test. *Psychiatry,* 1941, **4,** 547–566.

Zubin, J. A quantitative approach to measuring regularity of succession in the Rorschach experiment. *Character and Personality,* 1941, **10,** 67–78.

Zubin, J., & Barrera, S. E. Effect of electric convulsive therapy on memory. *Proceedings of the Society for Experimental Biology and Medicine,* 1941, **48,** 596–597.

Zubin, J., & Scholz, G. C. Negro mental defectives and epileptics in institutions in eighteen southern states and the District of Columbia, 1938. *American Journal of Mental Deficiency,* 1941, **45,** 617–623.

Zubin, J., & Taback, M. A note on Sheldon's method for estimating dysplasia. *Human Biology,* 1941, **13,** 405–410.

Zubin, J., & Thompson, W. J. *Sorting tests in relation to drug therapy in schizophrenia.* Ann Arbor, Mich.: Edwards Bros., 1941.

Fulcher, J. S., & Zubin, J. The item analyzer: a mechanical device for treating the four-fold table in large samples. *Journal of Applied Psychology,* 1942, **26,** 511–522.

Lewinson, T. S., & Zubin, J. *Handwriting analysis: A series of scales for evaluating the dynamic aspects of handwriting.* New York: Kings Crown Press, 1942.

Coyne, J. W., King, H. E., Zubin, J., & Landis, C. Accuracy of recognition of subliminal auditory stimuli. *Journal of Experimental Psychology,* 1943, **33,** 508–513.

Garrett, H. E., & Zubin, J. The analysis of variance in psychological research. *Psychological Bulletin,* 1943, **40,** 233–267.

Zubin, J. A proposed measure for social conformity. *Sociometry,* 1943, **6,** 72–93.

Zubin, J., Chute, E., & Veniar, S. Psychometric scales for scoring Rorschach Test responses. *Character and Personality*, 1943, **11**, 277–301.

King, H. E., Landis, C., & Zubin, J. Visual subliminal perception where a figure is obscured by the illumination of the ground. *Journal of Experimental Psychology*, 1944, **34**, 60–69.

Killinger, G. G., & Zubin, J. Psychobiological screening procedures in the War Shipping Administration. *Annals of the New York Academy of Sciences*, 1945, **46**, 559–569.

Zubin, J., & Peatman, J. G. Testing the pulling power of advertisements by the split-run copy method. *Journal of Applied Psychology*, 1945, **29**, 40-57.

Killinger, G. G., & Zubin, J. The psychobiological program of the War Shipping Administration. In B. Glueck (Ed.), *Current therapies of personality disorders*. New York: Grune & Stratton, 1946. Pp. 262–274.

Goodman, G., & Zubin, J. The training-station records and post-graduate assignments of trainees of The Maritime Service Training School, Sheepshead Bay, New York. In G. G. Killinger (Ed.), *The psychobiological program of the War Shipping Administration. Applied Psychology Monographs*, 1947, **12**, 263–266.

Zubin, J. Manual of projective and cognate techniques. Madison, Wis.: College Typing Company, 1948.

Zubin, J. Memory functioning in patients treated with electric shock therapy. *Journal of Personality*, 1948, **17**, 33–41.

Zubin, J. Objective studies of disordered persons. In T. G. Andrews (Ed.), *Methods of psychology*. New York: Wiley, 1948. Pp. 595–623.

Zubin, J. The problems of quantification and objectification in personality measurement: A Symposium. I. Introduction. *Journal of Personality*, 1948, **17**, 141–145.

Zubin, J. Recent advances in screening the emotionally maladjusted. *Journal of Clinical Psychology*, 1948, **4**, 56–63.

Zubin, J. The design of the psychologic investigation. In F. Mettler (Ed.), *Selective partial ablations of the frontal cortex*. New York: Paul B. Hoeber, 1949. Pp. 173–176.

Zubin, J. Personality research and psychopathology as related to clinical practice. *Journal of Abnormal and Social Psychology*, 1949, **44**, 14–21.

Zubin, J. Rorschach test. In F. Mettler (Ed.), *Selective partial ablations of the frontal cortex*. New York: Paul B. Hoeber, 1949. Pp. 283–300.

Landis, C., Zubin, J., & Mettler, F. A. The functions of the human frontal lobe. *Journal of Psychology*, 1950, **30**, 123–138.

Zubin, J. Discussion I. Part II. Diagnostic use of psychological tests. In P. H. Hoch & J. Zubin (Eds.), *Relation of psychological tests to psychiatry*. New York: Grune & Stratton, 1950. Pp. 96–104.

Zubin, J. *Quantitative techniques and methods in abnormal psychology*. New York: Columbia University Bookstore, 1950.

Zubin, J. Symposium on statistics for the clinician. Introduction. *Journal of Clinical Psychology*, 1950, **6**, 1–6.

Zubin, J. Test construction and methodology. In *Recent advances in diagnostic psychological testing.* Springfield, Ill.: Charles C Thomas, 1950. Pp. 99–120.

Landis, C., & Zubin, J. The alleged sedative effect of thonzylamine hydrochloride (neohetramine). *Journal of Laboratory and Clinical Medicine,* 1951, **38,** 873–880.

Landis, C., & Zubin, J. The effect of thonzylamine hydrochloride and phenobarbital sodium on certain psychological functions. *Journal of Psychology,* 1951, **31,** 181–200.

Zubin, J. Motivation and temperament in psychopathology. In J. Dailey (Ed.), *Conference report: Research planning conference on objective measurement of motivation and temperament.* San Antonio: Headquarters Human Resources Research Center, 1951. Pp. 113–118.

Zubin, J. Objective evaluation of personality tests. *American Journal of Psychiatry,* 1951, **107,** 569–576.

Zubin, J., & Windle, C. The prognostic value of the Metenym Test in a followup study of psychosurgery patients and their controls. *Journal of Clinical Psychology,* 1951, **7,** 221–223.

Cranston, R. E., Zubin, J., & Landis, C. The effect of small doses of thonzylamine-dexedrine and phenobarbital on test performance and self-ratings of subjective states. *Journal of Psychology,* 1952, **33,** 209–215.

Landis, C., & Zubin, J. Discussion of psychologic investigations. In F. A. Mettler (Ed.), *Psychosurgical problems.* New York: Blakiston, 1952. Pp. 275–278.

North, R. D., Lesser, G. S., Berg, E. A., & Zubin, J. Complex mental functions: Memory, learning, mental set, and perceptual tasks. In F. A. Mettler (Ed.), *Psychosurgical problems.* New York: Blakiston, 1952. Pp. 195–217.

Zubin, J. Abnormalities of behavior. *Annual Review of Psychology,* 1952, **3,** 261–282.

Zubin, J. Creativity in psychosurgery patients. In W. Overholser (Ed.), *Proceedings of the Second Research Conference on Psychosurgery.* (Evaluation of change in patients after psychosurgery). Washington, D. C.: U. S. Department of Health, Education, and Welfare, 1952. Pp. 96–101. (PHS Publication No. 156)

Zubin, J. The design of the psychologic investigation. In F. A. Mettler (Ed.), *Psychosurgical problems.* New York: Blakiston, 1952. Pp. 146–151.

Zubin, J. On the powers of models. *Journal of Personality,* 1952, **20,** 430–439.

Staudt, V., & Zubin, J. Evaluation of outcome of treatment in the somatotherapies. *American Psychologist,* 1953, **8,** 441. (Abstract)

Zubin, J. Design for the evaluation of therapy. In *Psychiatric treatment.* Vol. 31. Proceedings of the Association for Research in Nervous and Mental Disease. Baltimore: Williams & Wilkins, 1953. Pp. 10–15.

Zubin, J. Evaluation of therapeutic outcome in mental disorders. *Journal of Nervous and Mental Disease,* 1953, **117,** 95–111.

Zubin, J. How the psychologist helps the psychiatrist in the evaluation of therapy. *Journal of Brooklyn State Hospital Psychiatric Forum,* 1953, **6,** (3).

Zubin, J. Discussion II. Part II. Prognosis in relation to diagnosis and etiology. In P. H. Hoch & J. Zubin (Eds.), *Current problems in psychiatric diagnosis.* New York: Grune & Stratton, 1953. Pp. 112–118.

Zubin, J., Windle, C. E., & Hamwi, V. Retrospective evaluation of psychological tests as prognostic instruments in mental disorders. *Journal of Personality,* 1953, **21,** 342–355.

Crandell, A., Zubin, J., Mettler, F. A., & Logan, N. D. The prognostic value of "mobility" during the first two years of hospitalization for mental disorder. *The Psychiatric Quarterly,* 1954, **28,** 185–210.

Zubin, J. Presidential address—Biometric methods in psychopathology. In P. H. Hoch & J. Zubin (Eds.), *Depression.* New York: Grune & Stratton, 1954. Pp. 123–143.

Zubin, J. Failures of the Rorschach technique. *Journal of Projective Techniques,* 1954, **18,** 303–315.

Zubin, J. The measurement of personality. *Journal of Counseling Psychology,* 1954, **1,** 159–164.

Zubin, J., & Windle, C. Psychological prognosis of outcome in the mental disorders. *Journal of Abnormal and Social Psychology,* 1954, **49,** 272–281.

Zubin, J. Clinical vs. actuarial prediction: a pseudo-problem. In *Proceedings of the 1955 Invitational Conference on Testing Problems.* Princeton: Educational Testing Service, 1955. Pp. 107–128.

Burdock, E. I., & Zubin, J. A rationale for the classification of experimental techniques in abnormal psychology. *Journal of General Psychology,* 1956, **55,** 35–49.

Crandell, A., Zubin, J., Mettler, F. A., & Kugelmass, N. "Mobility" in chronic schizophrenia with special regard to psychosurgery. *Psychiatric Quarterly,* 1956, **30,** 96–113.

North, R. D., & Zubin, J. Complex mental functions. In N. D. C. Lewis, C. Landis, & H. E. King (Eds.), *Studies in topectomy.* New York: Grune & Stratton, 1956. Pp. 75–88.

Zubin, J. The non-projective aspects of the Rorschach experiment. I. Introduction. *Journal of Social Psychology,* 1956, **44,** 179–192.

Zubin, J., Eron, L. D., & Sultan, F. A psychometric evaluation of the Rorschach experiment. *American Journal of Orthopsychiatry,* 1956, **26,** 773–782.

Burdock, E. I., Sutton, S., Cheek, F., & Zubin, J. Prognostic indicators in mental illness. *Public Health Reports,* 1957, **72,** 592–595.

Staudt, V., & Zubin, J. A biometric evaluation of the somatotherapies in schizophrenia. *Psychological Bulletin,* 1957, **54,** 171–196.

Zubin, J. A brief survey of the interview. In H. H. Gee & J. T. Cowles (Eds.), *The appraisal of applicants to medical school.* Evanston, Ill.: Association of American Medical Colleges, 1957. Pp. 2–8.

Zubin, J. Discussion of the introduction to facet design and analysis by Louis

Guttman. *Proceedings of the International Congress of Psychology,* Brussels, 1957, 135–138.

Zubin, J. (Ed.) *Experimental abnormal psychology.* New York: Columbia University Bookstore, 1957.

Zubin, J. Psychopathology without benefit of Freud. *Contemporary Psychology,* 1957, **2**, 185–186.

Burdock, E. I., Sutton, S., & Zubin, J. Personality and psychopathology. *Journal of Abnormal and Social Psychology,* 1958, **56**, 18–30; *Schweizerische Zeitschrift für Psychologie und ihre Anwendungen,* 1958, **17**, 258–284; *Revista De Psicologia General y Aplicada,* 1958, **13**, 693–721.

Zubin, J. A. biometric model for psychopathology. In R. A. Patton (Ed.), *Current trends in the description and analysis of behavior.* Pittsburgh: University of Pittsburgh Press, 1958. Pp. 22–47.

Zubin, J. Discussion of "1,000 prefrontal lobotomies," III, by H. S. Barahals. *Psychiatric Quarterly,* 1958, **32**, 683–690.

Zubin, J. Discussion of uses and abuses of statistics in biochemical investigations of psychotic patients by Max Reiss. In M. Rinkel & N.C.B. Denber (Eds.), *Chemical concepts of psychosis.* New York: McDowell Obolensky, 1958. Pp. 441–443.

Zubin, J. Discussion of paper by Anastasi. *Eugenics Quarterly,* 1959, **6** (2), 91–93.

Zubin, J. Epidemiological aspects of prognosis in mental illness. In B. Pasamanick (Ed.), *Epidemiology of mental disorders.* Washington, D.C.: American Association for the Advancement of Science, 1959. Pp. 119–142. (Publication No. 60)

Zubin, J. Report of the committee on patient selection and controls. In J. O. Cole & R. W. Gerard (Eds.), *Psychopharmacology: Problems in evaluation.* Washington, D. C.: National Academy of Sciences, National Research Council, 1959. Pp. 620–625. (Publication No. 583)

Zubin, J. Role of prognostic indicators in the evaluation of therapy. In J. O. Cole & R. W. Gerard (Eds.), *Psychopharmacology: Problems in evaluation.* Washington, D. C.: National Academy of Sciences, National Research Council, 1959. Pp. 343–354. (Publication No. 583)

Burdock, E. I., Cheek, F., & Zubin, J. Predicting success in psychoanalytic training. In P. H. Hoch & J. Zubin (Eds.), *Current approaches to psychoanalysis.* New York: Grune & Stratton, 1960. Pp. 176–191.

Burdock, E. I., Hardesty, A. S., Hakerem, G., & Zubin, J. A ward behavior rating scale for mental hospital patients. *Journal of Clinical Psychology,* 1960, **16**, 246–247.

Zubin, J. English psychiatry's revolution. Review of V. Morris, *Mental illness in London,* and M. Shepherd, *A study of the major psychoses in an English county. Contemporary Psychology,* 1960, **5** (7), 211–214.

Chase, R., Sutton, S., First, D., & Zubin, J. A developmental study of changes in behavior under delayed auditory feedback. *Journal of Genetic Psychology,* 1961, **99**, 101–112.

Sutton, S., Hakerem, G., Zubin, J., & Portnoy, M. The effect of shift of sensory modality on serial reaction times: A comparison of schizophrenics and normals. *American Journal of Psychology,* 1961, **74,** 224–232.

Zubin, J. Discussion of Part III: Psychophysiology and genetics. In P. H. Hoch & J. Zubin (Eds.), *Psychopathology of aging.* New York: Grune & Stratton, 1961. Pp. 223–226.

Zubin, J. From the point of view of biometrics. In J. Zubin (Ed.), *Field studies in the mental disorders.* New York: Grune & Stratton, 1961. Pp. 406–410.

Zubin, J. Measurement of changes in human behavior under the effects of psychotropic drugs. In E. Rothlin (Ed.), *Neuro-psychopharmacology,* 1961, **2,** 333–338.

Zubin, J., Sutton, S., Salzinger, K., Salzinger, S., Burdock, E. I., & Peretz, D. A biometric approach to prognosis in schizophrenia. In P. H. Hoch & J. Zubin (Eds.), *Comparative epidemiology in the mental disorders.* New York: Grune & Stratton, 1961. Pp. 143–203.

Salzinger, S., Salzinger, K., Portnoy, S., Eckman, J., Bacon, M., Deutsch, M., & Zubin, J. Operant conditioning of continuous speech in young children. *Child Development,* 1962, **33,** 683–695.

Zubin, J. A biometric approach to diagnosis and prognosis. In J. Nodine & J. Moyer (Eds.), *Psychosomatic medicine: The first Hahnemann symposium.* Philadelphia: Lea & Febiger, 1962. Pp. 71–80.

Zubin, J. Discussion of Part II: Future of psychologic, social, and educational approaches. In P. H. Hoch & J. Zubin (Eds.), *The future of psychiatry.* New York: Grune & Stratton, 1962. Pp. 83–90.

Zubin, J. Behavioral concomitants of the mental disorders: A biometric view. In B. Wigdor (Ed.), *Recent advances in the study of behavior change.* Montreal: McGill University, 1963. Pp. 5–49.

Hakerem, G., Sutton, S., & Zubin, J. Pupillary reactions to light in schizophrenic patients and normals. *Annals of the New York Academy of Sciences,* 1964, **105,** 820–831.

Sutton, S., & Zubin, J. Effect of sequence on reaction time in schizophrenia. In A. Welford & J. Birren (Eds.), *Behavior, aging and the nervous system: Biological determinants of speed of behavior and its change with age.* Springfield, Ill.: Charles C Thomas, 1964. Pp. 562–597.

Zubin, J. A biometric approach to psychopathology. *Annals of the New York Academy of Sciences,* 1964, **105,** 816–819.

Zubin, J. Discussion of Part II: Technical issues. In P. H. Hoch & J. Zubin (Eds.), *The evaluation of psychiatric treatment.* New York: Grune & Stratton, 1964. Pp. 122–128.

Zubin, J. Foreword: Can psychopathology be measured? *Annals of the New York Academy of Sciences,* 1964, **105,** 815.

Zubin, J. Problems and prospects of the biometric method. *Annals of the New York Academy of Sciences,* 1964, **105,** 919–925.

Zubin, J., & Fleiss, J. Taxonomy in the mental disorders: A historic perspective. In *Symposium: Explorations in typology with special reference to psychotics.* New York: Human Ecology Fund, 1964. Pp. 1–12.

Zubin, J., & Katz, M. Psychopharmacology and personality. In D. Byrne &

P. Worchel (Eds.), *Personality change.* New York: Wiley, 1964. Pp. 367–395.

Sutton, S., Braren, M., John, E. R., & Zubin, J. Evoked potential correlates of stimulus uncertainty. *Science,* 1965, **150,** 1187–1188.

Zubin, J. Comments on Eysenck. *International Journal of Psychiatry,* 1965, **1,** 153–155.

Zubin, J. Dermooptical perception: A cautionary report. Letter to the editor. *Science,* 1965, **147, 985.**

Zubin, J. Discussion of Part II: Psychopathology of pain, taste, and time. In P. H. Hoch & J. Zubin (Eds.), *Psychopathology of perception.* New York: Grune & Stratton, 1965. Pp. 189–192.

Zubin, J. Paul H. Hoch's contribution to the American Psychopathological Association. *Comprehensive Psychiatry,* 1965, **6,** 74–77.

Zubin, J. Psychopathology and the social sciences. In O. Klineberg & R. Christie (Eds.), *Perspectives in social psychology.* New York: Holt, Rinehart & Winston, 1965. Pp. 189–207.

Zubin, J. Research techniques and evaluative programs. In *Research in community mental health.* Asbury Park, N. J.: New Jersey Department of Institutions and Agencies, and New Jersey Association of Mental Hygiene Clinics, 1965. Pp. 9–22.

Zubin, J., & Burdock, E. I. The revolution in psychopathology and its implications for public health. *Acta Psychiatrica Scandinavica,* 1965, **41,** 348–359; *Revista De Psicologia General y Aplicada,* 1965, **20,** 845–861.

Zubin, J., Eron, L., & Schumer, F. *An experimental approach to projective techniques.* New York: Wiley, 1965.

Zubin, J. A cross-cultural approach to psychopathology and its implications for diagnostic classification. In L. D. Eron (Ed.), *The classification of behavioral disorders.* Chicago: Aldine, 1966. Pp. 46–85.

Zubin, J. Discussion of Leon Eisenberg: The classification of the psychotic disorders in childhood. In L. D. Eron (Ed.), *The classification of behavior disorders.* Chicago: Aldine, 1966. Pp. 115–122.

Zubin, J. Foreword. In J. Inglis (Ed.), *The scientific study of abnormal behavior.* Chicago: Aldine, 1966. Pp. vii–viii.

Zubin, J., & Katz, M. M. Psychopharmacology and personality. *International Journal of Psychiatry,* 1966, **2,** 640–675.

Zubin, J., & Kietzman, M. A cross-cultural approach to classification in schizophrenia and other mental disorders. In P. H. Hoch & J. Zubin (Eds.), *Psychopathology of schizophrenia.* New York: Grune & Stratton, 1966. Pp. 482–514.

Sutton, S., Tueting, P., Zubin, J., & John, E. R. Information delivery and the sensory evoked potential. *Science,* 1967, **155,** 1436–1439.

Zubin, J. Classification of the behavior disorders. *Annual Review of Psychology,* 1967, **18,** 373–406.

Zubin, J. Review of the *Annual Review of Psychology,* Vol. 17, 1966. *American Journal of Psychiatry,* 1967, **123,** 1156–1162.

Zubin, J. Sorting out variables. *International Journal of Psychiatry,* 1967, **4,** 250–251.

Hammer, M., & Zubin, J. Evolution, culture and psychopathology. *Journal of General Psychology,* 1968, **78,** 151–164.

Hannes, M., Sutton, S., & Zubin, J. Reaction time: Stimulus uncertainty with response certainty. *Journal of General Psychology,* 1968, **78,** 165–181.

Zubin, J. Biometric assessment of mental patients. In M. Katz, J. O. Cole, & W. E. Barton (Eds.), *The role and methodology of classification in psychiatry and psychopathology.* Washington, D. C.: U. S. Department of Health, Education, and Welfare, 1968. Pp. 353–376. (PHS Publication No. 1584)

Zubin, J. Clinical, phenomenological, and biometric assessment of psychopathology with special reference to diagnosis. In S. B. Sells (Ed.), *The definition and measurement of mental health.* Washington, D. C.: U. S. Department of Health, Education, and Welfare, 1968. Pp. 67–98.

Zubin, J. The function of the assessment center in community mental health. In L. M. Roberts, N. Greenfield, & M. Miller (Eds.), *Comprehensive mental health: The challenge of evaluation.* Madison: University of Wisconsin Press, 1968. Pp. 169–193.

Zubin, J. Perspectives on the conference. In M. Katz, J. O. Cole, & W. Barton (Eds.), *The role and methodology of classification in psychiatry and psychopathology.* Washington, D. C.: U. S. Department of Health, Education, and Welfare, 1968. Pp. 556–558. (PHS Publication No. 1584)

Zubin, J., & Gosling, H. Review of J. Clausen, *Ability structure and subgroups in mental retardation. American Journal of Mental Deficiency,* 1968, **73,** 158–160.

Zubin, J., & Wolfson, R. Handwriting. *Encyclopedia Britannica,* 1968, **11,** 60–62.

Fleiss, J. L., & Zubin, J. On the methods and theory of clustering. *Multivariate Behavioral Research,* 1969, **4,** 235–250.

Zubin, J. The biometric approach to psychopathology—revisited. In J. Zubin & C. Shagass (Eds.), *Neurobiological aspects of psychopathology.* New York: Grune & Stratton, 1969. Pp. 281–309.

Zubin, J. Contributions of experimental and abnormal psychology to clinical psychology. *International Review of Applied Psychology,* 1969, **18,** 65–77.

Zubin, J. Cross-national study of diagnosis of mental disorders: Methodology and planning. Supplement to the *American Journal of Psychiatry,* 1969, **125** (10), 12–20.

Zubin, J. The role of models in clinical psychology. In L. L'Abate (Ed.), *Models of clinical psychology.* (Research Paper No. 22) Atlanta: Georgia State College, 1969. Pp. 5–12.

Zubin, J., & Endicott, J. From milestone to millstone to tombstone. Review of D. Rapaport, M. M. Gill, & R. Schafer, *Diagnostic psychological testing. Contemporary Psychology,* 1969, **14,** 280–283.

Zubin, J., & Sutton, S. Assessment of physiological, sensory, perceptual, psychomotor, and conceptual functioning in schizophrenic patients. In *Studies dedicated to Erik Essen-Möller*. Munksgaard, Copenhagen: *Acta Psychiatrica Scandinavica*, 1970, **46**, 247–263. (Suppl. No. 219)

Tueting, P., Sutton, S., & Zubin, J. Quantitative evoked potential correlates of the probability of events. *Psychophysiology*, 1971, **7**, 385–394.

Zubin, J. The aetiology of behavior in the year 2,000. In W. O. Evans & N. S. Kline (Eds.), *Psychotropic drugs in the year 2,000: Use by normal humans.* Springfield, Ill.: Charles C Thomas, 1971. Pp. 3–24.

Zubin, J. Contributions of biometrics to psychopathology. *Comprehensive Psychiatry*, 1971, **12** (3), 196–207.

Zubin, J. Research versus service. *Mental Hygiene News*, 1971, **42** (8), 2.

Zubin, J., & Fleiss, J. Current biometric approaches to depression. In R. R. Fieve (Ed.), *Depression in the 1970's. Modern theory and research.* Princeton: Excerpta Medica, 1971. Pp. 7–19.

Kietzman, M., Sutton, S., & Zubin, J. (Eds.) *Experimental approaches to psychopathology.* New York: Academic Press, in press.

Zubin, J. Problem of attention in schizophrenia. In M. Kietzman, S. Sutton, & J. Zubin (Eds.), *Experimental approaches to psychopathology.* New York: Academic Press, in press.

Proceedings of the American Psychopathological Association

Zubin, J. (Ed.) *Trends of mental disease.* New York: Kings Crown Press, 1945.

Hoch, P. H., & Zubin, J. (Eds.) New York: Grune & Stratton.
  1949   *Psychosexual development in health and disease.*
  1950   *Anxiety.*
  1952   *Relation of psychological tests to psychiatry.*
  1953   *Current problems in psychiatric diagnosis.*
  1954   *Depression.*
  1955   *Psychiatry and the law.*
  1955   *Psychopathology of childhood.*
  1957   *Experimental psychopathology.*
  1958   *Psychopathology of communication.*
  1958   *Problems of addiction and habituation.*
  1960   *Current approaches to psychoanalysis.*
  1961   *Comparative epidemiology of mental disorders.*

Zubin, J. (Ed.) New York: Grune & Stratton.
  1961   *Field studies in the mental disorders.*

Hoch, P. H., & Zubin, J. (Eds.) New York: Grune & Stratton.
  1961   *Psychopathology of aging.*
  1962   *The future of psychiatry.*
  1964   *The evaluation of psychiatric treatment.*

1965 *Psychopathology of perception.*

1966 *Psychopathology of schizophrenia.*

Zubin, J., & Hunt, H. (Eds.) New York: Grune & Stratton.

1967 *Comparative psychopathology: Animal and human.*

Zubin, J., & Jervis, G. (Eds.) New York: Grune & Stratton.

1967 *Psychopathology of mental development.*

Zubin, J., & Freyhan, F. (Eds.) New York: Grune & Stratton.

1968 *Social psychiatry.*

Zubin, J., & Shagass, C. (Eds.) New York: Grune & Stratton.

1969 *Neurobiological aspects of psychopathology.*

Zubin, J., & Freedman, A. M. (Eds.) New York: Grune & Stratton.

1970 *The psychopathology of adolescence.*

Zubin, J., & Freyhan, F. A. (Eds.) Baltimore: The Johns Hopkins Press

1972 *Disorders of mood.*

Acknowledgments

We are indebted to the following authors and publishers for the use of some of their material in this book:

Ádám, G. *Interoception and behaviour. An experimental study.* Budapest: Akadémiai Kiadó, 1967.

Aslanov, A. S. Correlation between cortical potentials in patients with obsessive neuroses. In A. S. Rusinov (Ed.), *Electrophysiology of the central nervous system.* New York: Plenum, 1970. Pp. 39–47.

Bagshaw, M. H., Kimble, D. P., & Pribram, K. H. The GSR of monkeys during orienting and habituation and after ablation of the amygdala, hippocampus and inferotemporal cortex. *Neuropsychologia, 3,* 1965, 111–119. Pergamon Press; Microforms International Marketing Corporation.

Bair, J. Development of voluntary control. *Psychological Review, 8,* 1901, 474–510. American Psychological Association.

Booth, J. H., & Hammond, L. J. Differential fear to a compound stimulus and its elements. Paper presented at the meeting of the Eastern Psychological Association, Philadelphia, 1969.

Carmon, A., & Benton, A. L. Patterns of impaired tactile sensitivity in unilateral cerebral disease. *Harefuah, 77,* 1969, 287–290. Israel Medical Association.

Carmon, A., & Benton, A. L. Tactile perception of direction and number in patients with unilateral cerebral disease. *Neurology, 19,* 1969, 525–532. American Academy of Neurology.

Cohen, H. *The nature, method and purpose of diagnosis.* Cambridge: University Press, 1943.

Dobzhansky, T. *Evolution, genetics and man.* 1955 by permission of John Wiley & Sons, Inc.

Eisenstein, M. E., & Cohen, M. J. Learning in isolated prothoracic ganglia. *Animal Behaviour, 13,* 1965, 104–108. Baillière, Tindall, & Cassell.

French, J. D. The reticular formation. In J. Field, H. W. Magoun, & V. E. Hall (Eds.), *Handbook of physiology.* Neurophysiology. Washington, D.C.: American Physiological Society, 1960. Section 1, Vol. II, Pp. 1281–1305.

Gavrilova, N. A. Spatial synchronization of cortical potentials in patients with disturbances of association. In V. S. Rusinov (Ed.), *Electrophysiology of the central nervous system.* New York: Plenum, 1970. Pp. 129–143.

Gilden, L., Vaughan, H. G., Jr., & Costa, L. D. Summated human EEG potentials with voluntary movement. *Electroencephalography and Clinical Neurophysiology,* **20**, 1966, 433–438. Elsevier Publishing Company.

Graham, F. K., & Clifton, R. K. Heart rate change as a component of the orienting response. *Psychiological Bulletin,* **65**, 1966, 305–320. Copyright 1966 by the American Psychological Association, and reproduced by permission.

Herrington, R. N., & Schneidau, P. Effects of imagery on waveshape of visual evoked response. *Experientia,* **24**, 1968, 1136–1137. Birkhäuser Verlag.

Hess, E. H. Ethology. In A. Freedman & H. Kaplan (Eds.), *Comprehensive textbook of psychiatry.* Baltimore: Williams & Wilkins, 1967. Pp. 180–189.

Horridge, G. A. Learning of leg positions by headless insects. Reprinted from *Nature,* **193**, 1962, 697. Macmillan Journals, Ltd.

Jasper, H. H., Proctor, L. D., Knighton, R. S., Noshay, W. C., & Costello, R. T. (Eds.). *Reticular formation of the brain.* London: Longmans, 1958. By permission.

John, E. R., & Morgades, P. P. Neural correlates of conditioned responses studied with multiple chronically implanted moving microlectrodes. *Experimental Neurology,* **23**, 1969, 417–475. Academic Press, Inc.

John, E. R., Shimokochi, M., & Bartlett, F. Neural readout from memory during generalization. *Science,* **164**, June 27, 1969, 1534–1536. Copyright 1969 by the American Association for the Advancement of Science.

King, H. E. The retention of sensory experience: I. Intensity. *The Journal of Psychology,* **56**, 1963, 283–290. The Journal Press.

King, H. E. The retention of sensory experience: IV. Short-delay versus long-delay intervals. *The Journal of Psychology,* **60**, 1965, 103–115. The Journal Press.

King, H. E. The retention of sensory experience: V. Variation of the standard stimuli. *The Journal of Psychology,* **62**, 1966, 15–22. The Journal Press.

Kleinsmith, L. J., & Kaplan, S. Paired associate learning as a function of arousal and interpolated interval. *Journal of Experimental Psychology,* **65**, 1963, 190–193. Copyright 1963 by the American Psychological Association and reproduced by permission.

Klinke, R., Fruhstorfer, H., & Finkenzeller, P. Evoked responses as a function of external and stored information. *Electroencephalography and Clinical Neurophysiology,* **25**, 1968, 119–122. Elsevier Publishing Company.

Lindsley, D. B. Psychophysiology and motivation. In M. R. Jones (Ed.), *Nebraska symposium on motivation.* Lincoln: University of Nebraska Press, 1957. Pp. 44–105.

Livanov, M. N. Information processing in the nervous system. *Proceedings of the 22nd International Congress of Physiological Science,* Leiden: Excerpta Medica Foundation, 1962, p. 899.

Miller, N. E., & Banuazizi, A. Instrumental learning by curarized rats of a specific visceral response, intestinal or cardiac. *Journal of Comparative and*

Physiological Psychology, **65**, 1968, 1–7. Copyright 1968 by the American Psychological Association, and reproduced by permission.

Miller, N. E., & Carmona, A. Modification of a visceral response, salivation in thirsty dogs, by instrumental training with water reward. *Journal of Comparative and Physiological Psychology,* **63**, 1967, 1–6. Copyright 1967 by the American Psychological Association and reproduced by permission.

Miller, N. E., DiCara, L. V., Solomon, H., Weiss, J. M., & Dworkin, B. Learned modifications of autonomic function: a review and some new data. Supplement I to *Circulation Research,* **26, 27**, 1970, I-3–I-11. By permission of the American Heart Association, Inc.

Ruchkin, D. S., & John, E. R. Evoked potential correlates of generalization. *Science,* **153**, July 8, 1966, 209–211. Copyright 1966 by the American Association for the Advancement of Science.

Siqueland, E. R., & Lipsitt, L. P. Conditioned head-turning in human newborns. *Journal of Experimental Child Psychology,* **3**, 1966, 356–376. Academic Press, Inc.

Slucki, H., Ádám, G., & Porter, R. W. Operant discrimination of an interoceptive stimulus in rhesus monkeys. *Journal of the Experimental Analysis of Behavior,* **8**, 1965, 405–414. Copyright 1965 by the Society for the Experimental Analysis of Behavior, Inc.

Stanford, W. B. *The Ulysses theme: A study in the adaptability of a traditional hero.* New York: Barnes & Noble Books, Harper & Row Publishers, Inc. 1964; Oxford: Basil Blackwell, 1963.

Sutton, S., Tueting, P., Zubin, J., & John, E. R. Information delivery and the sensory evoked potential. *Science,* **155**, March 17, 1967, 1436–1439. Copyright 1967 by the American Association for the Advancement of Science.

Thomas, D. R., Berman, D. L., Serednesky, G. E., & Lyons, J. Information value and stimulus configuring as factors in conditioned reinforcement. *Journal of Experimental Psychology,* **76**, 1968, 181–189. Copyright 1968 by the American Psychological Association, and reproduced by permission.

Zubin, J. Classification of the behavior disorders. *Annual Review of Psychology,* **18**, 1967, 373–406. Annual Reviews, Inc.

Author Index

Subject Index

Ability Structure Project, mental deficiency and, 289, 291
ACTH, hyperarousal and, 353–354
Africa, depression, increase in, 50, 51
Alcohol, use of, 361, 373
  amok syndrome and, 39
  anxiety and, 371
Alpha, mental deficiency and, 287–288, 291, 292
American Association for Mental Deficiency, 297
American Psychiatric Association, 61, 364
Amok syndrome, alcohol and, 39
  Batavia, occurrence in, 35–36, 39
  chronic dementia and, 38
  drugs and, 36, 38, 39, 40, 41
  epilepsy and, 39, 40
  febrile delirium and, 38, 40, 42
  historic change in, 33–42
  incidence, 37–38, 39–40
  interaction of tradition and modernizing influences and, 48, 49–50
  Java, occurrence in, 38, 39, 41
  malaria and, 40
  Malaysians, occurrence among, 34–42
  mata gelap, 37, 39
  narcoanalysis in, 41
  New Guinea, occurrence in, 41
  opiates and, 36, 38, 39, 40, 41
  organic brain syndrome and, 40
  Philippines, occurrence in, 41
  sakit hati, 39, 40
  Sarawak, occurrence in, 41
  schizophrenia and, 38, 40

  Straits Settlements, occurrence in, 38
Amphetamines, 372
Amygdala, skin conductance response and, 267–268
Anderson Index of mutual effect, 477–478
Anomie, 79–80
Anoxia, schizophrenia and, 349–350, 352–353
Antibody, 309, 310–311, 312, 313, 315–316
Anxiety, alcohol and, 371
  drug therapy in, 364, 366, 370–371
Aphasic disorders, hemispheric, cerebral dominance and, 227, 228
Apraxia, 227, 228
Arataeus of Cappodocia, 229
Army Specialized Training Program (ASTP), 444–449, 451–452
Arousal, ascending reticular activating system (ARAS) as substrate for, 285–287, 288–291
  autism and, 297
  autonomic indices of, 218–219
  degree of, and learning, 271–272
  memory, skin conductance responses and, 270–272
  mental deficiency and theory of, 285–299
  neurosis and, 298
  psychophysiology of, and mental deficiency, 291–297
  psychosis and, 298
  reactivity, 216, 220–221
  research needs in mental deficiency, 298–299

575

thought disorder, 209
twin studies, 65, 66, 99–100
verbal stimuli, responsiveness to, 114–115
Wechsler Adult Intelligence Scale (WAIS)
    responses, 122
Schizophrenia and Psychopharmacology
    Joint Research Project, 420
Second-signal system, 163, 169
Self-Insight Test (of MMPI), responses to
    of schizophrenics, 114–115
Semantic transfer, 159
Sensory impairment, brain lesions and, 231–
    240
Sensory retaining, 243–257
    adjustment method of successive com-
        parison, 246–247
    delayed matching, 246, 247–250
    engrams, 255
    as experimental method, 245–247
    memory, human, and, 243–257
    psychopathology and flaws in mechanism
        of, 256–257
    recognition tests, 246
    substrate, sensorial, 253–254, 255–257
    "Time errors," 246, 251
Serology, cancer and, 313–315
Shock therapy, 362
Skin conductance response, see Galvanic
    skin response
Sleep, arousal and, 294–295
    autonomic indices, 218, 219
    mental deficiency and, 287, 294–295
    REM, 294
Social breakdown syndrome (SBS), 84
Social change, and incidence and sympto-
    matology of mental disorders, 47–
    52
Social class, comparison of psychiatric dis-
    orders in, 13–29
    social network analysis, 94, 100–102
Social desirability, 24
Socialization, disorders, 84
    institutionalization and, 85, 88
    permanency of group and, 87–88
Social legitimacy, legitimate acts, 77–78
    legitimate rituals, 77
    nonlegitimate acts, 77–78, 79
    nonlegitimate rituals, 77
Social networks, 91–104
    behavior and, 96–97

enculturation and, 96–97
medical model of psychopathology, 103–
    104
methodology of analysis, 98
nature of, 92–93
schizophrenia and, 93–95, 99–100
social class analysis, 94, 100–102
structure, study of in ethnic groups, 94
twin studies, 99–100
value of studying, 93–98
Social science, deviance and, 79
Somatotherapy, 361–362; see also specific
    therapies
Somesthesis, hemispheric cerebral dominance
    and, 227–240
Soviet Union autonomic learning research,
    128
Speech, hemispheric dominance and, 228
    memory and, 244–245
    prosthetic environments for teaching, 182–
        184
    stimuli, schizophrenic responsiveness to,
        114–115
    symbolic cognition, 159–160
Speech Disorganization Scale, 209
Stanford-Binet intelligence test, 428
Startle reflex, mental deficiency and, 288
Statistical method of psychiatric classification,
    414–415
    clinical method versus, 415–416
Status groups, depression and, 18–19, 20,
    21–24
    manic-depressive psychosis and, 1–6
    personality disorders and, 16
    role performance and, 18, 20, 25–29
    schizophrenia and, 16
Stimuli, discriminative, 111
    desensitization, 112
    effects of, 112–115
    environment effects, 116–117
    galvanic skin response (GSR) to, 115
    identification, 112
    outside the laboratory, 112–115
    under experimental conditions, 115–117
Stimuli, verbal, responsiveness of schizo-
    phrenics to, 114–115
Straits Settlements, amok syndrome in, 38
    latah syndrome in, 43
Stress, 95
Stress film reactions, autonomic indices, 218